Administering Medications

Administering Medications
A Competency-Based Program for Health Occupations

Second Edition

Phyllis Theiss Bayt, R.N., B.S., C.M.A.

GLENCOE PUBLISHING COMPANY
Mission Hills, California

Dedicated to my husband Phillip and my mother Thelma Theiss

Copyright © 1989 by Glencoe Publishing Company, a division of Macmillan, Inc.
Copyright © 1982 by The Bobbs-Merrill Company, Inc.

All rights reserved. No part of this book shall be reproduced or transmitted in any form or by any means, electronic or mechanical, including photocopying, recording, or by any information storage or retrieval system, without written permission from the Publisher.

Send all inquiries to:
Glencoe Publishing Company
15319 Chatsworth Street
Mission Hills, California 91345

While the information, recommendations, and suggestions contained herein are accurate to the best of the author's and publisher's knowledge, health care, pharmacology, and drug use are rapidly changing areas. The reader should consult the manufacturer's package insert for current drug product information before administering any drug.

Printed in the United States of America

ISBN 0-02-685190-3 (Student Text)
ISBN 0-02-685191-1 (Mastery Tests and Answer Key)

3 4 5 6 7 8 9 10   92 91 90 89

CONTENTS

Preface vii
Acknowledgments viii
Introduction ix

UNIT 1
Orientation to Medications 2

UNIT 2
Pharmacodynamics 26

UNIT 3
Fundamentals of Medication Therapy 46

UNIT 4
Measurement and Dosage Calculation 70
    Math Review 80

UNIT 5
Routine Responsibilities 96
    Practice Procedure: Transcribe Medication Orders 125
    Practice Procedure: Write Down Verbal Medication Orders 125
    Practice Procedure: Count Controlled Substances 126
    Practice Procedure: Record the Use of Controlled Substances 127
    Practice Procedure: Set Up Medications on a Tray with Medicine Cards 127
    Practice Procedure: Dispense Unit-Dose Medications from a Cart 128
    Practice Procedure: Fill Out an Incident Report Form 129

UNIT 6
Drugs for Infection and Cancer 130
    Practice Procedure: Administer Medication to an Isolation Patient 151
    Product Information Table: Anti-Infectives 153
    Product Information Table: Antineoplastics 154

UNIT 7
Drugs for the Skin 156
    Practice Procedure: Apply Topical Medication to the Skin 171
    Product Information Table: Skin Drugs 173

UNIT 8
Drugs for the Cardiovascular System 176
    Practice Procedure: Administer Oral and Sublingual Medications 197
    Product Information Table: Cardiovascular Drugs 198

UNIT 9
Drugs for the Respiratory System 202
    Practice Procedure: Paint or Spray Medication onto Mucous Membrane of Mouth or Throat 219
    Practice Procedure: Instill Nose Drops or Nasal Spray 220
    Product Information Table: Respiratory Drugs 222

UNIT 10
Drugs for the Nervous and Sensory Systems 224
    Practice Procedure: Instill Eyedrops and Eye Ointment 246
    Practice Procedure: Instill Ear Drops 248
    Product Information Table: Nervous and Sensory System Drugs 249

UNIT 11
Drugs for the Gastrointestinal System **252**
    Practice Procedure: Insert a Rectal Suppository 274
    Practice Procedure: Administer Medication through an Installed Nasogastric
        or Gastrostomy Tube 276
    Product Information Table: Gastrointestinal Drugs 278

UNIT 12
Drugs for the Urinary System and Fluid Balance **280**
    Practice Procedure: Instill Medication into the Bladder through an
        Indwelling Catheter 296
    Product Information Table: Urinary Drugs 298

UNIT 13
Drugs for the Endocrine System **300**
    Product Information Table: Endocrine Drugs 318

UNIT 14
Drugs for the Reproductive System **320**
    Practice Procedure: Insert Vaginal Medication 332
    Product Information Table: Reproductive System Drugs 333

UNIT 15
Drugs for the Musculoskeletal System **334**
    Product Information Table: Musculoskeletal Drugs 345

UNIT 16
Medications and the Elderly **348**

UNIT 17
Administering Parenteral Medications **362**
    Practice Procedure: Draw Up Medication from a Vial 385
    Practice Procedure: Draw Up Medication from an Ampule 386
    Practice Procedure: Administer Intradermal Injection 387
    Practice Procedure: Administer Subcutaneous Injection 388
    Practice Procedure: Administer Intramuscular Injection 389

Bibliography **390**

Index **392**

PREFACE

The growing importance of long-term health care facilities such as nursing homes and convalescent centers has prompted an ever-increasing demand for persons trained in the administration of medications. To meet this demand, there is a need for a compact, self-contained program of instruction that can be studied in a variety of settings—either in school or on the job—and that provides in one place the necessary information for understanding drug actions and procedures of administration.

This text is designed to meet this need. It is written for a diverse group of students with varying preparations, including:

- students of the health occupations in high schools, vocational schools, and community colleges;
- nurses needing a refresher course to take on new job responsibilities;
- technicians, home care/day care workers, and medical clerks who need to be familiar with medications;
- persons in emergency medical technician training programs;
- trainees in specialized long-term and acute care facilities such as nursing homes, alcoholic centers, hospices, and adult day care centers;
- practitioners in hospital inservice programs; and
- students in state-approved programs for medication assistants.

We recognize that administering medications is a serious responsibility requiring a thorough understanding of the basic concepts of drug action. To grasp these concepts further requires a certain background in normal body functioning and the changes caused by disease. Through the use of simplified language, profuse illustrations, and structured learning experiences, we have attempted to provide the necessary background and to make complex concepts accessible to students at varying educational levels. It is understood that the study of this text is to be supervised by a licensed physician or registered nurse, who is expected to guide and evaluate performance on specific administration procedures.

It is our hope that this text will build the solid foundation of understanding that enables students to administer medications competently, safely, and with proper attention to the needs of their patients.

ACKNOWLEDGMENTS

A number of individuals and agencies have assisted at various stages in the preparation of this text. Special thanks go to:

Becky Adams, Linda Ealy, R.N., Dianne LaShorne, Claudia Sabo, and Cheryl Sandlin of Indiana Vocational Technical College, Indianapolis, and their students and staff, for help in field testing the modules;

Edward J. Rowe, Ph.D., of Butler University, Indianapolis, and William M. Heller, Ph.D., of USP Convention, Inc., for guidance in the early development of this text;

Louis Hefler, R.Ph., of Milwaukee Area Technical College, and James E. Berger, R.Ph., of Butler University, Indianapolis, for critiques of the pharmacology sections;

Mary C. Sundberg, R.N., Northern Michigan University, Marquette, Michigan, for a detailed review and suggested additions and illustrations;

Enid Errante Zwirn, R.N., M.P.H., of Indiana University School of Nursing, Indianapolis; Joan Moscati, R.N. of Hospital for Special Surgery, New York; Elizabeth Nye, R.N., of Robeson Technical Institute, Lumberton, North Carolina; Rita Huffer, R.N., of the United Health Careers Institute, San Bernardino, California; Dorothy G. Marshall, R.N.; Phyllis Bilger, R.N.; and Sarah Morris, R.N., of Indiana Department of Public Instruction, for reviewing portions of the text at various stages of development;

The staff of the Science Library, Butler University, Indianapolis, for the use of drug references;

Romma Woodward, R.N.; and Jeanette J. Tuttle, R.N., of Community Hospital, Indianapolis, for information on charting practices;

Angela Bowman, R.N., St. Vincent Hospital, Indianapolis, for information about hospital medication administration;

Kathy Lentz, R.N., programmer/analyst, and Rick Huddleston, R.N., Supervisor, Clinical Pharmacology, Eli Lilly Laboratory for Clinical Research, Wishard Memorial Hospital, for special assistance;

Marinetta Henby, Irma Dawson, Linda Ambroz, Joy Sherrill, and Ann Daloia for conscientious typing of the manuscript through several revisions;

The following agencies for granting permission to reproduce forms currently in use: St. Vincent Hospital and Health Care Center, Indianapolis (Figs. 3-8, 3-9, 5-1, 5-9, 5-11, 5-12, 5-13, 5-20, and 17-14); Hancock County Memorial Hospital, Greenfield, Indiana (Fig. 5-2); Physicians Record Company, Publishers (Figs. 5-11, 5-21, 5-23); Raymo Products, Inc. (Fig. 5-10).

INTRODUCTION

This textbook has been prepared to meet the requirements of competency-based education. This philosophy of learning and teaching has spread throughout the health fields. The term "competency-based" means making sure that all of you, as students, reach a certain level of ability (competence) in specific skills that are laid out as the goals of teaching and learning.

The specific skills you will learn are those required in the performance of certain duties and responsibilities. This contrasts with traditional instructional methods in which students are taught whatever the teacher feels is important and grades are assigned on the basis of how much they have learned.

However, in competency-based education, the goal is to make every student an "A" student. This is an appropriate goal in the health fields, where anything less than "A"-quality work is unacceptable.

You will notice the difference between competency-based and traditional instruction when you take the written and performance tests at the end of each unit. Competency-based education demands that you learn **everything** you need for the performance of your job. Therefore, to pass a written test, you must answer almost all the questions correctly. If you make too many errors, you will need to take the test again after additional study. The same is true of performance tests, in which you demonstrate practical skills for the instructor. You must carry out medication procedures correctly, efficiently, and with proper respect for the patient. Only when your work is of a high quality can you pass the performance test.

The aim of this textbook, then, is to ensure that you learn everything you need to know for the responsibility of administering medications.

ORGANIZATION OF LEARNING MATERIALS

The text is composed of 17 units, each one covering a major topic in the administration of medications. Units 1 through 5 cover basic background information and routine procedures that are important for anyone who is responsible for medications in a hospital or clinical setting.

Units 6 through 15 deal with specific body systems and the drugs that affect each system. In these units you will learn something about the structure and function of body parts, about major diseases, and about types of drugs. You will also receive detailed instructions on how to give medications.

Units 16 and 17 cover special topics—the problems and needs of the elderly and how to give drugs by injection.

Each unit is made up of several components, each having a different purpose. The components are described in the list that follows. Read through this section carefully to understand how the learning materials are organized.

Objectives

Following a brief general introduction to the content of each unit, specific learning objectives are listed. These are detailed statements of things you will need to know or be able to do after studying the unit.

Purpose: To alert you to key skills and facts to which you should pay particular attention as you read and study.

Vocabulary

This is a list of the medical terms and other key words necessary for your understanding of the chapter content. These terms should be memorized. Most of the words are also defined in the text; this list is merely a study aid and a reference in case of questions.

Purpose: To pull together medical vocabulary in one place so that it is easier for you to study.

Text Presentation

This is the main part of the unit. It is a complete presentation of the material you need to learn to prepare for the practice procedures and to pass the written mastery test. This part of the unit includes written text, tables, figures, and other study aids. The text gives background information to help you understand new ideas and procedures. The titles of the various sections of the unit serve as a guide to what is important to learn. Other key ideas and terms are printed in darker type or are summarized in tables and charts.

Purpose: To present the material to be learned in a brief, clear form. To give the necessary medical background for understanding procedures and ideas related to administering medications.

Exercises

The written exercises systematically cover all the important things you need to remember from the unit. They include "fill in the blanks," matching, short answer questions, and definitions. Some of the exercises require that you apply new ideas and procedures in realistic clinical situations.

Purpose: To reinforce the learning of new ideas and procedures and provide practice in applying certain procedures and skills in clinical settings.

Answers to Exercises

Answers are given following each set of exercises. The wording of the answers often differs from that of the text presentation, so that if something was not clear to you in the text, it may become clear when you read it in the answers.

Purpose: To give immediate feedback so that you know how well you are understanding the unit content and to help you spot areas in which you need extra study.

Practice Procedures

The practice procedures are a chance to practice the steps involved in administering medications. Your practice is guided by checklists that detail the steps in each procedure. The procedures are to be practiced under the supervision of an instructor or a nurse in charge. They can be carried out either in a teaching laboratory or on the job. It is expected that the supervisor will show you how to do the tasks and give you tips on doing them well.

Purpose: To practice administering medications, under supervision, until you demonstrate that you are competent to administer them on your own.

Mastery Test

This is your opportunity to show what you know. It is a written test covering the unit content. The 17 unit mastery tests are printed in a separate volume.

Purpose: To help you and your instructor find any weak spots in your knowledge that need extra study and to prepare you for any licensing test you may need to take in order to be permitted to administer medications.

Performance Test

Ten of the units call for a performance test, which is to be developed by your instructor or supervisor. The performance test is very important. It lets your instructor see whether you have reached the level of competence necessary for administering medications on your own to real patients. In the performance test, you should be able to administer medications skillfully and correctly.

Purpose: To make sure that you can perform the required tasks in a way that will benefit the patients who depend on your knowledge and skill.

HOW TO USE THIS TEXT

This textbook contains all the learning materials needed for you to learn at your own pace. By studying the learning objectives, reading the text, and doing the exercises and practice procedures, you will learn all you need to know to pass the mastery and performance tests. But to get the most out of the textbook, you need to know how to use it properly. Study this section very carefully, and refer to it often as you proceed through the book. The following list outlines the steps you should follow for each unit.

1. **Look at the learning objectives.** They spell out the topics you should look for during your readings of the unit. You may use the list of objectives as a sort of pretest to help you discover what you already know and what you need to learn. If you find you know most of the material in the unit already, you can skip to the exercises and the practice procedures and then take the mastery and performance tests.

2. **Read through the vocabulary list.** It contains important words that will be used to explain new ideas and procedures in the unit.

3. **Read through the text presentation** fairly quickly. Look for emphasized subjects and terms. Your aim on this first reading is to get an idea of the unit content.

4. **Now study the unit.** Reread the text slowly, trying to remember as much as you can. Pay particular attention to the tables and charts. Some of these will need to be memorized.

5. **Do the written exercises.** These will help you check how well you studied the unit. They also require you to put your knowledge to work in realistic situations. If you have trouble with the exercises, go back and reread the relevant sections of the unit. If you are still confused, consult your instructor, or look up the material in a reference book in the library. A list of useful references is included at the back of this book.

6. Arrange to **do the practice procedures** in the laboratory or on the job, under the supervision of an instructor or a nurse in charge. Check to see whether the laboratory has special times set aside for students who wish to practice. Read through the procedure checklists and then carry out the steps according to instructions.

Your "patient" may be a plastic doll, a friend, or a real patient (under supervision only). Practice as many times as you need in order to do the tasks smoothly and carefully. Practice patience and thoughtfulness, even if your patient is just a plastic doll. Make your practice session as much like the "real thing" as possible. That way you will feel prepared when you must administer medications on your own.

7. Tell your instructor when you are ready to **take the written mastery test.** Find out whether there are certain hours when you can take the test in the library or the laboratory. Sign up for one of those times and then keep your appointment. Your test should be graded within a short time. To pass the test, you must not miss more than a few questions. Check with your instructor or laboratory coordinator for the percentage correct you need for a passing grade.

After taking the test, find the answers to questions you missed. Remember, the idea is for you to learn everything you need to know to perform your job. If you missed more than the permitted number of questions, you will be required to repeat the test. Study the unit again. To solve specific problems, consult a reference book or your instructor. Then retake the test. Go to Step 8 only when you have passed the mastery test.

8. **Take the performance test.** Inform your instructor that you are ready to demonstrate your skills and be evaluated. Sign up for a testing time and keep your appointment. Discuss your performance with the instructor. The instructor will judge the quality of your work according to the steps on the checklist. You must perform each task at a high level of skill in order to pass the performance test. Check with your instructor for the performance standards by which you will be evaluated. When you have passed the performance test, you may proceed to the next unit and begin again at Step 1.

TIPS ON INDIVIDUALIZED STUDY

- **Set yourself goals for study.**
  Without a plan, studying can drag out and take much longer than necessary. Check with your instructor or laboratory coordinator to see if a specific plan is to be followed in your course. If you are studying on your own, decide how many units you would like to complete each week or month. Then follow your plan. You will feel more confident about studying if you make steady progress through the materials.

- **Study with a friend.**
  Test each other on the vocabulary, drug information, body systems, diseases, and procedures. Talking about new ideas and procedures together helps both of you remember the material.

- **Use resources in addition to the textbook.**
  No textbook can fill the needs of every individual. Occasionally there will be topics you do not fully understand after reading the text. You can find other learning aids in the library or ask the instructor for help. Ask about audiovisual materials that are widely available for students of nursing and the health occupations. These demonstrate nursing procedures and give helpful hints on administering medications.

- **Take the exercises and practice procedures seriously.**
  Do not dash through them or skip parts that seem hard or uninteresting. They are designed to give you needed practice in tasks that you will be performing on the job. They will also prepare you for the unit tests. The more you can rehearse the needed skills, the higher you will score on the unit tests and the more confident you will feel when you first take on your new responsibilities.

Unit 1

Orientation to Medications

In this unit you will learn where drugs come from, how they are standardized, and how their use is governed by law. You will also learn how to use drug references and drug cards to gather information about medications.

In this unit, you learn to:

- Define pharmacology, pharmacodynamics, pharmacy, anatomy, physiology, and pathology.
- List the major sources of drugs and give examples of each.
- List the six therapeutic uses of drugs.
- Define drug standards and tell how they are determined.
- Explain why drug standards are necessary.
- List and describe four types of names by which drugs are known.
- Name three drug references and show how to use at least one.
- Use drug references to prepare a drug card.
- Name three major drug laws and list their main features.
- Name the federal agencies that enforce the drug laws.
- Define the terms over-the-counter (OTC) drugs, prescription drugs, and controlled substances.
- Tell why health workers must be familiar with drug laws.

INTRODUCTION

Not long ago, only doctors and nurses were allowed to administer medications. But times are changing; many others in the health occupations are now also asked to give or know about medications. They also are expected to observe how patients react after taking their medications. These are important new responsibilities. They demand that you, a member on the allied health team working with medications, have knowledge of many health-related topics also. You must know the basic principles of **pharmacology,** which is the study of drugs and their uses. You must understand how drugs interact with the human body, or **pharmacodynamics**. This requires some knowledge of human **anatomy**, the structure of body parts, and also **physiology**, the functions of body systems, organs, tissues, and cells. You must know what goes wrong with body parts when there is disease, **pathology**, and how drugs change the course of disease. Attention must be given to **psychology**, the study of the mind, because the mental state of a patient influences the way the body reacts to drugs.

The units of this textbook will teach you step by step the basics of pharmacology pharmacodynamics, anatomy, physiology, and pathology. Tips on how to respond to patients' psychological needs will be included. The uses of specific drugs for treatment of disease are discussed in connection with the parts of the body on which they act. As you learn general principles, a number of you will also carry out practice tasks to give you experience in giving medications.

PHARMACOLOGY

A **drug** is any chemical that affects living things. Pharmacology (*fahr′mah-kol′o-je*) is the study of drugs: their sources, chemical makeup, preparation, and uses. Pharmacology includes the study of how specific chemicals affect the human body. In the field of medicine, we are concerned with drugs that help prevent, diagnose, and treat human disease. These are called **therapeutic** (*ther′ah-pu′tik*) drugs, or **medications**.

Pharmacology attempts to describe both the desired effects and the side effects of drugs. It focuses, too, on the proper amounts of drugs to be given and on how drugs are given. Knowledge of the laws and responsibilities surrounding drug use, along with practical experience in giving medications, will equip you to play a vital role in the health care team.

> **NOTE:**
> You may be confused by the terms "pharmacology" and "pharmacy." Pharmacology is the study of drugs. Pharmacy refers to the profession that prepares and dispenses chemical substances for use in therapy or to a place where a pharmacist works. A related word, pharmaceuticals, is simply another word for drugs.

DRUG SOURCES

Drugs come from four sources: plants, animals, minerals, and chemical synthesis/biogenic engineering in the laboratory (Figure 1-1).

Plants

Our human ancestors long ago discovered that the roots, leaves, and seeds of certain plants had the power to cure illnesses, ease pain, and affect the mind. Today many drugs are still extracted from parts of plants. An example is digitalis, which is used to treat certain heart conditions. Digitalis is made from a wildflower, purple foxglove. Other examples are opium, belladonna, vitamin C, and various gums and oils.

Animals

Drugs of animal origin are prepared by extracting natural substances, such as hormones, from animal tissues and organs. Insulin, for example, is extracted from the pancreas of cattle and pigs. Heparin, used to reduce the formation of blood clots, is taken from the intestinal linings of cattle and pigs.

Minerals

Iron, iodine, calcium, and sodium chloride (salt) are examples of minerals used in drug therapy. They come from rocks and crystals found in nature.

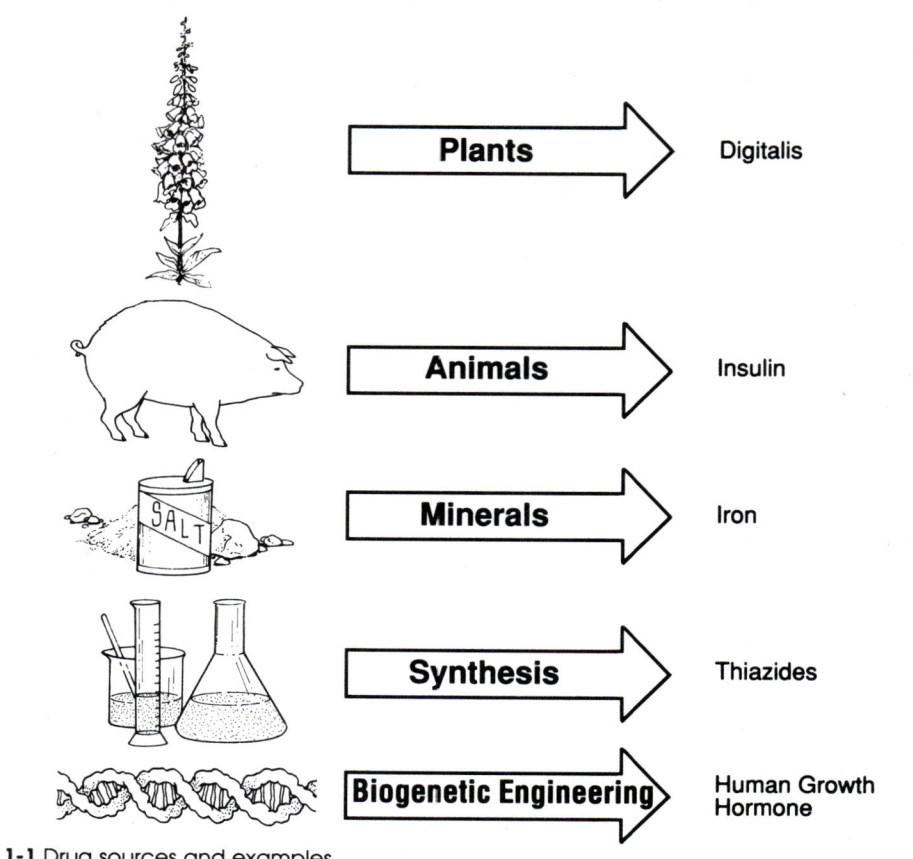

Figure 1-1 Drug sources and examples.

- Plants → Digitalis
- Animals → Insulin
- Minerals → Iron
- Synthesis → Thiazides
- Biogenetic Engineering → Human Growth Hormone

VOCABULARY

anatomy: the structure of body parts

assay: identifying and measuring ingredients of a drug product in a laboratory; test used to determine drug standards

bioassay: measuring the amount or biological activity of a drug by its effect upon a biological system

chemical name: describes the chemical structure of a compound

contraceptive: drug that prevents pregnancy

contraindications: conditions in which the use of a certain drug is dangerous or ill-advised

controlled substances: potentially dangerous or habit-forming drugs whose sale and use is strictly regulated by law

DEA: Drug Enforcement Agency; enforces the Controlled Substances Act of 1970

diagnosis: identifying the disease a patient has

DNA: deoxyribonucleic acid; the genetic information center of a cell

dose: how much of a drug is administered

drug: a chemical that effects the body

drug card: index card on which you write drug information for your own reference

drug legislation: laws governing the manufacture, sale, and use of drugs

FDA: Food and Drug Administration; enforcement agency for the FDCA

FDCA: Food, Drug, and Cosmetic Act of 1938

generic name: name provided for a new drug by the United States Adopted Names Council; a drug may have several trade names but only one generic name

generics: refers to products that are not trade-name preparations

health maintenance: developing a healthy lifestyle, keeping existing diseases under control, and getting regular checkups

indications: diseases and disorders for which a certain drug may be used

legend drugs: prescription drugs

medication: drugs used for medical therapy

metabolism: chemical processes that take place in a human cell

narcotics: drugs that act on the central nervous system to produce euphoria (false sense of well-being), drowsiness, and stupor; their use is subject to governmental control because they are dangerous and can cause chemical dependence or addiction

official name: drug name listed by FDA and printed in the *United States Pharmacopeia/National Formulary* (USP/NF)

over-the-counter (OTC) drugs: drugs available without a prescription

package insert: printed information about a drug included with the product

pathology: changes in the body caused by disease

PDR: *Physicians' Desk Reference*, reference book for drugs; uses product package inserts as sources

pharmaceuticals: drugs

pharmacodynamics: study of how drugs interact with body tissues

pharmacokinetics: the study of drug movement in the body; includes absorption, distribution, metabolism, and excretion

pharmacology: study of drugs (uses, preparation, routes, laws, etc.)

pharmacy: preparing and dispensing drugs; the place where a pharmacist works

physiology: functioning of the body parts

precautions: warnings to use care when giving drugs under certain conditions

prescription: a physician's written or verbal order that enables a person to purchase a drug from the pharmacy

psychology: study of the mind

references: books and other publications for looking up information

side effects: drug effects other than the desired beneficial ones

standards: rules ensuring uniform quality and purity

synthesis: method for creating drugs in the laboratory from various chemicals

therapeutic drugs: drugs used to prevent, diagnose, and treat disease and to prevent pregnancy

therapy: treatment of disease or disorder

trade name: licensed drug name under which a drug prepared by a specific manufacturer is sold; also called **brand name** or **proprietary name**

USAN: United States Adopted Names; system that adopts the generic name of a drug

USP DI: *United States Pharmacopeia Dispensing Information*; official reference containing dispensing information for pharmacists or persons administering medications

USP/NF: *United States Pharmacopeia/ National Formulary*; official book listing standardized drugs

Chemical Synthesis/Biogenetic Engineering

Many drugs are made, or **synthesized** (sin'the-sized), in the laboratory through chemical processes. An example is hydrochlorothiazide (*HydroDiuril*), a drug used to treat high blood pressure. Biogenetic engineering methods, patching together DNA material from different organisms, have made new drugs and drug products available. Insulin and vaccines can be produced this way.

DRUG USES

The study of drug uses will give you an understanding of one phase of health care, **drug therapy**. Drugs are helpful to both the healthy and the sick. The four most familiar uses of drugs relate to disease: **prevention, treatment, diagnosis,** and **cure**. The last two uses of drugs are **contraception**, or the prevention of pregnancy, and **health maintenance**.

Disease prevention involves the administration of drugs such as vaccines which inoculate the body against disease germs. Health maintenance is closely related to disease prevention. Drugs such as vitamins and insulin are given to help keep the body healthy and strong or to keep the body systems functioning normally.

Treating disease means relieving the symptoms while the body's natural disease-fighting mechanisms do their work. Aspirin and antihistamines are examples of drugs used to treat disease symptoms. Curing disease often means eliminating disease-causing germs. Antibiotics such as streptomycin and penicillin are drugs that help cure disease.

Diagnostic drugs are taken to enable physicians to determine whether disease is present. For example, radiopaque dye (a dye that shows up on fluoroscope or x-rays) is administered to detect gallbladder malfunctions.

The prevention of pregnancy is possible with the use of **contraceptives**, drugs that control fertility.

Drugs often have more than one use. The drug promethazine hydrochloride (*Phenergan*), for example, is used in a wide variety of ways. It can control allergic reactions, treat motion sickness, induce sleep, and prevent vomiting after surgery. Some drugs have the ability to prevent as well as cure or treat disease. The uses of different kinds of drugs are discussed in specific units.

DRUG STANDARDS

Drugs differ widely in strength, quality, and purity, depending on how they are manufactured. In order to control these differences, certain rules or **standards** have been set up that products must meet. Drug standards are required by law. The law says that all preparations called by the same drug name must be of a uniform strength, quality, and purity. A drug prepared in Indiana must meet the same standards for strength, quality, and purity as the same drug prepared in California or New Jersey. Because of drug standards, physicians who order penicillin, for example, can be sure that patients anywhere in the country will get the same basic substance from the pharmacist. Drug stan-

Figure 1-2 United States Pharmacopeia/National Formulary.

dards also help doctors prescribe accurate dosages and predict the results.

Drugs for which standards have been developed are listed in a special reference book called the **United States Pharmacopeia/National Formulary (USP/NF)** (Figure 1-2). The USP/NF is recognized by the U.S. government as the official list of drug standards, which are enforceable by the U.S. Food and Drug Administration.

Since 1975, USP has engaged in a program to include all drug substances, and to the extent possible, all drug products in the United States. The book is updated regularly and a new edition published every five years to keep the information up to date.

DRUG NAMES

All drugs have more than one name. In fact, most have four: a chemical name, a generic name, an official name, and one or more trade names. Figures 1-3 through 1-6 show the four names of one common drug.

Chemical Name

This name describes the chemical structure of the drug. It can be very long and complicated.

Generic Name

This is the name given a drug by the manufacturer with input from various regulatory agencies before the drug becomes officially recognized. It gives some information about the chemical makeup of the drug, but not as much as the chemical name. The generic name is established by the United States Adopted Names (USAN) Council. (The term "generic" has also come to mean any drug that is not sold under a particular trade name.)

Official Name

This is the name under which the drug is listed in the USP/NF. It is usually, but not always, the same as the generic name. If the USP/NF does change a name of one of its drugs, that name becomes the one and only allowable generic name in the United States.

Trade Name

Also known as the **brand name** or the **proprietary name**, this is the name under which the drug is sold by a specific manufacturer. The name is owned by the drug company, and no other company may use it. The symbol ® to the right of the name shows that its use is restricted. A drug that is manufactured by several companies may be known by several different trade names.

For example, the drug with the generic name nitroglycerin is sold by several manufacturers under such trade names as *Nitro-Bid, Nitrong,* and *Nitrostat.*

Trade Name Drugs Versus Generics

Most drugs are known to the general public by their trade names. *Librium*, for example, is much more familiar to most people than chlordiazepoxide hydrochloride. But you and your fellow health workers must be familiar with the generic names of many drugs. There are good reasons for

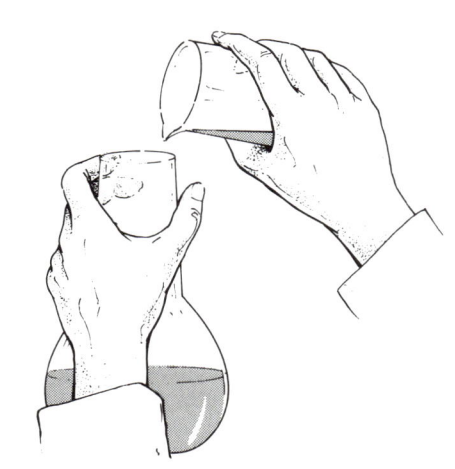

6-Chloro-3,4-dihydro-2H-1,2,4-benzothiadiazine-7-sulfonamide 1,1-dioxide

Figure 1-3 Chemical name.

Figure 1-4 Generic name.

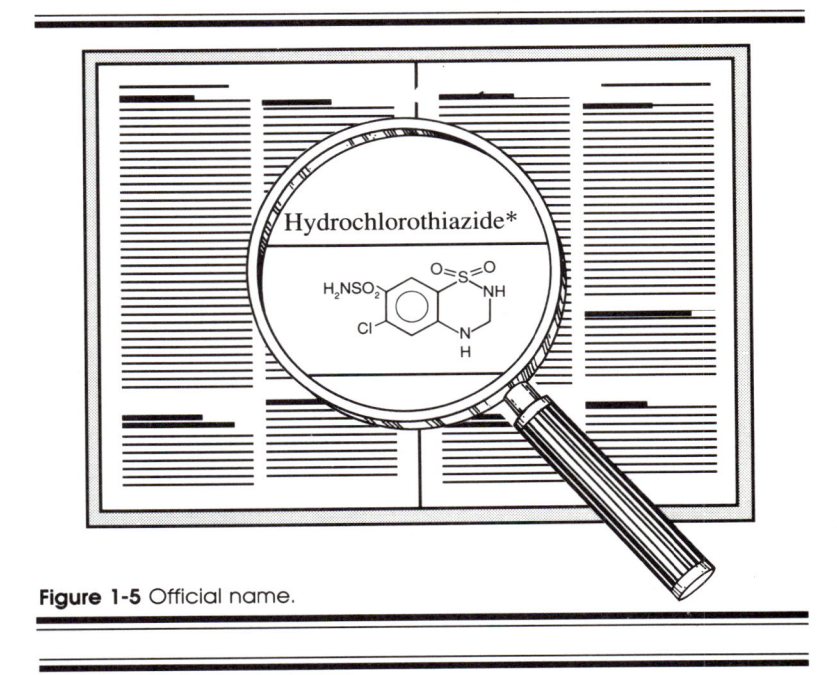

Figure 1-5 Official name.

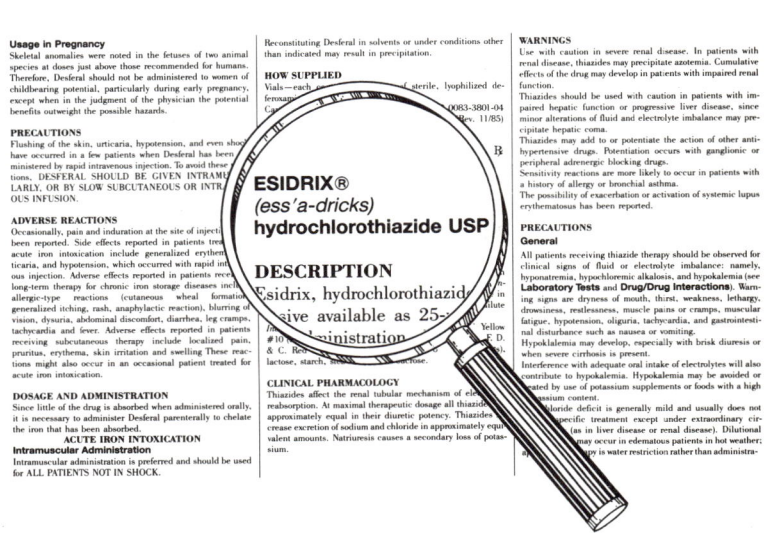

Figure 1-6 Trade or brand names. (© *Physicians' Desk Reference*, 1987 Ed. Medical Economics Co., Oradell, N.J. 07649).

this. First, drugs are frequently prescribed by their generic names rather than trade names. This is because the trade name preparations are more expensive, so there is a savings to the consumer in buying generic drugs. A prescription written for a generic product allows the pharmacist to choose among nonbranded drugs available from several companies. Bioavailability testing has helped assure that the patient gets the same benefits from taking the generic product as from the brand name product.

Another reason for knowing the generic name is that drugs often have several trade names but only one generic name. (Did you remember the USP/NF only allows one in the United States?) If you learn the generic names, you can organize information about several trade name drugs in your mind. Of course, it is not possible for you to memorize all of the generic and trade names for medications, but you should try to become familiar with both names of the drugs you handle daily in your work.

Where specific drugs are mentioned in this text, generic names are given first and are not capitalized. Trade names are capitalized and shown in parentheses in italic type following the generic names. Only one or two common trade names are given in each case. Keep in mind that there may be many other trade name products available.

DRUG REFERENCES

Several reference books provide useful information about drugs on the market. These are often referred to by doctors, nurses, and others in the health occupations when planning and administering drug therapy. Drug references can help you understand why and how a particular drug is administered. For each drug, they usually include information about:

- composition—what the drug is made of
- action—how the drug works
- indications—what conditions the drug is used for
- contraindications—conditions under which the drug should not be used
- precautions—special conditions that may alter the drug effects and that should be considered when prescribing the drug
- side effects and adverse reactions—unpleasant or dangerous effects of a drug other than the desired effect (see Unit 2)
- administration—how the drug is given
- how supplied—forms available

Learning how to use the drug references will help you meet the new responsibilities of health workers in administering medications.

A popular reference book is **Physicians' Desk Reference (PDR)**, which is available in most health facilities (Figure 1-7). The PDR gives information about the drug products of major pharmaceutical companies. It is useful for checking clinical pharmacology, mechanism of action, indications and uses, contraindications, warnings, precautions, adverse reactions, overdosage, dosage and administration, and how the product is supplied. It lists drugs by their trade names, generic names, uses, and manufacturers. Color photographs are included in a "Product Identification" section to help you identify some common drugs.

A new drug reference is the **United States Pharmacopeia Dispensing Information**, or the USP DI. The USP DI is written in everyday language. It provides pharmacists and other health workers with easy-to-follow information on over 4,000 official drugs and products available (Figure 1-8). You will find it particularly useful when you need to explain the use of a drug to a patient. Included are drug use categories, precautions, interactions, side effects, dosage and storage information, patient consultation guidelines, and sections on pharmacology and pharmacokinetics. It is a consensus of health care experts throughout the United States. The text is revised every year to update information on new and old drugs.

Another valuable reference is the **Handbook of Nonprescription Drugs**, published by the American Pharmaceutical Association. Pharmacology textbooks and articles in nursing journals are also helpful sources of information. Some health care facilities keep their own reference lists of the drugs they use most often.

ILOTYCIN®
[i-lo-ti'-sin]
(erythromycin)
Tablets, USP
(Enteric-Coated)

DESCRIPTION

Erythromycin is produced by a strain of *Streptomyces erythraeus* and belongs to the macrolide group of antibiotics. It is basic and readily forms salt with acids. The base, the stearate salt, and the esters are poorly soluble in water and are suitable for oral administration.

Tablets Ilotycin® (erythromycin, Dista) are specially coated to protect the contents from the inactivating effect of gastric acid and to permit efficient absorption of the antibiotic in the small intestine.

Each enteric-coated tablet contains 250 mg erythromycin. Each tablet also contains carboxymethyl cellulose, cellulose, dibasic calcium phosphate, hydroxypropyl cellulose, iron oxide, magnesium stearate, stearic acid, silicon dioxide, titanium dioxide, and other inactive ingredients.

ACTIONS

Erythromycin inhibits protein synthesis without affecting nucleic acid syntheses. Some strains of *Haemophilus influenzae* and staphylococci have demonstrated resistance to erythomycin. Some strains of *H. influenzae* that are resistant in vitro to erythromycin alone are susceptible to erythromycin and sulfonamides used concomitantly. Culture and susceptibility testing should be done. If the Bauer-Kirby method of disc susceptibility is used, a 15-mcg erythromycin disc should give a zone diameter of at least 18 mm when tested against an erythomycin-susceptible organism. Tablets Ilotycin® (erythromycin, Dista) are well absorbed and may be given without regard to meals. After absorption, erythromycin diffuses readily into most body fluids. In the absence of meningeal inflammation, low concentrations are normally achieved in the spinal fluid, but passage of the drug across the blood-brain barrier increases in meningitis. In the presence of normal hepatic function, erythromycin is concentrated in the liver and excreted in the bile; the effect of hepatic dysfunction on excretion of erythromycin by the liver into the bile is not known. After oral administration, less than 5 percent of the administered dose can be recovered as the active form in the urine. Erythromycin crosses the placental barrier, but fetal plasma levels are low.

INDICATIONS

Streptococcus pyogenes (Group A Beta-Hemolytic)—Upper and lower respiratory tract, skin, and soft-tissue infections of mild to moderate severity.

Injectable penicillin G benzathine is considered by the American Heart Association to be the drug of choice in the treatment and prevention of streptococcal pharyngitis and in long-term prophylaxis of rheumatic fever. When oral medication is preferred for treating the above-mentioned conditions, penicillin G or V or erythromycin is the alternate drug of choice.

The importance of the patient's strict adherence to the prescribed dosage regimen must be stressed when oral medication is given. A therapeutic dose should be administered for at least ten days. *Alpha-Hemolytic Streptococci* (Viridans Group)—Although no controlled clinical efficacy trials have been conducted, oral erythromycin has been suggested by the American Heart Association and the American Dental Association for use in a regimen for prophylaxis against bacterial endocarditis in patients hypersensitive to penicillin who have congenital heart disease or rheumatic or other acquired valvular heart disease when they undergo dental procedures and surgical procedures of the upper respiratory tract.[1] Erythromycin is not suitable for such prophylaxis prior to genitourinary or gastrointestinal tract surgery.

Note: When selecting antibiotics for the prevention of bacterial endocarditis, the physician or dentist should read the full joint statement of the American Heart Association and the American Dental Association.[1]

Staphylococcus aureus—Acute infections of skin and soft tissue which are mild to moderately severe. Resistance may develop during treatment.

S. (Diplococcus) pneumoniae—Infections of the upper respiratory tract (e.g., otitis media, pharyngitis) and lower respiratory tract (e.g., pneumonia) of mild to moderate severity.

Mycoplasma pneumoniae (Eaton Agent, PPLO)—In the treatment of respiratory tract infections due to this organism.

H. influenzae—May be used concomitantly with adequate doses of sulfonamides in treating upper respiratory tract infections of mild to moderate severity. Not all strains of this organism are susceptible at the erythromycin concentrations ordinarily achieved (see appropriate sulfonamide labeling for prescribing information).

Treponema pallidum—Erythromycin is an alternate choice of treatment for primary syphilis in penicillin-allergic patients. In primary syphilis, spinal-fluid examinations should be done before treatment and as part of follow-up after therapy.

Corynebacterium diphtheriae—As an adjunct to antitoxin, to prevent establishment of carriers, and to eradicate the organism in carriers.

C. minutissimum—In the treatment of erythrasma.

Entamoeba histolytica—In the treatment of intestinal amebiasis only. Extraenteric amebiasis requires treatment with other agents.

Listeria monocytogenes—Infections due to this organism.

Neisseria gonorrhoeae—In female patients with a history of sensitivity to penicillin, a parenteral erythromycin (such as the gluceptate) may be administered in conjunction with an oral erythromycin as alternate therapy in acute pelvic inflammatory disease caused by *N. gonorrhoeae*. In the treatment of gonorrhea, patients suspected of having concomitant syphilis should have microscopic examinations (by immunofluorescence or darkfield) before receiving erythromycin and monthly serologic tests for a minimum of four months.

Bordetella pertussis—Erythromycin is effective in eliminating the organism from the nasopharynx of infected individuals and in rendering them noninfectious. Some clinical studies suggest that erythromycin may be helpful in the prophylaxis of pertussis in exposed susceptible individuals.

Legionnaires' Disease—Although no controlled clinical efficacy studies have been conducted, in vitro and limited preliminary clinical data suggest that erythromycin may be effective in treating Legionnaires' Disease.

Chlamydia trachomatis—Erythromycins are indicated for treatment of the following infections caused by *C. trachomatis:* conjunctivitis of the newborn, pneumonia of infancy, urogenital infections during pregnancy (*see* Warning). When tetracyclines are contraindicated or not tolerated, erythromycin is indicated for the treatment of adults with uncomplicated urethral, endocervical, or rectal infections due to *C. trachomatis*.

CONTRAINDICATIONS

Erythromycin is contraindicated in patients with known hypersentivity to this antibiotic.

WARNINGS

Usage in Pregnancy—Safety of this drug for use during pregnancy has not been established. Therefore, the physician should consider carefully the benefits and risks of the use of this drug during pregnancy.

Pseudomembranous colitis has been reported with virtually all broad-spectrum antibiotics (including macrolides, semisynthetic penicillins, and cephalosporins); therefore, it is important to consider its diagnosis in patients who develop diarrhea in association with the use of antibiotics. Such colitis may range in severity from mild to life-threatening.

Treatment with broad-spectrum antibiotics alters the normal flora of the colon and may permit overgrowth of clostridia. Studies indicate that a toxin produced by *Clostridium difficile* is one primary cause of antibiotic-associated colitis. Mild cases of pseudomembranous colitis usually respond to drug discontinuance alone. In moderate to severe cases, management should include sigmoidoscopy, appropriate bacteriologic studies, and fluid, electrolyte, and protein supplementation. When the colitis does not improve after the drug has been discontinued, or when it is severe, oral vancomycin is the drug of choice for antibiotic-associated pseudomembranous colitis produced by *C. difficile*. Other causes of colitis should be ruled out.

PRECAUTIONS

Surgical procedures should be performed when indicated. Since erythromycin is excreted principally by the liver, caution should be exercised in administering the antibiotic to patients with impaired hepatic function. There have been reports of hepatic dysfunction, with or without jaundice, occurring in patients taking oral erythromycin products.

Drug Interactions—The use of erythromycin in patients who are receiving high doses of theophylline may be associated with an increase in serum theophylline levels and potential theophylline toxicity. In case of theophylline toxicity and/or elevated serum theophylline levels, the dose of theophylline should be reduced while the patient is receiving concomitant erythromycin therapy. There have been reports of excessive prolongation of prothrombin times in patients receiving erythromycin concurrently with chronic warfarin therapy. Such patients, particularly the elderly who generally exhibit slower warfarin clearance, may be at risk for developing bleeding due to this interaction. In patients receiving erythromycin during chronic treatment with warfarin, prothrombin times should be monitored closely and warfarin dosage adjusted accordingly.

ADVERSE REACTIONS

The most frequent side effeects of erythromycin preparations are gastointestinal (e.g., abdominal cramping and discomfort) and are dose related. Nausea, vomiting, and diarrhea occur infrequently with usual oral doses. During prolonged or repeated therapy, there is a possibility of overgrowth of nonsusceptible bacteria or fungi. If such infections arise, the drug should be discontinued and appropriate therapy instituted.

Mild allergic reactions, such as urticaria and other skin rashes, have occurred. Serious allergic reactions, including anaphylaxis, have been reported.

There have been isolated reports of reversible hearing loss occurring chiefly in patients with renal insufficiency and in patients receiving high doses of erythromycin.

DOSAGE AND ADMINISTRATION

Tablets Ilotycin® (erythromycin, Dista) are well absorbed whether given immediately after meals or between meals on an empty stomach.

Adults—The usual dosage is 250 mg every six hours. This may be increased up to 4 g or more/day according to the severity of the infection.

Children—Age, weight, and severity of the infection are important factors in determining the proper dosage. The usual regimen is 30 to 50 mg/kg/day in divided doses. For more severe infections, this dosage may be doubled. If administration is desired on a twice-a-day schedule in either adults or children, one-half of the total daily dose may be given every 12 hours.

Streptococcal Infections—In the treatment of group A beta-hemolytic streptococcal infections, a therapeutic dosage of erythromycin should be administered for at least ten days. In continuous prophylaxis of streptococcal infections in persons with a history of rheumatic heart disease, the dosage is 250 mg twice a day.

For prophylaxis against basterial endocarditis[1] in patients with congenital heart disease or rheumatic or other acquired valvular heart disease when undergoing dental procedures or surgical procedures of the upper respiratory tract, the dosage schedule for adults is 1 g (20 mg/kg for children) orally one and one-half to two hours before the procedure and then 500 mg (10 mg/kg for children) orally every six hours for eight doses.

Primary Syphilis—30 to 40 g given in divided doses over a period of ten to 15 days.

Acute Pelvic Inflammatory Disease Caused by N. gonorrhoeae—Ilotycin® Gluceptate (Sterile Erythromycin Gluceptate, USP, Dista), 500 mg intravenously every six hours for at least three days, followed by Ilotycin®, 250 mg every six hours for seven days.

Dysenteric Amebiasis—250 mg four times daily for ten to 14 days for adults; 30 to 50 mg/kg/day in divided doses for ten to 14 days for children.

Pertussis—Although optimum dosage and duration of treatment have not been established, the dosage of erythromycin utilized in reported clinical studies was 40 to 50 mg/kg/day, given in divided doses for five to 14 days.

Legionnaires' Disease—Although optimum doses have not been established, doses utilized in reported clinical data were those recommended above (1 to 4 g erythromycin base daily in divided doses).

Conjunctivitis of the Newborn Caused by C. trachomatis—Oral erythromycin suspension, 50 mg/kg/day in four divided doses for at least two weeks.[2]

Pneumonia of Infancy Caused by C. trachomatis—Although the optimum duration of therapy has not been established, the recommended therapy is oral erythromycin suspension, 50 mg/kg/day in four divided doses for at least three weeks.[2]

Urogenital Infections during Pregnancy Due to C. trachomatis—Although the optimum dose and duration of therapy have not been established, the suggested treatment is erythromycin, 500 mg orally four times a day for at least seven days. For women who cannot tolerate this regimen, a decreased dose of 250 mg orally four times a day should be used for at least 14 days.[2]

For adults with uncomplicated urethral, endocervical, or rectal infections caused by *C. trachomatis* in whom tetracyclines are contraindicated or not tolerated: 50 mg orally four times a day for at least seven days.[2]

Figure 1-7 The PDR is used in many health facilities. (© *Physicians' Desk Reference*, 1987 Ed. Medical Economics Co., Oradell, N.J. 07649).

ANTIHISTAMINES (Systemic)

This information applies to the following medicines:

Azatadine (a-ZA-ta-deen)
Bromodiphenhydramine (broe-moe-dye-fen-HYE-dra-meen)
Brompheniramine (brome-fen-EER-a-meen)
Carbinoxamine (kar-bi-NOX-a-meen)
Chlorpheniramine (klor-fen-EER-a-meen)
Clemastine (KLEM-as-teen)
Cyproheptadine (si-proe-HEP-ta-deen)
Dexchlorpheniramine (dex-klor-fen-EER-a-meen)
Dimenhydrinate (dye-men-HYE-dri-nate)
Diphenhydramine (dye-fen-HYE-dra-meen)
Diphenylpyraline (dye-fen-il-PEER-a-leen)
Doxylamine (dox-ILL-a-meen)
Phenindamine (fen-IN-da-meen)
Pyrilamine (peer-ILL-a-meen)
Terfenadine (ter-FEN-a-deen)
Tripelennamine (tri-pel-ENN-a-meen)
Triprolidine (trye-PROE-li-deen)

This information does *not* apply to Hydroxyzine, Promethazine, or Trimeprazine.

Listing of some commonly used brand names and other names.

Read the bold information first. Then go back and read the rest. If you do not recognize the names of medical conditions or medicines included in this information, check with your doctor, nurse, or pharmacist. Brand names for the generic drug names listed can also be found in the index. It is a good idea for you to learn both the generic and brand names of your medicines and to write them down for future use.

Antihistamines are used to relieve or prevent the symptoms of hay fever and other types of allergy. They work by preventing the effects of a substance called histamine, which is produced by the body.

Some of the antihistamines are also used to prevent motion sickness, nausea, vomiting, and dizziness. In patients with Parkinson's disease, diphenhydramine may be used to decrease stiffness and tremors. In addition, since antihistamines may cause drowsiness as a side effect, some of them may be used to help people go to sleep.

Antihistamines may also be used for other conditions as determined by your doctor.

Some antihistamine preparations are available only with your doctor's prescription. Others are available without a prescription; however, your doctor may have special instructions on the proper dose of the medicine for your medical conditions.

Remember:

- **Keep all medicines out of the reach of children.**

- In order for this medicine to work, it must be used as directed. **If you are using this medicine without a prescription, it is very important that you follow the directions on the label.**

- **It is also very important that you read and understand the following information.** If any of the information causes you special concern, check with your doctor before using this medicine without a prescription.

- If you are receiving this medicine by injection, some of the information about this medicine may not apply.

- Before you begin using any new medicine (prescription or nonprescription) or if you develop any new medical problem while you are using this medicine, check with your doctor, nurse, or pharmacist.

- **If you have any questions** about the following information or if you want more information about this medicine or your medical problem, **ask your doctor, nurse, or pharmacist.**

Before Using This Medicine

Before using this medicine check with your doctor or pharmacist:

—if you have ever had any unusual or allergic reaction to antihistamines.

—if you are on a low-salt, low-sugar, or any other special diet, or if you are allergic to any substance, such as foods, sulfites or other preservatives, or dyes. Most medicines contain more than their active ingredient, and many liquid medicines contain alcohol. Your doctor or pharmacist can help you avoid products that may cause a problem.

—if you are pregnant or if you intend to become pregnant while using this medicine. Although antihistamines have not been shown to cause problems in humans, the chance always exists since studies in animals have shown that some other antihistamines, such as meclizine and cyclizine, may cause birth defects. Studies have not been done in humans with terfenadine. However, studies in animals have shown that terfenadine, when given in doses several times the human dose, lowers the weight of the baby and increases the risk of death of the baby.

—if you are breast-feeding. Small amounts of antihistamines pass into the breast milk. Use is not recommended since the chances are greater for most antihistamines to cause side effects, such as unusual excitement or irritability, in the infant. Also, since these medicines tend to decrease the secretions of the body, it is possible that the flow of breast milk may be reduced in some patients. It is not known yet whether terfenadine may cause these same side effects.

Figure 1-8 The USP DI offers information for the health care provider and advice for the patient. (Reprinted with permission from United States Pharmacopeia Dispensing Information, ©1987, USP Convention, Inc.).

—if you have any of the following medical problems:
- Asthma attack
- Enlarged prostate
- Glaucoma
- Urinary tract blockage or difficult urination

—if you are now taking or receiving any of the following medicines or types of medicine:
- Amantadine
- Antimuscarinics (medicine for abdominal or stomach spasms or cramps)
- Aspirin or other salicylates
- Cisplatin
- Clonidine
- Guanabenz
- Haloperidol
- Ipratropium
- Maprotiline
- Methyldopa
- Metyrosine
- Paromomycin
- Phenothiazines (acetophenazine, chlorpromazine, fluphenazine, mesoridazine, perphenazine, prochlorperazine, promazine, promethazine, thioridazine, trifluoperazine, triflupromazine, trimeprazine)
- Procainamide
- Trazodone
- Tricyclic antidepressants (amitriptyline, amoxapine, clomipramine desipramine, doxepin, imipramine, nortriptyline, protriptyline, trimipramine)
- Vancomycin

—if you are now taking any central nervous system (CNS) depressants such as:
- Anticonvulsants (seizure medicine)
- Barbiturates
- Muscle relaxants
- Narcotics
- Other antihistamines or medicine for hay fever, other allergies, or colds
- Prescription pain medicine
- Sedatives, tranquilizers, or sleeping medicine

—if you are now taking or have taken within the past 2 weeks monoamine oxidase (MAO) inhibitors such as:
- Furazolidone
- Isocarboxazid
- Pargyline
- Phenelzine
- Procarbazine
- Tranylcypromine

Proper Use of This Medicine

Antihistamines are used to relieve or prevent the symptoms of your medical problem. Take them only as directed. Do not take more of them and do not take them more often than recommended on the label, unless otherwise directed by your doctor. To do so may increase the chance of side effects.

If you must take this medicine regularly and you miss a dose, take it as soon as possible. However, if it is almost time for your next dose, skip the missed dose and go back to your regular dosing schedule. Do not double doses.

For patients taking this medicine by mouth:
- Take it with food or a glass of water or milk to lessen stomach irritation if necessary.
- If you are taking the extended-release tablet form of this medicine, swallow the tablets whole. Do not break, crush, or chew before swallowing.

For patients taking dimenhydrinate or diphenhydramine:
- If you are taking this medicine for motion sickness, take it at least 30 minutes or, even better, 1 to 2 hours before you begin to travel.

For patients using the suppository form of this medicine:
- How to insert suppository: First remove foil wrapper and moisten the suppository with water. Lie down on side and push the suppository well up into the rectum with finger. If the suppository is too soft to insert because of storage in a warm place, before removing the foil wrapper chill the suppository in the refrigerator for 30 minutes or run cold water over it.

For patients using the injection form of this medicine:
- If you will be giving yourself the injections, make sure you understand exactly how to give them. If you have any questions about this, check with your doctor, nurse, or pharmacist.

How to store this medicine:
- Store away from heat and direct light.
- **Keep out of the reach of children,** since overdose may be very dangerous in children.
- Do not store the capsules or tablets in the bathroom medicine cabinet because the heat or moisture may cause the medicine to break down.
- Keep the liquid dosage form of this medicine from freezing.
- Do not keep outdated medicine or medicine no longer than needed. Flush the contents of the container down the toilet, unless otherwise directed.

Precautions While Using This Medicine

Tell the doctor in charge that you are taking this medicine before you have any skin tests for allergies. The results of the test may be affected by this medicine.

When taking antihistamines on a regular basis, make sure your doctor knows if you are taking large amounts of aspirin at the same time (as in arthritis or rheumatism). Effects of too much aspirin, such as ringing in the ears, may be covered up by the antihistamine.

Antihistamines will add to the effects of alcohol and other CNS depressants (medicines that slow down the nervous system, possibly causing drowsiness). Some examples of CNS depressants are sedatives, tranquilizers, or sleeping medicine; prescription pain medicine or narcotics; barbiturates; medicine for seizures; muscle relaxants; or anesthetics, including some dental anesthetics. **Check with your doctor before taking any of the above while you are using this medicine.**

This medicine may cause some people to become drowsy or less alert than they are normally. Even if taken at bedtime, it may cause some people to feel drowsy or less alert on arising. Some antihistamines are more likely to cause drowsiness than others (terfenadine, for example, produces this effect rarely). **Make sure you know how you react to the antihistamine you are taking before you drive, use machines, or do other jobs that require you to be alert.**

Antihistamines may cause dryness of the mouth, nose, and throat. For temporary relief of mouth dryness, use sugarless candy or gum, melt bits of ice in your mouth, or use a saliva substitute. However, if dry mouth continues for more than 2 weeks, check with your dentist. Continuing dryness of the mouth may increase the chance of dental disease, including tooth decay, gum disease, and fungal infections.

For patients using dimenhydrinate or diphenhydramine:

- This medicine controls nausea and vomiting. For this reason, it may cover up the signs of overdose caused by other medicines or the symptoms of appendicitis. This may make it difficult for your doctor to diagnose these conditions. Make sure your doctor knows that you are taking this medicine if you have other symptoms of appendicits such as stomach or lower abdominal pain, cramping, or soreness. Also, if you think you may have taken an overdose of any medicine, tell your doctor that you are taking this medicine.

Side Effects of This Medicine

Along with its needed effects, a medicine may cause some unwanted effects. Although not all of these side effects appear very often, when they do occur they may require medical attention. Check with your doctor as soon as possible if any of the following side effects occur:

Less common or rare
- Sore throat and fever
- Unusual bleeding or bruising
- Unusual tiredness or weakness

Signs of overdose
- Clumsiness or unsteadiness
- Drowsiness (severe)
- Dryness of mouth, nose, or throat (severe)
- Feeling faint
- Flushing or redness of face
- Hallucinations (seeing, hearing, or feeling things that are not there)
- Seizures
- Shortness of breath or troubled breathing
- Trouble in sleeping

Other side effects may occur which usually do not require medical attention. These side effects may go away during treatment as your body adjusts to the medicine. However, check with your doctor or pharmacist if any of the following side effects continue or are bothersome:

More common—rare with terfenadine
- Drowsiness
- Thickening of bronchial secretions

Less common or rare
- Blurred vision or any change in vision
- Confusion
- Difficult or painful urination
- Dizziness
- Dryness of mouth, nose, or throat
- Increased sensitivity of skin to sun
- Loss of appetite (increased appetite with cyproheptadine)
- Nightmares
- Ringing or buzzing sound in ears
- Skin rash
- Stomach upset or stomach pain (more common with pyrilamine and tripelennamine)
- Unusual excitement, nervousness, restlessness, or irritability
- Unusual increase in sweating
- Unusually fast heartbeat

Use of antihistamines is not recommended in premature or newborn infants. Serious side effects, such as seizures, are more likely to occur in children and would be of greater risk to these infants.

Children and elderly patients are usually more sensitive to the effects of antihistamines. Confusion, difficult and painful urination, dizziness, drowsiness, feeling faint, or dryness of mouth, nose, or throat may be more likely to occur in elderly patients. Also, nightmares or unusual excitement, nervousness, restlessness, or irritability may be more likely to occur in children and in elderly patients.

Other side effects not listed above may also occur in some patients. If you notice any other effects, check with your doctor or pharmacist.

December 1986

Coping with Technical Language

A problem with many drug references is that they are written in complex language. They use medical terms that may be unfamiliar, especially to new students. The descriptions of drugs assume that the reader has a background in anatomy, physiology, diseases, and pharmacology.

An important aim of this book is to help you learn enough so that you can understand what you find in drug references. You will learn important technical terms, basic principles to help you understand how drugs work, and enough about various diseases so that the reason for giving a particular drug will become clear.

At the end of this unit there is an exercise in using the PDR. It could be used for any drug reference your agency has on hand. This may be the first time you have looked at a drug reference. Do not be worried if the words and the descriptions seem completely unfamiliar. By the end of this course, you will probably be surprised at how much more material will make sense to you.

Coping with Changing Information

Information about drugs is constantly changing. New drugs appear all the time and old drugs are taken off the market. Drug research turns up better ways of using drugs and administering them. This means that drug references can become outdated very quickly. Some reference publishers send out regular supplements with information updates. These should be checked along with the drug reference. Another place to look for current information on drug administration is the **package inserts**. These are printed sheets of information found inside the boxes in which drugs are packaged. This is the same information that is in the PDR.

This book will help you cope with changing information on drugs. After studying the units, you will know general principles about groups or classifications of drugs. Any new information that becomes available should then fit easily into your general understanding of drugs.

PREPARING YOUR OWN DRUG CARDS

Because there are so many drugs and so much information about them, no one can expect to keep all of the important facts constantly in mind. Many health workers find it useful to prepare 5" x 7" index cards containing information about the drugs that they most often use in their work. This saves time, because they can find the information quicker in their card files than in a huge drug reference. Of course, the information on the cards must be updated regularly to keep them current. Drug cards can be designed according to your own needs. However, they should include at least these entries (discussed more fully in Units 2 and 3):

- Drug name, both generic and trade name.
- Drug classification, or the group a drug belongs to, such as analgesics (pain relievers), antipyretics (fever reducers), antacids, laxatives, and so on (you will learn the basic drug classifications in later units).
- Forms in which the drug is available (tablets, capsules, etc.).
- Action, or how the drug interacts with the organs or systems that it is supposed to affect.
- Uses of the drug.
- Side effects and adverse reactions.
- Signs of drug poisoning (toxicity).
- Route of administration.
- Dosage range and usual adult dose.
- Special instructions for giving the medication, including nursing care required, what to tell the patient about expected side effects and precautions, and so on.
- A note on where you got your information (specific drug reference, package insert, etc.).

A sample drug card is shown in Figure 1-9. Beginning in Unit 6, you will find product information tables listing representative drugs in the major drug categories. These tables can serve as a guide for what you should include on your drug cards. As you study the drugs in Units 6 through 15, make a habit of preparing drug cards for the medications you expect to be giving in your own health facility.

> Drug: bisacodyl (Dulcolax)
> Classification: Cathartic (laxative)
> Forms: 5-mg enteric-coated tablets, 10-mg suppositories
> Actions: Stimulates peristalsis by irritating the colon
> Uses: Relieves constipation
>   Cleanses bowel before surgery and bowel examination
> Dose: Usual dose 2 tablets (range 2-6 tablets); 1 suppository
> Side effects: Suppositories may cause burning sensation or local inflammation
> Special instructions/nursing implications:
>   Suppositories work within 15-60 minutes; tablets 6-12 hours
>   Enteric tablets should not be chewed, cut, or crushed;
>   may cause nausea; not to be taken orally within
>   1 hour of taking an antacid or milk
> Source: PDR, 1987, (41st Ed.)   R.B.j.

Figure 1-9 Sample drug card.

DRUG LEGISLATION

The U.S. government regulates the composition, uses, names, labeling, and testing of drugs. Since the early 1900s, many laws have been made to enforce the official drug standards and to protect the public from unreliable and unsafe drugs (Figure 1-10). Federal agencies have been set up to see that these laws are followed. Table 1-1 lists the major drug laws and their enforcing agencies.

The first law, the **Pure Food and Drug Act**, was passed in 1906. This law states that only drugs listed in the USP/NF may be prescribed and sold because these meet the required standards. Various amendments to this act regulate prescriptions, require the testing of new drugs, and call for complete information on drug effects and dangers. The **Food, Drug, and Cosmetic Act (FDCA)** of 1938 spells out added regulations concerning the purity, strength, effectiveness, safety, labeling, and packaging of drugs. It also states that the government must review safety studies on new drugs before they can be put on the market. This provision was added after more than 100 deaths resulted from a poorly tested and mislabeled sulfanilamide product. The FDCA is enforced by the **Food and Drug Administration (FDA)**.

Figure 1-10 Drug laws protect the public and you.

Since 1962, the FDA has required proof that new drugs are effective as well as safe.

Another important law is the **Controlled Substances Act of 1970** (officially, the Comprehensive Drug Abuse Prevention and Control Act of 1970). It identifies the drugs that are dangerous or subject to abuse, such as narcotics, depressants, stimulants, and psychedelic drugs. The law states that the manufacture, distribution, and dispensing of these drugs must be controlled. Otherwise, people might use these drugs carelessly and be injured physically or mentally.

Table 1-1 Major Drug Laws

LEGISLATIVE ACT	ENFORCEMENT AGENCY
Pure Food and Drug Act of 1906	None
Approves USP/NF and requires that drugs meet official standards	
Requires labeling of medicines containing morphine	
Amendment of 1912 prohibits making false claims about health benefits of a drug	
Food, Drug, and Cosmetic Act (FDCA) of 1938	**Food and Drug Administration (FDA)**
Regulates content and sales of drugs and cosmetics	Under the Department of Health and Human Services
Requires accurate labeling and warnings against unsafe use	Can investigate manufacturers, withdraw approval of drugs, and control shipment and testing
Requires government review of safety studies before selling new drugs	Enforces FDCA by prosecuting offending firms and seizing goods
Amendment of 1952 allows certain drugs to be dispensed by prescription only, and to be refilled only on a doctor's order; also recognizes OTC drugs as drugs that do not require a prescription	Drug manufacturers must register with the FDA and report to the FDA all adverse reactions resulting from the use of their products
Amendment of 1962 requires proof of effectiveness and safety before marketing new drugs and full information on advantages, side effects, and contraindications	Reviews studies of safety and effectiveness of new drugs
Certain drugs must carry the label "*Caution: Federal law prohibits dispensing without a prescription*"	
Controlled Substances Act of 1970	**Drug Enforcement Administration (DEA)**
Identifies and regulates manufacture and sale of narcotics and dangerous drugs	Under Department of Justice
Provides funding for education on drug abuse, rehabilitation of addicts and law enforcement	May punish violators by fines, imprisonment, or both
Classifies drugs into Schedules I-V according to medical usefulness and possible abuse (see Table 1-2)	

Controlled substances are grouped into five categories or schedules, and each schedule has its own special restrictions, as shown in Table 1-2. A record is kept each time a controlled substance is sold, noting how much of the drug was sold. There are restrictions on how often and how prescriptions can be refilled. All prescriptions must be written in ink. Oral emergency orders for Schedule II substances may be filled, but the physician must provide a written prescription within 72 hours.

Pharmacists must follow carefully the rules outlined in the Controlled Substances Act. Violation of the law is punishable by fine or imprisonment or both. The agency that enforces this act is the **Drug Enforcement Administration (DEA)**.

Doctors must also follow the law in prescribing controlled substances. They need a special license that is obtained from the

> **NOTE:**
> Be sure you understand these terms:
> - *OTC drugs*—can be bought and sold without a prescription
> - *prescription drugs*—must have a doctor's prescription (either oral or written) in order to be bought and sold; also called legend drugs.
> - *controlled substances*—drugs that have special restrictions on who can prescribe and sell them and on how often they can be prescribed.

Table 1-2 Drug classifications under the Controlled Substances Act of 1970[a]

Schedule I Drugs
High potential for abuse
To be used for research only
Not to be prescribed as lacks safety use in treatment
Examples: alfentanil, fenethylline, hashish, heroin, lysergic acid diethylamide (LSD), marijuana, methaqualone (*Quaalude*), peyote, psilocyn

Schedule II Drugs
High potential for abuse; severe physical and psychological dependence
Acceptable medical uses, with restrictions
Dispensed by prescription only
No refills without a new written prescription from the physician
Examples: amphetamines, cocaine, meperidine HCl (*Demerol*), methadone, methylphenidate hydrochloride (*Ritalin*), morphine, opium, pentobarbital (*Nembutal*)

Schedule III Drugs
Moderate potential for abuse, psychological dependence, low physical dependence
Acceptable medical uses
By prescription only, may be refilled 5 times in 6 months if authorized by the physician
Examples: barbiturates, butabarbital (*Butisol*), glutethimide (*Doriden*), phendimetrazine (*Bacarate, Bontril PDM*), secobarbital (*Seconal*), *Tylenol* with codeine

Schedule IV Drugs
Lower potential of abuse than Schedule III; limited psychological and physical dependence
Acceptable medical uses
By prescription only, may be refilled 5 times in 6 months if authorized by the physician
Examples: chloral hydrate (*Noctec*), chlordiazepoxide (*Librium*), diazepam (*Valium*), flurazepam HCl (*Dalmane*), oxazepam (*Serax*), phenobarbital, propoxyphene HCl (*Darvon*)

Schedule V Drugs
Low potential for abuse
Acceptable medical uses
OTC narcotic drugs, but sold only by registered pharmacist; buyer must be 18 years old and show ID
Examples: cough syrups with codeine, e.g., guaifenesin (*Naldecon DX*) and *Cheracol* with codeine, diphenoxylate HCl with atropine sulfate (*Lomotil*[b]), *Novahistine* expectorant, *Parepectolin*

[a] Source: Drug Enforcement Administration, U.S. Department of Justice. Check with your local DEA office for current regulations.
[b] Requires prescription.

DEA for each office from which they practice and must renew or register this license each year. They are given one tax stamp and number for each license. This number, called the DEA number, must be shown on any prescription for controlled substances.

In order to keep a supply of controlled substances in an office or a health facility, the staff must fill out special order forms and records. These forms show how many controlled substances are being kept at the facility and also who received doses of the drugs and how unused doses were disposed of. Every two years a physical inventory of all controlled substances in the office must be made. You will learn about these forms when you study Unit 5.

YOU AND THE LAW

As a member of the health care team, you are responsible for knowing the laws controlling drug use. Claiming ignorance of the law will not stand up in court if you are ever accused of irresponsible handling and administration of drugs.

How can you be sure you understand the law? As a first step, study carefully Tables 1-1 and 1-2. These summarize a great deal of information about the federal drug laws. You should be aware that the specific drugs under each schedule in the Controlled Substances Act may change. Your health facility will have an up-to-date list of controlled substances from the DEA.

Get copies of federal drug laws from the library or from the FDA.

As a next step, you should study the laws of your state. These regulate such things as who may give medications, what kinds of training and supervision are required, who may keep the records, and who may take down prescriptions over the phone.

Your own health agency will also have regulations for you to follow. There will be special rules, for example, if your agency receives Medicaid or Medicare funds from the government. You should also find out the lines of authority in your agency—in other words, who is in charge of what and who supervises whom. That way, you can go to the right person when you have a legal question about giving a certain drug.

By knowing the law, you protect yourself from errors and possible lawsuit. But there is a more important benefit—the safety of your patient. By showing your awareness of drug laws, you help to educate your patients. You also gain their cooperation in following the laws. Drug laws are designed to protect the public. They depend on your example and your support.

18 Administering Medications

EXERCISES

A. Define the following terms and abbreviations:

1. Drug _Chemical that affects body_
2. Pharmacology _Study of drugs_
3. Pharmacodynamics _study of how drugs interact c body tissues_
4. Anatomy _the structure of body parts_
5. Physiology _function of body parts_
6. Psychology _study of the mind_
7. Drug standards _all drugs c same name must be of uniform strength, purity, quality_
8. Drug references _helps to understand how/why_
9. PDR _Physicians Desk Reference_
10. USP DI _United States Pharmacopeia Dispensing Info_
11. USP/NF _United States Pharmacopeia National Formulary_
12. Pathology _Changes in body caused by disease_
13. Metabolism _Chemical process that takes place in cell_
14. USAN _United States Adopted Names_
15. Pharmacokinetics _Study of drug movement in body_

B. Name four sources of drugs and give an example of a drug that comes from each source.

Source	Example
1. plant - foxglove	digitalis
2. animals	insulin
3. minerals	iron
4. synthesis	thiazides

Orientation to Medications   19

C. From Column 2, select the term or phrase that best matches each item in Column 1.

Column 1

_e_ 1. chemical name
_c_ 2. generic name
_a_ 3. trade name
_f_ 4. assay
_b_ 5. bioassay
_d_ 6. routes of administration
_h_ 7. USP/NF
_g_ 8. PDR
_j_ 9. USAN
_i_ 10. official name

Column 2

a. *Visine* eye drops
b. finding the therapeutic dose by testing a drug in animals, human volunteers, or isolated tissue
c. hydrochlorothiazide
d. methods of giving drugs
e. 6-Chloro-3,4-dihydro-2H-1,2,4-benzothiadiazine-7-sulfonamide 1,1-dioxide
f. identifying and measuring ingredients in a laboratory
g. contains information about drug products provided by pharmaceutical companies
h. contains descriptions of official drugs and standards
i. name of drug listed in USP/NF
j. system that adopts generic names

D. Name the six therapeutic uses of drugs. Give examples.

Use	Example
1. disease prevention	vaccine
2. health maintenance	vitamins, insulin
3. relieving symptoms	aspirin/analgesics
4. cure	antibiotics
5. diagnosis	radiopaque dye
6. prevention of pregnancy	contraceptive

E. Food for thought: Why do you suppose we have drug standards and drug laws? Try to imagine what the medical field would be like without them.

F. Name the three major drug laws and the agencies that enforce them.

Law and Date	Enforcing Agency
1. Pure Food/Drug Act 1906	FDA
2. Food Drug Cosmetic 1938	FDA
3. Controlled Substance 1970	DEA

Review Table 1-1 and learn the main features of the three laws.

G. Match the drugs to their schedules or classes as spelled out in the Controlled Substances Act of 1970.

Schedule   Drugs

_e_ I   a. some barbiturates, *Doriden*, *Tylenol* with codeine

_b_ II   b. opium, morphine, *Demerol*, amphetamines, *Nembutal*

_a_ III   c. cough syrup with codeine, *Lomotil*, *Novahistine* expectorant

_d_ IV   d. *Librium*, *Valium*, phenobarbital, *Noctec*, *Dalmane*, *Darvon*

_c_ V   e. heroin, hashish, LSD, peyote, alfentanil

H. Define these legal classifications for drugs.

1. OTC drugs *no restrictions for buying or selling*

2. prescription drugs *must have license to prescribe, license to sell*

3. controlled substances *restrictions on who, how often can be prescribed*

I. Janie has just been hired for a new job in a nursing home. She wants to make sure she knows what she *is* and *is not* allowed to do with regard to giving medications.

What advice would you give her? _____

_____

_____

_____

J. Using a drug reference: the PDR: (This exercise could be adapted to other drug references.) The PDR is divided into seven sections:

Manufacturer's Index (white pages): Names and addresses of drug companies, along with a list of drugs manufactured by each company.

Product Name Index (pink): Drugs listed alphabetically by brand names.

Product Category Index (blue): Drugs grouped according to their effects (e.g., analgesics, anesthetics, decongestants).

Generic and Chemical Name Index (yellow): Brand names grouped under their generic or chemical names.

Product Identification Section (glossy): Full color photographs of selected medications, a quick reference for routine identification or in case of overdose or accidental poisoning.

Product Information (white): Main part of the book; gives detailed information about drug products, listed alphabetically by drug companies.

Diagnostic Product Information (green): Special section for drugs used to diagnose diseases.

The following exercises will help you learn how to use the PDR. Obtain a copy of the PDR from your school, nursing unit, or clinic. You will also need a medical dictionary to define technical terms.

1. You are giving Mr. Jones some *Tylenol* every few hours after surgery. You would like to know something more about the drug, so you consult the PDR. *Tylenol* is a brand name. Find the section in the PDR that lists drugs alphabetically by brand names. What color are the pages?

   pink

2. Look up *Tylenol* in the section you turned to in question 1. How many different forms of *Tylenol* are listed there? *8*

   Is there a small diamond to the left of any of the *Tylenol* forms? If so, that means there is a photograph of it in the "Product Identification" section. Find the photograph.

3. Using the page number given for *Tylenol* tablets, look them up in the "Product Information" section. The generic name is listed just after the word "*Tylenol*." What is it?

   acetaminophen

4. Read through the description of *Tylenol* tablets. What kinds of information are given about the product? List the main headings (shown in darker print).

   Description, action, indications, precautions, adverse reactions, usual dosage, how supplied

5. Under "Actions," *Tylenol* is described as an analgesic and an antipyretic. Look these words up in the dictionary. What do they mean?

   a. analgesic *relieves pain*

   b. antipyretic *relieves fever*

6. Look at the section marked "Indications." List the conditions for which *Tylenol* might be ordered. (Use the dictionary to help you understand the technical terms.)

   pain of arthritis, rheumatism, headache, muscle pain, nerve pain, menstrual pain, discomfort fever / colds

7. Look at the section called "Precautions and Adverse Reactions." What are the side effects of *Tylenol*?

   rare

22 Administering Medications

8. What is the usual adult dose of *Tylenol* tablets? _1-2 tablets - 4-6 hrs_
   no more than 12 a day

9. *Tylenol* tablets come in containers of various sizes. Find the section that tells you what sizes are available. List the sizes here.
   tins of 12, bottles 24, 50, 100, 200 tablets

10. Look up the drug **simethicone** in the "Generic and Chemical Name Index." Under it you will find a list of trade name products containing simethicone. Look up **one** of these trade name products. Then answer questions 4 through 9 for that product.

    Types of information: _____

    Actions (and definitions): _____

    Indications: _____

    Side effects: _____

    Dosage: _____

    How supplied: _____

11. Mrs. Allen has a skin condition called **eczema**. Her doctor has ordered some *Cordran* to help heal the dry, flaky sores (lesions) on her arms. You are not sure how to apply this ointment. Use the PDR to help you find out.

    Application of *Cordran*: _Clean area; apply cream_
    lotion or ointment sparingly bid or tid

12. *Tranxene* has been ordered for an elderly patient in the nursing home. What starting dosage is recommended in the PDR for an elderly patient?
    _15 mg_

K. Following the example in Figure 1-9, prepare drug cards for three drugs used often where you work. Or use the information from Part J to make drug cards for *Tylenol*, *Cordran*, and *Tranxene*.

ANSWERS TO EXERCISES

A. Definitions
   1. Any chemical that affects living things, including the human body.
   2. The study of drugs: sources, chemical makeup, uses, how to prepare them, and so on.
   3. What happens when drugs interact with the cells of the human body.
   4. The structure of the body and its parts.
   5. How body systems, organs, tissues, and cells work.
   6. The study of the mind, how people think, people's emotions, and so forth.
   7. Rules concerning the strength, quality, and purity of drugs.
   8. Books that give information about drugs.
   9. *Physicians' Desk Reference*, a drug reference.
   10. *United States Pharmacopeia Dispensing Information*, a drug reference.
   11. *United States Pharmacopeia/National Formulary*, a drug reference containing the standards for official drugs.
   12. Study of the changes in the body caused by disease.
   13. Chemical processes that take place in a cell.
   14. United States Adopted Names, a system for adopting generic drug names.
   15. The study of the drug movement in and out of the body.

B. Drug sources
   1. Plants: digitalis, opium, belladonna, vitamin C, gums, oils.
   2. Animals: insulin, heparin.
   3. Minerals: iron, iodine, salt, calcium.
   4. Chemical synthesis: hydrochlorothiazide (*HydroDiuril*); biogenetic engineering: insulin, vaccines.

C. Matching
   1. e   6. d
   2. c   7. h
   3. a   8. g
   4. f   9. j
   5. b   10. i

D. Drug uses (may be answered in any order)
   1. Prevent disease: vaccines
   2. Maintain health: insulin, vitamins.
   3. Diagnose disease: radiopaque dye, barium.
   4. Treat disease: aspirin, antihistamines.
   5. Cure disease: antibiotics
   6. Prevent pregnancy: contraceptives

E. Drug standards (no written answer required)

F. Drug laws and agencies
   1. Pure Food and Drug Act of 1906, no agency.
   2. Food, Drug, and Cosmetic Act of 1938, enforced by Food and Drug Administration.
   3. Controlled Substances Act of 1970, enforced by Drug Enforcement Administration.

24 Administering Medications

G. Matching
   I. e
   II. b
   III. a
   IV. d
   V. c

H. Legal terms
   1. Over-the-counter drugs can be bought and sold without a prescription.
   2. Prescription drugs need a doctor's written or verbal order to be bought and sold.
   3. Controlled substances have restrictions on who can prescribe, how, and how often.

I. Drug laws

   Janie should study the federal and state laws controlling medication administration. She should also study the nursing home's own regulations, and she should find out who is in charge so she knows to whom questions should be addressed.

J. Using the PDR
   1. Pink
   2. About eight (this will vary from year to year).
   3. Acetaminophen.
   4. Description, actions, indications, precautions, adverse reactions, usual dosage, overdosage, how supplied.
   5. a. Pain reliever.
      b. Fever reducer
   6. Pain of arthritis and rheumatism, headache, muscle pain (myalgia), nerve pain (neuralgia), menstrual cramps (dysmenorrhea), discomfort and fever of colds.
   7. Side effects are rare.
   8. One or two tablets every 4-6 hours, no more than 12 per day.
   9. Tins of 12; bottles of 24, 50, 100, and 200 tablets.
   10. (Answers depend on product selected.)
   11. Apply a thin film to affected area 2-3 times daily.
   12. Dosage 7.5-15 mg.

K. Drug cards

   Show your drug cards to your instructor or the nurse in charge.

Unit 2

Pharmacodynamics

In this unit you will learn what happens to drugs when they enter the human body and how they produce their effects. You will study how drugs are affected by normal body processes, by characteristics of individual patients, and by the method and time of administration. You will also become familiar with the adverse reactions that can occur with drug administration.

In this unit, you learn to:

- Define drug action and drug effect.
- State the four basic drug actions.
- Name and describe the four body processes that affect drug action.
- Identify at least 10 factors influencing drug action.
- State the difference between systemic and local drug effects.
- State the difference between the main effect and side effects.
- Recognize descriptions of major adverse reactions.
- Define drug dependence and explain the difference between psychological and physical dependence.
- List the symptoms of withdrawal.
- State the health worker's responsibilities with regard to adverse reactions, drug dependence, and drug abuse.

PHARMACODYNAMICS AND BODY CELLS

Pharmacodynamics (fahr'mah-ko-di-nam-iks) means the interaction between drugs and living things such as the human body. It refers to the chemical changes that drugs cause in the body cells, and how those chemical changes alter body functions. The term **drug action** is used to describe the way drugs cause chemical changes in body cells. **Drug effects** are the physical changes that occur in the body as a result of the drug action.

To understand pharmacodynamics, you need to know something about **cells**. Cells are the basic building blocks of all living things, including the human body. Although cells work together in groups, each individual cell does certain routine things on its own to keep itself alive. Like all living things, it needs food and needs to eliminate waste materials. Human cells take in oxygen and nutrients, and they eliminate carbon dioxide and waste liquids.

Cells are very tiny—there are millions of them in the human body. If you look at a cell under a microscope you can see the parts that carry out the routine jobs that keep the cell alive (Figure 2-1).

There are many different types of cells in the human body. Body organs and tissues are made up of similar cells held together by a special gluelike substance. These similar cells work together to carry out the jobs that organs and tissues must perform. For example, the liver is composed of specially designed cells that together perform the functions of the liver.

When a person takes a drug, the outcome depends on how that drug affects one or more groups of body cells. As you study pharmacodynamics, keep in mind that *drugs always act on body cells* in some manner.

DRUG ACTION

Drugs are chemicals that are known to have specific effects on the body. When one of the chemicals comes in contact with body cells, it causes changes in the cell molecules. That is, the chemical combines with or alters the molecules in body cells so as to change the way the cells work.

Drugs do not cause cells to function in entirely new and different ways, however. Usually they either slow down or speed up

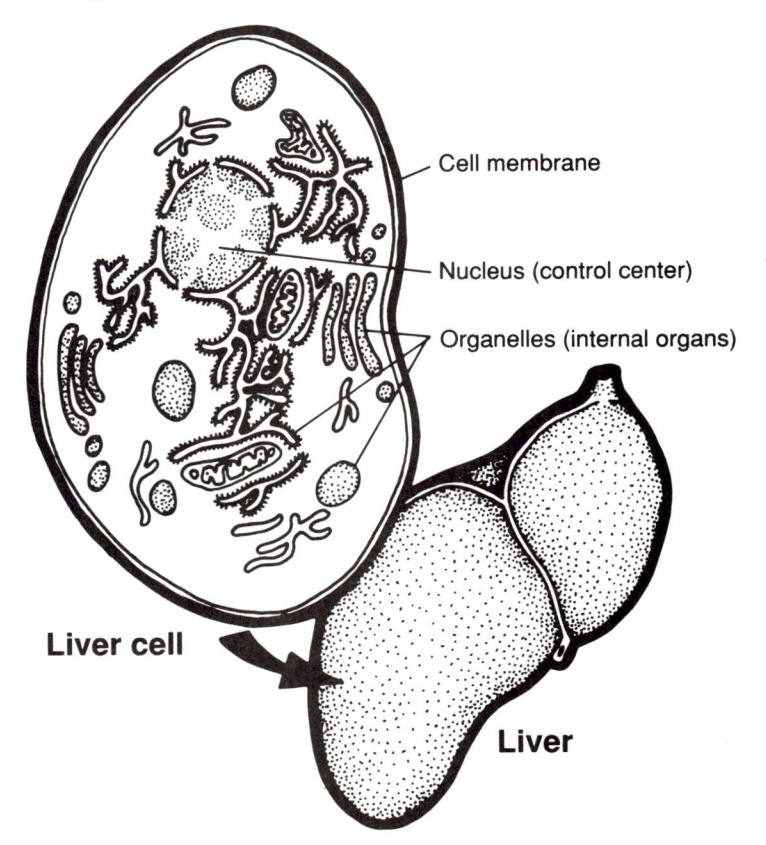

Figure 2-1 Diagram of a liver cell.

the ordinary processes that the cells carry out. For example, antihistamines slow the body's natural reactions to irritation, and stimulants speed up the energy-producing functions of cells.

Some drugs destroy certain cells or parts of cells. For example, some antibiotics kill disease germs, and fluorouracil and radioisotopes of cobalt kill cancer cells. Other drugs act to replace or supplement natural substances that the body lacks because of an organ malfunction or poor nutrition. Insulin is a drug taken by diabetics because they lack natural insulin.

Once a drug is taken, it enters into certain processes that go on in the body at all times. These processes are the body's normal means of using food and oxygen to produce energy. Energy is needed for cell growth and repair, for warmth, and for movement. Drugs are treated just like any other substance that enters the body, such as food, drink, and air. The only difference is that each drug interacts in a different way with the normal processes carried on by body cells.

VOCABULARY

absorption: passage of a substance into the bloodstream from the site of administration

action: the chemical changes in body cells and tissues caused by a drug

adverse reactions: dangerous or unexpected effects of drugs

allergy: reaction of the body cell to a foreign substance (antigen) to which it has previously developed antibodies; also called **hypersensitivity**

anaphylaxis: severe allergic reaction, often strong enough to produce shock (see also **shock**)

antagonism: two drugs acting together to cause a lesser response than the sum of their individual effects

antibody: a substance produced in the body that helps the body fight off "foreign" invaders like germs and antigens

antidote: drug that counteracts the effects of drug overdose or toxicity

antigen: substance that stimulates the production of antibodies and causes allergic reactions

biotransformation: normal body process by which substances are chemically broken down into a form that the body can excrete; part of the cells' work of burning fuel for growth and energy; also known as **metabolism**

capillaries: tiny blood vessels with very thin walls that let certain substances pass through them

cardiac arrest: sudden stoppage of the heart (heart attack)

cell: smallest living unit in the human body, able to carry out routine processes to keep itself alive

cumulation: collection of drugs in the body due to slow biotransformation or slow excretion

cyanosis: bluish color of the skin due to a lack of oxygen in the blood

depress: slow down

dependence: a compulsion to continue taking a drug; can be physical and/or psychological

distribution: transport of drugs to body cells and spaces between cells

drug abuse: taking drugs for their mind-altering effects or taking too many drugs or too much of a drug

dyspnea: difficult or labored breathing

edema: fluid collecting in body tissues

effect: a physical or psychological change in the patient brought about by a drug

enzyme: a chemical that speeds up biotransformation

euphoria: false sense of well-being

excretion: the removal of waste substances from the body

genetic: determined by heredity

habituation: drug dependence characterized by psychological dependence

hallucinogens: drugs that cause a person to see, hear, feel, taste, or smell things that aren't there (hallucinate)

histamine: substances released from injured cells during allergic reaction, responsible for allergic symptoms

hypotension: low blood pressure

idiosyncrasy: a peculiar, unusual individual response to a drug

local: having an effect in the nearby area; for example, eyedrops designed to affect only the eye

main effect: the therapeutic effect for which a drug is administered

overdose: drug dose that is too large for a person's age, size, or physical condition

pH: a measure of whether a substance is acidic or alkaline (basic)

placebo effect: a therapeutic effect that results from a patient's belief in the benefits of a medication (a **placebo** can be a pill containing sugar or an injection of sterile water)

potentiation: two drugs acting together to cause a greater response than the combined effects of each drug taken separately; also called **synergism**

reservoir: a tissue where drugs tend to collect; different drugs tend to collect in different tissues

shock: a serious condition in which blood circulation is very slow and body tissues suffer from a lack of oxygen

side effects: drug effects that are not part of the treatment goal

stimulate: to speed up

systemic: having an effect throughout the body

tolerance: resistance to the effect of a drug

sensitivity: allergic-type response to a drug that develops after several doses; also called **hypersensitivity**

toxic: poisonous

withdrawal symptoms: set of physical reactions that occur when a person stops taking a drug on which he or she is physically dependent

DRUG ACTION

- slowing down, or **depressing**, the normal work of cells
- speeding up, or **stimulating**, the work of cells
- **destroying** cells or cell parts
- **replacing** substances that the body lacks or fails to produce (Figure 2-2).

Figure 2-2 The four drug actions: depressing, stimulating, or destroying cells and replacing substances.

These interactions are determined by many things: the size and shape of the drug molecules, their ability to dissolve in water or fat, the pH balance of drugs and cells, and the electrical charges of molecules. The details need not concern you, but you should have an understanding of four basic body processes that affect drug action: **absorption, distribution, biotransformation,** and **excretion** (Figure 2-3).

Absorption

No matter where they enter the body, sooner or later most drugs pass into the bloodstream and then move throughout the body. The passage of a drug from the site of administration into the bloodstream is called **absorption**.

Unless the drug is properly absorbed, it may not reach the organs or tissues that it is supposed to affect. The speed of absorption and the amount of absorption are important in pharmacodynamics. Drug action depends on how quickly and completely the drug is absorbed. When an exact serum level is important, blood tests can be ordered to find out how much drug is present in the bloodstream after absorption.

The type of drug, the amount of drug given, and the method of administration all have an effect on absorption. Some drugs dissolve in the mouth and are absorbed into the bloodstream directly through the lining of the mouth. Some are swallowed and enter the bloodstream through the walls of the stomach or intestine. Drugs that are injected into skin or muscles pass into the bloodstream through nets of tiny blood vessels that nourish these areas.

Some drugs are not absorbed but are injected directly into the bloodstream. Drugs

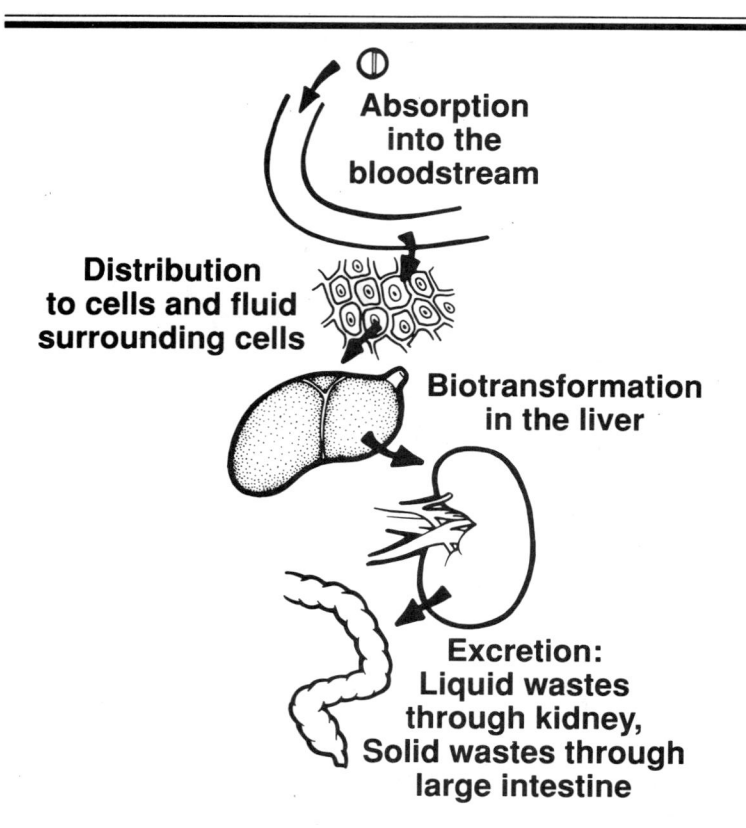

Figure 2-3 How a drug is handled by the human body.

ABSORPTION BEGINS	ROUTE	EXAMPLE
Mouth	sublingual	nitroglycerin
Stomach/intestine	oral	ibuprofen
In the muscle	IM	meperidine
Under the skin	SC	epinephrine, insulin
Bloodstream	IV	antibiotics, nalorphine

applied to the skin are usually intended *not* to be absorbed into the blood, but rather to affect only the cells in the skin layers.

The elderly tend not to have much difficulty with the process of absorption, but when they do, it may be due to reduction of cells and their function.

Distribution

After a drug is absorbed into the bloodstream, it is carried throughout the body by a complex network of blood vessels. Some of the drug passes out of the bloodstream through the thin walls of tiny vessels called **capillaries**. The drug then enters body cells through pores in the outer cell layers. It may also pass right through cells into the fluid-filled spaces between the cells. This movement of the drug into the body cells and into the spaces between cells is called **distribution**. The exact path that any given drug follows depends on the interaction between the drug and specific body tissues. Some tissues can combine with certain drugs and others cannot.

Distribution is affected by the chemical makeup of the drug, the amount of drug given, and cell conditions such as temperature and pH. If distribution is slow, the effect of the drug is not felt until some time after administration. If distribution is fast, drug effects are noticed almost immediately after administration. Some drugs tend to collect in certain organs or tissues, called **reservoirs**. If drugs do collect in reservoirs, they are released into the body more slowly than drugs that are evenly distributed at the start.

For the elderly, their growth of adipose tissue may cause drug accumulation in these reservoirs.

Biotransformation

Metabolism or biotransformation is a series of chemical reactions that break down the drug into different substances that are easier for the body to eliminate. This is a natural process much like the digestion of food. It is necessary so that the body can rid itself of the waste products that are left over after the cells make use of nutrients or drugs.

Enzymes are special body proteins that speed up the process of biotransformation, or metabolism. They cause chemical reactions to occur many thousands of times faster than they ordinarily would. Most of the biotransformation of drugs takes place in the liver. This very important organ, located in the abdominal cavity, is responsible for many body chemical reactions. Biotransformation also takes place to some extent in the lungs, the intestines, and the kidneys.

Some drugs cannot work on body cells *until* they are broken down chemically, so that biotransformation actually changes them into active drugs. Other drugs become inactive and lose their power to work on body cells when they are biotransformed. With some drugs this is good, because if these drugs were to remain unchanged in the body, they could collect and cause harm.

Some drugs do not need to be biotransformed in order to be eliminated. Ether, for example, passes out of the body in exactly the same chemical form as it entered. Its odor can be detected in the urine.

Here again, the elderly must be mentioned in regard to liver function. A decrease in size and function with age might interfere with the formation of body substances or enzymes necessary for biotransformation.

Excretion

Excretion is the body's way of removing the waste products of ordinary cell processes. Drugs are excreted in the same way as other waste products. Most drugs leave the body through the kidneys and the large intestine. In the kidneys, blood is filtered and liquid waste products collect in the form of urine. In the large intestine, undigested solid wastes collect in the form of feces.

Excretion also takes place in the lungs, where gaseous wastes, such as carbon dioxide and some types of drugs, are collected from the bloodstream. These are excreted when a person exhales. Anesthetic gases such as ether and chloroform are sometimes excreted through the lungs. Some drugs are excreted in the sweat, and some even in hair. Milk glands also excrete some types of drugs. This is an important fact to know when giving medications to nursing mothers. Drugs that leave the body in a mother's milk may cause harm to the baby.

If a drug is excreted quickly, its effects are short-lived. If it is excreted slowly, its effects last longer. The rate of excretion depends on the chemical composition of the drug, the rate of biotransformation, and how often the drug is administered. The condition of the excreting organs will also determine how quickly and completely excretion takes place.

For example, in the elderly more than 50 percent of the nephron units are nonfunctional. This reduces glomerular filtration by half. Reduced kidney function can also cause the problem of drug accumulation.

FACTORS AFFECTING DRUG ACTION

No two people are exactly alike, and no drug will affect every human body in exactly the same way. Body cells differ according to a person's age, size, sex, genetic inheritance, and physical and emotional condition. These personal characteristics may cause slightly different drug actions in several people given the same drug (Figure 2-4).

Age **Size** **Genes**

Sex **Emotions** **Disease**

Figure 2-4 Individual traits that affect drug action.

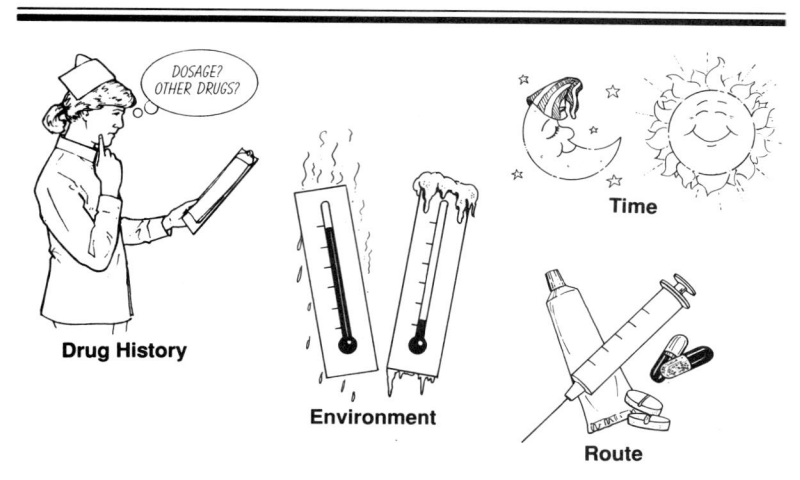

Figure 2-5 Administration factors that affect drug action.

Factors surrounding the administration of medications may also cause differences in people's responses to a drug. The route of administration, the time of day, the number and size of doses, and environmental conditions all play a role in drug action (Figure 2-5). Physicians take these factors into acccount before deciding *which* drug to prescribe and *how much* to prescribe.

Age

Most standard dosages are based on the amount of a drug that will cause the desired effect in an average adult. The bodies of very young and very old patients, however, do not function exactly like the average adult body.

In infants, the body systems are not fully developed. They may have trouble biotransforming or excreting drugs. Growing children must not take drugs that might affect their development. The body systems of the elderly may not function as efficiently as when they were middle-aged. The aging process slows down the work of certain organs, and older people are more prone to diseases that affect biotransformation and excretion. Therefore, smaller doses and different drugs are required in treating the young or the old.

Size

The size of a person and whether he or she is fat or lean have a bearing on drug action. An average dose given to a very tall person or to an obese person may have little effect. This is because there will be a low concentration of the drug in the bloodstream, body fluids, and cells. The same dose given to a small or very thin person may cause too high a concentration of the drug in the body. The proper dose is usually worked out according to a formula that takes into account body weight and/or age.

It should be mentioned though that with age some tissue is replaced by adipose tissue and this could cause a build up of some medications such as barbiturates in the cells. Therefore, you must always be watchful of your patient's response to long-term barbiturate therapy and report any unusual actions by them.

Sex

The sex of a person may influence drug action. Women may react more strongly to certain drugs than men do. This is partly because of their generally smaller size and the higher proportion of body fat. Pregnant women must be extremely careful about taking any medication. Some drugs may harm the fetus.

Genetic Factors

The individual makeup of each person causes slight differences in basic processes like biotransformation, which then affects drug action. Some people have very unusual drug reactions that may be linked to genetic factors.

Disease Conditions

Diseases can strongly affect how patients will respond to drugs. The organs necessary for biotransformation and excretion may be impaired. Diseases of the liver and kidneys will especially affect the processing and elimination of drugs. Heart disease, kidney failure, diabetes, and low blood pressure are disorders known to require special care in prescribing drugs. But any disease can change the effectiveness of a drug without warning.

Many older patients have diseases of both the liver and kidneys. Therefore, their responsiveness to drugs is greatly hindered. Often a drug simply cannot be used at all. Even though it may be specific for the patient's disease, the liver cannot change it to the therapeutically useful form, or elimination of the drug is impossible because the kidneys are damaged.

Cirrhosis (*sir-ro'sis*) of the liver and inflammation of the kidneys are two examples of diseases of the elderly that affect how patients respond to drugs.

Emotional Condition

The patient's mental state is an important factor in the success or failure of drug therapy. A patient with a positive attitude is likely to respond well to medication. A patient in a bad mood or in a state of depression or despair may not respond to some drugs. Strong feelings such as worry, jealousy, anger, or fear may have a noticeable effect on drug action.

Sometimes a positive drug effect arises just because the patient has taken something that is supposed to make him or her "feel better." This effect has nothing to do with the action of the drug itself. It is a psychological effect called the **placebo** (*plah-se'bo*) **effect**. If the patient understands the disease and its treatment and has a positive attitude, the placebo effect can add to the effectiveness of medication therapy.

As a member of the health care team, you can do much to create a positive attitude in the patient. One way is to review the important reasons for taking the medication. Another is to treat the patient in a cheerful and caring manner. And, finally, your own positive, confident attitude toward the drugs you administer will influence the patient's response to medication.

Route of Administration

Drugs are absorbed, distributed, and biotransformed differently when given by different means or routes (see Unit 3). This can affect drug action. A drug will act fastest when injected directly into the bloodstream. Drugs injected into or under the skin or into muscles take somewhat longer to take effect. Medications administered by mouth take the longest time to show their effects.

Time of Day

Care must always be taken to give drugs at the time of day ordered by the physician. There are many time-related factors that influence drug action. Drugs taken by mouth are usually given between meals, when the patient has an empty stomach. However, certain stomach-irritating drugs may be taken with meals to avoid patient discomfort. When possible, drugs that make the patient sleepy are ordered to be taken at bedtime. Drugs with stimulating effects are given at times when they will not interfere with sleep. Normal bodily functions also vary with the time of day, thus affecting drug action.

Drug-Taking History

Drug action depends on whether a patient has previously taken doses of the same or another drug. Some drugs tend to collect in the body. In this case, later doses must be made smaller to avoid overmedicating the patient. Repeated doses of a drug may also make a person less responsive to its effects. In that case, larger doses are required for the same effect.

Certain combinations of drugs can slow down or speed up drug effects, or they can show unusual and sometimes dangerous reactions. This is why patients' medical histories and charts must include careful records of the drugs they have recently taken. Doctors also check medical histories to find out whether a patient is allergic to particular drugs such as penicillin.

This area can be a problem for the elderly. They see several doctors who may be unaware of each other and the other drugs being prescribed. Each doctor prescribes what is needed in a patient's particular case, unaware of the medications other doctors have prescribed. Multiple doctors and multiple drugs can lead to serious drug interactions. "Elder-Ed: Using Your Medicines Wisely: A Guide for the Elderly" is part of a model education program for the prevention of medication misuse by the elderly. This information can be helpful, especially if you work with the elderly at home. It is available from the National Institute on Drug Abuse, 5600 Fishers Lane, Rockville, MD 20857.

Environmental Conditions

Extremes of weather affect the action of drugs because the body functions are influenced by heat and cold. Heat relaxes the blood vessels and speeds up circulation so drugs act faster. Cold slows their action by constricting the blood vessels and slowing the circulation. High altitude puts the body under stress because there is less oxygen in the air. This makes some drugs ineffective.

Table 2-1 Common side effects

Anxiety	Insomnia
Black (tarry) stools	Irritability
Blurred vision	Itching
Breast tenderness	Lightheadedness
Breathing difficulties	Loss of appetite
Bruising	Low blood pressure
Burning sensation	Menstrual irregularities
Chest pains	Nasal stuffiness
Confusion	Nausea
Constipation	Nervousness
Cramps	Palpitations
Depression	Rash
Diarrhea	Restlessness
Dizziness	Ringing in the ears
Drowsiness	Sweating
Dryness of mouth, nose, skin	Tingling
Edema (swelling)	Tremors
Fatigue	Twitching
Fever	Upset stomach
Flushing	Urinary frequency
Headache	Urine discoloration
Heartburn	Urine retention
Hiccups	Vaginal discharge
Hives	Weakness
Impotence	Weight gain

DRUG EFFECTS

The term **drug action** means the way the drug produces chemical changes in cells and tissues. The **drug effect** is the combination of biological and physical changes that take place in the body as a result of the drug action.

A drug is usually prescribed on the basis of its **main effect**. This is the desired **therapeutic effect**, or the reason the drug was administered. However, most drugs have additional effects on the body that are not part of the goal of drug therapy. These are called **side effects**.

A physician must always take possible side effects into account when planning drug treatment. Side effects can be harmless, mildly annoying, or even dangerous. Sometimes unpleasant side effects are tolerated because of the therapeutic value of the main effect. For example, the drug morphine is administered for its pain-killing effect, but it also has the side effects of respiratory depression, constipation, and urine retention.

Many side effects can be controlled or lessened by using other drugs or special procedures. For example, the drug aspirin, taken orally, is very beneficial for the treatment of arthritis but tends to irritate the lining of the stomach. This side effect is controlled by giving the drug with a glass of milk or with large amounts of water. To cite another example, diuretics can help ease water retention, but they may cause the body to excrete too much potassium. This situation can be corrected by giving potassium chloride or suggesting the patient eat potassium-rich foods such as bananas.

A partial list of common side effects is shown in Table 2-1. The list is not for you to memorize, but to show you the wide range of side effects that are possible. Side effects are related to the actions of specific drugs. In later units you will learn which side effects go with which drugs.

Drug effects are classified as either **local** or **systemic**. Some drugs affect mainly the area where they enter or are applied to the body: for example, eyedrops, sunburn creams, suppositories, and throat lozenges. These drugs are given for their local effects. Other drugs travel through the bloodstream to affect cells or tissues in various parts of the body. These are given for their systemic effects.

Proper administration of medications requires both knowledge of drug effects *and* observation of the results in the patient. The prescribed dosage is the physician's best guess as to which drug and how much of the drug is needed to bring about the desired effect in a specific patient.

So when you are giving medications, consider whether the drug is given for a local or a systemic effect. Then, while observing the patient's reaction, determine whether you are seeing the drug's main effect or a side effect (Figure 2-6). Your knowledge of drug effects is important to the work of the entire health care team— and especially important to your patient.

Figure 2-6 Questions to ask yourself while observing for medication effects.

ADVERSE REACTIONS

With proper administration, a drug usually has the desired effect— the patient feels better, bodily functions are restored, and side effects are under control. However, occasionally the body will react to a drug in an unexpected way that may endanger a patient's health and safety. These unexpected conditions are called **adverse reactions**. The most common adverse reactions will be described later, along with their causes, symptoms, and treatments.

As a person giving medications, you are expected to be aware of these possible reactions and notify your supervisor as soon as you notice any tell-tale signs. You may find it helpful to review this section again after studying the remaining units. By then you will have a better understanding of how these adverse reactions come about and how to recognize them.

Drug Allergy

This is an abnormal response that occurs because a person has developed **antibodies** against a particular drug (Figure 2-7). When a person takes the allergy-causing drug, called the **antigen**, the antibodies attack it. The reaction between antigen and antibodies causes damage to the body tissues. The injured cells release a substance called **histamine**, which is responsible for the symptoms usually seen in allergic reactions.

Figure 2-7 Drug allergy.

Mild allergic symptoms can occur either immediately after the drug is taken, or they can show up hours, days, or even weeks later. Severe allergic reactions, which can be fatal, usually begin within minutes of exposure and may require immediate emergency treatment.

In drug references, you may read warnings about **drug hypersensitivity**, which is an allergic reaction that develops over time, for example, when a person is taking a course of antibiotics. When this occurs, the person must be switched to another drug.

To avoid the problem of drug allergy, physicians try to find out whether patients have a history of allergies, such as hay fever, asthma, or skin rashes. They also ask whether patients have shown unusual reactions to any drugs taken in the past.

SYMPTOMS OF DRUG ALLERGY

- Mild: skin rashes, swelling or puffiness, nasal drainage, itchy eyes or skin, fever, and wheezing.
- Severe: shock reaction (called anaphylactic shock or anaphylaxis, an'ah-fi-lak'sis), shown by severe breathing problems (dyspnea, disp'ne-ah), extreme weakness, nausea or vomiting, and a bluish color to the skin (cyanosis, si'ah-no'sis)
- Severe low blood pressure (hypotension) and stopping of the heart (cardiac arrest) can also develop.

TREATMENT OF DRUG ALLERGY

- Notify supervisor immediately and follow instructions.
- Emergency treatment will be required for anaphylactic shock and hypotension.
- Antihistamines, epinephrine, and drugs that relieve dyspnea may be ordered by a physician.
- For milder symptoms, similar drugs are used but in smaller doses, and the patient is advised to avoid the allergy-producing drug in the future. Skin tests may be ordered to pinpoint the source of the allergy.

Unusual Effect (Idiosyncrasy, id'e-o-sin'krah-se)

Some people have strange or unique responses to certain drugs (Figure 2-8). These unusual effects or idiosyncrasies are thought to be caused by genetic factors that change the way particular drugs are biotransformed.

SYMPTOMS OF IDIOSYNCRASY
- Over- or underreaction to a drug.
- An effect completely opposite to that expected.
- Any other unexplainable and unpredictable effect that cannot be linked to drug allergy.

TREATMENT OF IDIOSYNCRASY
- STOP MEDICATION.
- Notify supervisor and follow instructions.

Figure 2-8 Unusual effect (idiosyncrasy).

Tolerance

Drug tolerance is a resistance to the effect of a drug (Figure 2-9). The exact way in which tolerance develops is not yet understood. It is known to occur in some people after repeated dosages of the same or a similar drug. In order to get the full effect of the drug, those patients have to take increasingly larger doses.

Figure 2-9 Tolerance.

SYMPTOMS OF TOLERANCE
- Lessened effect of a drug after several doses.

TREATMENT OF TOLERANCE
- Notify supervisor and follow instructions.
- The patient's physician will decide whether to increase the dosage or switch to another drug that has the same therapeutic effect.

Cumulation

Cumulation occurs when the body cannot biotransform and excrete one dose of a drug completely before the next dose is given (Figure 2-10). With repeated doses, the drug starts to collect in the blood and body tissues. This can be dangerous because high concentrations of many drugs are poisonous, or **toxic**, and can damage body cells.

Figure 2-10 Cumulation.

SYMPTOMS OF CUMULATION
- Stronger and stronger drug effects on the body with each additional dose given.

TREATMENT OF CUMULATION
- Notify supervisor as soon as this stronger effect is noticed, and follow instructions.
- Lower doses may be ordered by the physician, or another drug may be substituted.

Overdose and Toxicity

Through error, poor judgment, or attempted suicide, a patient may receive an overdose—a dose that is too large for his or her age, size, and physical condition. This can be dangerous because any drug can act like a poison if taken in too large a dose. Toxicity means the drug's ability to poison the body (Figure 2-11).

SYMPTOMS OF OVERDOSE AND TOXICITY
- Depend on the drug and are related to extremes of normal drug action. For example, there are drugs that slow down the nervous system (e.g., central nervous system (CNS) depressants.) Taken in overdose, these drugs slow the nervous system so much that it may "forget" to make the heart beat and the lungs breathe.
- Drug references often describe symptoms of overdose for each drug, so you can be aware when this occurs.

TREATMENT OF OVERDOSE AND TOXICITY
- STOP MEDICATION.
- NOTIFY SUPERVISOR IMMEDIATELY.
- Emergency measures may be needed to keep the person alive.
- There may be an antidote for the poison. This is a drug that has the opposite effect and can reverse the overdose symptoms.

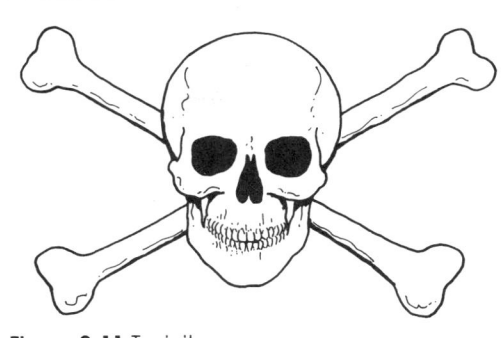

Figure 2-11 Toxicity.

Drug Interactions (Synergism and Antagonism)

Sometimes two or more drugs are given to a patient as part of drug therapy, or a patient may be taking an OTC medication at home for some other ailment. Whenever more than one drug is taken, the possibility of drug interaction has to be considered. Two or more drugs may interact, with the result that the degree and kind of effects produced may be altered. This is called a **drug interaction**.

When two drugs administered together produce a more powerful response than the sum of their individual effects, this is called **synergism** (sin'er-jizm) or **potentiation** (Figure 2-12). Patients who take sedatives, for example, are advised to avoid drinking alcoholic beverages. This is because alcohol causes sedatives to have a much stronger, possibly fatal, effect. When two drugs interact to cause a lesser response than the sum of their individual effects, this is called **antagonism** (Figure 2-13). Antacids such as *Gelusil* should not be given to patients who are on oral tetracycline, an antibiotic, because they work against the absorption of tetracycline through the intestines.

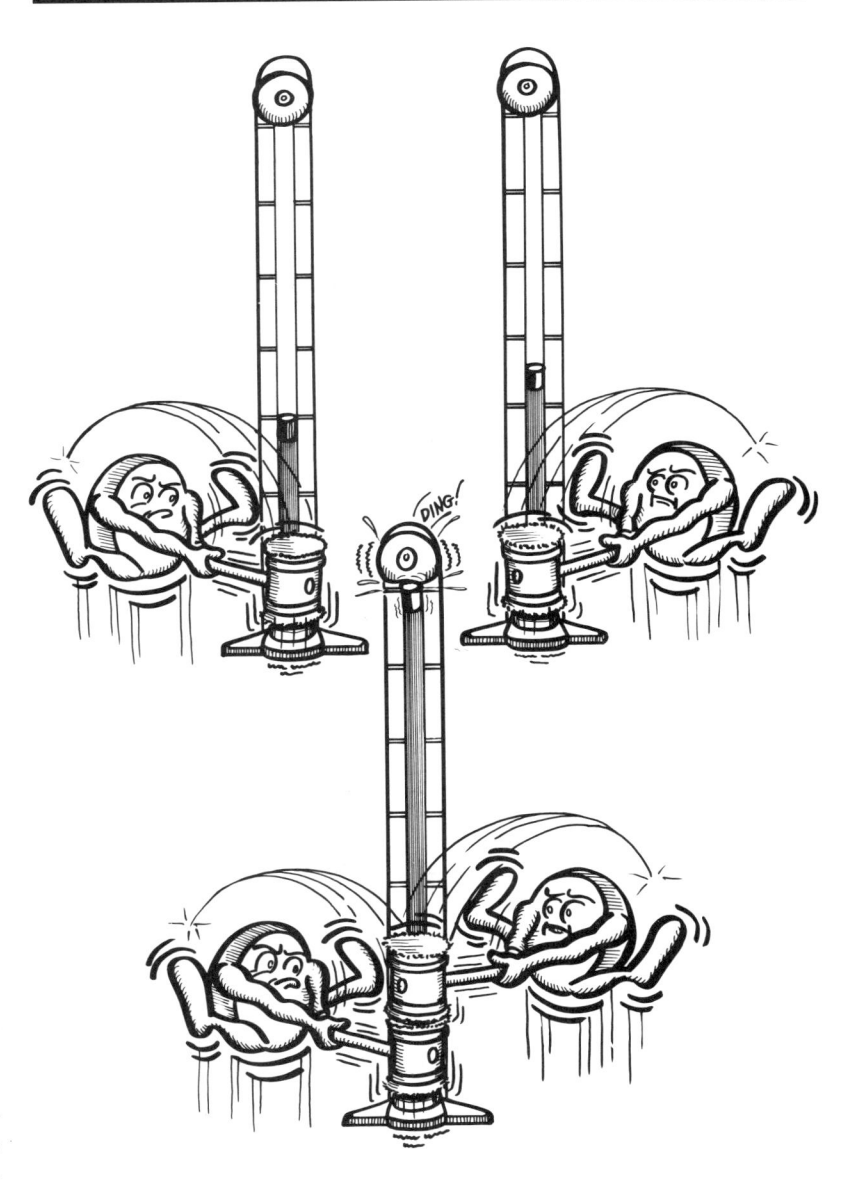

Figure 2-12 Synergism or potentiation (combined drug effects are more than individual effects).

Food can also affect drug absorption and can interact with drugs. Food-drug interactions can occur and you should be aware of them.

There are many other ways in which drugs interact. Some of these interactions are bad, but not all of them are. In fact, doctors sometimes make use of the known drug interactions to control unwanted side effects or to increase the therapeutic effect of a particular drug. Probenecid is sometimes given with penicillin G. Probenecid slows the excretion of the antibiotic. This effect results in higher blood levels or allows a smaller dose of penicillin to be given.

It is the *unplanned* drug interactions that are of concern in administering medications. It takes the cooperation of every member of the health care team to guard against patients receiving drugs that interact in unplanned ways.

SYMPTOMS OF DRUG INTERACTIONS
- Synergism: Unusually strong drug effect when patient is taking more than one drug.
- Antagonism: Unusually weak drug effect when patient is taking more than one drug.
- Other drug interactions: Symptoms vary.
- Lists are published of all known interactions between specific drugs. When any unusual symptoms occur, a nurse or a physician may consult such a list to see if a drug interaction is responsible.

TREATMENT OF DRUG INTERACTIONS
- STOP MEDICATION if dangerous signs develop, such as labored breathing or rapid heartbeat.
- Report all suspicious symptoms to supervisor and follow instructions.

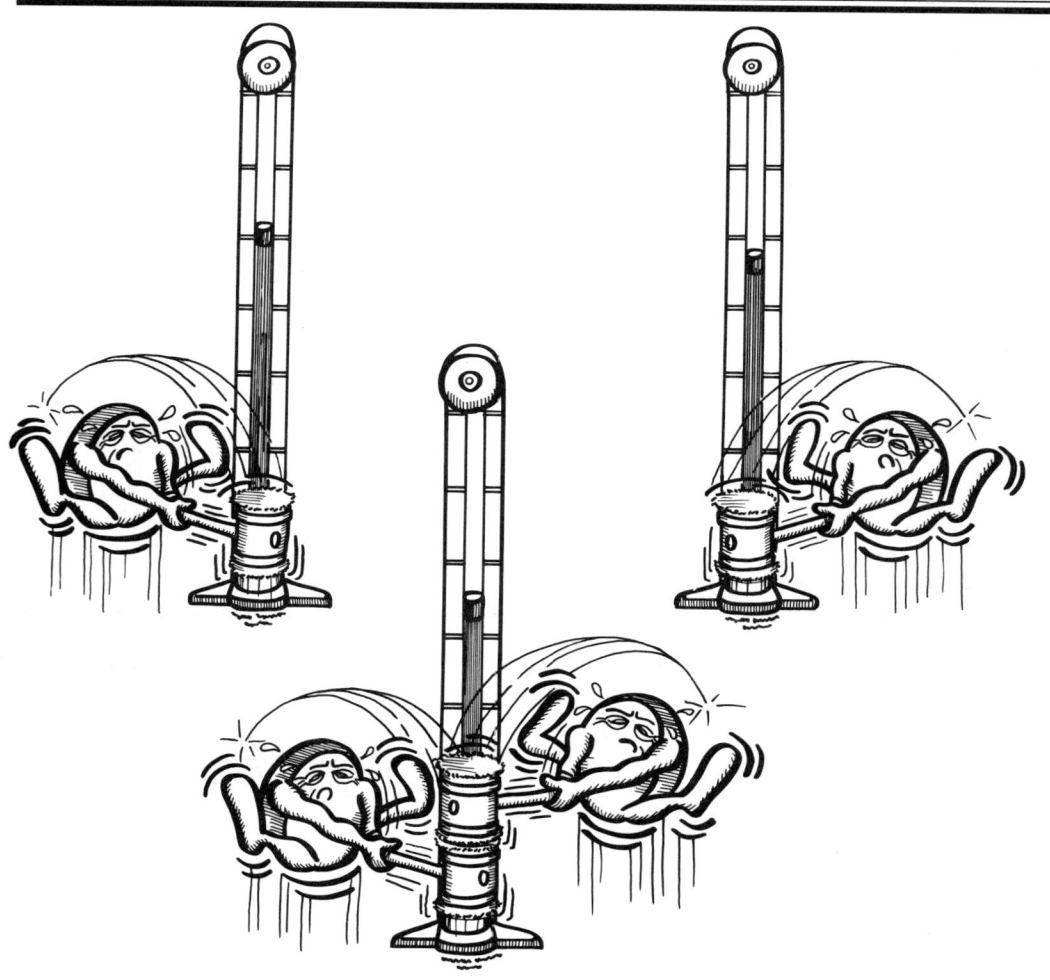

Figure 2-13 Antagonism (combined effects are less than the two individual effects).

Other Drug-Related Disorders

Some drugs, when administered over a period of time, can cause changes in body functioning or damage to certain organs. Bone marrow disease and a lower production of blood cells may result from fluorouracil therapy in cancer patients. Diseases of the liver and kidney may be caused by certain drugs. Drugs can also have negative effects on behavior and emotions. Antianxiety drugs such as *Valium* have been known to disturb sleep and cause nightmares. Irritability and nervousness are common problems with many drugs.

SYMPTOMS OF OTHER DRUG-RELATED DISORDERS

- Depend on condition.

TREATMENT OF OTHER DRUG-RELATED DISORDERS

- Report all suspicious symptoms to supervisor and follow instructions.

Drug Dependence

Drug dependence is a strong psychological and/or physical need to take a certain drug (Figure 2-14). This need develops when a person takes a drug over a period of time. Usually the drug was prescribed to relieve pain or to control some physical or emotional problem. Eventually, some people find they cannot seem to get along without the drug. They keep on taking it just to avoid the discomfort they would feel if they stopped.

Drug dependence can be either psychological or physical. In **psychological** or **emotional dependence** or **habituation**, a person has a drive or a craving to take a certain drug for pleasure or to relieve discomfort. There are no physical symptoms if the drug is taken away, but the person may feel anxious about not having the psychological "crutch."

In **physical dependence** (also called **addiction** or **chemical dependence**), the body has grown so accustomed to the drug that it *needs* the drug in order to function. When the drug is taken away, the person develops **withdrawal symptoms** involving extreme physical discomfort. Eventually, if no further dose of the drug is administered, the body returns to normal functioning.

SYMPTOMS OF DRUG DEPENDENCE

- Physical dependence: craving for a drug. If the drug is not administered, the patient develops symptoms of withdrawal, such as nausea, vomiting, tremors, sweating, and extreme physical discomfort.
- Psychological dependence: psychological craving for a drug. (This is present in physical dependence, too.) Patient displays anxiety and fear of physical discomfort when the drug is not administered.

TREATMENT OF DRUG DEPENDENCE

- Notify supervisor and follow instructions.
- With physical dependence, the physician may substitute another similar drug to ease the withdrawal symptoms and then gradually reduce the dosage of the substitute drug.
- With both physical and psychological dependence, counseling may be needed to help a person get along without the drug.
- In the case of the dying or terminal patient who is in a great deal of pain, drug dependence may be allowed to develop so that the patient can be as comfortable as possible.

Figure 2-14 Drug dependence.

DRUG DEPENDENCE OR DRUG ABUSE?

Drug dependence is a problem any health care worker may have to deal with in giving medications. The time may come when a patient asks for more pain medication, for example, and you may be worried that the patient is becoming too dependent on the drug. Is this drug abuse?

In this situation, your main responsibility is to consult the nurse in charge. The decision of whether to further medicate the patient must be made together by the members of the health care team. Your own concerns may be eased, however, if you understand something about the difference between drug dependence and drug abuse.

Drug **abuse** usually refers to a person's taking a certain drug, not for medical reasons, but for the psychological or emotional effects it produces. Feelings of euphoria or calmness or a heightened awareness of the senses (feeling "high") are some of the reasons people take these drugs. Some experts define drug abuse as taking any drug to the point where it interferes with health and daily living patterns.

COMMONLY ABUSED DRUGS
- narcotics and opium
- barbiturates ("downers"), sedatives or hypnotics, alcohol, and other depressants
- amphetamines, cocaine, and other stimulants ("uppers," "speed")
- LSD and other hallucinogens
- marijuana ("pot," "dope")

Most of the commonly abused drugs are controlled substances, which you studied in Unit 1. All of these drugs can create psychological dependence, and the barbiturates and narcotics can create physical dependence as well. However, drug abuse does not necessarily mean drug dependence.

Drug abuse is really part of an even larger and more widespread problem—drug **misuse** (Figure 2-15). This is overuse or careless use of any drug. Drug misuse is most often a problem with people who are taking their own medications at home. Tranquilizers, stimulants, and pain-killing drugs are frequently misused, and so are such common OTC drugs as laxatives. Nicotine and alcohol are widely misused, and both, in fact, can create serious physical as well as psychological dependence. As you can see, there is little difference between drug abuse and drug misuse.

The important thing to remember is that both *drug abuse* and *drug misuse* endanger people's health and well-being. This includes the medical staff as well as patients. As a health care worker, you can help by keeping medicines locked up when not in use, administering only prescribed medications, and watching for signs of drug dependence and improper use of drugs.

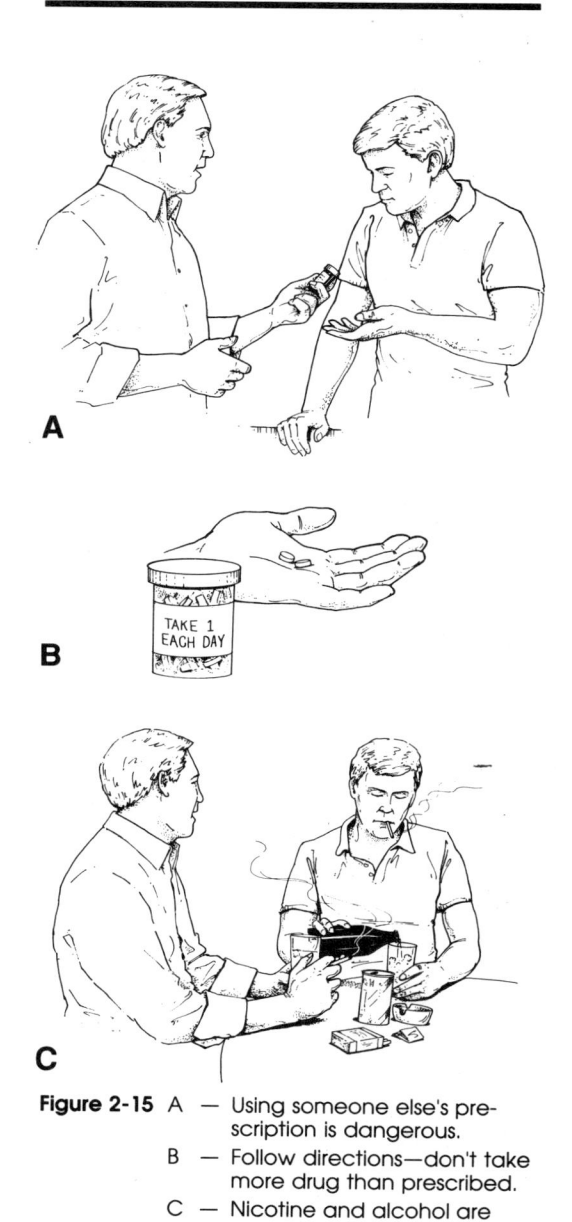

Figure 2-15   A — Using someone else's prescription is dangerous.
           B — Follow directions—don't take more drug than prescribed.
           C — Nicotine and alcohol are drugs too.

EXERCISES

A. Complete the following:

1. The way a drug changes the chemistry of body cells is called the drug __action__.

2. The physical changes that occur because of the drug action are called the drug __effects__.

3. Drugs act by __stimulating__, __depressing__, or __destroying__ the work of the cells.

4. Drugs also act by __replacing__ substances that the body fails to produce.

5. Drug action is affected by four bodily processes: __absorption__, __distribution__, __biotransformation__, and __excretion__.

6. The organs that excrete wastes are the __kidneys__, __large intestine__, __lungs__, and __milk glands__.

7. Absorption is __the passage of a drug from the site of administration into bloodstream__.

8. Distribution is __movement of the drug into the body cells/spaces between cells__.

9. Biotransformation is __metabolism__.

10. Excretion is __body's way of removing waste production__.

11. Drug effects that result from a drug circulating throughout the body are called __systemic__ effects.

12. Drug effects that are confined to the area where the drug was administered are called __local__ effects.

13. Drugs used in therapy have main effects and side effects. Main effects are __what the drug is supposed to do__.

14. Side effects are __unexpected reactions__.

15. A placebo effect can be produced by a sugar pill or an __injection of sterile water__.

42 Administering Medications

B. The following is a list of patient characteristics. Circle those that you think might influence drug action.

1. physical strength
2. (kidney disease) ✓
3. deafness
4. (old age) ✓
5. (inherited genes) ✓
6. (sex) ✓
7. food likes and dislikes
8. popularity
9. (infancy) ✓
10. (anger) ✓
11. (obesity) ✓
12. (poor circulation) ✓
13. (nervousness) ✓
14. (tallness) ✓
15. (cheerful mood) ✓
16. political affiliation
17. (drug-taking history) ✓
18. hair color
19. oral hygiene

C. Select the term that best completes each sentence and write in the blank.

~~antagonism~~   ~~drug dependence~~   ~~potentiation~~
~~drug allergy~~   ~~drug interaction~~   ~~tolerance~~
~~cumulation~~   ~~unusual effect~~   ~~toxicity~~

1. After taking several doses of medicine, little Billy no longer seems to be affected by the drug. This may be a symptom of
   __tolerance__.

2. Mrs. Jones gets a stronger drug effect with each additional dose of her medication. She may be showing signs of
   __cumulation__.

3. Two drugs producing a greater effect than the sum of their individual effects is referred to as
   __potentiation__.

4. The doctor has just canceled Ms. Williams' order for a sedative that helped her sleep after her operation. As the medication hour approaches, Ms. Williams expresses the worry that she will not be able to sleep without her medication. You see this as a possible sign of
   __drug dependence__.

5. Two drugs interacting to produce a lesser effect than the sum of the individual effects is called
   __antagonism__.

6. Annie Peterson is reacting in a peculiar way to her medication. You have never seen a person react this way to the medication she is taking. Drug allergy has been ruled out. Annie's response to the drug will probably be classified as a(n)
   __unusual effect__.

Pharmacodynamics 43

7. An adverse reaction resulting from an antibody attacking an antigen is called a(n) _drug allergy_

8. You have recently given Mr. Smith a medication ordered by his doctor. Mr. Smith is not reacting to the drug the way you expected. In talking with him, you discover that he has also been taking medication he brought with him from home. You suspect that his adverse reaction is due to a(n) _drug interaction_

9. Miss Grimes seems very sleepy and confused after receiving her medication. You check her records and discover that someone misread the doctor's order and gave Miss Grimes a dose that was much too large. You notify the supervisor immediately because you think Miss Grimes is showing signs of _toxicity_.

D. What would you do if you suspected an adverse reaction in a patient?
Stop medication immediately. Call doctor.

E. Complete the following:
1. Drug abuse is _using a drug a way that is no medically sound_
2. Drug misuse is _using a drug in a way that isn't intended_
3. Withdrawal symptoms include _sweating, nausea, tremors, vomiting_
4. Five groups of drugs that are often abused are: (a) _narcotics, opium_, (b) _barbiturates_, (c) _amphetamines_, (d) _hallucinogens_, and (e) _marijuana_.
5. If you suspect drug abuse, your obligation is to _consult nurse in charge_
6. Physical drug dependence is _addiction_
7. Psychological drug dependence is _using a drug for pleasure, feeling that you can't function without drugs_

8. Adipose tissue, which increases in the elderly, can become _a resivoir for drug accumulation_

9. A decrease in size of the liver and its function in the elderly might _interfere c̄ enzyme formation / biotransformation_

10. Glomerular filtration is reduced in the elderly because _50% of nephron units maybe nonfunctional_

ANSWERS TO EXERCISES

A. Completion
1. action
2. effects
3. speeding up (stimulating), slowing down (depressing), stopping or destroying
4. replacing
5. absorption, distribution, biotransformation, excretion
6. kidneys, large intestine, lungs, milk glands
7. passage of a substance into the bloodstream from the site of administration
8. movement of drugs into cells and into spaces between cells
9. breaking down drugs into different substances that can be excreted
10. removal of waste products from the body
11. systemic
12. local
13. desired therapeutic effects; the reason the drug is given
14. other effects besides the desired therapeutic effect
15. injection of sterile water

B. Patient characteristics
2, 4, 5, 6, 9, 10, 11, 12, 13, 14, 15, 17

C. Adverse reactions
1. tolerance
2. cumulation
3. potentiation (or synergism)
4. drug dependence
5. antagonism
6. unusual effect (or idiosyncrasy)
7. drug allergy
8. drug interaction
9. toxicity

D. Immediately consult the nurse in charge or the supervisor.

E. Completion
1. using a drug for other than medical reasons, or in such a way that it interferes with daily life
2. overuse or improper use of any drug
3. nausea, vomiting, tremors, sweating, and extreme physical discomfort
4. (a) narcotics and opium, (b) barbiturates, sedatives or hypnotics, and alcohol, (c) amphetamines, cocaine, and other stimulants, (d) LSD and other hallucinogens, (e) marijuana (*Any five is correct.*)
5. consult the nurse in charge
6. a condition in which the body must have a drug in order to function because it is so used to having the drug
7. a feeling of not being able to get along without a drug
8. a reservoir for drugs to accumulate in
9. interfere with enzyme formation and biotransformation
10. 50% of the nephron units may be nonfunctional

Unit 3

Fundamentals of Medication Therapy

In this unit you will learn about various forms of medications and the routes by which they are given. You will learn how to translate medication orders so that you can give medications in the proper form at the correct time and by the right route.

In this unit, you learn to:

- List the various forms of medication, ranging from liquids to solids.
- Follow correct procedures for storing and using tinctures, fluidextracts, elixirs, spirits, and suspensions.
- Tell how lotions, liniments, and ointments should be applied.
- Explain what delayed-release tablets and capsules are and how they should be given to patients.
- Define enteric coating and state the rule for giving enteric-coated tablets and capsules.
- List and describe the routes for administering medications.
- Tell who is allowed to give medications by the parenteral route.
- Give meanings of abbreviations for medication forms, routes, administration times, and general medical abbreviations.
- Follow the 24-hour clock in giving medications (in health facilities that use it).
- Tell the difference between a physician's order sheet and a prescription blank.
- Name the parts of a medication order.
- Define self-terminating orders and tell what types of drugs usually carry them.
- Translate physician's orders into plain English.
- Explain what to do if you cannot read or do not understand a medication order.

Fundamentals of Medication Therapy   47

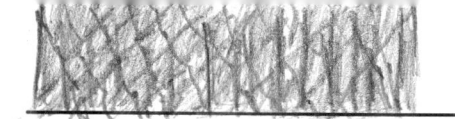

FORMS OF MEDICATION

Drugs are mixed with various ingredients to make them suitable for patients to take. There are ingredients to make oral medicines taste good. Old as well as young patients will take these medications better. There are ingredients to thin out a drug mixture so that the dosage can be controlled. Other ingredients allow drugs to be applied on the skin or placed into body parts such as the eyes, ears, or rectum. These combinations of drugs with various ingredients are called drug **preparations** or **products**.

Different forms of drugs are appropriate for different routes of administration, so it is very important to use the correct form. Using an incorrect form can cause damage to body cells. Therefore, you will need to learn something about the various drug preparations and their uses. You should memorize the abbreviations given in Table 3-1.

Medication forms are loosely classified as either liquids or solids. But many forms are really closer to semiliquids or semisolids. And some are gases (e.g., anesthetic agents and amyl nitrite).

Liquids and Semiliquids

Many drugs are administered in liquid form. They may be given by mouth, rubbed onto the skin, or dropped or **instilled** into eyes, ears, or other parts of the body. Liquid preparations are useful because they allow rapid absorption of the drug. For children and elderly patients who have trouble swallowing solid capsules or tablets, liquid oral medicines are especially helpful.

Some drugs are able to dissolve in liquids, and others are not. When **active ingredients** are mixed with water, alcohol, or both, the resulting preparations are either **solutions** or **suspensions**. In solutions, the drug is **dissolved** in the alcohol or water. In suspensions, the drug is not dissolved, but tiny particles or droplets of the drug are held, or **suspended**, in an even distribution throughout the liquid.

In suspensions that are left standing for a while, particles settle to the bottom of the bottle (oils rise to the top). A clear liquid portion is then visible. This situation is normal and can be corrected by shaking the bottle well before giving the medication (Figure 3-1). Solutions, on the other hand, rarely separate when left standing. If they do, it is because they have been stored improperly. Separated solutions must be discarded.

Within the broad categories of solutions and suspensions, there are several specific liquid forms of medication. These are described below. Tinctures, fluidextracts, elixirs, spirits, and syrups are all types of solutions. Emulsions, magmas, gels, and lotions are types of suspensions.

Figure 3-1 Shake suspension before use.

Table 3-1
Abbreviations for medication forms

Abbreviation	Form
cap., caps.	capsule
elix.	elixir
ext.	extract
fld. ext.	fluidextract
oint., ung.	ointment (unguent)
sol.	solution
sp.	spirit
supp.	suppository
syr.	syrup
tab.	tablet
tinct., tr.	tincture

VOCABULARY

active ingredient: the ingredient in a product that produces the therapeutic effect

concentration: amount of drug in a certain amount of liquid

counterirritant: a drug that irritates tissues so as to relieve some other problem

enteric coated: coated with a substance that dissolves in the intestine but not in the stomach (**enteric**—pertaining to the small intestine)

extract: a solution or powder made by removing and concentrating drug ingredients from a plant or an animal

gelatin: a stiff substance that dissolves in water; used for making capsules

infusion: placing a tube into a vein for the purpose of slowly adding fluids to the body (e.g., sugar water, plasma); also called **intravenous (IV) drip**

irrigation: rinsing a body cavity with water or other solutions

inhalation: administering drugs by way of droplets or mist that is breathed in

insertion: placing an object into a body cavity (e.g., putting a suppository into the rectum)

instillation: placing drops of liquid into the eyes, ears, nose, or some other body cavity

insufflation: blowing a powder into a body cavity

lanolin: an ointment base made from fine oil in the skin of sheep

mixture: two or more ingredients that retain their identities

mucous membrane: moist, glossy lining of tubes inside of the body (e.g., mouth, sinuses, rectum) that lets some liquids pass through into the body tissues

outpatient: patient who is not hospitalized or institutionalized; a "walk-in" (or **ambulatory**) patient

paste: stiff, thick ointment

petrolatum: an ointment base of petroleum jelly (like *Vaseline*)

physician's order sheet: a form for writing out medication orders, located in the patient chart

preparation: the form in which a drug is made; either a liquid, solid, or something in between

prescription: a written order for a drug

saliva: digestive juice produced by glands inside of the mouth to aid chewing and swallowing

self-terminating order: drug order that stops at a certain time or after a certain number of doses; also called **automatic stop order**

soluble: capable of being dissolved

solution: a liquid containing a dissolved drug

standing order: drug order that is to be continued until further notice

stat order: drug order carried out immediately and only once

sterile: germ free

suspension: a liquid containing undissolved particles of a drug

---

Tinctures—Tinctures (*tink'turz*) are solutions made with alcohol or alcohol with water. The active ingredients make up 10-20% of the solution. Examples are tincture of iodine, belladonna tincture, paregoric, and Tincture of Merthiolate.

Fluidextracts—Fluidextracts (*floo'id-ek'straktz*) are very concentrated alcohol solutions that contain drugs from plant sources.

Elixirs—These are solutions of alcohol and water containing 10–20% of a drug. Elixirs (*e-lik'serz*) have special added ingredients to make them sweet-tasting and pleasant-smelling. They are often used as oral medications for children and the elderly. Phenobarbital elixir and *Benadryl* elixir are examples.

Spirits—Spirits are alcohol solutions of volatile oils, or oils that evaporate. For example, camphor oil mixed with alcohol is called camphor spirit. Spirits contain 5–20% active ingredients.

Fundamentals of Medication Therapy 49

ADMINISTRATION REMINDER

Tinctures, fluidextracts, elixirs, and spirits are highly concentrated forms of drugs (Figure 3-2). They contain much higher amounts of drug per unit of liquid than do other liquid forms. These preparations must be measured very carefully using a dropper or a medicine glass. The medicine may be added to water, juice, or another solution suggested by the doctor. The patient then drinks this mixture.

Caution: *Tinctures, fluidextracts, elixirs, and spirits contain alcohol. Do not administer to a diagnosed alcoholic.* Storage is very important with these alcohol solutions. They must be kept tightly stoppered so that the alcohol cannot evaporate. Store them in a dark place, as stated on labels. Otherwise, the drug may separate out from the alcohol. If this should happen, *do not use* the preparation, but order another.

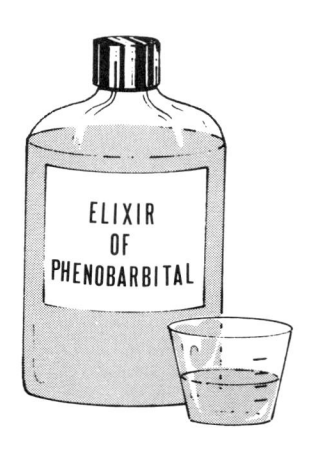

Keep tightly capped

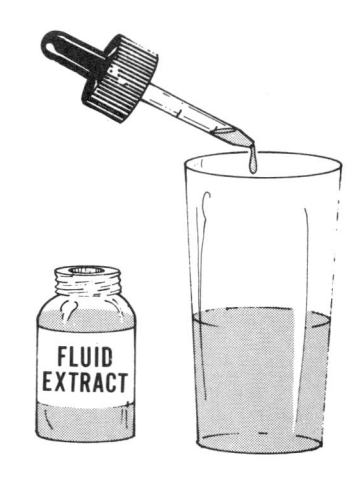

Small doses — measure carefully

Do not use if separated

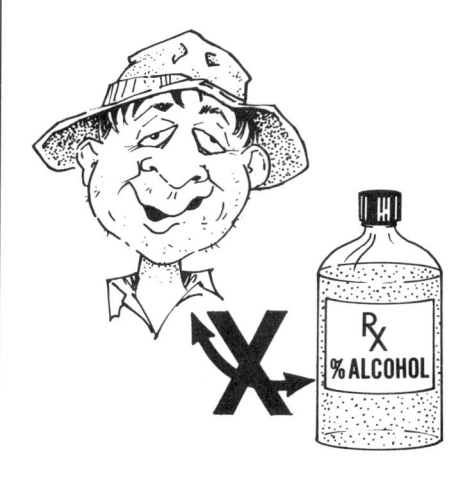

Not for alcoholics

Figure 3-2 Rules for alcohol solutions.

Syrups—Syrups are heavy solutions of water and sugar, usually with a flavoring added. They are mixed with a very small amount of a drug. Syrups are useful for masking the bitter taste of certain drugs (e.g., orange and cherry syrups).

Emulsions—Emulsions (*e-mul'shunz*) are suspensions of oils and fats in water. Cod liver oil emulsion is an example.

Magmas—A magma (*mag'mah*) contains heavy particles mixed with water which forms a milky liquid or paste. Milk of magnesia is a familiar example of a magma.

Gels—Gels are similar to magmas, but they contain finer particles.

ADMINISTRATION REMINDER
Emulsions, magmas, and gels are given in very small amounts because they contain large portions of active drug ingredients. Since they are suspensions, they must be shaken before use.

Liniments—These are mixtures of drugs with water, alcohol, oil, or soap for external use. Liniments are rubbed onto the skin to promote absorption. They are used as soothing preparations or as counterirritants (drugs that mask pain in nearby muscles or skin by creating a different kind of irritation).

Lotions—These are suspensions of drugs in a water base for external use. Lotions are *patted* onto the skin, rather than being rubbed in (Figure 3-3). Lotions tend to settle out and must be shaken well before use. Calamine lotion is a common example. Lotions have many uses: to protect, cool, lubricate, cleanse, or stimulate the skin.

Ointments—Ointments are drugs mixed in lanolin, a fine oil taken from the skin of the sheep, or in petrolatum, a jelly made from petroleum. They are usually applied to skin surfaces, but some ointments can be placed into the eyes. Eye ointments must always bear the label: "*STERILE—FOR OPHTHALMIC USE*" (Figure 3-4). Thick, stiff ointments that do not melt at body temperature are called **pastes**.

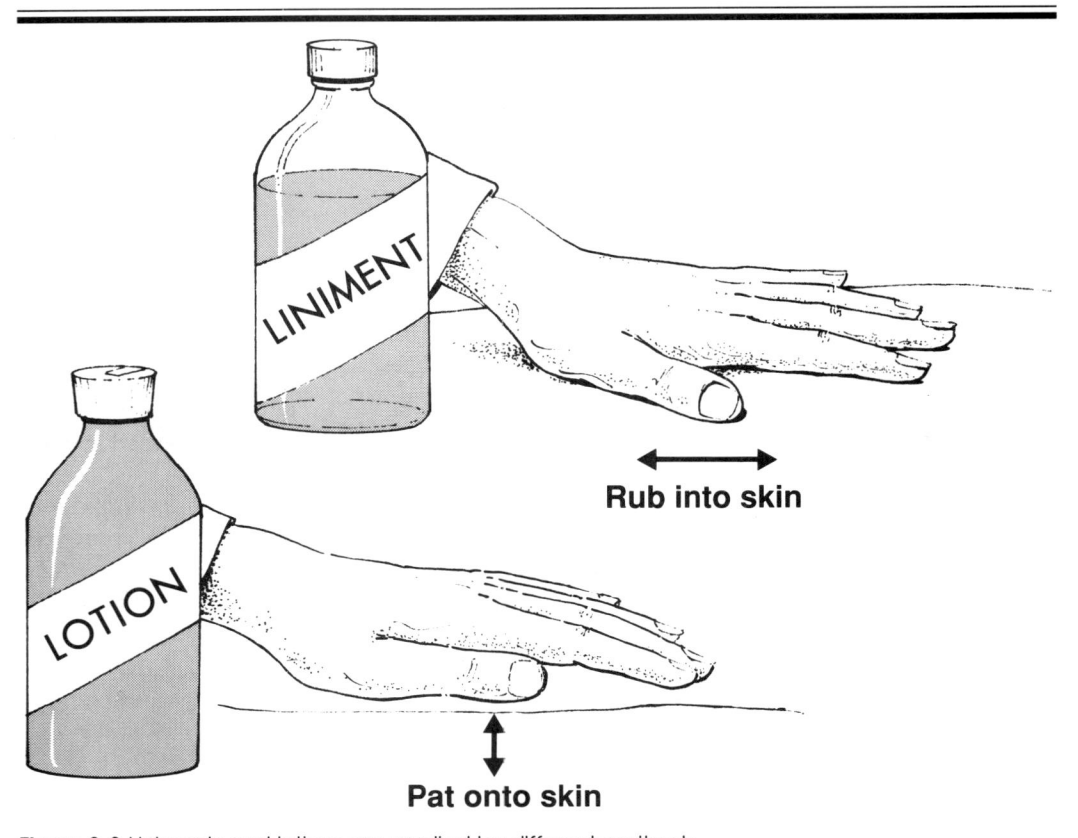

Figure 3-3 Liniments and lotions are applied by different methods.

Fundamentals of Medication Therapy 51

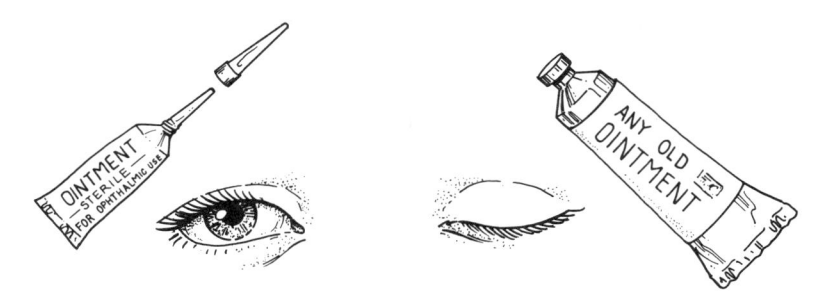

Figure 3-4 Ointments for the eyes are specially labeled.

Sprays—Liquid medications are sometimes prepared as sprays for application to the skin or mucous membranes. A special device sprays small droplets evenly across the surface to be medicated. Some sprays may be inhaled into the lungs.

Solids and Semisolids

Solid forms of drugs are widely used in drug treatment (Figure 3-5). There is no mixing, shaking, and measuring to be done as there is with many liquids. The solid forms are also a convenient way to take unpleasant-tasting or irritating drugs.

Powders—Powders are fine, dry particles of drugs. They may be dissolved in liquids or used as is, depending on a physician's orders. Powders have both internal and external uses.

Tablets—Tablets are drug powders that have been pressed or molded into small disks. They are designed to be swallowed either alone or with a liquid. Tablets come in a variety of sizes, shapes, and weights. Some have colored coatings, flavorings, and printed labels showing the manufacturer. Many tablets are **scored**, which means that they have one or more grooves down the middle. These make it possible to break the tablets into halves or quarters if needed.

Capsules—A capsule is a gelatin sheath that contains one dose of medication. The drug inside of the capsule can be either a powder, an oil, or a liquid. When the capsule is swallowed, the gelatin quickly dissolves and releases the medicine into the stomach.

Many different types of capsules are available. They come with hard or soft coverings in various sizes ranging from 7/16

Figure 3-5 Solid forms of medication come in many shapes, sizes, and colors.

to 1 inch. Many of them have special shapes and colorings that tell which company produced them.

Delayed-Release Tablets and Capsules—These forms contain several doses of a drug. The doses have special coatings that dissolve at different rates, so that medicine is released into the stomach gradually. Some doses are released immediately. Others are released up to 12 hours later. Delayed-release tablets and capsules allow for drug effects to continue at the same level over a long period of time. **Sustained release** and **timed release** are other terms used to describe these products.

Caution: *Never crush, open, or empty a delayed-release tablet or capsule into food or liquid.* Such actions could cause the patient to receive an overdose.

Enteric-Coated Tablets and Capsules—These are tablets and capsules with

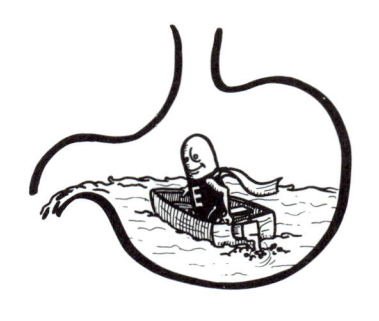

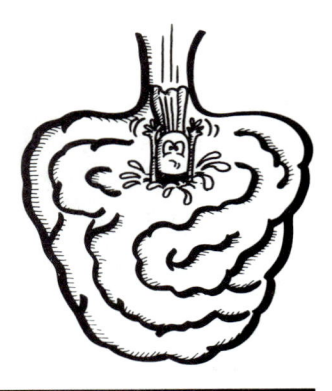

Figure 3-6 Enteric coating dissolves in the intestine.

a special coating that keeps them from dissolving in the stomach (Figure 3-6). They do not dissolve until they reach the intestine. The enteric coating prevents an irritating drug from upsetting the stomach. It also prevents the stomach juices from interacting with the drug to change its effect.

ADMINISTRATION REMINDER

If your patient is taking an enteric-coated product, watch carefully to see that the drug is taking effect. Some patients' intestines are not able to dissolve the enteric coating. Also, enteric-coated tablets and capsules must not be crushed or mixed into food or liquid. This would destroy the enteric coating and cause the medication to be released in the stomach instead of the intestine.

Table 3-2 Abbreviations for routes

Abbreviation	Route	Meaning
buc	buccal	inside the cheek
hypo, h, H, (h)	hypodermic	under the skin (same as subcutaneous)
ID	intradermal	into the skin
IM	intramuscular	into the muscle
IV	intravenous	into the vein
PO, p.o., O., "o"	oral	by mouth
p.r., r, "R."	rectal	by rectum
p.v.	vaginal	by vagina
SC, sub-Q, SQ, subcu	subcutaneous	under the skin (into fatty layer)
subling, subl	sublingual	under the tongue

Troches and Lozenges—These are tablets designed to dissolve in the mouth rather than being swallowed. They may be flat, round, or rectangular and are used for their local effects. As they dissolve, they bring a high concentration of drug into contact with the mouth and throat. They can help to relieve pain or soothe irritation in those areas.

Suppositories—These are drugs mixed with a firm substance that melts at body temperature. The drug mixture is molded into a shape suitable for insertion into the vagina, rectum, or urethra. After insertion, the suppository dissolves against the warm mucous membranes of these openings and releases the drug. The active ingredients take effect locally or are absorbed into the bloodstream for systemic effects.

ROUTES OF ADMINISTRATION

Drugs can be administered to patients through several methods or routes. Each route has its advantages and disadvantages. The route chosen will depend on the type of medication, the dosage form, and the desired effects (Figure 3-7). Abbreviations for routes of administration that you should know are given in Table 3-2.

Oral

In oral administration, a drug is given by mouth and swallowed, either alone or with a glass of liquid. The drug is then absorbed into the bloodstream through the lining of the stomach and intestine.

Oral administration is the easiest, safest, and most economical way for a patient to take medicine. However, it is also the slowest way for a drug to reach the cells of the body. The drug can be broken down by

Fundamentals of Medication Therapy 53

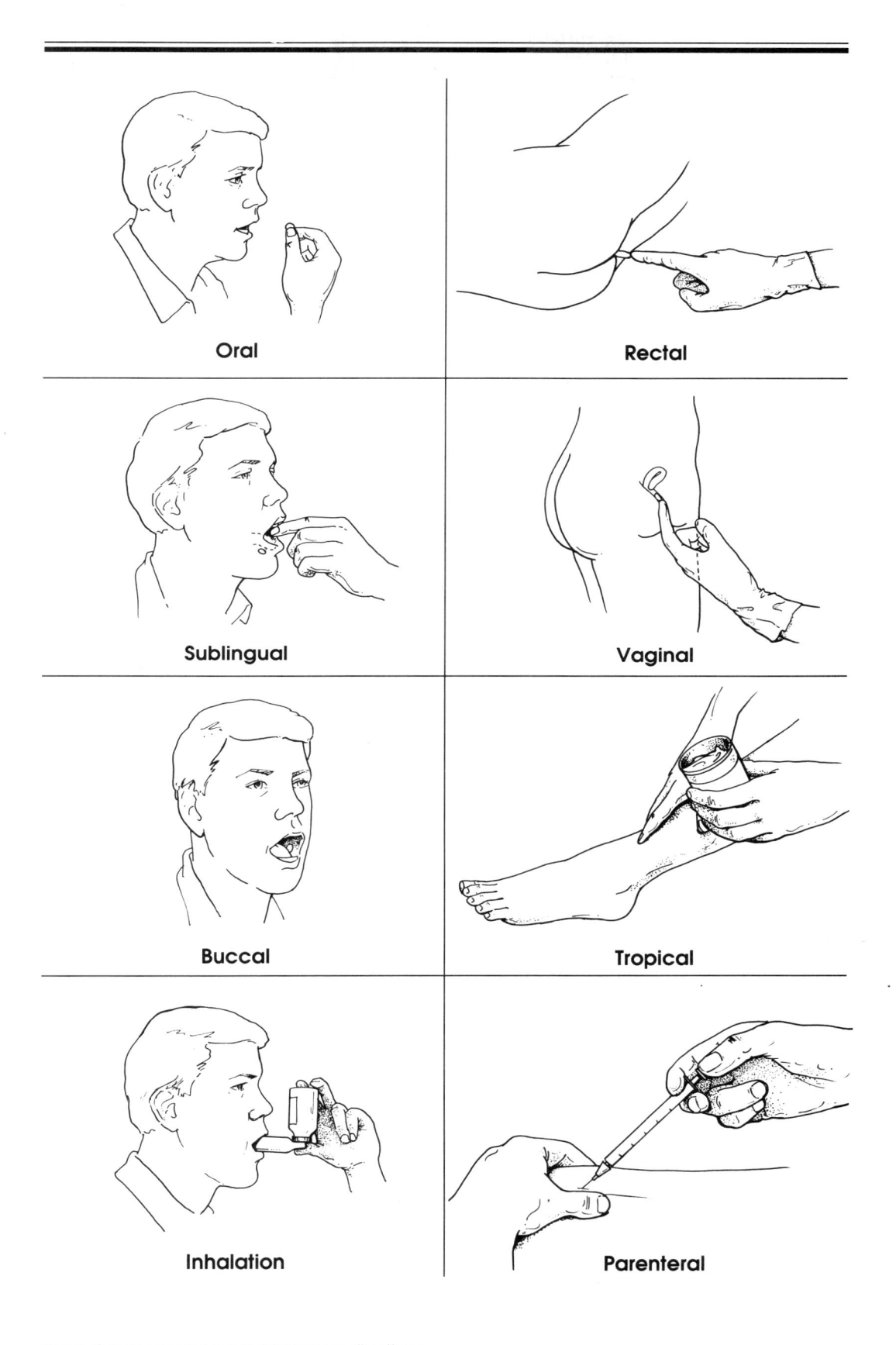

Oral	Rectal
Sublingual	Vaginal
Buccal	Tropical
Inhalation	Parenteral

Figure 3-7 Routes for administering medications.

enzymes in the digestive system. Its absorption can be affected by the presence of food. Irritating medicines may cause nausea and stomach discomfort. Nevertheless, the oral route is well acccepted and often used in drug therapy. Oral medications are usually in liquid, tablet, or capsule form.

Sublingual

Sublingual (*sub-ling'gwal*) administration means placing a drug under the tongue, where it dissolves in the patient's saliva. It is quickly absorbed through the mucous membrane that makes up the lining of the mouth. The patient is not permitted to drink or eat until all of the medication is dissolved.

Compared to the oral route, the sublingual route has the advantage of more rapid absorption. It also yields a higher concentration of the drug in the blood, because the drug does not have to pass through the digestive system first. This is a convenient route as long as drugs are not irritating or bad tasting.

Medications for sublingual administration are in the form of tablets. They are usually given for their systemic effects. Nitroglycerin, a drug that stimulates the heart muscle, is often administered sublingually. Ergotamine tartrate (*Ergostat*) may be given sublingually for migraine headache.

Buccal

Buccal (*buk'al*) administration is similar to sublingual, except that the medication is placed in the mouth next to the cheek. The drug is absorbed through the mucous membrane that lines the inside of the cheek. Buccal medications are in the form of tablets. These should not be swallowed, and no food or drink is permitted until they are dissolved. Oxytocin, a drug that brings on labor in pregnant women, may be administered buccally.

Topical

Topical administration is the method of applying a drug directly to the skin or mucous membrane, usually for a local effect. Drugs for topical use are often designed to soothe irritated tissues or to prevent or cure local infections. They are in the form of creams, liniments, lotions, ointments, liquids, and powders. Liquids may be sprayed, swabbed, or painted onto the desired surfaces. Powders may be blown onto the skin or into body cavities (**insufflation**) (*in'su-fla'shun*). Other forms are rubbed or patted on or held against skin surfaces with a bandage. Absorption through the skin is slow, while absorption through mucous membranes is rapid.

Topical medications can be dropped or instilled into the eyes, ears, and nose (**instillation**), and they can be inserted into the vagina, urethra, urinary bladder, and rectum (**insertion**). Any of these areas may also be rinsed with water containing drugs (**irrigation**). These applications are very easy to perform, but correct procedure must be followed to avoid damaging the tissue.

Rectal

Inserting medication into the rectum in the form of a suppository is called rectal administration. Absorption through the lining of the rectum is slow and irregular. However, this may be the best route when a patient cannot take medications orally. For example, a vomiting patient or an unconscious patient may require rectal administration.

Vaginal

This route of administration requires inserting a cream, foam, tablet, or suppository into the vagina. Medications inserted vaginally are usually given for their local effects, as in the treatment of a vaginal infection with *Mycostatin*.

Inhalation

In inhalation administration, medicine is sprayed or inhaled into the nose, throat, and lungs. The drug is absorbed through the mucous membranes in the nose and throat or through the tiny air sacs that fill the lungs. Drugs to be inhaled are in the form of gases or fine droplets (sprays, mists, steam, etc.)

The lungs contain a large surface area, so there is good absorption. However, it is hard to regulate the dose. The inhalation method is also awkward and not suitable for drugs that might irritate the lungs.

Inhalation is widely used for the rapid treatment of asthma symptoms. Special devices (e.g., inhalers, nebulizers, atomizers) are available that make inhalation therapy more convenient than in the past. Because germs can easily enter the body through the linings of the lungs, the equipment used for inhalation therapy must be very clean.

Parenteral

Parenteral administration means injecting a drug into the body with a needle and syringe. This method gives much more rapid absorption and distribution than does oral administration. The dosage can also be controlled very carefully. The parenteral route is especially useful in emergencies, when a drug effect is needed immediately.

There are several disadvantages to the parenteral route. All injection equipment and medicines must be **sterile**, or free of germs. The method is expensive, sometimes painful, and not easy for patients to administer to themselves. Most important, there is the danger of injecting a drug incorrectly into a vein, which could cause serious harm and even death.

Caution: *Parenteral administration requires special training, special safety precautions, and special equipment. State regulations allow only certain licensed health workers to administer medications parenterally; for instance, nurses and certified nursing assistants.*

Medicine for injection must be in liquid form. Often it must be prepared as a suspension of a powder in distilled water.

The parenteral route is divided into four main categories, according to where the injection is given.

In **intradermal (intracutaneous)** administration, a small amount of medicine is injected just beneath the outer layer of skin. The dose is usually less than 0.3 milliliters (ml). The injected drug forms a small bubble (bleb) under the skin. Intradermal injections are used in tuberculin tests, allergy tests, and vaccinations. The drug is absorbed very slowly in this type of injection.

In the **subcutaneous** route, medication is injected into a layer of fatty tissue that lies right below the skin. This is called the **subcutaneous** (under the skin) tissue. The dose is approximately 1–2 ml. Insulin, hormones, and local anesthetics are among the medications administered by subcutaneous injection.

Intramuscular administration is the injection of drugs deep into the muscles. Because the muscles are well supplied with blood, absorption from the muscles is faster than absorption from the skin layers. Muscles can also absorb a greater amount of fluid without discomfort to the patient—the usual dose is 1–3 ml. Intramuscular injection is also preferred for substances that would irritate the skin layers. Penicillin is often injected in this manner. During intramuscular administration, care must be taken to inject only large, healthy muscles and to avoid hitting major nerves, bones, and blood vessels.

In **intravenous** injection, a sterile drug solution is placed directly into a vein. This is the *least safe* method, but it may be necessary when medication is needed quickly. Dosages vary according to the situation.

Intravenous injection differs from **intravenous infusion**, or **IV drip**, mainly in speed of action. Infusion is the insertion of a tube or a needle into a vein through which fluids are slowly added to the bloodstream over a period of time. Infusion is used often in nursing care to keep the body's fluid level in balance. Drugs can be added to IV fluids for a continuous drug effect. Or they can be injected into the IV tube that leads into the vein, which is almost the same as injecting directly into the vein.

Intracardiac, intra-arterial, intrathecal *(in-trah-the'kal)* or **intraspinal**, and **intraosseous** *(in'trah-os'e-us)* are types of injections that only physicians are permitted to perform. In these methods, a drug is injected into the heart muscle, into an artery, into the spinal spaces, or into a bone, respectively.

THE MEDICATION ORDER

When a physician tells a nurse or another health care worker which drug or drugs to administer to a patient, the physician is giving a **medication order**. It may be expressed in writing or verbally.

Written orders are stated in a special book for doctors' orders or on a **physician's order sheet** in a patient's chart (Figure 3-8).

56 Administering Medications

LAKESIDE HOSPITAL AND HEALTH CARE CENTER

PHYSICIAN'S ORDER SHEET

DATE	DIAGNOSTIC PROCEDURES AND TREATMENTS	MEDICATIONS - INFUSIONS	ADDRESSOGRAPH
6/18/88	Obtain sputum culture	Chloral hydrate caps. 600 mg h.s. Dimetane elix. 2 tsp t.i.d. Aspirin gr V p.o. q. 4h. p.r.n. Ampicillin 250 mg p.o. q. 6h. x 10 days *Thomas Moore* M.D.	7209 347841-6 m28-447 TIMMONS, RALPH DR. THOMAS MOORE 1-PROT 5/06/20 ADMISSION: POSSIBLE PNEUMONIA
6/19/88	Chest x-ray stat. Postural drainage w/ percussion q.i.d. Magnesium sulfate sol. compresses t.i.d.	Kolantyl 2 tsp p.r.n. *Thomas Moore* M.D.	
6/20/88	Increase postural drainage & percussion q. 2h—	Disc. Dimetane elix. *Thomas Moore* M.D.	

USE BALL-POINT PEN — PRESS FIRMLY   **3A**

Figure 3-8 Physicians' order sheet.

A **prescription blank** is used to write medication orders for patients who are being discharged from the hospital or who are seeing the doctor in a clinic (Figure 3-9). These patients are called **outpatients**.

Orders may be given verbally in an emergency when there is no time to write them down, or verbal orders may be given over the phone when the doctor is away from the health facility. Some doctors routinely give verbal orders even when they are at the facility. In each case, the verbal order is written down and signed as soon as practical.

Physicians are usually the only people allowed to prescribe medicines, but in some states nurse-practitioners and physician's assistants are permitted to prescribe. These two new members of the health care team frequently practice in Health Maintenance Organizations (HMOs) and free-standing emergency health facilities. They prescribe drugs under the direct supervision of a physician with whom they work.

The person who is allowed to take down verbal orders differs according to each agency's policies. You should ask about your agency's specific policies regarding the writing and receiving of medication orders.

The medication order includes several important pieces of information. All of this information must be read and understood by you, the health care worker, so that you may correctly prepare and administer the medication. The basic parts of a medication order are:

- **The patient's full name**
  For proper identification, the first and last names and the middle initial are needed. The patient's admission number is included in some health facilities. The patient's age should be included, especially if the dosage needs to be checked (e.g., for children and elderly patients).

- **Date of the order**
  The day, month, and year are included. Often the time of day when the order was written is also shown. This helps avoid confusion when the staff changes shifts. The 24-hour clock is used in some facilities to lessen the chance of error. For example, 9:15 a.m. would be written as 0915 hours, and 5:45 p.m. would be 1745 hours. Study Figure 3-10 to understand how to use the 24-hour clock.

- **Name of the drug**
  On a prescription blank, this is preceded by "Rx," which means "take." The drug's generic name or trade name is written out. For reasons of cost, it is becoming more common for doctors to order drugs by their generic names. There may be a special line on the prescription blank even for writing in the generic name, or one that says "may substitute generic drug." If a drug name is not familiar to you, consult a drug reference such as the USP DI or the PDR.

- **Dosage**
  This includes the amount of the drug and the strength of the preparation (e.g., two 100-mg tablets as opposed to 50-mg tablets or 250-mg tablets). It also includes when and how often the drug is to be taken (e.g., with meals or twice a day). The dosage portion of the order should tell whether it is a standing order or a self-terminating order (see below). You will learn more about dosages in Unit 4.

- **Route of administration**
  This is important because some medicines can be given by several different routes. If no special route is ordered, you can usually assume that the medication is to be taken *orally*. If in doubt, ask your supervisor.

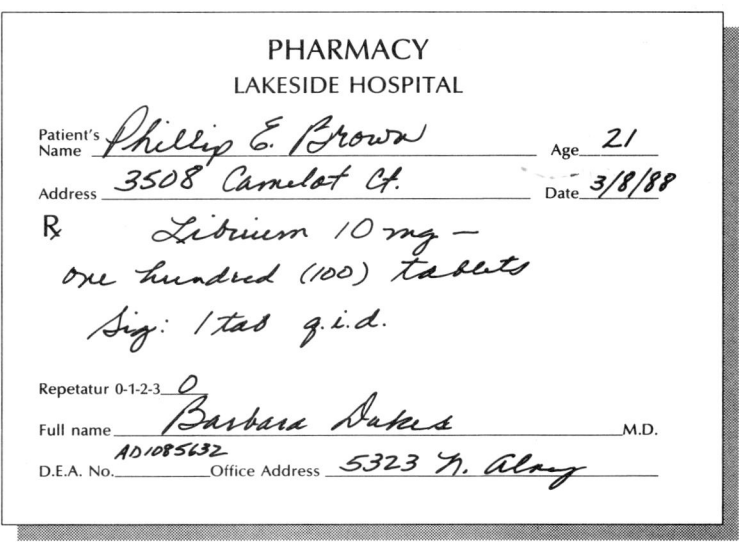

Figure 3-9 Prescription blank for an outpatient.

THE 24 - HOUR CLOCK

When using the 24-hour clock, time is given in four digits. The first two digits stand for hours. The second two digits stand for minutes. The day begins at 0001 (12:01 am) and ends at 2400 hours (12:00 midnight).

In the clock shown above, the am hours are numbered on the outer circle, as on regular clocks. The pm hours are numbered on the inner circle. These numbers are used after 1:00 pm. The hour 12:59 pm is expressed as 1259, and 1:00 pm is expressed as 1300 (thirteen-hundred hours). Note that no punctuation marks are used.

SAMPLE CONVERSIONS

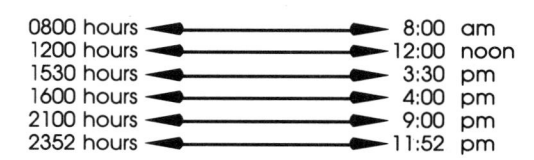

0800 hours	8:00 am
1200 hours	12:00 noon
1530 hours	3:30 pm
1600 hours	4:00 pm
2100 hours	9:00 pm
2352 hours	11:52 pm

An easy method to remember: To convert from regular time to the 24-hour clock, simply add 12 to the hour (starting at 1:00 pm):

3:30 pm → (think 3 + 12 = 15) → 1530 hours
11:52 pm → (think 11 + 12 = 23) → 2352 hours

To convert from the 24-hour clock to regular time, subtract 12 from the hour:

2100 hours → (think 21 - 12 = 9) → 9:00 pm
1745 hours → (think 17 - 12 = 5) → 5:45 pm

Figure 3-10 Introduction to the 24-hour clock.

- **Physician's signature**
  Without the signature of the physician, the medication order is not legal. When a nurse or other staff member must take an order by phone, the nurse signs the order, and the physician co-signs it the next time he or she visits the health facility.

  When a physician prescribes drugs for clinic outpatients or private patients, the medication order will also include:

- **Number of refills**
  Some drugs, especially Schedule II drugs, may not be refilled without another prescription. For other drugs, the order may show a certain number of refills. Figure 3-9 shows the number of refills, following the Latin word *repetatur*, meaning "repeat."

- **Labeling instructions**
  These tell the pharmacist what instructions to put on the bottle for the patient—for example, "Take one tablet daily at bedtime." Labeling instructions are preceded by the abbreviation "**sig**," meaning "signature" or "write on label."

- **Physician's DEA number**
  This is a registration number from the U.S. Drug Enforcement Administration. It is required on all prescriptions for controlled substances.

STANDING OR SELF-TERMINATING?

There are two basic types of medication orders: standing orders and self-terminating orders. A **standing** order is one that remains in force for an indefinite period of time. The medication may continue to be given until one of three things happens: (1) the physician writes a new order that cancels the old standing order; (2) the patient's condition improves to some specified level (e.g., the order may state, "Give aspirin 650 mg every 4 hours until fever drops below 101°F"); or (3) the order is canceled automatically by agency policy. Some health facilities have a policy of canceling all standing orders after a certain amount of time, say, 4 weeks. This is to make sure physicians regularly recheck the medication needs of their patients.

Standing orders sometimes include the instruction to "give as necessary," abbreviated PRN (for the latin phrase *pro re nata*, meaning "according to circumstances, also p.r.n., prn, or P.R.N."). A PRN order gives the nurse or other health worker some choice in deciding when and how often to give the medication.

The other type of medication order is the **self-terminating** order, also known as the **automatic stop** order. This type of order puts a limit on how long the medication may be given. It states either a set amount of time or a set number of doses, for example:

Ergotrate maleate 0.2 mg, 1 tab. q8h X 48 h

or

Demerol 100 mg IM q4h X 12 and then PRN

Another example of a self-terminating order is a **stat** order (from the Latin term *statim*). This is an order to be carried out immediately and only once.

In some hospitals, orders are automatically terminated after surgery or when moving a patient to another clinic (e.g., from intensive care into a regular ward). The patient's medications must be reviewed at this time and new orders written. In addition, certain types of drugs carry automatic stop orders as a matter of hospital policy. These drugs are antibiotics, narcotics, corticosteroids, anticoagulants, and barbiturates.

QUESTIONING A MEDICATION ORDER

There will be times when you have questions about a medication order. Perhaps you cannot read the doctor's handwriting. The prescribed dosage may seem unusually high or not quite right for your patient. You may find that a certain drug is not tolerated well by a patient. Or the patient may have trouble taking the drug by the prescribed route. When these questions come up, it is your right and your duty to **check the order with the doctor or supervisor. In no case should you give a medication unless the orders are clearly written or stated**.

What if your supervisor and the physician have explained the medication order to you, and still you are not satisfied that the medication is safe for the patient? **You have the right to refuse to give any medication that you feel would endanger the patient.** But ask your questions first. In most cases, the reasons behind the medication order will become clear.

It is also important to know your agency's policies concerning which staff members are allowed to carry out which procedures. You should not be asked to carry out any procedure that is against agency policy.

STANDARD MEDICAL ABBREVIATIONS

Abbreviations are a kind of "shorthand" for writing medication orders. They are a quick, convenient way to summarize instructions on what drug to give and how to give it. Certain standard abbreviations are familiar to most people in the medical field.

It is traditional for doctors to write medication orders in Latin, the language of medicine. Most of the standard abbreviations they use on medication orders are shortened versions of Latin words. At times this has led to confusion for those who had to interpret the instructions. Many people in the medical profession are now urging doctors to write out medication orders in plain English, and without abbreviations. Nevertheless, the Latin abbreviations are still used by many physicians as well as nurses and other health care workers.

Table 3-3 Time abbreviations

Abbreviation (Latin[a])	Meaning	Times Given[b]
a.c. (ante cibum)	before meals	1/2 hour before a meal
ad lib. (ad libitum)	at pleasure	given freely, as much as wanted
AM, A, a.m. (ante meridiem)	before noon	morning
BID, b.i.d. (bis in die)	twice a day	10 a.m. and 4 p.m.
h. (hora)	hourly	on each hour
h.s. (hora somni)	hour of sleep	at bedtime
n., noc. (nocte)	night	in the night
o.d. (omni die)	every day	10 a.m.
o.n. (omni nocte)	every night	8 p.m.
p.c. (post cibum)	after meals	1/2 hour after a meal
PM, P, p.m. (post meridiem)	after noon	afternoon
PRN, p.r.n. (pro re nata)	according to circumstances; occasionally	repeat whenever necessary
q.d., qq.d. (quaque die)	every day	10 a.m. or as ordered
q.h., qq.h. (quaque hora)	every hour	on each hour
q2h, q.2h.	every 2 hours	6 a.m. and on even hours
q3h, q.3h.	every 3 hours	6, 9, 12, 3, day and night
q4h, q.4h.	every 4 hours	8, 12, 4, day and night
QID, q.i.d. (quater in die)	4 times a day	8 a.m., 12 noon, 4 p.m., 8 p.m.
q.o.d.	every other day	10 a.m. or as ordered
s.o.s. (si opus sit)	if necessary	one dose given only if the patient seems to need it
stat (statim)	immediately	given once as ordered
TID, t.i.d. (ter in die)	3 times a day	usually given with meals

[a] The Latin words are included only to show where the abbreviations come from. You do not need to memorize them.
[b] Medication schedules vary with different health facilities, so the specific times may vary according to where you work.

It is important for you to memorize standard medical abbreviations to enable you to read and understand any medication order that you are expected to carry out. At some time, you may also have to translate a prescription into simple language for a patient's family. Tables 3-3 and 3-4 show some abbreviations commonly used in the medical profession.

You may find abbreviations capitalized on some orders and not capitalized on others. You may also find differences in punctuation. The use of capital letters and periods is inconsistent in the profession. Check to see if your agency has its own list of approved abbreviations, and follow that list.

Table 3-4 Medical abbreviations

Abbreviation (Latin[a])	Meaning
a (ante)	before
AD (aura dexter)	right ear
AS (aura sinister)	left ear
AU (aura uterque)	both ears
$\bar{c}$ (cum)	with
°C	degrees Celsius (Centigrade)
dil. (dilue)	dilute
°F	degrees Fahrenheit
♀	female
M. (misce)	mix
♂	male
n.p.o. (nil per os)	nothing by mouth
non rep. (non repetatur)	do not repeat
OD (oculus dexter)	right eye
ophth., op. (ophthalmicus)	ophthalmic
OS (oculus sinister)	left eye
OU (oculus uterque)	both eyes
per (per)	by
$\bar{p}$ (post)	after
pH	acid/base balance (on a scale of 0 to 14)
PO, p.o. (per os)	by mouth
q., qq. (quaque)	every
q.s. (quatum satis)	a sufficient amount; as much as necessary
®	registered trade name
Rx (recipe)	take
$\bar{s}$ (sine)	without
sig. (signa)	write on label
$\overline{ss}$	one-half

[a] Latin words are for reference only. You do not need to memorize them.

62 Administering Medications

EXERCISES

A. Matching. Match the forms of medication to their descriptions.

____ 1. ointment
____ 2. gel
____ 3. emulsion
____ 4. fluidextract
____ 5. spirit
_a_ 6. syrup
____ 7. tincture
____ 8. elixir
____ 9. magma
____ 10. liniment
____ 11. lotion

a. heavy sugar and water solution with flavoring
b. alcohol mixed with a volatile oil
c. 10–20% drug solution in alcohol and/or water
d. highly concentrated alcohol solution
e. 10–20% drug solution in alcohol and water *plus* sweeteners and aromatics
f. oils and fats suspended in water
g. mixture of heavy particles with water; looks like milk
h. thick mixture of fine particles with water
i. a soothing or counterirritant preparation for external use, designed to be rubbed in
j. a soothing or counterirritant preparation for external use, designed to be patted on
k. a topical or ophthalmic preparation in a base of lanolin or petrolatum

B. Practice decoding abbreviations. Give the term that the abbreviation stands for:

1. ext. _____
2. syr. _____
3. tinc. _____
4. sp. _____
5. supp. _____
6. fld.ext. _____
7. cap. _____
8. elix. _____
9. tab. _____
10. sol. _____
11. susp. _____

C. Describe the following solid forms:

1. troche _____
_____

2. suppository _____
_____

3. delayed-release capsule _____

_____

4. scored tablet _____

_____

D. Fill in the blanks with the word or phrase that best completes each statement.

1. Because of their high drug concentrations, spirits, tinctures, and fluidextracts must be measured with a _____.

2. To prevent alcohol solutions from separating, store them in _____.

3. Bottles containing tinctures, fluidextracts, elixirs, and spirits are kept tightly closed so that the _____ cannot evaporate.

4. All suspensions must be _____ before use.

5. When a drug dissolves in water or alcohol, the resulting preparation is called a(n) _____.

6. When a drug does not dissolve in liquid, the preparation is called a(n) _____.

7. _____ - coated capsules and tablets prevent stomach irritation by dissolving only when they reach the intestine.

8. Highly concentrated powders of drugs are known as dry _____.

9. Suppositories may be inserted into the _____, the _____, or the _____.

10. A diagnosed alcoholic should not be given any _____ solutions.

11. Delayed-release capsules are also called _____.

12. Oral medicines are made to taste good to help _____ as well as _____ take them.

13. Elixirs of phenobarbital or *Benadryl* have _____ to make them _____ to help the elderly take them.

64 Administering Medications

E. What is the important rule to remember when administering delayed-release tablets and capsules? Why is this rule important?

_____

_____

F. Match the route to the proper abbreviation.

_____ 1. under the tongue   a. buc

_____ 2. under the skin   b. O, p.o.

_____ 3. into the skin   c. ID

_____ 4. into the muscle   d. IV

_____ 5. into the vein   e. subl

_____ 6. by mouth   f. subcu

_____ 7. inside the cheek   g. IM

G. Fill in the blanks.

1. In sublingual and buccal administrations, no _____ is permitted until the medication is dissolved.

2. Applying local medications to the skin or the mucous membranes is known as the _____ route.

3. Injecting medications into the body with a needle and syringe is known as the _____ route.

4. Parenteral medications and equipment must be _____; otherwise, there is danger of infection.

H. List six items of information that must be included on *any* written medication order.

1. _____

2. _____

3. _____

4. _____

5. _____

6. _____

I. Define these terms:

1. standing order _____

   _____

2. self-terminating (automatic stop) order _____

   _____

J. 1. What should you do if you have a question about a medication order?

   _____

   _____

2. What two new members of the health team are allowed to prescribe medications

   as well as doctors in some states? _____

   _____

K. Fill in the blanks by converting from the 24-hour clock to the regular clock and vice versa.

	Regular Clock	**24-Hour Clock**
1.	7:00 a.m.	_____
2.	_____	1100 hours
3.	_____	1330 hours
4.	2:00 p.m.	_____
5.	_____	2000 hours

L. Matching. Choose the abbreviations that best match each phrase.

____ 1. eye medication orders   a. stat

____ 2. medications given as necessary b. B I D, Q I D, q4h, h.s., a.m.

____ 3. administration times   c. a.c., p.c.

____ 4. before or after meals   d. HCl, NaCl, H_2O

____ 5. medications given once a day   e. ad lib., PRN, s.o.s.

____ 6. immediate, one-time order   f. o.d., o.n., q.d.

____ 7. nothing by mouth   g. N P O

____ 8. chemical symbols   h. OD, OS, OU, ophth.

66 Administering Medications

M. Translate the doctor's orders. Use your knowledge of medical abbreviations to give the meanings of the following orders. (The dosage abbreviations you need are provided below. You will study these abbreviations in Unit 4.)

mg = milligram   tsp = teaspoon

1. Darvon caps 65 mg q4h PRN for pain _____

2. Phenobarbital elix. 1 tsp (20 mg) h.s. _____

3. Keflex 250 mg caps q6h P O _____

4. Lotrimin 1% cream bid x 2 weeks. _____

5. Bacitracin ophth. oint. OD TID for conjunctivitis _____

6. Propantheline bromide tabs. 15 mg a.c. _____

7. Heparin 5000 units IV stat _____

8. Acetaminophen 120 mg r supp. QID _____

ANSWERS TO EXERCISES

A. Matching
 1. k
 2. h
 3. f
 4. d
 5. b
 6. a
 7. c
 8. e
 9. g
 10. i
 11. j

B. Form abbreviations
 1. extract
 2. syrup
 3. tincture
 4. spirit
 5. suppository
 6. fluidextract
 7. capsule
 8. elixir
 9. tablet
 10. solution
 11. suspension

C. Solid forms
 1. pleasant-tasting tablet made to dissolve in the mouth for a local effect
 2. drug held in a firm substance that melts at body temperature; designed for insertion in vagina, rectum, or urethra
 3. capsule containing multiple doses of medicine that are released gradually for a sustained effect
 4. tablet with a groove down the middle for easy dividing

D. Fill in the blanks
 1. medicine dropper or medicine glass
 2. a dark place
 3. alcohol
 4. shaken
 5. solution
 6. suspension
 7. Enteric
 8. extracts
 9. rectum, vagina, urethra
 10. alcohol
 11. sustained release or timed release
 12. old as well as young
 13. added ingredients, tasting better

E. Do not dissolve the contents of a delayed-release capsule in food or drink. In doing so, you might overdose the patient.

F. Route abbreviations
 1. e
 2. f
 3. c
 4. g
 5. d
 6. b
 7. a

G. Fill in the blanks
 1. food or drink
 2. topical
 3. parenteral
 4. sterile

H. Medication order items
 1. patient's full name
 2. date of the order
 3. drug name
 4. dosage (frequency, amount, strength)
 5. route of administration
 6. signature of physician

I. Definitions
 1. medication order that stays in effect until further notice
 2. medication order that stops after a certain number of doses, after a certain period of time, or after a specified change in the patient's condition.

J. Medication orders
 1. If you question a medication order, ask the doctor or the nurse in charge to explain the reasons for the order.
 2. Physician's assistants and nurse practitioners

K. Twenty-four hour clock
   1. 0700 hours
   2. 11:00 a.m.
   3. 1:30 p.m.
   4. 1400 hours
   5. 8:00 p.m.
L. Abbreviations
   1. h
   2. e
   3. b
   4. c
   5. f
   6. a
   7. g
   8. d
M. Doctor's orders
   1. *Darvon* capsules, 65 milligrams every 4 hours as necessary for pain.
   2. Phenobarbital elixir, 1 teaspoon (20 milligrams) at bedtime.
   3. *Keflex* 250 milligram capsules every 6 hours orally.
   4. *Lotrimin* 1% cream twice a day for 2 weeks.
   5. *Bacitracin* ophthalmic ointment in the right eye 3 times a day for conjunctivitis.
   6. Propantheline bromide tablets, 15 milligrams before meals.
   7. Heparin 5000 units intravenously immediately.
   8. Acetaminophen 120-milligram rectal suppository 4 times a day.

Unit 4

Measurement and Dosage Calculation

In this unit you will learn about three systems used in measuring doses of medication. You will learn how to solve simple dosage problems and how to convert doses from one system of measurement to another. A review of fractions is included to help you brush up on your math skills.

In this unit, you will learn to:

- Write and define the abbreviations for units of measurement in the metric, apothecaries', and household systems.

- State the most common equivalents between apothecaries', metric, and household measures, and use a conversion table to find less common equivalents.

- Convert grams to milligrams and vice versa.

- Convert milliliters to teaspoons and vice versa.

- Calculate number of tablets or capsules to give when the available dose differs from the ordered dose.

- Calculate doses using a procedure for converting between different units of measurement.

- Tell the difference between a "child" and an "adult" in dose calculation.

- Calculate drops per minute for IV therapy.

SYSTEMS OF MEASUREMENT

Measurement has always been an important part of prescribing and administering medications. This is so because different amounts of a drug give different effects. Some drugs are deadly poisons, but when given in tiny amounts can help relieve disorders. Other drugs are useless for therapy unless given in large amounts.

Most drugs have a certain **dosage range**; that is, different amounts that can produce therapeutic effects (Figure 4-1). Doctors prescribe an amount within the dosage range depending on how strong an effect is needed and on the patient's age and physical condition. Doses below the dosage range will not produce the desired therapeutic effect. Doses above the dosage range can be harmful to the body and may be fatal.

To get the drug effects they want, physicians and pharmacists try to make dosages very exact by measuring drugs carefully. However, they have not always used the same units of measurement. There are different measurement **systems**, each having its own units of weight and volume.

Today, three different systems of measurement are commonly used in the medical field. You should be familiar with the units of weight and volume found in each system. Dosages on a medication order may be expressed in anything from milliliters (or cubic centimeters) to drops, teaspoons, drams, or minims. You need to know what each of these quantities means so that you can measure out the doses properly. In addition, you may be asked to convert (change) from one unit or system to another in the course of your daily routine. You need to know how to use conversion tables to convert from milligrams to grams, from milliliters to teaspoons, from grains to milligrams, and so forth.

The three systems of measurement used in ordering medications are the **apothecaries'** (ah-poth'e-ke-rez) system, the **metric** system, and the **household** system.

Apothecaries' System

The apothecaries' system of measurement is very old. It was brought to the United States from England during the eighteenth century. Colonial pharmacists (apothecaries) used it when compounding and measuring their medicinal preparations. The system is gradually being phased out in favor of the easier-to-use metric system.

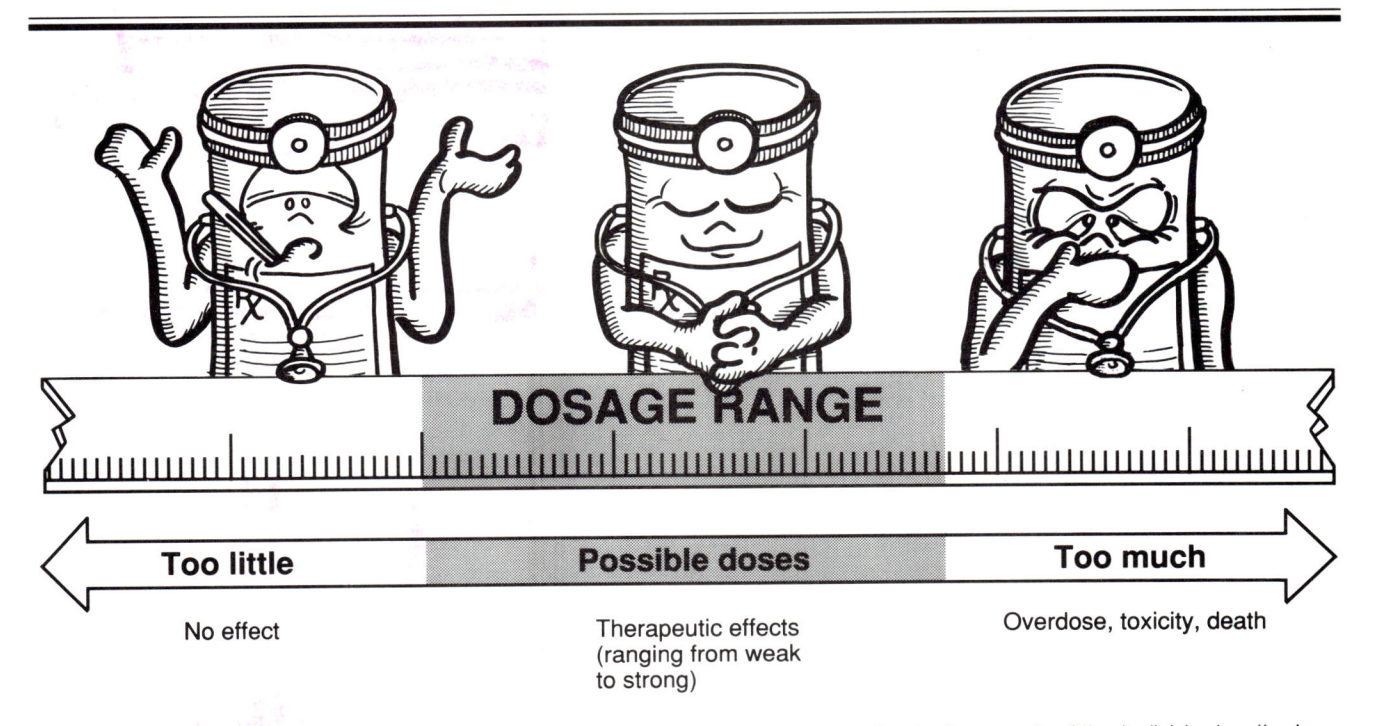

Figure 4-1 The physician chooses a certain dose within the dosage range according to the needs of the individual patient.

VOCABULARY

apothecary: old word for pharmacist

Arabic numerals: 1, 2, 3, 4, and so on

calculation: figuring out a mathematical problem

centimeter: one-hundredth of a meter

conversion: changing from one unit of measurement to another

dosage range: the different amounts of a drug that will produce therapeutic effects but not serious side effects or toxicity

dram: 60 grains (1 fluidram = 60 minims)

drop factor: number of drops per IV tubing, stated on the tubing box by the manufacturer

equivalents: things that are equal in amount or value

formula: a mathematical rule for doing a certain kind of math problem

fraction: a mathematical way of talking about an amount that is part of a whole or a ratio between two numbers

grain: basic unit of weight in the apothecaries' system

gram: basic unit of weight in the metric system

kilogram: 1000 grams

liter: basic unit of volume in the metric system

metric: system of measurement based on the meter in which all units are multiples of 10

microgram: one-millionth of a gram

milligram: one-thousandth of a gram

milliliter: one-thousandth of a liter (same as cubic centimeter)

minim: basic unit of volume in the apothecaries' system

Roman numerals: I, II, III, IV, V, and so forth

unit: (1) basic quantity in a measurement system; (2) a way of telling the strength of hard-to-measure drugs such as antibiotics (e.g., 100,000 units of penicillin)

volume: amount of space taken up by a substance

The basic unit of weight in the apothecaries' system is the **grain** (gr). It was originally supposed to be the weight of one grain of wheat. The basic unit of volume is the **minim** (min). A minim is the space taken up by a quantity of water that weighs the same as a grain of wheat.

Table 4-1 lists all of the units of weight and volume in the apothecaries' system. Note especially the abbreviations for these units. You need to be able to recognize them on a medication order and write them on a medication chart.

In the apothecaries' system, dosage quantities are written out in **lowercase Roman numerals** (see Table 4-2). By convention the Roman numerals are written with a bar over them *after* the unit of measurement; e.g., ʒ ii meaning 2 drams.

If the quantity of units is higher than 15, Arabic numerals can be used (15, 16, 17, etc.). Arabic numerals are usually written *before* the unit of measurement; for example, 25 gr, although many people prefer to write them after the unit to avoid confusing grains with grams in the metric system.

Table 4-1 The apothecaries' system

WEIGHT (DRY)	VOLUME (LIQUID)
grain (gr)	minim (min, ♏)
dram (dr or ʒ)	fluidram (fl dr, ʒ or fʒ)
ounce (oz or ʒ)	fluidounce (fl oz, ʒ or fʒ)
pound	pint (pt)
ton	quart (qt)

EQUIVALENTS

A minim of liquid weighs 1 grain
60 grains or 60 minims = 1 dram or fluidram
8 drams or fluidrams = 1 ounce or fluidounce

Table 4-2 Lower-case Roman numerals

1	i	9	ix
2	ii	10	x
3	iii	11	xi
4	iv	12	xii
5	v	13	xiii
6	vi	14	xiv
7	vii	15	xv
8	viii	(ss	= 1/2)

Quantities less than one (1/2, 3/4) and mixed fractions (2 3/4, 4 1/2) are also usually written with Arabic numerals before the unit. The only exception is the quantity one-half, for which the symbol $\overline{ss}$ is used with Roman numerals after the unit.

Here are some examples:

f℥ vii = 7 fluidounces

℈ iv = 4 drams

gr iss = 1 1/2 grains

5 1/4 dr = 5 1/4 drams

1/150 gr (also gr 1/150) = 1/150 grain

15 gr (also gr 15) = 15 grains

30 min = 30 minims

Metric System

The metric system is used throughout the world and is gradually becoming accepted in the United States, especially in medicine. It is a simple, logical system of measurement based on units of 10.

A unit of length, the **meter**, is the foundation of the metric system. It is actually one 10-millionth of the distance between the North Pole and the Equator. Metric volume is measured in fractions of a **liter** (L,l). Weight is measured in **grams** (g).

Prefixes added to the words "meter," "gram," and "liter" indicate smaller or larger units in the system (see Table 4-3). All units are a result of either multiplying or dividing by 10, 100, or 1000. The centimeter, for example, is 1/100 of a meter. A millimeter is 1/1000 of a meter. A kilometer is 1000 meters.

Table 4-3 Prefixes in the metric system

GREEK (MULTIPLY)	LATIN (DIVIDE)
deca ⟶ × 10	deci ⟶ ÷ 10
hecto ⟶ × 100	centi ⟶ ÷ 100
kilo ⟶ × 1000	milli ⟶ ÷ 1000
	micro ⟶ ÷ 1,000,000

In the metric system, units of length, weight, and volume are related to each other in systematic ways. The unit of volume most often used in preparing medications is the **milliliter** (ml), which is one-thousandth of a liter. One milliliter is the liquid contents of a cube measuring 1 centimeter (cm) on a side, or 1 **cubic centimeter** (cc). One liter is the liquid contents of a cube measuring 10 cm on a side, or 1000 cc. One gram is equal to the weight of 1 ml (or cc) of water. One liter contains 1000 ml of water, and so it weighs 1000 g (1 kilogram). These relationships are shown in Figure 4-2.

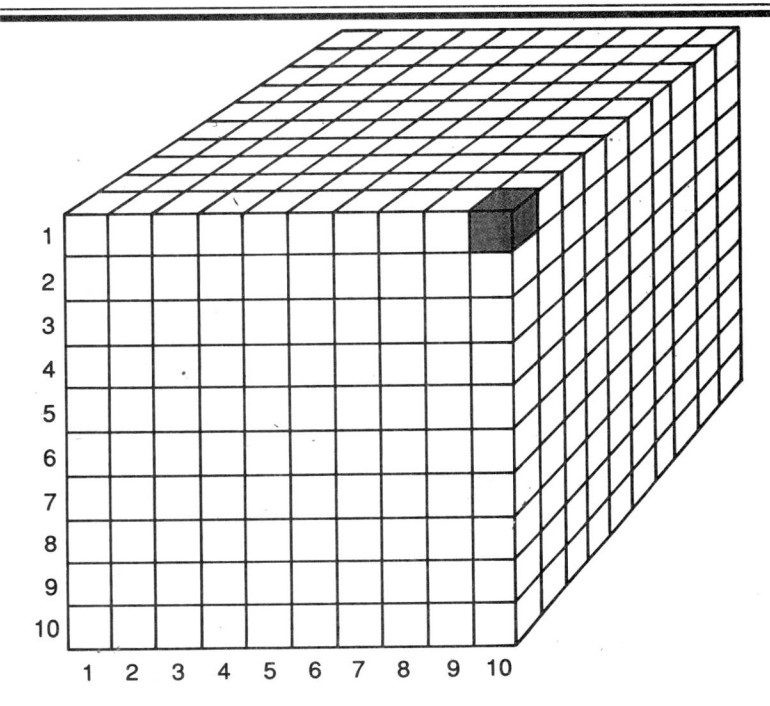

1000 cc = 1 L = 1 kg

1 cm { 1 cc = 1 ml = 1 gr

Figure 4-2 Relationships among units of length, volume, and weight in the metric system.

Metric doses are always written out in Arabic numerals. Fractions of metric doses are written as decimal fractions. For example, one-half gram is 0.5 g. In reading medication orders, pay special attention to where the decimal point is placed. The differences between 0.05 g, 0.5 g, and 5.0 g are huge when it comes to doses of medicine. A mistake could be dangerous.

Table 4-4 lists the basic units of volume and weight in the metric system and their equivalents. The bottom of the table shows how to change from milligrams to grams and vice versa. Note especially the instructions, because these are simple conversions you will probably make often on the job. The conversions are easy if you remember the hints shown in Table 4-4.

Table 4-4 The metric system

WEIGHT	VOLUME
microgram (μg, mcg)	milliliter (ml)
milligram (mg, Mgm)	cubic centimeter (cc, cm³)
gram (g, Gm, gm)	liter (L, l)
kilogram (kg),	

EQUIVALENTS

One milliliter (1 ml) is the same as 1 cubic centimeter (1 cc), and for water, both weigh 1 gram

1000 milliliters = 1 liter = 1000 cubic centimeters
1000 micrograms = 1 milligram
1000 milligrams = 1 gram
1000 grams = 1 kilogram
100 milligrams = 0.1 gram
10 milligrams = 0.01 gram, etc.

SIMPLE CONVERSIONS

From grams to milligrams:

g × 1000 = mg

Hint: Move decimal point three places to the right

0.25 g = **250** mg

From milligrams to grams:

mg ÷ 1000 g

Hint: Move decimal point three places to the left

500 mg = **.500** g = 0.5 g

Household System

The household system of measurement is actually more complicated than the metric and apothecaries' systems. However, most of us have grown up using its basic units—feet, inches, miles, pints, quarts, pounds, and so on—so the household system is quite familiar to us.

For medical purposes, household measures are not as accurate as apothecaries' or metric measures. So why use them at all? The reason is that medicine orders sometimes have to be translated into terms that patients can understand and use on their own. Particularly in home care, patients need to be able to take medicines in doses that can be measured with utensils they have on hand (teaspoons, tablespoons, medicine droppers, etc.).

The basic units of the household system are listed in Table 4-5. All household doses are written out in Arabic numerals.

Table 4-5 The household system

WEIGHT (DRY)	VOLUME (LIQUID)
ounce (oz)	drop (gt); drops (gtt)
pound (lb)	teaspoon (t, tsp)
ton	tablespoon (T, tbsp)
	teacup (6 oz)
	cup (c) or glass (8 oz)
	pint (pt)
	quart (qt)
	gallon (gal)

EQUIVALENTS

16 ounces = 1 pound
3 teaspoons = 1 tablespoon = 1/2 ounce
16 tablespoons = 1 cup = 8 fluidounces
2 cups = 1 pint
2 pints = 1 quart
4 quarts = 1 gallon

Drugs That Are Hard to Measure

Certain antibiotics and hormones from animal sources are impossible to weigh and measure in ordinary ways. Their strength is judged by the quantity shown to cause certain effects in laboratory animals and human volunteers—the bioassay technique. Rather than being dispensed in grams or grains, these drugs are dispensed in solutions labeled with a certain number of **units** (U) per cubic centimeter or milliliter. Examples of these drugs are penicillin and insulin.

CONVERTING BETWEEN MEASUREMENT SYSTEMS

From time to time you will find it necessary to change, or **convert**, from one system of measurement to another. A physician will order medicine in grains, but the hospital pharmacy may send up the medication in grams. Or perhaps an order written for milliliters will have to be converted into teaspoons for a patient who will be taking the medicine at home. These types of conversions are usually performed by the

Measurement and Dosage Calculation 75

pharmacist or the nurse in charge. But other health workers should also know how to make simple conversions by referring to a conversion table. Table 4-6 shows the equivalents between measures in the apothecaries', metric, and household systems. As you can see, the equivalents are not exact, but approximate. A 10% error usually occurs in making conversions.

You can make most of the conversions you need if you know these basic equivalents:

1 mg = 1/60 gr
60 mg = 1 gr
1 g = 15 gr

If you can remember these, it is easy to work out other equivalents (Table 4-7).

A close look at Figure 4-3 should also be helpful. It shows the relative sizes of containers you might use to measure out doses in the various systems.

Table 4-6 Commonly used measurement system equivalents[a]

APOTHECARIES'	METRIC	HOUSEHOLD
Liquid volume		
1 minim (m̧ or min)	0.06 ml (or cc)	1 drop
15 minims	1 ml	15 drops (gtt)[b]
1 fluidram (f ʒ)	4-5 ml	1 teaspoon (60 gtt)
4 fluidrams	15 ml	1 tablespoon
1 fluidounce (f ℥)	30 ml	2 tablespoons (1 oz)
	180 ml	1 teacup (6 oz)
	240 ml	1 cup or glass (8 oz)
	500 ml	1 pint (16 oz)
	750 ml	1.5 pints (24 oz)
	1000 ml (1 L)	1 quart (32 oz)
Dry weight		
1/60 gr	1 mg	
1 gr	60 mg	
7 1/2 gr	500 mg (0.5 g)	
15 gr	1000 mg (1 g)	
60 gr (1 dram)	4 g	
1 oz	30 g	1 oz
	500 g	1.1 lb
	1000 g (1 kg)	2.2 lb

[a] Equivalents are approximate. For example, some institutions set 1 grain equal to 64 or 65 mg for grain/milligram conversions.
[b] This figure varies. The number of drops per milliliter depends on the substance being measured.

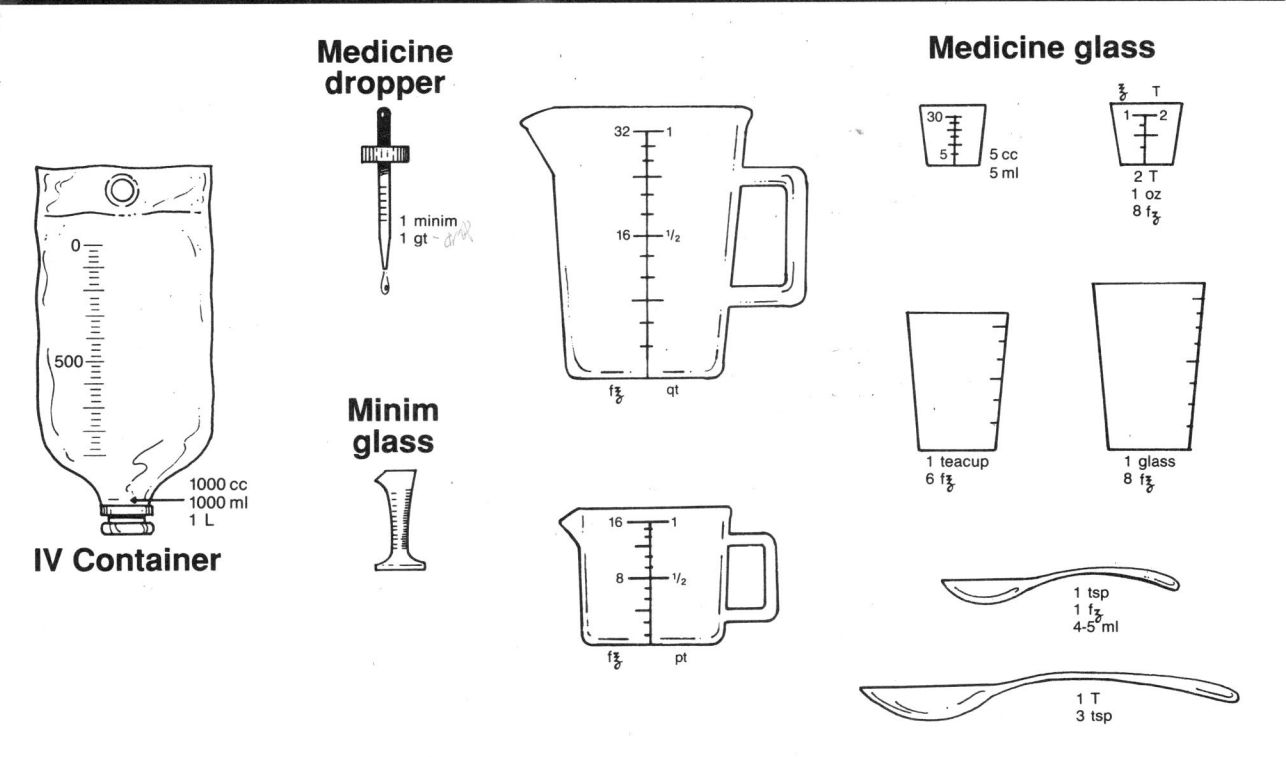

Figure 4-3 Relative sizes of measuring containers.

Table 4-7 Approximate conversions between the metric and apothecaries' systems

2 g (2000 mg)	=	30 gr
1 g (1000 mg)	=	15 gr
600 mg (0.6 g)	=	10 gr
100 mg (0.1 g)	=	1 1/2 gr
60 mg (0.06 g)	=	1 gr
30 mg (0.03 g)	=	1/2 gr
1 mg (0.001 g)	=	1/60 gr
0.1 mg (0.0001 g)	=	1/600 gr

Hints:

grains × 60 = milligrams
milligrams ÷ 60 = grains
grams × 15 = grains
grains ÷ 15 = grams

DOSAGE CALCULATION

The job of calculating dosages is much easier today than in the past. Now in some health facilities pharmacists do all of the calculating. They prepare drugs in unit packages that contain the correct amount of a drug for a single dose. In your facility, however, you may have to make simple dosage calculations as part of your daily routine. You will need to know how to do this correctly and confidently. In medication administration there is no room for error!

In this section, you will learn two simple procedures that can be used to calculate almost any type of dosage problem. The only math you need to know is how to multiply and divide using whole numbers and fractions. Use paper and pencil to do your calculations, and check them over carefully for errors. Some of the calculations are easy to do in your head. But practice with paper and pencil until you have mastered the techniques presented.

A brief review of fractions is included in this unit. To refresh your memory, turn to that review now, before reading the next section. If your arithmetic skills are weak, you will need some extra practice. There are many books available in the library or bookstore to help you brush up on your basic skills. Some of these are listed among the references at the back of this book.

Calculating Number of Tablets, Capsules, or Milliliters

A type of calculation you will probably run into often is the following:

Problem 1—The doctor orders 200 mg of a drug to be given three times a day. The pharmacy sends up a bottle of 50-mg capsules. You have to decide how many capsules to give for each dose.

A simple formula can be used to help you figure this out. The formula is:

Desired dose (what you WANT) ÷ Available dose per tablet, capsule, ml (what you HAVE)

= Number of tablets, capsules, ml's

or:

$$\frac{\text{WANT}}{\text{HAVE}} = \text{Number of tablets or capsules, liquids}$$

What this formula does is help you set up a fraction that you can **simplify** using the rules for fractions (see **Math Review**). Applying the formula to Problem 1, you get:

Dose ordered (WANT): 200 mg

Available packaging (HAVE): 50-mg caps

$$\frac{\text{WANT}}{\text{HAVE}} = \frac{200 \text{ mg}}{50 \text{ mg}} = \frac{\cancel{200}\cancel{\text{mg}}^{4}}{\cancel{50}\cancel{\text{mg}}_{1}} = 4 \text{ capsules}$$

Note that the units, mg, is also crossed out above and below the divider line when simplifying. The correct dose, then, would be four capsules three times a day.

Problem 2—The doctor orders 350 mg to be given once a day. All you have on hand are 100-mg tablets. How many tablets should you give? (If the drug ordered is a liquid, ml's or cc's can be used in place of tablets or capsules.)

$$\frac{\text{WANT}}{\text{HAVE}} = \frac{350 \text{ mg}}{100 \text{ mg}} = \frac{\cancel{350}\cancel{\text{mg}}^{3.5}}{\cancel{100}\cancel{\text{mg}}_{1}} = 3\ 1/2 \text{ tablets}$$

Note that your answer includes a fraction of a tablet. You may administer a half or a quarter of a tablet if the tablet is **scored** so that it breaks easily. If it is anything other than a scored tablet, ask the nurse in charge what to do. Dividing an unscored tablet is risky, and of course you should not attempt to divide capsules or specially coated tablets.

Problem 3—Now try a problem involving another unit of measurement. You are to give 20 gr of aspirin to an arthritis patient. The aspirin tablets you have are 5 gr each. How many tablets do you give?

$$\frac{\text{WANT}}{\text{HAVE}} = \frac{\overset{4}{\cancel{20}\,\cancel{gr}}}{\cancel{5}\,\cancel{gr}} = 4 \text{ tablets}$$

Note that both WANT and HAVE must be in the same unit of measurement (e.g., both milligrams or grains, etc.). This formula does *not* apply to a problem like:

$$\frac{100 \text{ mg}}{5 \text{ gr}}$$

Problem 4—What if the dosage ordered is a fractional dosage? For example, let's say the doctor orders 1/2 gr and your tablets are 1/4 gr. Setting up the WANT/HAVE formula, you get:

(Remember, this line means "divided by") $\longrightarrow \dfrac{1/2 \text{ gr}}{1/4 \text{ gr}}$

To work this out, use what you know about dividing fractions. You invert the bottom fraction and turn it into a multiplication problem:

$$\frac{1}{2} \div \frac{1}{4} = \frac{1}{\cancel{2}} \times \frac{\overset{2}{\cancel{4}}}{1} = 2 \text{ tablets}$$

Problem 5—The same procedure can be applied to situations where drugs are mixed into solutions. For example, the label on a bottle of elixir says it contains 5 gr of medication per teaspoon. The doctor has ordered 15 gr of medication.

$$\frac{\text{WANT}}{\text{HAVE}} = \frac{\overset{3}{\cancel{15}\,\cancel{gr}}}{\cancel{5}\,\cancel{gr} \,/\, \text{tsp}} = 3 \text{ tsp}$$

Problem 6—It also works for units of penicillin mixed in sterile water for injection. A vial states that it contains 100,000 units of penicillin per cubic centimeter. You are to inject 300,000 units.

$$\frac{\text{WANT}}{\text{HAVE}} = \frac{\overset{3}{\cancel{300,000}\,\cancel{\text{units}}}}{\underset{1}{\cancel{100,000}\,\cancel{\text{units}}\,/\,cc}} = 3 \text{ cc}$$

Dosage Calculations with Conversions

Suppose that the doctor orders a dose in grams, but your capsules are labeled in milligrams. Perhaps the order is in grains and your tablets are labeled in milligrams. Or suppose that the order is in milliliters and you want to instruct the patient how much to take at home using a teaspoon.

Dosage calculations in which you need to convert from one system or unit of measurement to another cannot be handled by the simple WANT/HAVE formula. A more complex formula is needed, but it is easy to use and can be adapted to a variety of situations. The formula is:

Dosage in ordered unit (KNOWN) X Conversion fraction (relation of UNKNOWN to KNOWN units)

= Dose in desired unit (UNKNOWN)

or:

KNOWN X conversion fraction = UNKNOWN

This formula is best explained in the context of some sample problems.

Problem 7—The doctor orders 0.5 g of ampicillin to be given four times a day. You want to know how many milligrams one dose would be. Your problem is:

0.5 g = ? mg (KNOWN unit is 0.5 g; UNKNOWN unit is ? mg)

To solve the problem, set up a calculation that will allow you to **cancel** the gram unit and give you the answer in milligrams.

$$\frac{0.5 \text{ g} \quad \text{x} \quad ? \text{ mg}}{? \text{ g}} = \text{answer in milligrams}$$

78 Administering Medications

You do this by means of a "conversion fraction." This fraction differs according to the particular problem. It is designed to show the equivalence between the known and unknown units of measurement. The known type of unit should be in the denominator. For this problem, the conversion fraction is

$$\frac{?\ mg}{?\ g}$$

You must fill in the missing quantities.

First you set the quantity of either unit to 1. Then you find out how many of the other units are contained in that quantity. In this case, let us set the quantity of grams at 1. One gram contains 1000 mg, so you fill in the fraction like this:

$$\frac{1000\ mg}{1\ g}$$

Note that this fraction is equal to 1, because the numerator and the denominator both represent the same quantity, only in different units. **Remember, the denominator must be in the same unit of measurement as the KNOWN dose.**

Now you can solve the problem by first canceling the gram unit and multiplying:

$$0.5\ g \times \frac{1000\ mg}{1\ g} = 0.5 \times 1000\ mg = 500\ mg$$

Problem 8—Take another example, this one involving a conversion between household measures. You are to give a patient 6 tsp of milk of magnesia as necessary for constipation. How many tablespoons would that be? In other words, 6 tsp = ? T (KNOWN unit is 6 tsp, UNKNOWN is ? T).

Set up the calculation so that you can cancel out the teaspoons and get the answer in tablespoons:

$$6\ tsp \times \frac{?\ T}{?\ tsp} = \text{answer in tablespoons}$$

You know that 3 tsp = 1 T, so you can fill in the conversion fraction as $\frac{1\ T}{3\ tsp}$

Proceed to solve as follows:

$$\overset{2}{\cancel{6\ tsp}} \times \frac{1\ T}{\cancel{3\ tsp}} = 2\ T$$

Problem 9—Next, try a problem that involves converting from one measurement system to another. The order is *Pro-Banthine* gr $\bar{ss}$. You have tablets that are labeled in milligrams. Can you use the described procedure to find out how many milligrams equal 1/2 gr?

$$\frac{1}{2}\ gr \times \frac{?\ mg}{?\ gr} = \text{answer in mg}$$

From memory (or looking at Table 4-7), you know that 1 gr = 60 mg, so:

$$\overset{}{\cancel{\tfrac{1}{2}}}\ \cancel{gr} \times \frac{\overset{30}{\cancel{60}}\ mg}{1\ \cancel{gr}} = 30\ mg$$

Now, suppose that your tablets of *Pro-Banthine* are 15 mg each. How many 15-mg tablets would it take to make 30 mg? Some quick mental figuring tells you that you should give the patient two tablets. If in doubt, you can use the WANT/HAVE formula, now that you have already converted from grains to milligrams.

$$\frac{\text{WANT}}{\text{HAVE}} = \frac{\overset{2}{\cancel{30}}\ mg}{\underset{1}{\cancel{15}\ mg}} = 2\ tablets$$

Children's Doses

As you learned in Unit 2, children need smaller doses of medicine than adults. There are two ways to adjust dosages for children: by age and by weight. In both cases, you can use the basic KNOWN/UNKNOWN procedure you have just learned. But first, here is the way children and adults are defined for the purpose of calculating doses.

	Age	Weight
Infant	0—24 months (up to 2 years)	Less than 40 lb
Child	25—150 months (2 to 12 1/2 years)	Less than 150 lb
Adult	More than 150 months (more than 12 1/2 yrs)	150 lb or more

Adjusting Doses by Age—You should know how to check or verify pediatric doses. A 6-month-old infant is to be given tetracycline. The usual adult dose is 250 mg. You should set up the problem like this:

$$\frac{\text{Patient's age (in months)}}{1} \times \frac{\text{Usual adult dose}}{\text{Adult age (in months)}} = \text{Child's dose}$$

The adult age is always 150 months (12-1/2 years) in this way of calculating. After filling in the proper numbers for your problem, you would get:

$$\cancel{6 \text{ months}} \times \frac{250 \text{ mg}}{150 \cancel{\text{ months}}} = \frac{1500 \text{ mg}}{150} = 10 \text{ mg}$$

The infant would therefore be given 10 mg of tetracycline.

Suppose that you were giving tetracycline to an 8-year-old. Eight years is the same as 96 months (8 x 12 = 96), so your problem would look like this:

$$\cancel{96 \text{ months}} \times \frac{250 \text{ mg}}{150 \cancel{\text{ months}}} = \frac{24{,}000 \text{ mg}}{150} = 160 \text{ mg}$$

Adjusting Doses by Weight—You can figure out a child's dose by weight just as you did by age. An adult is considered to weigh 150 lb in this formula:

$$\text{Patient's weight} \times \frac{\text{Usual adult dose}}{\text{Adult weight (always 150 lb)}} = \text{Child's dose}$$

A doctor orders *Dilantin* for a 30-lb child. The usual adult dose is 100 mg. Your calculation would look like this:

$$\overset{1}{\cancel{30 \text{ lb}}} \times \frac{100 \text{ mg}}{\cancel{150 \text{ lb}}_{5}} = \frac{100 \text{ mg}}{5} = 20 \text{ mg}$$

Parenteral Therapy

Another formula that is important to know is one used with intravenous or IV therapy. You will work here with one simple formula, but books are available covering this subject in detail. This formula will allow you to calculate drops per minute for most physician's orders relating to this type of patient care. However, there are IV pumps and controllers that will figure rates.

Suppose the doctor orders an infusion for a patient and specifies the amount of solution and amount of time to be given. You will need to calculate the rate of flow or drops per minute after you select the size of the IV tubing or drop factor. (The drop factor of the tubing for the adult is either 15 or 16 drops per 1 ml and for the child is 60 microdrops per 1 ml.) You will need the fraction 1 hr/60 minutes to complete the problem. The IV container will give you one of these drop factors.

Problem 10—The doctor orders 120 ml of 5% D/W to be given over a 6-hour period. The drop factor is 60 microdrops per 1 ml. How many microdrops would you administer in 1 minute?

$$120 \text{ ml in a 6-hour period} = \frac{120 \text{ ml}}{6 \text{ hour}}$$

Convert ml per hour to microdrops per minute:

$$\frac{120 \text{ ml}}{6 \text{ hour}} = \frac{? \text{ microdrops}}{? \text{ minutes}}$$

Write in one line as follows:

$$\frac{120 \text{ ml}}{6 \text{ hour}} \times \frac{60 \text{ microdrops}}{1 \text{ ml}} \times \frac{1 \text{ hour}}{60 \text{ minutes}}$$

Cancel the labels and the numbers that are equal:

$$\frac{\overset{20}{\cancel{120 \text{ ml}}}}{\underset{1}{\cancel{6 \text{ hour}}}} \times \frac{\overset{1}{\cancel{60 \text{ microdrops}}}}{1 \cancel{\text{ ml}}} \times \frac{1 \cancel{\text{ hour}}}{\underset{1}{\cancel{60 \text{ minutes}}}}$$

$$= \frac{20 \text{ microdrops}}{1 \text{ minute}}$$

The order of 120 ml given over a 6-hour period would be administered at the rate of **20 microdrops per minute** after you cancel and then multiply across terms.

Problem 11—How many drops per minute would you administer if the doctor ordered 1000 cc of 5% D/W in a 12-hour period?

$$1000 \text{ ml in a 12-hour period} = \frac{1000 \text{ cc}}{12 \text{ hour}}$$

Convert ml per hour to microdrops per minute:

$$\frac{1000 \text{ cc}}{12 \text{ hour}} = \frac{? \text{ gtt}}{? \text{ minutes}}$$

Write in one line as follows:

$$\frac{1000 \text{ cc}}{12 \text{ hour}} \times \frac{15 \text{ gtt}}{1 \text{ cc}} \times \frac{1 \text{ hour}}{60 \text{ minutes}}$$

Cancel the labels and the numbers that are equal:

$$\frac{\overset{250}{\cancel{1000 \text{ cc}}}}{12 \cancel{\text{ hour}}} \times \frac{\overset{1}{\cancel{15 \text{ gtt}}}}{1 \cancel{\text{ cc}}} \times \frac{1 \cancel{\text{ hour}}}{\underset{\underset{1}{4}}{\cancel{60 \text{ minutes}}}} \times \frac{250}{12}$$

$$= 20.8 \text{ or } \frac{21 \text{ gtt}}{1 \text{ minute}}$$

The order of 1000 cc given over a 12-hour period would be administered at the rate of 21 drops per minute.

When in Doubt

As a giver of medications, you share in the health care team's responsibility for making sure that the patient gets the correct dose. To meet this responsibility, you are learning all you can about dosage calculation and conversions between measurement systems. If you study hard and do the practice exercises until you have mastered them, you will be prepared to handle most routine dosage questions. However, you must also recognize your limitations. If you are the least bit confused about a conversion, or if you are unsure about a particular calculation, get some help. Ask the physician, the nurse in charge, or the pharmacist to check your work. There should be no shame in asking for assistance in this area. After all, the main concern is the welfare of the patient. What could be more important than getting the dose right?

MATH REVIEW: FRACTIONS

DEFINITIONS
A fraction is a way of expressing an amount that is part of a whole:

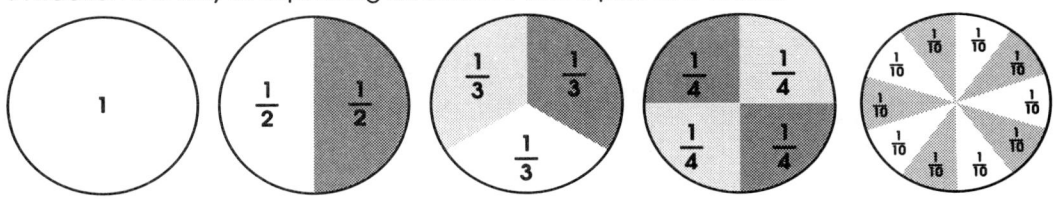

The more parts the whole is divided into, the smaller each part has to be:

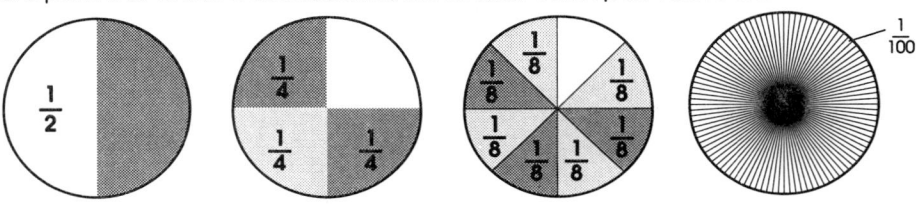

The whole can be a set of things, for example, nine dots or 100 mg:

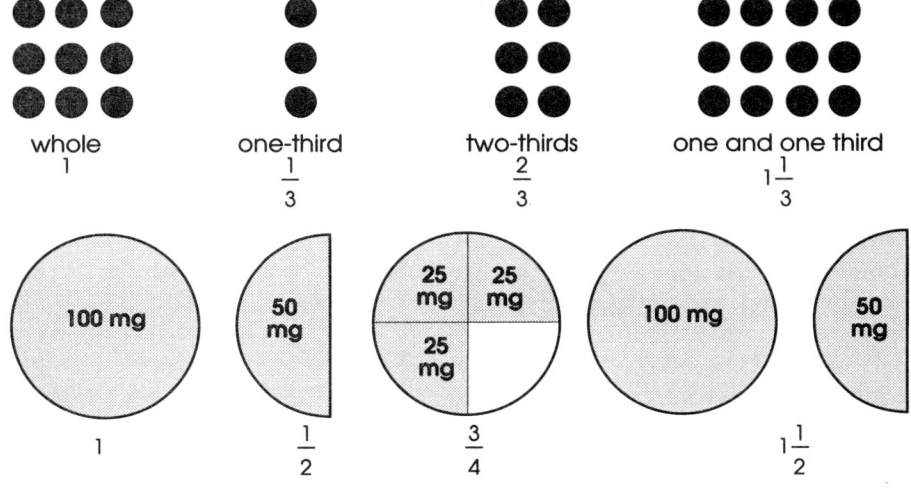

whole	one-third	two-thirds	one and one third
1	$\frac{1}{3}$	$\frac{2}{3}$	$1\frac{1}{3}$

A fractional amount of a whole is expressed like this:

NUMERATOR: how many parts of the whole you are taking → $\dfrac{3}{5}$

DENOMINATOR: how many equal parts the whole is divided into

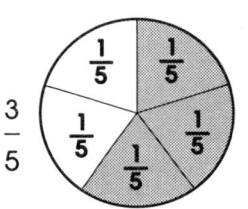

A fraction is also a way of expressing a *relationship between two numbers* or quantities; for example $3/4$ means "3 divided by 4," which can also be expressed as:

$$3 \div 4 \quad \text{or} \quad 4\overline{)3} \quad \text{or} \quad 3:4 \quad (\text{ratio})$$

A relationship like $\dfrac{350 \text{ mg}}{25 \text{ mg}}$ means the same as:

$$350 \text{ mg} \div 25 \text{ mg} \quad \text{or} \quad 25 \text{ mg}\overline{)350 \text{ mg}} \quad \text{or} \quad 350 \text{ mg} : 25 \text{ mg}$$

Simplifying fractions

To make calculations easier, fractions may be reduced to lowest terms:

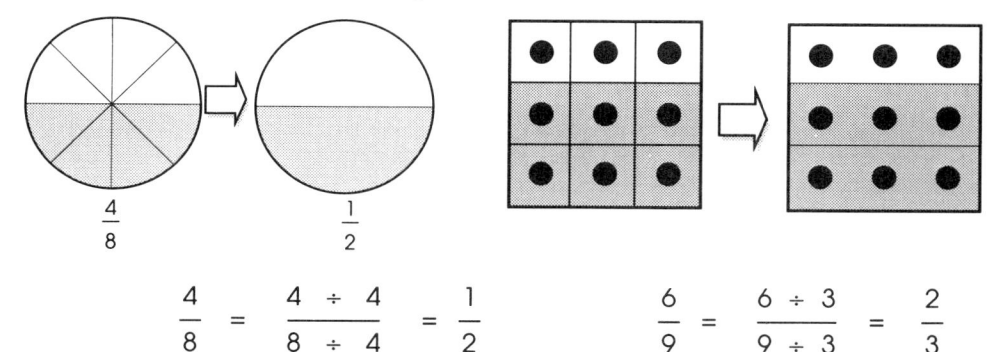

$$\frac{4}{8} \qquad \frac{1}{2}$$

$$\frac{4}{8} = \frac{4 \div 4}{8 \div 4} = \frac{1}{2} \qquad \frac{6}{9} = \frac{6 \div 3}{9 \div 3} = \frac{2}{3}$$

To reduce a fraction to lowest terms, *divide* both the numerator and the denominator by the largest number that will go into both of them evenly. *(Note: If there is no number that goes into both the numerator and denominator evenly, you cannot reduce the fraction: it is already in lowest terms.)*

When you reduce a fraction, the amount stays the same, but the fraction is easier to work with.

Canceling is a short cut way of showing that you have divided the top and bottom of the fraction by the same number. Here is how it is shown in written work:

$\dfrac{3}{15}$ You wish to reduce 3/15 to the lowest terms, so you divide the top and bottom by the largest number that will go into both of them evenly, or 3.

$\dfrac{\cancel{3}^{1}}{\cancel{15}_{5}}$ Three goes into 3 once, so you cancel out the 3 and write 1.
Three goes into 15 five times, so you cancel out the 15 and write 5.

$\dfrac{1}{5}$ Thus, after reducing to lowest terms, the fraction is 1/5.

Units of measurement can be canceled too, as long as the same type of unit appears in both the numerator and the denominator.

$$\frac{18 \cancel{\text{ mg}}}{25 \cancel{\text{ mg}}} \quad \text{or} \quad \frac{3 \cancel{\text{ gr}}}{5 \cancel{\text{ gr}}} \quad \text{but not} \quad \frac{3 \text{ gr}}{50 \text{ mg}}$$

To simplify a "top heavy" fraction (or **improper** fraction) where the numerator is larger than the denominator, turn it into a **mixed number** (whole number and fraction) as follows:

Such top-heavy fractions are changed to mixed numbers *only* in giving the final answer to a problem. During calculations, mixed numbers are awkward to work with and must be changed to improper fractions.

Divide the numerator by the denominator. Express the remainder as a fraction with the same denominator.

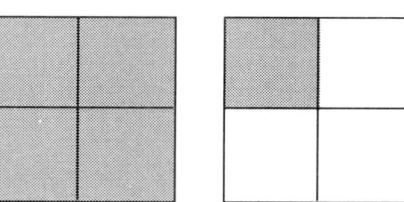

$$\frac{5}{4} = 1\frac{1}{4} \quad \left(4\overline{)5}^{\,1 \text{ rem } 1} \right)$$

Multiplying Fractions

To multiply a fraction by another fraction, multiply *numerator x numerator* and *denominator x denominator* (x = times):

$$\frac{3}{10} \times \frac{1}{10} = \frac{3 \times 1}{10 \times 10} = \frac{3}{100}$$

$$\frac{5}{8} \times \frac{2}{3} = \frac{5 \times 2}{8 \times 3} = \frac{10}{24}$$

Remember to reduce the answer to lowest terms.

$$\frac{\cancel{10}^{5}}{\cancel{24}_{12}} = \frac{5}{12} \quad \text{(divided top and bottom by 2)}$$

To multiply a fraction by a whole number, multiply *whole number x numerator*.

(You may express the whole number as a fraction by giving it the denominator "1.") Then place the product over the denominator and simplify.

$$\frac{7}{9} \times 2 = \frac{7}{9} \times \frac{2}{1} = \frac{14}{9} = 1\frac{5}{9}$$

In multiplying fractions, you are allowed to cancel across the times sign as follows:

$$\frac{3}{\cancel{4}_{1}} \times \frac{\cancel{4}^{1}}{5} = \frac{3 \times 1}{1 \times 5} = \frac{3}{5}$$

$$\frac{\cancel{8}^{4}}{9} \times \frac{5}{\cancel{14}_{7}} = \frac{4 \times 5}{9 \times 7} = \frac{20}{63}$$

You divide the denominator of one fraction and the numerator of the opposite fraction by the same number. This makes your job easier because you work with smaller numbers.

In the same way, you may cancel identical units of measurment across the times sign. This is important for certain formulas in dosage calculation:

$$2 \, \cancel{tsp} \times \frac{5 \, ml}{1 \, \cancel{tsp}} = 10 \, ml$$

$$\cancel{7.5}^{.5} \, \cancel{gr} \times \frac{1 \, g}{\cancel{15}_{1} \, \cancel{gr}} = 0.5 \, g$$

Dividing fractions

Flip over (invert) the divisor and then *multiply* the two fractions:

$$\frac{1}{2} \div \overset{\text{invert}}{\underset{\downarrow}{\frac{2}{3}}} = \frac{1}{2} \times \frac{3}{2} = \frac{3}{4}$$

$$\frac{5}{8} \div \frac{5}{9} = \frac{\cancel{5}^{1}}{8} \times \frac{9}{\cancel{5}_{1}} = \frac{9}{8}$$

$$\frac{4}{5} \div 3 = \frac{4}{5} \times \frac{1}{3} = \frac{4}{15}$$

Decimal fractions

In working with metric measures, fractions are expressed as decimals. Here is how the decimal system works:

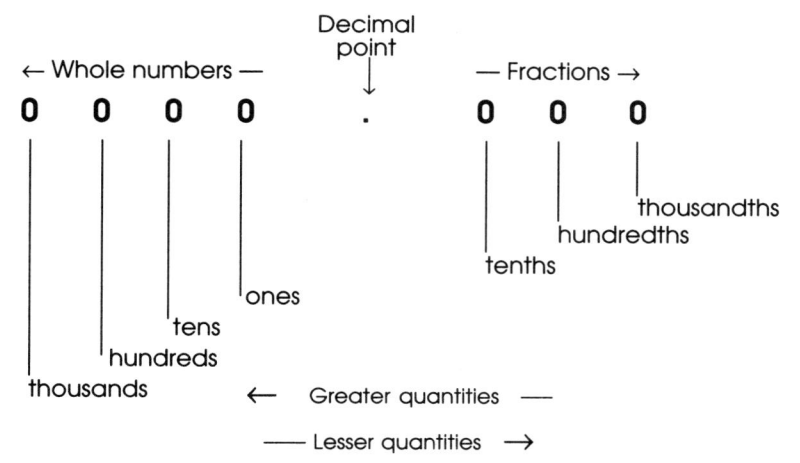

```
← Whole numbers —     Decimal     — Fractions →
                       point
  0    0    0    0   .   0    0    0
  │    │    │    │       │    │    │
  │    │    │    │       │    │    └ thousandths
  │    │    │    │       │    └ hundredths
  │    │    │    │       └ tenths
  │    │    │    └ ones
  │    │    └ tens
  │    └ hundreds
  └ thousands         ← Greater quantities —
                      — Lesser quantities →
```

The placement of numbers in relation to the decimal point tells their values are multiples of 10.

Here are some examples of various whole numbers and fractions expressed as decimals:

$1.0 \rightarrow 1\frac{0}{10} \rightarrow 1$ $0.33 \rightarrow \frac{33}{100} \rightarrow \frac{1}{3}$

$0.75 \rightarrow \frac{75}{100} \rightarrow \frac{3}{4}$ $0.25 \rightarrow \frac{25}{100} \rightarrow \frac{1}{4}$

$0.66 \rightarrow \frac{66}{100} \rightarrow \frac{2}{3}$ $0.125 \rightarrow \frac{125}{1000} \rightarrow \frac{1}{8}$

$0.5 \rightarrow \frac{5}{10} \rightarrow \frac{1}{2}$

As just shown, any decimal fraction can be expressed as a regular or **common** fraction. Note the position of the final digit relative to the decimal point:

$0.48 \rightarrow \frac{48}{100} \rightarrow \frac{\cancel{48}^{12}}{\cancel{100}_{25}} \rightarrow \frac{12}{25}$
↑
hundredths

$1.6 \rightarrow 1\frac{6}{10} \rightarrow 1\frac{\cancel{6}^{3}}{\cancel{10}_{5}} \rightarrow 1\frac{3}{5}$
↑
tenths

Any common fraction can be changed to a decimal fraction by dividing the numerator by the denominator:

$$\frac{1}{3} \rightarrow 3\overline{\smash{\big)}\,1.00}^{\,0.333,\text{etc.}} \rightarrow 0.33$$

```
        0.333,etc.
      ┌─────────
    3 │ 1.00
        9
        ──
        10
         9
        ──
         1
```

To multiply decimal fractions: 1.5 x 0.35 = ?

Set up your multiplication like a normal multiplication problem:

$$\begin{array}{r} 1.5 \\ \times\, 0.35 \\ \hline 75 \\ 45 \\ \hline 0.525 \end{array}$$

To decide where the decimal point goes, look at the original problem and count the total number of places shown to the right of the decimal point, in this case 3.

1.5 x 0.35 = 0.525
 1   2 3   3 2 1

Then, starting from the last digit of the answer, count that many places to the left, and place the decimal right after that digit.

More examples:

100 x 0.01 = 1.00
         1 2   2 1

3.25 x 0.002 = 0.00650
 1 2   3 4 5   5 4 3 2 1

2.5 x 1.4 = 3.50
 1   2   2 1

Placing the decimal point correctly is *very* important. A misplaced decimal means a huge error in the dose.

Divide decimal fractions as follows: 30 ÷ 1.5 = ?

If there is a decimal fraction in the divisor, move it to the right past the rightmost digit, making the divisor a whole number. Count how many places you moved it. Then move the decimal in the dividend the same number of places to the right. The decimal should be placed directly above the point in the quotient (answer).

$$ 20. \quad \leftarrow \text{quotient}$$
divisor → 1.5) 30.0   ← dividend

If there is no decimal fraction in the divisor, the quotient gets a decimal point directly above the one in the dividend.:

$$ 2.0$$
15) 30.0

---

84 Administering Medications

EXERCISES

A. Write abbreviations for these units of measurement.

1. minim — m
2. grain — gr
3. dram — ʒ
4. fluidram — fʒ
5. ounce — ℥
6. drops — gtt
7. pint — pt
8. teaspoon — tsp
9. tablespoon — tbsp
10. pound — lb
11. milligram — mg
12. milliliter — ml
13. cubic centimeter — cc
14. liter — l
15. gram — g

B. Practice decoding abbreviations. The following dosage orders are given using Roman numerals and abbreviations for the apothecaries' system of measurement. Write them out in full, using Arabic numerals.

1. ʒ iv — 4 drams
2. gr iss — 1½ grains
3. f℥ vii — 7 fluid oz
4. m ii — 2 minims
5. fʒ ix — 9 fluid drams

C. Practice with measurement systems. Use Tables 4-4, 4-6, and 4-7 to find the equivalents. See how many you can memorize.

1. A grain weighs the same as 300 minim(s) of liquid.
2. One minim is the same as 1 drop(s).
3. One milliliter is approximately equal to 15 drop(s).
4. Fifteen grains is about 1 gram(s).
5. One grain is about 60 milligram(s).
6. One gram is equal to 1000 milligrams.
7. One milliliter is the same as 1 cubic centimeter(s).
8. One teaspoon is about 4-5 milliliter(s).
9. One-half of a gram equals 500 milligram(s).
10. One glass (8 oz) contains about 240 milliliter(s).

86 Administering Medications

11. One milligram is about __1/60__ grain.

12. One-tenth of a milligram is about ____ grain.

13. One liter (1000 cc) is about __1__ quart(s).

D. Reduce these fractions to lowest terms.

1. $\frac{4}{8}$ __1/2__   5. $\frac{21}{28}$ __3/4__   9. $\frac{225}{500}$ __9/20__

2. $\frac{3}{9}$ __1/3__   6. $\frac{250}{1000}$ __1/4__   10. $\frac{36}{48}$ __3/4__

3. $\frac{50}{100}$ __1/2__   7. $\frac{12}{18}$ __2/3__   11. $\frac{18}{36}$ __1/2__

4. $\frac{24}{32}$ __3/4__   8. $\frac{25}{45}$ __5/9__   12. $\frac{15}{60}$ __1/4__

E. Change these improper fractions to mixed numbers.

1. $\frac{8}{3}$ = __2 2/3__   5. $\frac{18}{4}$ = __2 1/2__   9. $\frac{60}{15}$ = __4__

2. $\frac{5}{2}$ = __2 1/2__   6. $\frac{68}{3}$ = __22 2/3__   10. $\frac{83}{20}$ = __4 3/20__

3. $\frac{17}{12}$ = __1 5/12__   7. $\frac{350}{100}$ = __3 1/2__   11. $\frac{45}{7}$ = __6 3/7__

4. $\frac{55}{20}$ = __2 3/4__   8. $\frac{27}{5}$ = __5 2/5__   12. $\frac{600}{60}$ = __10__

F. Multiply these fractions. Reduce the answers to lowest terms.

1. $\frac{3}{10}$ × $\frac{1}{10}$ = __3/100__   7. $\frac{3}{4}$ × $\frac{4}{5}$ = __3/5__

2. $\frac{5}{8}$ × $\frac{2}{3}$ = __5/12__   8. $\frac{8}{9}$ × $\frac{5}{14}$ = __20/63__

3. 2 × $\frac{5}{8}$ = __1 1/4__   9. $\frac{4}{9}$ × $\frac{4}{5}$ = __16/45__

4. $\frac{5}{4}$ × $\frac{7}{6}$ = __1 11/24__   10. 250 mg × $\frac{1 \text{ gr}}{60 \text{ mg}}$ = ____

5. $\frac{11}{12}$ × 3 = __2 3/4__   11. 3 gr × $\frac{60 \text{ mg}}{1 \text{ gr}}$ = ____

6. 7 × $\frac{2}{5}$ = __2 4/5__   12. 45 gr × $\frac{1 \text{ g}}{15 \text{ gr}}$ = ____

Measurement and Dosage Calculation 87

G. Divide these fractions. Reduce the answers to lowest terms.

1. $\frac{1}{2} \div \frac{2}{3}$ = **1 1/3**
2. $\frac{5}{8} \div \frac{5}{9}$ = **8/9**
3. $\frac{1}{60} \div 3$ = _____
4. $\frac{1}{60} \div \frac{1}{2}$ = _____
5. $\frac{1}{12} \div \frac{3}{24}$ = _____
6. $2 \div \frac{4}{15}$ = _____
7. $1 \div \frac{1}{600}$ = _____
8. $\frac{1}{60} \div \frac{1}{12}$ = _____
9. $\frac{2}{6} \div \frac{3}{12}$ = _____
10. $\frac{3}{8} \div \frac{5}{8}$ = _____
11. $\dfrac{\frac{2}{15}}{\frac{1}{60}}$ = _____
12. $\dfrac{\frac{3}{5}}{\frac{2}{3}}$ = _____

H. Write these as decimal fractions:

1. $\frac{1}{2}$ = **.5**
2. $\frac{1}{3}$ = **.3**
3. $\frac{1}{4}$ = **.25**
4. $\frac{2}{3}$ = **.6**
5. $\frac{3}{4}$ = **.75**
6. $\frac{6}{10}$ = **.6**
7. $\frac{2}{5}$ = **.4**
8. $\frac{12}{100}$ = **.12**
9. $\frac{25}{100}$ = **.25**
10. $\frac{89}{100}$ = **.89**
11. $\frac{23}{1000}$ = **.23**
12. $\frac{225}{1000}$ = **.225**
13. $1\frac{2}{10}$ = **.102**
14. $3\frac{3}{4}$ = **.225**
15. $5\frac{78}{1000}$ = _____

I. Write these as common fractions and reduce to lowest terms:

1. 0.75 = **3/4**
2. 0.2 = **1/5**
3. 0.33 = **1/3**
4. 1.5 = **1 1/2**
5. 23.02 = **23 1/50**
6. 5.66 = **5 33/50**
7. 0.25 = **1/4**
8. 0.005 = **1/200**
9. 0.375 = **1/8**

J. Practice with decimal fractions:

1. 1.5 × 3 = _____
2. 1.5 × 0.3 = _____
3. 1.5 × 0.03 = _____
4. 2.75 × 0.1 = _____
5. 7.5 ÷ 25 = _____
6. 7.5 ÷ 2.5 = _____
7. 7.5 ÷ 0.25 = _____

8. 4 ÷ 0.4 = _____
9. $\dfrac{1.2}{0.03} \div \dfrac{2}{3}$ = _____
10. 2.25 g ÷ $\dfrac{15 \text{ gr}}{1 \text{ g}}$ = _____
11. 3.2 L × $\dfrac{1000 \text{ cc}}{1 \text{ L}}$ = _____
12. 0.5 ml × $\dfrac{15 \text{ m}\ell}{1 \text{ ml}}$ = _____

K. Change from grams to milligrams:

1. 0.1 g = _____ mg
2. 2.5 g = _____ mg
3. 0.03 g = _____ mg
4. 0.125 g = _____ mg
5. 3.45 g = _____ mg

L. Change from milligrams to grams:

1. 325 mg = _____ g
2. 1200 mg = _____ g
3. 3000 mg = _____ g
4. 5 mg = _____ g
5. 75 mg = _____ g

M. Use Table 4-7 if necessary to convert these dosages. But first try to do them in your head.

1. 0.1 mg = _____ gr
2. 0.5 mg = _____ gr
3. _____ mg = 1/60 gr
4. 4 mg = _____ gr
5. _____ mg = 1 gr

6. 150 mg = _____ gr
7. _____ mg = 5 gr
8. 1 g = _____ gr
9. _____ g = 7 1/2 gr
10. 3 g = _____ gr

N. Use the WANT/HAVE formula to solve these dosage problems:

1. The doctor orders 250 mg of a drug. You have 100-mg scored tablets on hand. You will give the patient _____ tablets.

2. The medication order calls for a dose of 1 1/4 gr aspirin. Aspirin comes in scored tablets of 5 gr each. You will give the patient _____ tablet. (Hint: 1 1/4 = 5/4.)

3. The physician orders 75 mg of a drug. You have capsules of 25 mg each. You give the patient _____ capsules.

4. An injectable antibiotic is packaged 100,000 units/cc. The doctor orders 400,000 units. A certified nurse assistant will administer _____ cc to the patient parenterally.

5. A solution contains 25 mg of a drug per teaspoon. The doctor orders 50 mg. You give _____ tsp.

6. You have 1/2-gr tablets. You want to give 1/4 gr. You administer _____ tablet(s).

7. The doctor's order says to give gr $\overline{xv}$. The medicine bottle says each 5-ml teaspoon contains 7 1/2 gr. You give _____ tsp. (Hint: 7 1/2 gr = 15/2 gr.)

O. Use the KNOWN/UNKNOWN formula or Table 4-7 to solve these dosage problems involving conversions:

1. The doctor orders 600 mg. The dosage form on hand is gr $\overline{x}$ tablets. You give _____ tablet(s). (Hint: Find 600 mg = ? gr, then use the WANT/HAVE formula.)

2. You have 1/4-gr tablets on hand, and the doctor has ordered 15 mg of the drug. You give _____ tablet(s).

3. The doctor ordered 3/4 gr. The tablets on hand contain 30 mg each. You give _____ tablet(s). (Hint: Find 3/4 gr = ? mg, then use the WANT/HAVE formula.)

4. An order is for 45 minims of a drug, but you do not have a measuring container marked in minims. You do have a container marked in milliliters. You administer _____ ml.

P. Practice with dosage calculations; translate each medication order and then answer the dosage questions:

1. An order reads: Hybephen f ℥ ī t.i.d. (p.o.) X 5 days.

   a. You do not have a glass container marked in fluidounces. What household measure could you use? _____

   b. How many tablespoons are there in f ℥ ī (f ℥ ī = ? T)? _____

   c. How many fluidounces do you need for a 1-day supply of *Hybephen*? _____

   d. How many fluidounces of *Hybephen* are needed in 5 days? _____

   e. How many pints do you order from the pharmacy to have a 5-day supply of *Hybephen* (15 f ℥ = ? pt)? _____

2. An order reads: Fer-In-Sol 18 mg q.d.p.c. One teaspoon supplies 18 mg of iron. The pharmacy sends up an 8-oz bottle of *Fer-In-Sol*.

   a. How many teaspoons are there in an 8-oz bottle (8 oz = ? tsp)? _____

   b. About how many days will the bottle of *Fer-In-Sol* last? _____

Q. Practice calculating dosages for children. The usual adult dose of *Dilantin* is 100 mg.

   1. How much *Dilantin* would you give to a child 9 months old? _____

   2. How much *Dilantin* would you give to a child who weighs 34 lb? _____

   3. How much would you give to a 10-year old? _____

   4. How much would you give to a 16-year old? _____

R. Extra practice with conversions.

   1. How many grams would you give if the order is 10 mg of *Valium*? _____

   2. How many cubic centimeters do you give when the order is 2 L of Ringer's lactate? _____

   3. How many tablespoons would you give if the order is 8 oz of *Gelusil*? _____

   4. How many drops do you give when the order is 1/2 tsp? _____

   5. How many milligrams of phenobarbital would you give if the order was for 2 gr? _____

   6. You have capsules containing 0.5 g of a drug. The doctor ordered 500 mg. How many capsules do you give? _____

S. Practice calculating IV therapy doses.

   1. How many drops per minute will you give if the order is 500 ml of 5% D/W in 5 hours? The drop factor is 15 gtt = 1 ml. _____

   2. You are ordered to give the patient 500 cc of blood in 5 hours. Calculate the rate of flow. The drop factor is 20 gtt = 1 cc. (Remember, the tubing gives the drop factor and for blood it can be 20 gtt = 1 cc instead of 15 or 16 gtt = 1 cc.) _____

   3. The physician orders 1500 ml of 5% D/W in 24 hours. The drop factor is 15 gtt = 1 cc. How many drops per minute will you give? _____

4. Order: give 2000 cc of 5% D/W in 20 hours. Calculate the infusion rate if the drop factor is 15 gtt = 1 ml._____

5. The nurse has an order for 240 ml of normal saline. The infusion rate must be calculated with the drop factor 60 microdrops = 1 ml for 6 hours._____

ANSWERS TO EXERCISES

A. Abbreviations
1. min, m
2. gr
3. dr, ʒ
4. fl dr, f ʒ
5. oz, ʒ
6. gtt
7. pt
8. tsp, t
9. T, tbsp
10. lb
11. mg
12. ml
13. cc, cm³
14. L, l
15. g, Gm

B. Decoding
1. 4 drams
2. 1 1/2 grains
3. 7 fluidounces
4. 2 minims
5. 9 fluidrams

C. Equivalents
1. 1
2. 1
3. 15
4. 1
5. 60
6. 1000
7. 1
8. 4-5
9. 500
10. 240
11. 1/60
12. 1/600
13. 1

D. Reduce fractions
1. $\frac{1}{2}$
2. $\frac{1}{3}$
3. $\frac{1}{2}$
4. $\frac{3}{4}$
5. $\frac{3}{4}$
6. $\frac{1}{4}$
7. $\frac{2}{3}$
8. $\frac{5}{9}$
9. $\frac{9}{20}$
10. $\frac{3}{4}$
11. $\frac{1}{2}$
12. $\frac{1}{4}$

E. Mixed numbers
1. $2\frac{2}{3}$
2. $2\frac{1}{2}$
3. $1\frac{5}{12}$
4. $2\frac{3}{4}$
5. $4\frac{1}{2}$
6. $22\frac{2}{3}$
7. $3\frac{1}{2}$
8. $5\frac{2}{5}$
9. 4
10. $4\frac{3}{20}$
11. $6\frac{3}{7}$
12. 10

92 Administering Medications

F. Multiply fractions

1. $\dfrac{3}{10} \times \dfrac{1}{10} = \dfrac{3}{100}$

2. $\dfrac{5}{\cancel{8}_4} \times \dfrac{\cancel{2}^1}{3} = \dfrac{5}{12}$

3. $\cancel{2}^1 \times \dfrac{5}{\cancel{8}_4} = \dfrac{5}{4} = 1\dfrac{1}{4}$

4. $\dfrac{5}{4} \times \dfrac{7}{6} = \dfrac{35}{24} = 1\dfrac{11}{24}$

5. $\dfrac{11}{\cancel{12}_4} \times \cancel{3}^1 = \dfrac{11}{4} = 2\dfrac{3}{4}$

6. $7 \times \dfrac{2}{5} = \dfrac{14}{5} = 2\dfrac{4}{5}$

7. $\dfrac{3}{\cancel{4}_1} \times \dfrac{\cancel{4}^1}{5} = \dfrac{3}{5}$

8. $\dfrac{\cancel{8}^4}{9} \times \dfrac{5}{\cancel{14}_7} = \dfrac{20}{63}$

9. $\dfrac{4}{9} \times \dfrac{4}{5} = \dfrac{16}{45}$

10. $\cancel{250}^{25} \text{ mg} \times \dfrac{1 \text{ gr}}{\cancel{60}_6 \text{ mg}} = \dfrac{25 \text{ gr}}{6} = 4\dfrac{1}{6} \text{ gr}$

11. $3 \text{ gr} \times \dfrac{60 \text{ mg}}{1 \text{ gr}} = 180 \text{ mg}$

12. $\cancel{45}^3 \text{ g} \times \dfrac{1 \text{ g}}{\cancel{15}_1 \text{ gr}} = 3 \text{ g}$

G. Divide fractions

1. $\dfrac{1}{2} \times \dfrac{3}{2} = \dfrac{3}{4}$

2. $\dfrac{\cancel{5}^1}{8} \times \dfrac{9}{\cancel{5}_1} = \dfrac{9}{8} = 1\dfrac{1}{8}$

3. $\dfrac{1}{60} \times \dfrac{1}{3} = \dfrac{1}{180}$

4. $\dfrac{1}{30} \times \dfrac{\cancel{2}^1}{1} = \dfrac{1}{30}$ (with $\cancel{60}$)

5. $\dfrac{1}{\cancel{12}_1} \times \dfrac{\cancel{24}^2}{3} = \dfrac{2}{3}$

6. $\dfrac{\cancel{2}^1}{1} \times \dfrac{15}{\cancel{4}_2} = \dfrac{15}{2} = 7\dfrac{1}{2}$

7. $\dfrac{1}{1} \times \dfrac{600}{1} = 600$

8. $\dfrac{1}{\cancel{60}_5} \times \dfrac{\cancel{12}^1}{1} = \dfrac{1}{5}$

9. $\dfrac{2}{\cancel{6}_1} \times \dfrac{\cancel{12}^2}{3} = \dfrac{4}{3} = 1\dfrac{1}{3}$

10. $\dfrac{3}{\cancel{8}_1} \times \dfrac{\cancel{8}^1}{5} = \dfrac{3}{5}$

11. $\dfrac{2}{\cancel{15}_1} \times \dfrac{\cancel{60}^4}{1} = 8$

12. $\dfrac{3}{5} \times \dfrac{3}{2} = \dfrac{9}{10}$

Measurement and Dosage Calculation

H. Decimal fractions
1. 0.5
2. 0.33
3. 0.25
4. 0.66
5. 0.75
6. 0.6
7. 0.4
8. 0.12
9. 0.25
10. 0.89
11. 0.023
12. 0.225
13. 1.2
14. 3.75
15. 5.078

I. Common fractions

1. $\dfrac{75}{100} = \dfrac{3}{4}$

2. $\dfrac{2}{10} = \dfrac{1}{5}$

3. $\dfrac{33}{100} = \dfrac{1}{3}$ (approx.)

4. $1\dfrac{5}{10} = 1\dfrac{1}{2}$

5. $23\dfrac{2}{100} = 23\dfrac{1}{50}$

6. $5\dfrac{66}{100} = 5\dfrac{2}{3}$ (approx.)

7. $\dfrac{25}{100} = \dfrac{1}{4}$

8. $\dfrac{5}{1000} = \dfrac{1}{200}$

9. $\dfrac{375}{1000} = \dfrac{3}{8}$

J. Practice with decimal fractions
1. 4.5
2. 0.45
3. 0.045
4. 0.275
5. 0.3
6. 3
7. 30
8. 10

9. $\dfrac{\cancel{1.2}\ 0.6}{\cancel{0.03}\ 0.01} \times \dfrac{\cancel{3}\ 1}{\cancel{2}\ 1} = \dfrac{0.6}{0.01} = 60$

10. $2.25\,\cancel{g} \times \dfrac{15\text{ gr}}{1\,\cancel{g}} = 33.75\text{ gr}$

    or $33\dfrac{3}{4}$ gr

11. $\dfrac{3.2\,\cancel{L} \times 1000\text{ cc}}{1\,\cancel{L}} = 3200\text{ cc}$

12. $\dfrac{0.5\,\cancel{ml} \times 15\,m\ell}{1\,\cancel{ml}} = 7.5\,m\ell$

    or $7\dfrac{1}{2}\,m\ell$

K. Grams to milligrams
1. 100
2. 2500
3. 30
4. 125
5. 3450

L. Milligrams to grams
1. 0.325
2. 1.2
3. 3
4. 0.005
5. 0.075

M. Conversions
1. 1/600
2. 1/120
3. 1
4. 4/60 = 1/15
5. 60
6. 2 1/2
7. 300
8. 15
9. 0.5
10. 45

94 Administering Medications

N. Dosage problems

    Answer: **Procedure:**   **Answer:**   **Procedure:**

1. $2\frac{1}{2}$ $\frac{250}{100} = \frac{5}{2} = 2\frac{1}{2}$ tabs   5.   2 $\frac{50}{25} = 2$ tsp.

2. $\frac{1}{4}$ $\frac{5/4}{5} = \frac{5}{4} \times \frac{1}{5} = \frac{1}{4}$ tab   6. $\frac{1}{2}$ $\frac{1/4}{1/2} = \frac{1}{4} \times \frac{2}{1} = \frac{1}{2}$ tab

3. 3 $\frac{75}{25} = 3$ caps

4. 4 $\frac{400{,}000}{100{,}000} = 4$ cc   7.   2 $\frac{15}{15/2} = 15 \times \frac{2}{15} = 2$ tsp

O. Dosage problems with conversions

1.   1 $600 \text{ mg} \times \frac{1 \text{ gr}}{60 \text{ mg}} = 10 \text{ gr}$ (or gr $\bar{x}$)

            $\frac{10 \text{ gr}}{10 \text{ gr}} = 1$ tab

2.   1 $15 \text{ mg} \times \frac{1 \text{ gr}}{60 \text{ mg}} = \frac{1}{4}$ gr

3. $1\frac{1}{2}$ $\frac{3}{4}$ gr $\times \frac{60 \text{ mg}}{1 \text{ gr}} = 45$ mg

           $\frac{45 \text{ mg}}{30 \text{ mg}} = \frac{3}{2} = 1\frac{1}{2}$ tab

4.   3 $45 \text{ min} \times \frac{1 \text{ ml}}{15 \text{ min}} = 3$ ml

P. Practice dosage problems

1. a. **tablespoon**   See conversion table.
   b. **2 T**   See conversion table.
   c. **f ℥ iii**   t.i.d. means three times a day, 3 x f ℥ i = f ℥ iii
   d. **f ℥ xv**   f ℥ iii per day times 5 is f ℥ xv
   e. **approx. 1 pt.**   15 fl. oz. x $\frac{1 \text{ pt}}{16 \text{ fl oz}} = \frac{15}{16}$ pt

2. a. **48 tsp**   8 fl oz contains 16 T (see Table 4-6); to get teaspoons, multiply by 3 (or 16 T x $\frac{3 \text{ tsp}}{1 \text{ T}} = 48$ tsp)
   b. **48 days**   given q.d. or once every day

Q. Children's dosages

1. **6 mg**

$$9 \text{ mos} \times \frac{\overset{2}{\cancel{100}} \text{ mg}}{\underset{3}{\cancel{150}} \cancel{\text{ mos}}} = \frac{18 \text{ mg}}{3} = 6 \text{ mg}$$

2. **23 mg**

$$34 \cancel{\text{ lb}} \times \frac{\overset{2}{\cancel{100}} \text{ mg}}{\underset{3}{\cancel{150}} \cancel{\text{ lb}}} = \frac{68 \text{ mg}}{3} = 22\frac{2}{3} \text{ mg, or about } 23 \text{ mg}$$

3. **80 mg**

10 yr = 120 mos;

$$120 \cancel{\text{ mos}} \times \frac{\overset{2}{\cancel{100}} \text{ mg}}{\underset{3}{\cancel{150}} \text{ mos}} = \frac{240}{3} \text{ mg} = 80 \text{ mg}$$

4. **100 mg** Anyone over 12 1/2 years old is considered an adult.

R. Extra practice

1. **0.01 g**

$$\underset{100}{\overset{1}{\cancel{10}} \cancel{\text{ mg}}} \times \frac{1 \text{ g}}{\cancel{1000} \cancel{\text{ mg}}}$$

= 0.01 g or move decimal three places to the left: 0̰0̰1̰0. mg

2. **2000 cc**   1 L = 1000 cc, so 2 L = 2000 cc

3. **16 T**

$$8 \cancel{\text{ fl oz}} \times \frac{2 \text{ T}}{1 \cancel{\text{ fl oz}}} = 16 \text{ T}$$

4. **30 gtt**

$$\frac{1}{2} \times \frac{\overset{30}{\cancel{60}} \text{ gtt}}{1 \cancel{\text{ t}}} = 30 \text{ gtt}$$

5. **120 mg**

$$2 \cancel{\text{ gr}} \times \frac{60 \text{ mg}}{1 \cancel{\text{ gr}}} = 120 \text{ mg}$$

6. **1 cap**   0.5̰0̰0̰0 g = 500 mg

S. IV therapy

1. **25 gtt/minute**

$$\frac{\overset{100}{\cancel{500}} \cancel{\text{ cc}}}{\underset{1}{\cancel{5} \cancel{\text{ hour}}}} \times \frac{\cancel{15} \text{ gtt}}{1 \cancel{\text{ cc}}} \times \frac{1 \cancel{\text{ hour}}}{\underset{4}{\cancel{60}} \text{ minutes}} = \frac{100}{4} \text{ or } 25 \text{ gtt/minute}$$

2. **33 gtt/minute**

$$\frac{\overset{100}{\cancel{500}} \cancel{\text{ cc}}}{\underset{1}{\cancel{5} \cancel{\text{ hour}}}} \times \frac{\overset{1}{\cancel{20}} \text{ gtt}}{1 \cancel{\text{ cc}}} \times \frac{1 \cancel{\text{ hour}}}{\underset{3}{\cancel{60}} \text{ minutes}} = \frac{100}{3} \text{ or } 33 \text{ gtt/minute}$$

3. **16 gtt/minute**

$$\frac{\overset{250}{\cancel{1500}} \cancel{\text{ ml}}}{\underset{4}{\cancel{24} \cancel{\text{ hour}}}} \times \frac{\overset{1}{\cancel{15}} \text{ gtt}}{1 \cancel{\text{ cc}}} \times \frac{1 \cancel{\text{ hour}}}{\underset{4}{\cancel{60}} \text{ minutes}} = \frac{250}{16} \text{ or } 15.6 = 16 \text{ gtt/minute}$$

4. **25 gtt/minute**

$$\frac{\overset{100}{\cancel{2000}} \cancel{\text{ cc}}}{\underset{1}{\cancel{20} \cancel{\text{ hour}}}} \times \frac{\overset{1}{\cancel{15}} \text{ gtt}}{1 \cancel{\text{ ml}}} \times \frac{1 \cancel{\text{ hour}}}{\underset{4}{\cancel{60}} \text{ minutes}} = \frac{100}{4} \text{ or } 25 \text{ gtt/minute}$$

5. **40 microgtt/minute**

$$\frac{\overset{40}{\cancel{240}} \cancel{\text{ ml}}}{\underset{1}{\cancel{6} \cancel{\text{ hour}}}} \times \frac{\overset{1}{\cancel{60}} \text{ microgtt}}{1 \cancel{\text{ ml}}} \times \frac{1 \cancel{\text{ hour}}}{\underset{1}{\cancel{60}} \text{ minutes}} = 40 \text{ gtt/minute}$$

Unit 5

Routine Responsibilities

In this unit you will learn how to do the routine tasks involved in giving medications: how to order, store, and dispose of drugs; how to keep track of medication orders; how to set up medications; and how to chart medications after giving them. You will also learn how to give drugs safely by following the basic rules of medication administration.

In this unit, you learn to:

- Order drugs from the pharmacy using the physician's order sheet or a pharmacy requisition.
- Identify single-dose and multiple-dose packaging of drugs.
- Store medicines properly as stock supplies or patient supplies in the medicine room.
- Tell how a medicine cart and a medicine tray are used in giving medications.
- Tell how the Kardex, medicine card, and medication record are used to communicate medication orders.
- Transcribe medication orders onto the Kardex, medicine cards, and/or medication records.
- Count controlled substances at the beginning of each shift and tell why this is done.
- Set up medications following proper procedure.
- State the rules for giving medications and explain each one.
- Fill out a proof-of-use record and tell why this is done.
- Describe the patient chart and fill out related forms.
- Describe the problem-oriented medical record and the subjective–objective–assessment–plan method of charting.
- Follow the principles of proper charting.
- Report medication errors and skipped medications on the proper forms.

ORDERING DRUGS FROM THE PHARMACY

After a physician writes a medication order for a patient, the proper drugs must be obtained. The way this is done depends on the type of facility in which you work.

In the Hospital

Most hospitals have a pharmacy located within the building. They may also have satellite or minipharmacies on each ward.

Pharmacy requests can be made in several ways. The physician's order sheet usually has a second page that makes a carbon copy of the medication order (Figure 5-1). This second page can be torn out and sent to the pharmacy. It tells the pharmacist which drugs, and in which form, to send back to the ward for the patient. In some facilities, the entire patient chart is sent to the pharmacy. The chart includes the original physician's order sheet. This is the safest method of ordering drugs because the pharmacist can follow the doctor's original order in preparing the medication.

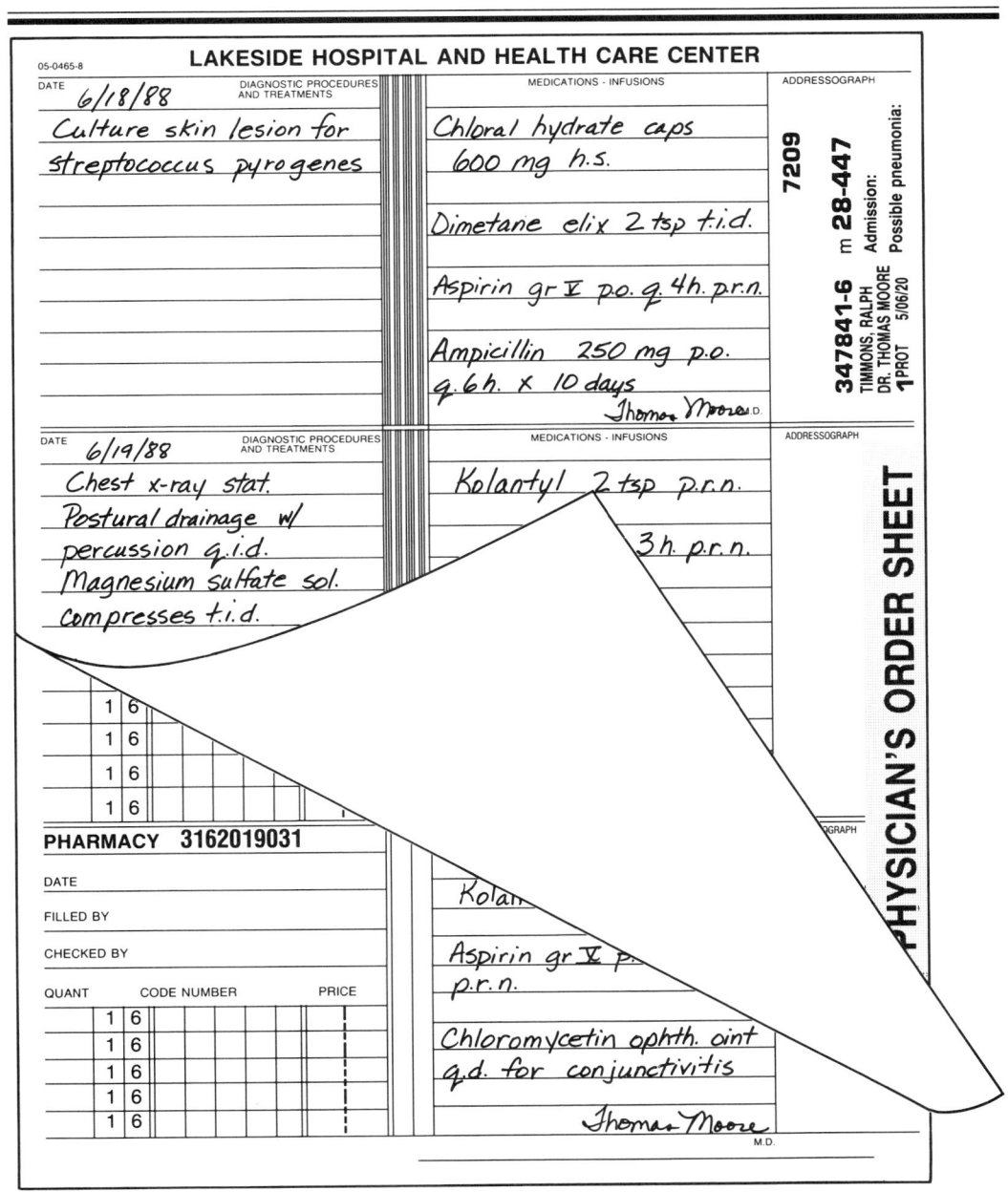

Figure 5-1 Physician's order sheet and carbon for pharmacy.

VOCABULARY

ampule: a small, sealed glass container holding medication for injection; a vial

chart: a collection of forms on which all of a patient's medical and nursing care is permanently recorded

charting: keeping records of all patient care on appropriate forms

contaminated: exposed to germs

expiration date: date after which a drug should not be used

external: outside of the body

incident report: a form used for giving information about a drug error, patient injury, or accident; also called **medication error form**

Kardex: portable card file listing daily medication orders and treatments for all patients on the unit

medication record: form showing routine and PRN medications ordered for a patient; each dose is checked off after it is given

medicine cards: small cards used for setting up medications when a unit-dose system is not used

medicine cart: movable unit for dispensing medications

medicine room: area where drugs are stored

multiple: more than one

nurses' notes: form for charting observations, stat and PRN medications, and special treatments given

observation: watching the patient for signs and symptoms of progress or distress

patient history: a form describing the development of the patient's symptoms and the course of the disease

pharmacy requisition: form on which to order supplies and medications from the pharmacy

POMR: problem-oriented medical record

proof-of-use record: form for keeping track of the administration of controlled substances; shows doses available and doses administered

routine drugs: drugs given on a regular schedule

satellite pharmacy: minipharmacy on the hospital ward

set up: to organize the drugs for administration by arranging the proper doses on a tray or a cart

SOAP: structured plan for charting; stands for subjective–objective–assessment–plan

stock supply: a collection of drugs commonly used by patients, such as lotions, milk of magnesia, and aspirin

strip label: part of a medication label that can be torn off and placed on a reorder sheet

vial: small bottle containing one or more doses of a liquid or powdered drug for injection; an ampule

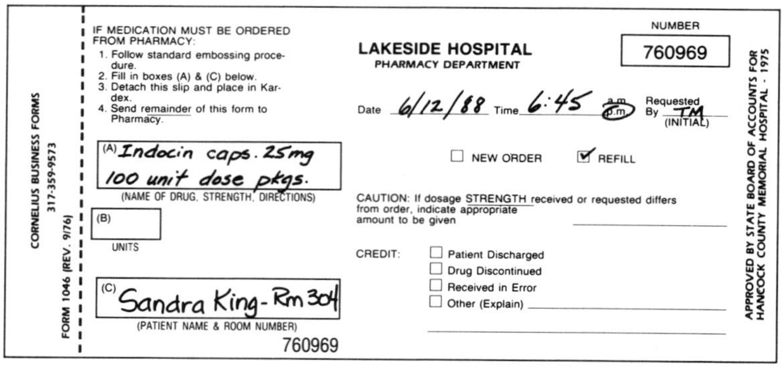

CORNELIUS BUSINESS FORMS
317-359-9573
FORM 1046 (REV. 9/76)

IF MEDICATION MUST BE ORDERED FROM PHARMACY:
1. Follow standard embossing procedure.
2. Fill in boxes (A) & (C) below.
3. Detach this slip and place in Kardex.
4. Send remainder of this form to Pharmacy.

(A) Indocin caps. 25mg
100 unit dose pkgs.
(NAME OF DRUG, STRENGTH, DIRECTIONS)

(B)
UNITS

(C) Sandra King - Rm 304
(PATIENT NAME & ROOM NUMBER)
760969

LAKESIDE HOSPITAL
PHARMACY DEPARTMENT

NUMBER 760969

Date 6/12/88 Time 6:45 a.m. (p.m.) Requested By TM (INITIAL)

☐ NEW ORDER ☑ REFILL

CAUTION: If dosage STRENGTH received or requested differs from order, indicate appropriate amount to be given

CREDIT:
☐ Patient Discharged
☐ Drug Discontinued
☐ Received in Error
☐ Other (Explain)

APPROVED BY STATE BOARD OF ACCOUNTS FOR HANCOCK COUNTY MEMORIAL HOSPITAL - 1975

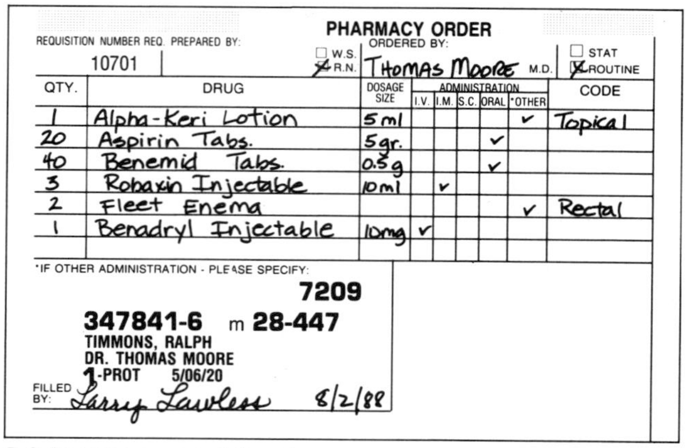

PHARMACY ORDER

REQUISITION NUMBER 10701 | REQ. PREPARED BY: ☐ W.S. ☒ R.N. | ORDERED BY: Thomas Moore M.D. | ☐ STAT ☒ ROUTINE

QTY.	DRUG	DOSAGE SIZE	I.V.	I.M.	S.C.	ORAL	*OTHER	CODE
1	Alpha-Keri Lotion	5 ml					✓	Topical
20	Aspirin Tabs.	5 gr.				✓		
40	Benemid Tabs.	0.5 g				✓		
3	Robaxin Injectable	10 ml		✓				
2	Fleet Enema						✓	Rectal
1	Benadryl Injectable	10 mg	✓					

*IF OTHER ADMINISTRATION - PLEASE SPECIFY:

7209
347841-6 m 28-447
TIMMONS, RALPH
DR. THOMAS MOORE
1-PROT 5/06/20

FILLED BY: Larry Lawless 8/2/88

Figure 5-2 Pharmacy requisition forms.

If a chart or a copy of the physician's order sheet cannot be used, the nurse must write out the drug orders on a pharmacy requisition form (Figure 5-2). This is sent to the pharmacist, and the orders are filled from it. There may be more than one drug order on each requisition form. When filling out a pharmacy requisition form, it is extremely important to copy all of the information correctly from the doctor's order. Be sure to fill in every item on the form. Study Figure 5-2 to see what information is included.

Using the physician's order sheet for ordering drugs is safer than using a requisition form because no copying is required. There is less chance of a medication error. When and if there is an error, it is much easier to find the source. State laws have helped to establish this single-entry ordering system because they require the order to go from the doctor directly to the pharmacy.

> **NOTE:**
> State laws and agency policies regulate who may carry out the routine responsibilities in medication administration. Check the policy manual of your health facility to find out who may: calculate and measure doses; set up and administer medications; transcribe medication orders; count and handle controlled substances; order, reorder, and receive drugs from the pharmacy; observe patients and chart progress; report to the physician; give patient's health instruction; and so on.

In the hospital, routine and stat drugs are requested every day as soon as they are ordered. The pharmacy sends up medicines three times a day. Usually it sends up enough of each drug to last 8 hours. At some facilities the pharmacist checks the medicine supplies in the ward three times a day. When a patient's supply is low, the pharmacist informs the ward supervisor, and a physician can reorder the needed drugs. If the doctor's order or reorder must be taken over the phone, it is written out on a special form with two copies, one for the patient chart and one for the pharmacy. The original top sheet is mailed out to the physician for signature.

In some hospitals, drug orders are entered into a computer either by the doctor or by a nurse or ward clerk following the doctor's verbal or written orders.

In some facilities, drugs are reordered by sending the empty containers to the pharmacy along with appropriate requisition forms.

In the Nursing Home

Some nursing homes have their own pharmacies, but most do not. They must order drugs from an outside pharmacy. The ordering system is somewhat different from the one used in hospitals. Drugs can be ordered using either a carbon copy of the physician's order sheet or a pharmacy requisition form. These forms are sent to the pharmacy at a certain time each day. The drugs are prepared at the pharmacy and sent back within 24 hours. When they come in, they are checked by comparing the delivery ticket with the doctor's orders.

Reorders are listed on a special reorder sheet. To make up the list, part of the original drug label called the **strip label** is pulled off of each container and pasted onto the reorder form (Figure 5-3). The form then goes to the outside pharmacy where the orders are filled.

Most drugs for nursing home patients are ordered for an indefinite period of time. In other words, they are standing orders. For that reason, drugs are ordered in large batches and are reordered only every 30–60 days.

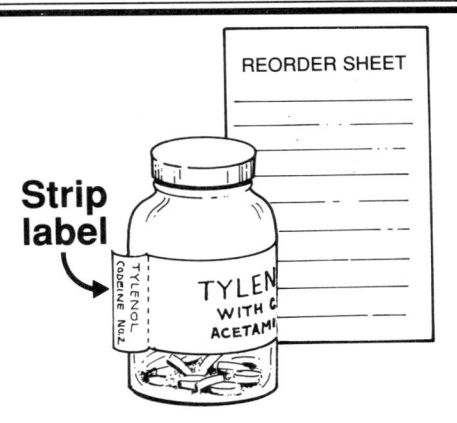

Figure 5-3 Strip label and reorder sheet.

DRUG PACKAGING

The pharmacy supplies drugs in one of two forms: single-dose packages or multiple-dose packages.

Single or Unit Dose

In single-dose or unit-dose packaging, each dose of medication is individually wrapped or bottled. Single-dose ampules, vials, and prefilled syringes are supplied for some parenteral medications. Each single-dose package contains the proper dose for one administration. It is labeled with the drug name, strength, expiration date, and sometimes the patient's name (Figure 5-4).

Unit-dose packaging provides the safest and most convenient means of administering medicines. The drugs require little handling and no special preparation before being taken to the patient. Unused doses can be returned to the pharmacy for credit. The individual wrappings ensure that they will not become contaminated in handling.

Multiple Dose

Many drugs are sent from the pharmacy in multiple-dose bottles or vials (Figure 5-5). The person who is to administer the drug must measure and pour out single doses of liquid medications or count out tablets or capsules from a bottle. Because these drugs require more handling, there is more chance for error than with unit-dose packages. Unused drugs from multiple-dose containers cannot be credited to the patient's account. They are destroyed in the pharmacy because they may have been contaminated.

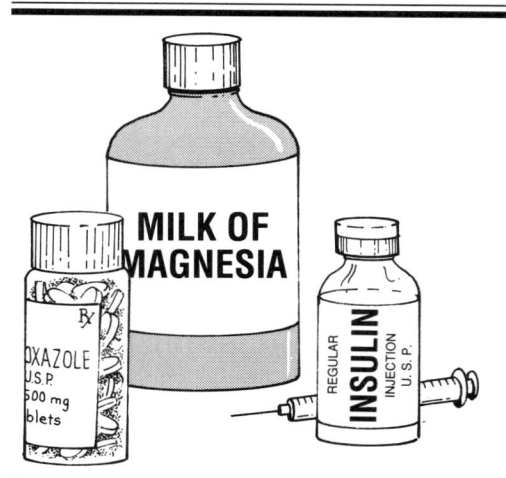

Figure 5-4 Unit dose packages.

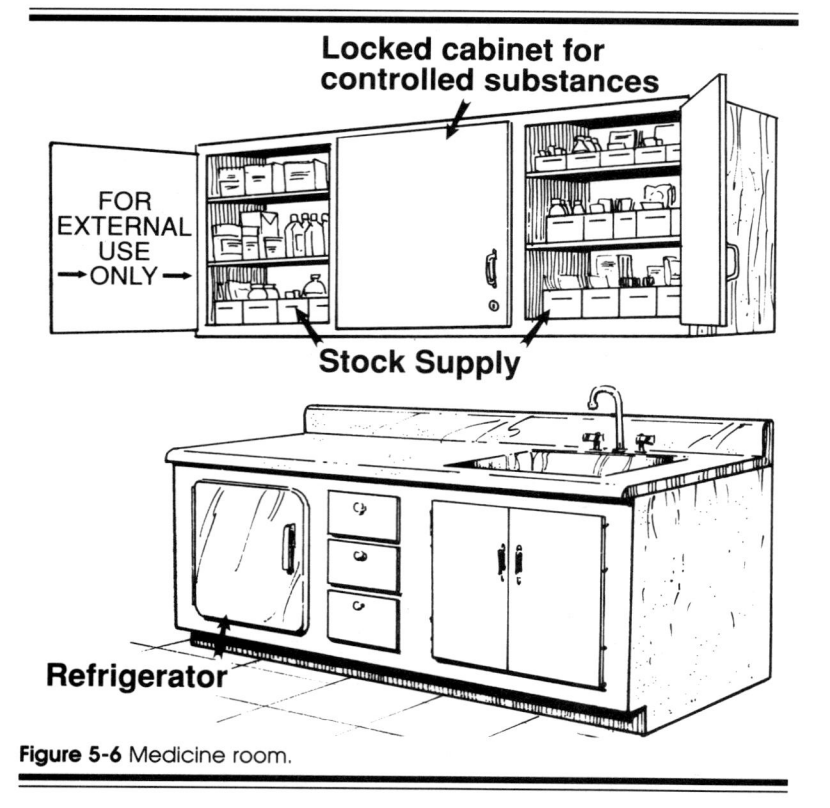

Figure 5-5 Multiple dose packages.

Figure 5-6 Medicine room.

STORAGE AND DISPOSAL OF DRUGS

Medicine Room

All medications are stored in a special area, usually located behind the nurses' station of each unit. This is known as the **medicine room** (Figure 5-6). It is open only to authorized personnel.

The medicine room contains a sink, a refrigerator, and a number of cabinets. The refrigerator is needed because some drugs must be stored in a cool place; otherwise they lose their effectiveness. Drugs that need refrigeration are so labeled. Among them are insulin, antibiotics, suppositories, eyedrops, and tetanus vaccine.

There is a special cabinet in the medicine room for controlled substances. It is kept locked so that the use of these restricted drugs can be monitored.

Another cabinet may hold **stock supply** drugs, or drugs commonly used by many patients. Some stock supply drugs are also kept in the refrigerator. Drugs like aspirin, milk of magnesia, penicillin, lotions, and emergency medications are often part of the stock supply. Because of the new unit-dose system, stock supplies are not as common as they used to be.

Cabinets in the medicine room should be kept closed at all times. Many drugs break down if they are exposed to light. Drugs that are for external use only are always kept in separate cabinets or compartments.

Keep the medicine room and refrigerator clean and tidy at all times. This is vital in helping to prevent medication errors.

Medicine Cart

For convenience, doses of routine drugs are often stored in a medicine cart. It is kept locked when not in use. This cart has drawers marked off for different patients. A supply of unit-dose packages is kept in each patient's drawer. When it is time for a dose to be given, the cart can be wheeled from room to room. The medications are then dispensed right out of the drawers (Figure 5-7).

Within the drawers, sections may be divided and labeled to hold routine medications, bedtime medications, and PRN medications. A special locked drawer in the cart contains the Schedule II, III, and IV drugs. (Schedule II drugs *must* be kept in double-locked drawers. Schedule III and IV drugs *may* be kept there.) The health care worker unlocks this drawer only when a dose of a controlled substance is needed. The drawer is relocked immediately, before giving the medication to the patient.

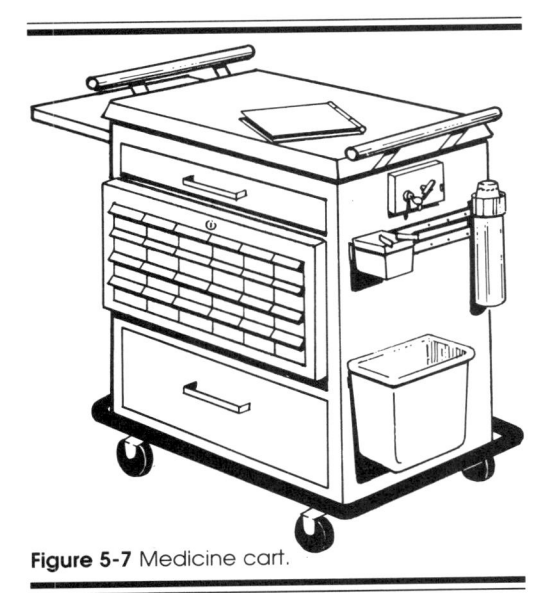

A folder on top of the medicine cart contains the paperwork that tells which drugs are to be administered at which times.

Medicine Tray

Another way of carrying drugs from room to room at administration time is the medicine tray. There are two types of trays. One is a flat tray on which you would place the medicine cups with a medicine card next to each of them. (These cards are described in the next section.) The other is a Styrofoam or plastic tray with molded recesses for holding cups and medicine cards. The molded tray is better than the flat tray because the cards and cups cannot move about and get mixed up (Figure 5-8).

Figure 5-8 Medicine tray.

Disposing of Unused Drugs

Unused doses of medications should never be returned to stock supply bottles. Discard the unused doses in the proper manner. Each health facility has it own policy regarding drug disposal. Usually the drugs must be returned to the pharmacy. In some cases, they must go to a certain person or storage area. They are then held until there is a batch of drugs to return to the pharmacy. The disposal of controlled substances must be witnessed by another staff member. It must then be noted on the proper form.

Figure 5-7 Medicine cart.

KEEPING TRACK OF MEDICATION ORDERS

Whenever more than one patient is being cared for, it is necessary to keep track of which patient is supposed to get which medicine at what time. In a ward of 20 patients, some of whom are to receive several drugs, careful preparation is needed to keep their medications straight. Medical facilities and nursing homes have various ways of handling this problem. Three common aids—the **Kardex file, medicine cards**, and the **medication record**—are helpful.

Start	TREATMENT ORDER	DAY	EVE.	NIGHT	Nurse Initial	LAB. REQ. (USE PENCIL)	DATE TO BE DONE	X-RAY REQ. (USE PENCIL)	DATE TO BE DONE
8/2	B/P	9-12	3-6	9	PB	EKG	8/2	P-A Lateral Chest	8/3/88
8/2	Fleet Enema	8			PB	CBC	8/2	P-A Lat. Chest	8/10/88
8/2	Force Fluids	9-11	1-3		PB	Serum Enzymes	8/2		
8/2	Vital Signs	9-12	3-6	9	PB	Blood Gases	8/3		
8/2	Oxygen 3L PRN				PB				
8/2	Record Output	6	3	12	PB			DAILY THERAPY (USE PENCIL)	
								Range of Motion (passive)	8/6

BED REST ___ UP AD LIB ___
SIT ON SIDE OF BED ✓
CHAIR ✓
WALK ___
BRP (YES) (ASSIST) NO
BATH O (A) C SHO/TUB
BED (OCC) UNOCC
FEED (ASSIST) SELF

SPECIAL INSTRUCTIONS
No visitors except husband
No phone calls except husband

DAILY LAB (USE RED PENCIL): Serum Enzymes

DIET: Soft Low Caloric, Decaffeinated Coffee, No Cola Beverages

DIAGNOSIS: 1. Myocardial Infarction

Room	Bed	Adm. Date	Last Name	First Name	Age	Religion	Doctor
621	1	8/2/88	Terry,	Cheryl	52	Cath.	T. Lorn

MED. ALLERGIES: None

START DATE	MEDICINE	INSTRUCTIONS AND/OR NOTES	DOSAGE	Route	FREQUENCY	DAY	EVE.	NIGHT
8/2	Morphine	severe pain	10 mg	IM	q.4h.p.r.n.			
8/2	Meperidine	moderate pain	100 mg	IM	q.3h.p.r.n.			
8/2	Nitroglycerin	sublingual for angina	gr 1/150	O	p.r.n.	q.2h.	q.2h.	q.2h.
8/2	Colace	soften stool	50 mg.	O	h.s.			8
8/5	Nembutal	repeat one time	100 mg.	O	h.s.			
8/5	Librium	mod. anxiety	10 mg	O	q.3h.	9-12	3-6	

MEDICATION CARD

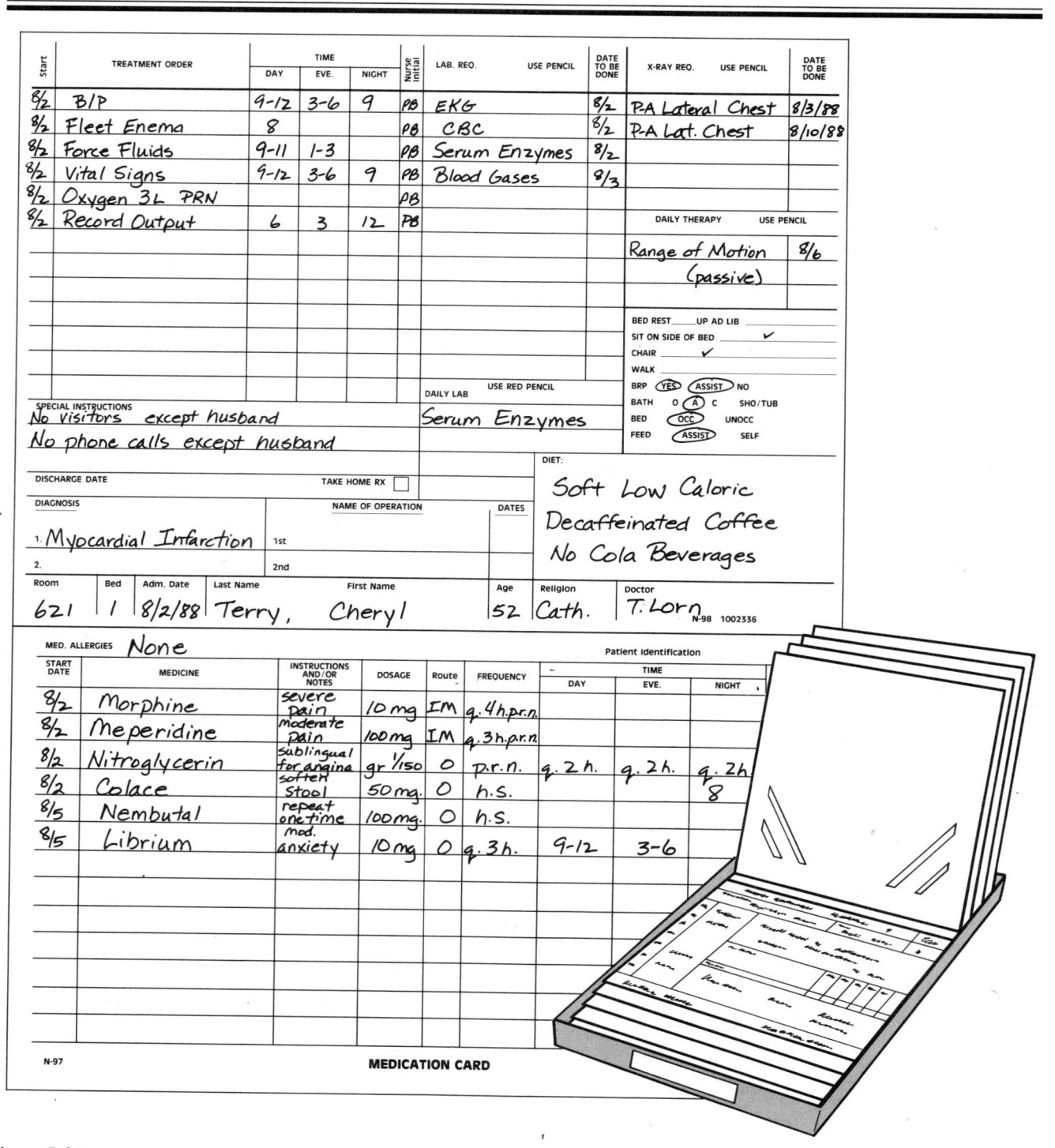

Figure 5-9 Kardex.

Kardex

The Kardex file is a handy means of communication among doctors and the nursing staff (Figure 5-9). It consists of a set of index cards in a portable file. A card for each patient gives up-to-date information about medications and treatments ordered. Each time new orders are given, the old ones are erased and the new ones penciled in. The Kardex is a quick reference when any member of the health team needs to know about a patient's daily course of treatment. Health workers can use the Kardex to help organize their own work day. They can also use it to "set up" medications. This means to organize the drugs for administration by arranging the proper doses on a tray or a cart.

Medicine Cards

Medicine cards are another aid in keeping track of medications (Figure 5-10). They are not used as often today as in the past because the unit-dose system has cut down on the need for them. Where they are still used, information is transcribed or copied onto a set of medicine cards from the Kardex. One medicine card is written out for each type of drug that a patient is to receive. Each card states the patient's name; room and bed number; name of the drug, dose, route, time at which the drug is to be given; and other notes in regard to specific medications. Sometimes the card also includes the signature of the nurse or clerk who copied the information from the Kardex.

Medicine cards are kept in the medicine room and picked up each hour just before setting up the drug tray.

If the information on a medicine card seems unclear to you, be sure to recheck the Kardex and the physician's order sheet. A mistake may have been made in copying this information. Never try to read through a card that has medicine spilled on it. You may make a medication error. Go back to the patient's chart and the Kardex and make a new medicine card. However, be sure that *you* copy the information correctly onto the new card! If you need more help, consult the nurse in charge or the drug references on your unit.

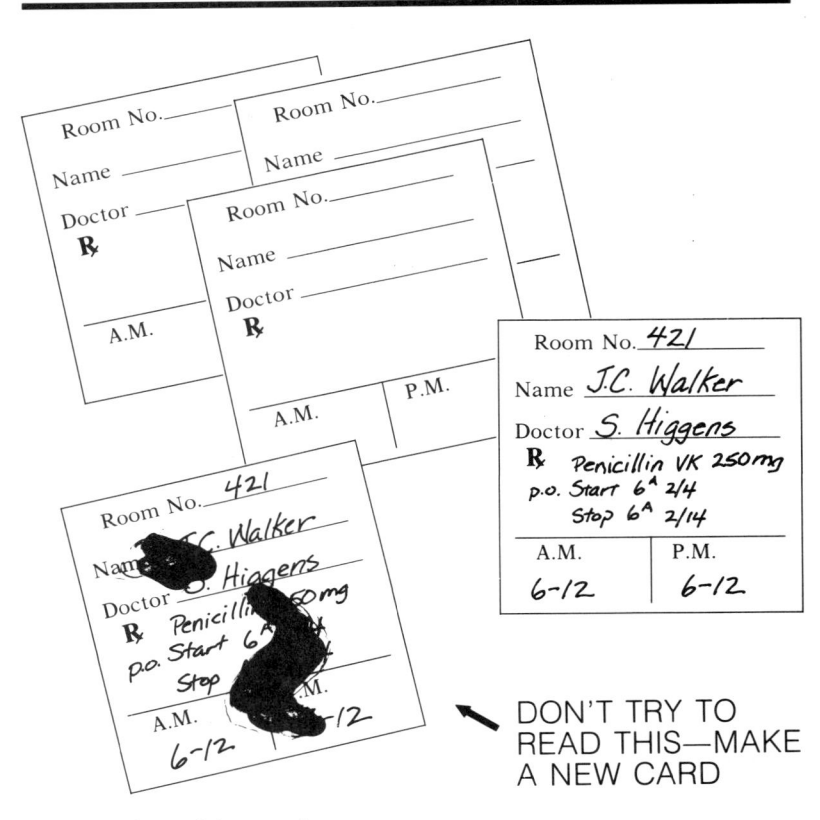

Figure 5-10 Medicine cards.

Medication Record

The medication record is a convenient way of keeping track when more than one drug is being administered to a particular patient every day. It is especially helpful when several drugs are to be given at different times. The name of each drug is written down once on a patient's medication record (Figures 5-11 and 5-12). There are separate sections for routine and PRN medications. The amount, strength, and route are also noted.

If a drug is to be given regularly, a complete schedule is written out of all the administration times for that drug. Then, each time a dose is administered, the health care worker checks off the time it was given and initials it. The full name of each person dispensing medications is listed somewhere on the sheet. This is so the initials can be identified, if needed.

The medication record is prepared by the clerk, pharmacist, or other health care worker as drugs are ordered. The nurse

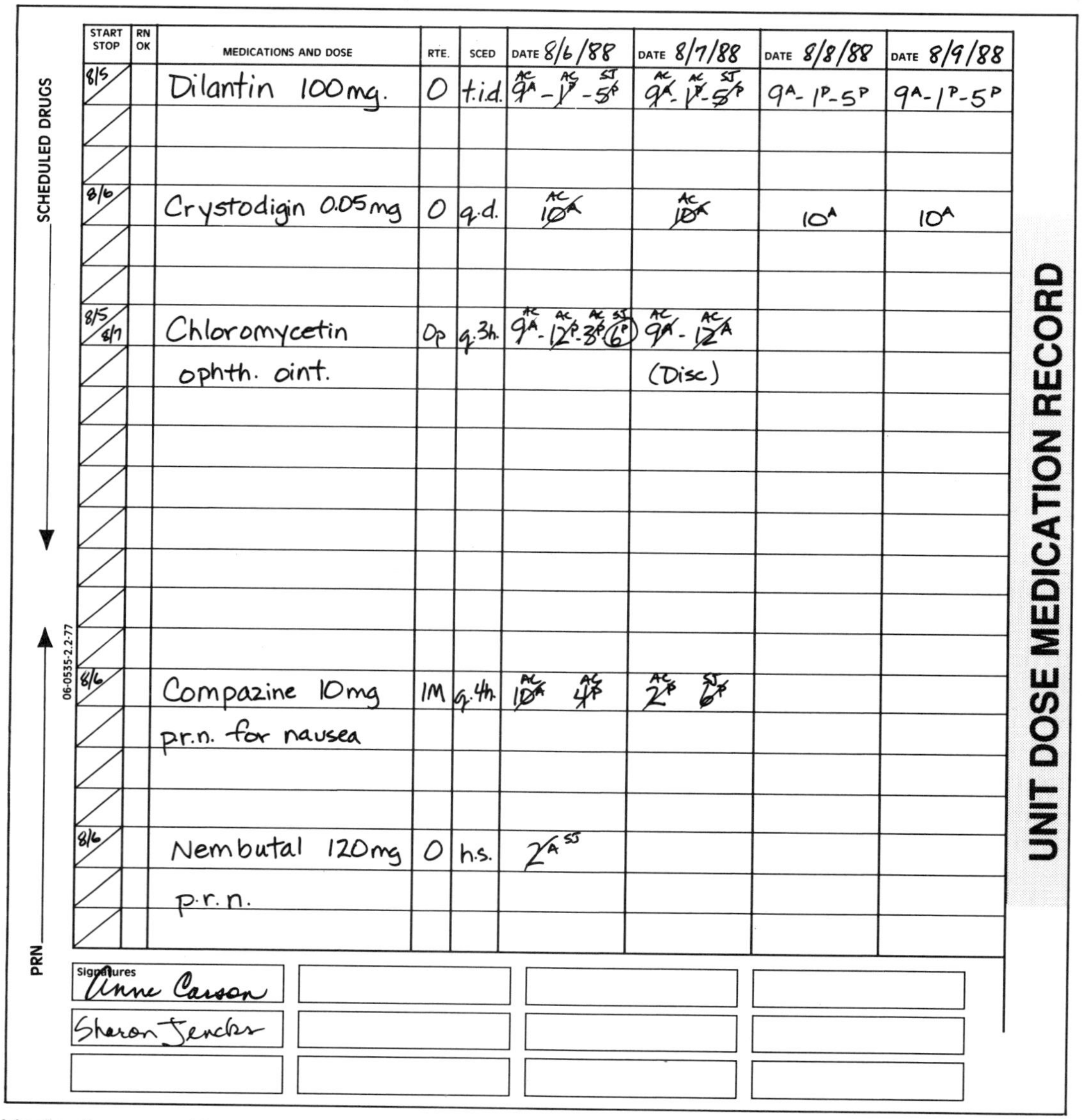

START STOP	RN OK	MEDICATIONS AND DOSE	RTE.	SCED	DATE 8/6/88	DATE 8/7/88	DATE 8/8/88	DATE 8/9/88
8/5		Dilantin 100mg.	O	t.i.d.	AC AC SJ 9A-1P-5P	AC AC SJ 9A-1P-5P	9A-1P-5P	9A-1P-5P
8/6		Crystodigin 0.05mg	O	q.d.	AC 10A	AC 10A	10A	10A
8/5 8/7		Chloromycetin ophth. oint.	Op	q.3h.	AC AC AC SJ 9A-12P-3P-(6P)	AC AC 9A-12A (Disc)		
8/6		Compazine 10mg p.r.n. for nausea	IM	q.4h.	AC AC 10A 4P	AC SJ 2P 6P		
8/6		Nembutal 120mg p.r.n.	O	h.s.	2A SS			

Figure 5-11 Medication record form.

then checks the form against the doctor's order and signs it. Medication records for all patients may be kept in a special folder on the medicine cart. Or they may be kept in individual patient charts.

Self-Terminating Orders

Self-terminating or automatic stop orders mean that the drug is only to be given until a certain date or time. When this type of order is copied from the physician's order sheet, the nurse or clerk makes a special note or mark on the Kardex, medicine cards, or medication record. This shows the date and time when the drug should stop being given. In Figures 5-11 and 5-12, the orders for chloromycetin show examples of such notes. When that time comes, the nurse or clerk will notify the patient's doctor that the order has terminated. If the doctor decides the patient needs to continue receiving the drug, a new order will be written. Remember that automatic stop orders usually cover antibiotics, narcotics, corticosteroids, anticoagulants, and barbiturates.

Controlled Substances

Controlled substances are drugs whose use is restricted. This group of drugs includes narcotics, stimulants, and depressants (see Unit 1).

Figure 5-12 Medication record form using 24 hour clock.

Because of legal restrictions, these medications must be counted or measured at the beginning of each shift. As the shift changes, the person coming off duty and the person coming on duty do the counting and measuring together. They record the quantity of each controlled substance on forms for that purpose. They then sign a special form so there is a record of who counted the drugs on each shift (Figure 5-13). If the count is found to be incorrect at a later shift, the error can be traced to the proper persons.

Controlled substances are sometimes sent to the ward in special containers that allow easy counting. They are packaged in either single doses or multiple doses. The packages are given a special seal at the pharmacy. Only medications in packages

Figure 5-13 Count controlled substances at beginning of each shift.

on which the seal is broken (showing that they have been used) need to be measured and counted.

Each time a controlled substance is administered to a patient from the stock supply, the health worker must sign a **proof-of-use record**, such as the one shown in Figure 5-14. Each health facility has its own form for this purpose. The form usually shows the number of doses sent to the ward stock supply from the pharmacy. As each dose is used, the date, time, patient, room number, amount given, physician, and person administering the dose must be written down. If a dose *less* than the prepared individual dose is given, the amount actually given is noted. The unused portion must be destroyed in front of a witness, who must also sign the form.

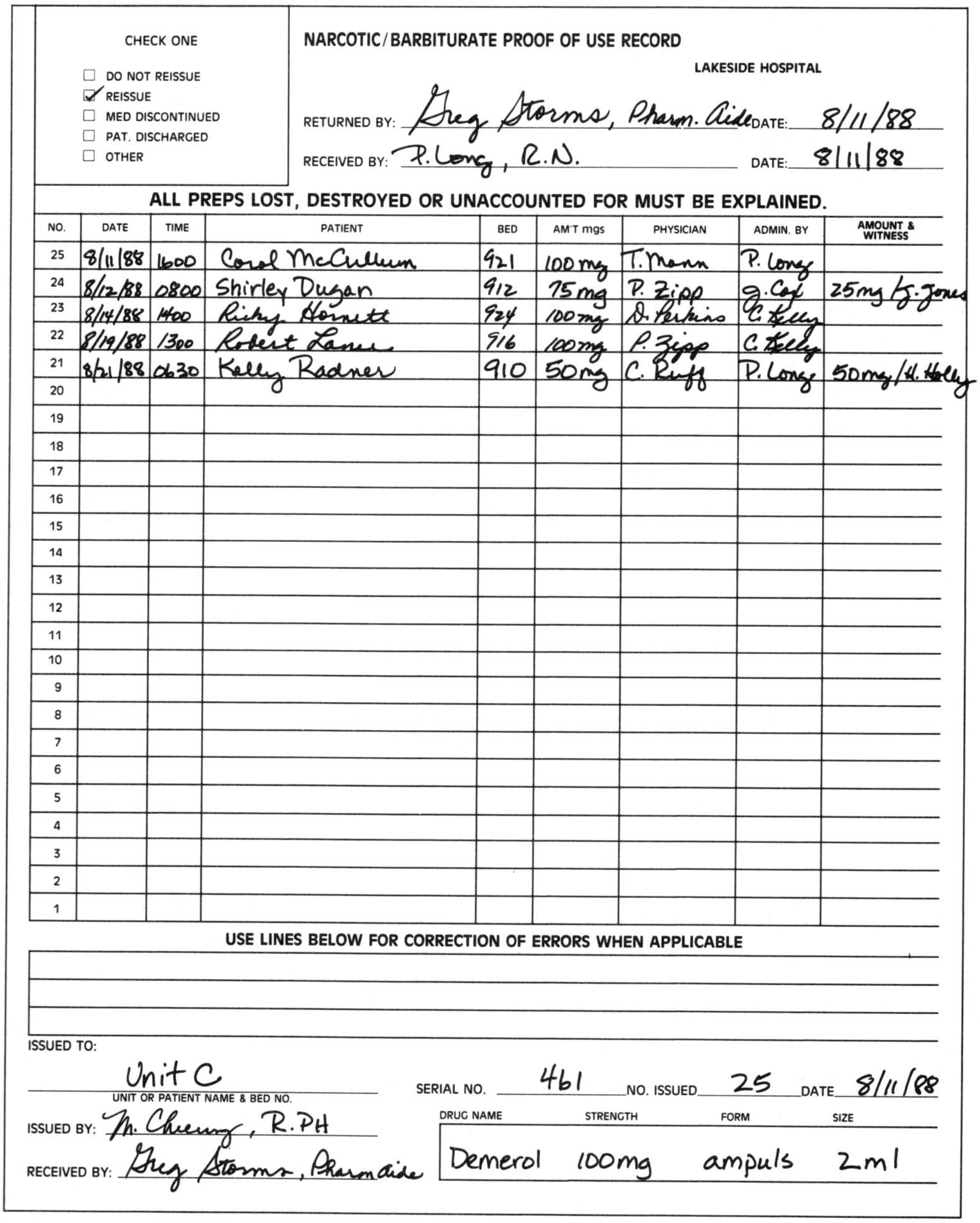

CHECK ONE

- ☐ DO NOT REISSUE
- ☑ REISSUE
- ☐ MED DISCONTINUED
- ☐ PAT. DISCHARGED
- ☐ OTHER

NARCOTIC/BARBITURATE PROOF OF USE RECORD

LAKESIDE HOSPITAL

RETURNED BY: Greg Storms, Pharm. Aide DATE: 8/11/88

RECEIVED BY: P. Long, R.N. DATE: 8/11/88

ALL PREPS LOST, DESTROYED OR UNACCOUNTED FOR MUST BE EXPLAINED.

NO.	DATE	TIME	PATIENT	BED	AM'T mgs	PHYSICIAN	ADMIN. BY	AMOUNT & WITNESS
25	8/11/88	1600	Carol McCullum	921	100 mg	T. Mann	P. Long	
24	8/12/88	0800	Shirley Dugan	912	75 mg	P. Zipp	g. Cox	25 mg/g. Jones
23	8/14/88	1400	Ricky Hornett	924	100 mg	D. Perkins	C. Kelly	
22	8/19/88	1300	Robert Lanes	916	100 mg	P. Zipp	C. Kelly	
21	8/21/88	0630	Kelly Radner	910	50 mg	C. Ruff	P. Long	50 mg/H. Holly
20								
19								
18								
17								
16								
15								
14								
13								
12								
11								
10								
9								
8								
7								
6								
5								
4								
3								
2								
1								

USE LINES BELOW FOR CORRECTION OF ERRORS WHEN APPLICABLE

ISSUED TO: Unit C
UNIT OR PATIENT NAME & BED NO.

SERIAL NO. 461 NO. ISSUED 25 DATE 8/11/88

ISSUED BY: M. Cheung, R.PH

RECEIVED BY: Greg Storms, Pharm Aide

DRUG NAME	STRENGTH	FORM	SIZE
Demerol	100mg	ampuls	2ml

Figure 5-14 Proof-of-use record for controlled substances.

ROLE OF COMPUTERS

Computers are playing a greater and greater role in our society. So it is not surprising that they are being used more frequently and extensively in health care. Computers can make some functions more efficient and less expensive. They could well save you time and help your patients get better faster.

When you begin working in a hospital, you may find computers at the nurses' station (Figure 5-15). In some hospitals, much of the drug ordering and record-keeping are done by computer. (You will be trained on the job for those computer-related activities, but a computer course will greatly increase your understanding of the system and how it operates.)

Computer systems used in different hospitals vary and improvements are being made all the time. But let's look at some kinds of information that can be processed by computer.

Let us take the example of John Smith, who has already been hospitalized for a while. His current medications of insulin and *Lanoxin* have already been entered into the system. Now his doctor wishes to add a PRN order for codeine. The physician can do this in the usual way by writing a medication order. The nurse or unit clerk then enters it into the computer system as a new medical order (Figure 5-16a). A label for this prescription is then printed out in the pharmacy (Figure 5-16b). The prescription is filled and brought to the floor.

Based on the information entered, the computer will print out at regular intervals, usually hourly, the medications scheduled for a particular floor (Figure 5-16c). Also at regular intervals, the computer will print a listing of unscheduled or miscellaneous drugs (Figure 5-16d). When the drugs on either of these printouts are given, that information is entered. Figure 5-16e shows all the charting done for a specific patient, John Smith, over the past 24 hours.

Whether you chart information in writing in the patient's record or enter it into the computer, you must be very careful and accurate. And be sure you do your recording when you are supposed to.

SETTING UP MEDICATIONS

The medications are ordered by the physician, requested from the pharmacy, and stored in the proper area. Now comes the time when you, the giver of medications, must be most alert — setting up medications. Setting up medications means taking information given on the Kardex, medication record, or medicine card and preparing an actual dose of medication for a patient. You will be setting up several drugs at a time, and you must be aware of all of the possibilities for error. Here are some guidelines to help you prepare a medicine tray or drug cart for your rounds.

Figure 5-15 Inputting drug administration data.

1. **Clear your mind of all thoughts except getting your medications set up properly.** Do not try to carry on a conversation with someone while you work—the task at hand needs your full attention.

2. **Before handling any medications, think about cleanliness and the possibility of spreading germs.** Germs can be transmitted to patients on tablets and other medications, so follow aseptic procedure (see a fuller discussion in Unit 6). Wash your hands before touching any drug product. Try not to touch them at all, but pour them directly into paper or plastic medicine cups. Never give a pill that has fallen on the floor—throw it out. Do not cough or sneeze on the medications. Keep unit doses sealed until you are ready to give them.

3. **When you take the medication from the storage area, check the expiration date and notice if there is any change in color, smell, or texture.** Any physical change may mean that the drug has lost its effectiveness, perhaps because of improper stor-

108 Administering Medications

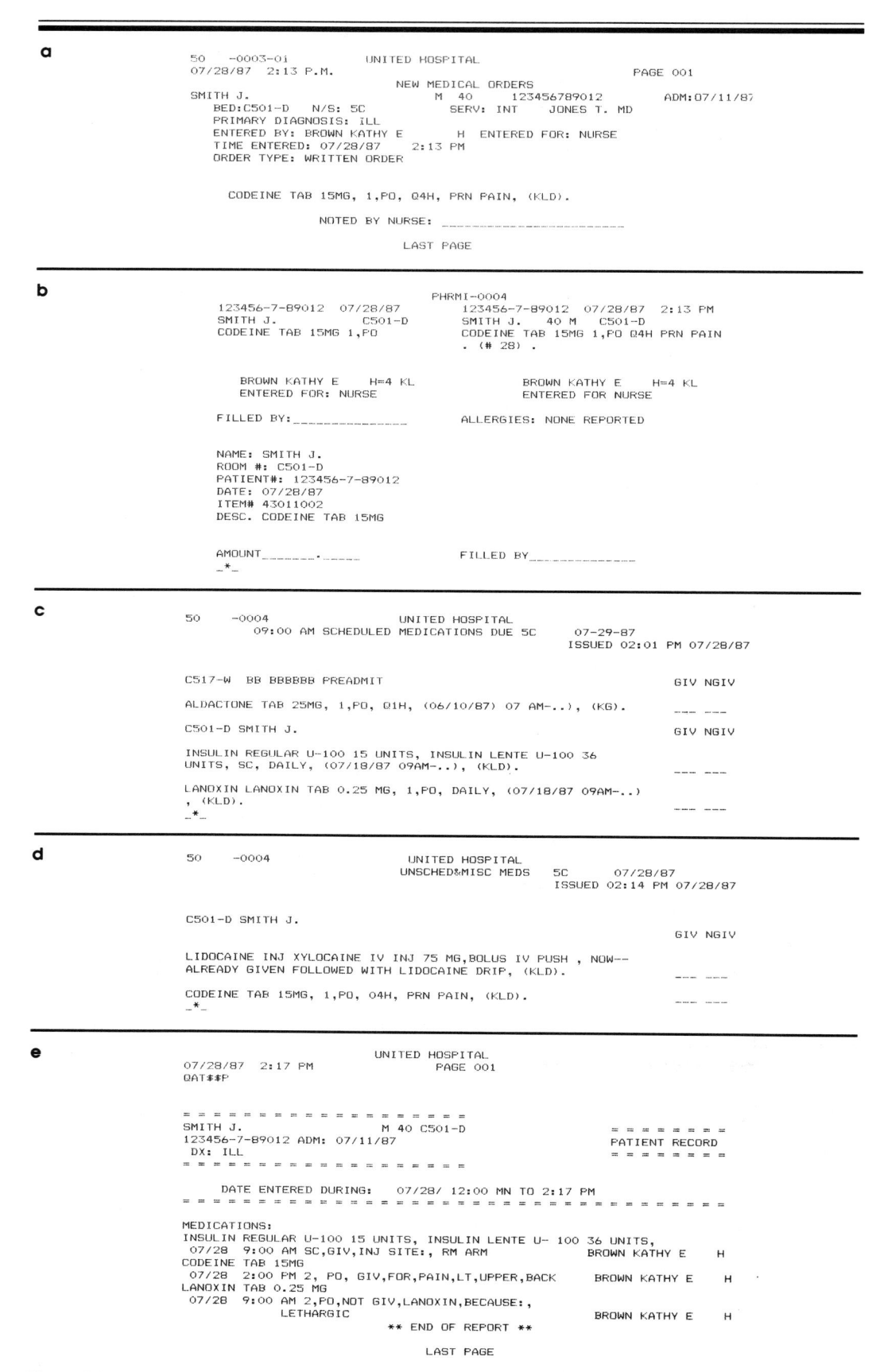

Figure 5-16 Examples of computer generated forms and information.

age or extremes of temperature. If you note anything unusual about the appearance of a drug, do not give it to the patient. Send it back to the pharmacy for replacement.

4. Setting up is the time when you need to decide whether you must calculate a dose. You will notice whether the pharmacist's order is in a unit of measurement different from that of the physician's order. At this point the skills you learned in Unit 4 will come in handy. Remember to use conversion tables and have your work checked if you have any doubts at all.

If you should need to divide a tablet, place the tablet on a clean paper towel or tissue. Use a knife edge to press down hard on the scored part to make a quick, clean break.

5. When you pour liquid medication from a bottle, pour it on the side away from the label. Then if there is a drip from the mouth of the bottle, it will not smudge the label. The label is very important in helping you choose the right drug next time your patient needs it.

Hold the measuring container at eye level so you can see that you are getting the exact amount. The liquid will tend to curve up along the sides of the container—the lowest part of the curve should be even with the marked measure you want (Figure 5-17).

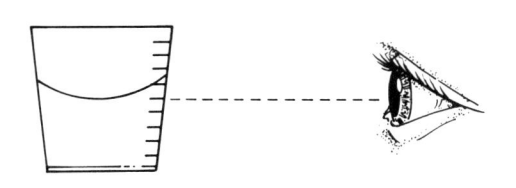

Figure 5-17 Measure liquid at eye level.

6. After removing the desired dose from a bottle, recap the bottle tightly. Then replace the bottle in the cabinet, refrigerator, or cart, taking care to keep the medication area neatly arranged.

7. Decide whether the medication is to be mixed with a liquid or food. Drugs are sometimes mixed with food or drink to hide their taste. Tablets may be crushed and capsules opened and mixed to make them easier for a patient to swallow. If the doctor's order does not give special instructions, check the package insert.

Drugs cannot be mixed with just any liquid. Some drugs are broken down by acids, others by alkalis, so the correct juice or other liquid must be selected. For example, fruit juices are acid, whereas milk is alkali. Some possible liquids with which medications may be taken are orange juice, apple juice, lemonade, cranberry juice, grape juice, milk, soup, cocoa, and coffee. Applesauce is a common choice when drugs must be mixed with food. If you do mix a medication with liquid or food, do not let the mixture stand a long time. Give it to the patient immediately.

Further guidelines for setting up are included in the "five rights" of medication administration discussed in the next section.

RULES FOR GIVING MEDICATIONS: THE "FIVE RIGHTS"

The rules for giving medications are the same no matter who is giving them. Special problems and situations may exist, and individual answers are needed for these. But the basic rules and regulations never change. They are:

- Give the medicine to the **Right Patient**
- Give the **Right Drug**
- Give the **Right Dose**
- Give the medicine by the **Right Route**
- Give the medicine at the **Right Time**

Right Patient

Always identify the patient in some way. Make absolutely certain that you know who the patient is. Read the identification wristband that all hospital patients wear. Ask patients their names or greet a patient by name and observe the response. (This is not foolproof, however.) Get the nurse in charge to help you identify a patient, if necessary.

Check the patient's name against the name on the medicine card or medication record *each time* you administer medication.

Right Drug

Give only medicine that *you* have prepared. Give drugs only from *labeled* containers. Keep unit-dose packages wrapped until ready to use so the label stays with the medication. Read the label *three times* as you prepare the medicine (Figure 5-18).

1. As you *take it* from the shelf or drawer where it is stored.
2. As you *pour* or measure the drug.
3. As you *replace* the bottle or package from which you measured or poured the drug.

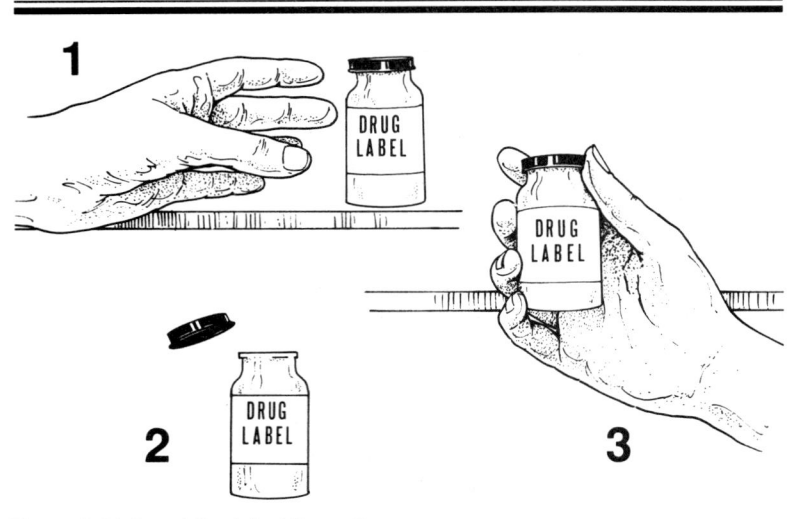

Figure 5-18 Read the label three times.

Be aware of the different names for the same drug—the generic name and various trade names. Also be aware that very different drugs can have very similar names. *Orinase* and *Ornade*, for example, might be mistaken for each other, but one is for diabetes and the other for a stuffy nose. This means you should notice very carefully the spelling of the drug name, and be sure to verify an order if the handwriting is unclear.

Know the abbreviation for the different dosage forms.

Recheck any medicine that the patient feels is the wrong medicine. Be sure the label corresponds to the name of the drug written on the medicine card or medication record. And recheck to see that you have the right patient!

Right Dose

Read the package insert. It tells how to dilute or mix medications, if necessary. Also read the package label carefully to make sure that the drug is of proper strength.

Know the correct dosage symbols and abbreviations. Use properly marked measuring containers: a minim glass for minims, medicine glasses marked with metric or apothecaries' units, and a medicine dropper if drops are ordered. If you must calculate a medicine dose, double-check your work. Recheck any drug dose that the patient feels is wrong.

Be sure that the amount the patient receives matches the amount stated on the medicine card or chart. **Stay with each patient until he or she takes the medicine.**

Help weak patients take medication to be sure they get the full amount.

Open capsules or crush large tablets for those who have difficulty swallowing.

Right Route

Always write the route on the medicine card or medication record. Package inserts, drug references, and the patient chart can give you information about the right route. Call the nurse in charge if you still have questions after checking these references.

Know the correct abbreviations for the routes.

Be aware of factors or changes in the patient's condition that would affect the route of administration. For example, the rectal or parenteral route probably makes more sense for a patient who is vomiting than an oral dosage form. Have the doctor write a different order when these changes arise.

Right Time

Know the correct abbreviations for times of administration.

Check the medication record or medicine card for the correct time to give a medication.

Give the drug as close as possible to the stated time.

Never leave a drug at the patient's bedside unless this is ordered by the doctor.

Organize your work time at the beginning of each shift so you can get medications to each patient on schedule. Review all of the day's nursing activities and your own duties. Plan accordingly, taking into account the times when patients are to receive medications (Figure 5-19).

Check whether an oral drug should be taken on an empty stomach or with food. Drugs to be taken on an empty stomach should be given 1 hour before meals or 2 hours after. Drugs to be taken on a full stomach should be given immediately before, with, or after a meal.

CHARTING MEDICATIONS

Any time a patient is given some form of treatment, such as medication, a record is kept of that treatment. Special problems or circumstances are also written down, such as new symptoms, the patient's own statements, laboratory tests performed, and so on. All of the "events" in the course of a patient's treatment are written down in the **patient chart**, which is a permanent record of care received.

The chart is an important document. First, it is a form of communication between the patient, doctor, and other members of the health care team. The patient chart is also a legal document. It is the official record of the care given to a patient. The patient or the patient's family may question the quality of treatment. The health facility can evaluate the situation by referring to the chart. If there is a lawsuit, the chart can be used in court to decide whether the patient received good or bad care. The chart is taken as proof of the care the patient received.

The chart may also be used by researchers to study certain diseases or drugs. It may serve as a teaching aid for medical students. Or it may be used to gather facts and figures about the overall performance of a certain health facility.

For all of these reasons, it is important for you to learn how to write down the necessary information on a patient chart. This is called **charting**.

First, you should know that not all charts look alike. Different health facilities have their own forms for keeping records. The traditional patient chart consists of a collection of different forms (Figure 5-20). Each form is filled out separately by a different member of the health care team. Individual staff members chart the problems for which they are responsible and the treatment or care that they give. Other team members refer to these specific reports as needed.

The traditional patient chart contains a form you have already seen: the physician's order sheet. This is filled out by the patient's doctor. It contains orders for tests, procedures, and drugs to treat the patient's condition. The doctor also fills out a **patient history sheet**, describing the patient's medical problems in more detail. Various other forms are used to record such things as laboratory tests, x-rays, reports of specialists, and patient progress. Two

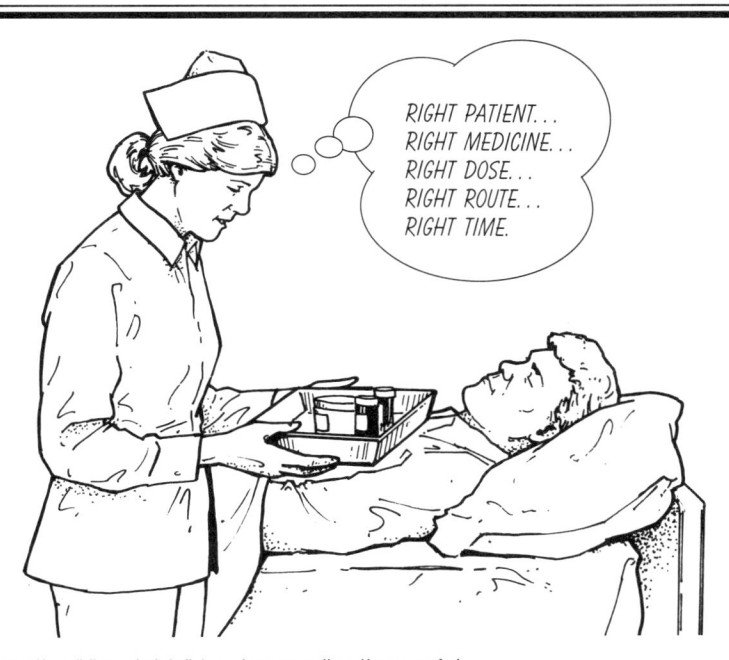

Figure 5-19 Follow the "five rights" to give medications safely.

112 Administering Medications

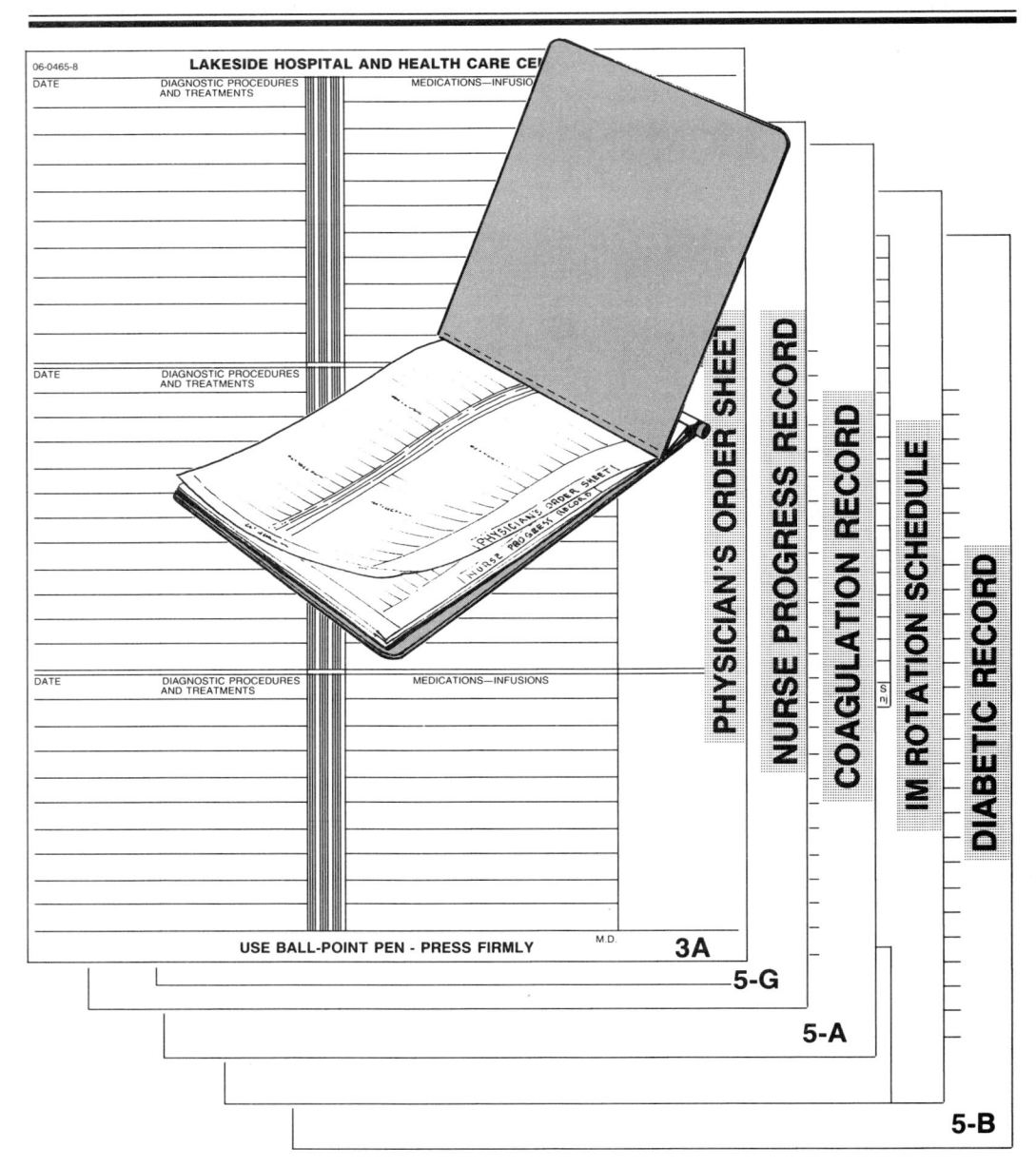

Figure 5-20 Patient chart and traditional forms.

forms that you will deal with in administering medications are the **medication record** and the **nurses' notes.**

Medication Record

You learned what the medication record is in an earlier section. Here you will learn how to chart after the medication has been given. The following facts must be included on the medication record:

- Name of the drug
- Strength and/or amount of the drug
- Times at which the drug is to be given
- Route by which the drug is given
- Initials of the health worker who administered the drug

For routine medications, most of this information has been written out ahead of time. Only your initials need to be charted each time a drug is administered. Look back at Figures 5-11 and 5-12 to see two different ways of charting on medication records.

In case a dose of medicine is *not* given at a scheduled time, you should indicate that fact on the chart. Usually this is done by

NURSES' NOTES

Family Name	First Name	Attending Physician	Room No.	Hosp. No.
Powers	G. Frederick	Dr. Stephens	321	43-586

Date	Time	REMARKS - TREATMENT	Nurses' Signature
8/1/88	0100	Demerol 100 mg/2 cc IM for right knee pain	B. Cassel, LPN
8/1/88	1800	Declomycin 150 mg. p.o. not given. Refused medication due to upset stomach. Supervisor notified.	J. West, Med Aide
8/2/88	1015	Allerest 2 tabs. given stat for hayfever symptoms	F. Strum, LPN Student

Figure 5-21 Nurses' notes.

circling the skipped time on the medication record and initialing it. You should also explain *why* the drug was not given on the nurses' notes.

If the medication record has a section for PRN medications, you will need to chart both the time of administration and your initials. If there is no place to chart PRN medications, you should chart them on the nurses' notes.

Nurses' Notes

This form is called by several names, including progress notes and nurses' progress notes. It is used by the nurse to chart observations of the patient and nursing care provided (Figure 5-21). Stat medications and sometimes PRN medications are also charted on the nurses' notes.

The following information must be charted in the nurses' notes each time a stat medication is given:

- Name of the drug
- Strength and/or amount of the drug administered
- Route
- Time of administration
- Results of checking vital signs (blood pressure, temperature, respiration, pulse) if required for specific drugs

- Any other special information regarding the drug or the patient (e.g., problems getting the patient to take the drug, unusual reactions)
- Signature (first initial and last name) and title of the person who administered the drug

In addition to recording stat medications, the form includes other information. Any time you notice something unusual with *any* medication, you should chart it on the nurses' notes. You should also make a note on the nurses' notes any time a scheduled medication is *not* given. The second entry in Figure 5-21 shows a case like this.

The POMR

Many hospitals and other health facilities use a chart called the **problem-oriented medical record (POMR)**. In this system the chart is organized according to a numbered list of problems (Figure 5-22). All health team members chart on the same form. They chart their observations, plans of action, treatments, and results, with a number telling which particular problem they are working on. The list of problems includes any social and psychological factors in the patient's life that may have an effect on treatment. The POMR is designed to make sure that all members of the health care team are aware of what the others are

LAKESIDE HOSPITAL AND HEALTH CARE CENTER
Patient Record

7209
347841-6 m 28-447
TIMMONS, RALPH
DR. THOMAS MOORE
1-PROT 5/06/20
ALLERGIES: Penicillin
BLOOD TYPE: AB+

PROBLEM NUMBER	DATE	PROBLEM DESCRIPTION	DATE RESOLVED
#1	3/25/88	Diabetes mellitus, insulin-controlled	
#2	3/25/88	Left hand 2nd degree burn	
#3	3/25/88	Wife seriously ill	

Progress Notes

PROBLEM NO. & DESCRIPTION	SUBJECTIVE(S)-OBJECTIVE(O)-ASSESSMENT(A)-PLAN(P)
#2 - LH burn	S: Complains of insomnia, "tossed and turned all night"; LH painful.
	O: Dark circles under eyes, bed sheets rumpled; no change in burn wound appearance.
	A: No pain relief from analgesic. May need larger dose and/or a sedative.
	P: Give back rub. Notify Dr. Moore.
	L. Parker, LPN

Figure 5-22 Problem-oriented medical record (POMR), problem list, and progress notes.

doing and planning for the patient. In this way, the patient receives coordinated care.

Where the POMR is in use, patient progress is often charted by the **subjective–objective–assessment–plan (SOAP)** method. This is a way of organizing the information to be charted. If you wanted to make a note about an unusual reaction to a medication, you would write the information in the order S–O–A–P, as follows:

- **Subjective data**—the patient's complaints and feelings in his or her own words
- **Objective data**—your own observations or measurements (e.g., blood pressure, appetite)
- **Assessment**—what you think may be wrong with the patient
- **Plan**—treatments, diagnostic tests, medications, or patient education that might help the patient's current problem

Figure 5-22 shows how a health worker might chart the fact that a patient appears to be in pain.

Nursing Home Clinic Charts

In the clinic of a nursing home, the forms used for charting are different from those used on a hospital ward. Usually there is no medication record. Rather, any drugs administered will be charted on a patient history sheet or on the nurses' notes. Again, all of the important information must be charted: drug name, strength and/or amount, route, time of administration, your signature and title, and any other notes about the patient or the drug.

PRINCIPLES OF CHARTING

Because the chart is a record of treatment of a patient, it must *record only facts*. This means that you must write down only things you did or saw or heard the patient say. Your own conclusions and opinions about a patient's behavior are *not* to be charted. The only exception to this rule is in the SOAP method of charting, which calls for your assessment of the patient's problem. In this case it is clear that you are giving your own conclusions.

Why are facts better than opinion in charting? Let us take an example. If you found Mrs. Smith in her room crying, you would not write on the chart "depressed about upcoming operation." Instead, you would write "was crying," since there could be many reasons. Suppose that Mr. Jones gagged on a tablet this morning. If you wrote down "doesn't like medicine" on the chart (your *opinion* of the situation), your information would be misleading. Perhaps there was a physical problem developing that caused Mr. Jones to have trouble swallowing. The chart would better show the problem if you wrote simply "gagged on tablet."

Another important feature of charting is that it is a **summary of events.** It has to be concise and to the point. There is simply not enough room to record every detail. This is the reason why abbreviations are useful. They allow you to say a great deal in a small amount of space. Learn them well and use them carefully so others can understand what you have written. It is also useful to learn the proper medical terms for symptoms and body functions. These are understood by most people in the health care field, and they are a kind of shorthand for complicated explanations.

Charting is not difficult, but it requires some practice. Your own charting will be successful if you follow a few simple rules:

- Before you begin, make sure you have the right chart.
- Chart medications directly from a medicine card or a medication record. If neither of these forms is being used, chart directly from the patient chart.
- Chart only *after* you have given a drug, never before.
- Be specific. Do not write "Gave Demerol for pain in the evening." Instead, write "8 p.m., Demerol 100 mg I.M. for pain in left arm."
- Write down events in the order that they occurred.
- Mark "disc." for discontinued after the last dose of a drug is given (see Figure 5-11 or 5-12), or cross out the remaining scheduled times, as required by your agency. The doctor will have specified the day and time of the last dose.
- Do not leave gaps or skip lines. If a note does not fill up a complete line, draw a straight line to fill the gap. Put your signature at the right-hand side directly after the note.

ALL BLOCKS WITH RED HEADINGS MUST BE COMPLETED
CHECK OUT ONLY ONE BOX IN EACH SECTION

CONFIDENTIAL REPORT OF INCIDENT (Not part of medical record)

NAME AND ADDRESS OF PERSON INVOLVED. GIVE MEDICAL RECORD NUMBER. USE ADDRESSOGRAPH IF AVAILABLE. (1-18)

IDENTIFICATION	SEX	AGE	TIME LOST (Employees Only)	NURSES STA. NO
☐ 1-Patient ☐ 2-Employee ☐ 3-Visitor	☐ 1-Female ☐ 2-Male		☐ 1-Yes (If unknown, check "No.") ☐ 2-No	
(19)	(20)	(21-23)	(24)	(25-29)

INCIDENT DATE	REPORT DATE	INCIDENT SHIFT	INCIDENT TIME	HOSPITAL CODE NOS.
(Digits Only)	(Digits Only)	☐ 01-1st ☐ 02-2nd ☐ 03-3rd	: A.M. : P.M.	STATE (2 Digits) HOSP. NUMBER (3 Digits)
(30-35)	(36-41)	(42-43)		(44-48)

CONDITION BEFORE	BED ADJUSTMENT	LOCATION OF INCIDENT		NATURE OF INJURY (Injury sustained as a result of incident)
(Patients Only)	(Not Bed Rails) (Patients Only)	☐ 400 Admitting	☐ 510 Patients Bathroom	☐ 100 Asphyxia, Strangulation, Inhalation
1-Normal	1-Not Applicable	☐ 410 Offices	☐ 520 Nurses Station	☐ 110 Burn or Scald
2-Senile	2-Up	☐ 420 Elevators	☐ 530 Surgery and Recovery	☐ 120 Chemical Burn
3-Disoriented	3-Down	☐ 430 Corridors	☐ 540 Delivery, Labor & Recovery	☐ 130 Concussion
4-Sedated		☐ 440 S		
5-Unconscious		☐ 450 C		
6-Other		☐ 460 H		
		☐ 470 D		
		☐ 480 L		
		☐ 490 E		
		☐ 500 P		
(49)	(50)			

INCIDENT CAUSE (57-58) If more than one
(† Use only for patient incidents.)

A-Falls	B-Medication
☐ 1-Bed, Rail Up	☐ 7-Patient Iden
☐ 2-Bed, Rail Down	☐ 8-Dosage
☐ 3-From Chair or Equip.	☐ 9-Route
☐ 4-From Different Level	☐ 10-Unordered
☐ 5-On Same Level	☐ 11-Duplication
☐ 6-Fainting	☐ 12-Omission

IF PATIENT
Out-Of-Bed Privileges? ☐ Yes ☐ No
Cause for Hospitalization:
Room No. Attending Physician:

GIVE BRIEF DESCRIPTION OF INCIDENT.

INJURY:
PREDOMINANT AND CONTRIBUTING CAUSE

EQUIPMENT INVOLVED:

STATE CORRECTIVE ACTION TAKEN, INDI

List all patients in the room. Give names

Was person seen by a physician? ☐ Yes
If Yes , time seen: A.

Name and Address of HOSPITAL

ACCIDENT OR INCIDENT REPORT

(Report all accidents or incidents even if no apparent injury)

Family Name	First Name	Middle Name	Room No.	Bed No.	Admission No.

Date of accident or incident ______ 19 ____ Time ______ a.m. p.m. Place ______

Was it neccessary to notify physician? yes ____ no ____ Time of notification ______ a.m. p.m.

Name of physician ______ Name of supervising nurse ______

Describe nature of accident or incident and injuries received: ______

Illustrate on the diagram position or place of injury, if any: ______

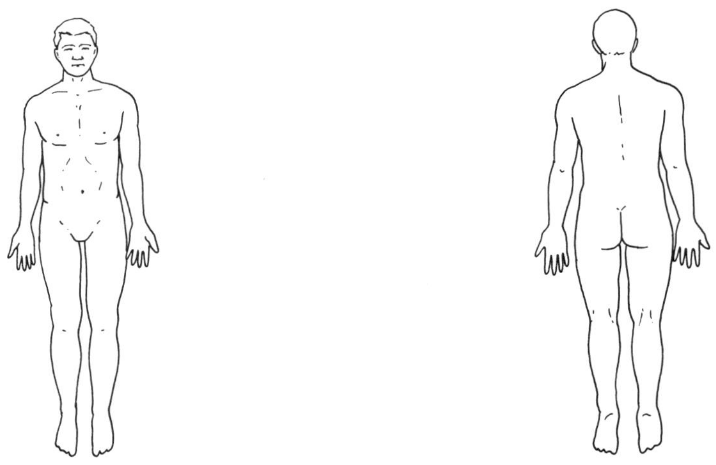

Date report written ______ 19 ____ Time ______ a.m. p.m. Signed ______
PHYSICIAN OR NURSE

FORM NH-310(X) PHYSICIANS' RECORD CO., BEDWYN, ILLINOIS - PRINTED IN U.S.A. ACCIDENT OR INCIDENT REPORT

Figure 5-23 Incident report forms.

- If you make an error, **do not erase it**. Draw a line through the mistake. It should still be visible—do not black it out! Initial it, and write the word "error" on the line. Then rechart the information correctly.
- Never use ditto marks in charting.
- Write with a pen, *not* a pencil. Only pen will ensure a permanent record. Some agencies require you to use a certain color of ink.
- Always print or write legibly when charting. You may print *or* you may write neatly in longhand.
- Always use proper abbreviations and symbols when charting. **This is very important.**
- Chart **anything** that seems important to you in regard to medication administration.
- Consult the nurse in charge when in doubt about a charting rule.
- The patient chart is to be kept strictly confidential. Do your part to make sure that only authorized people see the chart or discuss its contents. Find out what your agency's policy is, and follow it.

Reporting Medication Errors

A medication error is a serious concern. A medication error occurs when you:

- Give a drug to the **Wrong Patient**
- Give the **Wrong Medicine**
- Give the **Wrong Dose**
- Give the drug by the **Wrong Route**
- Give the drug at the **Wrong Time**

Any of these five situations must be reported immediately to the nurse in charge. The error must be noted in the nurses' notes in the patient chart. An **incident report** or a **medication error form** must also be filled out (Figure 5-23). This form is to be signed by the health worker who made the error and by the nurse in charge. Many health facilities require that the patient be seen by a doctor after the medication error. In this case, the doctor must fill out a section on the form and sign it. The doctor's orders for further patient care must be followed carefully. Remember, telling the truth about an error is better from a legal standpoint than trying to cover it up or make excuses. *Not* reporting an error at all may seriously harm your patient.

As a final step, review the events that led to the error. Errors may occur for many reasons: copying orders incorrectly, not paying close attention while setting up medications, carrying out procedures automatically without thinking, or failing to communicate with other members of the health care team. Figure out how the error happened and avoid that situation the next time you administer medications.

EXERCISES

A. Complete the following:

1. Two forms that can be used to order drugs from the pharmacy are _____ and _____.

2. Unit-dose packages contain _____ dose(s) of medication.

3. Multiple-dose packages contain _____ dose(s) of medication.

4. _____ must be counted or measured at the beginning of each shift.

5. Two examples of controlled substances are _____ and _____.

6. Controlled substances are kept in a _____ cabinet.

7. Two types of drugs that often require refrigeration are _____ and _____.

8. A clean medicine room helps avoid _____.

9. A portable file that contains current information about daily medications and treatments ordered for patients on the ward is called a _____.

B. Short answers.

1. Stock supply drugs are _____
_____

2. Why do some drugs have to be kept in a dark place? _____
_____

3. How will you know whether a drug should be refrigerated? _____
_____

4. What should you do with unused doses from a stock supply bottle? _____
_____

5. Two advantages of single-dose packaging are:

   a. _____

   b. _____

6. Where should drugs labeled "for external use only" be kept?
_____
_____

C. Fill in the blanks.

1. When setting up medications, check the _____ date to make sure that the medication is usable.

2. A change in the _____ of the medication may mean it was stored improperly.

3. To avoid spreading germs, always _____ before setting up or counting medications.

4. Pour bottled medications on the side away from the _____.

5. Use a _____ to make a clean break when dividing a scored tablet.

D. Match the medical forms to their descriptions.

a. problem-oriented medical record
b. proof-of-use record
c. medicine card
d. nurses' notes
e. doctor's order sheet
f. patient history sheet
g. prescription blank
h. incident report form
i. Kardex
j. medication record

_____ 1. medications ordered by the physician in a hospital

_____ 2. details of the development and symptoms of a patient's disease

_____ 3. observations of the patient, nursing care, stat and PRN medications

_____ 4. form for charting medications administered on a regular schedule

_____ 5. one form used to chart care given by all health team members

_____ 6. doctor's orders for an outpatient

_____ 7. signed after administering narcotics

_____ 8. placed next to each dose of medication on a medicine tray

_____ 9. summary of daily medications and treatments for all patients on the ward

_____ 10. used to record medication errors

E. Fill in the blanks.

1. Name the "five rights" of medication administration.

   Right _____

   Right _____

   Right _____

   Right _____

   Right _____

2. The correct time to chart is _____ you have given a drug.

3. After giving the last dose of a medication, write _____ on the medication record or mark out the remaining times.

4. When administering drugs in a clinic or office, you chart them on the
   _____

5. Two rules for administering medications to the right patient are:

   a. Check the patient's _____ band.

   b. Ask _____
   _____

6. Two rules for giving the right medicine are:

   a. Give medicine from _____ containers.

   b. Read the label _____ times.

7. Two rules for giving the right dose of medicine are:

   a. Use properly marked _____

   b. Know dosage _____ and _____

8. Two rules for using the right route are:

   a. Be aware of _____ in the patient's condition that may affect the route.

   b. Know the abbreviations for _____

9. Three rules for giving the patient's medicine at the right time are:

   a. Organize your _____

   b. Know the abbreviations for _____

   c. Check whether the medication should be given on a full or empty _____

F. Short answers.

1. Give three reasons why the patient chart is an important document:

   a. _____

   b. _____

   c. _____

2. What information must be charted whenever a medication is given?

   a. _____

   b. _____

   c. _____

   d. _____

   e. _____

   f. _____

3. When are the three times you should read the label as you prepare a medication for your patient?

   a. _____

   b. _____

   c. _____

4. What is the SOAP system of charting? _____
   _____
   _____

5. On a medication record, how would you show that a dose of medicine was *not* given when scheduled? (Check the procedure in your own agency.)

   _____
   _____
   _____

6. How would you show that a dose of medicine *was* given? (Check the procedure in your own agency.)

   _____
   _____

122 Administering Medications

G. Charting practice. Show how you would chart the following events in the nurses' notes. Be sure to include all of the required information. Remember that only facts are to be charted, not assumptions or opinions.

Mr. Schwartz is under treatment for a blood clot in the leg. He has been taking *Coumadin*, an anticoagulant, for several days. He is also taking a diuretic, *Diuril*, to reduce the swelling in his leg. The doctor has confined Mr. Schwartz to bed. This is because any movement of the leg might cause the clot to break off and travel in the bloodstream, which could be dangerous.

1. At 0800 on October 5, 1987, you give Mr. Schwartz two 5-mg tablets of *Coumadin* to swallow with a glass of water. You chart it on the medication record. As you refill the water pitcher, Mr. Schwartz asks if you happen to have something for an upset stomach. He says his stomach hurts like the time he had an ulcer 20 years ago. Because the anticoagulant can cause internal bleeding (e.g., from an old ulcer), you have been alert for signs of this side effect. You notify your supervisor, who asks the doctor to order a test for internal bleeding. The test results are negative. The supervisor then directs you to give Mr. Schwartz two teaspoons of *Maalox* to calm his stomach.

   Your chart entry is _____

   _____

   _____

   _____

   _____

2. It is 1200 hours and time for Mr. Schwartz' next dose of *Diuril*. Mr. Schwartz complains again about his upset stomach, but this time he tells you it is worse right after he takes the *Diuril*. You skip this dose of *Diuril* and notify the supervisor. The supervisor tells you to continue giving the *Diuril* but to keep an eye out for signs of internal bleeding.

   Your chart entry is _____

   _____

   _____

   _____

   _____

3. It is 2000 hours the next evening and time to give Mr. Schwartz a laxative. The laxative (*Dulcolax*) has been ordered by the doctor because bedridden patients often develop constipation, which can lead to impaction (blockage of the intestine). Straining at stool might cause the blood clot to break off and become an embolism (traveling clot). Mr. Schwartz tells you he has been having regular bowel movements and doesn't want the laxative. He asks why he needs it when he has been in bed only 2 days. You explain that it is preventive medicine to avoid the problems of impaction and embolism. But Mr. Schwartz doesn't seem to listen to your explanation. He seems nervous about his condition. He refuses the laxative. You then notify the supervisor. After consulting with the doctor, the supervisor instructs you to give Mr. Schwartz 10 milligrams of *Valium* intramuscularly right away. *Valium* is a tranquilizer that will ease Mr. Schwartz' anxiety so he can cooperate with the treatment.

Your chart entry is: _____

_____
_____
_____
_____
_____

ANSWERS TO EXERCISES

A. Completion
1. copy of the doctor's order sheet, pharmacy requisition
2. one
3. several
4. Controlled substances
5. narcotics, barbiturates, amphetamines, hallucinogens, etc. (name two)
6. locked
7. vaccines, eye drops, suppositories (name two)
8. medication errors
9. Kardex

B. Short answers
1. Drugs that are commonly used, such as aspirin, laxatives, penicillin, and so on, and therefore are kept on hand in the medicine room
2. Because light causes chemical breakdown
3. The drug label will say if it should be refrigerated
4. Dispose of them according to agency policy
5. a. There is less chance of error because no mixing, pouring, or handling of drugs is needed
   b. Unused doses can be returned to the pharmacy for credit
6. In a labeled cabinet separate from the drugs for internal use

C. Setting up
1. expiration
2. color, smell, or texture
3. wash your hands
4. label
5. knife edge

D. Matching
1. e
2. f
3. d
4. j
5. a
6. g
7. b
8. c
9. i
10. h

E. Five rights
1. patient, drug, dose, time, route
2. after
3. "disc." (discontinued)
4. patient history sheet
5. a. wrist identification
   b. the nurse in charge to help identify the patient (or ask the patient his/her name, but this is not foolproof if patients are groggy and confused)
6. a. labeled
   b. 3
7. a. measuring containers
   b. measurements and abbreviations

124 Administering Medications

       8. a. changes or factors
         b. routes
       9. a. time or workday
         b. administration times
         c. stomach
   F. Short answers
       1. a. form of communication among members of the health care team
         b. legal document, official record of health care given
         c. used for research, teaching, and evaluation of health facilities
       2. a. drug name
         b. strength and/or amount of the drug
         c. time of administration
         d. route
         e. anything else that seems important about the patient or administration
         f. signature (or initials) of the health care worker
       3. a. while taking it from the storage area
         b. just before opening it
         c. when putting it away
       4. Charting *subjective* comments of the patient, *objective* tests of the patient's condition, the health worker's *assessment* of the problem, and a *plan* of action.
       5. This depends on your agency. One way is to circle the scheduled time and initial it.
       6. This depends on your agency. One way is to cross out the scheduled time and initial it.
   G. Charting practice

      1. *10/5/88 0800 — Complained of abdominal pain & requested med. for upset stomach. Stated pain is like ulcer pain experienced previously. Supervisor notified. Hematest ordered — negative. Maalox 2T given as ordered. Your name, Title*

      2. *10/5/88 1200 — Said stomach pain most severe after taking Diuril. Withheld Diuril & notified supervisor. Orders given to continue Diuril and observe for bleeding. Your Name, Title*

      3. *10/6/88 2000 — Refused Ducolax. Possible complications such as impaction & embolism explained. Notified supervisor. Valium 10 mg IM given stat for agitation. Your Name, Title*

PRACTICE PROCEDURE

TRANSCRIBE MEDICATION ORDERS

Equipment:

- Physician's order sheet with at least five drugs ordered
- Kardex and medicine cards or medication record (the forms used by your agency)

_____ 1. Read the medication orders on the physician's order sheet.

_____ 2. Transcribe each order onto the Kardex, if used by your agency. Use proper medical terms and abbreviations. Be sure to record all necessary information, including:
- Name of patient, room number, and bed number.
- Name of drug.
- Route.
- Dosage (strength and frequency of administration).
- Time(s) of administration.
- Special administration or nursing instructions, if any.

_____ 3. Transcribe each order onto a medicine card or medication record. Include the same information as in 2.

_____ 4. Check off each order as you finish transcribing it to the medication record or medicine card.

_____ 5. Sign or initial the doctor's order after each set of orders is transcribed.

Show your work to the instructor or the nurse in charge.

PRACTICE PROCEDURE

WRITE DOWN VERBAL MEDICATION ORDERS

Note: *Agency policy determines which staff members are allowed to write down doctor's verbal orders.*

Equipment:

- Oral or tape-recorded statements of at least five medication orders
- Physician's order sheet (in a patient chart) or doctor's order book

_____ 1. Listen closely to the verbal medication orders.

_____ 2. Record the orders onto the physician's order sheet or order book. Be sure to:
- Include all the necessary information (patient name, date, drug name, dosage, route).
- Use proper medical terms and abbreviations.
- Skip a line between orders.
- Write neatly with a ballpoint pen.

_____ 3. Read the orders back to the physician (or the instructor) afterward.

_____ 4. Record the physician's name and then your name. State how you received the orders, in person or by phone (e.g., Dr. E. S. MacLean/phone order taken by P. T. Bayt). Remember that for the order to be legal, the physician will have to sign it personally as soon as possible.

Show your work to the instructor or the nurse in charge.

PRACTICE PROCEDURE

COUNT CONTROLLED SUBSTANCES

Note: *In a laboratory setting, this procedure should be practiced with a partner. Pretend that one of you is going off duty and the other is coming on duty.*

Equipment:

- Controlled substance folder with the forms used by your agency (sign-in/out form, proof-of-use records for several drugs)
- Locked box, cabinet, or drawer and keys
- Sample containers of controlled substances (divided containers, multiple-dose bottles (tablet or capsules *and* liquids), unit-dose packages, etc.)

_____ 1. The person coming on duty obtains the key to the controlled-substance storage area from the person going off duty. Some areas have double doors and require two keys.

_____ 2. Unlock the controlled-substance cabinet, box, or drawer in the medicine room. Remove the containers.

_____ 3. Count the amount of medicine in each container.

- *Divided containers (tablets or capsules).* Look for the slot that has the last tablet or capsule in it. The number of this slot is the number of tablets left.
- *Unit-dose packages.* Unit doses will be numbered. The package with the highest number tells how many doses are left.
- *Multiple-dose bottles (tablets or capsules).* Tip the bottle on its side and count the contents.
- *Multiple-dose bottles (liquids).* The bottle should be marked off in cubic centimeters or milliliters. Hold the bottle at eye level and note how many cubic centimeters or milliliters are left.

_____ 4. As you finish counting each drug, write the quantity on the appropriate form. Each drug will have a form to go with it. If the form is a proof-of-use record, check that your count matches the amount of drug shown as still available. Different facilities will have different ways to do this. Sign your name where requested.

_____ 5. If your count differs from the number shown in the records, do a recount. If there is still a difference, look at the Kardex and other forms to locate the source of error. Notify the nurse in charge if the source of error cannot be found.

_____ 6. Correct errors on your forms according to the policy of your health facility.

_____ 7. Sign any of the forms required by your agency (sign- in/out, key count, etc.).

_____ 8. Return medications to the lock-box and close and lock the doors. Return the controlled-substance folder to the place where it is kept.

_____ 9. The person who has just come on duty keeps the key(s) for use in administering controlled substances during the next shift.

Show your work to the instructor or the nurse in charge.

PRACTICE PROCEDURE

RECORD THE USE OF CONTROLLED SUBSTANCES

Equipment:

- Locked storage area (box, cabinet, or drawer) and keys
- Medication record, medicine cards, or Kardex with several orders for controlled substances
- Proof-of-use records for several controlled substances
- Sample containers of controlled substances (unit dose, multiple dose)

_____ 1. Unlock storage area and read medication orders. Follow Steps 2 through 7 for one medication at a time.

_____ 2. Read the label as you remove a container from the storage area.

_____ 3. Pick out the proof-of-use form that goes with that drug. Fill out the form, giving: date of administration, time of administration, patient's full name, room and bed number, amount of medication taken from the container, patient's physician, name of the person giving the medication, and the amount of medication given to the patient.

_____ 4. Get someone as a witness if you have to discard some of the medication. You might have to discard medication if:

- You must give a smaller amount than the smallest unit-dose size.
- You suspect that a drug is contaminated.

The witness should sign the proof-of-use record and state how much of the drug was destroyed.

_____ 5. Set up the medication as you would any other. Be sure to read the label again as you open the container.

_____ 6. Replace the container in the storage area. Read the label one last time as you do so.

_____ 7. Repeat these steps for the remaining controlled substances.

_____ 8. Lock the storage area and replace the controlled substance folder. Keep the keys in your pocket for use on duty.

Show your work to the instructor or the nurse in charge.

PRACTICE PROCEDURE

SET UP MEDICATIONS ON A TRAY WITH MEDICINE CARDS

Note: *This same procedure may be used to set up a medicine cart when you have multiple-dose packages. If the drawers of the cart are marked with patients' names, you may set up from a medication record rather than medicine cards.*

Equipment:

- Medicine cards
- Medicine tray (either flat or molded)
- Containers of medicine (unit dose and multiple dose)
- Paper cups for tablets or capsules, plastic cups for liquids
- Supplies (water and water cups, tongue blades, spoons, blood pressure cuff, applesauce or juice for mixing medications, if necessary)

_____ 1. Set up one medication at a time. Place one card on the tray. You need the medicine card to be able to tell which medicine goes to which patient.

_____ 2. Read the label as you take the appropriate medicine container from the cabinet, refrigerator, or medicine cart. Hold the label at eye level.

_____ 3. Before opening the container, check the label against the medicine card.

_____ 4. Pour or count out the drug into plastic or paper cups. Double-check the dose against the medicine card after you have poured or counted out the medication.

_____ 5. Set the medicine cup on the tray right next to its medicine card. By setting up only one drug at a time, you make sure that you will put the right card with the right medication. (Refer back to Figure 5-8 to see how a typical tray is set up.)

_____ 6. Measure liquids at eye level. Pour with the label away from the side on which you are pouring.

_____ 7. Read the label again as you put away the container. Be sure to wipe off any spilled medication.

_____ 8. Place any needed supplies on the tray for administering the medications.

_____ 9. Follow Steps 1 through 8 as you set up the remaining medications, one at a time.

Show your work to the instructor or the nurse in charge.

PRACTICE PROCEDURE

DISPENSE UNIT-DOSE MEDICATIONS FROM A CART

Equipment:

- Folder with medication records
- Medicine cart, drawers labeled with names of patients
- Unit doses of medicine placed in appropriate drawers of medicine cart
- Medicine cart supplies (water, cups, spoons, etc.)

_____ 1. Open folder to first patient's medication record.

_____ 2. Go to that patient's room and identify the patient by:
- Checking the name on the wristband or on the bed.
- Asking the patient his or her name.
- Asking personnel to help you identify any patient who seems confused or who does not have a wristband or a bed tag.

_____ 3. Open the appropriate patient's drawer, identify the right medication, and give it to the patient, following these steps:
- Read the medication record and identify the medication.
- Read the label of unit-dose package and compare it with the medication record.
- Read the label of unit-dose package as you give it to the patient.
- Read the label of unit-dose package as you discard it.

_____ 4. Chart administration of each drug on the medication record.

_____ 5. Make the patient comfortable.

_____ 6. Go to the next patient's room. This should be the patient whose medication record is next in the medication folder.

Show your work to the instructor or the nurse in charge.

PRACTICE PROCEDURE

FILL OUT AN INCIDENT REPORT FORM

Equipment:
- Incident report form (the form that is used by your agency)
- Written or oral summary of an actual or made-up medication error (a tape recording or a written story)

_____ 1. Read or listen to the report of a medication error.

_____ 2. Record all information requested on the appropriate incident/accident form. Usually this includes:
- Name, room number, and bed of patient.
- Date, time, and location of the incident.
- Name of doctor or supervisor who was notified of the incident.
- Nature of the incident or accident and injuries received.
- Diagram of the location of the injury on the body.
- Date and time of this report.
- Your signature.

_____ 3. Obtain signatures of all persons involved as required on the form.

Show your work to the instructor or the nurse in charge.

Unit 6

Drugs for Infection and Cancer

In this unit you will learn basic facts about cells, tissues, organs, and systems. This is your introduction to the study of specific body systems in later units. You will then learn about two types of disorders that can affect any system of the body: infection and cancer. You will learn how these disorders affect the body and how drugs are used to treat them. You will also learn how health workers can stop the spread of germs.

In this unit, you will learn to:

- Use proper terms for discussing cells, tissues, organs, and body systems.
- Name the four types of body cells.
- List substances that the body must take in.
- Describe three ways the body defends itself against harmful germs.
- Explain why infection is more dangerous in a hospital or long-term care unit than elsewhere.
- State the two main actions of anti-infectives on germs.
- State the main difference between antibiotics and sulfonamides.
- Explain why drug resistance, drug sensitivity, and superinfection are important concerns in anti-infective drug therapy.
- Name at least two problems that may arise in giving penicillin.
- List the most common uses of sulfonamides and gamma globulin.
- Name the three characteristics of all cancers.
- Explain the difference between a benign tumor and a malignant tumor.
- Explain how chemotherapy works.
- List the signs to look for when working with patients on chemotherapy.
- Name at least three groups of antineoplastic drugs and give examples.
- Define the most commonly used medical terms for discussing infection and cancer.
- Define isolation and explain why it is necessary.
- Describe the correct procedure for washing your hands before and after giving medications.

INTRODUCTION TO BODY SYSTEMS

The human body is a marvelously complex machine. In Unit 2 you learned something about how it responds to the actions of drugs. Beginning with this unit, you will learn about the various parts of the body and their **structure** and **function**. Your knowledge of how different parts of the body work will help you in administering medications. You will understand what goes wrong with body parts during disease or malfunction. You will also understand why doctors prescribe certain specific drugs for each condition. Armed with this knowledge, you will be a more responsible member of the health care team.

Cells

The basic building blocks of all living things are cells. There are millions of them in every human body. Each cell carries out certain routine functions to keep itself alive—absorbing food; creating energy for heat, growth, or movement; excreting waste products; and reproducing itself when conditions are right. But each cell works with other cells, too, to carry out more complex activities that keep the whole body working smoothly.

For efficiency, cells are **specialized** to do certain jobs. Some are designed to form protective coatings and linings for body parts. Some specialize in producing chemicals that control body processes. Others are specialized for connecting body parts together or creating body movement. Still others have the job of sending messages to and from the body's main control center, the brain.

There are four types of cells in the human body, each with its own special job: **epithelial** (*ep′i-the′le-al*) cells, **connective** cells, **muscle** cells, and **nerve** cells (Figure 6-1).

Cells have the ability to split in two when they have reached a certain size. This is called **cell reproduction**. The two cells that result from this division are exactly alike. They will do the same job in the body as the original cell. Cell reproduction enables living things to grow. As cells divide and redivide, the body grows larger. At some point this process stops: the human body reaches its full adult size. From then on,

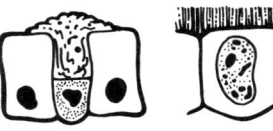

Epithelial cells
Linings of body tubes and cavities
Glands
Skin

Connective cells
Bones, ligaments, cartilage
Scar tissue

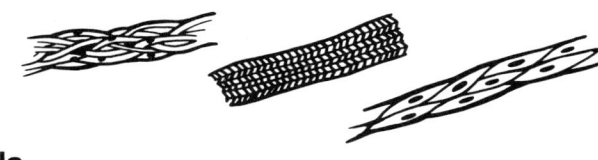

Muscle cells
Muscles that move bones
Smooth muscles in internal organs
Heart muscle

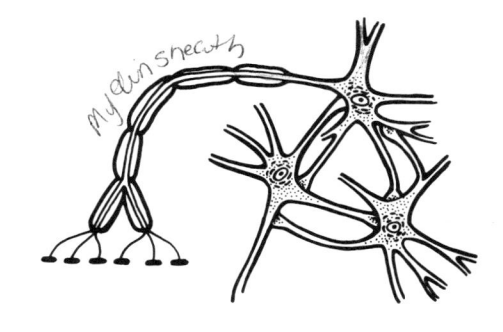

Nerve cells
Brain
Spinal cord
Sense receptors
Nerves

Figure 6-1 The four types of cells, with some of the body parts they make up.

cells reproduce themselves only to replace worn out or damaged cells.

During disease and trauma, many cells may be damaged. But because cells can reproduce themselves, the body can often replace the damaged cells. This is called **healing**.

VOCABULARY

alopecia: loss of hair

anaphylaxis: severe, possibly fatal systemic hypersensitivity reaction to a sensitizing agent; i.e., a drug, food, or chemical

antibiotic: substance produced by a living microorganism that kills or stops the growth of other organisms (can also be produced in the laboratory)

antibody: a proteinlike substance produced in the body to fight germs

anti-infective: drug that kills germs or keeps them from growing

antineoplastic: drug that suppresses cancer cells and other growing cells

aseptic: free of pathogens

autoclave: sterilizing machine

bactericidal: destructive to bacteria

bacteriostatic: an agent that inhibits the growth or multiplication of bacteria

benign: harmless; unable to spread to other parts of the body

biocidal activity: the ability to kill microorganisms

biostatic activity: the ability to inhibit the growth of a microorganism

biosynthesis: making a compound by physiologic processes in a living organism

broad spectrum: affecting a wide variety of pathogens

chemotherapy: drug therapy for cancer symptoms (also refers to drug therapy of other types)

culture and sensitivity test: laboratory technique for finding out which microbes are present, if any, and which anti-infective will be effective against a specific pathogen

cytoplasm: fluid inside the cells

cytostatic: able to suppress cell growth and replication

cytotoxic: poisonous to cells

disinfectant: substance for sterilizing tools and equipment

extravasation: discharge of blood or other substances into tissues

gamma globulin: a class of protein in the bloodstream which includes antibodies

Gram stain: laboratory test to help identify microbes

hepatotoxicity: the potential of a drug or other chemical to cause liver damage

hypersensitivity: an exaggerated response to a drug or other foreign agent through allergic mechanisms and causing symptoms

immunity: ability to withstand disease germs because the body has produced antibodies against them

immunization: a way of stimulating production of antibodies by exposing the body to weakened or killed germs

infection: an invasion by pathogens that causes symptoms

infectious disease: disease caused by pathogens that can often be spread from one living being to another

inoculation: immunizing by injection of a vaccine

isolation: keeping a patient in an environment where pathogens cannot spread from patient to health worker and/or vice versa

leukocytes: white blood cells specialized to destroy germ cells

leukopenia: reduction in the number of the leukocytes in the blood; i.e., 4,000 or less

malignant: cancerous; able to spread to other parts of the body or to invade locally

metastasis: spread of a cancer by "seeding" cancer cells to other parts of the body

microorganisms: tiny, one-celled plants and animals; some are beneficial to humans, and others are harmful; also called **microbes**

narrow spectrum: affecting only specific pathogens

organ: group of tissues working together to perform some function

pathogens: harmful microorganisms

penicillinase: enzyme that microbes produce that makes them resistant to natural penicillin by destroying the penicillin molecule

photosensitivity: rash that appears after exposure to strong light; a side effect of some drugs

remission: disappearance of disease symptoms

resistance: a germ's developed ability to withstand drug effects after a period of drug therapy

rhabdomyosarcoma: highly malignant tumor of the striated muscle

sulfonamide: synthetic anti-infective; "sulfa drug"

superinfection: second infection that starts while an antibiotic is destroying the first infection

synthetic: developed in a laboratory; opposite of natural

system: group of organs and tissues that carry out one set of important life processes (e.g., eating, breathing, elimination)

tissue: group of cells of the same type, working together to perform some function

tissue fluid: fluid found in spaces between cells; also called **intercellular fluid**

tumor: abnormal lump or mass of tissue

TSH: thyroid-stimulating hormone (thyrotropic hormone)

vaccination: immunizing by puncturing the skin and introducing into the body weakened or killed microbes

---

As the body grows older, its cells begin to slow down. They are not able to replace themselves as easily as they did in youth. Consequently, the body takes a longer time to heal after an accident or an illness. The routine processes of digesting, producing energy, and excreting waste all slow down, too. This is why older people have special medical needs and why drug doses have to be adjusted for age.

Tissues, Organs, and Systems

Cells are specialized to do certain jobs, but they do not do these jobs alone. They work together with other cells that have the same specialty. These groups of cells that together perform a certain task are called **tissues**.

Four basic types of tissues, corresponding to the four types of cells, make up all of the body parts. They are epithelial tissue, connective tissue, muscle tissue, and nerve tissue. Each type of tissue has a different structure and function.

After cells and tissues, organs are the next most complex structures in the human body. Organs are made up of two or more types of tissues, organized to carry out a particular function. The heart, the liver, the stomach, and the kidneys are all familiar examples of organs. Some people consider skin and blood to be organs, too.

The important functions that keep the body alive—breathing, eating and digesting, elimination, thinking, and regulating the body processes—are performed by well-organized groups of organs and tissues called body **systems**. Each system is responsible for one important body function.

There are 10 major systems in the human body. You will learn more about these systems as you study the remaining units of this text. You will learn what their parts are; how they function; and what can go wrong with them when they are injured, diseased, or aged. This will give you a better understanding of how they are affected by drugs and why specific drugs are given.

NECESSARY SUBSTANCES

The body is built of living cells, and it can make many substances that it needs. However, there are some materials that the body must take in.

Water is the most important of these substances. In fact, the body is composed largely of water, about 66%. Water is the largest component of the fluid inside cells or **cytoplasm**.

Water also surrounds the cells, bathing every tissue in fluid. This is important because water is the medium through which most of the body's chemical activities take place. Gases, liquids, and solids are dissolved in water before traveling through the body. The processes of absorption, distribution, biotransformation, and excretion all involve water. The water that surrounds the cells is known as **tissue fluid**.

Other substances that the body depends on for its life processes are **minerals** such as salt (tissue fluid is slightly salty) and calcium (for the hardness in bones and teeth), **vitamins**, **fats**, **carbohydrates**, and **proteins**. A well-balanced diet ensures that the body takes in a good supply of these necessary substances.

INFECTION AND IMMUNITY

We are literally surrounded by tiny, one-celled plants and animals—called "germs," or, more properly, **microorganisms** or **microbes**. They are in the air we breathe, on the food we eat, and on the things we touch. Many of them are harmless. Some are even beneficial—for example, certain bacteria that live in the intestine help create important vitamins out of the waste products of digestion. But some are able to produce infection and disease in the human body. These harmful germs—known as **pathogens**—are responsible for everything from the common cold to malaria, Colorado tick fever, and spinal meningitis (Figure 6-2). When they get a foothold in the body, they reproduce themselves rapidly and start to affect healthy tissue, causing symptoms.

Infectious diseases have distinct sets of symptoms that help in diagnosis. Fever, chills, headache, nausea, vomiting, diarrhea, and pus formation at the infection site are some of the signs that a physician takes into consideration. Laboratory tests confirm the diagnosis by identifying the specific germ that caused the disease. Identifying the germ is very important because different drugs are effective against different types of germs. For your information, Table 6-1 lists the major types of infectious diseases.

The Immune System

Luckily, the body can defend itself against most germ invaders (Figure 6-3). There are three lines of defense against infection.

Skin

The skin and the mucous membranes (see Unit 8) are the first line of defense. They provide a tough physical barrier to the entry of germs. In addition, both the skin and the mucous membranes are moistened with substances that discourage the growth of germs.

However, these body coverings cannot provide complete protection. Many germs enter the body through broken skin (cuts and other injuries). Others are inhaled into the lungs. A great many are passed from the hands to the mouth after touching contaminated objects or persons.

Leukocytes

This special group of white blood cells is designed to surround and digest germ

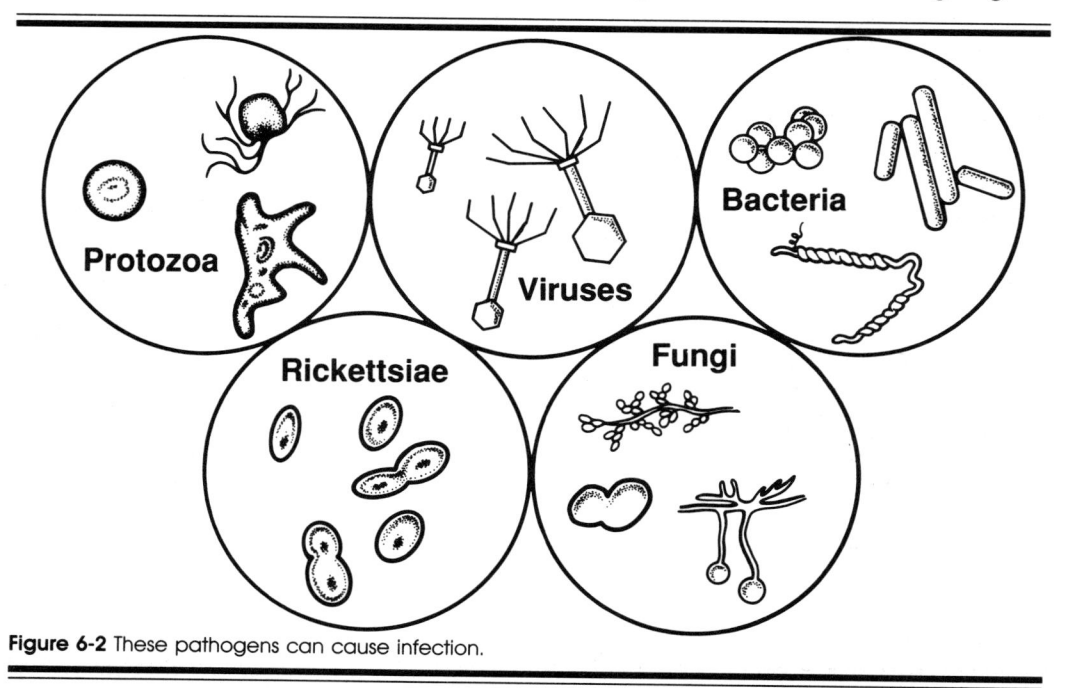

Figure 6-2 These pathogens can cause infection.

Table 6-1 Infectious diseases

Bacterial infections	Fungus infections (mycoses)	Spirochetal infections
Anthrax	Actinomycosis	Syphilis
Bacillary dysentery	Candidiasis (moniliasis)	
Bacterial endocarditis	Coccidioidomycosis	**Virus infections**
Blood poisoning	Histoplasmosis	AIDS
Boils		Chickenpox
Botulism	**Parasitic infections**	Cold sores (herpes simplex)
Brucellosis (undulant fever)	Flukes	Common cold
Cholera	Hookworm	Encephalitis
Diphtheria	Pinworm	Genital herpes
Gastroenteritis (food poisoning)	Roundworm	Influenza (flu, grippe)
Gonorrhea	Schistosomiasis	Lymphogranuloma
Meningitis	Tapeworm	Measles
Osteomyelitis	Trichinosis	Mononucleosis
Plague		Mumps
Pneumonia	**Protozoan infections**	Poliomyelitis
Strep throat	Amebic dysentery (amebiasis)	Psittacosis (parrot fever)
Tetanus	Malaria	Rabies
Trench mouth	Toxoplasmosis	Shingles (herpes zoster)
Tularemia	Trypanosomiasis (sleeping sickness)	Viral hepatitis
Typhoid fever		Yellow fever
	Rickettsial infections	
Chlamydial infections	Rocky Mountain spotted fever	
	Typhus	

cells. The pus that builds up in infected wounds is made up in part of dead leukocytes (lou'ko-sitz). When the invasion is on a large scale, the body steps up production of leukocytes to provide an extra measure of defense.

Antibodies

The body's third line of defense, antibodies, are substances that either destroy or stop the growth of certain types of germs. They are carried in the bloodstream and can readily move to the site of germ entry.

Specific antibodies act against specific germs. When an unfamiliar germ enters the body, proteins in the blood are stimulated to produce a special antibody to act against it. The next time that same germ enters the body, the specific antibody "remembers" it and proceeds to destroy the germ. Antibodies make the body **immune** to a great many infections.

Immunity can be either temporary or permanent, depending on the type of antibody. People who cannot form antibodies are at risk because they cannot defend themselves against the infections to which we are all constantly exposed.

Skin and mucous membranes
Unbroken

Leukocytes

Antibodies

Figure 6-3 The body's defenses against germ invasion.

Despite all of these defenses, germs sometimes get the better of us. They multiply and spread in the body, and the result is infection. The infection can be local, such as in a cut or a surgical wound, or it can be systemic and affect the whole body, as in measles.

Immunization

Because of the pioneering work of Edward Jenner, Jonas Salk, and others, today we are able to prevent many deadly or debilitating infectious diseases that in the past affected many lives. Through **immunization**, we are able to stimulate the body to produce antibodies against the dreaded disease germs. This is done by placing a small amount of dead or weak disease germs into the body, called inoculation or vaccination. Because the germs are not at full strength, they do not cause a full-blown disease, but they provide enough material so the body can manufacture the necessary antibodies. Thus, when living germs come along, the antibodies are already there to fight them off. Immunization has been so successful that diseases that used to kill thousands of people during sweeping epidemics, such as measles and yellow fever, are now very rare.

Patients at Risk

Most individuals can fight off infection successfully. If they are in good health, their natural defenses hold down the number of germs so there are few disease symptoms. Even if the diseases do take hold, healthy people are able to survive while the infection runs its course. It is the people who are *not* healthy who are at risk.

Patients with surgical wounds or with lowered resistance because of other conditions, such as acquired immune deficiency syndrome (AIDS), are especially prone to infections. Weak, unhealthy patients are apt to have more serious disease symptoms. They also have a harder time shaking off infections and avoiding complications. Very young and very old people also have less resistance to infection.

Hospitals and other health care facilities have large numbers of these at-risk patients located in one place. Once started, an infection can spread very rapidly through such groups. For this reason, medical personnel must be especially concerned with avoiding the spread of pathogens. They are trained in **aseptic** (*a-sep-tik*) or germ-free techniques of caring for patients. They learn to wash their hands before and after caring for each patient. They learn to sterilize equipment, change bed linens frequently, and wear protective clothing when handling certain infected patients.

There are pathogens that seem to lurk in hospitals waiting to attack weakened patients. Each hospital has its own problem infections caused by antibiotic-resistant germs that gain a foothold in the building. Staph (staphylococcal, *staf'i-lo-kak'al*) infections are a common danger for hospitalized patients. People who develop such infections (e.g., in a surgical wound) must be kept in **isolation**. No one may enter or leave these patients' rooms without special precautions against spreading the staph germs. A practice procedure at the end of this unit will show you how to prepare to administer medications to an isolation patient.

ANTI-INFECTIVE DRUGS

The discovery of the so-called "miracle drugs"—the antibiotics and the sulfonamides (*sul-fon'ah- mid*)—changed the practice of medicine radically. These are drugs that destroy microorganisms. The antibiotics are natural substances produced by certain living cells against others—for example, penicillin comes from mold cells and destroys many bacteria. The sulfonamides are synthetic substances produced in the laboratory. Many antibiotics are now synthesized as well.

How do these drugs bring about their miracles? Anti-infectives either kill germs directly (indicated by the suffix **-cide**, as in fungicide) or keep them from growing (suffix = **static**, as in bacteriostatic). Some interfere with cell wall production in the germs. Others inhibit (slow down) protein synthesis. Still others mix up the chemical messages for producing nucleic acid, a major substance in cell growth. Some act better on rapidly multiplying pathogens, whereas others are more effective with slowly growing organisms.

Administration Considerations

Before prescribing antibiotics or sulfonamides for specific ailments, a physician must consider three things:

- **The condition of the patient's own defense system.**

  The physician must note whether the patient's immune system is working properly. Some antibiotics kill germs directly and others slow the growth or reproduction of germs. Both types depend on the body's natural defenses (leukocytes and antibodies) for help in eliminating an infection.

- **The type of infection and its cause.**

  The organism causing the infection is important. Some infectious diseases have distinct symptoms, but many have similar symptoms. When in doubt, an attempt must be made to identify the germ. The identity of the pathogen determines the choice of a specific antibiotic or sulfonamide. That choice often depends on how the germ behaves in a laboratory test called a **Gram stain**.

  When placed on a microscope slide along with a stain, some microbes turn blue and others turn red. The blue-staining germs are called **gram-positive** microbes and the red-staining ones, **gram-negative**. **Acid-fast** germs do not turn either color in gram staining. These terms are used in drug references to tell which drugs are effective against which microbes. For example, penicillin is effective against most gram-positive microbes, and tobramycin is effective against most gram-negative microbes.

- **The type of drug and its effects.**

  The physician must consider the type of antibiotic because these drugs have varying effectiveness and varying side effects. Another laboratory procedure called a **culture and sensitivity** test helps in deciding which drug to use. A sample of fluid (e.g., pus obtained from throat scraping) is taken from an infected person's body and used to start a culture of bacteria in the laboratory. Then pieces of paper saturated with samples of different anti-infectives are placed on the culture. The results show which drug can kill the bacteria, and this is the drug the doctor will prescribe.

Sometimes it is hard to isolate the germ that is causing an ailment. In these situations a physician might prescribe a **broad-spectrum** antibiotic. This is an antibiotic that destroys a great variety of microorganisms. The tetracyclines are one group of broad-spectrum antibiotics. In contrast, **narrow-spectrum** antibiotics are effective against only a few types of pathogens (Figure 6-4).

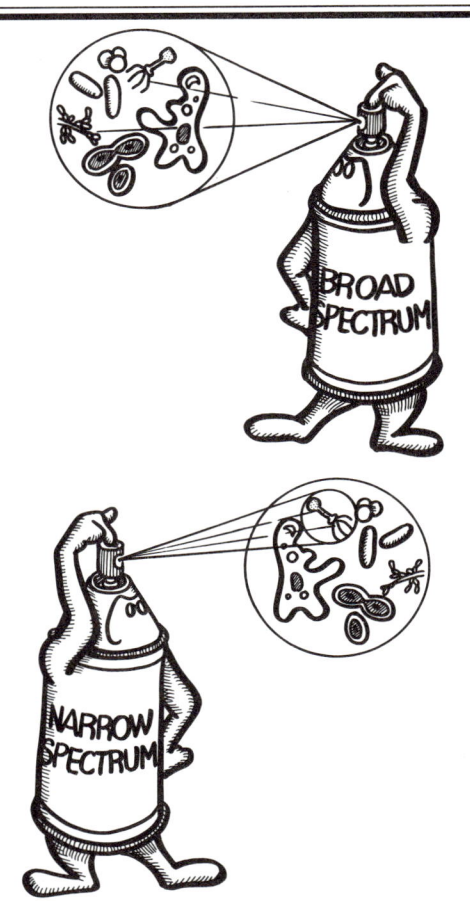

Figure 6-4 Two types of anti-infectives. When a pathogen can be identified, a narrow-spectrum anti-infective is better.

Resistance—If the disease-producing organism can be identified, a narrow-spectrum drug is usually a better choice than a broad-spectrum drug. This is because pathogens are able to develop **resistance** to antibiotics. After being exposed to a certain antibiotic for a while, a particular pathogen is no longer sensitive to its action.

Once this happens, it is useless to continue giving that antibiotic to the patient. (But note that the *germ*, not the *person*, becomes resistant to an antibiotic.) Use of broad spectrum antibiotics gives more types of organisms a chance to develop resistance. Because of resistance, the overuse of antibiotics is now recognized as an important public health problem. The results are seen in hospitals where certain strains of resistant bacteria have appeared, causing hospital-acquired infections.

Sensitivity—Another problem the doctor considers in prescribing anti-infectives is drug **hypersensitivity**. After a few doses of some antibiotics and sulfonamides, certain patients become especially sensitive to the drugs and show allergiclike reactions. The doctor must then switch them to another drug that kills the same germs but perhaps has more side effects.

Antibiotics and sulfonamides have some serious side effects (see Figure 6-5). Some antibiotics are especially toxic to the kidneys and are thus dangerous for people with kidney problems. The physician weighs the benefits of the drug against the dangers of not giving the drug. Usually the physician has several drugs to choose among, with some more dangerous than others. A more dangerous drug is chosen only when a less dangerous one has failed to stop an infection or when the patient has become hypersensitive or resistant to it.

Schedules

Timing is also important. It takes time to wipe out infection, and pathogens may be present long after symptoms are gone. The physician must order the anti-infective for the proper length of time, and those who give medications must see that all doses are taken. This is an important teaching point for patients who will be taking these drugs on their own.

Time of day is also important because doses of anti-infectives must be scheduled with mealtimes in mind. Oral anti-infectives can cause gastric irritation. Giving them on a full stomach or with milk can help soothe the irritation. However, some are made less effective when food or milk is present in the stomach. It is important to find out if oral anti-infectives should be given with food or milk or on an empty stomach. Instructions to "give between meals" means that the drug is to be given at least 1 hour before or 2 hours after meals, when the stomach is assumed to be empty.

Antibiotics

An antibiotic is a substance with the ability to destroy life. It is produced by a microorganism and has **bactericidal** (bak-ter'i-si'dal) activity or **bacteriostatic** (bak-te're-o-stat'ik) activity on other microorganisms.

Penicillins—The penicillins are a large group of anti-infective drugs. They come in many forms to be given by different routes according to the therapeutic aim. Natural penicillins are made from a mold that grows on bread and fruit. Penicillin G potassium (*Pentids*) and penicillin V (*Pen-Vee, V-Cillin K*) are the most common natural penicillins. They are used against gram-positive cocci (round-shaped bacteria) and some gram-negative cocci. They are used to treat gonorrhea, syphilis, and meningitis. Natural penicillins are also given before some surgeries to ward off in-

Figure 6-5 Dangers to watch for in administering antibiotics and sulfonamides.

fections in patients with heart disease and rheumatic fever. To improve usefulness, semisynthetic forms of penicillin have been developed in the laboratory. Ampicillin (*Principen, Omnipen*) and amoxicillin (*Amoxil, Larotid*) are other popular semisynthetic penicillins.

Unfortunately, there are some cocci (especially staphylococci, the deadly "staph germs") that "fight back" when attacked by penicillin. They secrete a substance called **penicillinase** that cancels out penicillin's effects. The microbes are then resistant. For these germs, there are special semisynthetic forms of penicillin that are not affected by penicillinase. Examples are methicillin (*Staphcillin*), oxacillin (*Prostaphlin*), and nafcillin (*Unipen*).

The greatest danger with penicillin use is allergy. Severe skin rashes can occur as a result of penicillin allergy. Other reactions can be life threatening. A person can go into **anaphylaxis** (an'ah-fi-lak'sis), which is signaled by difficulty in breathing, swelling of the throat so as to cause suffocation, and shock symptoms. Persons who have penicillin allergies are asked to wear a medical ID to alert the medical staff in case emergency treatment is needed.

Cephalosporins—These are broad-spectrum, semisynthetic drugs related to penicillin. They can substitute for penicillin when germs have developed resistance. But people who are allergic to penicillin may be allergic to cephalosporins, too. Examples are cephalexin (*Keflex*) and cephalothin (*Keflin*).

Tetracyclines—The tetracyclines are effective against a wide variety of pathogens—in other words, they are broad-spectrum antibiotics. Examples of this drug group are tetracycline hydrochloride (*Achromycin V, Sumycin*) and doxycycline (*Vibramycin*).

Like the penicillins, the tetracyclines carry the danger of allergic reactions, superinfection, and the development of resistant organisms. They may also permanently discolor the developing teeth of children, cause stomach and liver problems, and cause skin rash in patients exposed to sunlight (**photosensitivity**). Oral tetracyclines should not be given when a person is taking antacids or eating dairy products such as milk. Milk and antacids for stomach upset prevent the proper absorption of tetracyclines from the gastrointestinal tract.

Chloramphenicol—This is an example of an antibiotic with a serious side effect: blood disorders. It has a wide range of uses but is rarely selected unless other, less risky antibiotics have not worked. It is the best drug for treating typhoid fever and one form of meningitis. When it is used, blood tests must be made at least every 48 hours to check for signs of blood disorders caused by the drug.

Erythromycins—These drugs work against many gram-positive cocci and bacilli and rickettsiae. Because they kill many of the same microbes as penicillin, erythromycins are good substitutes to use for people with penicillin allergies. They are also used in the treatment of "Legionnaires' disease." Allergic reactions to erythromycins are rare, and side effects are limited to stomach upset, with a slight danger of liver disorder. Examples of brand name preparations of erythromycins are *Ilosone, Erythrocin, E-Mycin*, and *E.E.S.*

Aminoglycosides—These are a group of broad-spectrum antibiotics that keep germ cells from building proteins they need for growth. Examples are amikacin (*Amikin*), neomycin, streptomycin, and gentamicin (*Garamycin*). All of them are given parenterally for systemic effects. They are also available as one ingredient in creams and ointments for topical use (e.g., *Neosporin, Cortisporin Otic*), and in oral forms for a local antibacterial effect (e.g., preparing the intestines for bowel surgery). When given by injection, there is danger of nerve damage that can cause deafness. These drugs also can damage the kidneys.

Sulfonamides

Members of this family of antibiotics were developed in the laboratory. Sulfonamides have the same effect on microbes, however, which is to slow their growth or destroy them. They do this by taking the place of substances that germs need for nourishment.

When first discovered in 1935, the sulfonamides, or "sulfa drugs," were hailed as miracle drugs that could destroy disease germs of many different kinds, including those that cause meningitis, strep throat, and gonorrhea. However, because of the wide use of sulfa drugs, many germs have become resistant. Many people have also developed hypersensitivity to these drugs. Today, therefore, their use is confined to the treatment of urinary tract infections, conjunctivitis, and some forms of intestinal disorders. Examples of sulfonamides are sulfisoxazole (*Gantrisin*), sulfadiazine, sulfamethoxazole (*Gantanol*), and combinations (e.g., *Bactrim*).

Sulfonamides are usually given orally, and a few preparations are available for topical use (e.g., *Sulfamylon* for burns). Side effects are more common with long-acting sulfonamides than with fast-acting ones. Common side effects are fever, skin rash, nausea, vomiting, and diarrhea.

Sulfonamides may cause crystals to form in the urine. These crystals can block the tubes that carry the urine away. For this reason, patients taking sulfa drugs should be given plenty of fluids each day. Sulfonamides may also cause blood disorders such as anemia. Blood cell counts must be made often if a person is on long-term sulfonamide therapy.

Gamma Globulin

Gamma globulin is a protein that circulates in the bloodstream and contains the antibodies that make people immune to specific diseases. Because gamma globulin contains many different specific antibodies, it is sometimes given in large doses to patients in the hope of preventing an infection. For example, if a person has been exposed to viral hepatitis, a liver disease, the doctor might order several injections of gamma globulin to ward off the infection. Gamma globulin is also given to people whose bodies lack these substances from birth.

You should be familiar with drugs given in the table of representative anti-infectives at the end of this unit. Product information tables such as this appear in many of the remaining units of this text. You are not expected to memorize all of the information given. However, you should read them over carefully. Your study of drugs in this text is designed to enable you to read and understand the latest drug information provided in drug references.

CANCER AND CHEMOTHERAPY

Cancer is not one disease, but several hundred. The course of the disease and its treatment vary with the part of the body that is affected. In the remaining units, several forms of cancer are mentioned along with the body systems or organs they affect. However, the drugs used to treat cancer are described here because they are best understood by looking at processes that take place at the cell level. They are also similar to antibiotics because they, too, destroy living cells.

All cancers have several features in common.

- **Rapid cell growth and reproduction.**
  This growth is caused by a change in the genetic code (or "messages") governing normal cell reproduction. These changes cause cancer cells to reproduce at a much faster rate than normal.
- **Effects on adjacent cells.**
  Cancer cells can invade nearby tissues as they grow, causing destruction.
- **Seeding.**
  Cancer cells can "seed" (implant) themselves in other parts of the body and start new growths there. This is called **metastasis.** We say that a cancer has **metastasized** to another part of the body.

Rapid cell growth may give rise to **tumors**, which are lumps or masses of tissue. Not all tumors are cancerous, however. Noncancerous tumors are called **benign** tumors. They involve rapid cell growth, but the cells do not invade nearby tissues or spread to other parts of the body.

Cancerous tumors are called **malignant** tumors. As they grow, they put pressure on surrounding healthy tissues and organs and also invade them, causing destruction. Some cancers affect whole systems, such as the blood and lymph-forming organs, rather than causing a local tumor. In such cases the cancer cells are circulating throughout the body.

Early detection of cancer gives the best chance of curing the disease. The methods of treatment most often used first are surgery and radiation. Surgery is employed to remove tumors and nearby lymph glands, where cancer cells that have spread from the tumor may be trapped. Radiation may be focused on a specific spot to kill the cancer cells. It may also be implanted in nearby tissue or swallowed in a substance that is attracted to the site of the cancer.

Drugs for Chemotherapy

Drug treatment of cancer is called **chemotherapy**. Drugs can cure a few rare types of cancer, but they are more often used to control cancer symptoms after surgery and radiation have failed to bring about a cure. Or they are used in system-wide invasions of cancer cells, such as leukemia and Hodgkin's disease.

The drugs used for chemotherapy are powerful and have strong effects on healthy cells as well as cancer cells. They are dangerous drugs whose use has to be carefully planned and supervised by a physician. Some of them are specifically attracted to cells that are multiplying rapidly—thus they rush to the scene of a tumorous growth, killing cancer cells.

But at the same time they are attracted to the blood-forming centers of the body because there the cells are also multiplying rapidly. When the drugs kill blood cells, they weaken the body and destroy some of its defenses. Patients receiving chemotherapy often bruise easily because many platelets (parts of the blood that help stop bleeding) have been destroyed. They may be especially prone to infection because of the destruction of white blood cells. Their bones may heal slowly and also may break easily because the cancer drugs weaken the bone tissue where blood cells are produced.

Other areas of the body that have rapidly multiplying cells are the skin and the linings of the mouth, throat, stomach, and intestines. These areas, too, are affected by chemotherapy. Side effects such as nausea, vomiting, and hair loss are common.

Doses must be carefully controlled because large doses can be toxic to healthy cells. Often some toxic effects are necessary to achieve the benefit of a drug's cancer-suppressing ability. Rather than giving a low dose continuously over a long period of time, cancer drugs are sometimes given in cycles—intensive treatment followed by a recovery period of 4–6 weeks, followed by another intensive treatment, and so on. This gives the body time to recover from the toxic effects and to build blood cells back up to a normal level.

No drug is able to kill all cancer cells at one time. But each successive dose kills a few more so that the population is kept down to a level where the symptoms are under control. The effect of chemotherapy is shown in Figure 6-6, which depicts the reproductive life of a cancer cell. Without chemotherapy, after six generations this cell would have produced 64 cancer cells. With two waves of chemotherapy, it produced only six. During the same amount of time a normal cell might have reproduced itself only one or two times.

Remission means the disappearance of symptoms (not just of cancer, but of any disease). The object of cancer chemotherapy is to bring about a remission and to keep the symptoms from recurring. Chemotherapy is not guaranteed to cure cancer, but it can give the patient many more years of useful life.

Drugs used against cancer are called **antineoplastics** (Figure 6-7). The prefix **anti** means against, and **neoplasm** means tumor. They slow down or kill growing cells by interfering with chemical processes or by substituting for nutrients in the cells so the cells "starve" to death. Other terms used for anticancer drugs are **cytostatic**, which means that they stop all growth (**cyte** = cell; **stasis** = stop), and **cytotoxic**, which means poisonous to cells.

Alkylating Agents (Nitrogen Mustards)—These are drugs that chemically latch onto important cell parts so they do not work properly. This results in cell destruction. Nitrogen mustards are related to mustard gas first used in World War I as a chemical weapon. Applied to the skin, as in a "mustard bomb," they blister the skin. But used as cancer drugs they stop the growth of many cancer cells. Alkylating agents have toxic effects on the blood-building organs, the gastrointestinal system, and the sex glands. An immediate side effect is usually vomiting and nausea. But after a while, the patient's daily blood counts will reveal that fewer lymph cells are being produced in the bone marrow, signaling a remission. Examples of alkylating agents are mechlorethamine hydrochloride (*Mustargen*), chlorambucil (*Leukeran*), and cyclophosphamide (*Cytoxan*).

A newer type of alkylating agent is a group of drugs called nitrosoureas (carmustine and lomustine). These drugs are able to pass into the brain, making them useful for treating brain tumors.

Antimetabolites—These drugs interfere with metabolism. Metabolism is the cell process that burns nutrients to pro-

142 Administering Medications

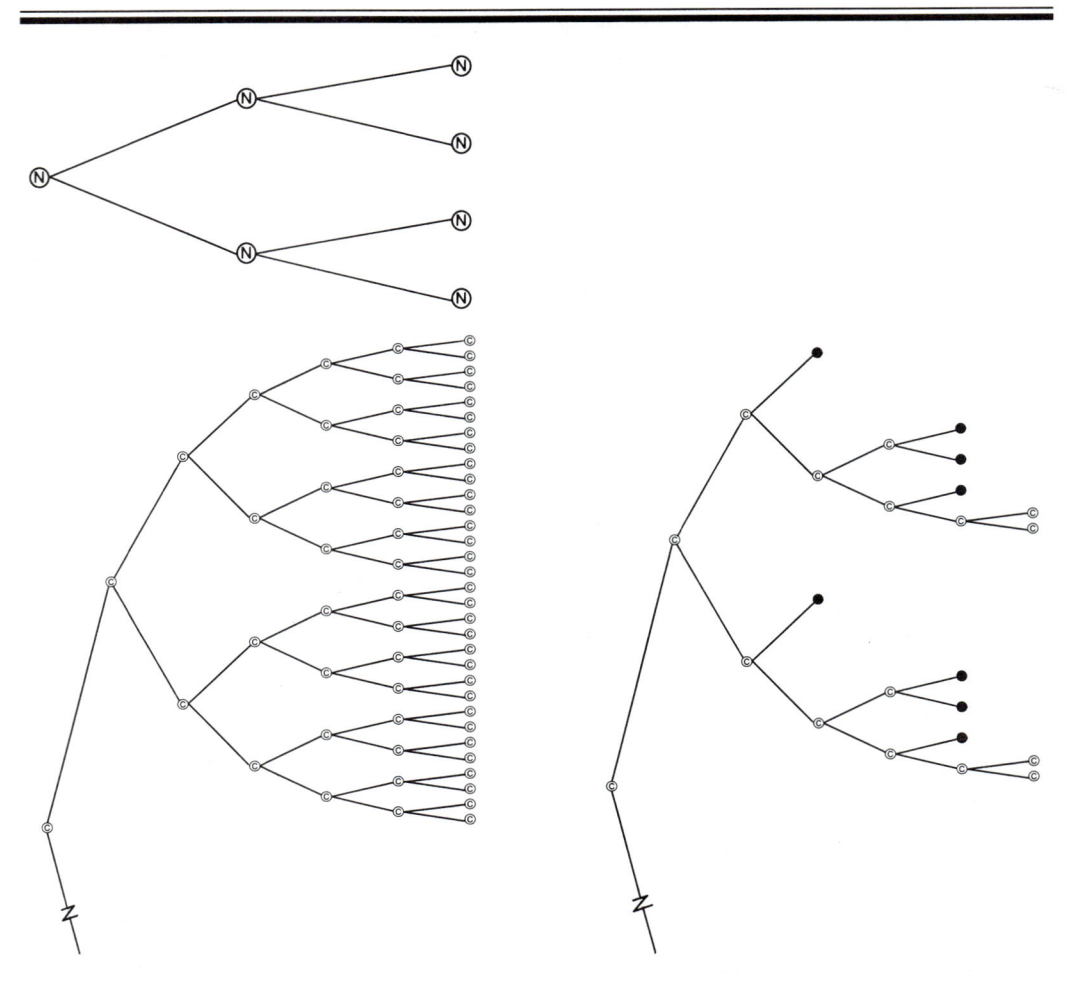

Figure 6-6 Compare the reproduction of cancer cells and normal cells. Chemotherapy slows reproduction by destroying some of the abnormal cells.

duce energy for growth and action. Antimetabolites look very much like the normal nutrients that cells use, but they cannot produce energy. The cancer cells consume them, but since the antimetabolites do not provide energy, the cell eventually dies. This is similar to the action of sulfonamides on bacteria and viruses. Examples of antimetabolites are fluorouracil, mercaptopurine, and cytarabine (*Cytosar-U*).

Antibiotics—Some antibiotics stop the growth of cancer cells and so are used in chemotherapy. Examples are dactinomycin (*Cosmegen*), bleomycin, doxorubicin (*Adriamycin*), and plicamycin (*Mithracin*).

Hormones—Sex hormones (e.g., estrogen, testosterone) are used to control specific cancers in the sex organs, such as cancer of the breast, prostate, and uterus. Examples of these are dromostanolone (*Drolban*) and fluoxymesterone (*Halotestin*). Other hormones suppress the production of lymph cells and make the patient feel better, so they are used in managing leukemia.

Figure 6-7 Antineoplastics destroy or slow the growth of cancer cells.

Note that the described antineoplastics may be given in various combinations. The drugs vincristine (*Oncovin*) and vinblastine (*Velban*) are sometimes included in these combinations. They are products of the periwinkle plant (vinca), and they work by interfering with cell division. See the product information table at the end of this unit for representative antineoplastics and their uses, actions, doses, and side effects.

Care of the Cancer Patient

Patients undergoing chemotherapy need special care and emotional support from you. They must deal not only with the threat of cancer itself, but also with the unpleasant, often dangerous side effects of chemotherapy. Many of the drugs given for cancer therapy must be administered parenterally by specially trained nurses or by physicians. However, you may be involved in giving some of the routine drugs for pain and nausea. You can provide emotional support by listening to your patients' fears and needs and by doing what you can to help make them comfortable. You should also observe them carefully for physical signs of drug side effects and disease effects, especially:

- Nausea and vomiting
- Irritation of the mucous membranes of the mouth and throat
- Signs of developing infections, especially around the eyes, nose, and rectum
- Pain caused by the disease that could be treated with analgesics (pain relievers)
- Fluid retention
- Diarrhea
- Fever

Chart these observations and follow the physician's orders.

Because antineoplastics irritate the gastrointestinal tract, from the mouth through the rectum, patients have trouble eating because it is uncomfortable. They may develop a painful inflammation of the mucous membranes of the mouth, called **stomatitis**. Encourage them to eat by providing a pleasant atmosphere and letting them select their own foods. Help with their oral hygiene by rinsing their mouth often with water or mouthwashes. Clean the teeth and gums gently with a soft brush.

Finally, take special care not to infect chemotherapy patients with germs from other patients. Remember, their bodies' natural defenses against infection may be seriously weakened by the antineoplastics they are taking.

ISOLATION PROCEDURES

There are two basic situations in which isolation procedures may be used:

- when a patient must be protected from any germs that you carry
- when you must be protected from any germs the patient is carrying (Figure 6-8).

Depending on the specific disease or germ danger, there are special types of isolation requiring different precautions.

Strict Isolation

The patient is kept in a separate room, with the door closed. All involved staff wear protective gowns, masks, and gloves. Hands must be washed upon entering and leaving the room. All equipment for drug administration must be discarded in special containers after use or must be disinfected and sterilized.

This type of isolation is ordered for hospital staph infections and serious infectious diseases that can be spread by touch and by air. It protects the medical staff (and other patients) from germs the patient is carrying.

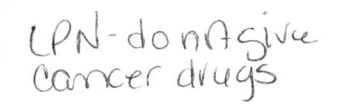

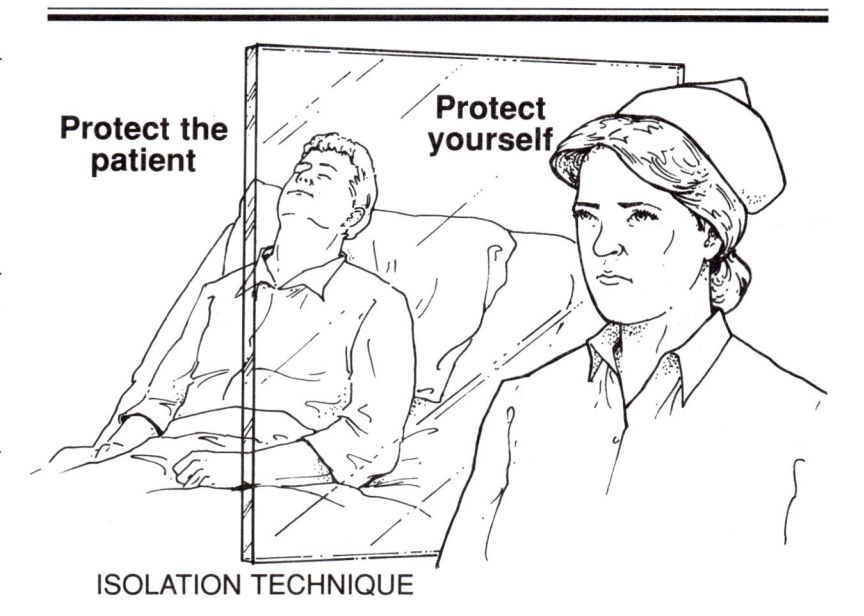

Figure 6-8 Isolation technique—hand washing, gown, gloves, mask, cap, and disinfection of equipment—forms a barrier to germs.

Respiratory Isolation

The patient is kept in a separate room, with the door closed. Staff members wear protective masks only. Hands must be washed upon entering and leaving the room. Gloves are not necessary, but any object that is contaminated with fluids from the patient's nose and lungs must be disinfected so the patient's germs are not spread to others. Meningitis, mumps, and tuberculosis are diseases requiring respiratory isolation.

Reverse Isolation (Protective Isolation)

The patient is kept in a separate room, with the door closed. Gown, mask, and gloves must be worn by the staff. Hands must be washed upon entering and leaving the room.

This type of isolation protects patients who have no immunity or who have weakened immunity because of leukemia or cancer chemotherapy; the patient is being protected from germs *you* are carrying.

Practice Pointers

Special procedures are also followed when handling patients with disease germs that pass out of the body in the feces (enteric precautions), burns and skin infections (wound and skin precautions), and open sores, blood infections, and draining wounds (discharge precautions). These do not require a separate room for the patient, but aseptic (germ-free) procedures must be followed to avoid causing or spreading infection.

Before administering drugs to any isolation patient, you should review isolation procedures in your agency's procedure manual or in a good nursing manual. The steps are specific and should be followed. There are usually instructions for putting on and taking off gowns, masks, and gloves and for disposing of materials and equipment.

The procedure you will most often be using, whether working with an isolation patient or not, is washing your hands. This is done both *before* and *after* administering a medication. The checklist at the end of this unit will help refresh your memory of the proper hand-washing technique.

When administering medications to an isolation patient, you may wonder just which items are considered contaminated. The answer is **everything that has been in direct or indirect contact with the patient**. An example of indirect contact would be your touching a glass that has remained near a coughing patient, even if the patient had never actually touched the glass. Your gown and mask protect you (or the patient) from indirect contact. Your gloves protect you from direct contact. For additional protection, you may ask patients to take their own medications and dispose of supplies while you watch, as long as they are able to do this.

When working with a patient who has an infectious disease, it may be helpful to know the main places that germs can be picked up. Germs leave the body of a diseased person in the secretions of the nose and mouth, in material coughed up from the lungs, in the feces or anything touched by feces (bedclothes, toilet, etc.), in the urine, in the vaginal area, in drainage from infected wounds, and in the blood (in the case of hepatitis). Those sources of contamination are the ones toward which aseptic and isolation procedures are directed.

You may take advantage of disposable materials to avoid carrying germs from one place to another. Where disposable materials are not available or not practical (as with permanent pieces of equipment), contaminated items must be washed and sterilized by using a special machine. Machines can kill germs by baking them at high heat, searing them with steam, or bombarding them with sound waves or ultraviolet rays. A common sterilizing machine is the **autoclave**, which uses steam. A variety of chemical germ killers called **disinfectants** are also available for sterilizing surgical tools and other pieces of equipment.

Disposal procedures are also important when you are working with infected patients. Equipment and disposable materials must be specially wrapped before being discarded or sent to the hospital's sterilization unit. Each agency usually has its own proper disposal procedures written up in a procedure manual. Study these carefully to learn the proper techniques.

Drugs for Infection and Cancer 145

EXERCISES

A. Matching.

_c_ 1. basic building blocks of all living things
_a_ 2. groups of cells working together
_b_ 3. substance that makes up two-thirds of the body
_d_ 4. groups of organs and tissues working together
_g_ 5. fluid found inside cells
_h_ 6. fluid surrounding cells
_f_ 7. ability of cells to split in two
_e_ 8. ability of the body to replace damaged cells
_j_ 9. biocidal activity
_i_ 10. biostatic activity

a. tissues
b. water
c. cells
d. systems
e. healing
f. reproduction
g. cytoplasm
h. tissue fluid
i. inhibit growth
j. kill

B. Define these medical terms.

1. antibody _fights a specific pathogen_
2. immunization _ability to resist disease - artificial_
3. pathogen _disease causing entity_
4. leukocyte _white blood cell_
5. superinfection _more than 1 infection_
6. biostatic _stays the same_
7. biocidal _kill_
8. extravasation _____
9. hypersensitivity _↑ sensitivity_
10. hepatotoxicity _toxic to liver_

C. Short answers.

1. Why are staph and other infections a special problem in hospitals and long-term care units? Give at least three reasons.

_____
_____
_____
_____
_____

146 Administering Medications

2. List the body's three lines of defense against invading germs. How does each one fight germs?

   a. _____

   b. _____

   c. _____

3. Anti-infective drugs fight infection in two basic ways. These are:

   a. _____

   b. _____

D. Matching.

   _c_ 1. laboratory test to identify germs
   _f_ 2. laboratory test to determine which drug will kill a specific germ
   _d_ 3. drugs that affect a great many pathogens
   _a_ 4. drugs that affect only a few pathogens
   _b_ 5. a germ's immunity to the effects of germ-killing drugs
   _e_ 6. allergiclike reaction to a drug after taking several doses

   a. narrow spectrum
   b. resistance
   c. Gram stain
   d. broad spectrum
   e. hypersensitivity
   f. culture and sensitivity test

E. 1. List at least three possible problems associated with the use of penicillin.

   _____
   _____
   _____

2. You have just administered penicillin to Mrs. Mosley. Within minutes she goes into shock, has difficulty breathing, and shows signs of swelling in the throat. What is probably the matter and what should you do?

   _____
   _____
   _____

3. Why should oral tetracyclines not be given to a patient taking antacids or dairy products (e.g., milk):

   _____
   _____
   _____

4. Which organs may be damaged by aminoglycosides?

   _____

5. What is the possible serious side effect of chloramphenicol?

_____

_____

6. What is the difference between antibiotics and sulfonamides?

_____

_____

_____

F. Match these anti-infectives to their descriptions.

___ 1. semisynthetic forms of penicillin
___ 2. broad-spectrum antibiotics that should not be taken with antacids or milk
___ 3. antibiotic which can lead to blood disorders
___ 4. broad-spectrum antibiotics which can cause nerve damage
___ 5. synthetic drugs used mostly for urinary tract infections
___ 6. blood protein containing antibodies, given to protect the body from infection
___ 7. substitute for penicillin, used in Legionnaires' disease

a. tetracyclines
b. chloramphenicol
c. sulfonamides
d. ampicillin, amoxicillin
e. kanamycin, gentamicin
f. erythromycins
g. gamma globulin

G. Short answers.

1. Name three characteristics of cancer cells:

a. _____

b. _____

c. _____

2. Antineoplastics harm healthy cells as well as cancer cells. Which parts of the body are especially affected by chemotherapy?

_____

_____

3. What signs should you look for when giving medications to cancer patients?

_____

_____

_____

H. Match these types of antineoplastics to examples and descriptions.

___ 1. alkylating agents
___ 2. antimetabolites
___ 3. antibiotics used against cancer
___ 4. sex hormones

a. used especially to fight cancer of the prostate, uterus, and breast
b. take the place of nutrients in cancer cells
c. bleomycin and dactinomycin
d. nitrogen mustard and mechlorethamine

I. Short answers. In the spaces provided, answer these questions about isolation procedures.

1. Isolation procedures protect the patient from _____ and protect you from _____.

2. List the three main types of isolation (in which patients are kept in separate rooms):

3. When should you wash your hands during medication administration?

4. List at least three ways in which germs leave the body of an infected person:

5. Where should you look (book, manual, etc.) to find the proper procedures for isolation and disposal of contaminated materials?

Drugs for Infection and Cancer

ANSWERS TO EXERCISES

A. Matching
   1. c
   2. a
   3. b
   4. d
   5. g
   6. h
   7. f
   8. e
   9. j
   10. i

B. Definitions
   1. substance produced in the body to kill specific germs
   2. shot or vaccination to stimulate antibody formation against a certain disease germ
   3. harmful germ; one that can cause infection
   4. white blood cell specialized to "swallow" germs
   5. one infection on top of another; caused by an antibiotic killing microbe in the body that acted as natural antibiotics
   6. ability to inhibit growth of microorganisms
   7. ability to kill microorganisms
   8. discharge of blood or other IV fluids into tissue surrounding needle in arm
   9. symptoms relating to anaphylaxis
   10. septicemia originating in the liver

C. Short answers
   1. Infections in hospitals are dangerous because drug-resistant germs that live in some health facilities cannot be killed by antibiotics. In hospitals, a large number of at-risk patients are gathered into one place. Patients with skin wounds and lowered resistance are easily attacked by germs. Medical staff can carry germs from patient to patient as they work.
   2. a. Skin and mucous membranes: prevent germs from entering the body.
      b. Leukocytes: swallow and digest germs in the body.
      c. Antibodies: kill certain germs that enter the body.
   3. a. By killing germs directly.
      b. By slowing the growth of germs.

D. Matching
   1. c
   2. f
   3. d
   4. a
   5. b
   6. e

E. Short answers
   1. Allergic reaction; superinfection; some penicillins poorly absorbed by oral route and/or excreted quickly; microbes develop resistance by secreting penicillinase.
   2. The patient is probably allergic to penicillin and is going into anaphylactic shock. You should get emergency help immediately.
   3. Antacids and dairy products prevent the proper absorption of tetracyclines from the gastrointestinal tract.
   4. There is a risk of nerve damage that can cause deafness; the kidneys.
   5. Blood disorders.
   6. Antibiotics are substances produced by organisms against other organisms; sulfonamides are substances synthesized in the laboratory. However, some antibiotics today are also synthetic.

F. Matching
   1. d
   2. a
   3. b
   4. e
   5. c
   6. g
   7. f
G. Short answers
   1. Cancer cells
      a. They grow and divide more rapidly than normal cells.
      b. They invade nearby healthy tissues.
      c. They metastasize (spread) to other parts of the body.
   2. Parts of the body where cells are dividing rapidly, such as the blood-forming areas of the bones.
   3. Gastrointestinal upset (nausea, vomiting, diarrhea), pain, fever, and infections.
H. Antineoplastics
   1. d
   2. b
   3. c
   4. a
I. Short answers
   1. Germs that you are carrying; germs that the patient is carrying.
   2. Strict, respiratory, and reverse (protective).
   3. Before and after leaving the room, or before and after giving medication.
   4. Secretions from nose and mouth; secretions coughed up from lungs; feces or anything touched by feces; drainage from wounds; infected blood.
   5. In your agency's procedure manual; or, if they do not have one, look in a good nursing manual.

Drugs for Infection and Cancer 151

PRACTICE PROCEDURE

ADMINISTER MEDICATION TO AN ISOLATION PATIENT

NOTE: *You may wish to practice the procedure several times using a different type of isolation each time.*

Equipment:
- Medication order for an oral medication to be taken with water
- Kardex, medication record, patient chart
- Oral medication (e.g., tetracycline capsule)
- Medication tray or cart with souffle cups
- Gown, mask, and gloves
- Instructions for basic isolation procedures in your agency's procedure manual
- Water pitcher and glass (next to patient's bed)

_____ 1. Assemble equipment. Use disposable equipment if possible.

_____ 2. Read medication order and set up medication. Check to see that you have the RIGHT DOSE of the RIGHT MEDICATION for the RIGHT PATIENT by the RIGHT ROUTE at the RIGHT TIME.

_____ 3. Check to see what kind of isolation the patient is under—respiratory, strict, reverse, or special precautions (enteric, skin wounds, discharge, etc.). There should be a sign on the door of the patient's room or on the Kardex telling the type of isolation.

_____ 4. Review isolation procedures for the specific type of isolation and decide what clothing you must wear—gown, mask, and/or gloves. Here is a brief reminder:
- *For reverse isolation.* Wear gown, mask, and gloves. This is protection for the patient.
- *For respiratory isolation.* Wear a mask only. This protects you from airborne bacteria that may be inhaled into the lungs.
- *For strict isolation.* Wear gown, mask, and gloves. This is protection for you since you must not touch anything contaminated.

But remember to wash your hands before you put on the protective clothing.

_____ 5 Wash your hands following standard nursing practice. In other words, use soap and water to make a lather and then scrub each finger and the front and back of each hand with a circular motion. Rinse, keeping hands lower than elbows so water flows from the cleaner area toward the dirtier area. Lather and rinse again. The washing process should last at least 1–2 minutes. Dry hands with a paper towel, using the same elbow-to-hand motion.

_____ 6. *Now* put on your gown, mask, and/or gloves following the proper procedure.

_____ 7. Carry the medication into the patient's room in a souffle cup or envelope (Figure 6-9). **Leave the drug cart or tray outside the door.**

_____ 8. Identify the patient following agency procedure. Explain what you are going to do (e.g., give the patient an antibiotic to help heal an infection or fight disease germs). **If necessary,** assist the patient into a comfortable position for taking the medication.

_____ 9. Administer the medication. Have the patient pour a glass of water from the bedside pitcher and then take the medication from the souffle cup and swallow it with water **while you watch.**

___ 10. Give any special instructions regarding the medication; for example, mild side effects that may be expected. Make the patient comfortable before leaving the room.

___ 11. Remove gown, mask, and/or gloves and discard according to the rules of your agency. Wash your hands following standard nursing practice. Use a paper towel to turn off the water faucet, unless there is a foot or knee pedal.

___ 12. Chart the medication, noting time, dose, and anything unusual that you may have noticed or that the patient may have mentioned.

Demonstrate this procedure for your instructor or the nurse in charge.

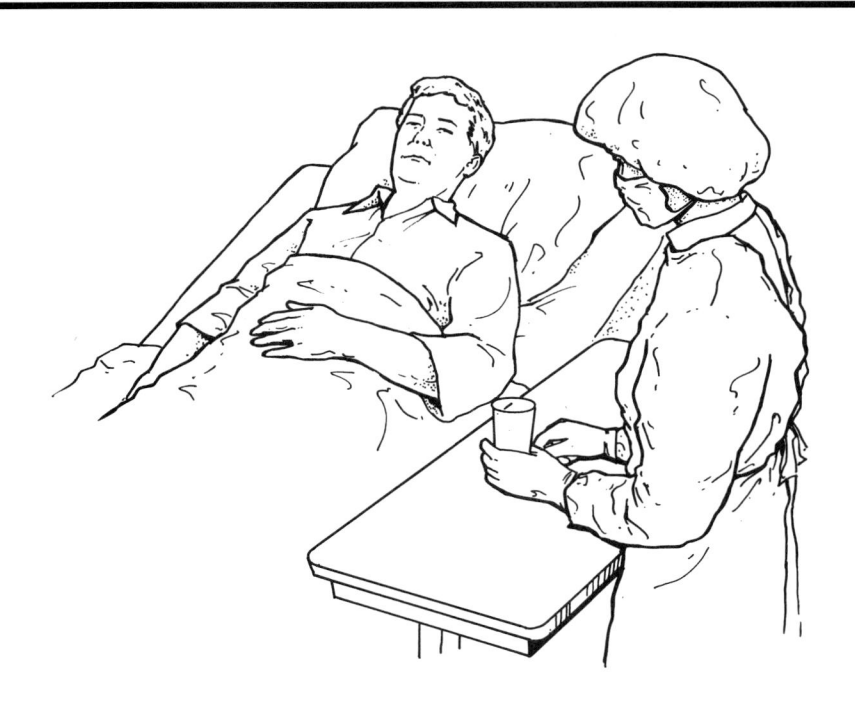

Figure 6-9 Administering medication to an isolation patient.

Drugs for Infection and Cancer 153

REPRESENTATIVE ANTI-INFECTIVES

CATEGORY, NAME[a], AND ROUTE	USES AND DISEASES	ACTIONS	USUAL DOSE[b] AND SPECIAL INSTRUCTIONS	SIDE EFFECTS AND ADVERSE REACTIONS
Antibiotics				
Penicillin G potassium (*Pentids*) Oral	Pneumonia; streptococcal pharyngitis, syphilis, gonorrhea	Inhibits biosynthesis of cell wall	5–20 million units/day PO, depending on infection and body weight; watch patient closely for anaphylaxis with first dose	Hypersensitivity reactions such as rash, chills, fever, edema, and possibly fatal anaphylaxis
Methicillin (*Staphcillin*) IM, IV	Penicillinase resistant	Inhibits biosynthesis of cell wall	1 g IM q 4–6 hours 1 g IV q 6 hours	Nausea, vomiting, diarrhea, glossitis, possibly fatal anaphylaxis
Cephalothin (*Keflin*) IM, IV	Pneumonia and urinary tract and skin infections	Inhibits biosynthesis of cell wall	500 mg–1 g IV or IM q 4–6 hours	Superinfection, hypersensitivity, hemolytic anemia, and abnormal liver and kidney function tests
Tetracycline HCl (*Cyclopar*) Oral, IM	Respiratory and urinary tract infections, rickettsial infections, syphilis, acne	Bacteriostatic, inhibits protein synthesis	1–2 g/day PO or IM in two to four doses; give between meals with full glass of water; do not give with antacids or dairy products; patients should avoid sunlight	Loss of appetite, nausea, vomiting, diarrhea, allergic reactions, photosensitivity, tooth discoloration in infants and children, superinfection, stomach cramps
Erythromycin (*E-Mycin, Ilotycin*)	Respiratory infections, prophylaxis for rheumatic fever and bacterial endocarditis, venereal disease, Legionnaires' disease, walking pneumonia	Bacteriostatic	250–500 mg PO q 6 hours, give between meals with ample water; do not give with fruit juice	Superinfection, allergic reactions, nausea, diarrhea, vomiting, stomach upset
Polymyxin B–neomycin–gramicidin–hydrocortisone (*Cortisporin Cream*)	Topical infections, burns, wounds, dermatitis	Bacteriocidal	Follow package directions	Skin rash, superinfection
Sulfonamides				
Sulfisoxazole (*Gantrisin*)	Urinary tract and ear infections, meningitis	Bacteriostatic	2–4 g PO initially, then 4–8 g/day in four to six doses; give between meals with plenty of water; given IV in meningitis	Hypersensitivity, photosensitivity, nausea, vomiting, diarrhea, dizziness, loss of appetite
Co-trimoxazole (*Bactrim, Septra*)	Chronic bronchitis, acute ear infections, urinary tract and intestinal infections	Bacteriocidal	1 double strength tablet PO q 12 hours (800 mg sulfamethoxazole and 160 mg trimethoprim); give with a full glass of water between meals	Nausea, vomiting, diarrhea, skin rash, kidney problems, photosensitivity

[a] Brand names given in parentheses are examples only. Check current drug references for a complete listing of available trade name products.
[b] Average adult doses are given. However, dosages are determined by a physician and vary with the purpose of the therapy and the particular patient. The doses presented in this text are for general information only.

REPRESENTATIVE ANTINEOPLASTICS

CATEGORY, NAME[a], AND ROUTE	USES AND DISEASES	ACTIONS	USUAL DOSE[b] AND SPECIAL INSTRUCTIONS	SIDE EFFECTS AND ADVERSE REACTIONS
Alkylating Agents				
Mechlorethamine (*Mustargen*)	Hodgkin's disease, lymphosarcoma	Inhibits rapidly growing cells	Intravenous dosage according to body weight, adjusted to highest non-toxic dose; assist patient with oral hygiene; give adequate fluid; follow physician's orders carefully; note length of time for IV infusion; watch for pain at infusion site	Nausea, vomiting, bleeding, bruising
Carmustine (*BiNCU*)	Brain tumor, Hodgkin's disease, lymphomas	Inhibition of cell synthesis	Intravenous dosage according to surface area, pain at injection site common	Blood and liver problems, nausea, vomiting
Antimetabolites				
Fluorouracil (*Adrucil*)	Cancer of the breast, colon, rectum, stomach, and pancreas	Slows reproduction of cells	Intravenous dosage according to body weight; avoid extravasation	Loss of appetite, nausea, vomiting, stomatitis, diarrhea, fever, bleeding, sore throat
Mercaptopurine (*Purinethol*)	Leukemias	Slows reproduction of cells	Oral dosage according to body weight, adjusted to highest nontoxic dose	Blood and liver problems
Antibiotics				
Dactinomycin (*Cosmegen*)	Cancer of the testes and uterus, Wilms' tumor	Inhibits cell reproduction	Intravenous dosage according to body weight, adjusted to highest nontoxic dose. Drug is corrosive; avoid contact with skin; avoid extravasation	Nausea, vomiting, fever, stomatitis, bleeding, bruising, loss of hair
Hormones				
Dromostanolone (*Drolban*)	Cancer of the breast	Tumor regression, promotes feeling of well-being in advanced cancer	100 mg IM three times per week	Mild virilism (deepening voice, growth of facial hair), hypercalcemia

[a] Brand names given in parentheses are examples only. Check current drug references for a complete listing of available trade name products.
[b] Average adult doses are given. However, dosages are determined by a physician and vary with the purpose of the therapy and the particular patient. The doses presented in this text are for general information only.

Unit 7

Drugs for the Skin

In this unit you will learn about the structure of the skin and its functions. You will study the major skin disorders, the medical terms for their symptoms, and the drugs used to treat them. You will learn to administer topical drugs to the skin with a proper understanding of their uses and action.

In this unit you will learn to:

- Name the three layers of skin tissue and the structures contained in each.
- List the main functions of the integumentary system.
- Name the secretions of the ceruminous, sebaceous, sudoriferous, and mammary glands.
- State the normal body temperature.
- Explain the process of inflammation.
- List and define the common symptoms of skin disorders.
- Describe the major skin disorders.
- State the actions and give examples of the following drug categories: keratolytics, protectives, astringents, topical corticosteroids, antifungals, antiseptics, topical anesthetics, and parasiticides.
- List five ways of increasing absorption of drugs into the skin layers.
- Follow general instructions for administering topical medications to the skin (psychological support, preparing the patient, bandaging, etc.).
- Follow the correct procedures for applying topical creams, lotions, liniments, ointments, and aerosol sprays.

INTEGUMENTARY SYSTEM

The integumentary (*in-teg-u-men'tar-e*) system consists of the skin (the **integument**), along with the hairs, nails, and glands that are embedded in it. The skin has been called the largest organ of the body because its surface area is so large. It forms a waterproof, protective covering for the entire body, but protection is not its only function.

The skin also senses changes in the environment, and it helps to regulate body temperature. The body's normal temperature is about 98.6°F (37°C). This is the temperature at which the cells maintain their normal functioning. Changes of even a few degrees above or below this normal temperature can disrupt body processes.

The skin is actually three distinct layers: the epidermis, the dermis, and the subcutaneous layer (Figure 7-1).

Epidermis

The outermost layer, the **epidermis**, is made of flat, tough epithelial cells that are constantly being shed and replaced. These cells contain the pigments that give a person's skin its characteristic color. The epidermis forms a barrier against bacteria and moisture. It also holds water *in* to keep body tissues from drying out.

Any break in the epidermis, such as a puncture or a cut, lets in bacteria that may attack the deeper tissues. For this reason, all skin wounds must be kept clean until they heal.

Dermis

Just beneath the epidermis lies a second layer, the **dermis**. The dermis is made up of connective tissue interwoven with tiny blood vessels and nerve endings. It also contains several other structures:

- **Hair follicles**, from which grow the tiny hairs that cover the body.
- **Sebaceous** (*se-ba'shus*) **glands**, or oil glands, that lubricate the hairs with oil or **sebum**.
- **Sudoriferous** (*su'do-rif'er-us*) **glands**, or sweat glands, that help regulate body temperature.
- **Sense receptors**, which send messages to the brain when they feel pain, pressure, heat, cold, touch, etc.

Two glands in the dermal layer have very specific locations: **ceruminous** (*se-roo'mi-nus*) glands in the ear secrete earwax, and **mammary** glands in the female breast secrete milk. These are both specialized forms of sweat glands.

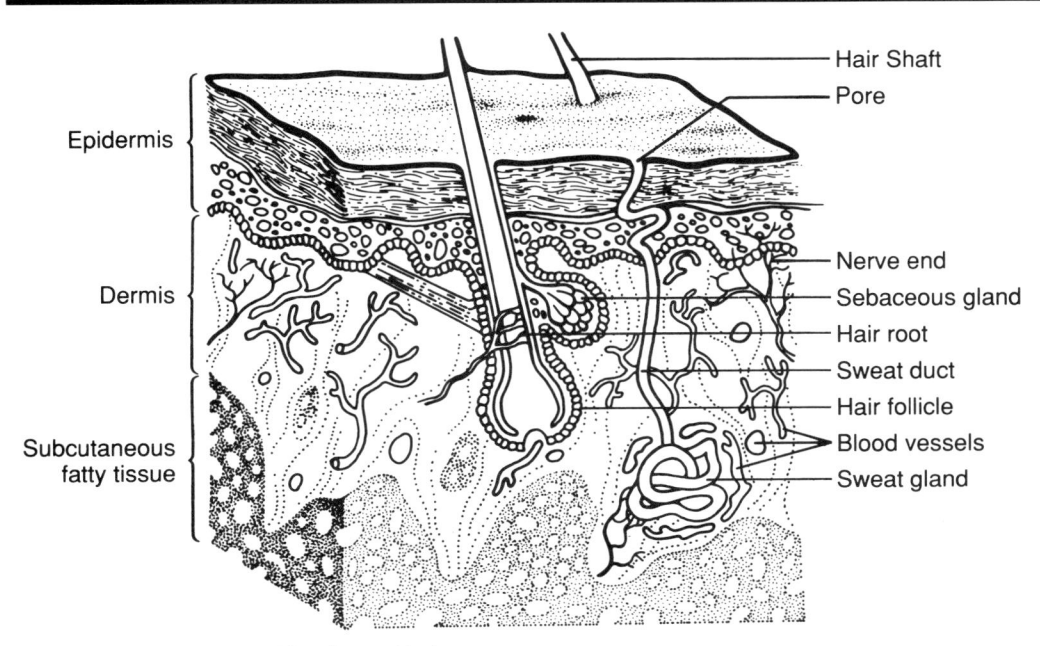

Figure 7-1 Cross section of the three skin layers.

VOCABULARY

acne: skin condition caused by pores plugged with sebum

analgesic: pain reliever

antifungal: drug that kills or prevents the growth of fungi; also called **fungicide**

antihistamine: drug that lessens the effects of histamine

anti-inflammatory: drug that suppresses inflammation

antipruritic: drug that relieves itching

antiseptic: drug that destroys germs on skin surfaces

astringent: solution that tightens skin pores

contact dermatitis: reaction to irritating substance that has touched the skin

corticosteroids: drugs used on the skin because they suppress inflammation, tighten the blood vessels, and relieve itching

dandruff: noninflammatory irritation of the scalp

decubitus: bedsore

dermatitis: inflammation of the skin causing bumps, blisters, scales, or scabs; also called **eczema**

dermatology: the branch of medicine concerned with skin disorders

dermis: middle layer of skin

disinfectant: agent used to kill germs on surgical instruments

ecchymosis: escape of blood into tissues from ruptured blood vessels; causes a bruise

edema: swelling

epidermis: outer skin layer

epithelial: type of cell that makes up body coverings (skin) and linings

erythema: reddening of the skin

follicle: structure of the skin out of which hair grows

forceps: surgical tweezers

fungus: one-celled, plantlike parasite (plural: **fungi**)

histamine: substance normally present in the body; actively released in response to tissue injury

inflammation: the body's reaction to irritation; a process that results in swelling, reddening, heat, and pain

integument: the skin

keratin: protein contained in cells of the epidermis, nails, hair, and horny tissue

keratolytic: drug that destroys keratin and promotes peeling

keratosis: build up and hardening of keratin in the skin

lesion: sore or break or any abnormal place on the skin (in general, any detrimental changes in the structure of a body part)

macerate: soften by moistening, causing increased absorption through the skin

mammary: gland that secretes milk, located in the breasts

nit: egg of a louse

occlusive dressing: bandage that seals in drug, body heat, and moisture

parasite: organism that lives on or in another organism (e.g., lice, mites, tapeworms)

parasiticide: drug that kills parasites

pediculicide: drug that kills lice

pediculosis: infection caused by lice

petechiae: tiny, purplish-red spots on the skin due to bleeding in the skin layers

photodermatitis: irritation caused by skin sensitivity to light

protective: drug that soothes, cools, and protects inflamed skin

pruritus: itching

psoriasis: chronic skin disease of unknown cause; involves drying and scaling skin

scabicide: drug that kills mites

scabies: infection caused by mites

sebaceous: gland in the skin that produces oil

seborrheic dermatitis: inflammatory irritation of the scalp, face, or groin, producing greasy scales

sebum: oil that lubricates the skin, produced by the sebaceous glands

sense receptor: structure that picks up sensations of hot, cold, touch, pain, or pressure in the skin

subcutaneous: deepest skin layer, made up of fatty tissue

sudoriferous: gland that produces sweat

ulceration: open sore

urticaria: raised, whitish patches that itch intensely; also known as hives or **welts**

Subcutaneous Layer

The **subcutaneous** (*sub'ku-ta'ne-us*) layer is a combination of fibrous and fatty connective tissue. The fibrous tissue attaches the upper skin layers to the skeletal muscles. The fatty tissue holds in body heat and acts as an insulator against cold. It also acts as a storage area for energy in the form of fat. Some of the glands, follicles, and sense receptors in the dermis extend down into this subcutaneous layer.

SKIN DISORDERS

The skin reflects the upheavals inside the body caused by infectious diseases, such as measles and chicken pox and by irritating substances that have been touched, swallowed, or inhaled. The skin is also a mirror of human emotions, which reveal themselves through blushing, paleness, and rashes.

This section describes disorders that are confined mainly to the skin area itself. However, the symptoms are similar, whether caused by systemic diseases or by local irritation. The symptoms are the result of the body's natural response to injury: **inflammation**.

Inflammation is a process that occurs wherever and whenever there is cell damage. The capillaries around the damaged area expand to bring in the white blood cells (the leukocytes), which are the germ fighters, and cell repair is begun. The "battle zone" is characterized by redness, swelling, heat, and pain. The person experiencing this may be very uncomfortable, but the inflammatory process is essential for survival.

Major Skin Diseases

The diseases and conditions that cause these symptoms are numerous. A few of the most common conditions will be described.

SYMPTOMS OF SKIN DISORDERS

- **itching (pruritus)** (*proo-ri'tas*)—caused by the release of histamine from the skin cells during allergic reactions.
- **reddening (erythema)** (*er'i-the'mah*)—caused by an expansion of the capillaries close to the skin surface.
- **swelling (edema)** (*e-de'mah*)—caused by a build up of fluid in the spaces between cells due to inflammation.
- **scaling**—an excess of a protein, **keratin** (*ker'ah-tin*), in the epidermis. When a layer of dead cells builds up and becomes hard, the resulting condition is called **keratosis** (*ker'ah-to'sis*).
- **lesions**—patches, rashes, tumors, and sores that are flat or raised and appear in various colors, shapes, and sizes.
- **ulcerations**—open lesions that are the result of tissue damage that starts below the skin and then "erupts" onto the skin surface.
- **hives** or **welts (urticaria)** (*ur'ti-ka're-ah*)—raised, whitish patches that look like large mosquito bites and itch intensely. Hives can appear on parts of the body or cover the whole body. They are caused by a sensitivity to some substance in the environment, or by various other factors such as fatigue and emotions.

Contact Dermatitis—Contact dermatitis (*der'mah-ti'tis*) is an inflammation resulting from direct contact with a substance to which the skin is sensitive. This could be an insect sting, poison ivy, cosmetics, soaps, or chemicals. The main symptom of contact dermatitis is urticaria. The treatment is a protective astringent lotion to prevent itching, dry up oozing, and guard against infections. For serious cases, an oral antihistamine may be given to counteract the allergic reaction and itching.

Eczema (Dermatitis)—This is an inflammation with eruptions of pimplelike bumps, blisters, scales, or scabs. The lesions may be dry or "weepy" (having a watery discharge).

Eczema (*ek'ze-mah*) is really more a set of symptoms than a disease in itself. It is characterized by redness, swelling, itching, and feelings of warmth to the touch. Eczema can be a reaction to a drug or a common substance. Creams, lotions, and ointments containing corticosteroids help suppress the inflammation of eczema. Oral antihistamines may be given instead, as eczema patients often develop sensitivity to the topical preparations.

Psoriasis—A chronic (long-term) skin condition, psoriasis (*so-ri'ah-sis*) is identified by its bright red, raised lesions covered with dry, silvery scales. The cause is unknown. It appears mainly on the knees, the elbows, the lower back, the scalp, the nails, the backs of the hands, the ears, the genitals, and the skin around the anus. Topical medications that are mildly irritating (keratolytics) are applied to the lesions. This mild irritation stimulates the healing of the underlying tissues. Psoriasis is also relieved by drugs that fight inflammation, such as corticosteroids.

Acne—Acne lesions develop in adolescence when growth hormones speed up the secretions of the oil (sebaceous) glands. The open pores of the skin become plugged with oil (sebum) and dead cells. This produces blackheads that can become inflamed. Treatment consists of cleansing with soap and water or an alcohol sponge. Topical preparations for acne include keratolytic drugs that produce peeling and open up the plugged pores. Tetracycline may be ordered by the physician to prevent infection or control the excess production of sebum.

Seborrheic Dermatitis—This is an inflammation of the scalp, face, or scrotum—areas that contain many sebaceous glands. Greasy scales are produced on lesions of the skin. Dry, white scales on the scalp are signs of a familiar **noninflammatory** variation of seborrhea called **dandruff**. Frequent washing and shampooing help to control seborrheic (*seb'o-re'ik*) dermatitis or dandruff. Selenium sulfide (*Selsun Blue*), keratolytics such as salicylic acid, zinc compounds (e.g., zinc pyrithione), and oral or topical corticosteroids are also used.

Burns—Burns can be mild or severe. They are caused by overexposure to sun, fire, steam, radiation, x-rays, chemicals, or electricity. Mild burns (first-degree burns) merely redden the skin. More severe burns can blister the skin (second-degree burns). The most severe types of burns (third-degree burns) destroy underlying tissues. These burns have a charred or pearly white appearance. The treatment of serious burns is difficult and complex. A physician must order the proper treatment.

Mild astringents and cooling medications such as aluminum acetate are used for minor burns such as sunburn. Topical anti-infectives used for burns are mafenide (*Sulfamylon*), silver sulfadiazine, and gentamicin sulfate (*Garamycin*). These are applied as protective creams.

Patients who are sensitive to the sun may develop skin cancer after long periods of exposure. To prevent this, sunscreen products are available, such as oxybenzone cream (*Solbar*). Para-aminobenzoic acid (*PABA*) is used for protection by individuals desiring a tan.

Decubitus Ulcers—Decubitus (*de-ku'bi-tus*) ulcers are bedsores caused by prolonged pressure between a body part and a hard or semihard surface. This condition occurs in patients who lie in bed for long periods of time without moving. The bedsores develop where the body is in contact with the bed (e.g., at the elbows, heels, and hips). The weight of the body presses down on these spots and shuts off blood circulation. Without oxygen and nutrients, the cells die and decay. The results are deep ulcerations.

Prevention is the best cure for bedsores. Once the tissues begin to break down, it becomes very difficult for the area to heal. Lotions may be rubbed into pressure spots to stimulate blood flow. Plastic coatings, substances that digest pus and clear wounds, and anti-inflammatory agents are sometimes administered topically around the sores.

Infections—Skin infections are caused by microbes invading the skin tissues. They may enter through a break in the skin. Or they may attack when the skin's natural protective chemistry is unbalanced. The signs of infection are the same as those of inflammation: reddening, swelling, warmth to the touch, and pain. In bacterial skin infections there is usually also pus, a thick, yellowish fluid made of dead white blood cells and debris. **Impetigo** and **boils** are examples of bacterial infections.

In fungus infections the skin is invaded by **fungi** (plural of fungus), which are one-celled parasitic plants. Some common fungus infections are *tinea pedis* ("athlete's foot"), *tinea capitis* (ringworm of the scalp), and *tinea cruris* (ringworm of the groin, or "jock itch").

Fungal organisms can also develop in the mouth, around the anus, and in the vagina, causing itching and burning. Sometimes this happens after an antibiotic has been given orally to treat another disease. The antibiotic kills the helpful bacteria that usually destroy the fungus in these areas, causing **superinfection**.

Topical antiseptics and anti-infectives (antibiotics and antifungals) are designed to kill invading microbes on skin surfaces. Oral anti-infectives are also used.

Scabies and Pediculosis—Small insects called **mites** and **lice** cause these infestations. The mites of the disease **scabies** burrow under the skin. A month later the patient begins to develop symptoms such as watery blisters between the fingers. The infestation spreads very quickly. Special topical insecticides called **scabicides** are used to destroy the mites. There is no easy or fast treatment for scabies, because the mites are very hard to get rid of. Bedding and clothing must be treated to help destroy the mites.

Pediculosis (*pe-dik'u-lo'sis*) is caused by lice. These are insect parasites that lay eggs at the base of the hair of the head, in the pubic area, or in the seams of undergarments. Drugs called **pediculicides** are available to kill the lice. But all clothing, combs, and bedding must also be cleaned to help cure the condition. Patients must practice good hygiene if they want to avoid a repeat infection.

TOPICAL MEDICATIONS
Major Categories

Each skin disorder has its own best treatment and drugs. But many of the drugs have things in common with each other. They belong to certain general categories or drug groups. If you learn what these categories are, you will understand how a great many drugs operate. For instance, suppose that you know that a particular drug is in the category "anti-infective." You then know that it works something like other anti-infectives you have studied in Unit 6. Memorize the technical terms for these drug categories. This will help you especially when you are looking up drugs in drug references.

Oral drugs such as sedatives, antihistamines, and analgesics are sometimes ordered to make patients with skin diseases more comfortable. These oral drugs are described in other units. Most topical drugs for the skin fall into one or more of the following drug groups.

Keratolytics—Keratolytic drugs soften and destroy the outer layer of skin so that it is sloughed off (shed) (Figure 7-2). The name of this drug category comes from **keratin**, the protein found in the dead cells of the outer skin. Strong keratolytics are effective for removing warts and corns. Milder preparations are used to promote the shedding of scales and crusts in eczema, psoriasis, and seborrheic dermatitis. Very weak keratolytics irritate inflamed skin, which speeds up healing. Common keratolytics are salicylic acid, resorcinol, sulfur, and urea.

Protectives and Astringents—These drugs work by covering, cooling, drying, or soothing inflamed skin (Figure 7-3). **Pro-**

Figure 7-2 Keratolytics.

Figure 7-3 Protectives and astringents.

tectives do not penetrate the skin or soften it, but form a long-lasting film. This protects the skin from air, water, and clothing while the natural healing processes go on. Astringents shrink the blood vessels locally, dry up secretions from weepy lesions, and lessen the sensitivity of the skin.

Antipruritics—These drugs relieve itching caused by inflammation (Figure 7-4). Some of the drug forms themselves (e.g., emollient oils, creams, lotions) are soothing and thus help to relieve itching. Corticosteroid drugs (described later) relieve itching by suppressing the inflammation itself. Antihistaminic drugs, such as trimeprazine (*Temaril*) and hydroxyzine (*Atarax*), lessen the effects of histamine, the cause of the itching.

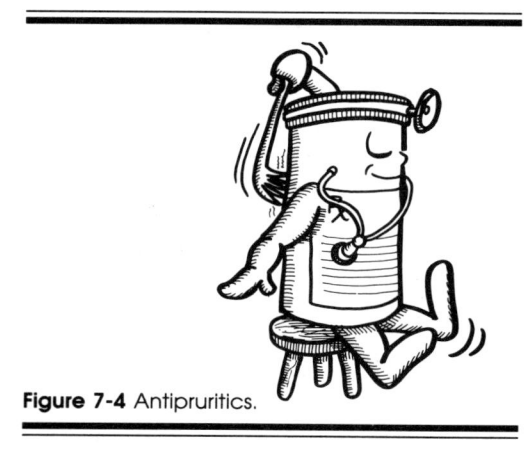

Figure 7-4 Antipruritics.

Anti-Inflammatory Drugs (Topical Corticosteroids)—The corticosteroids have three actions that relieve symptoms of skin disorders:

- **Antipruritic**—relieves itching.
- **Anti-inflammatory**—suppresses the body's natural reactions to irritation.
- **Vasoconstrictive**—tightens the blood vessels in the area of the inflammation. This reduces swelling.

Most of the top-selling prescription drugs for the skin are corticosteroids. Examples are hydrocortisone, betamethasone (*Valisone, Celestone, Diprosone*), triamcinolone (*Aristocort, Kenalog*), fluocinonide (*Lidex*), fluocinolone acetate (*Synalar*), and flurandrenolide (*Cordran*). The actions of corticosteroids are further described in Unit 13.

Anti-Infectives (Antibacterials and Antifungals)—These kill or inhibit microbes that cause skin infections. They also kill germs that enter the body through breaks in the skin surface and cause diseases. A few antibacterials are applied topically, but most are given systemically (see Unit 6). Many common topical antibacterials are combinations of neomycin sulfate, polymyxin B, and bacitracin (e.g., *Neosporin, Neo-Polycin, Cortisporin*). Two soothing anti-infective preparations for burns are mafenide acetate (*Sulfamylon*) and silver sulfadiazine (*Silvadene*).

Antifungals (fungicides) are anti-infectives that treat specific fungus infections by:

- stopping the growth of fungus organisms.
- changing the condition of the skin cells so that fungi can no longer grow there.

Different antifungals are effective for different types of fungi. Fungus infections of the mouth, anus, and vagina are treated with such drugs as amphotericin B (*Fungizone*), nystatin (*Mycostatin*), and nystatin–triamcinolone–gramicidin (*Mycolog*). Preparations for ringworm and athlete's foot include clotrimazole (*Lotrimin*), tolnaftate (*Tinactin*), zinc undecylenate (*Desenex, Cruex*), and benzoic and salicylic acids. Griseofulvin (*Fulvicin P/G*) is given orally for severe cases that do not respond to topical medication.

Antiseptics—Antiseptics, such as alcohol, benzalkonium chloride (*Zephiran*), thimerosal (*Merthiolate*), mercurochrome, and povidone-iodine (*Betadine*), destroy germs on skin surfaces. They are used topically, never given orally. Antiseptics prevent infections in cuts, scratches, and surgical wounds. (**Disinfectants** are very strong germ-killing drugs that are used only on nonliving objects such as surgical tools.)

Topical Anesthetics—For pain on the skin surfaces or mucous membranes, as in wounds, hemorrhoids, and sunburns, the physician may order a topical anesthetic. These relieve pain and itching by numbing the skin layers and mucous membranes. They are applied directly to the painful areas by means of sprays, creams, and suppositories. Examples are benzocaine (*Solarcaine*) and dibucaine (*Nupercainal*).

Parasiticides—These are drugs that kill insect parasites that infest the skin (Figure 7-5). Scabicides kill the mites that cause scabies. Pediculicides kill the lice that cause pediculosis. A parasiticide that is effective against both scabies and lice is lindane (*Kwell*).

The product information table at the end of this unit lists a few representative drugs for treating skin disorders. The chart lists the drug category to which each drug belongs, its uses, hints for application, and side effects. As a giver of medications, you will be administering these drugs frequently. Be sure to consult your drug references and package inserts when you have questions or need additional information.

Table 7-1 lists some skin preparations available without a prescription. This list is provided for your information, as you are certain to handle these drugs regularly.

Absorption of Drugs into the Skin Layers

Drugs for the skin are prepared in the form of powders, lotions, gels, creams, ointments, pastes, and plasters. To refresh your memory about these forms of topical applications, review Unit 3. The form that is chosen for a topically administered drug depends on the desired therapeutic effect.

Figure 7-5 Parasiticides.

The form affects the absorption of the drug into the deeper skin layers. Very few drugs used on the skin are supposed to be absorbed into the bloodstream. Some, like the protectives and the antiseptics, are supposed to remain only on the skin surface. Others are designed to sink into the dermal and subcutaneous layers to provide anti-inflammatory or soothing actions. The type of drug, its form, and the nursing treatment that goes with it must be chosen very carefully by the physician to achieve the proper effect.

When absorption into the underlying skin layers is desired, the following measures increase absorption:

Table 7-1 Selected OTC drugs for the skin

CONDITION	PRODUCTS	ACTION
Acne	*Cuticura Medicated, Clearasil, Stri-Dex Medicated Pads*	Keratolytic
Dandruff	*Selsun Blue, Head and Shoulders, Sebisol*	Keratolytic/Cytostatic
Diaper rash and prickly heat	*A & D Ointment, Desitin, Vaseline, Baby Magic, Johnson's Medicated Powder,* zinc oxide	Protective/Antimicrobial
Dry skin	*Keri, Corn Huskers*	Emollient
Eczema and psoriasis	*Tegrin, Psorex, Zetar*	Keratolytic/Antipruritic
Foot care	*Desenex, NP 27, Tinactin, Freezone*	Antifungal/Keratolytic
Insect bites and stings	*Dermoplast, Nupercainal*	Anesthetic/Antipruritic
Minor burns	*Medi-Quick, Solarcaine, Unguentine, Noxema*	Anesthetic/Antimicrobial
Minor wounds	*Betadine, Zephiran Chloride, Baciguent, Neosporin, Neo-Polycin, Mycitracin*	Antiseptic/Antibiotic
Poison ivy and poison oak	*Calamine, Caladryl, Ivy Dry Cream, Ziradryl*	Antipruritic/Antihistaminic

- **Apply wet dressings.**

  These bandages soften or macerate the skin. This permits the drug to pass through the epidermis, which is normally "waterproof."

- **Use a drug in an oil base.**

  The drug is absorbed easily through the pores of the sebaceous glands because the oil and the sebum blend together.

- **Rub the preparation into the skin.**

  This is done only when the skin is not covered with lesions that could be damaged by rubbing. Creams are rubbed in gently. Liniments are rubbed in vigorously. Hard rubbing also stimulates the skin, which draws blood to the area.

- **Keep medicine in contact with skin for a long time.**

  One way to achieve this is to cover the area with a dressing that prevents the drug from being rubbed off by sheets or clothing. Another way is to reapply the medication as soon as it seems to have worn off.

- **Apply an occlusive dressing if ordered by the physician.**

  An *occlusive* bandage does not permit evaporation of the drug. It holds the drug against the skin while at the same time holding in moisture so the skin becomes **macerated** and readily absorbs the drug. An occlusive dressing holds in body heat, too, which increases absorption into the skin.

- **Use a stronger concentration of the drug.**

  When a preparation has more of the drug in it, then there is more drug to be absorbed.

> **NOTE:**
> Mucous membranes are treated very differently than skin when administering medications. These membranes make up the linings of body tubes and openings such as the mouth, the eyes, the rectum, and the vagina. Unlike the skin, the mucous membranes do not have a tough outer layer of dead cells to protect the underlying tissues. Instead, their surfaces are moist and easily penetrated. Therefore, drug absorption through the mucous membranes is very rapid. Topical preparations for the skin are formulated differently than those for mucous membranes. Never apply skin medications on the mucous membranes, accidently or otherwise—this would invite the risk of overmedicating the patient.

Absorption into the skin is most complete when several of these techniques are used at the same time; for example, a strong preparation held against the skin for a long period of time under an occlusive dressing. Absorption is also deeper in young children and elderly patients because these groups have thinner layers of skin.

Drugs applied to the skin are rarely supposed to be absorbed into the bloodstream. However, if the skin is cut, scratched, or scraped, or if there are many open sores, the drug may readily enter the bloodstream. This is usually undesirable and can be dangerous. Thus, to avoid poisoning the body with too high a dose of the drug, you will sometimes need to apply a preparation only at the base of a lesion, or only *around* the infected area.

As you can see, the safe and effective absorption of each drug depends on a great many factors. For this reason, it is very important that you understand and follow instructions when applying each topical medication.

GENERAL INSTRUCTIONS FOR MEDICATING THE SKIN

Psychological Support

People who have skin conditions need your psychological support. Living with constant itching or pain is stressful. Patients may lose sleep because they just cannot get comfortable. They may become depressed about their condition, especially if it lasts for a long time. This may have an effect on their appetite and intake of fluids.

Because of the psychological problems with skin diseases, doctors sometimes prescribe sedatives and tranquilizers. Patients with conditions like psoriasis, for which there is no permanent cure, may need counseling to help them live with the disease.

You can help these patients by accepting their feelings and responding to their needs with patience and understanding.

Patient Considerations

If the condition is a painful one, the doctor may have ordered an analgesic (pain-killing) drug. It is a good idea to plan to apply topical medications *after* a dose of analgesic so that you cause as little discomfort as possible.

Before giving the medication, explain to the patient what you are going to do. Inform him or her of any unusual sensations the drug may cause. For example, some gels produce warmth or a burning sensation on the skin.

Find a position that is comfortable for the patient and that lets you easily reach the skin area you need to work on. Protective pads should be placed under the affected area to keep the bed and the patient's clothing clean. (Some skin medications cause stains.) If possible, position the affected area so that the patient does not see it while you are applying the medication. Afterward, be sure to help the patient back into a normal position.

Wound Preparation

As lesions heal, the fluids that are produced dry out and form granules or crusts on the skin surface. These may be removed before applying medications, if ordered. This can be done by gently swabbing the crusts with sterile water. Or it can be done by soaking the area with hydrogen peroxide and then lifting the crusts away with forceps (surgical tweezers). The best way to clean the skin depends on the specific disease. In some cases you will also need to remove some of the dead skin with sterile forceps or scissors. This lets the medicine come in contact with live tissues so as to promote healing.

Apply medications only on the affected area. In the case of irritating substances, such as corn and wart removers, the healthy skin surrounding the lesions needs to be protected. A film of petroleum jelly provides good protection against absorption and irritation.

Some drugs must be diluted (mixed with water or some other liquid) before being applied. Follow instructions carefully to prepare the drug. Check with the pharmacy if you do not understand the directions. A drug that is improperly diluted could cause irritation or poisoning or be ineffective.

Applying the Medication

Apply the drug as directed. In general, creams and liniments are rubbed in by hand. Lotions are patted on the skin with pieces of cotton. Ointments are applied with a wooden tongue blade or cotton swab (Figure 7-6). When infection or an open wound is present, you should use a sterile plastic glove. Apply the medication with a firm touch to avoid the sensation of itching.

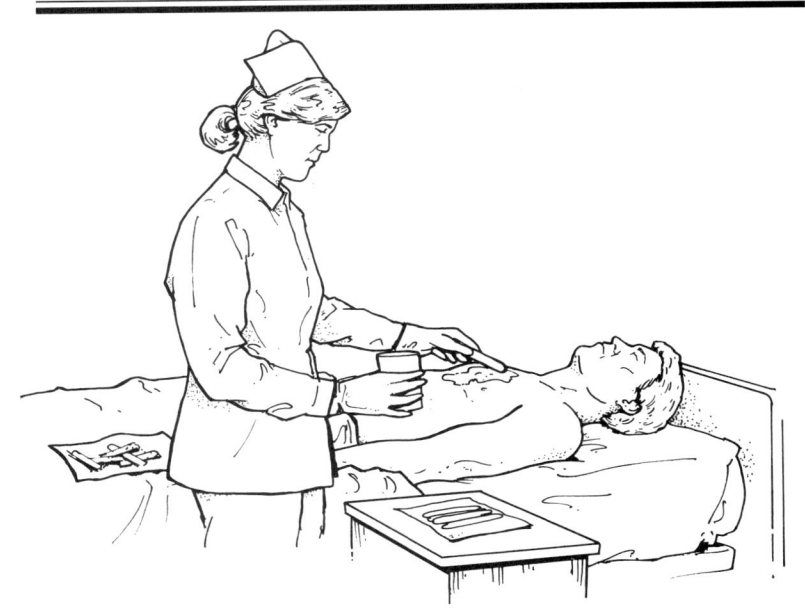

Figure 7-6 Applying medication with a wooden tongue blade.

When opening the container, place the cap upside down on the medicine tray or cart. Use a sterile tongue blade or cotton swab to dip out a quantity of medication from its container. Do *not* dip in and out with the same applicator you are using on the patient! Then apply the medication according to instructions (the physician's or those in the package insert).

When medicating large areas, work on one section at a time and drape the remaining parts of the body with sheets. Work systematically, using a pattern to help you cover the entire area. For example, you might use a circular motion or a back and forth motion.

A few skin drugs are administered by means of a medicated bath (e.g., a coal tar for a psoriasis patient), a special soap or shampoo (e.g., acne soaps, pediculicides), or an injection directly into a lesion. For specific instructions on the nursing care that goes with these drugs, refer to a manual of nursing procedures.

The instruction, "Apply as needed," is given only for drugs that carry no danger of overdose. It means to reapply the medication whenever the symptoms flare up, or when the thin film of drug has worn off or has been absorbed into the skin. A registered nurse or physician is frequently responsible for deciding when to reapply the medication. Others may do so if they have the permission of the physician or nurse.

Bandages and Dressings

Bandages and other coverings should be used only when ordered by the physician. This is because they hold in body heat and increase absorption. Some lesions must be covered to protect them from clothing and scratching. Others must be covered to keep the medication in constant contact with the affected skin. However, a bandage can be irritating rather than helpful. Many lesions heal better when left exposed to air.

Infected lesions that are actively producing pus are usually bandaged to soak up the fluids. The bandages must be changed frequently.

Care must be taken when removing bandages from a wound so as to avoid pulling away the scab. A dressing that is sticking to a lesion may be softened by moistening it with sterile water. To avoid removing and reapplying tape each time a dressing is changed, you may use butterfly tape strips.

Follow-Up

- **Charting Observations**

  Each time you prepare to apply a topical medication, make a note of the appearance of the skin. Has there been a change for better or for worse since you last saw it? If there is *no* change, then perhaps the medication is not working. Are there any signs of irritation? Be sure to chart your observations, since these will help in evaluating the patient's progress and pinpointing problems.

- **Side Effects**

  Be on the lookout for any signs of irritation that do not seem to come from the disease itself. Many persons are sensitive to certain drugs. They may develop rashes, dryness, redness, tiny purplish-red spots, and ruptures of surface blood vessels (**petechiae**, *pe-te'ke-e*; **ecchymosis**, *ek'i-mo'sis*), sensitivity to light (**photodermatitis**), and/or itching in the area where you applied the medication. These signs should be charted and reported to the nurse in charge. The strength of the drug may be changed or another drug or treatment may be ordered.

- **Patient Education**

  Instruct your patients in how to apply skin medications properly. If there is a long-lasting condition, they will be responsible for their own skin care. The USP DI (United States Pharmacopeia Dispensing Information) is a good place to look for information that will be useful to the patient.

Drugs for the Skin 167

EXERCISES

A. Match skin structures to the jobs they do.

a. secretes earwax
b. grows hair
c. secretes oil
d. secretes sweat
e. feels pressure or pain
f. secretes milk
g. insulates and stores energy
h. acts as a waterproof covering

_a_ 1. ceruminous gland
_h_ 2. epidermis
_b_ 3. follicle
_f_ 4. mammary gland
_c_ 5. sebaceous gland
_e_ 6. sense receptor
_g_ 7. subcutaneous
_d_ 8. sudoriferous gland

B. Define these medical terms:

1. pruritus _itching_
2. erythema _redden skin_
3. edema _swelling_
4. keratin _protein in skin_
5. urticaria _rash_
6. lesion _raised sore_

C. Select the skin disorder that best matches each description. Write the name of the disorder in the blank.

decubitus
eczema (dermatitis)
pediculosis
psoriasis
seborrheic dermatitis
tinea capitis

1. Mr. Yee has applied *Kwell* cream on his body to combat scabies. After a few hours his skin becomes dry and scaly. It is red, swollen, itchy, and warm to the touch. _eczema_

2. Miss Barnett has suffered from dry scales on the backs of her hands for many years. The symptoms are kept under control with *Celestone*. _psoriasis_

3. Fred Entler is annoyed to find dry, white, greasy scales on his scalp. _sebor_

4. Fran Graham is bedridden with a muscle disease. A sore is developing where her tailbone touches the sheets. _decubitus_

5. Mr. Chopra's doctor says this patient has ringworm of the scalp and orders griseofulvin to treat it. _____

6. While washing her children's hair, Mrs. Johnson discovers tiny eggs laid in their scalps at the base of the hairs. _____

D. Tell what these types of drugs do; for example:
Protectives *cover and soothe inflamed skin*

1. Antipruritics _____
2. Antiseptics _____
3. Topical corticosteroids _____
4. Antifungals _____
5. Keratolytics _____
6. Parasiticides _____

E. Which of the following are known to increase the absorption of a drug into the layers of the skin? Circle the number next to each one.

1. strong drug mixture
2. dry dressing
3. oil-base drug
4. unbroken skin
5. broken skin
6. wet dressing
7. occlusive dressing
8. very young or very old patient
9. patting drug on skin
10. rubbing drug into skin
11. giving an oral antihistamine
12. reapplying drug when worn off

F. Match drug names to drug categories

a. topical corticosteroids
b. parasiticide
c. topical anesthetics
d. oral antipruritics and antihistamines
e. topical antibacterials
f. topical antifungals
g. antiseptics
h. keratolytics
i. protectives and astringents
j. oral antifungal

____ 1. salicylic acid, resorcinol
____ 2. *Aristocort, Valisone, Cordran*
____ 3. *Tinactin, Mycostatin, Lotrimin*
____ 4. *Kwell*
____ 5. *Neosporin, Sulfamylon*
____ 6. zinc oxide, calamine
____ 7. *Temaril, Atarax*
____ 8. griseofulvin
____ 9. *Betadine*, alcohol, *Merthiolate*
____ 10. benzocaine, *Nupercainal*

G. True or false. Circle T if the statement is true, F if it is false.

- T F 1. For painful skin conditions, it is good to apply topical medications before giving a dose of pain reliever.
- T F 2. Patients with skin diseases need psychological support.
- T F 3. Try to position the patient so that he or she has a good view of the area you are medicating.
- T F 4. Do not explain medication procedures to patients unless they ask you to.
- T F 5. Remove crusts from lesions by rubbing them firmly with a cotton swab.
- T F 6. When using strong keratolytics on warts and corns, the surrounding healthy skin may be protected with petroleum jelly.
- T F 7. Creams and liniments should be rubbed in by hand.
- T F 8. If there is any ointment left on a wooden blade after application, you may scrape it off into the medication container.
- T F 9. When removing the cap of a medication jar or bottle, the cap should be placed upside down on the tray or cart.
- T F 10. Do not use a dressing unless ordered by the physician.
- T F 11. A sticky bandage should be softened with sterile water to avoid removing the scab.

H. Short answers.

1. Is it all right to use a skin medication on mucous membranes? Explain why or why not.

   _____

   _____

   _____

2. Before applying a topical medication, you are expected to examine the skin very carefully. What signs would you chart on the nurses' notes?

   _____

   _____

   _____

ANSWERS TO EXERCISES

A. Matching.
   1. a
   2. h
   3. b
   4. f
   5. c
   6. e
   7. g
   8. d

B. Definitions.
   1. itching
   2. redness
   3. swelling
   4. protein in cells of the epidermis
   5. hives or welts
   6. cut, scrape, or sore (any change in the structure of the skin due to disease or injury)

C. Skin disorders.
   1. eczema (dermatitis)
   2. psoriasis
   3. seborrheic dermatitis
   4. decubitus
   5. tinea capitis
   6. pediculosis

D. Drug functions.
   1. relieve itching.
   2. kill germs on skin surfaces.
   3. suppress inflammation, relieve itching, and reduce swelling.
   4. destroy or prevent the growth of fungus organisms.
   5. soften hardened skin and promote peeling and shedding.
   6. kill parasites such as mites and lice.

E. Absorption through skin.
   These numbers should be circled: 1, 3, 5, 6, 7, 8, 10, and 12.

F. Matching.
   1. h
   2. a
   3. f
   4. b
   5. e
   6. i
   7. d
   8. j
   9. g
   10. c

G. True or false.
   1. F
   2. T
   3. F
   4. F
   5. F
   6. T
   7. T
   8. F
   9. T
   10. T
   11. T

H. Short answers.
   1. Skin medications should not be used on mucous membranes because absorption is much quicker through mucous membranes than through skin.
   2. Chart any changes in the condition of the skin since you last applied medication. Note dryness, rashes, redness, ecchymosis, petechiae, or any other sign of irritation that is not a symptom of the disease itself. Also, make a note if there seems to be *no* change for the better after several applications of the drug.

Drugs for the Skin 171

PRACTICE PROCEDURE

APPLY TOPICAL MEDICATION TO THE SKIN

Equipment:
- Sterile gloves
- Sterile scissors, forceps
- Sterile dressings and coverings
- Sterile applicators: tongue blades, gauze, cotton balls, or swabs
- Medication (lotion, ointment, cream, liniment, or aerosol spray)
- Bag or newspapers for disposal
- Medication record, Kardex, medicine card, or the form used by your agency

____ 1. Assemble equipment, medications, and patient records.

____ 2. Read Kardex, medication record, or medicine card. Check this against the medication label. Be sure you have the RIGHT DRUG and the RIGHT DOSE for the RIGHT PATIENT at the RIGHT TIME by the RIGHT ROUTE.

____ 3. Read the instructions on application in the package insert.

____ 4. Identify the patient and explain the procedure. Check wrist ID or follow agency policy for identifying patients.

____ 5. Administer systemic analgesic (if ordered) to relieve pain caused by applying topical medication. Wait for 10–20 minutes.

____ 6. Position patient and affected area comfortably. Protect clothing and bed linen with pads, if necessary.

____ 7. Wash your hands.

____ 8. Open gloves, dressings, applicators, and medication needed. The lid of the medication container should be placed upside down on the table or tray to avoid contaminating the medication. Then put on sterile gloves to prevent wound contamination.

____ 9. Remove old, soiled dressings. Discard in newspaper or disposal bag. Be careful not to pull the scab off a newly healed area. If the dressing sticks to the wound, apply sterile water. Let it soak for 5–10 minutes.

____ 10. Cleanse and remove dead tissue or crusts from lesions if ordered. Use cleansing liquid ordered by physician. Remove dead tissue with sterile scissors or forceps. Remove crusts with cotton swabs or forceps.

____ 11. Reread the label to make sure that you have the right drug.

____ 12. Take medication from its container using a sterile applicator (tongue blade or swab). Try to dip out the entire amount you will need for one application.

____ 13. Apply the medication using the correct procedure for the medication form.
- *Creams*: rub in gently
- *Lotions*: pat or dab on skin
- *Liniments*: rub in vigorously
- *Ointments*: apply with wooden blade or cotton swab
- *Aerosol sprays*: hold can upright and spray area from a distance of 3–6 inches; spray a second and third time
- *Foam medication*: hold can inverted next to skin and spray

____ 14. Apply a thin or thick film, as ordered by the physician or as stated on package directions. Be systematic in covering the affected area. Do not further damage the lesion, as this may aggravate the condition.

_____ 15. Cover area with wet or dry dressings, if ordered. (See doctor's orders, package insert, or procedure manual for instructions.) Secure dressings with adhesive tape or butterfly tape strips.

_____ 16. Instruct the patient in further care of the skin. See package directions or doctor's orders. Remove your gloves.

_____ 17. Make the patient comfortable before leaving. Fluff pillows, return patient to normal position, secure call button, and so forth.

_____ 18. Remove, clean, and/or discard equipment and supplies. Put away medications, rereading the labels as you do so. Dispose of used supplies in appropriate area. Wash your hands.

_____ 19. Record the application of medication. Note:
- Condition of the skin or skin lesions (on nurses' notes).
- Reactions of the patient (on nurses' notes).
- Date, time, medication, and dosage (on medication record).

Demonstrate this procedure for the instructor or the nurse in charge.

REPRESENTATIVE DRUGS FOR THE SKIN

CATEGORY, NAME[a], AND ROUTE	USES AND DISEASES	ACTIONS	USUAL DOSE[b] AND SPECIAL INSTRUCTIONS	SIDE EFFECTS AND ADVERSE REACTIONS
Keratolytics				
Salicylic acid Topical	Seborrheic dermatitis, psoriasis, warts, corns, calluses	Swells and softens excess keratin for easy removal or shedding	Dosage depends on form and strength of preparation. Soaking skin before use assists drug action. Apply dressing as ordered. Do not put drug in contact with eyes, mucous membranes, or normal skin	Irritation, burning
Carbol-fuchsin (Castellani's Paint) Topical	Antifungal agent for athlete's foot and ringworm infections	Kills fungus on contact	Apply to affected area once or twice a day	Irritation of affected area
Astringents				
Calamine and diphenhydramine (Caladryl) Lotion	Itching from poison ivy or oak, insect bites, or other skin irritations; mild sunburn	Relief of itching; soothes mild sunburns drying action	Apply topically 3 or 4 times daily. Clean and dry area before applying	Burning or itching; consult doctor
Antipruritics				
Trimeprazine tartrate (Temaril) Oral	Urticaria, atopic and contact dermatitis, pityriasis rosea, and drug rash	Relief of itching, is an antihistamine and antipruritic, has a drying effect and sedative effect	2.5 mg 4 times daily; 1 spansule q 12 hour	*Short-term therapy:* Drowsiness, hypotension, bradycardia, faintness, and very rarely, anorexia, nausea, and vomiting, dry mouth *Long-term therapy:* skin pigmentation, extrapyramidal reactions (dyskinesia)
Anti-inflammatory drugs (topical corticosteroids)				
Betamethasone valerate (Valisone) Topical	Contact dermatitis, dermatoses, psoriasis	Suppresses inflammation, relieves itching and swelling	Dosage depends on form and strength of preparation. Apply ointment, lotion, or cream sparingly and gently massage into affected area. Do not apply in or near eyes. Also available as aerosol—do not inhale spray. Check skin regularly for signs of irritation. Use occlusive dressing as ordered	Irritation, burning, itching, blistering, peeling
Triamcinolone (Aristocort) Topical	Contact dermititis, oral lesions	Suppresses inflammation, relieves itching and swelling	Dose varies depending on condition	Irritation, burning, itching, blistering, peeling

REPRESENTATIVE DRUGS FOR THE SKIN

CATEGORY, NAME[a], AND ROUTE	USES AND DISEASES	ACTIONS	USUAL DOSE[b] AND SPECIAL INSTRUCTIONS	SIDE EFFECTS AND ADVERSE REACTIONS
Anti-inflammatory drugs (topical corticosteroids) —*continued*				
Hydrocortisone				
OTC: *Hytone* 0.5% ointment *Delacort* 0.5% lotion *Bactine* 0.5% cream *Aeroseb HC* 0.5% spray *Cortef Rectal Itch* 0.5% ointment	OTC: Temporary relief of many minor skin, genital, and anal itching and rashes; anorectal products used for severe inflammation and swelling have other ingredients such as belladonna and benzocaine	Anti-inflammatory, antipruritic, and vasoconstrictive actions	Use sparingly and rub in lightly. Cover *only as directed* with occlusive dressing. Protect patient's face when spraying with aerosols and avoid inhalation as well when using this form of medication	Burning and itching sensations, irritation, dryness and skin maceration, especially if used with occlusive dressings. Systemic effects may occur if used excessively or for a prolonged time
Prescription: *Dermacort* 1.0% lotion *Synacort* 2.5% cream *Sensacort* 0.5% spray *Nutracort* 1.0% gel *Cort-Dome* 15 mg suppositories *Proctofoam* 1.0% aerosol foam	Prescription: Relief of inflammatory and pruritic manifestations of corticosteroid-responsive dermatosis			
Anti-Infectives, Antibacterials, Antifungals				
Mafenide acetate (*Sulfamylon*) Topical	Burns	Antibacterial, soothes and protects	Cleanse area of debris before application. Apply with sterile tongue-blade or gloved hand to a thickness of 1/16 inch. Keep area covered with medication at all times. Apply dressing as ordered	Pain, burning, stinging, allergic reactions, fungal superinfection
Clotrimazole (*Lotrimin*) Topical	Fungus infections, ringworm, athlete's foot	Antifungal, relieves itching	Gently massage into affected area twice a day, morning and night	Redness, urticaria, irritation
Griseofulvin (*Fulvicin*) Oral	Severe fungus of infections of hair, skin, and nails	Antifungal	500–1000 mg/day (microsize) PO in single or divided doses. Caution patient to avoid sunlight. Give after meal with high fat content to increase absorption	Headache, photosensitivity
Nystatin (*Mycostatin*) Topical	Cutaneous or muco-taneous mycotic infections caused by *Candida* (Monilia) *albicans*	Fungistatic and fungicidal against a wide variety of yeast fungi	Apply cream and ointment liberally to affected area twice daily or as indicated until healing is complete; powder should be applied to the lesion 2 or 3 times daily until lesion is healed	Irritation possible but well tolerated even by infants

REPRESENTATIVE DRUGS FOR THE SKIN

CATEGORY, NAME[a], AND ROUTE	USES AND DISEASES	ACTIONS	USUAL DOSE[b] AND SPECIAL INSTRUCTIONS	SIDE EFFECTS AND ADVERSE REACTIONS
Anti-Infectives, Antibacterials, Antifungals —continued				
1% silver sulfadiazine (*Silvadene*) Topical Cream	Adjunct for prevention and treatment of wound sepsis in second- and third-degree burns	Antibacterial and antimicrobial	Cleanse and debride; cover with drug at all times. Reapply 1 or 2 times daily using sterile technique to a thickness of 1/16 inch	Itching, burning, or rash; adverse reactions attributed to sulfonamides
Antiseptics				
Povidone-iodine (*Betadine*) Topical	Surface infections, burns, minor wounds, vaginitis	Kills germs	Apply as ordered; avoid contact with eyes	Irritation, redness, swelling
Anesthetics				
Benzocaine (*Solarcaine*) Topical	Pruritus, minor burns; the oral, nasal, and gingival mucous membranes	Inhibits conduction of nerve impulses from sensory nerves	Give smallest effective dose according to age	Sensitization

[a] Brand names given in parentheses are examples only. Check current drug references for a complete listing of available trade name products.

[b] Average adult doses are given. However, dosages are determined by a physician and vary with the purpose of the therapy and the particular patient. The doses presented in this text are for general information only.

Unit 8

Drugs for the Cardiovascular System

In this unit you will learn about the organs and functions of the cardiovascular system and what goes wrong with them during common cardiovascuular disorders. You will study the types of drugs used to treat each disorder and learn to classify common generic and brand name drugs according to their drug categories. And you will practice step-by-step procedures for administering oral and sublingual medications.

In this unit, you will learn to:

- Name the parts of the cardiovascular system and state their functions.
- Recognize the names of instruments used to measure blood pressure and to record the heartbeat.
- State the average blood pressure and pulse rate.
- List the main components of blood.
- State the functions of the lymphatic system.
- Give the proper medical terms for common symptoms of cardiovascular disorders.
- Recognize descriptions of the major disorders for which cardiovascular drugs are given.
- Describe the actions and give examples of the following drug groups: vasoconstrictors, vasodilators, antihypertensives, heart stimulants (digitalis products), heart depressants (antiarrhythmics), anticoagulants, coagulants, and hematinics.
- State the difference between a maintenance dose and an initial dose.
- Follow proper procedure for administering oral and sublingual medications to patients with cardiovascular disorders.
- State the special nursing procedures for administering vasoconstrictors, vasodilators, antihypertensives, digitalis, antiarrhythmics, anticoagulants, coagulants, and hematinics.

CARDIOVASCULAR SYSTEM

The cardiovascular system consists of the heart, the blood vessels, and the blood. It is designed to transport vital substances to and from various parts of the body. Among these substances are nutrients, waste products, oxygen, carbon dioxide, minerals, hormones, drugs, and body heat. The blood plays an important role in the body's defense against disease (see Unit 6).

Think of the circulatory system as a network of pipes with a pump to keep liquid flowing through them. The liquid is the blood. The pipes or tubes that carry the blood are the blood vessels. The heart is the pump that keeps the blood circulating through the system.

Blood Vessels

There are two types of vessels: **arteries** and **veins**. Arteries carry blood away from the heart; veins carry blood back toward the heart. As arteries get farther away from the heart, they branch into increasingly smaller arteries. The same is true of veins. At their smallest points, arteries and veins are connected by very thin-walled vessels called **capillaries** (Figure 8-1).

The capillaries are where the blood's most important functions are carried out. Nutrients from digestion, oxygen, and other substances (such as drugs) from the arteries pass through the capillary walls into the tissue fluid that surrounds the body cells. The substances then enter the cells, where they are used in energy production and other vital cell processes. At the same time, waste products and carbon dioxide are released from the cells. They pass through the capillary walls into the veins, which return the blood to the heart. These processes are shown in Figure 8-1.

The Heart

The heart is a hollow muscle about the size of a fist. It is designed to pump blood into the arteries under pressure. There has to be enough pressure to keep the blood moving all the way out to the tips of the toes and fingers and back again. Muscle tissue in the arteries and special valves in the veins help the blood along too, but the heart does the most important work.

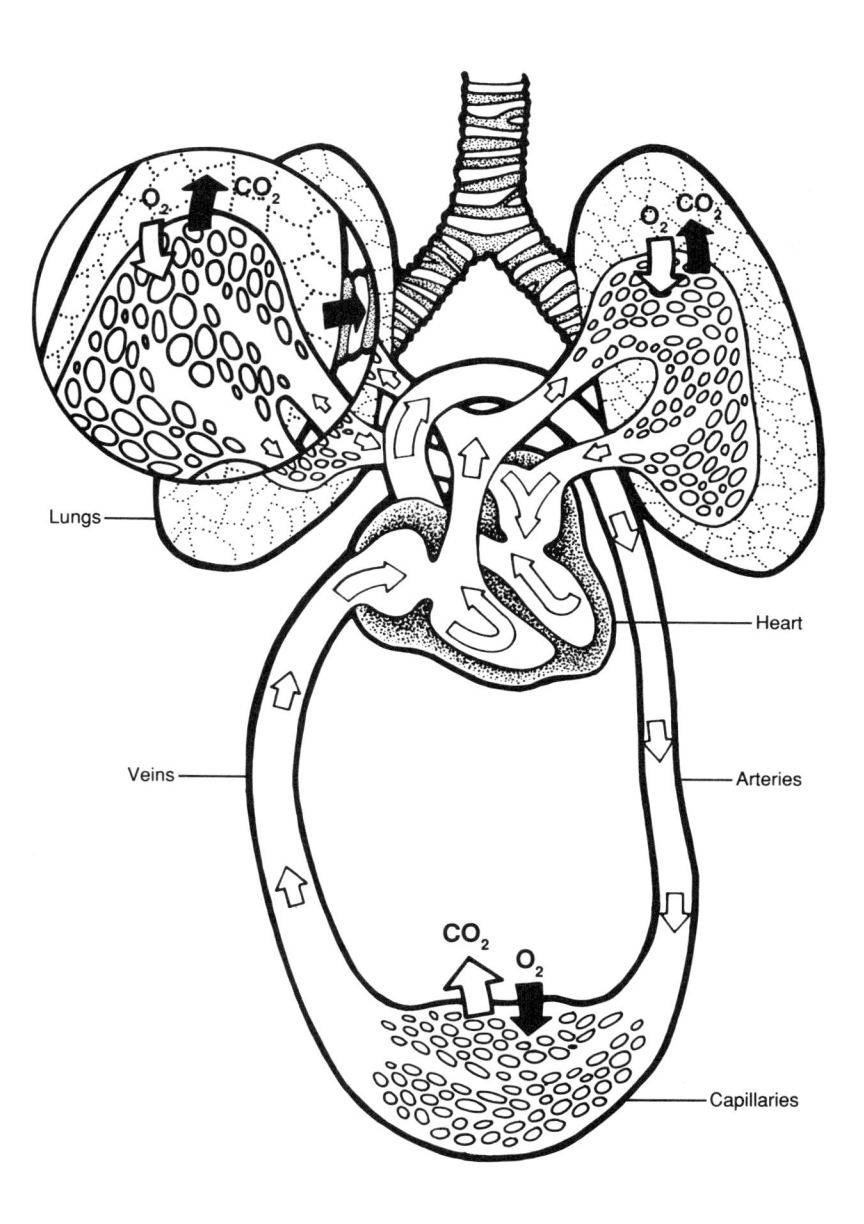

Figure 8-1 Blood circulation and gas exchange in the cardiovascular system.

Cardiac drugs are designed to affect specific parts of the heart:

- **Myocardium**—the heart muscle has four sections or **chambers**, two to receive blood and two to pump it back out. Heart stimulants such as digitalis make the heart stronger.

VOCABULARY

adjunctive: something added as a helper

anemia: insufficient red blood cells or hemoglobin

angina pectoris: chest pain thought to be due to a lack of oxygen in the heart tissue

anticoagulant: drug that keeps blood from clotting

antihypertensive: drug that combats high blood pressure

antilipemics: drug that promotes the breakdown and excretion of cholesterol, thus lowering the level of cholesterol in the bloodstream

apical pulse: heart rate taken over heart in chest

arrhythmia: an irregularity of the heartbeat; also called **dysrhythmia**

arteriosclerosis: hardening of the arteries

artery: blood vessel that carries blood away from the heart

atherosclerosis: buildup of fat in the blood vessels

blood pressure (BP): force of the blood against vessel walls

bradycardia: very slow heartbeat (below 60 beats per minute)

capillaries: tiny, thin-walled vessels that link arteries to veins and allow gases and nutrients to pass into and out of the bloodstream

carbon dioxide: a gaseous waste product of body metabolism

cardiac: pertaining to the heart

cardiac arrest: stopping of the heartbeat

cardiac glycoside: a heart stimulant that increases the force of the heartbeat

chambers: hollow parts of the heart

coagulant: drug that aids blood clotting; also called **hemostatic**

contraction: tensing or tightening action of a muscle

coronary: pertaining to the heart vessels

corpuscles: solid elements of the blood

cutdown: incision into a vein for intravenous infusion (a sterile procedure)

cyanosis: bluish color of the skin due to lack of oxygen

diastolic pressure: blood pressure between contractions of the heart

digitalization: initial part of digitalis therapy, during which larger doses are given to bring up the blood level

diuretic: drug that helps the kidneys eliminate excess fluids

dyspnea: shortness of breath

edema: swelling due to buildup of fluids in tissues

elasticity: ability of blood vessel walls to stretch

electrocardiogram ("EKG"): a chart of the heartbeat recorded on an electrocardiograph

embolism: sudden blocking of an artery by a clot, bubble, or foreign material (**embolus**)

hematinic: drug that stimulates production of red blood cells and increases the hemoglobin content in the blood; also called **antianemic**

hemoglobin: iron-containing substance that carries oxygen and is located in red blood cells

hemoptysis: coughing up blood

hemorrhage: internal or external bleeding

hematoma: a collection of blood in the tissues

Hg: chemical symbol for mercury

hypertension: high blood pressure

hypotension: low blood pressure

injection point: the top end of a needle, covered by rubber tubing, that is inserted into a patient's arm and used for injection of heparin

leukemia: condition in which there is excess production of white blood cells

lymph: fluid drained off from the spaces between cells by lymph vessels

myocardial infarction: "heart attack" or death of a part of the heart muscle due to lack of oxygen

myocardium: the heart muscle

orthostatic hypotension: a condition of low blood pressure that occurs when a person stands up from a sitting or lying position

palpitations: irregular heartbeats that can be felt by the patient, such as pounding or skipping beats

phlebitis: inflammation of a vein

plasma: the liquid part of blood

platelets: solid elements in the blood that are responsible for blood clotting

pulse: spurts of blood resulting from heartbeats; can be felt by touching arteries

sphygmomanometer: device for measuring blood pressure

spleen: organ of the lymphatic system

systolic pressure: blood pressure during a heart contraction

tachycardia: rapid heartbeat (over 100 beats per minute)

thiazides: group of diuretics

thrombophlebitis: inflammation of a vein blocked by a thrombus

thrombosis: condition in which a blood clot (**thrombus**) is closing off all or part of a blood vessel

transdermal: through the skin, i.e., nitroglycerin pads taped to the skin area which will absorb nitro continuously for relief of angina

varicose veins: condition in which blood backs up in the veins and they become enlarged and knotted

vasoconstrictor: drug that tightens the vessel walls so that they become narrower

vasodilator: drug that relaxes the walls of blood vessels so that they become wider

vein: vessel that carries blood toward the heart

- **Coronary arteries**—This special network of arteries and veins wrap around the heart and provide it with needed oxygen and food. (The heart does not absorb these materials from the blood that is pumped through it.)

  If these arteries are narrowed, pain usually occurs. If one or more is blocked, part of the heart muscle dies. Vasodilators such as nitroglycerin produce a general opening or expansion of the arteries and veins. This effect reduces the work and oxygen use of the heart.

  The heartbeat is controlled by "pacemaker" cells that stimulate the heart muscle when it is supposed to contract. Each heartbeat is caused by a wave of electricity that passes from the pacemaker cells to the heart muscle. The signals can be picked up by a machine called an **electrocardiograph ("EKG")**. The EKG records these signals so that they can be used in diagnosing heart problems (Figure 8-2).

- **Electrical conduction system**—The heart alternately contracts and then relaxes about 72 times a minute (the normal range at rest is 60–80 beats per minute). The heartbeat you hear is the sound of the heart valves opening and closing during these contractions.

  Heart depressants such as propranolol keep the system from becoming too excitable or irregular.

  After the blood has transported oxygen through the arteries, capillaries, and veins and has picked up waste products, it must go through the lungs. There it picks up new oxygen and gets rid of carbon dioxide wastes (see Figure 8-1). In this way, the cardiovascular system is linked to the respiratory system, which is described in Unit 9. The cardiovascular system is closely linked to all the other body systems, for blood is important in all body functions.

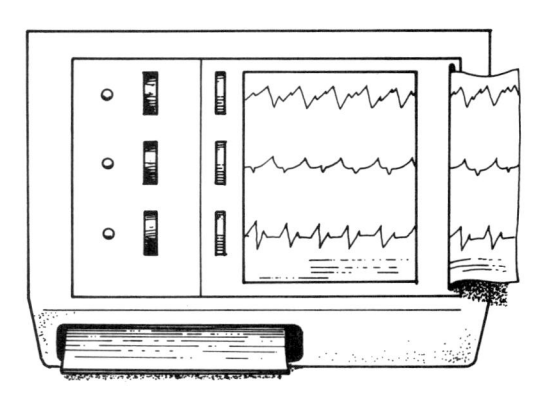

Figure 8-2 The readout from an EKG shows the electrical signals from the heart.

Blood Pressure and Pulse

One way to tell if the heart and vessels are working properly is by measuring a patient's **blood pressure**. This is the force of the blood against the walls of the blood vessels.

A person's blood pressure results from a combination of two factors:

- **the force of the heartbeat**
- **the condition of the vessels**

The walls of normal blood vessels give and take with each spurt of blood that is pumped out of the heart. This ability to give and take is called **elasticity**. If the vessels lose their elasticity because of disease, the heart has to pump against stiff, narrow vessel walls, which makes its job harder. The heart also has to pump harder if the vessels are partially blocked by deposits of fat. Either situation results in a higher blood pressure.

To measure blood pressure, you will use an inflatable rubber cuff and an instrument called a **sphygmomanometer** (*sfig'mo-mah-nom'e-ter*) (Figure 8-3). When the cuff is inflated, it tightens around the patient's arm, and you will listen for two types of sounds:

- **systolic**—the amount of pressure when the heart has just contracted
- **diastolic**—the amount of pressure when the heart is at rest between contractions.

Blood pressure is recorded as two numbers: systolic pressure over diastolic pressure. The numbers stand for the amount of mercury (Hg) that is displaced on the sphygmomanometer, measured in millimeters. The average blood pressure measures about 120/80 mm Hg ("120 over 80"). However, variations from 140/90 to 90/60 are common and are usually considered normal. An unusually high blood pressure (**hypertension**) or low blood pressure (**hypotension**) is a danger signal.

The **pulse** rate is another way to tell how well the cardiovascular system is working. The pulse is measured by placing the fingers gently over an artery, usually one in the wrist (Figure 8-4). The blood "spurts" that are felt in the artery are counted for 1 minute. Each spurt of blood

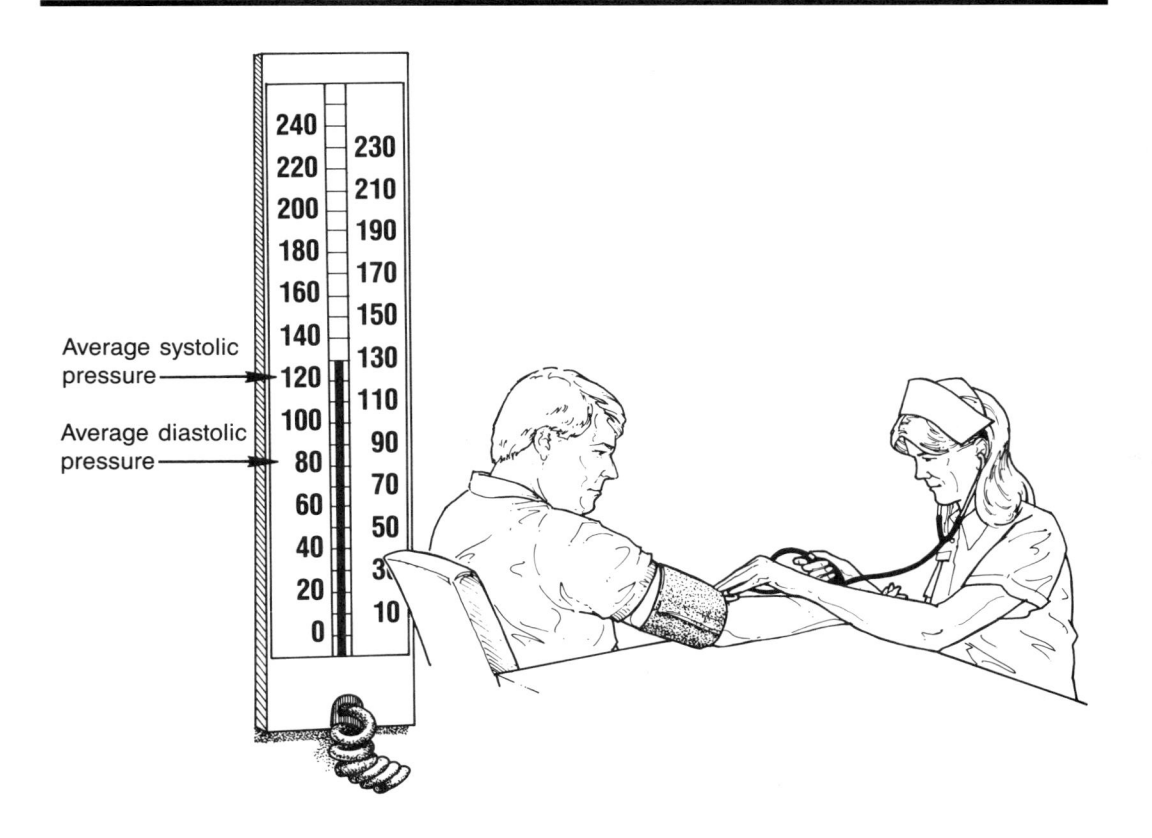

Figure 8-3 Measuring blood pressure with a sphygmomanometer and cuff.

indicates one beat of the heart. The normal pulse is strong and full and about 60–80 beats per minute.

Figure 8-4 Taking the pulse to check on the heart's pumping action and the condition of the blood vessels.

If the heart or blood vessels are diseased, or if there is too little blood in the system, the pulse may be weak and irregular. A weak pulse taken at the wrist but a strong one taken elsewhere (foot or neck) may mean the vessels in the area are narrowed or blocked.

Often, it will be required that you take your patient's pulse and/or blood pressure before administering a cardiac drug. Such requirements will be included on the physician's order. Review your nursing procedures to be sure you know how to do these tasks. The results must be charted each time. Unless there is a special form for this, the pulse and blood pressure (abbreviated "*BP*") are usually charted on the nurses' notes.

Blood

The purpose of the cardiovascular system is to put blood in close contact with every tissue in the body. This is a critical function, since the blood has such important jobs to do.

Blood has two component parts: fluid called **plasma** and solid elements called **corpuscles**, which float in the plasma. Plasma is about 90% water, with nutrients and other substances (proteins, carbohydrates, fats, and minerals) dissolved in it.

Each type of corpuscle has a special function:

- **red blood cells (erythrocytes)**—carry oxygen. They contain a substance called **hemoglobin**, made partly of iron, which combines with oxygen in the lungs and then releases the oxygen at the capillaries.
- **white blood cells (leukocytes)**—consume bacteria and other foreign matter that enter the body. In cases of disease or wounds, the body produces extra leukocytes to fight off infection.
- **platelets**—are critical in clotting. When a blood vessel is cut or punctured, the platelets release a substance that causes fibers to form over the wound. These fibers eventually harden into a scab.

Arterial blood
- bright red
- full of oxygen
- going from heart to capillaries

Venous blood
- dark red
- contains carbon dioxide/wastes
- going from capillaries to heart to lungs

Lymphatic System

In addition to the cardiovascular system, a network of **lymph vessels** extends throughout the body. The lymphatic system drains away extra fluid that enters the spaces between cells from the capillaries. The extra fluid is called **lymph**. The system carries away waste products that the blood cannot carry, such as dead cells and debris. These wastes are removed at the **lymph nodes**, which are like small filtration stations. They are located mainly in the groin, the armpits, and the neck. After being filtered, the lymph is poured back into the veins near where they enter the heart.

Unlike the blood, the lymph is not pumped but merely collected from the various body parts through open-ended lymph vessels. The movements of the body help to push the lymph through its vessels.

Besides draining the lymph fluid, the lymphatic system is responsible for producing some of the white blood cells and the disease-fighting antibodies.

These jobs are performed by the **spleen**, a soft, purplish organ in the upper left side of the abdomen. The spleen is made of lymphoid tissue similar to that in the lymph nodes. While lymph nodes filter the lymph, the spleen filters the blood. The spleen removes and destroys used-up red blood cells and other foreign matter.

Effects of Aging

Heart disease is a major problem that increases with age. Most deaths due to cardiovascular disease are in the aged population. There are changes in the heart associated with aging. The heart may become smaller, and it has a deeper color. The endocardium becomes thicker and sclerotic, and the aorta and the arteries are less elastic. The valves thicken and are more rigid. These changes lead to problems in filling and emptying the heart which result in decreased oxygen intake and output. Even with these changes, the heart is able to meet most demands. Under stress, however, declining heart function is apparent. Now let us look at heart disorders that affect the elderly and sometimes the younger patient.

CARDIOVASCULAR DISORDERS

Anything that interferes with the functioning of the heart and the vessels deprives the body of the vital nutrients that circulate in the blood. Any change in the rate, rhythm, and force of the heartbeat or in the force and the quantity of blood running through the vessels thus endangers the entire body.

Symptoms

The presence of cardiovascular disorders is revealed by the following symptoms (Figure 8-5):

- **Breathlessness (dyspnea,** *disp'ne-ah*)— difficult breathing, which can occur while at rest or exercising. Knowing when the dyspnea began (e.g., when the patient was lying down, sitting, or doing some strenuous physical activity) gives clues to the type of heart problem.
- **Chest pain**—a symptom of some types of heart diseases. It can be caused by a lack of blood in the heart muscle, by inflammation of the heart, or by simple nervous tension.
- **Edema** (*ĕ-de'mah*)—the swelling of body tissues due to a leaking of fluid into the spaces between cells. It occurs in cardiovascular disorders when the blood is not being pumped quickly or strongly enough. Some of the blood fluid "backs up" in the tissues, and swelling results. Even the abdominal cavity or the lungs may become filled with fluid.
- **Irregular heartbeats or palpitations**— may indicate a heart problem. Patients may complain that their heart is pounding or jumping or missing a beat. Disturbances of the heartbeat are tachycardia (very rapid heartbeat—pulse above 100 per minute) and bradycardia (very slow heartbeat—pulse below 60 per minute).
- **Coughing up blood (hemoptysis,** *hemop'ti-sis*)—may indicate serious cardiovascular disease where blood is leaking into the lungs. **Hemorrhage** indicates internal bleeding caused by ruptured organs or faulty blood clotting processes.
- **Fainting and fatigue**—When the heart or vessels are not functioning at their best, the tissues do not receive all the oxygen they need. This can cause pain in the oxygen-starved tissues. When the oxygen content in the blood is low, the skin may turn bluish, a condition called **cyanosis**.
- **Cardiac arrest**—a sudden and unexpected stopping of the heart and circulation. It can be brought on by myocardial infarction, electric shock, severe allergic reactions, drug overdose, or surgery.

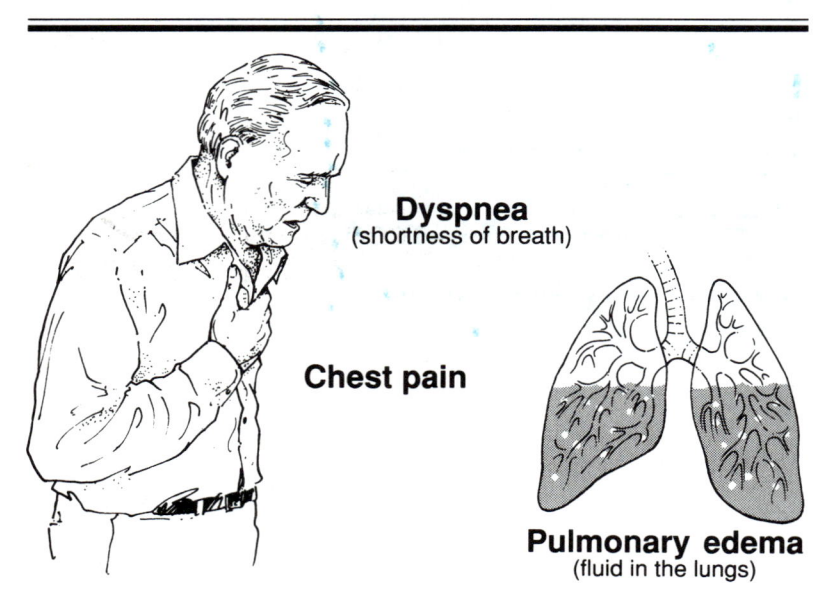

Figure 8-5 Some symptoms of cardiovascular disorders.

Dyspnea (shortness of breath)

Chest pain

Pulmonary edema (fluid in the lungs)

Unless immediate steps are taken to restore the heartbeat, cardiac arrest is fatal.

The specific diseases that bring on these common symptoms are many and varied. The major heart, vessel, and blood disorders are described very briefly now.

Congestive Heart Failure

Congestive heart failure results from the inability of the heart to pump strongly enough. This can be caused by aging, high blood pressure, dead or injured heart muscle, damaged heart valves, kidney malfunction, or blood vessel disease. The heart pumps so weakly that blood backs up in the veins and body organs. Important organs like the liver and kidneys can be badly affected. Blood pressure is high and fluids leak into the spaces between cells, causing edema. The legs and ankles may become swollen or "waterlogged" (edematous). If the swelling extends to the lungs, dyspnea and hemoptysis may result.

Congestive heart failure is treated by giving digitalis to slow and strengthen the heartbeat. Diuretic drugs are also given to help the kidneys eliminate excess fluids.

Cardiac Arrhythmias (Dysrhythmias)

Arrhythmias or dysrhythmias are conditions in which the entire heart or parts of the heart muscle do not beat properly. Instead, they may vibrate (fibrillate), skip contractions, or beat very rapidly (tachycardia). This endangers the body because it affects the heart's ability to pump blood. Arrhythmias occur because the electrical signals that control the heart rate and rhythm are disturbed. Antiarrhythmic drugs are given to slow and steady the heart contractions.

Coronary Artery Disease

When blood vessel diseases develop in the arteries that supply the heart (coronary arteries), the functioning of the heart itself is endangered. **Angina pectoris** is a clutching pain in the chest caused by oxygen starvation due to narrowed coronary arteries. It is usually relieved by giving nitroglycerin. Chest pain that lasts for more than 20–30 minutes may be a sign of "heart attack" or **myocardial infarction**. Myocardial infarction means that a part of the heart muscle dies because its supplying artery is completely blocked. This severely weakens the heart.

Blood Vessel Diseases

Problems related to the blood vessels fall into four main areas and are illustrated in Figure 8-6.

Thrombosis—This condition involves the formation of a blood clot (**thrombus**) in a blood vessel. This can be due to injury, inflammation, or narrowed vessels. The thrombus blocks the flow of blood to the part of the body served by that particular vessel. The body part becomes pale and cold and sometimes bluish (cyanotic). A vein that is partially blocked by a blood clot may become inflamed, resulting in the condition called **thrombophlebitis** [phlebitis *(flĕ-bi'tis)* means an inflammation of a vein]. If a thrombus breaks off into the blood vessel, it can circulate

Thrombus

Embolus

Atherosclerosis

Hypertension

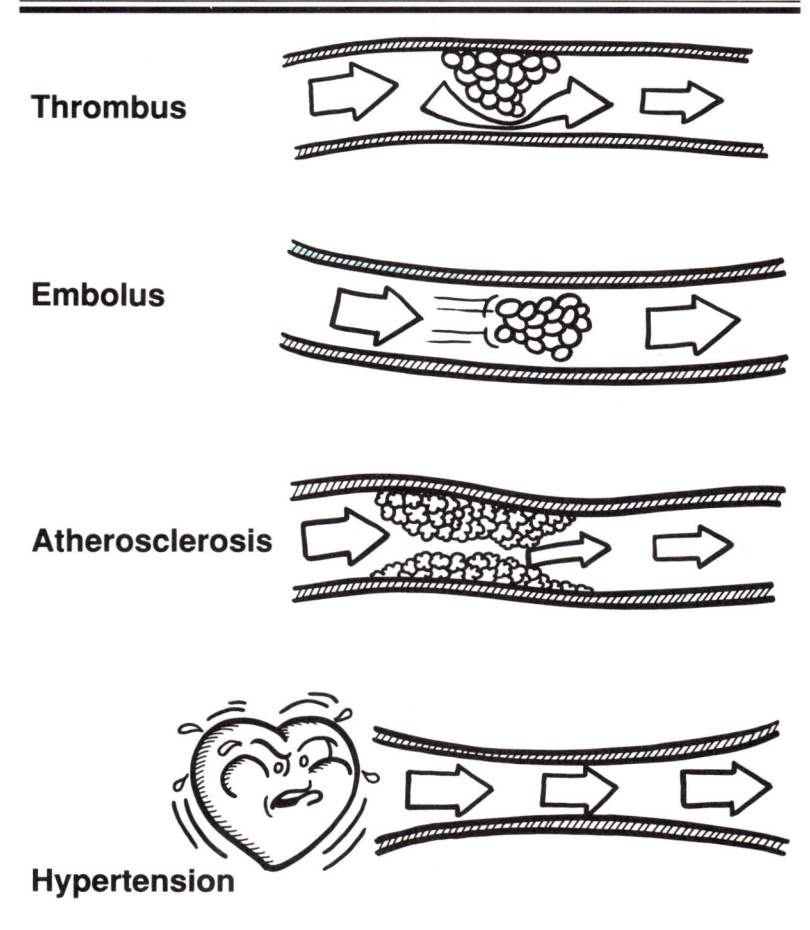

Figure 8-6 Blood vessel disorders.

through the blood. It is then called an **embolus**. An embolus can also be an air bubble or any kind of particle that can block a vessel. It may travel to another part of the body and cut off the blood circulation to a vital area, such as the brain. This condition is known as **embolism**.

Arteriosclerosis—"Hardening of the arteries" is due to changes in the blood vessel walls that cause them to lose their elasticity. The vessel walls can then become clogged with fatty deposits (**atherosclerosis**), which, in turn, affects circulation. Arteriosclerosis is a serious problem because it can lead to heart attack if it affects the coronary arteries. Medications for this condition are given to expand the blood vessels (vasodilators) or to eliminate excess fat in the bloodstream (**antilipemics**).

Hypertension—High blood pressure is a chronic (long-term) disease whose causes are not well understood. In hypertension, the small vessels stay tightened instead of expanding and contracting as spurts of blood are pumped into them by the heart. Over time, hypertension can badly weaken the heart and affect the vital organs. It also weakens the vessels themselves, so that one of them may burst. If an artery in the brain bursts, it can cause a "stroke," which damages brain cells. Hypertension can result from several diseases, but the most common type of hypertension has no known cause. It can be controlled by antihypertensive drugs and diet and stress management.

Varicose Veins—This blood vessel disorder affects about 10% of the population. The veins near the skin surface become stretched because of either a loss of elasticity or an inherited vessel weakness. There are valves in the veins that usually keep the blood from flowing backward. But when the veins are overstretched, the valves do not close properly and blood backs up, causing veins to become enlarged. Infections and open sores may result if the condition is not treated. The effects of varicose veins can be reduced by wearing support hosiery and elevating the legs several times a day to give the veins a rest.

Shock

Shock is the collapse of the circulatory system. It occurs because blood is lost from hemorrhage or because too many of the small arteries and capillaries dilate all at once. There is not enough blood in the system to maintain circulation when this happens. The blood "pools" in the capillary areas. Blood pressure drops very low and tissues are inadequately nourished.

Shock can be brought on by severe blood loss, surgery, sudden infections, allergic reactions, or heart failure. **Some signs of shock are low blood pressure; high pulse rate; pale, clammy skin; and mental confusion.** Shock requires emergency treatment because without an adequate blood supply, the vital organs can be damaged. Patients can die rapidly from shock. Drugs that tighten the blood vessels (vasoconstrictors) are used to treat shock. Blood transfusions are also given to restore the proper volume of blood in the system.

Diseases of the Blood and Lymph

Blood and lymph diseases involve abnormal blood clotting processes, excessive bleeding, or disturbances in the production of blood cells.

Anemia—With anemia, there are fewer red blood cells than the body needs and thus less hemoglobin. The body needs a good supply of hemoglobin because this is the substance that holds oxygen so that it can be carried to all parts of the body. The entire body is affected by fatigue and other symptoms when too little oxygen is delivered to body tissues. Anemia can be caused by lack of iron or cyanocobalamin (vitamin B_{12}) in the diet, by severe bleeding, by diseases in which red blood cells are destroyed (hemolytic diseases), or by failure to produce red blood cells. Its treatment varies with the cause, but iron supplements, proper diet, control of the underlying diseases, vitamin B_{12}, folic acid, and transfusions are useful.

Leukemia—This cancer affects the blood-forming tissues in the bone marrow, spleen, and lymph system. There is excessive production of white blood cells, which results in anemia and a tendency toward infections and bleeding. The drugs used to treat leukemia interfere with the abnormal production of white blood cells (see Unit 6).

Hodgkin's Disease—This disease is a cancer that affects the lymphatic system. Tumors develop in the lymph nodes and spread to other parts of the body.

Hodgkin's is treated with a combination of chemotherapy (drugs) and radiotherapy (radiation treatment).

DRUGS FOR CARDIOVASCULAR AND BLOOD DISORDERS

Vasoconstrictors

Vasoconstrictors raise the blood pressure by causing the blood vessels to contract. They are used in the treatment of shock, heart block (failure of electrical impulses to stimulate the heartbeat), and adverse reactions to medications. Vasoconstrictors are very powerful drugs. Patients must be watched carefully to make sure they are not getting too strong a reaction—in other words, hypertension. Their blood pressure must be checked regularly and often. Norepinephrine (*Levophed*) is a vasoconstrictor used in hospital emergency treatment. Metaraminol (*Aramine*) is a less powerful vasoconstrictor. Both are given parenterally with great care.

An IV line must be established as soon as possible or even a **cutdown** may be necessary when profound shock is present and infusion cannot be started by venipuncture.

Other vasoconstrictors are mephentermine (*Wyamine*), methoxamine (*Vasoxyl*), and phenylephrine (*Neo-Synephrine*).

Vasodilators

These drugs relax or dilate the walls of the arteries, so that less force is needed to push the blood through them (Figure 8-7). They are used especially in the control of angina pectoris. They dilate the arteries so that the heart receives more blood and more oxygen. Sublingual nitroglycerin (*Nitrostat*) is the most common vasodilator. Taken at the beginning of an angina attack, it takes effect within about 2 minutes. Timed-release tablets and capsules and topical preparations (nitroglycerin transdermal systems) are available for longer-lasting effects. With transdermal systems, read directions carefully as each system is different. Isosorbide dinitrate (*Isordil*) is another vasodilator used to treat angina.

Nitroglycerin may be left at the patient's bedside to be taken whenever the patient feels an angina attack coming on. If this is done, you must keep track of how many tablets are left each time you check on the patient—and chart the number taken. If there is no improvement, the nurse in charge should be notified.

Diuretics

These drugs help the body eliminate excess fluids through urinary excretion (see Unit 12). In so doing, they reduce the amount of blood that the heart has to pump. Because some also help to dilate the blood vessels, certain diuretics are often given along with antihypertensive drugs in the treatment of high blood pressure. Diuretics commonly used in the treatment of congestive heart failure are:
- the thiazides chlorothiazide (*Diuril*) and hydrochlorothiazide (*HydroDiuril, Esidrix*)
- the potassium-sparing diuretics spironolactone (*Aldactone*), triamterene (*Dyrenium*), and amiloride
- "loop" diuretics furosemide (*Lasix*), metolazone (*Zaroxolyn*), ethacrynic acid (*Edecrin*), and bumetanide (*Bumex*)

Antihypertensives

These drugs are used on a daily basis to control high blood pressure or hypertension (Figure 8-8). Some work by relaxing the vessel walls themselves. Others interfere with the nerves that cause the vessel walls to become tense. Hydralazine (*Apresoline*), captopril (*Capoten*), nifedipine (*Procardia*), propranolol (*Inderal*), methyldopa (*Aldomet*), and metoprolol (*Lopressor*) are some of the major antihypertensive drugs.

Antihypertensive therapy is often done by a "stepwise" approach. This means

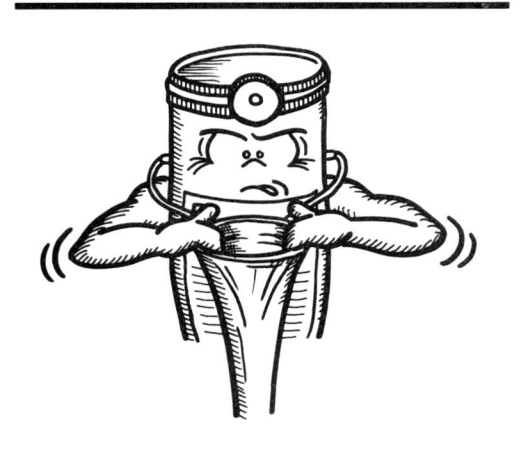

Figure 8-7 Vasodilators.

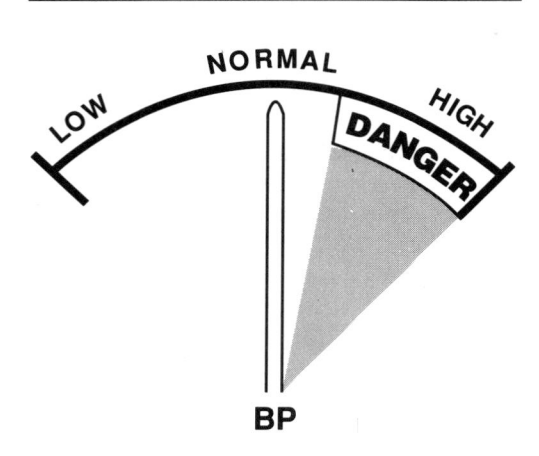

Figure 8-8 Antihypertensives.

starting with a less potent drug and then moving up to a more potent drug or adding additional drugs, depending on the patient's response.

Because they act on the nervous system, which is what controls muscle tension, most antihypertensives have some unwanted side effects such as diarrhea, dizziness, fainting, mental depression, headache, and water retention (edema). Each antihypertensive has its own set of side effects, which you should check in a drug reference. However, a sign to watch for with most of them is extreme low blood pressure when the patient stands up quickly, or **orthostatic hypotension**. This may indicate too high a dose for the individual. Caution your patient to rise slowly from a sitting or lying position to avoid dizziness or fainting. Hot showers and baths can also bring on orthostatic hypotension. Some patients may need help in walking if they get dizzy spells from the antihypertensive.

Antihypertensives are used for long-term control of high blood pressure. Their use must be supervised closely by a physician so that the dosage can be adjusted properly and because of the many side effects. Patients may need encouragement to keep on taking their blood pressure medications over a long haul. Because there are no dramatic symptoms of high blood pressure, patients easily forget how important the medication is for avoiding serious damage to vital organs. Therefore, patient education is a needed aspect of antihypertensive therapy.

Antilipemics

Although the link between high cholesterol levels and heart disease is not completely understood, lowering cholesterol levels is usually considered. Diet and exercise are frequently all that is necessary. However, several drugs can help lower cholesterol levels. Several antilipemics (or anticholesteremics) are dextrothyroxine sodium (*Choloxin*), clofibrate (*Atromid-S*), cholestyramine (*Questran*), colestipol (*Colestid*), niacin (*Nicobid*), and lovastatin (*Mevacor*).

Heart Stimulants (Digitalis Products)

These drugs directly stimulate the heart muscle (**myocardium**). They also stimulate the pacemaker cells that control the rate (not the force) of the heartbeat (Figure 8-9). Also known as **cardiac glycosides**, they are products of the digitalis "leaf." Digitalis is given to relieve some arrhythmias. It increases the force of the heart's pumping action and regulates its beat. This relieves edema, brings more oxygen to the tissues, and restores kidney function. The major digitalis products are digitoxin (*Crystodigin*) and digoxin (*Lanoxin*).

Digitalis therapy is begun with large doses to bring the blood level up to a certain point. This is called the period of **digitalization**. Thereafter, smaller doses are given—just enough to maintain the proper

Figure 8-9 Heart stimulants (digitalis).

level of digitalis in the blood. Doses are adjusted carefully according to the needs of the individual patient.

Before giving digitalis, the patient's pulse must be checked, as digitalis doses are cumulative. If it is below about 60 (see doctor's order), or if it has noticeably changed in any way, the drug must not be given. Instead the nurse in charge should be notified. The nurse may want an **apical pulse** taken since it is more accurate.

Patients on digitalis are weighed every day. A careful record is also kept of their fluid intake and output (see Unit 12). These measures tell the medical team whether digitalis is taking effect and whether the kidneys are working properly. If the body loses too much potassium in the urine (a condition called **hypokalemia**), the action of digitalis is much stronger, and possibly dangerous. For this reason, potassium supplements may be given, such as *Slow-K*, *Micro K*, or *K-Lyte*.

Digitalis therapy is usually long term, so patient education is important. Low-salt diets are commonly ordered along with the therapy.

Heart Depressants (Antiarrhythmics)

Heart depressants also act on the heart's pacemaker cells. They are used mainly to treat arrhythmias. They "calm down" the heart muscle so that it does not flutter or beat too rapidly (Figure 8-10). Examples are quinidine (*Quinora*), propranolol (*Inderal*), and procainamide (*Pronestyl*). Propranolol is also used in the control of both hypertension and angina pectoris.

If not used properly, antiarrhythmics can have serious side effects. The dosages must be adjusted individually to each patient. When an order for antiarrhythmics says "give three times a day," check with the physician or pharmacist for the correct timing. These drugs should be given every 8 hours to ensure a constant blood level. Before administering antiarrhythmics, the pulse and blood pressure usually must be taken. Response to the drug may be checked on the EKG.

Anticoagulants

Anticoagulants prevent blood from clotting (Figure 8-11). This helps prevent or reduce the formation of a thrombus or embolus in narrow or inflamed arteries and

Figure 8-10 Heart depressants (antiarrhythmics).

Figure 8-11 Anticoagulants.

veins. Warfarin (*Coumadin*) and dicumarol are examples of anticoagulants. Another anticoagulant, heparin, is given only parenterally.

Heparin is frequently administered into the patient's vein (usually in the forearm) using an intermittent infusion set. A loop of the infusion tubing and the injection port are anchored to the arm with tape that states the date and time the set was inserted. After patency has been checked, ordered heparin is injected onto the port which has been wiped with an antiseptic such as alcohol. (Patency is checked by drawing back on the syringe and needle that has been injected into the port. If blood does not backflow into the tubing, then the heparin is not injected. But, if there is a backflow, heparin, usually undiluted, is administered slowly as ordered.)

If the physician wants continuous IV infusion of heparin to control rate and volume, the prescribed amount of heparin is added to 1000 ml of isotonic sodium chloride and an infusion pump is used.

For subcutaneous administration, use a 20–22-gauge needle to withdraw heparin from the container. Then replace this needle with a 1/2 inch 25–26-gauge needle for administration usually into the fatty layer of the abdomen. Pinch up skin fold and insert needle at 90 degree angle; do not aspirate syringe but inject drug slowly. If you do not use a 90 degree angle, there is pain resulting from the injection, and a greater possibility of a hematoma formation. After injection, apply pressure for 1 minute. Be sure to rotate administration sites.

Anticoagulants are very strong drugs. The dosages must be adjusted very carefully because they can lead to hemorrhage inside the body. Patients taking such drugs must regularly be given blood clotting tests (prothrombin time) to determine the proper dosage. They must also be observed for signs of blood in the urine and feces (red or dark brown urine and tarry stools) and bleeding from the skin or mucous membranes, which indicate overdosage. Other drugs (including OTC drugs such as aspirin, oral contraceptives, and antacids) affect the action of anticoagulants. Careful records should be kept of the various drugs a patient is taking.

Coagulants (Hemostatics)

These help the formation of blood clots. This is useful when much blood is being lost due to injury or disease, or when a patient has an overdose of an anticoagulant. Vitamin K, a necessary ingredient in blood clotting, helps stop internal bleeding. It is sometimes given before surgery or childbirth. One form of Vitamin K is phytonadione (*Mephyton*). Thrombin, an enzyme that stimulates clotting, can be given topically as a powder or solution to stop external bleeding (Figure 8-12). It may be applied with a gelatin sponge (*Gelfoam*).

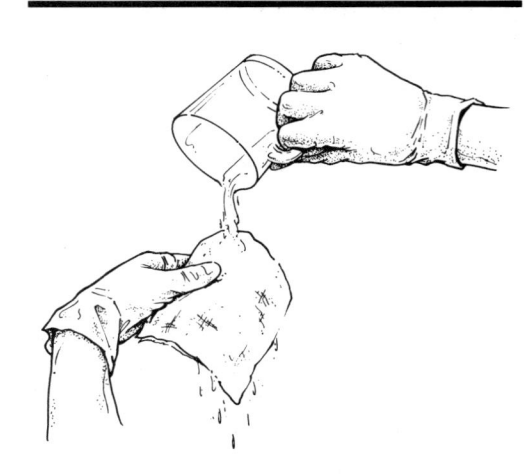

Figure 8-12 Coagulant solution for topical application.

Hematinics (Antianemics)

Hematinics are used where there is a lowered red blood cell count or a lack of hemoglobin, in conditions such as anemia. Hematinics provide the necessary ingredients for the production of red blood cells, such as iron and cyanocobalamin (vitamin B_{12}). Meanwhile, the physician must look for the underlying cause of the iron deficiency, such as poor diet and effects of other drugs. Cyanocobalamin is used to treat pernicious anemia. Popular iron preparations are ferrous sulfate (*Feosol, Fer-In-Sol*), given orally, and iron dextran (*Imferon*), given parenterally.

Iron taken orally can irritate the mucous membranes. Tablets must be given with plenty of liquid. Patients who have trouble swallowing may need a liquid preparation. Iron supplements can stain skin and clothing, so they must be handled carefully. Liquid preparations should be well diluted with the liquid called for in the package insert. They should be taken with a straw and the mouth rinsed afterward to avoid staining the teeth. Patients should be warned to expect their stools to be dark and tarry-looking. This is a harmless side effect of taking iron. However, they should report any trouble with diarrhea or constipation.

The major cardiovascular drugs with which you need to be familiar are shown at the end of this unit.

GIVING CARDIOVASCULAR MEDICATIONS

Many of the patients to whom you will be giving medications suffer from some form of cardiovascular disorder. The best way to prepare yourself is to learn as much as you can about how the medications work and about how the cardiovascular system works. Read package inserts and drug references to become familiar with all the common drugs for this system.

Note that more than one dose is sometimes given in the dosage column of the product information table. The dosage depends on whether a person is just beginning to take the drugs or has been taking them for several days. When a disorder has just been discovered, the doctor may order a fairly large dose to start the drug therapy. This quickly builds up the level of medication in the patient's bloodstream. It is called the **initial** or **loading** dose. After one or more initial doses, the dosage is lowered to a **maintenance** dose. This is the amount that maintains the level of drug in the blood without overdosing the patient. The maintenance dose will continue to be given for as long as the doctor orders. Anticoagulants and digitalis products are both given in this way, but a loading dose of an anticoagulant is used less frequently now.

Occasionally an initial dose is lower than the maintenance dose. This is true, for example, of some antihypertensives. They must be given in small doses at first to let the body adjust gradually to them. Once the body is adjusted, the normal larger dose can be given.

Side effects and adverse reactions are of special concern when giving cardiovascular drugs. The medications are strong and can be dangerous. The dosages must be absolutely correct. Most side effects of these drugs come from overdosage. Side effects from cardiovascular drugs are generally as follows:

- **too high blood pressure**—headache, nervousness, "pounding" pulse, and high blood pressure reading.
- **too low blood pressure**—weakness, flushing of skin, fainting (especially when the person stands up after lying down), and low blood pressure reading.
- **interference with heart action**—weak, thready, and/or irregular pulse; weakness; and shortness of breath.

The logical side effects and the symptoms they produce are further summarized in Table 8-1. Be alert for signs of pain, fatigue, and breathing difficulties while you are giving the medications. Chart any unusual signs in the nurses' notes and report them to your supervisor. Remember also to take and chart the pulse and/or blood pressure as ordered.

Because the cardiovascular system is so important for life, patients who have trouble with this system may be very anxious. They need all the emotional support you can give. Explain procedures carefully and answer their questions as best you can. Do not rush them. Try to gain their confidence so that they will cooperate in any special nursing procedures you need to do.

Many patients with cardiovascular diseases must change their lifestyles if they wish to survive. The doctor has probably ordered them to give up life-long habits like smoking or eating rich and salty foods. They may have to start on exercise programs to lose weight and strengthen the heart. These new ways of doing things are sometimes hard to accept. Patients may be depressed or fearful. You can help by teaching them, by reassuring them, and by focusing on the benefits of these changes.

Table 8-1 Summary of drugs for the cardiovascular system

DRUG GROUP	INTENDED ACTION	LOGICAL SIDE EFFECTS
Vasoconstrictors	Raise blood pressure	Blood pressure may go too high
Vasodilators	Dilate arteries and veins	May over-dilate arteries, causing low blood pressure
Antihypertensives	Lower high blood pressure	Blood pressure may go too low
Diuretics	Eliminate excess body fluid	Loss of too many valuable body elements along with body water
Heart stimulants	Cause heart to beat slower and stronger	Too slow a heartbeat, or an irregular heartbeat
Heart depressants	Make heart less "excitable"	May make heart more excitable and irregular
Anticoagulants	Prevent the clotting of blood	May cause bleeding because blood cannot clot
Coagulants	Make blood clot faster	Almost none because used topically, or limited dose given.
Hematinics (oral)	Improve quality of red blood cells	Stools resemble a condition of intestinal hemorrhage

EXERCISES

A. Fill in the blanks.

1. The main parts of the cardiovascular system are the _____ and the _____.

2. The tiny vessels that connect arteries to veins are called _____.

3. Veins carry blood _____ (to or from) the heart.

4. Arteries carry blood _____ (to or from) the heart.

5. Blood picks up oxygen in the _____ before being pumped out into the body.

6. The average blood pressure is about _____.

7. The average pulse rate is between _____ and _____ per minute.

8. The system that collects excess fluids from the spaces between cells is called the _____ system.

9. The heart muscle itself is nourished by _____ arteries and veins.

10. Blood is composed of _____ and _____.

B. Matching.

____ 1. "give and take" of vessel walls
____ 2. force of the blood against vessel walls
____ 3. surge of blood with each heartbeat
____ 4. blood pressure instrument
____ 5. instrument for recording signals from pacemaker cells

a. sphygmomanometer
b. elasticity
c. pulse
d. blood pressure
e. electrocardiograph (EKG)

C. More matching.

____ 1. white blood cells
____ 2. red blood cells
____ 3. platelets
____ 4. spleen
____ 5. plasma
____ 6. lymph

a. important in clotting process
b. carry oxygen attached to hemoglobin
c. excess fluid carried away from spaces between cells
d. surround and destroy germs and foreign matter
e. liquid portion of blood
f. filters blood and produces antibodies

D. Define these medical terms for cardiovascular symptoms:

1. dyspnea _____

2. edema _____

3. tachycardia _____

4. bradycardia _____

5. hemoptysis _____

6. hemorrhage _____

7. cyanosis _____

8. cardiac arrest _____

9. hypertension _____

10. hypotension _____

11. adjunctive _____

12. cutdown _____

13. transdermal _____

14. thiazides _____

E. Select the cardiovascular disorder that best matches each description. Write the name of the disorder in the blank.

congestive heart failure   phlebitis
arrhythmias   leukemia
angina pectoris   arteriosclerosis
myocardial infarction   atherosclerosis
thrombosis   shock
embolism   anemia

1. Collapse of the circulatory system, signaled by severe hypotension, high pulse rate, pale, clammy skin, and mental confusion.

   _____

2. Fat is deposited along vessel walls so that circulation is reduced.

   _____

3. Vessel walls lose their elasticity so that the heart has to work harder to pump blood through them. This disease is known as hardening of the arteries.

   _____

4. A blood vessel becomes inflamed.

   _____

5. Injury, inflammation, or narrowing of a vessel causes a blood clot to form on the vessel wall. This cuts off circulation to a part of the body.

   _____

6. A blood clot or air bubble travels through the bloodstream and cuts off circulation to a vital organ.

   _____

7. Chest pain that is usually relieved by giving nitroglycerin.

8. Death of a part of the heart muscle due to lack of blood circulation to that area.

9. Heart vibrations or missed heartbeats due to faulty signals from the pacemaker cells.

10. The heart beats weakly and ineffectively so that blood backs up into the veins and vital organs, causing edema.

11. The blood lacks red blood cells or hemoglobin. Not enough oxygen is carried to body tissues.

12. The blood-forming organs produce too many white blood cells, resulting in serious anemia and an abnormal tendency for infections and bleeding.

F. Tell what these types of drugs do; for example, Diuretics *help the body eliminate excess fluids through the urine.*

1. Vasoconstrictors _____

2. Vasodilators _____

3. Antihypertensives _____

4. Heart stimulants (digitalis) _____

5. Heart depressants (antiarrhythmics) _____

6. Anticoagulants _____

7. Coagulants _____

8. Hematinics _____

G. Match drug names to drug categories.

____ 1. *Coumadin*, dicumarol, heparin
____ 2. vitamin K, thrombin, *Mephyton*
____ 3. iron, cyanocobalamin, *Feosol*
____ 4. *Levophed*, norepinephrine, *Aramine*
____ 5. *Crystodigin, Lanoxin*, digoxin, digitoxin
____ 6. quinidine, propranolol, *Inderal*
____ 7. metoprolol, hydralazine, methyldopa
____ 8. *Isordil, Nitrostat*, nitroglycerin
____ 9. triamterene, *Aldactone*

a. antihypertensives
b. antiarrhythmics
c. heart stimulants, cardiac glycosides
d. vasoconstrictors
e. anticoagulants
f. coagulants
g. hematinics
h. vasodilators
i. potassium-sparing diuretics

H.
1. Patients taking heparin or warfarin (*Coumadin*) must be watched for signs of _____ in the urine, feces, and mucous membranes.

2. _____ may be left at a patient's bedside for angina pain.

3. Before giving vasoconstrictors, you must take the patient's _____.

4. Because digitalis slows as well as strengthens the heartbeat, an adult patient's pulse rate must be at least _____ in order to give the drug.

5. Patients on antihypertensives may feel _____ when they get up from bed because of orthostatic hypotension.

6. Some hematinics can _____ clothing and skin, and so they must be handled with care.

7. A topical _____ can be used to stop external bleeding.

8. The first dose or two of a medication is sometimes a greater or lesser amount than the patient will be taking later. This first dose is called the _____ dose.

9. The usual amount of medication that a patient takes after the first doses is called the _____ dose.

10. Daily _____ tests are needed to determine the proper dose of an anticoagulant.

I. Short answers.

1. The intake of oxygen and the output of carbon dioxide represent a link between the cardiovascular and respiratory systems. Explain.

2. Why must the fluid intake and output of a digitalis patient be carefully recorded every day?

3. Put yourself in the shoes of a cardiovascular patient. What are some of the psychological problems you would experience? Tell what the person who gives your medications could do to make you feel better.

ANSWERS TO EXERCISES

A. Fill in the blanks
1. heart, vessels, blood
2. capillaries
3. to
4. from
5. lungs
6. 120/80
7. 60 and 80
8. lymphatic
9. coronary
10. plasma, corpuscles (solid elements)

B. Matching
1. b
2. d
3. c
4. a
5. e

C. More matching
1. d
2. b
3. a
4. f
5. e
6. c

D. Definitions
1. difficulty breathing, shortness of breath
2. swelling of tissues
3. very rapid heartbeat
4. very slow heartbeat
5. coughing or spitting up blood
6. bleeding
7. bluish color of the skin due to lack of oxygen
8. stopping of the heart
9. high blood pressure
10. low blood pressure
11. something added as a helper
12. incision into a vein for intravenous infusion
13. across or through the skin
14. group of diuretics

E. Cardiovascular disorders
1. shock
2. atherosclerosis
3. arteriosclerosis
4. phlebitis
5. thrombosis
6. embolism
7. angina pectoris
8. myocardial infarction
9. arrhythmias
10. congestive heart failure
11. anemia
12. leukemia

F. Drug categories
1. tighten the blood vessel walls and raise blood pressure.
2. relax the blood vessel walls, dilate the arteries and veins.
3. relax the vessel walls and lower blood pressure.
4. make the heart beat more strongly and regularly.
5. calm the heart muscle to make it beat regularly.
6. slow or prevent the blood clotting process.
7. promote blood clotting.
8. replace iron needed for red blood cell production.

G. Matching drug names to categories
1. e
2. f
3. g
4. d
5. c
6. b
7. a
8. h
9. i

H. Fill in the blanks
1. bleeding, hemorrhage
2. Nitroglycerin
3. blood pressure
4. 60 per minute
5. faint, dizzy
6. stain
7. coagulant
8. initial
9. maintenance
10. blood clotting (prothrombin)

I. 1. Before the blood is pumped out from the heart and into the arteries, it takes a detour through the lungs to pick up new oxygen and get rid of carbon dioxide wastes.
2. Fluid level indicates whether the kidneys are working properly and whether the digitalis is taking effect.
3. See text section entitled "Giving Cardiovascular Medications." Also write your own ideas.

PRACTICE PROCEDURE

ADMINISTER ORAL AND SUBLINGUAL MEDICATIONS

Equipment:

- Medication orders for three patients

    Patient No. 1: digoxin 0.25 mg PO q.d.

    Patient No. 2: ferrous sulfate 220 mg PO QID with juice

    Patient No. 3: nitroglycerin 0.4 mg subl PRN

- Medications

    Lanoxin (0.125- or 0.25-mg tablets)

    Feosol elixir (220 mg ferrous sulfate per teaspoonful)

    Nitrostat (0.4-mg sublingual tablets)

- Apple juice, water, cups
- Medication tray or cart with appropriate charts and records

___ 1. Set up medications one at a time. Read drug labels as you reach for bottles, then again as you pour, and again as you put drugs away. Check and double check the medication orders for the "five rights."

___ 2. Wash your hands.

___ 3. Proceed to Patient No. 1. Identify patient. Explain what you are going to do. Assist patient into position for oral administration.

___ 4. Administer digoxin (*Lanoxin*).
   a. Check pulse first to make sure that it is over 60 (or the rate specified on the patient chart).
   b. Administer one 0.25-mg tablet or two 0.125-mg tablets.
   c. Give water to drink. Assist patient if necessary.
   d. Chart administration.
   e. Make patient comfortable before leaving.
   f. Wash your hands.

___ 5. Proceed to Patient No. 2. Identify, explain, and assist (as in Step 3).

___ 6. Administer ferrous sulfate (*Feosol*).
   a. Mix one teaspoonful of *Feosol* elixir with apple juice.
   b. Administer to patient (use a straw). Assist patient if necessary.
   c. Chart administration.
   d. Make patient comfortable before leaving.
   e. Wash your hands.

___ 7. Proceed to Patient No. 3. Identify patient. Explain that you are leaving a packet of nitroglycerin tablets by the bedside. As you leave, patient complains of angina pain.

___ 8. Administer nitroglycerin (*Nitrostat*).
   a. Place one tablet (0.4 mg) of *Nitrostat* under the patient's tongue. Instruct the patient not to swallow until tablet is completely dissolved.
   b. Do not give liquids.
   c. Chart administration.
   d. Make patient comfortable before leaving.
   e. Wash your hands.

___ 9. Return equipment and charts to proper location.

Demonstrate this procedure for the instructor or the nurse in charge.

REPRESENTATIVE DRUGS FOR THE CARDIOVASCULAR SYSTEM

CATEGORY, NAME[a], AND ROUTE	USES AND DISEASES	ACTIONS	USUAL DOSE[b] AND SPECIAL INSTRUCTIONS	SIDE EFFECTS AND ADVERSE REACTIONS
Vasoconstrictors[c]				
Metaraminol bitartrate (Aramine) SC, IM, IV	Shock; hypotension due to medical/surgical complications; hemorrhage, trauma	Constricts blood vessels; raises systolic and diastolic BP	2–10 mg IM or SC; higher doses in IV infusion. Watch patient closely.	Hypertension, restlessness, headache, arrhythmias, nausea, cardiac arrest possible
Norepinephrine (Levophed) IM	Acute hypotensive states, myocardial infarction, cardiac arrest	Powerful peripheral vasoconstrictor; increase in systemic blood pressure and coronary artery blood flow	Dilute 4 mg/1000 ml of 5% dextrose injection. Adjust dosage to maintain normal blood pressure of 80–100 mm Hg. Maintenance dose is 2–4 micrograms/minute	Headache, bradycardia
Vasodilators				
Nitroglycerin (Nitro-Bid, Nitrostat) Sublingual, buccal, oral, topical, IV	Angina pectoris	Relaxes smooth muscle; dilates coronary arteries; relieves angina pain	Dosage individualized, usually 0.15–0.6 mg sublingual or buccal every 5 minutes up to three times; consult supervisor or physician if pain persists; instruct patient to rest 15–20 minutes to let headache pass and avoid dizziness. Given sublingual for immediate effect (e.g., *Nitrostat*); timed-release caps for sustained effect (e.g., *Nitro-Bid*); sublingual tablets may be left at patient's bedside for self-administration as needed; check often to see how much taken and chart. Topical ointment for systemic absorption. Do not apply with fingers. Do not rub in.	Headache, dizziness, flushing, orthostatic hypotension, nausea, rapid pulse
Isosorbide dinitrate (Isordil) Sublingual, oral	Angina pectoris	Relaxes smooth muscle; dilates coronary arteries; relieves angina pain	5–10 mg q 2–3 hours sublingual. Also available in chewable and sustained-release forms.	Headache, dizziness, flushing, orthostatic hypotension, nausea, rapid pulse
Heart Stimulants (Cardiac Glycosides)				
Digitoxin (Crystodigin, Purodigin) Oral, IV, IM	Congestive heart failure; arrhythmias	Slows and strengthens the heartbeat; increases cardiac output	Initial doses given every 4–6 hours during digitalization. Daily maintenance dose 0.05–0.3 mg PO; usually 0.15 mg. Must take pulse before giving medication. (Adult pulse must be at least 60; child's at least 90.)	Nausea, vomiting, slow or irregular pulse, loss of appetite, extreme fatigue, distortion of color perception (may be signs of overdose)

REPRESENTATIVE DRUGS FOR THE CARDIOVASCULAR SYSTEM

CATEGORY, NAME[a], AND ROUTE	USES AND DISEASES	ACTIONS	USUAL DOSE[b] AND SPECIAL INSTRUCTIONS	SIDE EFFECTS AND ADVERSE REACTIONS
Heart Stimulants (Cardiac Glycosides) — continued				
Digoxin (Lanoxin) Oral, IV, IM	Congestive heart failure; arrhythmias	Slows and strengthens the heartbeat; increases cardiac output	Daily maintenance dose 0.125–0.5 mg PO; usually 0.25 mg.	Nausea, vomiting, slow or irregular pulse, loss of appetite, extreme fatigue
Antihypertensives/Diuretics				
Methyldopa (Aldomet) Oral	Moderate to severe hypertension	Lowers blood pressure; exact mechanism of action unknown	Initial dose: 250 mg BID or TID; maintenance: 125–500 mg BID or TID	Drowsiness, headache, edema of legs and feet, fever, anemia
Atenolol (Tenormin) Oral	Management of hypertension	Beta blocker, lowers BP	50 mg/day as one tablet; may go to 100 mg/day	Respiratory distress, bradycardia, dizziness, fatigue, diarrhea, nausea
Metoprolol tartrate (Lopressor) Oral	Management of hypertension; most effective used with a thiazide diuretic or other antihypertensive	Beta blocker, lowers BP	100 mg/day in single or divided doses; maintenance dose: 100–450 mg/day	Respiratory distress, bradycardia, dizziness, fatigue, diarrhea, nausea
Propranolol (Inderal) Oral	Management of moderate to severe hypertension	Beta blocker, lowers BP	Usually 40 mg BID initially; usual dosage is 160–640 mg/day	Breathing difficulties, upset stomach
Nifedipine (Procardia) Oral, sublingual	Vasospastic angina; coronary artery spasm; hypertension	Inhibits calcium ion influx across the cell membrane of cardiac and vascular smooth muscle, in turn causing modest hypotension	Titrate doses: give 10–30 mg TID over a 7–10-day period; obtain blood pressure and pulse immediately before administration. (Use same arm and have patient in the same position each time also).	Dizziness, lightheadedness, flushing, peripheral edema, nausea, and weakness
Diltiazem hydrochloride (Cardizem) Oral	Angina and hypertension	Inhibits calcium ion influx across the cell membrane during depolarization of cardiac and vascular smooth muscle	30–120 mg (up to 240 mg/day)	Edema, arrhythmias, drowsiness, nausea, lightheadedness
Verapamil hydrochloride (Calan) Oral, IM, IV	Angina and hypertension; paroxysmal atrial tachycardia	Inhibits calcium ion influx and slows AV conduction; reduces supraventricular tachycardia due to atrial flutter or fibrillation	Titrate doses: 80 mg three or four times a day; up to 240–480 mg; obtain blood pressure, pulse, and respirations immediately before giving drug	Peripheral edema, bradycardia, dizziness, headache
Chlorothiazide (Diuril) Oral	Management of hypertension	Vasodilation	Initial: 250 mg/day; adjust dosage to patient response; may need potassium supplement	Hypokalemia, weakness, dizziness, fatigue, dry mouth, confusion
Triamterene (Dyrenium) Oral	Used to counteract potassium-losing effect of thiazides	Potassium sparing	50–100 mg/day; do not give potassium supplement	Hyperkalemia, renal stones, nausea, vomiting
Heart Depressants (Antiarrhythmics)				
Quinidine Oral, IV, IM	Arrhythmias (fibrillation, flutter)	Lessens excitability of the myocardium; slows heart rate; lowers BP	200–300 mg PO TID or QID; take pulse and BP before administering. Give with meals to avoid gastrointestinal irritation	Gastrointestinal distress, bitter taste, hypersensitivity (esp. fever or skin rash), hypotension, severe headache, blurred vision, dizziness, hearing disturbances

REPRESENTATIVE DRUGS FOR THE CARDIOVASCULAR SYSTEM

CATEGORY, NAME[a], AND ROUTE	USES AND DISEASES	ACTIONS	USUAL DOSE[b] AND SPECIAL INSTRUCTIONS	SIDE EFFECTS AND ADVERSE REACTIONS
Heart Depressants (Antiarrhythmics) — continued				
Propranolol (Inderal) Oral, IV	Arrhythmias (esp. tachycardia)	Lessens excitability of the myocardium; slows heart rate; lowers BP	Arrhythmias: 10–30 mg PO TID or QID. Give before meals and at bedtime. Take pulse and BP before administering	Diarrhea, nausea, dry mouth, dyspnea, hypotension, confusion, slow pulse
Procainamide (Pronestyl) Oral, IM, IV	Premature ventricular contractions, ventricular tachycardia; atrial fibrillation and paroxysmal atrial tachycardia	Lessens excitability of the myocardium; slows heart rate; lowers BP	Oral: 0.5–1 g q 4–6 hours IV: 25–50 mg/min; depends on patient's condition; blood tests needed when on maintenance dose	Hypotension, anorexia, nausea, urticaria, chills, fever, agranulocytosis, lupus syndrome after prolonged use
Anticoagulants				
Warfarin sodium (Coumadin) Oral	Thrombus, pulmonary (lungs) embolism, phlebitis, coronary occlusion	Prevents or slows formation of blood clots; prevents enlargement of existing thrombus	Dosage must be adjusted individually; 2–10 mg PO daily for maintenance (initial dose may be given IM, IV, or PO)	
			Blood coagulation (prothrombin time) tests are given daily (or more often) until the desired effect is achieved and less frequently to monitor effect thereafter	
			Not to be used when there is a risk of hemorrhage (e.g., surgery, ulcers, pregnancy). Watch for signs of bleeding.	Hemorrhage (blood in urine, feces, and tissues, bruising, nosebleed, bleeding gums)
Dicumarol Oral	Thrombus, pulmonary (lungs) embolism, phlebitis, coronary occlusion	Depleted clotting factors	Dosage is individualized. Initial: 200–300 mg; maintenance: 25–200 mg after prothrombin time has stabilized	Hemorrhage
Heparin calcium (Calciparine) IV, SC, IV bolus	Thrombosis, embolism	Inhibits reactions that lead to clotting	5,000–40,000 units; do not give IM due to pain or hematoma; doses adjusted to individual patient	Hemorrhage, chills, fever, hypersensitivity reactions, alopecia
Hematinics				
Ferrous sulfate (Feosol, Fer-in-Sol) Oral	Iron-deficiency anemia	Replaces iron needed in red blood cell production	90–300 mg iron PO daily in divided doses, tablets or liquid. Give between meals with ample fluids. Mix liquid with fruit juice or water, according to package instructions. Use a straw to prevent staining of teeth. Avoid spilling on clothes.	Black, tarry stools, nausea, loss of appetite, diarrhea, constipation

REPRESENTATIVE DRUGS FOR THE CARDIOVASCULAR SYSTEM

CATEGORY, NAME[a], AND ROUTE	USES AND DISEASES	ACTIONS	USUAL DOSE[b] AND SPECIAL INSTRUCTIONS	SIDE EFFECTS AND ADVERSE REACTIONS
Coagulants				
Phytonadione, Vitamin K (*Mephyton, Aqua-Mephyton*) Oral, SC, IM, IV	Poor clotting, overdose of anticoagulant	Promotes blood clotting, reverses effects of *Coumadin*	Blood tests determine proper dose (dosage range is 2.5–25 mg). Protect drug from light.	Flushing, odd taste, allergic reactions, gastric upset, headache
Gelatin Hemostatics Gelatin Film OTC	Used in neurosurgery, thoracic surgery, and ocular surgery	Promotes blood clotting	Immerse in saline; soak until pliable; can be cut to size and shape needed.	Completely absorbed in 1–6 months

[a] Brand names given in parentheses are examples only. Check current drug references for a complete listing of available trade name products.

[b] Average adult doses are given. However, dosages are determined by a physician and vary with the purpose of the therapy and the particular patient. The doses presented in this text are for general information only.

[c] All patients receiving vasoconstrictors must be monitored constantly and blood pressure and pulse taken every 2–5 minutes.

Unit 9

Drugs for the Respiratory System

In this unit you will review the parts and functions of the respiratory system. You will learn how breathing takes place and how common respiratory disorders affect this process. You will study the types of drugs used to treat respiratory disorders and their actions and the nursing care that goes with them. You will learn to administer drugs in the form of nose drops and sprays to the mucous membranes of the nose and throat.

In this unit, you will learn to:

- Name and describe the parts of the respiratory system.
- Explain how gases are exchanged in the lungs.
- Give the normal respiration rate for an adult.
- Explain why coughing is important.
- List and describe common symptoms of respiratory disorders, using correct medical terms.
- Recognize descriptions of the major respiratory disorders.
- Describe the actions and give examples of the following drug groups: antitussives, expectorants, decongestants, antihistamines, and bronchodilators.
- Recognize the names of physical and mechanical techniques and devices used in respiratory therapy.
- Follow nursing procedures for making respiratory drugs work better.
- Observe patients for symptoms of breathing problems.
- Administer nose drops and paint or spray mucous membranes, using correct procedures.

RESPIRATORY SYSTEM

The respiratory system is a continuous, open pathway from the mouth and the nose through the head, the neck, and the chest to the lungs. This pathway allows the outside air to penetrate deep into the lungs, where a vital exchange of gases takes place. Inhaling and exhaling air for the purpose of this gas exchange is called **respiration**.

Figure 9-1 shows the various parts of the respiratory pathway. Air enters the body through either the mouth or the nose. Just inside the nostrils are the **nasal cavities**, which are lined with mucous membranes that warm and moisten the air and also trap dust particles and bacteria. The nasal cavities join the **pharynx** *(far'inks)*, a part of the air passage that is shared with the digestive system. At its lower end, the pharynx divides into two tubes, one that goes on to the stomach and one that goes into the **larynx** *(lar'inks)* and eventually into the lungs.

The larynx is responsible for the sounds a human can make. It is a person's "voice box." The entrance to the larynx closes automatically when a person swallows, thanks to a flap of tissue called the **epiglottis** *(ep'i-glot'is)*. The epiglottis keeps food and saliva from going down "the wrong way" into the lungs.

The larynx joins a tube that leads into the lungs, called the **trachea** *(tra'ke-ah)* or the windpipe. C-shaped pieces of cartilage line the trachea and keep it open at all times. The trachea branches off into two tubes, the **bronchi**, which lead to the right and left lungs. The bronchi branch into increasingly smaller tubes, the **bronchioles**, that extend deep into the lungs.

At the tips of these many branches are clusters of **alveoli** *(al-ve'o-li)*, or **alveolar sacs**. These are tiny air sacs with very thin walls. They are in close contact with many blood capillaries. This is where inhaled oxygen is picked up from the air by the red blood cells. At the same time, carbon dioxide is released from the blood into the air sacs and travels back up the air passages. During exhalation the carbon dioxide and other waste gases pass out of the body.

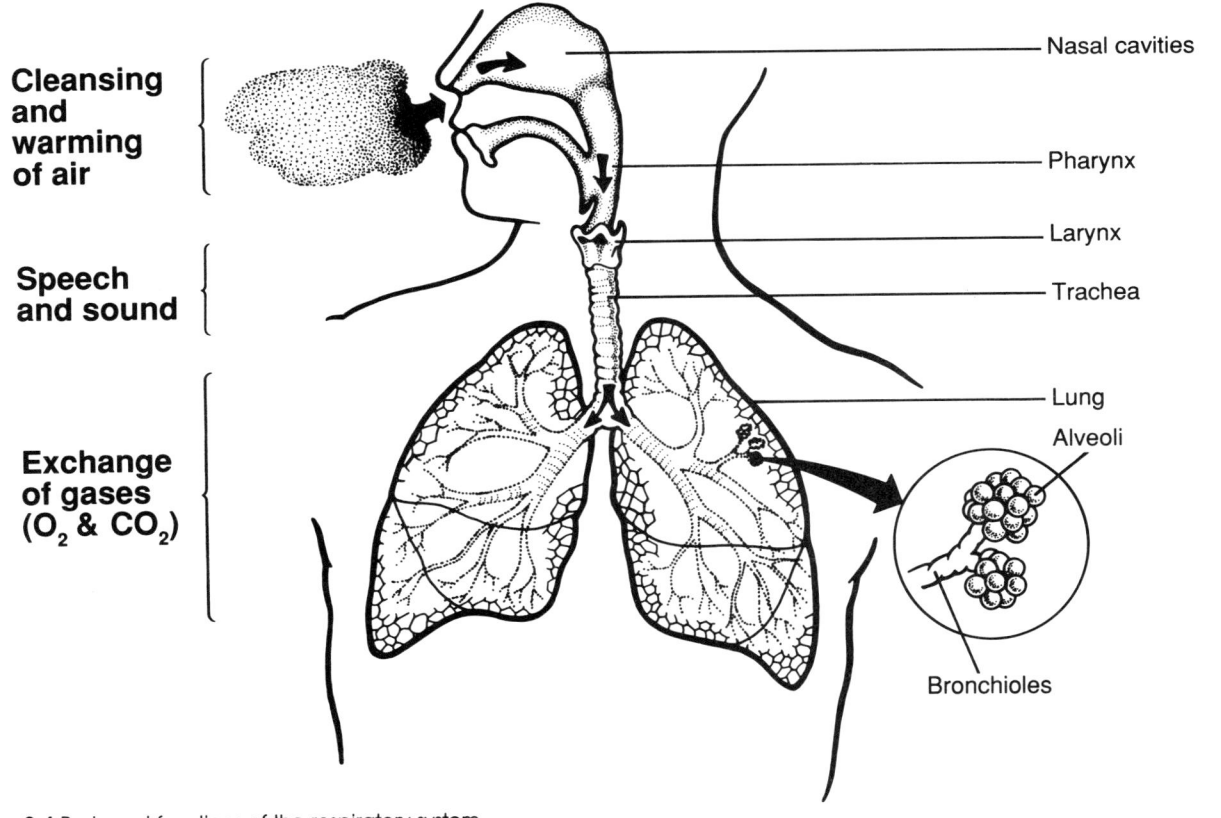

Figure 9-1 Parts and functions of the respiratory system.

VOCABULARY

aerosol: a mist administered from a pressurized container, used for spraying or inhaling drugs

allergen: irritating substance that stimulates an allergic reaction in the body

alveoli: tiny air sacs in the lungs that permit the exchange of oxygen and carbon dioxide through capillary walls (singular: alveolus, alveolar sac)

antihistamine: drug that lessens the effects of histamine, relieving allergy symptoms

antitussive: drug that decreases coughing

apnea: stoppage of breathing; may be temporary or fatal

asthma: condition marked by wheezing in which the bronchioles tighten

atomizer: device that produces a drug mist for inhalation therapy

bronchi: air passages leading from the trachea to the bronchioles in the lungs (singular: bronchus)

bronchiole: branch of the bronchi leading to alveoli deep in the lungs

bronchodilator: drug that expands the bronchioles by relaxing the smooth muscles

bronchopulmonary: pertaining to the lungs and the air passages

decongestant: drug that shrinks and dries the mucous membranes to reduce congestion in the air passages

emphysema: air-filled expansion of lung tissue with deterioration of alveolar walls

epiglottis: flap of tissue at the entrance to the larynx that prevents food from being swallowed into the air passages

exhale: breathe out

expectorant: drug that thins and breaks up mucus so it can be coughed up

expectorate: cough up sputum

hyperpnea: breathing too rapidly or deeply; also called **hyperventilation**

inhale: breathe in

IPPB: intermittent positive pressure breathing, a means of administering respiratory therapy

larynx: voice box, a part of the respiratory tract

mucolytic: drug that breaks down the proteins and carbohydrates in mucus and thins it out; called **proteolytic** if only proteins are broken down

mucus: thick fluid secreted by the mucous membrane lining of body cavities

nasal: pertaining to the nose

nasal cavities: hollow parts of the skull through which air passes when inhaled through the nose

nebulizer: device that produces a drug mist for inhalation

orthopnea: difficulty in breathing in any position except upright

percussion: physical therapy for respiratory patients; unclogs mucus by thumping or vibrating the chest area

pharynx: part of the respiratory passageway shared with the digestive system; connects the mouth and the nose to the larynx

phlegm: mucus produced by the lining of the respiratory tract

pleura: membranes lining the lungs and lung cavities

postural drainage: physical therapy for respiratory patients; helps to unclog mucus through force of gravity by tilting the entire body with the head down

productive cough: cough that brings up sputum

pulmonary: pertaining to the lungs

rebound effect: reappearance of symptoms in even stronger form after a drug dose has worn off

respiration: breathing

saliva: clear, viscous fluid secreted from salivary and mucous glands that is excreted into the mouth

spasm: an abnormal, uncontrollable muscle contraction

sputum: mucus and/or pus coughed up from the respiratory passages

stethoscope: instrument for listening to the heartbeat and breathing sounds

tachypnea: rapid breathing

trachea: part of the respiratory tract; connects larynx to bronchi

ventilator: machine that assists breathing

The average person breathes in and out about 18 times per minute. The normal **respiration rate** varies between 12 and 25 times per minute. Children tend to breathe more quickly and elderly patients more slowly than the average adult.

Breathing is accomplished by the muscles around the ribs and by the **diaphragm**, a layer of muscle tissue that separates the chest cavity from the other internal organs. When a person inhales, the respiratory muscles contract to lift the rib cage and the diaphragm flattens out. Both of these actions create a downward and outward pull on the lungs that forces them to draw in air (inhalation). When the muscles relax, the lung cavity collapses and forces the air back out (exhalation). Inside the lungs, the elastic walls of the bronchioles and the alveoli expand and contract with each breath. This elasticity is very important, for when it is decreased by disease, proper breathing is no longer possible.

RESPIRATORY SYSTEM DISORDERS

Respiration is crucial to sustaining life. A person cannot live more than a few minutes without oxygen. Brain damage begins after only 6 minutes without oxygen. This is why the respiration rate is one of the four vital signs that medical staff keep a close watch on in serious diseases and emergency treatment. (The other three vital signs are body temperature, blood pressure, and pulse.)

When a respiratory disorder is suspected, the doctor will examine the patient with a **stethoscope**. This is an instrument that amplifies the sounds of breathing. By holding the stethoscope against the chest at various points, the doctor can hear whether there is fluid in the lungs, whether the lungs are expanding properly and so forth. Different breathing sounds give clues to different types of diseases.

There are several other tests that help in diagnosing respiratory diseases. A chest x-ray may be taken. Coughed-up mucus may be sent to the laboratory for microscopic examination. Blood tests are done on the patient to check oxygen and carbon dioxide content. The chest cavity may be drained and the fluid examined in the laboratory. Finally, there are tests of lung capacity that can be done while a patient is inhaling and exhaling (Figure 9-2). By measuring the amount of air taken in and given out with each breath cycle, the medical staff can identify problems that may be developing deep inside the lungs.

Symptoms

Coughing—This main symptom is the body's attempt to rid itself of matter that blocks the air passages. Respiratory diseases often cause secretion of mucus, pus, or other fluids in the lungs. Coughing can be persistent or it can come in uncontrolled fits. The special sound of a patient's cough is a sign that helps in diagnosing the underlying disease (Figure 9-3).

Sputum—Coughing brings up secretions known as **sputum** *(spu'tum)*. This unclogs the air passages. The sputum itself contains clues to the patient's disease. It varies from thin and watery to thick and yellowish to pink and frothy. Blood in the sputum (**hemoptysis**) is usually a signal that blood is leaking into the lungs through hemorrhage or pulmonary edema.

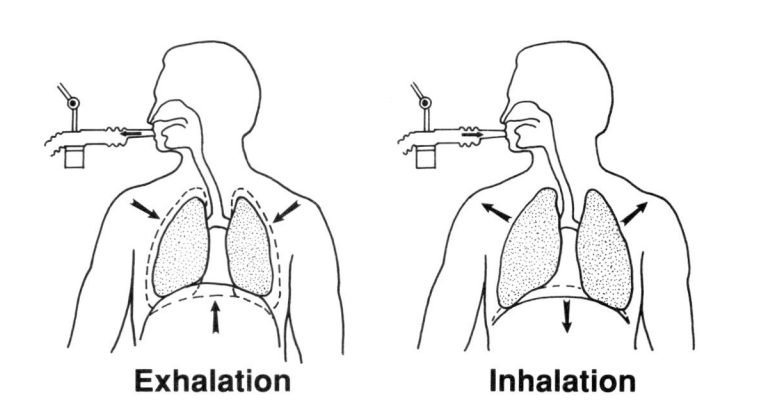

Figure 9-2 Testing lung capacity.

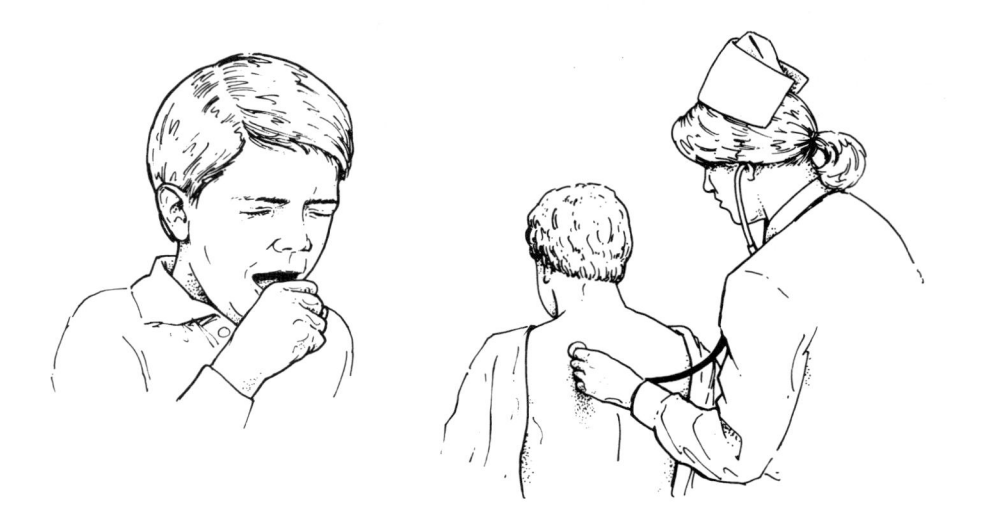

Figure 9-3 Coughs and breathing sounds give clues to respiratory problems.

Hoarseness—This symptom may be caused by an abnormal growth on the larynx, or it may be the result of an infection in the throat.

Breathing Disturbances—These are signs of changes in lung capacity or of changes in the nerve centers that control breathing.

---

dyspnea *(disp'ne-ah)*—Shortness of breath, or labored breathing
tachypnea *(tak'ip-ne'ah)*—rapid breathing
apnea *(ap-ne'ah)*—stopped breathing
hyperpnea *(hi'perp-ne'ah)*, or **hyperventilation**—breathing too rapidly or deeply
orthopnea *(or'thop-ne'ah)*—breathing comfortably only in an upright position

---

Abnormal Sounds—Unusual sounds during breathing are common with many diseases. Wheezing, musical sounds, and grating sounds signal chest congestion, obstruction of the air passages, and infection of the lung linings, respectively.

Chest Pain—Pains in the chest area occur in various forms during respiratory disorders; for example, chest tightness, pain when taking a deep breath, or stabbing pain that comes unexpectedly.

More general symptoms of respiratory disorders are loss of appetite (**anorexia**, *an'-o-rek'se-ah*), weight loss, fever, fatigue, cyanosis, clubbing of the fingers, and sweats and chills.

Major Diseases

Some respiratory problems are caused by disturbances in the control centers of the brain or in the nerves that send messages to the respiratory muscles in the ribs and the diaphragm. These problems, and the drugs used to treat them, are discussed in Unit 10. This unit focuses on disorders that affect the air passages and the lungs, or **bronchopulmonary** disorders (**pulmonary** = pertaining to the lungs).

The Pneumonias—There are many types of pneumonia, each named for the agent (bacteria, virus, fungus, etc.) that causes it. All pneumonias are infections of the lower respiratory tract (bronchi, bronchioles, and alveoli). Some are caused by bacteria that normally live in the human air passages. In times of low resistance (e.g., from other diseases, exposure to cold, poor nutrition), these bacteria sometimes multiply and infect the lungs.

Such bacteria may also crop up after surgery, anesthesia, diseases that interfere with lung drainage, and drugs that suppress the body's immune system. As a result of the bacterial infection, the lungs fill up with pus, which must be drained off quickly. As soon as the type of bacteria is identified, antibiotics can be given to fight the infection. Meanwhile, the nursing staff must use special techniques to help drain the lungs of pus so breathing can be maintained.

Bronchitis—Bronchitis is an inflammation of the air passageways caused by irritants (e.g., smoke or chemicals), allergic reactions, flu, or viruses. It can be acute (short term) or chronic (long term). In bronchitis treatment, the main objective is to keep the air passages open. They are easily plugged by the great quantities of sputum and pus that are produced by the infected bronchi. In chronic bronchitis, hard coughing is a problem. Sometimes it becomes so severe that it may break a rib or rupture a lung or a blood vessel. Because most forms of bronchitis are caused by viruses or outside irritants, antibiotics are seldom given. The patient must drink lots of fluids and take drugs that keep the sputum moist and thin (expectorants).

Emphysema — Emphysema (*em-fi-se' mah*) is a narrowing of the bronchioles because of disease or repeated bronchial infections. The narrowed bronchioles are able to take in air during inhalation, but they do not let all of the air pass back out. As a result, "stale" air gets backed up in the alveoli. This in turn makes it impossible to take in much new air on the next breath. The alveoli expand with the backed-up air, causing the lungs to swell and giving the patient a "barrel chest." There is no cure for emphysema, although breathing exercises are sometimes helpful. Antibiotics can be given for specific infections. Drugs that thin the sputum (expectorants) and drugs that expand the bronchioles (bronchodilators) are given to promote the coughing up of sputum that may be clogging the air passages.

Pleurisy—Pleurisy (*ploor'i-se*) is an inflammation of the linings (the **pleura**) of the lungs and lung cavities. The patient feels knife-sharp pains in the chest area along with a mild fever. This condition usually clears up with rest, mild sedatives, pain medication, and treatment of the primary disease.

Asthma—Asthma attacks can be caused by irritating substances in the environment as well as other factors such as exercise, allergy, illness, or emotional upset. The "attacks" may occur from time to time or may last for several days (the most dangerous form). During an attack, the muscles around the bronchioles contract, narrowing the air passages. Inhaled air cannot be exhaled properly. The alveoli become plugged with unusually thick sputum which is hard to cough up. There is wheezing, shortness of breath, and coughing. Most patients are able to obtain quick relief by inhaling epinephrine, a drug that opens up the bronchial passages (bronchodilator). Expectorants and postural drainage treatments (explained later) are also helpful. Some patients receive allergy treatments to make them less sensitive to irritants that start the asthma attacks.

Cancers of the Respiratory Tract—The most frequent form of cancer in the upper respiratory tract is cancer of the larynx. Persistent hoarseness is one of the first signs of this form of cancer. It is treated by removing the growth surgically. Cancer of the lung is common in the lower respiratory tract. Often lung cancer is a sign that a cancer has spread from some other place in the body. It is difficult to detect until symptoms become very severe. It starts as coughing, wheezing, and hemoptysis (*he-mop'ti-sis*). Surgery to remove the cancerous tissue is the major form of treatment.

Pulmonary Embolism—This is the result of an embolus blocking a branch of the pulmonary artery that goes from the heart to the lungs. With the pulmonary artery blocked, a part of the lungs receives little or no oxygen. This can cause sudden death. Less severe pulmonary embolisms are treated with anticoagulants as described in Unit 8.

Tuberculosis—Tuberculosis is an infectious disease caused by **Mycobacterium tuberculosis**. The body becomes sensitive to this bacteria when it is first exposed (e.g., from the coughing of a person with active tuberculosis). After initial infection, the TB germs can be dormant for long periods and then reactivate. The patient weakens, coughs up blood, and eventually dies unless treated early. Treatment consists of drugs that attack the tubercle bacillus (e.g., isoniazid, rifampin, ethambucol, streptomycin), combined with long-term rest. In many parts of the world today, tuberculosis is under control because of new testing procedures that allow early detection of "carriers" of the bacteria. However, in other parts of the world tuberculosis is still widespread.

Inflammations of the Nose, Sinuses, and Throat—Rhinitis, sinusitis, and **strep throat** are some of the most common inflammations of the upper respiratory tract. They are caused by bacterial infections, allergies, or irritating substances. "Seasonal rhinitis," for example, is an allergic reaction to the pollen in the air during the late summer and fall. Signs of rhinitis and sinusitis include a runny nose, sneezing, headache, sore throat, watery eyes, fever, and redness and swelling of mucous membranes. The symptoms can be controlled with decongestants and antihistamines. To treat a strep throat, the disease-causing bacteria may need to be identified by means of a throat culture. Then a systemic antibiotic that kills that specific bacteria is prescribed.

DRUGS FOR RESPIRATORY DISORDERS

Antitussives

Antitussive drugs are cough suppressants (Figure 9-4). They act on the control center in the brain that stimulates coughing. There are narcotic antitussives (codeine) and nonnarcotic antitussives, e.g., dextromethorphan (*Benylin DM*). Remember that not all coughing is harmful or undesirable. It clears the lungs and bronchial tubes of foreign objects and sputum that interfere with breathing. A cough that brings up sputum is called a **productive** cough. A cough that brings up nothing is called "dry" or **nonproductive**. Nonproductive coughing occurs when the mucus is clogged in the lower respiratory tract or when irritation in the throat stimulates repeated coughing. Despite the fact that no mucus is being brought up, a person may have a repeated urge to cough. Coughing of this sort is exhausting and robs the patient of needed sleep. In such cases antitussives are given to suppress the cough reflex somewhat (never completely). Antitussives have a sedative effect as well, so they help patients get the needed rest.

Expectorants

These drugs are believed to break up thick mucous secretions of the lungs and bronchi so they can be coughed up (Figure 9-5), but there is controversy concerning their effectiveness. They also are thought to increase the amount of fluid in the respiratory tract. This would have the effect of moistening the sputum so that it thins out. Examples of expectorants are guaifenesin (*Triaminic*), potassium iodide (*SSKI Solution*), acetylcysteine (*Mucomyst*), and terpin hydrate. Expectorants that act by breaking up the protein molecules in mucus are referred to as **proteolytics**.

Decongestants

Decongestants act against congestion in the respiratory tract. They reduce the swelling by shrinking the blood vessels in the mucous membranes. Some also have the effect of drying up the mucous membranes (Figure 9-6).

Decongestants only relieve symptoms; they do not cure the underlying cause of congestion. They are available in many forms for oral and inhalation use. Examples are phenylephrine hydrochloride (*Neo-Synephrine*), propylhexadrine (*Benzedrex*), phenylpropanolamine hydrochloride (*Propagest*), and oxymetazoline (*Afrin*). Most of these are available OTC, but patients should not overuse them.

A **rebound effect** can occur with decongestants after continued use—when the drug effect wears off, the mucous membranes swell up even worse than before.

Figure 9-4 Antitussives.

Figure 9-5 Expectorants.

Decongestants can also irritate the nasal passages.

Antihistamines

These drugs work against the effects of histamine (Figure 9-7), which is why they are used in allergic conditions such as hay fever. Recall that histamine is released by certain cells whenever there is a foreign "invader" such as an irritating substance, a germ, or an injury. Histamine causes the blood vessels to dilate and the smooth muscle in the bronchi to contract. Antihistamines, in contrast, shrink the blood vessels and relax the bronchial muscles.

Antihistamines are administered orally because they are easily absorbed through the intestinal lining. The major antihistamines used for respiratory problems are diphenhydramine (*Benadryl*), promethazine (*Phenergan*), terfenadine (*Seldane*), chlorpheniramine maleate (*Chlor-Trimeton, Teldrin*) and related drugs (*Dimetane, Actidil*), and cyproheptadine (*Periactin*).

Older antihistamines have the side effects of drowsiness, sedation, and occasionally dry mouth and insomnia. They interact with many other drugs (especially alcohol, sedatives, and tranquilizers), so their use must be carefully controlled. Patients who are just starting on an older

Figure 9-6 Decongestants.

> **NOTE:**
>
> **Drugs for the respiratory system are often given in combination with each other. For example, a medicine might contain a bronchodilator to open the air passages and an expectorant to loosen the sputum so that it can be coughed up. Many cold remedies are combinations of antitussives, expectorants, and decongestants. Elixir of terpin hydrate and codeine, for example, has a combined antitussive and expectorant action. *Tedral* combines two bronchodilators, theophylline and ephedrine, with a sedative, phenobarbital. Popular brand name products for allergies and colds combine antihistamines with decongestants, expectorants, and antitussives—for example, *Actifed, Benylin, Dimetapp, Ornade, Drixoral, Phenergan Expectorant with Codeine*.**

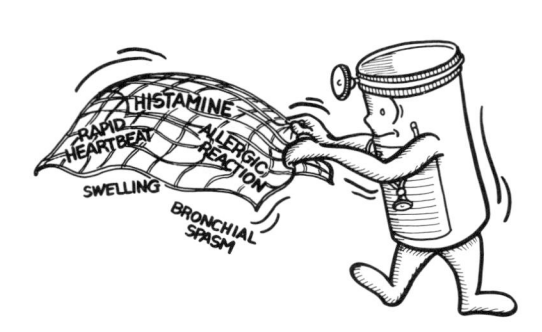

Figure 9-7 Antihistamines.

antihistamine should be warned not to undertake tasks that require good physical coordination (e.g., driving a car)—at least until their response to the drug is known.

The newer, nonsedating antihistamines (e.g., terfenadine) do not produce drowsiness or adverse psychomotor effects and do not have the interaction potential of traditional antihistamines.

Bronchodilators

Bronchodilators cause the bronchioles to relax and expand (dilate) (Figure 9-8). This is very useful in conditions like asthma, where the muscles surrounding the bronchioles go into spasm. By relaxing these muscles, bronchodilators permit normal breathing and end the asthmatic attack. The main bronchodilators are epinephrine (*Primatene Mist*), isoproterenol (*Isuprel*), ephedrine (*Quibron Plus*), theophylline (*Elixophyllin*), aminophylline (*Somophyllin*), terbutaline (*Brethine*), and various combination products.

Bronchodilators are given by inhalation or orally, depending on the drug (and by injection in some emergencies). Besides dilating the bronchioles, these drugs have other effects such as stimulating the heart and respiration and stopping the release of histamine. For this reason, some of these drugs are used in emergency treatment of cardiac arrest and allergic reactions. They must be used with great care, in the proper dosages, and with close attention to side effects. Epinephrine, for example, can cause anxiety, restlessness, dizziness, weakness, pallor (pale skin), palpitations, and breathing difficulty. Patients can develop tolerance to bronchodilators, and rebound effects are also possible.

The product information table at the end of this unit lists uses, side effects, dosages, and special instructions for representative drugs used in treating respiratory disorders. Popular OTC drugs for colds, hay fever, and asthma are listed in Table 9-1.

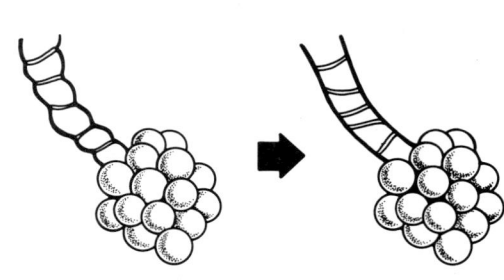

Figure 9-8 Bronchodilators.

Table 9-1 Selected OTC drugs for the respiratory system

Condition	Products	Actions
Cough	Benylin, Cheracol, Romilar, Triaminic, Vicks Formula 44	Antitussive/expectorant/demulcent/analgesic/antihistaminic
Colds and allergic rhinitis	Allerest, Chlor-Trimeton, Contac, Coricidin D, Comtrex, Dristan, Neo-Synephrine, Sinarest, Sudafed	Decongestant/antihistaminic/analgesic
Asthma	Bronkaid, Primatene Mist	Bronchodilator

GIVING RESPIRATORY DRUGS

The goals of therapy in respiratory diseases are to control the rate and depth of breathing, to remove anything that may be blocking the air passages, and to clear out the sputum so that it does not lead to infection. Drugs are only one part of the treatment; other important parts are to remove the source of irritation (e.g., have the patient stop smoking and avoid allergens) and to use physical techniques that promote normal mucus drainage and breathing.

You may be called on to assist in certain physical procedures when you administer medications to respiratory patients. Oxygen inhalation therapy may be ordered to make up for the lungs' poor oxygen intake. A **ventilator** may be needed to help the patient breathe regularly by mechanical means. **Postural drainage** may be ordered. The postural drainage technique consists of placing the patient in one of several positions so that gravity helps to pull the mucus out of the lungs and the air passages. This helps the patient cough it up.

Percussion is another technique for loosening up the clogged mucus. It involves gently clapping or vibrating the area where the mucus is lodged. Percussion is usually combined with postural drainage. Sometimes patients have to be encouraged to cough, even if it hurts, so that excess mucus does not build up in the lungs.

Psychological factors are important in administering respiratory medications. It is threatening and frightening to a patient not to be able to breathe properly. But this is exactly what happens with diseases of the respiratory tract, even with the common cold. For the sake of the patient, you need to be supportive and calm.

With respiratory medications, it is especially important to watch the patient's symptoms closely. Each time you are with the patient, make a note of the rate and depth of breathing. This helps you decide which PRN drugs are needed, if any, or whether new drugs need to be ordered:

- Has the patient's breathing changed since you last saw him or her?
- Has the respiration rate increased?
- Is it hard for the patient to take in a breath?

You can tell by looking at the chest to see whether it is sucked in with each breath. Holding the mouth open while breathing, spreading the nostrils, and making unusual sounds while breathing are other signs of respiratory problems. Some signs are so subtle that the patient may not be aware of them. Does the patient move more slowly, get excited easily, or have muscle twitches? Even stomach movements or changed speech patterns can be clues to the need for respiratory medications. Naturally, you should chart your observations.

Clinical Considerations

There are ways you can make the respiratory medications work better and help patients breathe. Here are a few suggestions:

- Explain to patients the effects of the drugs and the breathing exercises that are a part of their treatment. The instructions that come with the drugs will help you do this.
- Assist patients into sitting or leaning positions. These positions help them breathe by allowing the lungs to expand fully.
- Be sure to give drugs on time. Many respiratory drugs are ordered just before busy times of the day to prevent the fatigue that comes with extra activity. When getting a breath of air is an effort, any added activity can be tiring.
- Be sure to remove mucus from the nose and throat (Figure 9-9). Encourage the

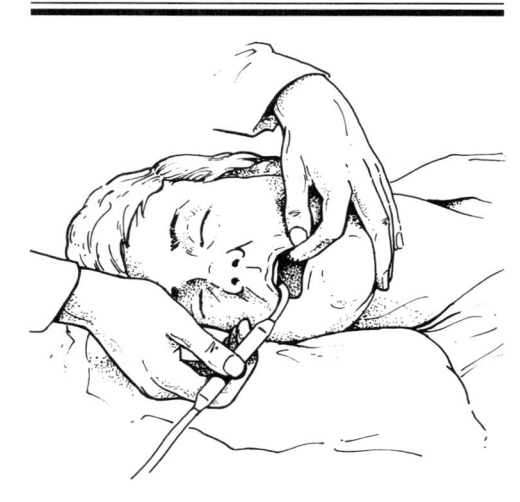

Figure 9-9 Suctioning to remove mucus.

Figure 9-10 Four ways to help a nonproductive cough.

- patient to cough. Regardless of the number of respiratory drugs a patient is taking, mucus in the respiratory tract can still prevent the needed air exchange.
- Ask the patient to let you know whenever breathing begins to get difficult. Catching the problem early makes the drug treatment more effective.
- Do not rush the patient while giving drugs. This only increases the patient's anxiety. The patient is already anxious because of the effort of catching a breath.
- Give the proper amounts of fluids (e.g., juice, water), with respiratory medications. Expectorants and antitussives should be given with extra fluids. The fluids help to thin out respiratory secretions so they can be coughed up and eliminated. No fluids should be given with soothing syrups (demulcents) because they are designed to coat the respiratory tract.
- To help a patient with a nonproductive cough, remove him or her from irritating fumes, dust, and smoke. Provide hard candy or a demulcent to get rid of tickling in the throat (Figure 9-10).
- Add moisture to the air with a humidifier. Dry mucous membranes can become irritated. They are also more prone to infection.
- Recall that some respiratory drugs, especially some antihistamines, may cause drowsiness (Figure 9-11). Patients should be warned not to drive a car or operate heavy equipment while taking them. This is true of many OTC products as well as prescription drugs. Some doctors avoid antihistamines because they tend to dry secretions.
- Instruct the family in measures they can take to assist the patient's breathing. Well-informed family members can encourage a patient to cooperate in treatment.

Respiratory Therapy

Many patients with lung disorders are treated with some sort of respiratory therapy. They inhale from machines that produce mists containing tiny droplets of

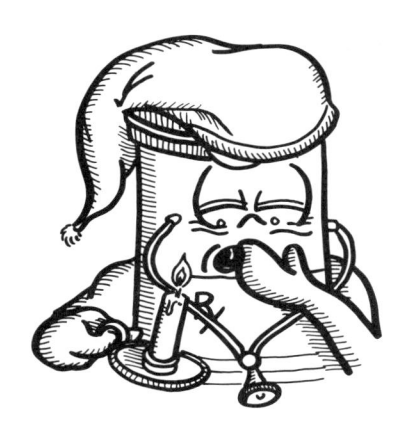

Figure 9-11 Caution patients about this side effect of antihistamines.

drugs. The drugs suited to this method of administration are bronchodilators, mucolytics, corticosteroids, and antibiotics.

Drugs inhaled as a mist are able to travel deep into the lungs. They are absorbed directly through the linings of the respiratory tract or through the alveoli, depending on the size of the droplets. Drugs that are absorbed by the alveoli have a rapid systemic effect because of the richness of the blood supply. The absorption of drugs through the linings of the respiratory tract is like topical applications to mucous membranes.

There are several types of machines and equipment used for inhalation therapy [e.g., intermittent positive pressure breathing (IPPB) apparatus, slipstream nebulizer]. They are operated by specially trained health care workers called **respiratory therapists**. Small, hand-held devices called **atomizers** or **nebulizers** are also available for self-medication.

After inhaling a mist, the patient should rinse out the mouth to avoid swallowing the medication.

Use of Oxygen

Oxygen is essential in sustaining all forms of life and is in every body cell. Without it, the cell dies within a few minutes. Lack of oxygen is called **hypoxia**. Emphysema and other lung problems, anemia, and heart problems deprive the body of oxygen to the point that tissues may not respond to replacement therapy.

Too much oxygen, **hyperoxygenation**, can cause irreversible damage. Careful assessment of the patient's needs can prevent hyperoxygenation. Symptoms of oxygen toxicity are substernal distress, nausea and vomiting, malaise, fatigue, and numbness and tingling of the extremities.

Oxygen should be considered a drug and prescribed and administered as such. There must be specific, written orders for the flow rate and the method of administration. The initial dose, as well as any changes in administration and dose, including discontinuation, should be based on blood gas analysis.

Methods of administration include the nasal catheter, oxygen mask, and oxygen tent. The catheter is usually used for restless or uncooperative patients. The oxygen tent is used mainly with children or those patients who will not tolerate other modes of administration or with patients who need oxygen and humidity or just humidity. Inspired air must be moisturized to prevent drying of the respiratory mucosa and thickening secretions that could then inhibit air flow through the passages.

Oxygen therapy is never ended abruptly. You must gradually wean your patient by alternating periods of oxygen-supplemented inspiration with periods of breathing without the oxygen.

Direct Applications, Sprays, and Nose Drops

Drugs may be painted, sprayed, or dropped onto the mucous membranes of the mouth, nose, and throat. They penetrate directly into the linings of the respiratory tract, but treat only the area sprayed rather than traveling into the lungs. These topical applications are useful for localized inflammations and symptoms such as sinus infections, stuffy nose, injuries of the mucous membranes, and sore throat. Decongestants, for example, may often be sprayed or dropped into the nasal cavities to reduce swelling so a patient can breathe more easily.

Nose drops should not be swallowed, as they are meant to give a local rather than systemic effect. The dropper should be rinsed with hot water after use. This is to avoid spreading germs to the medicine bottle.

Practice procedures are available at the end of this unit to show you how to administer topical medications to the respiratory passages.

EXERCISES

A. Fill in the blanks.

1. Inhaling and exhaling air so that gases can be exchanged in the lungs is called _____.

2. The nasal cavities warm and moisten the air we breathe. They also trap _____.

3. The part of the respiratory tract that is shared with the digestive system is the _____.

4. The part of the respiratory system that produces speech sounds is called the _____.

5. The flap of tissue that keeps food from going down into the lungs when it is swallowed is the _____.

6. The tube that leads to the lungs and is known as the windpipe is the _____.

7. The two tubes that branch from the windpipe and lead into the right and left lungs are the _____.

8. The small branched tubes that carry air to and from the air sacs deep inside the lungs are known as _____.

9. The tiny sacs where gases are exchanged between the blood and inspired air are the _____.

10. The gases that are exchanged in the lungs are _____ and _____.

11. The average respiration rate is about _____ breaths per minute.

12. The layer of muscle that flattens out during inhalation and pulls downward on the lungs is the _____.

13. The instrument used to listen to breathing sounds is the _____.

14. Secretions coughed up from the air passages are known as _____.

15. A hand-held device that produces a drug mist for inhalation is called a(n) _____.

B. When administering respiratory medications, part of your job is to observe the patient for changes in symptoms. List five symptoms that you would look for as clues to respiration problems.

_____

_____

_____

C. Define these medical terms.

1. pulmonary _____

2. dyspnea _____

3. tachypnea _____

4. apnea _____

5. hyperpnea _____

6. hyperventilation _____

7. pleura _____

8. rebound effect _____

D. Select the disorder that best matches each description. Write the name of the disorder in the blank.

bronchitis   asthma
pneumonia   rhinitis
tuberculosis   emphysema

1. In a small town in Asia, Grandfather Kim has had a lung disease for a long time. He is very weak and is coughing up blood. The public health worker is worried that Kim's grandchildren will catch the disease from him.

   _____

2. Nancy Epstein suffers from frequent attacks of wheezing, coughing, and shortness of breath. She can control these attacks by inhaling epinephrine and by avoiding dust and mold.

   _____

3. Mr. Smith can never get a good breath because he cannot exhale completely. He does breathing exercises every day and takes expectorants and bronchodilators to help his condition.

   _____

4. Sue Bosworth has a virus infection of the upper respiratory tract. Her doctor gives instructions to drink plenty of fluids so that she can cough up the great quantities of sputum that are clogging her air passage.

   _____

5. Frank Fernandez was recoving from the flu when he developed a bacterial infection. The infection now has clogged the alveoli with pus, making it difficult for him to breathe.

   _____

6. Brad Katz gets a bad stuffy nose every autumn when there is much pollen in the air.

   _____

E. Tell what these types of drugs do; for example, Demulcents *coat mucous membranes and soothe irritation that causes coughing.*

   1. Antitussives _____

   2. Expectorants _____

   3. Decongestants _____

   4. Bronchodilators _____

   5. Antihistamines _____

F. Match the drug names to drug categories.

   ____ 1. aminophylline, *Isuprel, Brethine*　　　　　a. antitussives
   ____ 2. dextromethorphan, codeine, benzonatate　　b. decongestants
   ____ 3. phenylephrine, *Benzedrex,*　　　　　　　c. tuberculosis drugs
          phenylpropanolamine, *Afrin*　　　　　　　d. bronchodilators
   ____ 4. *Benadryl,* chlorpheniramine,　　　　　　e. expectorants
          Teldrin, Periactin　　　　　　　　　　　f. antihistamines
   ____ 5. guaifenesin, acetylcysteine, potassium
          iodide
   ____ 6. streptomycin, isoniazid, *INH*

G. 1. What are some things you can do to make respiratory drugs work better? Name at least five. Be sure you know *how* they help.

   _____
   _____
   _____
   _____

2. Extra fluids should be given with most antitussives and expectorants. Why?

   _____
   _____
   _____
   _____

Drugs for the Respiratory System 217

H. Matching.

___ 1. positioning the patient so that clogged mucous is drawn out by gravity
___ 2. clapping the patient's back or chest to loosen mucous
___ 3. machine that helps a patient breathe by artificial means
___ 4. device that produces a mist for inhalation
___ 5. may cause drowsiness as a side effect
___ 6. to be given with lots of fluids
___ 7. should not be swallowed

a. expectorants
b. antihistamines
c. nebulizer
d. percussion
e. postural drainage
f. ventilator
g. nose drops and mists

ANSWERS TO EXERCISES

A. Fill in the blanks
  1. respiration
  2. dust and bacteria
  3. pharynx
  4. larynx
  5. epiglottis
  6. trachea
  7. bronchi
  8. bronchioles
  9. alveoli
  10. oxygen (O_2), carbon dioxide (CO_2)
  11. 18 (or 16–20)
  12. diaphragm
  13. stethoscope
  14. sputum or phlegm
  15. nebulizer or atomizer

B. Respiratory symptoms
  You would look for coughing, appearance of sputum (e.g., hemoptysis), hoarseness, breathing disturbances, abnormal sounds, chest pain, anorexia, fatigue, fever, flaring nostrils, sucking in of the chest with each breath, or similar symptoms.

C. Definitions
  1. pertaining to the lungs
  2. breathlessness or difficulty in breathing
  3. rapid breathing
  4. stopped breathing
  5. breathing too rapidly or deeply, hyperventilation
  6. same as hyperpnea
  7. membranes lining the lungs and lung cavities
  8. symptoms returning in worse form after a drug dose has worn off

D. Respiratory disorders
  1. tuberculosis
  2. asthma
  3. emphysema
  4. bronchitis
  5. pneumonia
  6. rhinitis

E. Fill in the blanks
   1. suppress coughing.
   2. thin and break up sputum so that it can be coughed up.
   3. dry the mucous membranes and reduce swelling.
   4. relax the smooth muscles and expand the bronchioles.
   5. block the effects of histamine (i.e., shrink blood vessels, relax bronchial muscles).
F. Matching
   1. d
   2. a
   3. b
   4. f
   5. e
   6. c
G. Short answers
   1. Give medications on time. Explain effects to patients. Put patients in sitting or leaning position. Remove mucus from the air passages. Catch changes in the patient's condition early. Do not rush patients, causing added anxiety. Give the proper amounts of fluids, especially with antitussives and expectorants. Humidify the air. Give hard candy or other demulcents to soothe the throat. Eliminate smoke, dust, fumes.
   2. Most expectorants and antitussives work more effectively when the respiratory secretions are thinned out or diluted.
H. Matching
   1. e
   2. d
   3. f
   4. c
   5. b
   6. a
   7. g

PRACTICE PROCEDURE

PAINT OR SPRAY MEDICATION ONTO MUCOUS MEMBRANE OF MOUTH OR THROAT

Equipment:
- Physician's medication order, Kardex, medicine card, or medication record
- Medication in atomizer, plastic spray bottle, or tube applicator
- Flashlight, tongue blade, and cotton-tipped applicator
- Medication tray or cart with appropriate charts and records.

_____ 1. Set up medications. Check for the "five rights."

_____ 2. Wash your hands.

_____ 3. Identify the patient, explain the procedure, and assist the patient into position for medication administration (either sitting up or lying down).

_____ 4. Apply medication as follows (Figure 9-12):
- Tilt head backward and open mouth.
- Locate affected area visually. Use a tongue blade and small flashlight to find the area.
- Spray or paint on the medication directly on the affected area. For painting, use a cotton-tipped applicator. Do not apply medication blindly, but confine it to the affected area.

_____ 5. Assist patient back into a comfortable position.

_____ 6. Instruct patient not to eat or drink for a certain period of time. Allow patient to gargle with a mouthwash after a sufficient period of time for absorption.

_____ 7. Chart the administration of medications.

_____ 8. Wash your hands.

_____ 9. Return equipment and charts to proper location.

Demonstrate this procedure for the instructor or the nurse in charge.

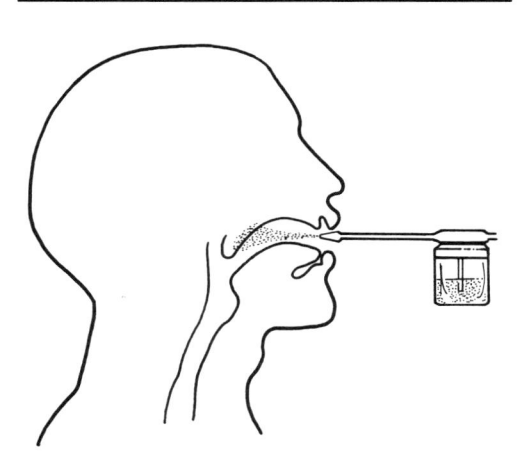

Figure 9-12 Spraying medication on the back of the throat.

PRACTICE PROCEDURE

INSTILL NOSE DROPS OR NASAL SPRAY
Equipment:
- Medication orders for nose drops or nasal spray
- Medication record, medicine cards, or Kardex
- Nose drops, nasal spray
- Cart or tray with appropriate charts and records.
- Tissue wipes

____ 1. Set up medications. Check for the "five rights."

____ 2. Wash your hands.

____ 3. Identify the patient. Explain the procedure. Warm the nose drops to body temperature by holding them in your hand or placing them in a bottle of warm water.

____ 4. Assist the patient into the proper position for administration. For nose drops, the patient should lie on his or her back, with the head extended beyond the edge of the bed or with a pillow under the shoulders. Support the head with your hand to avoid straining the neck muscles. The head should be either tilted back at a right angle to the body or tilted back and to one side, depending on the affected area (Figure 9-13).

____ 5. Administer nasal medication.

Nose drops
- Measure correct dosage on marked dropper.
- Hold the dropper upright just above the nostril.
- Drop the medication into one nostril. Repeat with the other nostril if ordered.
- Keep the patient in the same position for at least 5 minutes for proper absorption.
- Assist the patient back into a comfortable position. Give tissue wipes to catch any flow from the nose.

Nasal spray
- Place patient in sitting position. Have the patient breath through the nose with the mouth open.
- Insert the tip of the bottle into the nose, taking care not to touch the mucous membrane. Sqeeze the bottle 2 or 3 times quickly.
- Wipe any excess medication from the nose.

Figure 9-13 Positions for instilling nose drops.

___ 6. Give further instructions to the patient according to package directions or physician's orders.
___ 7. Chart medication administration. Tell whether you treated one or both nostrils.
___ 8. Wash your hands.
___ 9. Return equipment and charts to proper location.

Demonstrate this procedure for the instructor or the nurse in charge.

REPRESENTATIVE DRUGS FOR THE RESPIRATORY SYSTEM

CATEGORY, NAME[a], AND ROUTE	USES AND DISEASES	ACTIONS	USUAL DOSE[b] AND SPECIAL INSTRUCTIONS	SIDE EFFECTS AND ADVERSE REACTIONS
Antitussives/Expectorants				
Narcotic:				
Codeine Oral IM IV SC	Antitussive	Suppresses cough	10–20 mg q 4–6 hours. Do not exceed 120 mg in 24 hours.	Nausea, vomiting, constipation, dizziness, palpitations, drowsiness
Nonnarcotic:				
Diphenhydramine hydrochloride (Benylin) Oral	Temporary relief of cough due to minor throat and bronchial irritation	Suppressant for minor coughs due to the common cold	10 ml (two tsp) every 4 hours not to exceed 12 tsp in 24 hours	Drowsiness, excitability, especially in children
Benzonatate (Tessalon) Oral	Coughing in acute and chronic respiratory conditions	Inhibits cough reflex, relieves tightness of chest	100 mg TID to be swallowed whole; do not chew or break perles (beads). To stimulate productive cough, give ample fluids, moisten air, avoid smoke and fumes	Sedation, nasal congestion, headache, mild dizziness, numbness in chest
Acetylcysteine (Mucomyst) Inhalant	As adjuvant therapy for patients with abnormal, viscid, mucous secretions	Lowers the viscosity of mucus	Dosage individualized	Stomatitis, nausea, vomiting, drowsiness, clamminess, bronchoconstriction
Decongestants				
Phenylephrine (Neo-Synephrine) Topical	Nasal congestion, allergic rhinitis, sinusitis	Shrinks blood vessels to reduce swelling of mucous membranes	Nasal spray: 1 or 2 sprays into each nostril q 3–4 hours, depending on strength of solution. Drops: 2 or 3 drops into each nostril q 3–4 hours, depending on strength	Irritability, insomnia, rebound congestion, dizziness, nervousness, palpitations, dryness of mucous membranes
Phenylpropanolamine (Propagest) Oral	Nasal congestion	Vasoconstriction and nasal decongestion	25 mg q 3–4 hours or 50 mg q 6–8 hours, not to exceed 150 mg/day; 75-mg sustained-release tablet q 12 hours	Headache, nervousness, nausea, rapid pulse, dizziness
Oxymetazoline (Afrin) Nasal spray	Nasal congestion	Vasoconstriction, mucous membrane constriction	2 or 3 drops or sprays of 0.05% solution in each nostril two times a day, morning and evening	Stinging, headache, restlessness, arrhythmias
Antihistamines				
Promethazine (Phenergan) Oral	Symptoms of hay fever and allergy	Provides antihistaminic action	25 mg at bedtime or 12.5 mg before meals and at bedtime; dosage can be individualized	Sedation, blurred vision, dryness of mouth, possible confusion, hypotension

REPRESENTATIVE DRUGS FOR THE RESPIRATORY SYSTEM

CATEGORY, NAME[a], AND ROUTE	USES AND DISEASES	ACTIONS	USUAL DOSE[b] AND SPECIAL INSTRUCTIONS	SIDE EFFECTS AND ADVERSE REACTIONS
Antihistamines — continued				
Chlorpheniramine (Teldrin) Oral	Symptoms of hay fever, colds, and allergies	Dries mucous membranes	2–4 mg q 4–6 hours; included in many combination products (e.g., Alerest, Contac, Ornade)	Dryness of mouth, drowsiness, dizziness, nausea
Terfenadine (Seldane) Oral	Symptoms of colds and allergies	Provides antihistaminic action	60 mg twice daily	Fewer side effects than many other antihistamines
Bronchodilators				
Theophylline (Elixophyllin) Oral	Bronchial asthma, bronchitis, emphysema	Relaxes smooth muscle of bronchioles, dilates pulmonary vessels, stimulates respiration	400–900 mg daily in divided doses; give oral form with full glass of water; may be given with food to avoid upset stomach	Headache, restlessness, nausea, insomnia, irritability
Isoproterenol (Isuprel) Inhalation Oral IV Sublingual	Bronchial asthma, bronchitis, emphysema	Relaxes smooth muscle of bronchioles	Sublingual: 10 mg TID or QID, up to 60 mg per day, adjusted individually. Inhalation: 1 or 2 inhalations 4–6 times daily; start with one inhalation, follow with second inhalation in 3–5 minutes if no relief. Rinse mouth with water between doses to prevent throat irritation	Flushing, palpitations, chest pain, dry mouth, restlessness, insomnia, pinkish color of saliva
Epinephrine (Primatene Mist) Inhalation	Bronchodilation	Relaxes smooth muscles of bronchioles, dilates pulmonary vessels	1 inhalation, wait at least 1 minute; if not relieved, use once more; do not repeat for at least 4 hours; if still no relief, call physician	Nervousness, restlessness, tachycardia
Antitubercular Drugs				
Isoniazid (INH) Oral	Tuberculosis	Bactericidal, interferes with lipid and nucleic acid biosynthesis	Used in conjunction with effective antitubercular agents, rifampin, streptomycin; 5 mg/kg/day (up to 300 mg total) in a single dose	Peripheral neuropathy most common adverse effect (dose related), nausea, vomiting, and epigastric distress, hepatitis
Streptomycin Oral	Mycobacterium tuberculosis	Interferes with normal protein synthesis	IM only, 1 g/day with other antitubercular drugs	Ototoxicity, nausea, vomiting, vertigo, numbness of face, rash, fever, edema involving skin, blood problems

[a] Brand names given in parentheses are examples only. Check current drug references for a complete listing of available trade name products.

[b] Average adult doses are given. However, dosages are determined by a physician and vary with the purpose of the therapy and the particular patient. The doses presented in this text are for general information only.

Unit 10

Drugs for the Nervous and Sensory Systems

In this unit you will learn how the nervous system coordinates the systems of the body and responds to changes inside and outside the body. You will learn how the sense receptors pick up information about the environment, and what organs and structures are involved. You will become familiar with the disorders that affect the nervous and sensory systems, the types of drugs that are used to treat them, and how to administer the drugs properly.

In this unit, you will learn to:

- Name the two main divisions of the nervous system and their parts.
- State the basic functions of the autonomic nervous system.
- List the major sense receptors and tell what they do.
- Identify the external parts of the eye and ear.
- Give the correct medical terms for symptoms of nervous and sensory system disorders.
- Recognize descriptions of the major nervous system disorders and disorders of the eye and ear for which medications are given.
- Describe the actions and give examples of the following drug groups: cerebral stimulants, respiratory stimulants, antidepressants, analgesics, sedative/hypnotics, anticonvulsants, antipsychotics, and antianxiety drugs.
- Tell whether each drug group above is a type of CNS stimulant or CNS depressant.
- Follow general instructions for administering sedative/hypnotics, pain medications, long-term medications, stimulants, emergency drugs, and eye and ear medications.
- Identify drugs that are often involved in drug abuse.
- Follow proper procedures for instilling eyedrops, eye ointments, and ear drops.

THE NERVOUS AND SENSORY SYSTEMS

The brain, the spinal cord, and the nerves coordinate body functions. Together they make up the nervous system. Closely related to the nervous system is the sensory system. This is composed of the eyes, the ears, the nose, the tongue, and several other structures that pick up sensory information.

The function of the nervous and sensory systems is to note changes within the body and in the outside environment. The nerves and special sense organs feel these changes and send messages about them to the brain. The brain interprets the messages and decides on an appropriate set of actions. The brain then sends out "action messages," which are relayed by the nerves to various parts of the body. The brain's messages can involve voluntary actions (walking, talking, etc.), feelings (fear, anger, love, etc.), or automatic actions (breathing, heartbeat, blood vessel contraction, etc.). In this way, the body is able to respond in a coordinated way to the constantly changing conditions, both within and without.

The nervous system has two main parts: the **central nervous system** (CNS) and the **peripheral nervous system** (Figure 10-1). The CNS consists of the brain and the spinal cord. The peripheral nervous system is made up of the nerves which connect the CNS to all parts of the body.

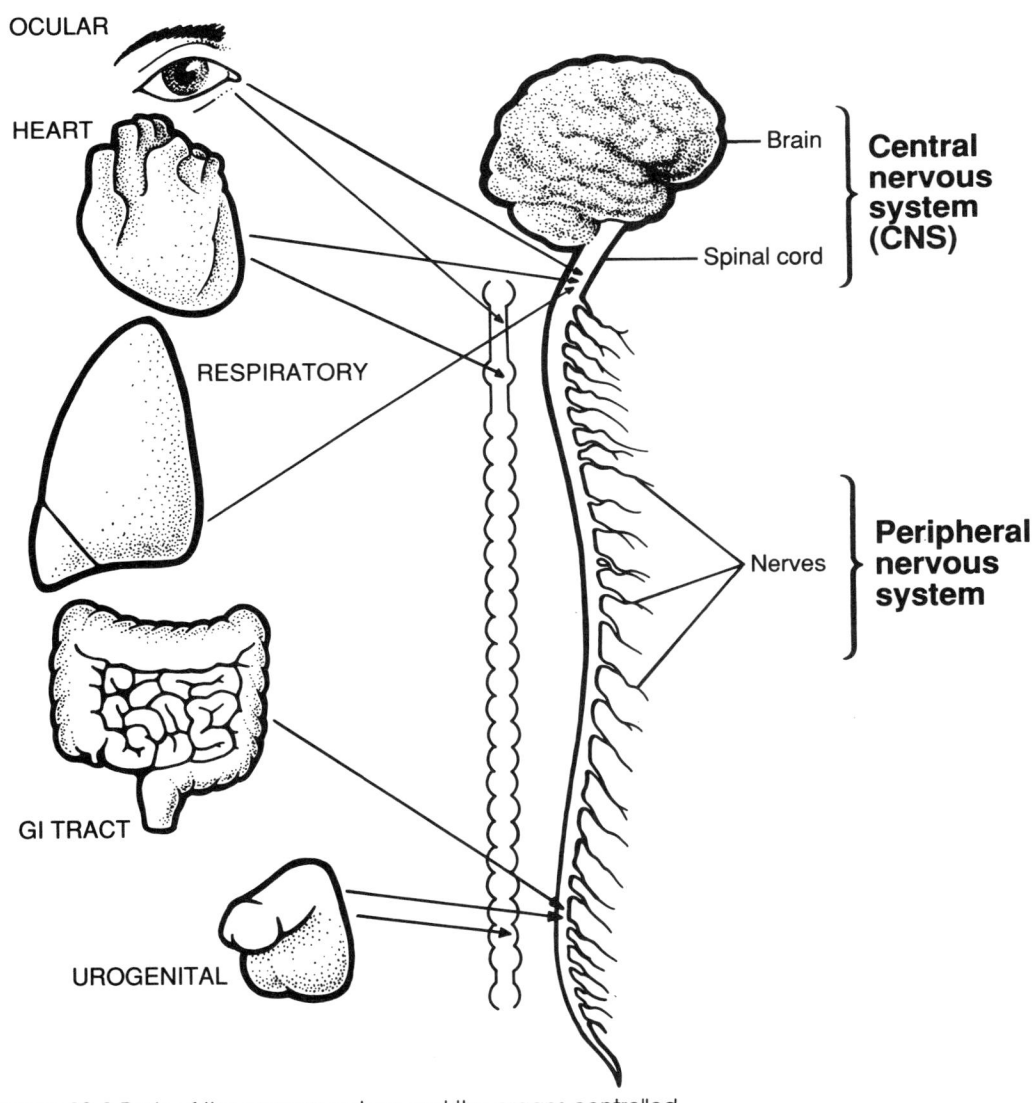

Figure 10-1 Parts of the nervous system and the organs controlled.

VOCABULARY

acetylcholine: special chemical in the end of neurons

acoustic: pertaining to hearing or sound

amphetamines: group of stimulant drugs that are often abused

analgesic: drug that relieves pain

anesthesia: unconsciousness or numbness brought on by drugs in preparation for surgery

anticonvulsant: drug that prevents seizures

antipsychotic: depressant drug that calms agitated, destructive psychotic behavior

antipyretic: drug that reduces fever

autonomic: automatic, reflexlike

barbiturates: group of depressant drugs used as sedative/hypnotics and anesthetics

benzodiazepines: group of antianxiety drugs

bradykinesia: slowness of movement

cerebral: pertaining to the brain

cerebrovascular accident (CVA): hemorrhage or thromboembolism in the brain; also called **stroke**

cerumen: earwax

CNS: central nervous system

coma: sleeplike state from which the patient cannot be awakened

conjunctiva: mucous membranes lining the eye sockets and eyelids

conjunctival sac: gutter or pouch formed by the eyelid

convulsion: seizure involving uncontrolled large-muscle movements

cranial: pertaining to the skull

depression: psychological condition involving sense of worthlessness or hopelessness, resulting in inability to carry out normal activities

diplopia: double vision

dyskinesia: impairment of power of voluntary movements

eardrum: round disk that vibrates and transmits sound from the outer ear to the middle ear

extrapyramidal: refers to a group of clinical disorders that are characterized by abnormal involuntary movements of the muscles; e.g., Parkinson's disease

hypnotic: drug that produces sleep by depressing the CNS

hypoxia: lack of oxygen in the tissues, revealed by tremors or convulsions

impulse: electrochemical message transmitted by nerve cells

insomnia: sleeplessness, or inability to fall asleep or stay asleep

lacrimal gland: gland that produces tears

meninges: three layers of membranes covering the brain and spinal cord

myelin sheath: insulating covering of the nerve cells

narcotics: group of analgesic drugs whose use can lead to physical dependence

neuron: nerve cell

olfactory: pertaining to the sense of smell

optic: pertaining to the eyes or sight

otic: pertaining to the ear

paralysis: inability to move the muscles

parasympathetic nervous system: that part of the autonomic nervous system concerned with the conservation of body energy and bringing the body back to normal conditions

peripheral nervous system: the thoracolumbar (sympathetic) and craniosacral (parasympathetic) divisions of the autonomic nervous system as well as the sensory and motor nervous system and all the nerves of the body that come and go to the brain and spinal cord

psychosis: severe psychological disorder in which the patient loses touch with reality

receptor: receiver of sensory information about changes inside and outside the body

sedative: drug that calms by depressing brain activity

seizure: temporary loss of consciousness during which there is overactivity of part of the brain

sensory: pertaining to the senses (smell, taste, hearing, sight, feeling)

spinal cord: part of the CNS; carries messages between the brain and the peripheral nerves

stupor: state of mental dullness, confusion, or being in a daze

sympathetic nervous system: that part of the autonomic nervous system concerned with the expenditure of energy

synapse: gap between neurons

tardive: late appearing

tinnitus: ringing in the ears

tranquilizer: depressant drug that produces feelings of calm without dulling brain activity

tremor: trembling, shaking

vertigo: dizziness, whirling feeling in the head

visceral: pertaining to the internal organs in the abdominal cavity

The Nerves

Nerves are bundles of nerve cells bound together by connective tissue. The individual nerve cells, called **neurons**, have rounded cell bodies containing a nucleus, but their cytoplasm stretches out into long, thin fibers with many branches (Figure 10-2). Neuron fibers can be as long as 3 feet (about 1 meter). They connect with other neurons to form a complex wiring system linking the CNS to all parts of the body.

Like an elaborate set of telephone lines, neurons have the ability to transmit messages or **impulses**. This is done by means of special chemicals (**acetylcholine**, *as'e-til-ko'len*, and **norepinephrine**, *nor'ep-i-nef'rin*) in the ends of neurons and in the gaps (**synapse**, *sin'aps*) between them. Many of the drugs that affect the nervous system are designed to increase or decrease the concentration of these chemicals.

Nerve impulses travel along the nerve pathways at all times so that the brain and body parts are in constant communication. Some neurons are specialized for transmitting messages *to* the CNS; others are specialized for carrying messages *away from* the CNS to various tissues and organs of the body.

The Brain and the Spinal Cord (CNS)

The brain is the control center for all body functions. It consists of the **cerebral** (*ser'e-bral*) **cortex**, the **cerebellum** (*ser'e-bel'um*), and the **brain stem** (Figure 10-3). As Figure 10-3 shows, different parts of the brain have special functions to carry out. Most of our conscious thought processes—plus our speech, hearing, and sight—are controlled by the cerebrum. The unconscious brain activity, balance, muscle coordination, and gland stimulation are regulated in the brain stem and the cerebellum.

The spinal cord is attached to the brain stem and passes from the neck down to the

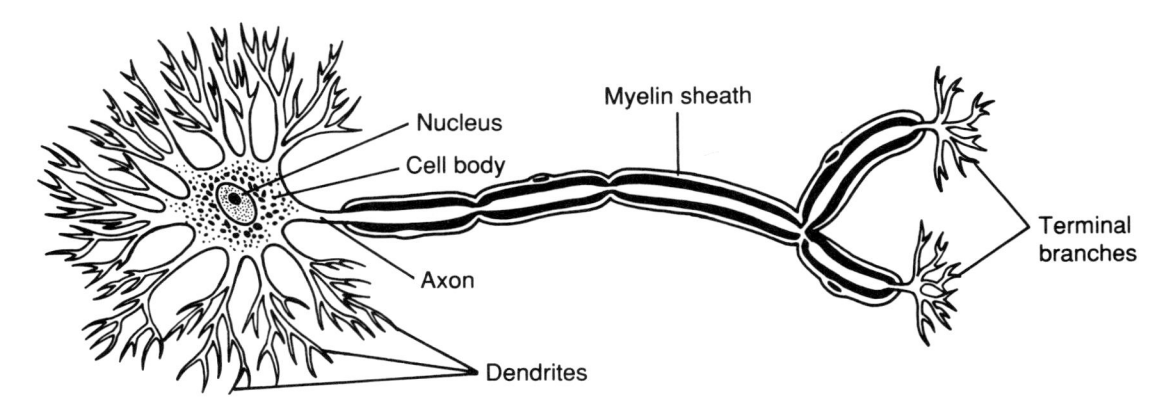

Figure 10-2 Parts of a nerve cell.

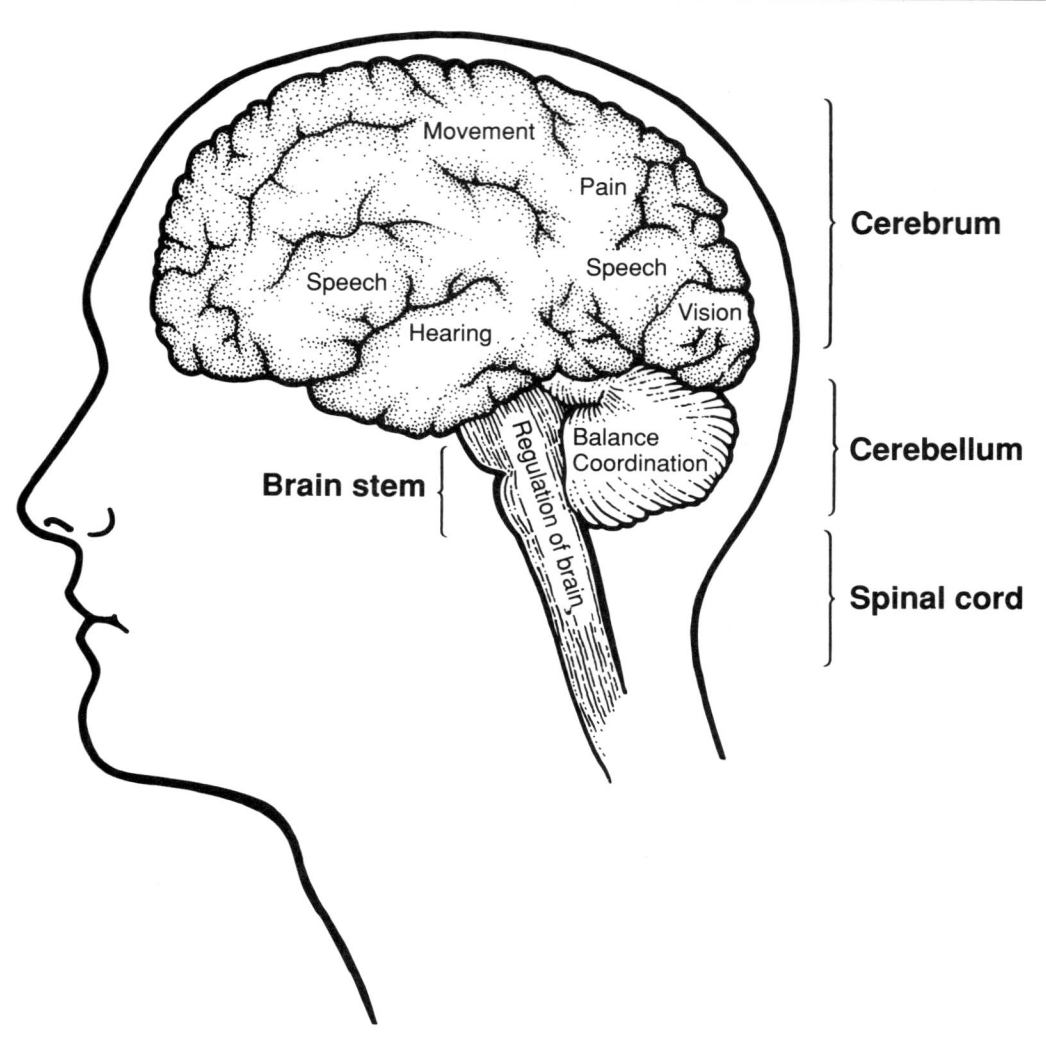

Figure 10-3 The brain as control center.

lower back. It acts as a reflex center and as a pathway for impulses to and from the brain.

The Autonomic Nervous System

Many of the brain's functions are carried on automatically without our being aware of them. It would be distracting, to say the least, if we had to remind ourselves to breathe 18 times a minute, or if we were constantly aware of the clothing touching our skin. The brain is continually receiving impulses from these areas, but it shuts off our attention from most of them so that we can focus on more important matters. Some functions are regulated, not by the brain, but by a network of peripheral nerves called the **autonomic nervous system**. The primary function of this system is to regulate the heartbeat and the smooth muscles in our blood vessels and gastrointestinal tract.

The autonomic nervous system (ANS) includes six visceral systems: digestive, respiratory, urinary, genital, endocrine, and vascular. The ANS is made up of the peripheral system and the central control centers. The peripheral system is composed of the thoracolumbar (sympathetic) and craniosacral (parasympathetic) divisions.

Sympathetic or Thoracolumbar Division—This part of the ANS is concerned with the use of energy. Under conditions of stress, it prepares the body for meeting an emergency by producing epinephrine. This agent speeds up the heart rate and raises the blood pressure. The bronchial tubes dilate to allow more oxygen to enter the body and the digestive system is slowed by the inhibition of peristalsis. With these changes, the body is ready for action. For this reason, the sympathetic portion of the ANS is called the "flight or fight" system.

Parasympathetic or Craniosacral Division—This part of the system restores and conserves body energy and brings the body back to normal conditions. It works just the opposite of the sympathetic division.

The Senses

Our ability to feel, see, hear, taste, and smell things around us is due to very special nerve cells called **sense receptors**. They are specialized to pick up only specific sensory messages. For example, some pick up color, some pick up feelings of pressure, others respond only to odors. It is up to the brain to figure out what the messages mean, according to which receptors sent the messages.

We are used to thinking of only five senses—sight, hearing, smell, taste, and touch. But there are other senses as well, including pressure, pain, temperature, body position, thirst, and hunger. Some types of sensory receptors are found in only certain parts of the body or in specialized organs such as the eyes and the ears. Other types of sensory receptors are spread throughout the body.

The Eye—The eye is a group of tissues that are specialized to permit vision. It is housed in a bony eye socket and is surrounded by fatty tissue and muscles that serve to protect and move the eye. An **eyelid** covers the outer eye. Lashes on the eyelid help to keep dust and dirt from entering the eye. At the edge of the eyelid is a **lacrimal** (*lak'ri-mal*) **gland**, which produces tears to keep the eye moist and wash away dust particles. Tears are drained off through the tear **ducts** into the nose. The eye sockets and the eyelids are lined with mucous membranes called the **conjunctiva** (*kon'jawk-ti'vah*).

The eye itself is made up of three cell layers: the **sclera**, the **choroid layer**, and the **retina**. Within these layers there are many parts that work together to produce sight (Figure 10-4). Special encased fluids (the *humors*) give the eyes their round shape and allow light to pass through them. The **cornea**, the **iris**, the **pupil**, and the **lens** act like a camera and project patterns of light and dark onto the retina at the back of the eye. The **optic nerves** (one from each eye) carry information about these patterns to the brain. The brain then codes the information into moving pictures.

The Ear—The ear is a complex organ designed for hearing. It also plays a part in the body's sense of balance. It has three basic parts: the external ear, the middle ear, and the inner ear (Figure 10-5). The

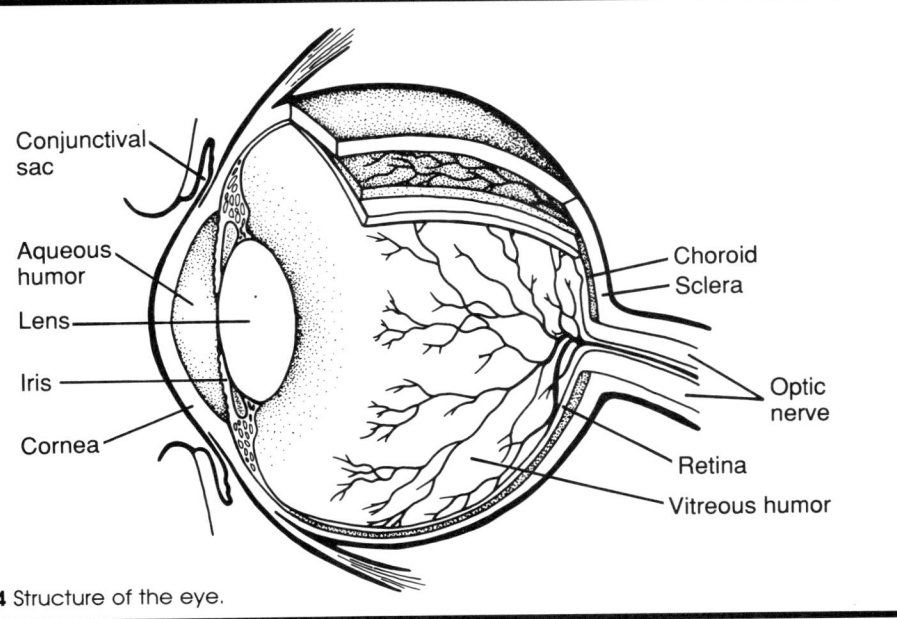

Figure 10-4 Structure of the eye.

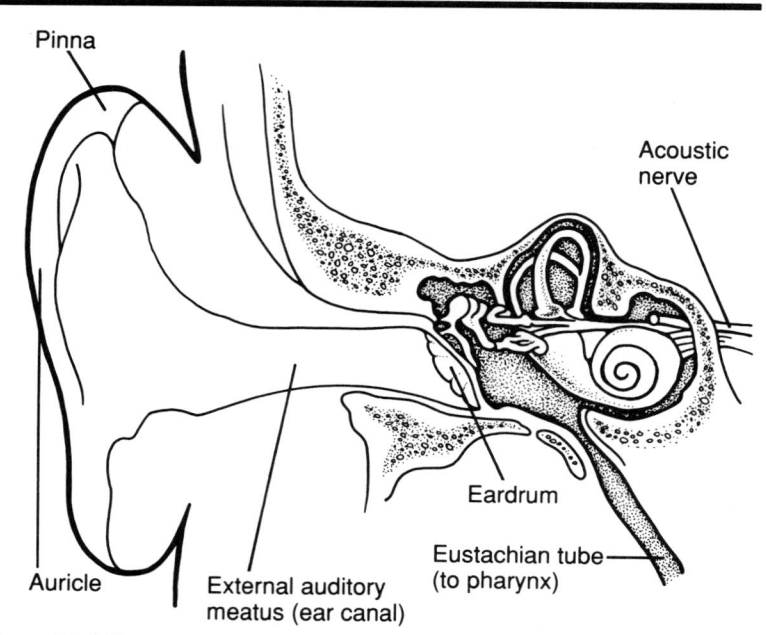

Figure 10-5 Structure of the ear.

external ear consists of an outer **auricle** that projects from the head and an ear canal called the **external auditory meatus**. Ceruminous glands in the external ear produce wax, or **cerumen** (*se-roo'men*). Small hairs in the canal move this wax toward the outer opening. The wax protects the ear by trapping foreign materials and dust.

Hearing begins when the external ear picks up sound waves from the environment. The ear canal carries the sound waves to the **eardrum**, which vibrates with the sounds. The vibrations of the eardrum are picked up by three tiny bones in the middle ear. These bones transmit the vibrations to specialized hearing cells in the inner ear. These cells are linked to the brain by means of the **acoustic nerve**. Other cells in the inner ear detect changes in body position and therefore help to regulate balance.

The Nose—The upper part of the nasal cavity is lined with **olfactory** cells that perform the function of smelling. These cells are connected to the **olfactory nerve** leading to the brain. The brain interprets messages from the olfactory cells as odors.

The Tongue—The tongue contains taste-sensitive cells inside oval-shaped **taste buds**. Dissolved foods and liquids stimulate the taste buds to send messages to the brain by way of the **glossopharyngeal nerves** and **facial nerves**. Taste buds on different parts of the tongue detect different tastes: sweet, sour, salty, and bitter. The olfactory cells of the nose also assist in the sense of taste because the aroma of foods is an important part of taste. A person who cannot smell properly also cannot taste properly.

Other Sense Receptors—Receptors for hunger are located in the stomach ("hunger pangs" come from these receptors). Receptors for thirst seem to be centered in the mouth, nose, and throat. A number of other sense receptors are widely spread throughout the body. These are the receptors that feel pressure, touch, heat and cold, pain, and body position.

Aging of the Nervous System

For healthful living, there must be functional nerve pathways and responsive receptors within the CNS and the peripheral nervous system. But, unfortunately, aging brings structural and functional changes to the human nervous system. Changes develop, and some nerve cells may die. Therefore, there are decreases in reception and conduction and reflex reaction. Reflexes first may become sluggish and then may disappear completely. These changes result in varying degrees of muscular incoordination, paralysis, and asthenia (weakness). Sensory preceptors are less reactive unless the stimulus is much stronger.

NERVOUS AND SENSORY SYSTEM DISORDERS

Almost any disease or body injury is liable to affect the nervous system in some way. There are many signs that show that the nervous system is being affected (Figure 10-6). These signs do not always mean that the nervous system itself is malfunctioning or diseased. They can signal a drug overdose or side effects, a psychological disorder, or a problem elsewhere in the body. Pain, for example, is a danger signal picked up by sensory receptors to alert the brain of a possible injury.

Some other signs that the nervous system is being affected by disease or drugs are: trembling (**tremor**); dizziness (**vertigo**); loss of muscle control; dry mouth; blurred vision; inability to move (**paralysis**); unusual postures and body movements; convulsions; deep sleep from which a person cannot be roused (**coma**); being

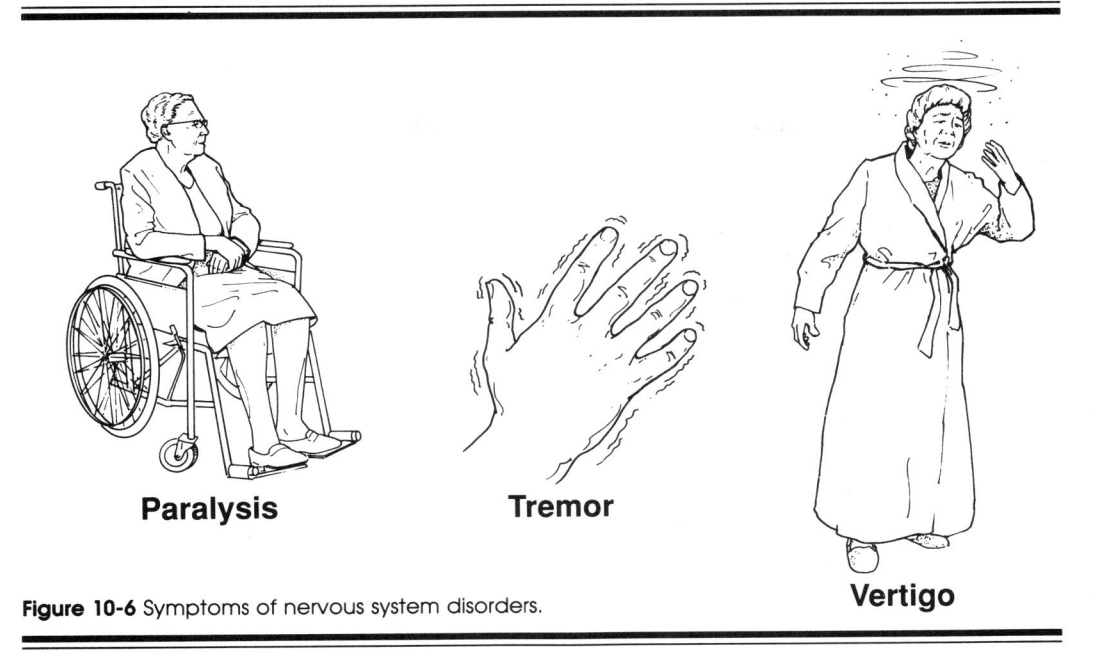

Figure 10-6 Symptoms of nervous system disorders.

"in a daze" (**stupor**); irritability, excitation, agitation, restlessness, and/or sleeplessness (**insomnia**); nausea; headache; speech difficulties; and changes in pulse, respiration, and pupil size.

The major nervous system disorders for which drugs are given are described below. The causes of many of these diseases are unknown or poorly understood, and drug treatment in many cases is based on what seems to work best for particular patients. Research is underway to find better drug treatments that will cure or control symptoms without harmful side effects.

Parkinson's Disease

This disease slowly destroys a small nerve center at the base of the brain that is responsible for body movement. The classic symptoms are shaking of arms and legs (**tremor**), stiffness (**rigidity**), and slowness of movement (**bradykinesia**). Tremor makes it hard to do simple tasks like eating and writing. Rigidity can lead to a bent posture, difficulty in walking, deformities of the hands and feet, and problems with keeping balance. There are treatments in the form of special medicines (antiparkinsonian agents) and physical therapy. Physical therapy is important to keep the muscles functioning despite their stiffness. Massage, stretching, and overall exercise help to keep the disease from completely crippling the patient.

Myasthenia Gravis

This is a chronic disease in which the muscles, especially those of the eyes and throat, become tired easily and take a long time to recover. It is thought to be caused by a chemical deficiency in the junction between these muscles and the nerves that control them. Removal of the thymus and use of the drug neostigmine seem to restore some muscle power, but a cure for this disease is still being sought.

Multiple Sclerosis

Multiple sclerosis (MS) is a disease that attacks the outer covering (**myelin sheath**) of the nerves. Once the myelin sheath is gone, the nerves are unable to conduct impulses. Multiple sclerosis can attack anywhere in the body: brain, spinal cord, or peripheral nerves. The symptoms depend on which nerves are damaged and are usually intermittent with lengthy remissions. They include paralysis, blurring of vision, speech problems, unsteady walk, and numbness. The cause and cure of MS remain unknown. Corticosteroids may help for unclear reasons.

Epilepsy

Epilepsy is a set of disorders that cause periodic **seizures**. Seizures are temporary losses of consciousness caused by overactivity of the nerve signals in a part of the brain. The origins of these seizures can be injuries, infections, irritations, or interrupted blood flow to the brain. In "grand mal" epilepsy, the epileptic patient suffers **convulsions** during seizures. During convulsions, the large muscles tighten and twitch uncontrollably. There are several other types of epilepsy with less severe types of seizures, depending on which part of the brain is affected. Most epilepsy is controllable with medications that prevent seizures (anticonvulsants).

Epileptic patients must take their medications regularly and on time. A missed or late dose may result in a seizure. Teaching the patient the importance of regularity is part of your responsibility as a giver of medications.

Cerebrovascular Accident (CVA)

This condition is more commonly known as **stroke**. It is a loss in the supply of blood to a part of the brain. The cause can be a cerebral thrombus or embolus or a hemorrhage in a part of the brain.

Signs of Stroke

- memory loss
- dizziness (vertigo)
- headache
- fainting
- blurred vision
- speech difficulty
- partial paralysis

Stroke is treated with surgery or with anticoagulants and vasodilators to prevent further clotting and increase the blood flow to the brain (see Unit 8).

Tumors

Any abnormal growth in the brain is dangerous, even though it might not be cancerous (malignant). This is because the brain is encased in a hard covering, the skull. Any growth or swelling presses on the healthy parts of the brain, causing damage or malfunctions. Surgery, antineoplastics, and radiation (see Unit 6) are three possible treatments for brain tumors. Diuretics and corticosteroids may be used to reduce edema.

Infections and Inflammations

Infections and inflammations have specific names depending on which part of the nervous system they attack. Inflammation of the brain is called **encephalitis** (*en'sef-ah-li'tis*). Inflammation of the linings of the brain and the spinal cord (meninges) is called **meningitis** (*men'in-ji'tis*). Nerve inflammations are called **neuritis** and are characterized by weakness, abnormal sensations, temporary paralysis, and loss of reflexes. **Neuralgia** is a painful condition of the nerves caused by inflammation or irritation. These conditions are treated with pain relievers (analgesics) and with antibiotics if the infection can be identified as not viral.

Eye Disorders

The symptoms of eye disorders include blurred vision or loss of eyesight, pain, bloodshot eyes, abnormally dilated pupils, and more general problems such as nausea and vomiting. Another symptom, **diplopia** (double vision), is frequently a symptom of nervous system disorder. A diagnosis is made using instruments that test vision, measure fluid pressure in the eye, or permit the physician to look inside the eye.

Other than infections of the eye (**conjunctivitis, stye**, etc.), most disorders of the eye call for surgery rather than drug therapy. You may be called on to instill eyedrops or eye ointment (e.g., *Neosporin Ophthalmic* or *Neo-Cortef*) as part of routine care after surgery or in the elderly. Or you may need to instill eyedrops to dilate or constrict the pupil.

Drugs that constrict the pupil are used in the treatment of **glaucoma**, a disorder in which the fluid pressure builds inside the eye and causes blindness. The main drug for the treatment of glaucoma is pilocarpine (*Isopto Carpine*), which promotes drainage of eye fluids (humors). Another drug for lowering intraocular pressure is timolol (*Timoptic*). It is well tolerated and produces fewer and less severe side effects than pilocarpine. A type of diuretic (acetazolamide) is also used to lessen the production of humors.

Drugs that dilate the pupil (mydriatics, such as atropine) are used in preparation for ophthalmic (eye) examinations. They open the pupil so that the physician can look into the eye with a special instrument. The appearance of the retina gives clues to the presence of diseases like atherosclerosis and diabetes, which affect the whole body.

Ear Disorders

Earache, headache, fever, difficulty in hearing, ringing in the ears (**tinnitus**), and dizziness can all signal problems with the ear. Common complaints are "running ear," "impacted ear," swelling, and pain on touching. Hearing tests, special instruments, and looking into the ear with a magnifying apparatus are methods that help determine the cause of the problem.

The main ear disorders for which medication is required are **otitis** (external or middle) and **Meniere's disease**. Otitis is an inflammation of the ear, with pain, congestion, and possibly hearing loss. Such infections and congestion of the middle ear are treated with systemic drugs such as antihistamines and antibiotics.

Meniere's disease is characterized by attacks of dizziness, hearing loss, and tinnitus. Its cause is unknown, and drug therapy is aimed at controlling symptoms.

Topical medications for the outer ear are used to relieve earache, dry up any discharge, soften earwax, or kill insects that enter the ear canal. *Cortisporin Otic* is a topical anti-infective preparation used to reduce inflammation in the outer ear.

Psychological Disorders

Disorders of the thought processes and emotions account for many uses of drugs that affect the nervous system. Psychological disorders range from mild depression or anxiety to severe changes in behavior. Drugs that energize, tranquilize, and control mood swings are among the types used for these diseases. They act by stimulating or depressing the central nervous system (CNS) or specific parts of the brain. Mild tranquilizers, sedatives, and antidepressants are prescribed for people with temporary emotional problems or anxiety. For example, patients who are worried about upcoming surgery or about their disease might be given a mild sedative to help them sleep.

Much more powerful antipsychotic drugs are used to control symptoms in patients with severe behavior changes. These changes include psychotic depression, manic-depressive psychosis, and schizophrenia, which keep the patient from functioning in daily life.

DRUGS THAT AFFECT THE CENTRAL NERVOUS SYSTEM

Nervous system drugs often affect the whole body, since they act on the body's control systems. The way they work is not well understood. They appear to influence the chemical changes that allow nerve impulses to be transmitted between nerve cells.

This unit focuses on drugs that affect mainly the CNS. These are divided into two major categories: **CNS stimulants** and **CNS depressants** (Figure 10-7). Stimulants speed up the cell processes and make it easier for nerve cells to transmit messages. Depressants slow down cell activity and inhibit the passing of nerve impulses. Within these two broad categories are many specific types of drugs.

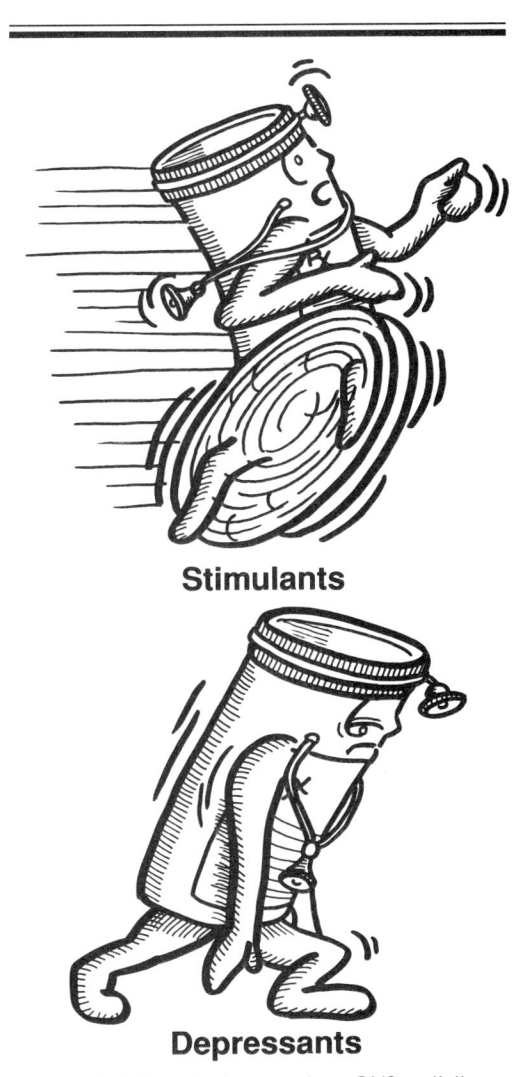

Figure 10-7 Stimulants speed up CNS activity; depressants slow it down.

Some drugs affect the peripheral autonomic nervous system and the automatic regulation of internal organs. These drugs (e.g., epinephrine and atropine) are described in other units (e.g., Units 8 and 9) because they are used in treating disorders affecting other body systems. You will see these drugs referred to in drug references as **sympathomimetic, sympatholytic, parasympathomimetic** or **cholinomimetic** and **parasympatholytic** or **anticholinergic**. The names of the drug categories may be confusing, but just keep in mind that they all affect the unconscious, automatic processes that keep the body functioning.

CNS Stimulants

These stimulants are used for a variety of purposes. They help wake people up in the morning (e.g., caffeine in coffee), relieve depression, counteract overdoses of depressant drugs, counteract sluggishness and apathy in the elderly, and help emphysema patients breathe more effectively. These drugs fall into three categories: cerebral stimulants, respiratory stimulants, and antidepressants. All the CNS stimulants have important side effects, mainly overstimulation or excitement, dizziness, dry mouth, constipation, palpitations, restlessness, and tremors. They are also subject to abuse because they cause euphoria, a false sense of well-being.

Cerebral Stimulants—These drugs speed up brain activity, which in turn speeds up the activities of the whole body. Because of their hazards and abuse potential, amphetamines, a family of stimulants, have extremely limited therapeutic applications. They are used to treat hyperactive children and narcolepsy (recurrent attacks of unwanted and inappropriate sleep).

Another CNS stimulant similar to the amphetamines is methylphenidate (*Ritalin*). It is used to treat hyperactive children as well as withdrawal and apathy in the elderly.

Respiratory Stimulants—These drugs act on the respiratory control center in the brain. They increase the rate and depth of breathing. This effect is desired in such cases as barbiturate overdose, narcotic and carbon dioxide poisoning, shock, and emphysema. Respiratory stimulants are often administered intravenously since a quick response is needed in such emergencies. The main drugs in this category are doxapram hydrochloride (*Dopram*) and spirits of ammonia (used for fainting).

Antidepressants—These drugs intervene in the chemical processes in the brain (Figure 10-8). In so doing, they relieve deep depression. Their mechanism of action is poorly understood.

Figure 10-8 Antidepressants.

One group of antidepressants is called **monoamine oxidase (MAO) inhibitors**. These drugs prevent an enzyme, monoamine oxidase, from metabolizing certain chemicals needed for nerve impulses to pass between neurons. Thus they aid the passage of nerve impulses, which appears to counteract depression. These drugs have dangerous side effects and do not mix well with other drugs and some foods (e.g., cheese, liver, Chianti wine). An example is phenelzine sulfate (*Nardil*).

Another chemical group of antidepressants, the **tricyclic antidepressants**, helps increase the concentration of impulse-transmitting chemicals between neurons. Examples of this group are imip-ramine (*Tofranil*) and amitriptyline (*Elavil*).

Patients should be educated to avoid alcohol, OTC drugs, and restricted foods while on antidepressants. A close watch must be kept for serious side effects, especially changes in blood pressure, and dosages must be carefully individualized.

CNS Depressants

Drugs in this category can either depress the whole CNS (e.g., sedatives) or selectively depress only parts of the nervous system (e.g., pain relievers, tranquilizers, anticonvulsants). Central nervous system depressants are used in the treatment of both physical and mental problems. Like CNS stimulants, these drugs have a high potential for abuse. In addition, many of them can cause physical dependence.

Analgesics—Analgesics are pain-relieving drugs. They relieve pain by either affecting the brain itself or interfering with the ability of pain receptors around the body to send pain messages to the brain. One large group of analgesics is the **narcotics** (Figure 10-9). Along with pain relief, these drugs bring euphoria and a sense of calm; therefore, they are often abused. Examples of narcotic analgesics are morphine, codeine, oxycodone (one ingredient in *Percodan*), meperidine (*Demerol*), methadone, and pentazocine (*Talwin*).

Figure 10-9 Narcotic analgesics.

A common group of **analgesics** has the ability to reduce fever (antipyretic) as well as relieve pain (Figure 10-10). This group includes the familiar drugs aspirin and acetaminophen (*Tylenol*). They reduce fever by eliminating heat through vasodilation and increased respiration. Aspirin also has anti-inflammatory effects, which are put to use in treating musculoskeletal disorders. Analgesic antipyretics are often combined with narcotic analgesics or sedatives in prescription pain relievers—for example, *Tylenol with Codeine*, *Empirin Compound with Codeine*, and *Fiorinal* (butalbital with aspirin and codeine). More re-

Figure 10-10 Analgesics/antipyretics.

cently, ibuprofen, a nonsteroidal anti-inflammatory prescription drug (e.g., *Motrin*) has become available as a nonprescription product (e.g., *Nuprin* and *Advil*). Ibuprofen acts by inhibiting the release of prostaglandin, a substance involved with pain in the body. Ibuprofen is considered one of the three major pain-relieving drugs available without prescription: aspirin, acetaminophen, *and* ibuprofen. Each has analgesic and antipyretic activity, with aspirin and ibuprofen also having anti-inflammatory activity to help reduce swelling.

Nonprescription Pain Relievers: Cautions

aspirin
- may cause GI upset and bleeding
- allergies to aspirin (shortness of breath, skin rash, swelling, hives, asthma, or shock)

acetaminophen
- risk from overdose greater than from either aspirin or ibuprofen
- individuals who have alcoholism, cirrhosis, or other serious liver disease should exercise caution in taking acetaminophen

ibuprofen
- should not be taken by individuals who have had a severe allergic reaction to aspirin

---

Antianxiety and Sedative/Hypnotic Drugs—These drugs have a quieting, calming effect (Figure 10-11).

An older group of sedative/hypnotics is the **barbiturates** (phenobarbital, pentobarbital, secobarbital) which have generally

Figure 10-11 Sedative/Hypnotics.

Figure 10-12 Tranquilizers.

been replaced by newer and more effective drugs. Some uses of barbiturates are to produce sleep, tranquilize, and control seizures (as in epilepsy). They are also used in surgical **anesthesia**.

When used for sleep, barbiturates sometimes cause a drug "hangover" on waking the next morning. This means that the effects of the barbiturates have not yet worn off. Barbiturates very often cause mental confusion in elderly persons.

Antianxiety agents produce feelings of calm without causing confusion or dullness of the thought processes (Figure 10-12). They do not depress the whole CNS, but act selectively on the centers that control a person's mood. They are given in different doses depending on their purpose. Benzodiazepines are important drugs for the management of anxiety and more popular now than the previously used barbiturates. They are used in the management of short-term anxiety, anxiety associated with depression, preoperative apprehension, alcohol withdrawal, insomnia due to anxiety, and irritability in older patients. Some examples are alprazolam (*Xanax*), chlordiazepoxide (*Librium, Libritabs*), lorazepam (*Ativan*), diazepam (*Valium*), halazepam (*Paxipam*), oxazepam (*Serax*), and prazepam (*Centrax*). These drugs may cause drowsiness, so the patient must avoid tasks requiring alertness.

There are many other drugs in the sedative/hypnotic category. Some of the better known drugs are chloral hydrate (*Noctec*), ethchlorvynol (*Placidyl*), meprobamate (*Miltown*), flurazepam (*Dalmane*), and triazolam (*Halcion*).

Antipsychotics—The **antipsychotics** are used to control agitated, hyperactive, destructive mentally ill patients. Examples of antipsychotics are the phenothiazines, including thioridazine (*Mellaril*), trifluoperazine (*Stelazine*), fluphenazine (*Prolixin*), and chlorpromazine (*Thorazine*). Lithium carbonate (*Eskalith, Lithonate, Lithane*) is used for manic depressive psychoses.

The main side effects of antipsychotics are drowsiness, dizziness, and blurred vision. Patients who take tranquilizers must not drink alcoholic beverages because alcohol potentiates (increases the strength or effect of) these drugs. The results can be fatal.

Long-term use of antipsychotics can result in **tardive dyskinesia**, a syndrome of abnormal involuntary stereotyped movements of the face, mouth, tongue, and limbs. This **extrapyramidal** reaction begins with fine wormlike movements of the tongue at rest and facial tics or jaw movements and progresses to such actions as lip smacking, chewing motions, and mouth openings and closings. To prevent the development of tardive dyskinesia, the antipsychotic drug is discontinued, if possible. Most symptoms will usually disappear over several months. The benefits of antipsychotic therapy must be carefully weighed against the risks of developing tardive dyskinesia, which can be permanent.

The product information table at the end of this unit lists uses, actions, doses, and side effects of several representative drugs affecting the nervous and sensory systems.

Anticonvulsants—Anticonvulsants are used to control convulsions and other less serious seizures (Figure 10-13). Convulsions are violent muscle contractions that are not under conscious control. They involve the large muscles of body movement. Convulsions occur as reactions to high fever, to drug overdose, to injury, and for unexplained reasons. (Remember, a disorder in which there are recurring seizures is called **epilepsy**.)

Figure 10-13 Anticonvulsants.

Anticonvulsants work by blocking the nerve impulses that cause convulsions. Anticonvulsants often cause drowsiness, and stimulants can be given to counteract this side effect. Phenytoin (*Dilantin*) is the major anticonvulsant drug. Others are primidone (*Mysoline*), ethosuximide (*Zarontin*), valproic acid (*Depakene*), and carbamazepine (*Tegretol*). Phenobarbital also is commonly used to control seizures.

Antiparkinsonian Agents—Several types of drugs are used to treat Parkinson's disease. Some of them control tremors by interrupting the nerve messages that cause it. Others are especially used for relaxing rigid muscles. Gentle stimulants help to counteract slowness. Levodopa (*Dopar, Larodopa*) appears to work by replacing missing chemicals that transmit messages between nerve cells. A combination of levodopa and carbidopa, *Sinemet*, is widely used because it can be given in smaller doses with fewer side effects than levodopa alone. Other drugs for Parkinson's disease are benztropine (*Cogentin*), trihexyphenidyl (*Artane*), procyclidine (*Kemadrin*), and amantadine (*Symmetrel*).

Dizziness, drowsiness, and blurred vision are common side effects of antiparkinsonian agents. Those that have an antihistaminic effect can cause the mucous membranes of the mouth to dry out. This is helped by giving the patient hard candy or gum or by rinsing the mouth with water.

GIVING MEDICATIONS FOR THE NERVOUS AND SENSORY SYSTEMS

To give medications that affect the nervous system, you will need to know how to administer drugs efficiently and courteously by all the usual routes. In addition, there are specific principles to follow in administering certain types of drugs.

Sedative/Hypnotics

When prescribing these drugs, the physician's concern is to order the right amount so that the patient is quieted and comfortable, but not so much that he or she is in a daze and unable to function normally.

You can make sedatives more effective if you:

- Reduce the noise level in the patient's room. Avoid loud talking. Turn down the television or radio.
- Relax the patient by giving a warm bath or a back rub.
- Listen to the patient's concerns and fears with sympathetic understanding.
- Make sure the patient gets enough exercise. Napping and lack of physical or mental exercise during the day can cause sleep problems at night. You may reduce the need for hypnotics simply by keeping the patient as active as he or she is able to be.

When sedatives are ordered PRN, be sure to ask the patient *why* when he or she requests a sedative. If the reason is pain, sedatives will not help. The patient will need an analgesic to relieve the pain that is interfering with sleep.

Do not be too concerned about the possibility of drug dependence with sedative/hypnotics if a patient is hospitalized for an illness. This is a period of great concern and tension. The patient's worries may be greater because of the unfamiliar surroundings of the hospital ward. Do not withhold PRN medications unless you have made a careful study of the situation. Withholding PRN medications when they are really needed is as bad as giving them too often.

On the other hand, you want to avoid overuse of sedatives. Do not give sedatives just to avoid having to listen to the patient's complaints and worries. Sedatives are no substitute for good nursing care. Also, do not leave sedatives at the bedside to take as needed. Overdose is possible if these drugs are taken too often or all at one time.

Be observant of patients who are taking CNS depressants. Check their vital signs (pulse, blood pressure, respirations, etc.) often and report any great changes. The dosage will need to be changed if a medication depresses the nervous system too much. Drugs such as the narcotics and barbiturates that depress the whole CNS tend to cause respiratory depression (very slow breathing) when an overdose is taken or given.

Look for idiosyncratic responses and drug interactions. Elderly people often become confused while under sedation. Depressant drugs given during the day may unexpectedly potentiate a sedative given at night.

Allow the proper amount of time for drugs to show their effects. The long-acting sedative/hypnotics such as phenobarbital may take 30–60 minutes to give the desired results.

Help protect patients from complications if they are confined to bed and are taking sedatives. Their medication will keep them from moving about. You will need to change their positions often to prevent bedsores and pneumonia. The medications may also dry up the mucous membranes. Lubricate the eyes, the mouth, and the nose to prevent sores caused by dryness. Sugarless chewing gum and rinsing the mouth with water also help to relieve dryness.

Long-Term Medications

Patients on long-term drug therapy to control seizures, Parkinson's disease, or psychological disorders must be watched carefully for signs of toxicity (drug poisoning). Your observations may suggest that the patient needs blood and urine studies, and this may help avoid serious overmedication. Patients need to be educated as to the importance of taking their medicines regularly over a long period of time, even after their symptoms disappear. Patients with Parkinson's disease may have tremors that make it difficult for them to care for themselves and even to take their medicines. You should stress the importance of continued drug treatment despite their difficulties.

Drugs for Pain

To be effective, analgesics must be given on time. The objective is to keep the patient as comfortable as possible. If you wait too long to give the next dose of analgesic, the last dose will have worn off, the patient will suffer needlessly, and the pain will be much harder to control.

Let patients know that the medication you are giving is for pain. The psychological effect of telling them this will make the drug work better (this is the **placebo effect**).

If the pain reliever is a narcotic, remember to discard the unused portion (chart this properly!) and the equipment used to administer it. There should be no chance of anyone else using the leftover medication.

Some of the analgesics have antipyretic (fever-reducing) effects. With these drugs, take the patient's temperature often, give extra liquids, and chart these procedures so that the doctor can review the patient's progress.

Pain medications ordered before surgery must be given on time so that they take effect before the procedure begins. Insist on undisturbed bedrest for the patient after giving a preoperative medication. This will help the medication take effect. Encourage the family to cooperate with your instructions. After surgery, check on the patient often and administer pain medications as needed. The anesthetic does not eliminate the pain of surgery. It just makes the patient drift in and out of consciousness. During conscious moments, the patient may feel pain.

Giving Drugs to Alcoholics

Be conscientious about giving medications to alcoholic patients. The medications provide for their nutritional and psychological needs so that they can recover from their alcoholism. Be sure to explain what drugs you are giving and what they are supposed to do. This will calm the patients' fears and gain their support for the treatment.

Stimulants

Stimulants are often given to drug overdose patients. Some of these patients have taken an overdose of CNS depressants to commit suicide. They must be watched carefully for further suicide attempts.

Dryness in the mouth is a side effect of some stimulants and other CNS drugs. To counteract dryness, suggest the use of hard candy or sugarless gum, or rinse the mouth with water.

Emergency Drugs

Many medical emergencies are treated with drugs that affect the nervous system. Emergency drugs are very powerful, and errors in dosage can be extremely hazardous to the patient. Be certain to check the dosage strength and the route before administering them. As a matter of routine, the supply of emergency drugs should be reviewed often to be sure that they are in good condition and not discolored or expired.

Explain the possible effects of the emergency nervous system drugs to the patient to avoid fear and worry when new symptoms appear. Support the patient's family in emergency situations.

Emergency patients often receive IV infusions. Be careful when moving these patients to avoid letting the fluids pass into surrounding body tissues. Check often to be sure the needle is in the vein.

Psychiatric Patients

The care of psychiatric patients requires special training and knowledge. Medication handlers must fully understand the actions and the long-term side effects of antipsychotic drugs. Along with drug therapy, these patients often receive psychological therapy. As they begin to respond to drug therapy, there is a danger that they may attempt to commit suicide. You must be sure they do not manage to "pocket" their medications inside their cheeks and then spit them out when you are not looking. They may try to save pills in this way in order to take a fatal overdose later. Stay with patients until they have swallowed their oral medications, and watch carefully for signs of toxicity. Never forget to treat these patients kindly and with respect, despite any strange behaviors they may show.

Drug Abuse

Nervous system drugs are very prone to abuse. This is true of aspirin as well as narcotics, sedative/hypnotics, and stimulants. Help to educate patients about the dangers of drug overuse. Support their efforts to understand and cope with their disease so that they do not depend on drugs for their support. Be aware, too, of opportunities for misuse of alcohol and amphetamines in school and industry. Keep informed about how to handle these situations. The most commonly abused drugs are listed here for your information:

- **Hallucinogens (psychedelics)**—LSD, marijuana (e.g., "grass," "pot," "dope"), mescaline, STP, DMT
- **Narcotics**—heroin, methadone, morphine, opium, *Demerol*
- **Sedatives and tranquilizers**—alcohol, barbiturates (e.g., "barbs," "phennies," "sleepees"), *Nembutal, Seconal*
- **Stimulants**—amphetamines (e.g., "pep pills," "bennies"), cocaine, glue

Eye Medications

The linings of the eyelids and eye sockets (conjunctiva) are among the most sensitive mucous membranes in the human body. Absorption through them is rapid, and only mild medications may be used. The lacrimal sac can absorb medication systemically, but this can be avoided by putting pressure on it with your finger for one minute. This is called **digital pressure**.

Eye medications are often given in the form of ophthalmic solutions. These solutions are administered as eyedrops, eyewashes, or baths (irrigations), or on dressings applied over the eyes. Ophthalmic ointments are also common. Ointments keep the medication in contact with the eye for a longer time than the solutions, but they also cause blurriness for a while after application. So as to disturb vision as little as possible, solutions may be given during the day and ointments at night.

Note that some eyedrops require refrigeration. Check the drug label for instructions. Remember, do not put *anything* into the eye unless the container is labeled **"Sterile—for Ophthalmic Use."**

Care must be taken to avoid contaminating eyedrops and ointments. To keep them sterile, do not let the eyedropper or the ointment tube touch a part of the eye. Handle only the rubber part of the dropper. Disposable plastic eyedroppers are available to prevent contamination. Each patient should have a separate bottle or tube of eye medication.

Some eye medications cause stinging and discomfort to the patient. Explain these effects before instilling medications so that the patient does not become alarmed. Medications that dilate the pupils cause sensitivity to light (photophobia). Suggest that patients wear dark glasses until the drug effects have worn off if they are going outside.

Watch for adverse reactions to eye medications: swelling of skin and lids, watery eyes, redness of the eye, dryness of skin surfaces, and cracks in the skin at the corners of the eyes. Chart these signs and report them to the supervisor.

Ear Medications

The outer ear is lined with epidermis and has a protective coating of cerumen (earwax). For this reason, topical ear medications can be stronger than those used on other body cavities. However, if an eardrum is damaged (perforated), the ear must be treated as if it were a mucous membrane.

There are several ways to apply medications to the ear. Drops can be instilled directly into the ear canal, powders can be blown into the ear, and medications can be mixed into ear washes or irrigations. For constant medication, a piece of gauze can be dipped in medicating solution and then placed in the ear. It remains there for several days. The gauze acts as a wick. The outer end is moistened with medicine every so often, and the medicine is drawn through the gauze toward the inner ear.

Before instilling ear medications, the ear canal must be cleaned. This can be done by wiping the surfaces gently with a sterile cotton-tipped applicator. Or it can be done by washing the ear with a syringe and a saline (salt) or alcohol solution. The ear must then be dried thoroughly with warm air.

EXERCISES

A. Fill in the blank with the word or phrase that best completes the statement.

1. The two main divisions of the nervous system are the __central__ nervous system and the __peripheral__ nervous system.

2. The ~~neurons~~ __spinal cord__ carries messages from the peripheral nerves to the brain.

3. The organs of the chest and the abdomen are regulated automatically by a part of the peripheral nervous system called the __autonomic__ nervous system.

4. The __sense__ receptors pick up information about the environment inside and outside the body.

5. Neurons carry __impulses__ to and from the CNS.

B. Match the parts to their definitions.

__e__ 1. tube that drains moisture from the eye
__b__ 2. mucous linings of the eye socket and eyelid
__c__ 3. ear canal
__d__ 4. earwax
__a__ 5. part of the ear that stands out from the head
__f__ 6. gland that produces tears

a. auricle
b. conjunctiva
c. external auditory meatus
d. cerumen
e. tear duct
f. lacrimal

C. Define these terms for nervous system symptoms.

1. tremor __shaking__
2. vertigo __dizziness__
3. paralysis __inability to move__
4. coma __unresponsive__
5. stupor __dazed condition__
6. insomnia __inability to sleep__
7. bradykinesia __slow movements__
8. tinnitus __ringing in ears__
9. diplopia __double vision__

242 Administering Medications

D. Select the disorder that best matches the description. Write the name of the disorder in the blank.

epilepsy
Meniere's disease
Parkinson's disease
stroke or CVA
multiple sclerosis (MS)

meningitis
conjunctivitis
glaucoma
otitis
depression

1. Jackie Palmer went swimming last week in a polluted stream and developed an infection in his right eye. _conjunctivitis_

2. Mr. Brown has trouble getting dressed in the morning because his hands shake so badly. When he walks, he moves very slowly and has trouble keeping his balance. _Parkinson's disease_

3. Dick Fox has blurred vision in his left eye and his left leg is paralyzed. The doctor says it is because the disease has destroyed some of the myelin sheath that covers the nerves. _MS_

4. Mrs. Poston has a sudden hemorrhage in a part of the brain. This causes her to feel dizzy and have difficulty speaking. _CVA_

5. Joan Weiss is taking *Dilantin* regularly. If she were to skip a dose, she knows she might go into convulsions. _epilepsy_

6. Mr. Crane is having an operation to relieve the build up of fluid pressure inside his eye. Without this surgery, he may become blind. _glaucoma_

7. Little Danny has chronic inflammation and congestion in his ears. The doctor is giving him antihistamines and antibiotics to try to clear the ears and prevent hearing loss. _otitis_

8. George Thompson has a serious inflammation of the coverings of the brain and the spinal cord. _meningitis_

9. Alma West has a psychological disorder that keeps her from fully living her life. Without medication, she sits with her head buried in her hands most of the day. But when she takes amitriptyline (e.g., *Elavil*), she is able to function almost normally. _depression_

10. Mrs. Gonzalez has attacks of dizziness, ringing in the ears, and hearing loss. _Meniere's disease_

Drugs for the Nervous and Sensory Systems 243

E. Tell what these types of drugs do; for example, Cerebral stimulants *speed up brain activity which speeds up the whole body.*

1. Respiratory stimulants __increase respirations__
2. Antidepressants _____
3. Analgesics __relieve pain__
4. Antipyretics __reduce fever__
5. Hypnotics _____
6. Anesthetics _____
7. Anticonvulsants _____
8. Antianxiety agents _____
9. Antipsychotics _____

F. Place an S next to the CNS stimulants and a D next to the CNS depressants.

__D__ 1. hypnotics
__D__ 2. sedatives
__S__ 3. antidepressants
__D__ 4. anticonvulsants
__D__ 5. analgesic antipyretics
__D__ 6. narcotics
__D__ 7. barbiturates
__S__ 8. amphetamines
__S__ 9. caffeine
__D__ 10. antianxiety agents
__D__ 11. anesthetics
__D__ 12. antipsychotics

G. Match drug names to drug categories.

__d__ 1. caffeine, methamphetamine, *Ritalin*
__f__ 2. doxapram, spirits of ammonia
__c__ 3. MAO inhibitors, *Elavil*, imipramine
__e__ 4. *Demerol, Percodan*, morphine
__a__ 5. aspirin, acetaminophen
__h__ 6. *Placidyl, Dalmane, Noctec*
__b__ 7. *Dilantin*, valproic acid, phenobarbital
__i / k__ 8. meprobamate, *Librium, Valium*
__g__ 9. *Cortisporin Otic, Neosporin Ophthalmic*, pilocarpine
__j__ 10. levodopa, *Artane*, benztropine
__k__ 11. alprazolam, oxazepam, prazepam
__l__ 12. lithium
__m__ 13. *Prolixin, Stelazine, Mellaril*

a. analgesic antipyretics
b. anticonvulsants
c. antidepressants
d. cerebral stimulants
e. narcotic analgesics
f. respiratory stimulants
g. ear and eye medications
h. sedative/hypnotics
i. antianxiety agents
j. antiparkinsonian agents
k. benzodiazepines
l. antimanic
m. antipsychotic agents

244 Administering Medications

H. List at least three things you can do to make sedative/hypnotics more effective.

_____

_____

_____

I. Fill in the blanks with the word or phrase that best completes the statement.

1. Patients on long-term drug therapy should be encouraged to _____ *med. recs.*

2. They should also be watched for signs of drug *toxicity*.

3. To keep the patient as comfortable as possible, analgesics must be given *on time*.

4. Always *discard* any leftover narcotic and the equipment used to administer it.

5. With analgesic antipyretics, take the patient's *temp*.

6. Emergency drugs are usually potent and errors in dosage can be *fatal*.

7. Eye ointment may cause *blurriness* for a while after application.

8. Before instilling ear medications, the ear canal must be *clean/dry*.

9. For patient comfort, ear drops should be *warmed* in the hand or in warm water.

10. To soothe a dry mouth caused by stimulants or antiparkinsonian agents, give the patient *hard candy* or rinse the mouth with water.

11. Never administer a topical medication to the eyes unless it is labeled *State*.

J. List as many drugs as you can that are prone to drug abuse.

_____

_____

_____

_____

ANSWERS TO EXERCISES

A. Fill in the blanks
 1. central, peripheral
 2. spinal cord
 3. autonomic
 4. sense
 5. impulses or messages

B. Matching
 1. e
 2. b
 3. c
 4. d
 5. a
 6. f

C. Definitions
 1. shakiness, trembling
 2. dizziness
 3. inability to move
 4. deep sleep out of which a person cannot be roused
 5. dazed condition, mental sluggishness
 6. sleeplessness
 7. slowness of movement
 8. ringing in the ears
 9. double vision

D. Nervous system disorders
 1. conjunctivitis
 2. Parkinson's disease
 3. multiple sclerosis
 4. stroke or CVA
 5. epilepsy
 6. glaucoma
 7. otitis
 8. meningitis
 9. depression
 10. Meniere's disease

E. Functions of drugs
 1. increase the rate and depth of breathing.
 2. relieve depression.
 3. relieve pain.
 4. reduce fever.
 5. produce sleep.
 6. create numbness or unconsciousness in preparation for surgery.
 7. control or prevent seizures.
 8. produce feelings of calm in tense or nervous (but not psychotic) patients.
 9. produce feelings of calm in patients with severe mental illness.

F. Stimulants or depressants
 1. D
 2. D
 3. S
 4. D
 5. D
 6. D
 7. D
 8. S
 9. S
 10. D
 11. D
 12. D

G. Matching
 1. d
 2. f
 3. c
 4. e
 5. a
 6. h
 7. b
 8. i
 9. g
 10. j
 11. k
 12. l
 13. m

H. Reduce the noise level. Give a warm bath or a back rub. Listen to patient concerns. Give the patient enough exercise.

I. Fill in the blanks
 1. take their medication regularly
 2. toxicity or poisoning
 3. on time
 4. discard
 5. temperature
 6. hazardous
 7. blurriness
 8. cleaned and dried
 9. warmed
 10. candy or sugarless gum
 11. "Sterile—for Ophthalmic Use"

J. See section on *Drug Abuse*.

PRACTICE PROCEDURE

INSTILL EYEDROPS AND EYE OINTMENT

Equipment:
- Physician's orders for eyedrops and eye ointment
- Kardex, medicine cards, medication record, patient chart
- Medication tray or cart
- Bottle of eyedrops and eyedropper
- Tube of ophthalmic ointment
- Sterile cotton balls or gauze
- Tissues to wipe up spills

____ 1. Set up medications on tray or cart. Check for the "five rights."

____ 2. Wash your hands.

____ 3. Identify patient and explain procedure.

____ 4. Instill eyedrops:

Under lower eyelid:
- Position patient either sitting up or lying down with head back, chin tilted up.
- Using a piece of sterile cotton or gauze, gently pull down the lower lid to form a gutter or pouch (eye sac), as shown in Figure 10-14.
- Hold the dropper close to the eye without touching it. Use your little finger to steady the dropper as you hold it.
- Release 1 or 2 drops into the eye sac (or the measured amount ordered). Let the eye close gently.

Under upper eyelid:
- Have the patient lie down on his or her back. Ask the patient to keep both eyes open and look down.
- With gauze or cotton, gently pull up the upper eyelid and release 1 or 2 drops at the top of the eye. Let the eye close gently.

____ 5. Wipe up any liquid overflow with cotton or tissue.

____ 6. With a fingertip and a sterile cotton or tissue, press gently against the inner corner of the eye and the nose bone. This keeps the medication from entering the tear ducts and the nose. Do this for just 1–2 minutes.

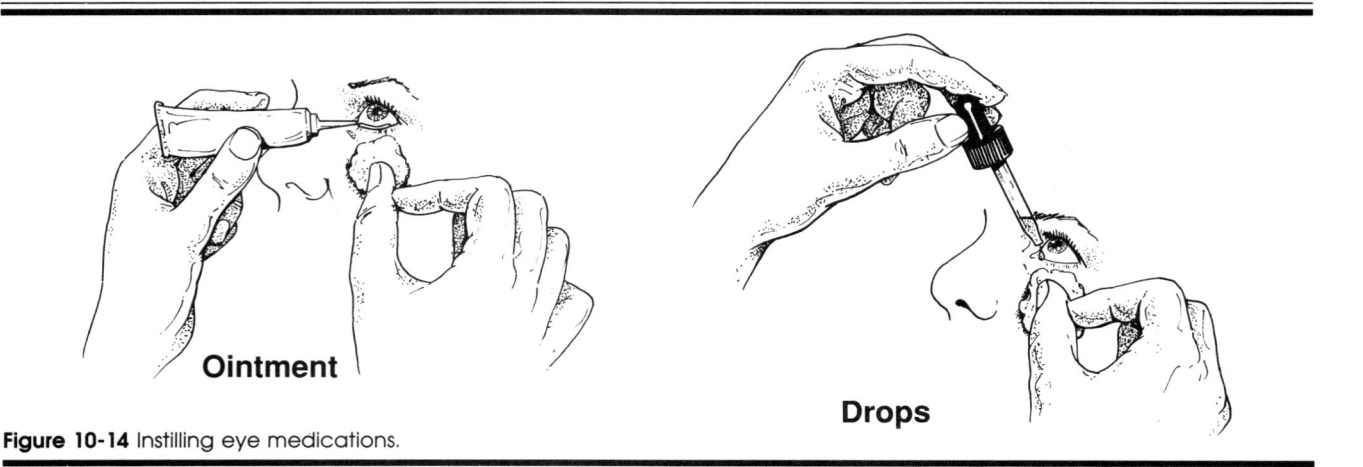

Ointment

Drops

Figure 10-14 Instilling eye medications.

_____ 7. Instill eye ointment:
- First cleanse eyelids to prevent entry of germs and dust.
- Gently pull down the lower eyelid with cotton or gauze. Instruct the patient to look up.
- Place a thin line of ointment along the inside of the lower eyelid, moving smoothly from one end to the other. Twist the tube slightly to release the ribbon of ointment.
- Close the eye and instruct the patient to roll the eyeball from side to side. This spreads the ointment over the eye. If the eye is not injured, it may be massaged gently to spread the ointment.

_____ 8. Wipe up excess ointment with tissue or cotton.

_____ 9. Help patient back into a comfortable position.

_____ 10. Wash your hands.

_____ 11. Chart the procedure.

Demonstrate this procedure for the instructor or the nurse in charge.

PRACTICE PROCEDURE

INSTILL EAR DROPS

Equipment:

- Medication order for ear medication
- Medication record, medicine cards, and chart
- Ear medication in bottle with dropper (marked with drops or milliliters)
- Medication tray or cart
- Sterile cotton

_____ 1. Set up medication. Make sure it is at room temperature or warmed to body temperature, according to instructions. Check for the "five rights."

_____ 2. Wash your hands.

_____ 3. Identify patient, explain procedure, and position patient lying on back with head turned to side.

_____ 4. Clean and dry the ear canal with cotton swabs or a saline syringe and warm air.

_____ 5. Instill ear drops.

- Grasp outer ear and pull gently to straighten ear canal, as shown in Figure 10-15. In children, pull down and back on earlobe; in adults, grasp upper part of ear and pull up and back.
- Place 3 or 4 drops (or measured amount) of medication into ear without touching the dropper to the ear canal.
- With sterile cotton, press on the forward part of the ear several times to help the medication flow down the ear canal.

_____ 6. Wipe up any spills with tissue.

_____ 7. Place a piece of sterile cotton or pack in the ear canal to trap the medication inside. Leave this in for about 15–20 minutes.

_____ 8. Ask the patient to remain in the same position for at least 5 minutes.

_____ 9. Wash your hands.

_____ 10. Chart the procedure. Be sure to record the number of drops instilled and which ear was treated.

Demonstrate this procedure for the instructor or the nurse in charge.

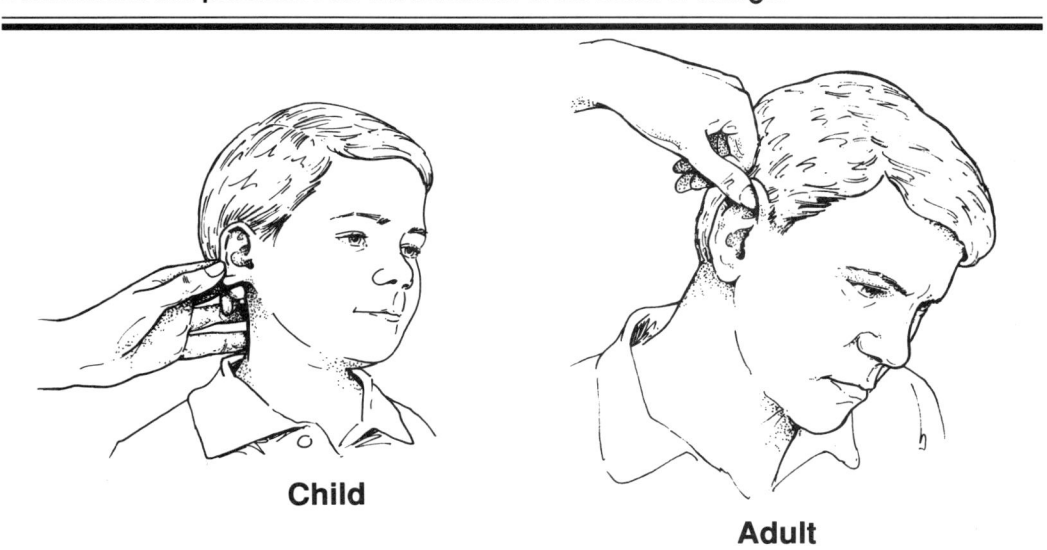

Child

Adult

Figure 10-15 Straightening the ear canal in preparation for ear drops.

REPRESENTATIVE DRUGS FOR THE NERVOUS AND SENSORY SYSTEMS

CATEGORY, NAME[a], AND ROUTE	USES AND DISEASES	ACTIONS	USUAL DOSE[b] AND SPECIAL INSTRUCTIONS	SIDE EFFECTS AND ADVERSE REACTIONS
Stimulants				
Methylphenidate (*Ritalin*) Oral	Hyperactivity in children, narcolepsy	Cerebral stimulant	20–30 mg/day in divided doses for adults; 10 mg/day for children; adjusted individually	Anorexia, nervousness, insomnia, hypersensitivity, arrhythmias
Antidepressants				
Amitriptyline (*Elavil*) Oral, IM	Depression	Action poorly understood; elevates mood, sedates	50–200 mg/day in divided doses or in single dose given at bedtime; caution patient to avoid alcohol, OTC drugs, and prolonged exposure to sunlight	Drowsiness, dry mouth, blurred vision, tachycardia, constipation, urine retention, photosensitivity
Imipramine (*Tofranil*) Oral, IM	Depression	Action poorly understood; elevates mood, sedates	50–150 mg/day in divided doses or in single dose given at bedtime; up to 300 mg given to hospitalized patients; same cautions as above	Drowsiness, dry mouth, blurred vision, tachycardia, constipation, urine retention, photosensitivity
Analgesics				
Oxycodone and aspirin (*Percodan*) PO	Moderate to severe pain	Relieves pain, sedates, reduces fever	One tablet q 6 hours PRN; give with food or with full glass of water or milk	Dependence, respiratory depression (esp. in elderly), dizziness, drowsiness
Pentazocine (*Talwin*) PO, IM, SC, IV	Moderate to severe pain; preparation for surgery	Relieves pain, sedates	50–100 mg q 3–4 hours PO; 30 mg IM; caution patient to avoid alcohol and OTC drugs	Dependence, dizziness, drowsiness, euphoria, nausea, dyspnea
Meperidine (*Demerol*) IM, SC, IV, PO	Moderate to severe pain; preparation for surgery	Relieves pain, sedates	50–100 mg q 3–4 hours PRN orally or parenterally; may cause drowsiness; caution patient to avoid alcohol	Dependence, dizziness, drowsiness, nausea, flushing, sweating, dry mouth, orthostatic hypotension
Antianxiety Agents and Sedative/Hypnotics				
Diazepam (*Valium*) Oral, IM, IV	Anxiety, tension before surgical procedures, alcohol withdrawal, muscle spasms	Relieves anxiety, relaxes skeletal muscles, controls spasms, sedates	2–10 mg BID to QID PO, adjusted individually to the lowest effective maintenance dose; caution patient to avoid alcohol; give with food to avoid upset stomach	Drowsiness, slurred speech, blurred vision, pain at injection site, unusual fatigue, dependence
Chlordiazepoxide (*Librium*) Oral, IM, IV	Anxiety, tension before surgical procedures, alcohol withdrawal	Relieves anxiety, sedates	5–25 mg 3 or 4 times daily PO; up to 100 mg IM or IV	Drowsiness, dizziness, clumsiness, confusion, lethargy, constipation
Meprobamate (*Equanil*) Oral	Anxiety	Relieves anxiety; promotes sleep in anxious patients	400 mg TID or QID; caution patient to avoid alcohol; may cause drowsiness	Drowsiness, clumsiness (ataxia), dependence

REPRESENTATATIVE DRUGS FOR THE NERVOUS AND SENSORY SYSTEMS

CATEGORY, NAME[a], AND ROUTE	USES AND DISEASES	ACTIONS	USUAL DOSE[b] AND SPECIAL INSTRUCTIONS	SIDE EFFECTS AND ADVERSE REACTIONS
Antianxiety Agents and Sedative/Hypnotics —continued				
Alprazolam (*Xanax*) Oral	Short-term anxiety	Relieves anxiety	0.25–0.5 mg TID	Drowsiness; avoid use of alcohol
Chloral hydrate (*Noctec*) Oral, Rectal	Insomnia	Sedates, promotes sleep	500–1000 mg h.s. for hypnotic effect; give with full glass of liquid; caution patient to avoid alcohol	Dependence, nausea, vomiting, stomach pain, headache, occasional skin rash, arrhythmias
Flurazepam (*Dalmane*) Oral	Insomnia	Promotes sleep	15–30 mg h.s. for hypnotic effect; dose individualized; may take 2 or 3 nights for medication to reach full effectiveness; caution patient to avoid alcohol	Dependence, clumsiness, dizziness, daytime drowsiness, staggering
Triazolam (*Halcion*) Oral	Insomnia	Promotes sleep	0.125–0.5 mg at bedtime	Headache, nausea, dizziness, lightheadedness
Antipsychotic Agents				
Chlorpromazine (*Thorazine*) Oral, IM, Rectal	Schizophrenia, severe agitation, behavior problems in children, severe nausea	Management of manifestations of psychotic disorders	10–25 mg TID or QID and increased as necessary	Drowsiness, anemia, dizziness, tachycardia, tremors, spasms of the neck, tardive dyskinesia, liver, eye, and bone marrow dysfunctions
Fluphenazine (*Prolixin*) Oral, IM	Schizophrenia	Management of clinical manifestations of schizophrenia	20–40 mg/day; outpatients should receive lower dosages	Dry mouth, constipation, fecal impaction, urinary retention, tardive dyskinesia
Trifluoperazine (*Stelazine*) Oral, IM	Schizophrenia, acute active psychoses	Relieves symptoms	2–4 mg/day	Drowsiness, dizziness, jaundice, tardive dyskinesia, dry mouth, blurred vision
Haloperidol (*Haldol*) Oral, IM	Schizophrenia, acute active psychoses	Relieves symptoms	0.5–5 mg BID or TID; may cause drowsiness; caution patient to avoid alcohol and OTC drugs	Tardive dyskinesia, orthostatic hypotension, dry mouth, dizziness
Anticonvulsants				
Phenytoin sodium (*Dilantin*) Oral, IV	Grand mal epilepsy; psychomotor seizures	Controls seizures	100 mg TID PO, adjusted individually; give with or after meals; caution patient to avoid alcohol; may cause drowsiness; good oral hygiene is important because drug may inflame gums (gingivitis)	Back-and-forth eye movements (nystagmus); swollen, tender gums; staggering walk (ataxia); constipation; dizziness; nausea and vomiting; rashes, anemia

REPRESENTATATIVE DRUGS FOR THE NERVOUS AND SENSORY SYSTEMS

CATEGORY, NAME[a], AND ROUTE	USES AND DISEASES	ACTIONS	USUAL DOSE[b] AND SPECIAL INSTRUCTIONS	SIDE EFFECTS AND ADVERSE REACTIONS
Anticonvulsants —continued				
Carbamazepine (*Tegretol*) Oral	Tonic-clonic seizures; other seizure types	Prophylactic treatment of seizures	200 mg BID increased to 800–1200 mg per day; should not be used by pregnant women or nursing mothers	Dizziness, drowsiness, nausea, vomiting; crosses placental barrier, appears in mother's milk
Antiparkinsonian Agents				
Carbidopa and levodopa (*Sinemet*) Oral	Parkinson's disease or Parkinson-like symptoms	Reduces rigidity of head and limbs	Initial dose 1 tablet (10 mg carbidopa/100 mg levodopa or 25/100) TID; maintenance dose 1 or 2 tablets (25/250) TID, individually adjusted; watch for symptoms of depression; give with food; may cause drowsiness	Mood changes, unusual uncontrolled body movements, palpitations, difficult urination, nausea, vomiting
Benztropine mesylate (*Cogentin*) Oral, IM	Parkinson's disease adjunct	Control extra-pyramidal disorders except tardive dyskinesia	0.5–2 mg/day	Dry mouth, blurred vision, skin rashes, tachycardia
Eye Medications				
Polymyxin B, bacitracin, neomycin (*Neosporin Ophthalmic*) Topical	Eye infections	Kills bacteria	Solution: 1 or 2 drops (gtt) BID or QID; ointment: 1-cm (1/3") strip q 3 hours or PRN	Stinging, itching, swelling, redness
Pilocarpine HCl (*Isopto Carpine*) Topical	Glaucoma	Reduces fluid pressure inside eye, contracts pupil (miotic action), neutralizes mydriatics used in eye exams	Dosage depends on strength of solution, usually 1 drop four times daily; give on time; gently press tear duct for 1–2 minutes to prevent systemic absorption	Blurred vision, eye pain, eye irritation
Ear Medication				
Polymyxin B, neomycin hydrocortisone (*Cortisporin Otic*) Topical	Bacterial infection of outer ear, postsurgical ear infection	Kills bacteria, suppresses inflammation and itching	3 or 4 drops (gtt) TID or QID	Superinfection, hypersensitivity

[a] Brand names given in parentheses are examples only. Check current drug references for a complete listing of available trade name products.

[b] Average adult doses are given. However, dosages are determined by a physician and vary with the purpose of the therapy and the particular patient. The doses presented in this text are for general information only.

Unit 11

Drugs for the Gastrointestinal System

In this unit you will learn about the organs of digestion and elimination. You will learn what they do, what happens to them when they are diseased, and how drugs are used to treat their disorders. You will also learn procedures to follow in giving gastrointestinal medications.

In this unit, you will learn to:

- State the five main functions of the gastrointestinal system.
- Name the major parts of the gastrointestinal system and tell what they do.
- Use correct medical terms to describe symptoms of gastrointestinal disorders.
- Recognize descriptions of major gastrointestinal disorders for which drugs are given.
- Describe the actions and give examples of the following drug groups: antacids, digestants, antiflatulents, emetics, antiemetics, anticholinergics and antispasmodics, antidiarrheals, cathartics (laxatives and purgatives), antiparasitics, and anorexiants.
- State three important things to remember when giving medications for the gastrointestinal system.
- Describe and follow proper procedure for inserting rectal suppositories.
- Describe and follow proper procedure for giving medications through a nasogastric or gastrostomy tube.

GASTROINTESTINAL SYSTEM

Food is vital to the survival of the body. Every cell requires nourishment to carry on its life functions. But no cell can use the food we eat just as it enters the body. The food must first undergo mechanical and chemical changes that break it down into particles small enough to pass through cell walls. This function is carried out by the gastrointestinal (GI) system, also known as the **digestive system**.

The GI system carries out five steps in the process of digestion:

Step 1. Breaking up food into smaller pieces. This is a mechanical action. It is performed by the mouth and its accessory parts, the tongue and the teeth, with the aid of the salivary glands.

Step 2. Transporting food through the GI tract. The GI tract (also known as the **digestive tract** or **alimentary canal**) is one long tube passing from the mouth to the rectum. Rhythmic contractions of the lining of the GI tract push the food along this passageway. These muscle movements are called **peristalsis** (*per'i-stal'sis*). By moving food along, peristalsis puts the food in contact with physical and chemical processes that take place in different parts of the system.

Step 3. Secreting digestive enzymes. Glands in the mouth, in the lining of the stomach, and in the accessory organs (liver, small bowel, and pancreas) all secrete **enzymes**, which are chemical substances that aid digestion. Digestion is a series of chemical changes that breaks down food particles into basic nutrients that can be used by cells: namely, amino acids (proteins), fats, minerals, vitamins, sugars, and water.

Step 4. Absorbing nutrients into the blood. After being broken down into its smallest parts, food is absorbed from the small intestine into the bloodstream. From there it circulates to all the cells of the body to supply fuel for energy production and growth.

Step 5. Excreting solid waste products. This function takes place in the large intestine and the rectum. Undigested substances like plant fibers are not absorbed into the blood but pass into the large intestine. The large intestine prepares these substances for elimination from the body.

Keeping in mind these five basic steps of digestion, let us explore the structure of the GI system in more detail (See Figures 11-1 and 11-2).

Organs of Digestion

Mouth—The teeth and the tongue work together to break food into smaller pieces. The tongue moves food into position so that it can be chewed by the teeth. Teeth have different shapes that make them suitable for cutting, tearing, and grinding the food. Even before chewing begins, the **salivary glands** start to produce a fluid called **saliva**. The saliva helps to dissolve the food and coats it so that it can easily be swallowed. Saliva also begins to act on the carbohydrates (starchy foods) to turn them into sugars.

Esophagus—Recall from Unit 9 that when a person swallows, the epiglottis closes to prevent food from entering the lungs. The food then passes into the **esophagus**, which is the part of the GI tract that links the mouth to the stomach. Chunks of food are pushed down the esophagus by peristaltic movements of the tube lining. At times when the stomach is irritated, peristalsis may take place in the opposite direction, and vomiting will probably result.

Stomach—The stomach is a gourd-shaped pouch that can expand to hold up to 2 quarts of food and liquid. Valves at the entrance and exit of the stomach control the intake and outlet of food. The lining of the stomach is dotted with over 35 million tiny glands that secrete gastric juice. Gastric juice consists of stomach acid and digestive enzymes. Stomach acid is an important factor in digestion. It dissolves the food, destroys bacteria, and breaks down the connective tissue in meats. After entering the stomach, the food is churned around by muscles in the stomach wall and mixed with gastric juice. It remains in the stomach for about 30–45 minutes. By this time it has become a well-dissolved, soupy liquid.

Small Intestine—The section of the small intestine closest to the stomach is called the **duodenum** (*du'o-de'num*). As soon as food enters the duodenum, it is doused with strong digestive enzymes from the liver and pancreas. These juices complete the breaking-down process that changes the food into molecules of protein,

VOCABULARY

adsorbent: designed to soak up fluids or chemicals

anal rectal ridge: a ring of muscle several inches inside the anal opening; suppositories must be inserted past this ridge

anorexia: loss of appetite;

anorexiant: drug that suppresses the appetite

antacid: drug that neutralizes stomach acid

anticholinergic: drug that acts on the autonomic nervous system to reduce intestinal motility and slow production of stomach acid

antidiarrheal: drug that slows intestinal motility and helps produce formed stools instead of loose, watery stools

antiemetic: drug that prevents or relieves nausea and vomiting

antiflatulent: drug that relieves gassiness and bloating; also called **carminative**

antiparasitic: drug that eliminates intestinal parasites (pinworms, roundworms, etc.)

antispasmodic: drug that acts on the smooth muscle of the intestines to relieve griping and cramping

anus: distal (far-end) opening of the gastrointestinal tract through which feces are eliminated

astringent: designed to shrink and dry swollen tissues

bile: digestive juice produced by the liver and stored in the gallbladder; helps digest fats

cathartic: drug that promotes defecation either to relieve constipation or to clear the bowel before surgery

defecation: passage of feces out of the body; bowel movement

digestant: drug that aids digestion by replacing missing digestive enzymes

duodenum: first portion of the small intestine, just past the stomach

emesis: vomiting; reversal of peristalsis

emetic: drug that causes vomiting

enzyme: substance that assists chemical changes (e.g., digestion)

eructation: belching, burping

esophagus: portion of the gastrointestinal tract leading from the mouth and pharynx to the stomach

feces: solid waste products remaining after food is digested and nutrients are absorbed; also called **stools**

gallbladder: storage pouch for bile

gastric: pertaining to the stomach

gastric gavage: tube feeding (not to be confused with gastric **lavage**, which means washing out the stomach)

gastrointestinal tract: body tube leading from the mouth through the anus, through which food passes, nutrients are absorbed, and solid wastes are eliminated; also known as **alimentary canal** or **digestive tract**

gastroscope: instrument for visual examination of the stomach

gastrostomy tube: tube inserted through a stoma into the stomach, used for tube feeding

hyperacidity: too much acid (e.g., in the stomach)

intestinal motility: movement or excitability of the smooth muscles lining the gastrointestinal tract; the speed of peristalsis

jaundice: yellowing of the skin; a symptom of liver problems and the presence of bile pigment in the bloodstream

laxative: mild cathartic that relieves constipation

liver: organ that filters blood, stores and releases nutrients into the blood, and is involved in biotransformation or excretion of some drugs and other substances

nasogastric tube: tube inserted through the nose and down the esophagus into the stomach, used for tube feeding; also called **Levin tube**

pancreas: organ that secretes strong digestive enzymes that empty into the duodenum; also secretes insulin that passes directly into the bloodstream

peptic: pertaining to digestion in the stomach

peristalsis: rhythmic contractions of the smooth muscles lining the gastrointestinal tract, designed to move food and waste materials through the system

proctoscope: instrument for visually examining the rectum

purgative: strong cathartic that clears out the intestines (e.g., in preparation for surgery)

rectum: distal (far-end) portion of the large intestine

saliva: digestive juice secreted by salivary glands in the mouth; breaks down certain sugars, moistens and coats food for easy swallowing

sigmoidoscope: used to visualize the rectum and sigmoid colon

stoma: surgically produced opening in the stomach or the abdomen

tarry stools: feces that have a black, tarlike appearance; may indicate bleeding in the gastrointestinal tract or may result from iron pills, milk of bismuth, charcoal, or spinach

ulcer: open sore or break in the lining of the stomach (peptic ulcer) or duodenum (duodenal ulcer); can break through the gastrointestinal lining into the abdominal cavity (perforated ulcer)

villi: small fingerlike projections of the intestinal lining that provide a large surface area for absorption

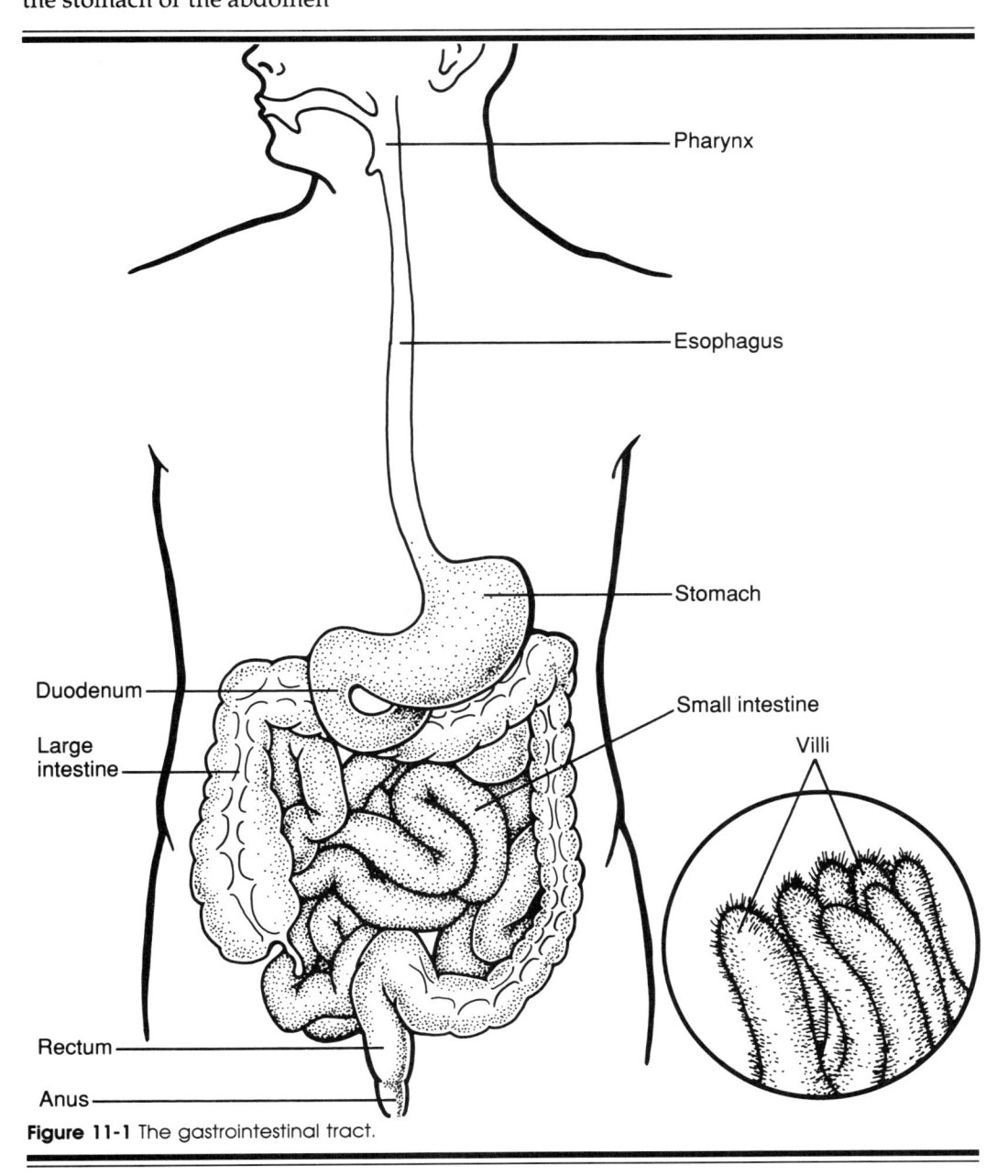

Figure 11-1 The gastrointestinal tract.

256 Administering Medications

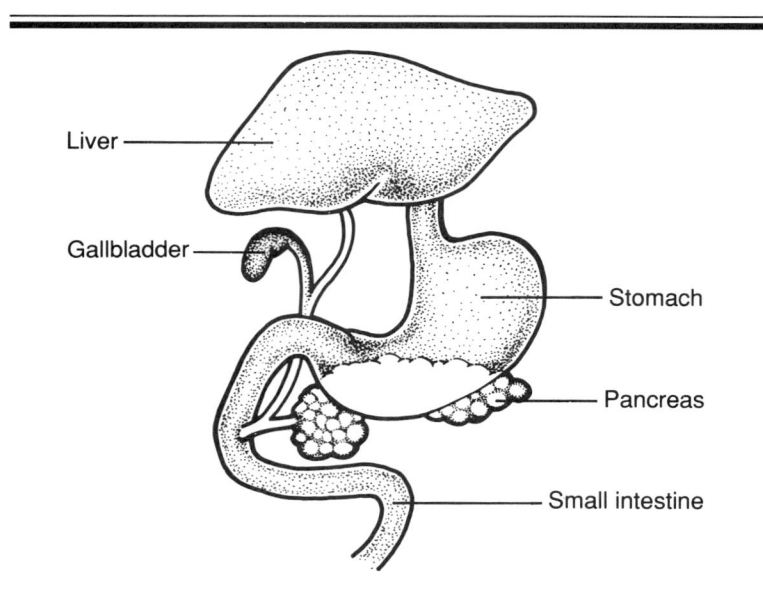

Figure 11-2 Accessory organs of the gastrointestinal system.

sugar, fat, minerals, and so on. The small intestine is a long, coiled tube about 20 feet in length. It also secretes a fluid rich in digestive enzymes that helps to break down fats, proteins, and carbohydrates. Its walls are lined with tiny fingerlike projections called **villi**. The villi are responsible for absorbing nutrients into the bloodstream. They have very thin walls, and, because of their shape, they provide a huge surface area for absorption to take place. Tiny capillaries and lymph ducts in the villi take in the nutrients and transport them to the liver. From there they are released into the bloodstream as needed by the body. By the time the food has passed through all 20 feet of the small intestine, most of the nutrients have been absorbed. All that is left is undigestible materials mixed with water.

Large Intestine—The large intestine is much shorter and wider than the small intestine. It is only about 4 or 5 feet long. In the large intestine, excess water is absorbed into the bloodstream, leaving the undigested wastes. These are collected and compacted into semisolid masses, called **feces** or **stools**. The feces leave the body by way of the **rectum** and its opening, the **anus**.

Liver and Gallbladder—The **liver** is a large glandular organ that serves many functions in the human body. Its role in the GI system is to secrete **bile**, a fluid that aids in digesting fats. The bile is collected in a storage pouch called the **gallbladder** until it is needed for digestion. The liver stores nutrients absorbed from the small intestine. The liver also removes certain waste products from the blood, and it produces important substances for blood clotting and the immune system. It is a very important organ—so important that the body cannot survive without it.

The liver is important in drug action because it breaks down or inactivates many drugs. Patients with poor liver function can become overdosed with some routinely administered drugs because their livers are unable to break down the drugs quickly enough.

Pancreas—The pancreas is another large glandular organ that has several functions. It produces digestive juices that complete the chemical changes that turn fats, proteins, and carbohydrates into particles that can be absorbed. The pancreas also secretes **insulin**, a hormone that regulates the amount of sugar used by the cells (see Unit 13). Insulin is released directly into the bloodstream. It does not enter into digestion.

Autonomic Control

Peristalsis and the secretion of digestive enzymes are both under control of the autonomic nervous system. This means that people cannot consciously control what goes on in their stomachs and intestines. It also means that digestion is affected by stress.

When the autonomic nervous system prepares the body to meet danger or stress, the muscular movements of the stomach and intestine slow down. Digestive enzyme production slows down, too. In other cases, peristalsis and enzyme secretion are stimulated needlessly by nervous tension. Therefore, chronically nervous or anxious people tend to have overactive digestion. Mild sedatives or tranquilizers are sometimes used to calm these reactions and restore normal digestion.

DISORDERS OF THE GASTROINTESTINAL SYSTEM

Symptoms

The symptoms of GI disorders are quite familiar. Hardly anyone has escaped occasional nausea, vomiting, constipation, diarrhea, indigestion, heartburn, gassiness, stomachache, and abdominal cramps. The symptoms have many causes. They can be the result of passing irritations, flu, mild food poisoning, psychological stress, or side effects of drugs. Or they can signal more serious underlying diseases. Drugs can relieve some GI symptoms, but the underlying diseases must be treated if permanent relief is desired.

Nausea is a queasy feeling in the stomach arising from many causes, such as infection, radiation treatment, psychological stimulation, reaction to a drug, pregnancy, poisoning, or stomach irritation. Sometimes this feeling leads to **vomiting**, or **emesis**. The contents of the stomach are emptied as peristalsis switches direction and carries food back up the esophagus. Emesis can be useful when it brings up substances that irritate the stomach. But too much vomiting is dangerous because it can remove too many fluids from the body. It is also dangerous because it keeps the body from digesting and absorbing needed nutrients.

Heartburn is a burning sensation in the pit of the stomach that may be felt in the esophagus and the throat as well. It is often felt along with sour belching. **Indigestion** is a gassy or bloated feeling in the stomach. Both heartburn and indigestion may be the result of poor eating habits or psychological tension. A bland diet, mild sedatives, and simple antacids help to relieve passing symptoms. Of course, if symptoms persist, an underlying cause must be looked for.

Burping, belching (eructation), and **passing gas** are common symptoms of GI irritation. The gas (**flatus**) comes from chemical reactions that release gases into the GI system. Or it comes from swallowing air along with food and drink. Excess gas can cause pressure, pain, and a bloated feeling. Cramping or **griping** of the digestive tract is also common with many disorders. Cramps are the result of muscle spasms in the walls of the stomach and intestines.

Constipation is the failure to have regular bowel movements. It can be due to hardened feces, slow movement of the intestine, lack of bulk in the diet, psychological factors, or lack of physical activity. Constipation is of concern when it causes straining at stool or when it threatens to block the intestines. Normally, people have a bowel movement about every 1–3 days. Different people have different schedules, and no one should be concerned if he or she does not have a bowel movement every single day. Laxatives are much overused. People who reach for a laxative when they do not have a daily bowel movement may become dependent on the drug, which can cause serious problems.

Diarrhea means passing loose, watery stools or passing stools too often. It is often accompanied by abdominal cramps, which signal irritation in the large intestine. Diarrhea is the result of peristalsis moving food through the intestines too quickly. It has many underlying causes, including infections, poisons, drugs, and nervousness.

As in the case of diarrhea, many disorders either result from or cause changes in the speed at which nutrients are carried through the GI tract. The terms used to refer to the speed of peristalsis is **intestinal motility** (Figure 11-3). Nervous tension, infections, drugs, and many other factors affect intestinal motility.

Intestinal motility = Peristalsis

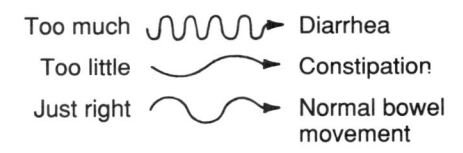

Too much ⟿ Diarrhea
Too little ⟿ Constipation
Just right ⟿ Normal bowel movement

Figure 11-3 Intestinal motility affects the speed and quality of digestion.

Abdominal or stomach pain sometimes accompanies GI disorders. The pain can be the result of gas pressure, irritation, or more serious problems. Especially in the case of abdominal pain, it is important not to give medications until a search has been made for an underlying cause. Treating abdominal pain with an analgesic may delay discovery of something serious like appendicitis.

Other symptoms to look for are difficulty in swallowing, loss of appetite (**anorexia**), sudden or severe weight loss, and change in the appearance of the stools (bloody, tarry, clay-colored, or containing excess mucus).

Major Disorders

Some of the major diseases and disorders for which drugs may be given will be discussed. GI symptoms can be about the same for minor problems as well as serious problems. Most digestive upsets and "bugs" run their course within a day or two. One should suspect a more serious problem when symptoms persist over many days. Usually in such cases a physician will order tests (x-rays, blood tests, etc.) to find an underlying cause for the symptoms. Special tubes (**gastroscope** or **proctoscope**) may be used to examine visually the walls of the stomach, intestine, or rectum.

Tooth and Gum Disorders—Problems with the teeth or gums can lead to GI problems. Unless the teeth and gums are in good condition, eating and drinking may be painful or inefficient. Patients may avoid hard-to-chew foods, including foods that would help keep their bowel movements regular (e.g., fruits, vegetables, and grain products high in bulk and fiber content). Some of the main tooth and gum disorders are **dental abscess** (which can result from neglect or severe tooth decay), **gingivitis, pyorrhea, trench mouth** (Vincent's infection), and **stomatitis**. They are treated with antibiotics, surgical removal of diseased tissue, or special cleaning procedures. Various pastes and powders are available for routine tooth cleaning, such as stannous fluoride and sodium monofluorophosphate. Elderly persons, patients in long-term care, and people who are being fed with a tube (i.e., by gastric gavage) may require your help in maintaining their oral hygiene with these products.

Gastritis—This is an inflammation of the stomach, signaled by a burning pain, nausea, and vomiting. It may be caused by accidentally swallowing caustic substances. Or it results from normal use of irritants such as coffee, alcohol, and tobacco. The condition may be temporary, or it may persist for months, causing damage to the stomach lining. Treatment involves removing the cause as well as treating the symptoms.

Ulcers—Ulcers may attack either the stomach (**peptic ulcer**) or, more frequently, the duodenum (**duodenal ulcer**). An ulcer is an open sore in the stomach or duodenal lining. The mucous membranes have been broken down by digestive acids so that the underlying tissue is exposed and can be destroyed by the acids. If the ulcer is left untreated, the tissue destruction eventually leads to perforation. A perforated ulcer is a hole that permits food and enzymes to enter the abdominal cavity and contaminate other organs.

The cause of ulcers is excess secretion of gastric acids (**hyperacidity**) due to prolonged use of alcohol, cigarettes, or coffee or due perhaps to chronic nervous tension. The treatment is to remove the source of irritation (psychological or food sources). Drug therapy is aimed at reducing the amount of stomach acid. Antacids neutralize acids in the stomach, while anticholinergics, sedatives, and tranquilizers calm nervous tension that stimulates acid production. Cimetidine (*Tagamet*) and sucralfate (*Carafate*) are newer anti-ulcer drugs. Surgery to repair stomach tissue is required in serious cases.

Liver Disorders—A symptom of many liver disorders is **jaundice**, a yellowing of the skin. This is due to bilirubin (a yellow-colored substance) entering the bloodstream, usually because the bile duct is blocked. **Cirrhosis** is a disorder in which the liver at first becomes enlarged and later contracted. This condition is accompanied, in late stages, by nausea, weight loss, vomiting, and difficulty in digesting fats. Jaundice, enlarged veins, hemorrhoids, and swelling of the abdomen may appear. Cirrhosis is thought to be related to poor nutrition and drinking too much alcohol. It is treated with a change in diet, rest, and diuretics. **Hepatitis** is a common and very serious infection of the liver. It is caused by a virus. Both treatment and recovery can take a long time.

Gallbladder Disorders—Gallstones are small granules of cholesterol in the gallbladder. They are thought to be the result of extra-concentrated bile. They are common in people over the age of 40, but they do not necessarily cause symptoms. Gallstones can cause trouble if they block the opening of the gallbladder or the tube that carries bile to the intestine. Infections of the gallbladder (**cholecystitis**) and bile duct (**cholangitis**) can result. These involve fever, vomiting, jaundice, and pain in the upper right portion of the abdomen. Surgery is necessary for severe gallbladder disorders. In elderly people, however, surgery may pose more risks than the gallstones themselves. In these cases, drugs that reduce abdominal spasms (anticholinergics or antispasmodics) are sometimes ordered to keep symptoms under control.

Pancreatitis—This is an inflammation of the pancreas that causes severe abdominal pain and shock symptoms. It is treated with analgesics to relieve the pain, IV fluids, bed rest, and withdrawing foods. Two other disorders of the pancreas, diabetes and hypoglycemia, are described in Unit 13.

Enteritis and Ulcerative Colitis—These are inflammations of the small and large intestine, respectively, resulting in diarrhea, fever, pain, anemia, and weight loss. They are treated with antidiarrheals, sulfasalazine, or corticosteroids, rest, and a bland diet.

Peritonitis—This is an acute inflammation of the membranes that line the abdomen. It is caused by a rupture in a part of the GI tract which allows the digestive juices and food matter to enter the abdominal cavity. Perforated ulcers, injuries to the intestine, malignancies, and a ruptured appendix are some of the causes that trigger peritonitis. The treatment is surgery to repair the damage and antibiotics to stop the infection.

Irritable Bowel—This condition, in which the lower intestine feels crampy, bloated, and gassy, is not due to an underlying disease. It seems to be an overreaction to certain foods or to nervous tension. Other names for irritable bowel are **spastic colon** and **spastic colitis** (ko-li'tis). The condition is generally harmless, and it may be relieved with mild sedatives and antispasmodics or anticholinergics.

Diverticulosis—This is a condition in which small, blisterlike pockets develop in the walls of the large intestine. This causes no trouble unless these growths become inflamed (**diverticulitis**). The treatment of diverticulitis consists of rest, a soft diet, and antibiotics.

Hemorrhoids—Hemorrhoids are enlarged veins around the anal opening. They can become swollen and painful, and blood clots may form in them. Problems with hemorrhoids can be avoided by preventing straining at stool, having bowel movements regularly, and keeping the anal area clean. Suppositories, ointments, and hot sitz baths (immersion of thighs, buttocks, and abdomen) are used to relieve pain in severe cases. Some hemorrhoid preparations, such as *Anusol-HC*, include anti-inflammatory ingredients as well as soothing and lubricating ingredients.

Tumors—Tumors, either benign or malignant, may grow in any part of the GI tract, causing obstruction, bleeding, pressure or rupture and producing some or all of the usual symptoms. Small outgrowths on the inside of the large intestines are called **polyps**. They are usually benign.

Intestinal Parasites—Intestinal parasites are worms that live in the intestines, such as tapeworms, hookworms, trichina worms, pinworms, and roundworms. Some of these parasites are quite common, and others are found only in certain parts of the world. Most may be prevented by eating properly cooked meats (especially pork) and by keeping the hands and nails clean.

DRUGS THAT AFFECT THE GASTROINTESTINAL SYSTEM

Antacids

Antacids relieve gastritis and ulcer pain by neutralizing stomach acid (Figure 11-4). Many people take OTC (over-the-counter) antacids to relieve indigestion as well. It should be remembered, however, that stomach acid is very necessary to digestion. Overuse of antacids may actually interfere with proper digestion.

The substances used to neutralize stomach acid are alkaline. When these substances are combined with acids, they cancel each other out chemically. Certain antacids are absorbable. If too much of these are taken, there will be excess alkali that can pass into the intestine and be absorbed. This may cause an imbalance in the body's natural chemistry called **alkalosis** (see Unit 12).

Sodium bicarbonate, better known as baking soda, is a fast-acting antacid that has a short-term effect. When it neutralizes acid, the chemical reaction releases carbon dioxide, which causes belching. Overuse often leads to alkalosis. Sodium bicarbonate interferes with the action of tetracycline.

Figure 11-4 Antacids.

Other common antacids are calcium salts (e.g., calcium carbonate), aluminum salts (e.g., aluminum hydroxide), and magnesium salts (e.g., magnesium hydroxide, oxide, carbonate, and trisilicate). Aluminum hydroxide is sold both generically and under the brand name *Amphojel*. Magnesium hydroxide is the familiar preparation, milk of magnesia.

Aluminum salts and calcium salts tend to cause constipation as a side effect. Magnesium salts, on the other hand, tend to cause diarrhea. It is generally believed that combining these substances will cancel out the side effects, so there are many preparations that contain both. *Maalox*, *Gelusil*, *Kolantyl*, and *Aludrox*, for example, are combinations of magnesium salts and aluminum hydroxide.

Digestants

This category includes a variety of drugs that replace or supplement the body's natural digestive juices or stimulate production of those juices (Figure 11-5). When the stomach fails to produce enough acid, for example, the situation can be remedied by giving hydrochloric acid or glutamic acid

Figure 11-5 Digestants.

hydrochloride (*Acidulin*). Liquid preparations of hydrochloric acid must be diluted and sipped through a straw to avoid damaging mucous membranes and tooth enamel.

Antiflatulents (Carminatives)

These drugs are a variety of digestants. Their main function is to reduce the feelings of gassiness and bloating (flatulence) that accompany indigestion (Figure 11-6). They facilitate the passing of gas by mildly stimulating intestinal motility. Simeth-

Figure 11-6 Antiflatulents (carminatives).

icone (*Mylicon*), a common antiflatulent, relieves bloating by gathering gas bubbles together so that they can be expelled more easily. It is an ingredient added to many antacid and digestant preparations, such as *Phazyme, Di-Gel, Maalox Plus,* and *Mylanta*. Small portions of whiskey or brandy are sometimes given with water to stimulate the intestines to pass gas.

Emetics

Emetics are drugs that produce vomiting in cases of poisoning. Syrup of ipecac is often kept in home medicine chests for accidental swallowing of pills, plant leaves, and noncaustic cleaning substances. Syrup of ipecac usually starts to work after 15–30 minutes. Give 8 oz. of water to assist in vomiting. If vomiting does not occur after the first dose, ipecac may be administered two more times. Another emetic is apomorphine hydrochloride, which stimulates the brain center that controls vomiting.

Antiemetics (Antinauseants)

These drugs suppress nausea and vomiting by acting on the brain control center to stop the nerve impulses (Figure 11-7). They have various uses, including motion sickness, "morning sickness" of pregnancy, dizziness caused by diseases of the inner ear, and nausea and vomiting that appear as side effects of other drugs.

The main antiemetics are antihistamines and phenothiazines. For example, dimenhydrinate (*Dramamine*), a familiar antinauseant for motion sickness, is an antihistamine. Other antiemetics are cyclizine (*Marezine*), buclizine (*Bucladin-S*), meclizine (*Antivert, Bonine*), and the phenothiazines (e.g., *Compazine, Thorazine, Phenergan*). Drowsiness is their main side effect. An anticholinergic, scopolamine, is especially effective against motion sickness.

Anticholinergics and Antispasmodics

These drugs act on the autonomic nervous system to slow peristalsis in the GI tract (Figure 11-8). They make the smooth muscle contract less often and less forcefully. This is useful in the treatment of ulcers and irritable bowel.

Figure 11-8 Anticholinergics and antispasmodics.

In addition to slowing intestinal motility, anticholinergics block the action of acetylcholine, a chemical substance that helps transmit nerve impulses, including those that stimulate the acid-secreting glands of the stomach. By blocking these nerve impulses, anticholinergics cause less stomach acid to be produced. This action is important in ulcer treatment.

The anticholinergics are a group of natural and synthetic alkaloids. The major natural alkaloids are atropine sulfate, belladonna, and scopolamine hydrobromide. Examples of synthetic anticholinergics are methantheline bromide (*Banthine*), propantheline bromide (*Pro-Banthine*), and isopropamide iodide (*Darbid*). Because

Figure 11-7 Antiemetics.

these drugs affect the entire autonomic nervous system, they have many side effects. Blurred vision, dilated pupils, dry mouth, heart palpitations, constipation, and inability to urinate are some of the effects.

Antispasmodics have more of an effect on the smooth muscle and very little on the secretion of acid. They also have less severe side effects than anticholinergics. An example is dicyclomine hydrochloride (*Bentyl*).

Many combinations of anticholinergics or antispasmodics with sedatives are available, including *Donnatal*, *Librax*, *Milpath*, and *Bellergal*. Changes in diet and eating habits are usually ordered along with these drugs.

Antidiarrheals

These drugs (Figure 11-9) work by:

- soaking up excess fluids and bacteria that cause the diarrhea (*adsorbent* action)
- lessening intestinal motility, which slows the movement of fecal material through the intestine so that there is more time to absorb the water and make formed stools.

Figure 11-9 Antidiarrheals.

Some antidiarrheals also contain ingredients that shrink swollen tissues (**astringent** action) or coat and soothe the tissues (**demulcent** action).

Among those preparations that soak up fluids are kaolin, bismuth (*Pepto-Bismol*), and pectin (ground apples). These are found in many combinations; for example, *Kaopectate* (kaolin and pectin).

The drugs that slow intestinal motility also have an effect on the central nervous system. The main group is the opiates, including paregoric, opium powder or tincture (laudanum), and diphenoxylate. The opiate antidiarrheals can lead to drug dependence if used too often.

Anticholinergics such as atropine are often used as adjuncts in the treatment of diarrhea because they relieve painful intestinal spasms. They are found in combinations along with adsorbents and opiates; for example, *Lomotil*, *Donnagel*, *Arco-Lase Plus*, and *Cantil*. Other preparations that help cure the underlying cause of diarrhea are antibiotics and intestinal bacteria that kill diarrhea-causing germs.

Cathartics (Laxatives and Purgatives)

These are drugs that promote **defecation** (bowel movement). In smaller doses they gently relieve constipation and are called **laxatives**. In larger doses they clean out the entire GI tract and are called **purgatives**. Purgatives are used before surgery or intestinal examinations. Cathartics work in several ways (Figure 11-10).

Stimulants—One group of cathartics stimulates peristalsis in the intestines so as to push the fecal material through faster. When intestinal motility is increased, there is less time for water to be absorbed by the large intestine, so the stools remain soft and moist. Drugs of this type include caster oil (*Neoloid*), prunes or prune juice, senna (*Fletcher's Castoria*, *Senokot*), cascara sagrada (*Cas-Evac*), and several synthetics including bisacodyl (*Dulcolax*) and phenolphthalein (*Phenolax*, *Ex-Lax*).

Saline—Another group of cathartics holds liquid in the large intestine so as to soften the feces and stimulate bowel movements. These are the saline cathartics, or salts of sodium, magnesium, and potassium. Milk of magnesia (taken in higher doses than when used as an antacid) and epsom salts are members of this group.

Bulk Formers—A third family of cathartics is the drugs that increase bulk. Some of them have the effect of swelling and lubricating the feces as well. The bulk-forming cathartics are indigestible substances. They merely add to the contents of the intestines, thus stimulating peristalsis. Their effects can take from 12 hours to 3

Drugs for the Gastrointestinal System 263

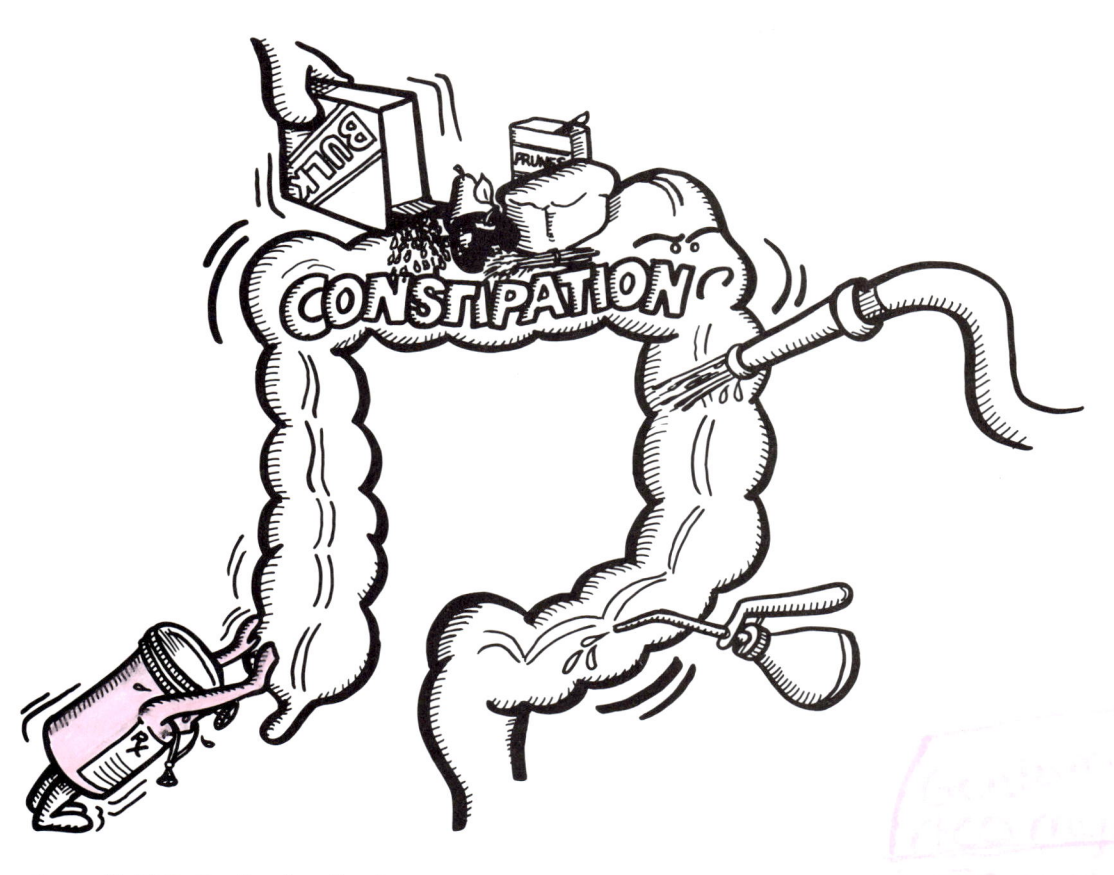

Figure 11-10 Cathartics (laxatives).

days to show up. Cereals and breads that contain bran and other fibers relieve constipation in this way. So do extracts of the plantain weed (psyllium) found in such preparations as *Metamucil* and *Effersyllium*. There are also several synthetic compounds. These should be taken with plenty of water and should not be chewed before swallowing because they might swell in the esophagus.

Emollients/Lubricants—A fourth group of laxatives does not increase intestinal motility but acts directly on the fecal matter. These are the lubricants and the detergents. Lubricants such as mineral or vegetable oil allow the feces to pass more easily through the intestine, but they are thought to interfere with the absorption of some vitamins. Detergents, or stool softeners, such as docusate sodium are found in several laxative products (*Colace, Peri-Colace, Senokot-S, Surfak*).

Antiparasitics

Antiparasitics are drugs that rid the body of intestinal parasites. These parasites belong to the animal group helminths (worms). The drugs are effective against worms, but they can be toxic to the body, so they must be used with care according to the doctor's orders. Usually the doctor will instruct the infected person to change underwear regularly, bathe and wash hands, keep fingernails trimmed, prepare food hygienically, and take similar precautions. Drugs used for pinworms and roundworms are piperazine (*Antepar*), pyrvinium pamoate (*Povan*), mebendazole (*Vermox*), pyrantel pamoate (*Antiminth*), and gentian violet.

Anthelminthics

Anorexiants

These are drugs that suppress the appetite so as to help the patient eat less and lose weight. (Recall that the term "anorexia" means loss of appetite.) The main anorexi-

Table 11-1 Selected OTC medications for gastrointestinal disorders

CONDITION	PRODUCTS	ACTIONS
Toothache, cold sores, canker sores	Benzodent, Blistex, Numzident, Orabase, Betadine	Anesthetic/Astringent
Diarrhea	Kaopectate, Pepto-Bismol, Donnagel	Antidiarrheal
Acid indigestion, heartburn	Amphojel, Di-Gel, Maalox, Gelusil, Mylanta, Bi-SoDol, Phillips' Milk of Magnesia, Rolaids, Tums, Kolantyl	Antacid/Antiflatulent
Constipation	Ex-Lax, Haley's M-O, Metamucil, Senokot, Cas-Evac, Colace, Dulcolax, Correctol	Laxative
Motion sickness	Bonine, Dramamine, Marezine	Antiemetic
Poisoning	Ipecac syrup	Emetic
Hemorrhoids	Anusol, Nupercainal, Preparation H	Antiseptic/Astringent/ Anesthetic/Protectant

ants are amphetamines or related drugs. These act by stimulating the central nervous system, which has an appetite-suppressing effect. Examples of these drugs are diethylpropion (*Tenuate*) and phentermine (*Fastin*). These drugs are not prescribed frequently because they work poorly and are potentially harmful and often abused. Many OTC diet products contain caffeine or phenylpropanolamine, both mild CNS stimulants.

The product information table at the end of this unit lists the uses, doses, and side effects of representative drugs given for GI disorders. Table 11-1 lists common OTC products that affect the GI system.

GIVING GASTROINTESTINAL MEDICATIONS

In most GI disorders, drug therapy is only an adjunct to physical measures. A person with constipation needs to get on a regular bowel-movement schedule; eat fresh fruits, prunes, or bran cereals that contain bulk; drink plenty of water; and get some exercise daily. Likewise, a person with diarrhea may get relief by eating small portions of bland foods, avoiding very hot or very cold drinks, resting, and replacing lost fluids. People with ulcers or gastritis must change their diet and give up irritating substances like tobacco, coffee, and alcohol. As a health care worker, your role is to make sure patients understand how these practices will help them feel better and make the drugs work better.

It is also important for good digestion to avoid nervous tension. Nervous tension can make constipation, nausea, ulcers, and many other disorders worse. You should strive to create a pleasant, nonstressful atmosphere around the patient. Arrange the environment for comfort and privacy with empathy to the patient's worries and fears, and offer instruction and encouragement.

Here are some general principles to remember when giving medications for the GI system:

- **Time.** Time of administration is particularly important (Figure 11-11). Medications that help digestion must be given before, during, or after mealtime as ordered. Otherwise, they may not be of any use. Other medications must be given between mealtimes when no food is present. Read the instructions carefully and follow them.

- **Liquids.** Give the recommended amount of liquids with each medication, according to the physician's instructions or the package insert. GI medications must be properly diluted to be effective and to avoid irritating the stomach.

Figure 11-11 Timing is important with gastrointestinal medications.

- **Abdominal Pain.** If the patient requests medication for abdominal pain, check with your supervisor before administering a PRN analgesic. Abdominal pain may signal some other undiagnosed GI disturbance that should be evaluated by a doctor.

Suppositories

Suppositories may be ordered when a patient is nauseated or unconscious and cannot take oral medication (Figure 11–12). They may also be ordered when a direct effect on the large intestine or feces is desired, such as with analgesics and cathartics.

The insertion of a suppository can be unpleasant and embarrassing for a patient. You need to be aware of the patient's needs. Give enough privacy. Explain what you are doing and why it is necessary. Remove the wrapper, and lubricate the suppository to make it enter the rectum as smoothly and gently as possible. The suppository must be inserted well into the rectum, beyond a ring of muscle called the **anal rectal ridge**. The length of your index finger—2–3 inches—should be deep enough. To be effective, the suppository must be placed along the wall of the colon rather than into fecal matter.

If the patient has pain or irritation in the rectal area after you have inserted the suppository, chart it and inform the nurse in charge or the physician. Either may be a sign of local inflammation caused by the drug. When the patient has a bowel movement, note and chart the appearance of the stools. If the bowel movement occurs shortly after the suppository is inserted, check with the physician. Another suppository may have to be inserted to get the full dose of medication.

Stomach Tubes

In certain severe conditions, such as coma or cancer of the throat, patients are unable to swallow food and drink. Therefore, they are fed through special tubes into the stomach. Tube feeding is called **gastric gavage**. There are two types of tubes: (1) a **nasogastric** or **Levin tube** is inserted through the nose or mouth and passes through the esophagus to the stomach (Figure 11-13) or (2) a **gastrostomy tube** is inserted directly into the stomach through a surgical opening in the abdomen called a **stoma**.

When these tubes are in place, oral medications are also given through them. These medications must be in liquid form. For this reason, tablets and capsules must

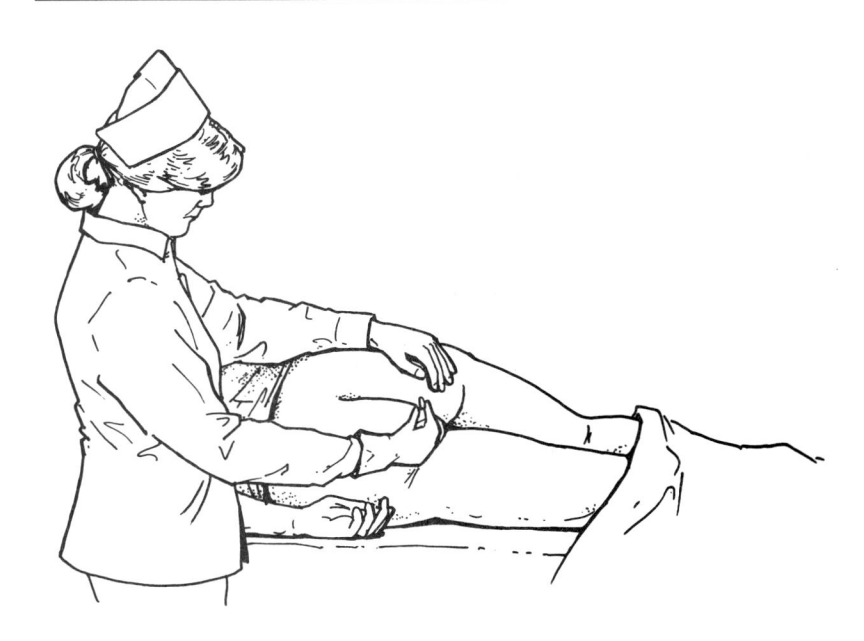

Figure 11-12 Administering a rectal suppository.

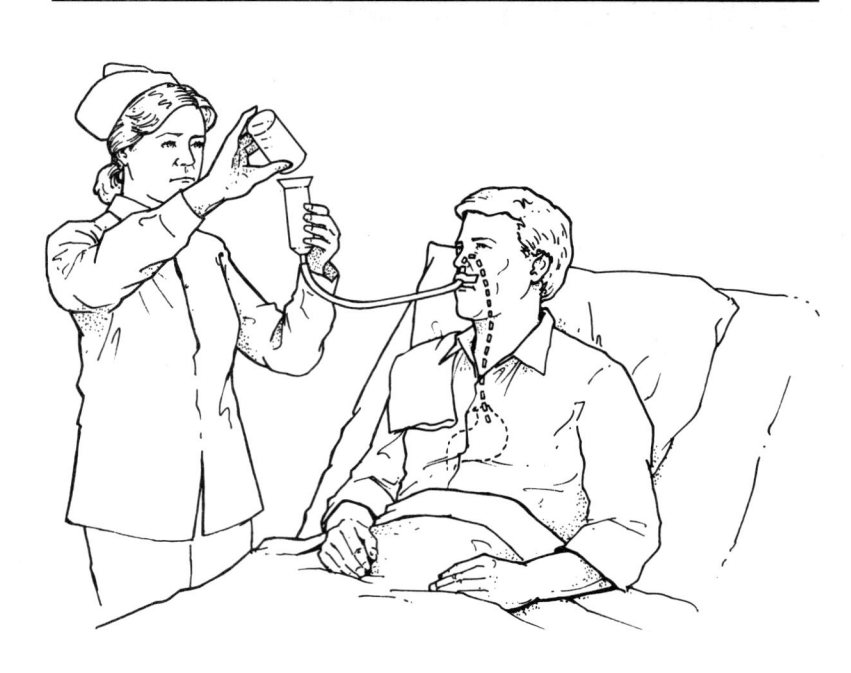

Figure 11-13 Administering medications through a nasogastric (Levin) tube.

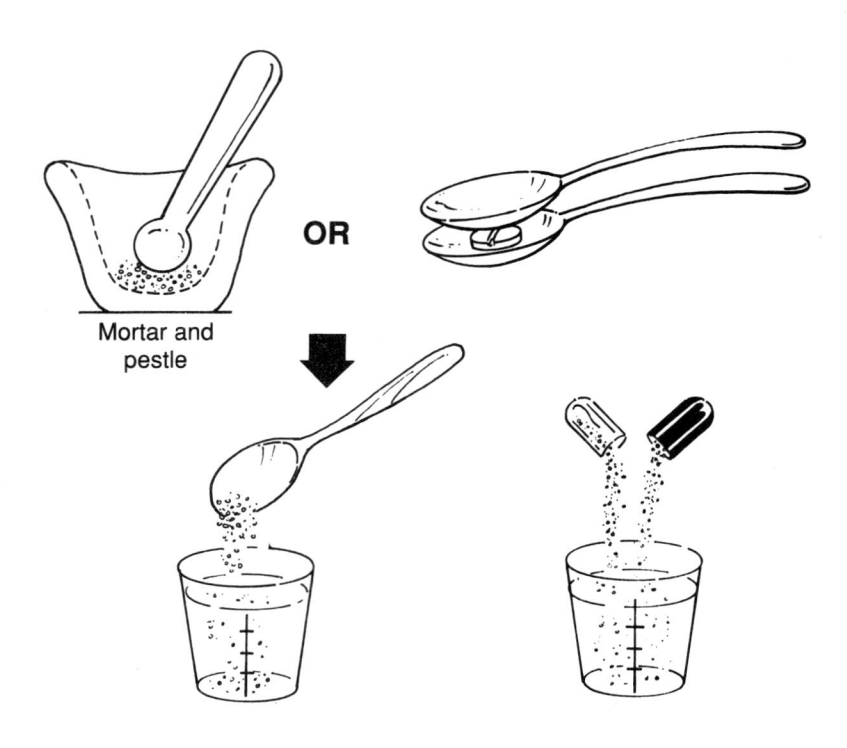

Figure 11-14 Crush tablets or open capsules and mix with water for tube administration (not timed-release products).

be crushed and mixed with water before administering. Crush them either with a mortar and pestle or between two nested spoons (Figure 11-14). They should be mixed with about 1 ounce of water. (**Remember, in no case should you crush or dissolve a timed-release or enteric-coated tablet or capsule**. If this is the prescribed medication, consult the doctor or the nurse in charge as to what to do.)

The dissolved medications are poured *very slowly* into the tube through a syringe. You can adjust the rate of flow by raising or lowering the hand that is holding the syringe. Then the medications are washed down into the stomach with water. To avoid shocking the system, the water should be at room temperature or a little warmer. It need not be sterile. Watch for any leakage around the gastrostomy opening and report it to the supervisor. Also be sure that the liquid is draining into the stomach. If not, there may be something blocking the tube. If there is any redness, pus, or pain around the stoma, notify your supervisor immediately.

Keep in mind that tube-fed patients are completely dependent on others for eating and taking medications. This is not a pleasant experience for them. Try to make them as comfortable as possible and maintain a calm, soothing atmosphere so as to avoid creating more tension.

Tube-fed or unconscious patients may need special care in oral hygiene. They may be lying with their mouths open, allowing the mucous membranes to dry out. Be alert to the need for rinsing their mouths and caring for their teeth. Lemon and glycerin swabs may be used to clean the teeth and moisten mucous membranes.

EXERCISES

A. Fill in the blanks.

1. Another name for the gastrointestinal system is the _digestive_ system.

2. The opening that passes through the body from the mouth to the rectum is the _digestive tract_.

3. The muscular movement that carries food through the gastrointestinal system is called _peristalsis_.

4. Glands in the mouth, stomach, liver, and pancreas secrete _enzymes_ that help break down food.

5. Nutrients are absorbed into the blood mainly from the _small intestines_.

6. The fluid that coats and dissolves food in the mouth is called _saliva_.

7. The body tube that connects the mouth to the stomach is the _esophagus_.

8. When peristalsis moves in the opposite direction, the result is _vomiting_.

9. Powerful juices from the pancreas and liver are mixed with food in the _duodenum_, which is the entryway to the small intestine.

10. Because of their fingerlike shape, the _villi_ of the small intestine provide a huge surface area for absorption.

11. Undigested waste products that collect in the large intestine are called _feces_.

12. The opening that allows material from the rectum to pass out of the body is the _anus_.

13. Bile, an enzyme that breaks down fat, is produced in the _liver_.

14. Bile is stored in the _gall bladder_.

15. Powerful digestive juices that complete the digestion of carbohydrates, fat, and protein are produced in the _pancreas_.

268 Administering Medications

B. Short answers.

1. What are the five functions of the gastrointestinal system?

   breakdown food, transport through GI tract, secretes enzymes, absorbs nutrients, remove waste

2. How is digestion related to psychological stress?

   Enzymes, peristalsis influenced by ANS

3. List all the symptoms you can think of that signal some disorder of the digestive tract.

   nausea, diarrhea, cramps, stool appearance, vomiting, constipation, belching, gas, bloating, anorexia

4. What is intestinal motility and what happens if it is too fast or too slow?

   speed/force of peristalsis

5. How can tooth and gum disorders lead to other gastrointestinal problems?

   interfere good nutrition

C. Choose the gastrointestinal disorder that best matches each description below and write it in the space provided.

| gastritis | gallstones | hepatitis | peritonitis |
| duodenal ulcer | cirrhosis | hemorrhoids | irritable bowel |

1. Mrs. Phillips has been straining at stool. The large veins around her anal opening are swollen, itching, and beginning to bleed. **hemorrhoids**

2. Following a transfusion of blood, Mr. Mann develops a liver infection. The doctor suspects that the blood donor also had the infection and passed it on to Mr. Mann through the transfusion. **hepatitis**

3. Mrs. Merriweather has small grains of cholesterol building up in her gallbladder. They cause mild spasms from time to time. The doctor will not remove them unless they begin to block the tube that leads to the intestine. The doctor prescribes a drug to reduce the intestinal spasms. _gall stones_

4. Mr. Hale is an alcoholic. His doctor has been warning him about the damage to his liver for years. Now Mr. Hale has developed a severe inflammation of the liver. The doctor orders rest, a change of diet, and anti-inflammatory drugs.

   cirrhosis

5. Ms. Yang has an inflammation of the stomach. The burning pain and nausea have been coming and going for several weeks. Her doctor suggests she cut out smoking and coffee to give her stomach relief. _gastritis_

6. Mr. Hruban has developed an open sore at the entrance of the small intestine. The doctor prescribes antacids to calm Mr. Hruban's nervous tension. She also orders Mr. Hruban to quit smoking. _duodenal ulcer_

7. Because of an injury to the Nelson boy's intestine, food and digestive juices have leaked into the abdominal cavity. This has caused a serious inflammation of the abdominal linings. Surgery and antibiotics are ordered at once.

   peritonitis

8. Miss Perez is troubled by abdominal cramping and a bloated, gassy feeling. She is under a great deal of stress in her job as a junior high school teacher. After careful examination, the physician reassures her that the condition is not serious and prescribes an antispasmodic to reduce the cramping.

   irritable bowel

D. Describe what each of the following drug groups does; for example, Emetics *cause vomiting*

   1. Antacids _neutralize HCl_
   2. Digestants _produce HCl - aid indigestion_
   3. Antiflatulents _prevent gas buildup in intestine_
   4. Antiemetics _prevent vomiting_
   5. Anticholinergics _prevent spasms_
   6. Antidiarrheals _prevent diarrhea_
   7. Cathartics _stimulate bowel_
   8. Antiparasitics _prevent, kill worms in digestive system_
   9. Anorexiants _↓ appetite_

E. Match these drugs to their categories:

   _f_ 1. piperazine, *Antiminth*, gentian violet

   _b_ 2. cascara sagrada, *Metamucil*, bisacodyl

   _e_ 3. kaolin, pectin, bismuth, paregoric, *Lomotil*

   _a_ 4. *Pro-Banthine*, atropine, *Bentyl*

   _h_ 5. *Antivert, Dramamine, Compazine*

   _d_ 6. simethicone, brandy

   _g_ 7. hydrochloric acid, pancreatin

   _c_ 8. *Maalox*, aluminum hydroxide, *Gelusil*, sodium bicarbonate

   a. anticholinergics and antispasmodics
   b. laxatives
   c. antacids
   d. antiflatulents (carminatives)
   e. antidiarrheals
   f. antiparasitics
   g. digestants
   h. antiemetics

F. Short answers.
   1. State the four ways that laxatives (cathartics) work.

   2. What are some of the physical measures that help gastrointestinal drugs work better?

   3. List three things to remember when giving gastrointestinal medications.

Drugs for the Gastrointestinal System 271

4. How can you ease the discomfort and embarrassment of the patient when you are inserting a rectal suppository?

_____

_____

_____

5. What signs should you look for, chart, and report after inserting a suppository?

_____

_____

6. How should you prepare a tablet or capsule for administration through a nasogastric or gastrostomy tube?

_____

_____

7. What signs should you look for, chart, and report when administering medications through a nasogastric or gastrostomy tube?

_____

_____

_____

G. Match the medical terms to their definitions.

__c__ 1. yellow color of the skin due to liver bile in the bloodstream

__f__ 2. instrument for looking into the stomach

__h__ 3. loss of appetite

__b__ 4. ring of muscle a few inches in from the anus

__e__ 5. tube inserted into the stomach through a hole

__d__ 6. tube inserted into the stomach through the nose and esophagus

__g__ 7. moving the bowels

__a__ 8. vomiting

a. emesis
b. anal rectal ridge
c. jaundice
d. nasogastric tube
e. gastrostomy tube
f. gastroscope
g. defecation
h. anorexia

ANSWERS TO EXERCISES

A. Fill in the blanks
   1. digestive
   2. digestive tract, gastrointestinal tract, or alimentary canal
   3. peristalsis
   4. digestive juices, or enzymes
   5. small intestine
   6. saliva
   7. esophagus
   8. vomiting, or emesis
   9. duodenum
   10. villi
   11. feces, or stools
   12. anus
   13. liver
   14. gallbladder
   15. pancreas

B. Short answers
   1. Breaking up food, transporting food through the system, secreting digestive enzymes, absorbing nutrients into the blood, and excreting solid wastes.
   2. Enzyme secretion and peristalsis are controlled by the autonomic nervous system, which is also influenced by emotional stress.
   3. Nausea, vomiting, indigestion, bloating, cramping, belching, flatus, constipation, abdominal pain, diarrhea, anorexia, weight loss, and changes in appearance of stools.
   4. Intestinal motility is the speed and force of peristalsis. Changes in motility lead to either diarrhea or constipation.
   5. If eating and chewing are painful because of these problems, people will not eat right, and poor nutrition and constipation will result.

C. Gastrointestinal disorders
   1. hemorrhoids
   2. hepatitis
   3. gallstones
   4. cirrhosis
   5. gastritis
   6. duodenal ulcer
   7. peritonitis
   8. irritable bowel

D. Gastrointestinal drugs
   1. neutralize stomach acid.
   2. supplement or replace digestive juices.
   3. reduce gassiness and bloating.
   4. stop vomiting and nausea.
   5. slow peristalsis and block secretion of stomach acid.
   6. relieve diarrhea by soaking up fluids or slowing peristalsis.
   7. stimulate bowel movements or clear out the intestines.
   8. destroy intestinal parasites (worms).
   9. suppress the appetite.

E. Matching
   1. f
   2. b
   3. e
   4. a
   5. h
   6. d
   7. g
   8. c

F. Short answers
   1. Softening feces, stimulating peristalsis, adding bulk to the diet, and coating or lubricating.
   2. Changes in diet; regular bowel movements; getting enough exercise; reducing nervous tension; and giving up smoking, coffee, and alcohol.
   3. Give medications at the proper time (before, after, or with meals or at bedtime). Give the right amount of liquid with each. Be wary of giving PRN medications for abdominal pain.
   4. Provide privacy, explain what you are going to do, lubricate the suppository, and insert it gently and smoothly.
   5. Signs of pain or irritation, appearance of stools, and bowel movement too soon after insertion.

6. Crush tablets between two spoons or in a mortar and pestle, and then mix with 1 ounce of water. Open capsules and dissolve in water. Do not crush and dissolve timed-release tablets or capsules.

7. Signs of inflammation or leakage around the stoma or poor tube drainage.

G. Matching definitions
   1. c
   2. f
   3. h
   4. b
   5. e
   6. d
   7. g
   8. a

PRACTICE PROCEDURE

INSERT A RECTAL SUPPOSITORY

Equipment:

- Physician's order for a rectal medication
- Kardex, medicine card, medication record, patient chart
- Medicine tray or cart
- Rectal suppository
- Plastic or rubber glove or finger cover (nonsterile)
- Lubricating jelly (water-soluble)
- Protective pad or paper towel

_____ 1. Assemble equipment and set up medication. Check for the "five rights."

_____ 2. Identify the patient according to agency policy. Explain the procedure. Make sure that the patient understands that the suppository must be held in. You will need the patient's cooperation for this.

_____ 3. Wash your hands. Unwrap the suppository and place it on the wrapper.

_____ 4. Assist the patient into a side-lying (lateral) position with the upper leg bent. Drape the patient so as to expose only the anal area. Place a paper towel or pad under the hip to protect the sheet. Help the patient relax in preparation for the procedure.

_____ 5. Put on a glove or finger cover. Lubricate the smooth or rounded tip of the suppository. Also lubricate your gloved index finger.

_____ 6. Insert the suppository (Figure 11-15).
   a. With the ungloved hand, spreads the buttocks apart and locate the anus.
   b. Instruct the patient to breathe through the mouth. This will help relax the anal sphincter.
   c. With the gloved hand, insert the suppository into the anal opening. Gently push it in to the length of your index finger. This will place it past the anal rectal ridge. Make sure that it lies along the wall of the colon and is not pressed into a mass of feces.
   d. Close the buttocks and press them together for a moment. The patient may have an urge to expel the suppository, and this will help keep it in until the urge passes.

_____ 7. Instruct the patient to remain quiet and avoid having a bowel movement for at least 20 minutes. This is to give the medication time to work. Assist the patient back into a comfortable position.

_____ 8. Remove the glove or finger cover by turning it inside out. Discard it in an appropriate place. If you use a nondisposable glove, wash the glove in soap and water. Also, wash your hands.

_____ 9. Chart the medication.

_____ 10. After this procedure has been completed, watch for signs of pain or irritation in the rectal area; chart and report them. When the patient has a bowel movement, chart the appearance of the feces.

Demonstrate this procedure for the instructor or the nurse in charge.

Drugs for the Gastrointestinal System **275**

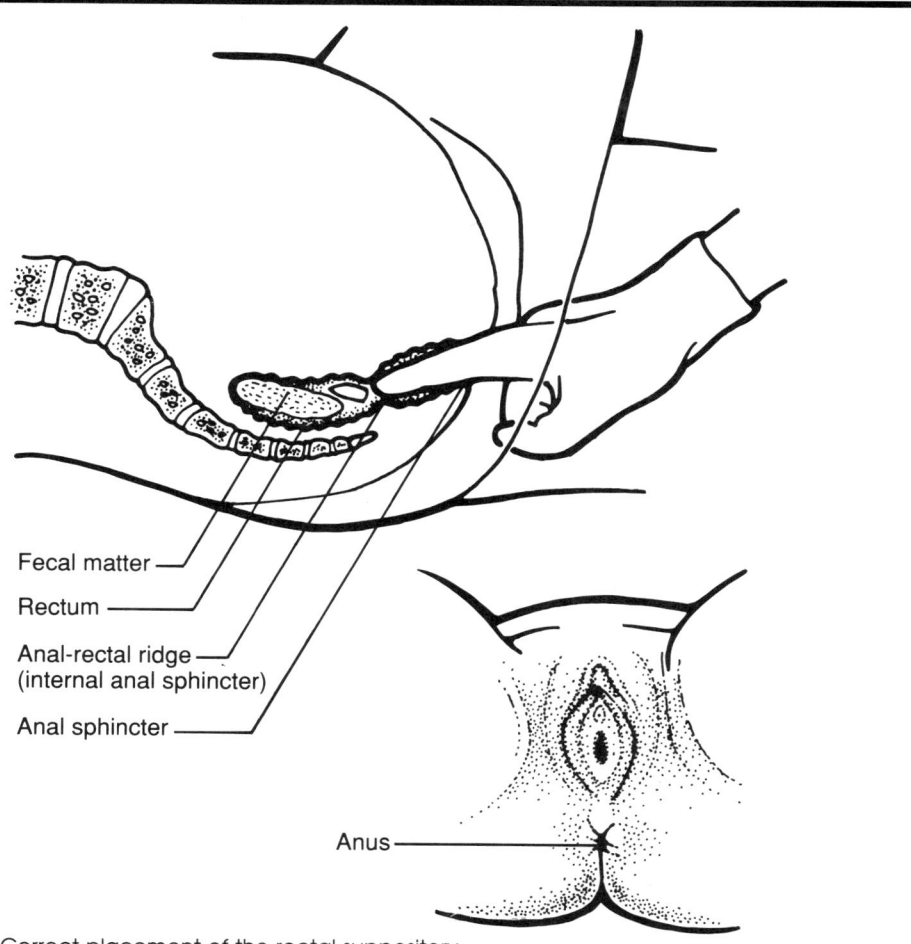

Figure 11-15 Correct placement of the rectal suppository.

276 Administering Medications

PRACTICE PROCEDURE

ADMINISTER MEDICATION THROUGH AN INSTALLED NASOGASTRIC OR GASTROSTOMY TUBE

Equipment:
- Physician's order for a gastrointestinal medication
- Medication (tablet, capsule, powder, or liquid—no timed-release or enteric-coated forms)
- Medication record, medicine card, Kardex, patient chart
- Medicine tray or cart
- Pitcher containing 2–4 oz of water at room temperature
- Plastic or glass bulbed syringe, with a tip the right size to fit into the tube
- Protective cover such as a small towel or disposable protective pad
- Tube clamp on patient tubing

_____ 1. Assemble equipment and set up medication. Check for the "five rights."

_____ 2. Wash your hands.

_____ 3. Prepare the medication. Crush tablets or pills with a mortar and pestle, or crush them between two spoons, using the top spoon to press down on the tablet. Then mix with 1 oz of water in a small glass. If the medication is in capsule form, empty capsule contents into water and mix. The water does not need to be sterile.

_____ 4. Identify the patient according to agency policy. Explain the procedure.

_____ 5. Place the patient in proper position for administration.
- In bed: semireclining (Fowler's) position
- In a chair or wheelchair: sitting position

_____ 6. **Nasogastric:** Place a towel over the patient's chest and remove the clamp from the tube.

Gastrostomy: Remove the dressing from the abdomen and unclamp the tube.

_____ 7. Insert the tip of a syringe into the end of the tubing. (Take off the syringe bulb first.) Hold the tubing and the syringe together with one hand (Figure 11-16). This prevents the syringe from coming out of the tube during administration. Hold both tube and syringe above the level of the stomach so as to prevent outward drainage.

_____ 8. Pour the liquid medication slowly into the open syringe. Follow it with 2–4 oz of water, also poured slowly. The water washes the medication into the stomach as it clears the tubing. *Do not* use the syringe bulb to force the medication into the stomach. Let gravity carry it down. Control the flow by raising or lowering your hand.

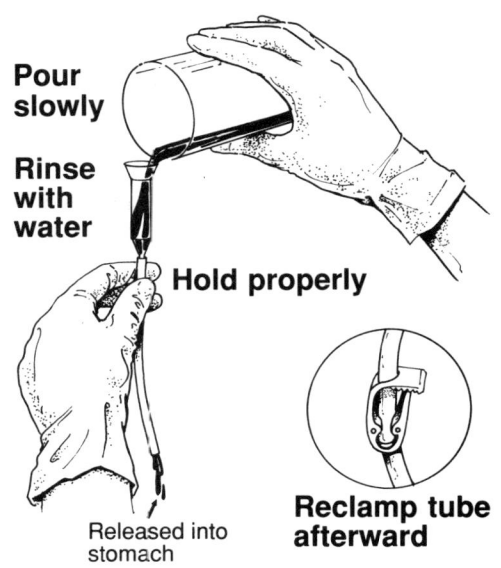

Pour slowly

Rinse with water

Hold properly

Released into stomach

Reclamp tube afterward

Figure 11-16 Principles of tube administration.

_____ 9. Take away the syringe, still holding the tubing with the free end up. Do not put the tube down until you have reclamped it; otherwise, medication may run out.

_____ 10. Clamp the tube. With a corner of the towel, wipe the end clean of any liquid.

_____ 11. **Nasogastric:** Tape the tube to the forehead or cheek.

Gastrostomy: Replace the dressing over the hole where the tube enters the stomach. Check for leakage around the hole and report it to the supervisor. Lay the tube down over the abdomen.

_____ 12. Assist the patient into a comfortable position and give any special instructions.

_____ 13. Wash your hands and clean the equipment.

_____ 14. Chart the medication. Chart any signs of leakage around the stoma (note the color), pain, pus, redness, or failure to drain into the stomach. If any of these signs are present, report them immediately.

Demonstrate this procedure for the instructor or the nurse in charge.

REPRESENTATIVE DRUGS FOR THE GASTROINTESTINAL SYSTEM

CATEGORY, NAME[a], AND ROUTE	DISEASES AND USES	ACTION	DOSAGE[b] AND SPECIAL INSTRUCTIONS	SIDE EFFECTS AND ADVERSE REACTIONS
Antacids Magnesium and aluminum combinations (*Aludrox, Gelusil, Maalox*) Oral	Heartburn, sour stomach, acid indigestion (with gas)	Neutralizes stomach acid, antigas	Two or more teaspoons or tablets 1 hour after meals and at bedtime; tablets may be chewed	Do not take more than 12 tablets in a 24-hour period because of a laxative effect; do not give to patients with kidney trouble
Antiflatulents Simethicone (*Mylicon*) Oral	Excess gas in the digestive tract	Defoaming action; added to antacid and digestants	1 or 2 tablets QID after meals and at bedtime, as needed	None
Antinauseants Dimenhydrinate (*Dramamine*) Oral, IM	Nausea, vomiting, and vertigo	Relieves vomiting, nausea, and vertigo	Give 30 minutes to 1 hour before activity; 50 mg q 4 hours	Dizziness, drowsiness
Prochlorperazine (*Compazine*) Oral, rectal	Severe cases of nausea and vomiting	Controls vomiting, reflex by depressing CNS, sedates	5–10 mg three or four times a day	Hypotension, drowsiness, dizziness, amenorrhea, blurred vision
Meclizine (*Antivert*) Oral	Motion sickness, dizziness, nausea, and vomiting; management of vertigo associated with diseases affecting vestibular system	Antihistamine properties	Vertigo: 25–100 mg per day in divided doses; motion sickness: 25–50 mg taken 1 hour before activity	Drowsiness, dry mouth, and blurred vision
Antispasmodics/ Anticholinergics Propantheline bromide (*Pro-Banthine*) Oral	Effective as adjunctive therapy in treatment of peptic ulcer	Inhibits GI motility and diminishes acid secretion	15 mg taken 30 minutes before meals and 30 mg at bedtime	Dry mouth, decreased sweating, blurred vision, mydriasis, urinary retention, tachycardia, headache, nervousness
Dicyclomine (*Bentyl*) Oral, IM	Irritable or spastic bowel	Relieves smooth muscle spasm, reduces intestinal motility	10–20 mg TID or QID PO	Constipation, drowsiness, dizziness
Antidiarrheals Diphenoxylate HCl and atropine sulfate (*Lomotil*) Oral	Diarrhea	Reduces intestinal motility	Initial dose 5 mg QID; maintenance dose lower; adjusted individually	Abdominal distension, rash, dry mouth, restlessness
Cathartics Bisacodyl (*Dulcolax*) Oral, rectal	Constipation, preparation of bowel for surgery or examination	Increases intestinal motility by stimulating nerves in colon	Tablets: 10–15 mg; give at bedtime or early morning (works in 6–12 hours); to be swallowed whole; do not give within 1 hour of an antacid or milk (these can dissolve enteric coating)	Abdominal cramps; rarely nausea, vomiting, diarrhea

REPRESENTATIVE DRUGS FOR THE GASTROINTESTINAL SYSTEM

CATEGORY, NAME[a], AND ROUTE	USES AND DISEASES	ACTIONS	USUAL DOSE[b] AND SPECIAL INSTRUCTIONS	SIDE EFFECTS AND ADVERSE REACTIONS
Psyllium hydrophilic mucilloid (*Metamucil*) Oral	Chronic constipation; irritable bowel syndrome and diverticulosis; management of patients with hemorrhoids and pregnant women	Provides bland, nonirritating bulk; promotes normal bowel elimination	Give 1 rounded tsp stirred into an 8-oz glass of cool water or liquid; give 1–3 times a day followed by another full glass of liquid	None
Docusate sodium (*Colace*) Oral	Constipation and hard stools, in patients with painful anorectal conditions, and in cardiac and other conditions where maximum ease in passage of the stool is desired	A surface-active agent that helps to keep the stool soft	50–240 mg/day; full effect may take 1–3 days; if liquid, give in half glass of milk or fruit juice	Rare; may be a bitter taste; throat irritation and nausea with liquid

[a] Brand names given in parentheses are examples only. Check current drug references for a complete listing of available trade name products.
[b] Average adult doses are given. However, dosages are determined by a physician and vary with the purpose of the therapy and the particular patient. The doses presented in this text are for general information only.

Unit 12

Drugs for the Urinary System and Fluid Balance

In this unit you will learn how the urinary system excretes liquid wastes from the body. You will study the way the kidneys keep the proper balance of fluids and salts to meet the needs of the cells. You will learn about the disorders that arise in the urinary system and how drugs are used to control them. You will learn how to administer drugs into an indwelling catheter and how to give diuretics.

In this unit, you will learn to:

- State three functions of the urinary system.
- Name the parts of the urinary system and tell what they do.
- Explain how urine gives clues to disorders in the urinary system.
- Give the correct medical terms for symptoms of urinary system disorders and fluid imbalances.
- Recognize descriptions of the main disorders that affect the urinary system.
- Define electrolytes, acidifiers, and alkalizers.
- Describe the actions and give examples of the following drug groups: urinary antiseptics, diuretics, replacement electrolytes and fluids.
- Describe the nursing care that goes with giving diuretics.
- State the purposes of a urinary catheter.
- Follow proper procedure for administering medications through an indwelling catheter.

URINARY SYSTEM

The urinary system includes two kidneys, two ureters (*u-re'terz*), a urinary bladder, and a urethra (*u-re'thrah*) (Figure 12-1). The system has three major functions:

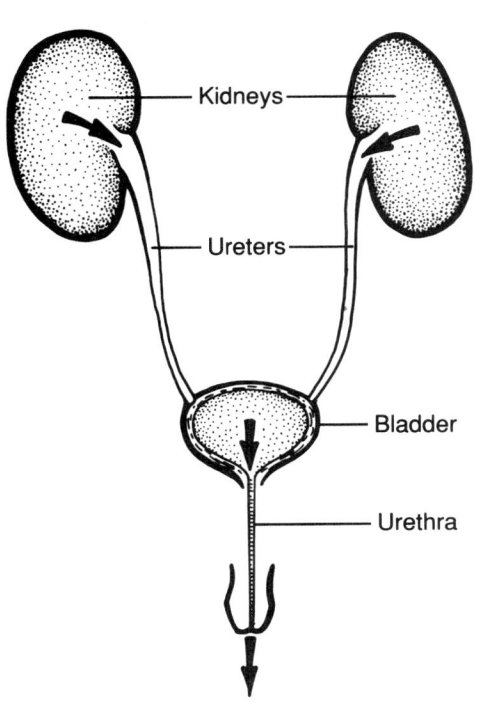

Figure 12-1 The urinary system.

- **Excretion of waste products.** The kidneys excrete waste products by filtering them out of the blood. The main waste products are **urea** (*u-re'ah*), a byproduct of the use of proteins by the body cells, certain mineral salts, and water.
- **Regulating the amount of water.** By eliminating excess water, the urinary system helps to maintain a proper balance of fluids in the body tissues.
- **Regulating the pH balance.** The body cells work best in a neutral or slightly basic environment. The kidneys help to maintain the proper balance of acids and bases no matter what types of foods are eaten.

All three functions of the urinary system are carried out through the same process of filtering the blood. This process takes place in the kidneys. Urine is produced and leaves the body by way of the ureter, the bladder, and the urethra, which are the organs of elimination.

The two **kidneys** are located at the back of the abdominal cavity high up under the diaphragm. They are supported by a layer of fatty connective tissue and are partially protected by the ribs. Each kidney has two layers, the **cortex** and the **medulla** (Figure 12-2). In the cortex, the important filtering of the blood takes place. This is done by over a million tiny coiled tubes called **nephrons** (*nef'ronz*). Each nephron has a bulb at one end, the **glomerulus** (*glo-mer'u-lus*), which contains many capillaries (Figure 12-3).

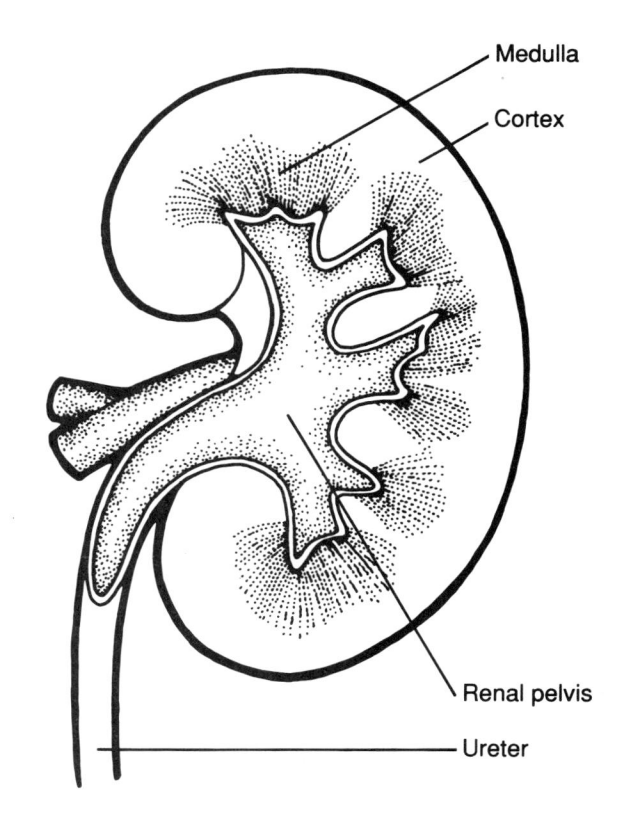

Figure 12-2 Close-up of kidney.

As the blood circulates through the glomerulus, water and dissolved substances pass out of the blood through the capillary walls and into the nephron. Then this liquid travels through the coils of the nephron tube, and some of the water, nutrients, and minerals are reabsorbed into the bloodstream through the nephron walls. This leaves only waste products, certain salts, and varying amounts of water. The

VOCABULARY

acid: substance with a low pH (below pH 7); opposite of base

acidifier: drug that makes the body's pH more acid

acidosis: condition in which the body tissues and fluids are too acid

alkalizer: drug that makes the body's pH more basic or alkaline

alkalosis: pH imbalance in which the body tissues and fluids are too basic or alkaline

anuria: no urine produced by the kidneys

base: substance with a high pH (above pH 7); opposite of acid; also called **alkali**

bladder: muscular pouch for storage of urine

catheter: tube inserted through the urethra into the bladder to allow urine drainage, bladder irrigation, or instillation of medication

cystitis: bladder infection

cystoscope: instrument for visually examining the bladder

dehydration: excessive loss of water from the tissues

dialysis: mechanical filtering of the blood in cases of kidney failure

diuretic: drug that increases production of urine by blocking reabsorption of salt and water in the nephrons

dysuria: difficult or painful urination

edema: swelling of tissues due to water retention

electrolyte: dissolved mineral salt that enters into chemical transport processes in body fluids

frequency (urinary frequency): the need to urinate more often than normal

glomeruli: tiny structures in the kidney that filter the blood

hematuria: blood in the urine

hypo- and **hypercalcemia**: calcium imbalances

hypo- and **hyperkalemia**: potassium imbalances; also called **hypo-** and **hyperpotassemia**

hypo- and **hypernatremia**: sodium imbalances

incontinence: inability to control urination

indwelling catheter: catheter designed to be held in place over a period of time; also called **anchored** or **retention** catheter

irrigation: flushing with liquid

nephritis: kidney inflammation

nephrons: tiny structures in the kidney that reabsorb certain salts and fluids after the blood has been filtered

oliguria: production of very little urine by the kidneys

pH: a measure of the acidity or basicity of a solution

pyelonephritis: kidney infection

pyuria: pus in the urine

retention: inability to urinate

urea: a waste product contained in urine

ureters: tubes that conduct urine from the kidneys to the bladder

urethra: tube leading from the bladder to the outside of the body

urgency: pressing need to urinate

urinary antiseptic: drug that kills germs or slows the growth of germs in the urinary tract

urination: release of urine through voluntary control of the bladder; also called **voiding** or **micturition**

urine: liquid wastes collected by the kidneys from the bloodstream

---

resulting liquid is called **urine**. The nephrons dip into the second layer of the kidney, the medulla. There the urine collects in a tube called the **ureter** that leads out of the kidney. The ureter is about 10–13 inches long.

The two ureters, one from each kidney, carry the collected urine to the **bladder**. The bladder is a storage bag for urine. Its muscular walls are able to stretch out and hold up to a pint of liquid. Nerve endings in the bladder signal to the nervous system when the bladder is full. This creates the urge to **urinate** or **void**.

During urination the urine passes out of the body by way of the **urethra**. The urethra is about 1-1/2 inches long in the female. It opens to the outside of the body between

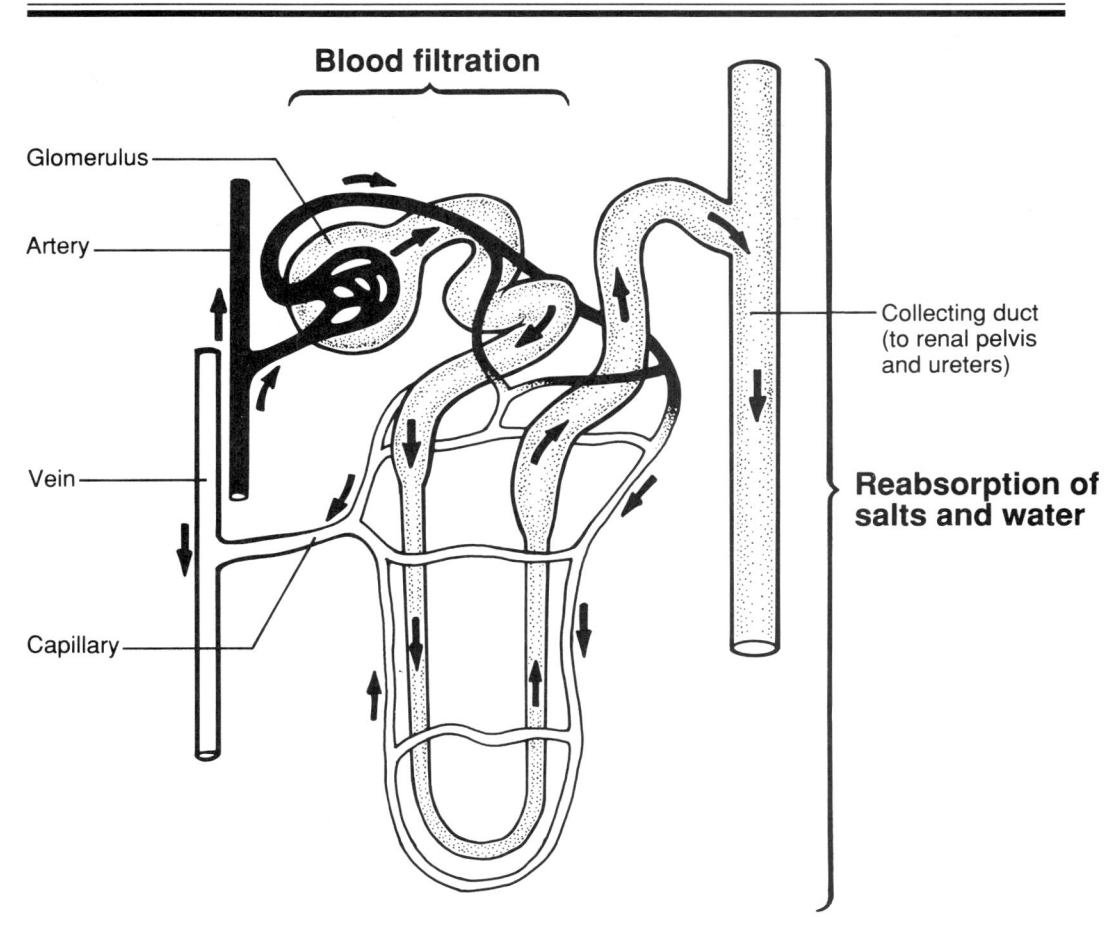

Figure 12-3 A kidney nephron, showing where filtration and reabsorption take place.

the labia in the female genital area, just above the vaginal opening. The urethra is about 8 inches long in the male and opens to the outside at the tip of the penis. The male urethra is shared between the urinary system and the reproductive system. The location of the urethra in relation to other parts of the male and female genitals is shown in Unit 14 (Figures 14-2 and 14-3).

The urine itself is a medically important substance. Examining and testing the urine gives clues to many types of diseases and disorders. It is about 90–95% water and 5–10% salts, urea, and other waste products. About 1500–2000 ml (or cc) of urine are produced by the kidneys in a 24-hour period. The bladder voids about 200–300 ml at a time. By studying the urine, doctors can determine how well the kidneys are functioning and whether there are imbalances in the body's water and pH levels. When there is an excess of water, the kidneys allow more water to be eliminated. This shows up in urine tests because there is a smaller percentage of waste products per unit of liquid.

DISORDERS OF THE KIDNEYS AND THE URINARY TRACT

Tests and Symptoms

There are several ways to tell if the kidneys and other parts of the urinary tract are not working properly. X-rays are used, and there is a tube with a lens that permits visual examination of the internal organs, called a **cystoscope** (*sis'to-skop*). These tools can be used to find growths or objects that might be blocking or putting pressure on parts of the system. They can also be used to check the condition of the bladder and ureters. A plastic tube called a **catheter** (*kath'e-ter*) may be inserted through the urethra into the bladder. The catheter causes the bladder to empty immediately. This tells the medical staff whether there is urine that a person is not able to void because of a bladder condition. Finally, much can be discovered just by examining the urine. A visual examination of a urine sample may reveal traces of blood (**hematuria**, *hem'ah-tu're-ah*) or pus (**pyuria**, *pi-u're-ah*) in the urine. Chemical analysis of the urine reveals if there is improper excretion of blood cells, protein, acids, or salts.

The outward signs of urinary tract disorders are changes in the act of urinating. Inability to urinate is called **retention**. Inability to control urination is **incontinence**. Having to urinate very often (**frequency**) or feeling a great urge to urinate even when the bladder is empty (**urgency**) are common symptoms of disorders. Urination may require effort or be painful (**dysuria**, *dis-u-re'ah*). There may be a **burning** sensation during urination. Or there may be little urine (**oliguria**, *ol'i-gu're-ah*) or no urine (**anuria**, *ah-nu're-ah*) produced at all.

These symptoms may be the result of urinary tract disorders. But they may also show up as side effects of drugs given for other disorders (drugs that affect the nervous system). When these conditions appear after giving a drug, they should be charted just like any unusual symptom (Figure 12-4).

Major Disorders

Obstructions—Physical obstructions of the urinary tract may be the result of malformed organs. Or they may be caused by tumors or injuries. **Kidney stones** are also responsible for some obstructions. These stones are formed out of salts in the urine. The salts form crystals that grow larger and larger, similar to the iciclelike mineral deposits in caves. Kidney stones may grow large enough to block the ureters. Sometimes they travel down the ureters, causing intense pain, and lodge in the bladder. When in the bladder, they may be easily crushed with special instruments and flushed out through the urethra.

Infections—The kidney, ureters, bladder, and urethra are prone to infection. This is because they are lined with mucous membranes and lie close to outer portions of the body that may carry germs. Personal cleanliness is important to prevent germs from entering the urinary tract. Once germs gain entry, they can cause infections that may travel up the urethra to the bladder and other parts of the system. Bladder infections cause spasms that make the patient urinate frequently. They resist drug treatment and tend to keep coming back.

Urinary Tract Infections

pyelonephritis (*pi'e-lo-ne-fri'tis*)—kidney infection

nephritis (*ne-fri'tis*)—inflammation of the kidney, also known as "Bright's disease"

cystitis (*sis-ti'tis*)—inflammation of the bladder

ureteritis (*u're-ter-i'tis*)—inflammation of the ureter

urethritis (*u're-thri'tis*)—inflammation of the urethra

Urinary tract infections are treated with anti-infectives (sulfonamides and antibiotics) and analgesics for pain.

Kidney Failure—Whenever the kidneys are physically unable to perform their regulating functions, the patient has some degree of kidney failure. The consequences may be grave.

Trouble signs:

Hematuria

Pyuria

Incontinence

Retention

Frequency

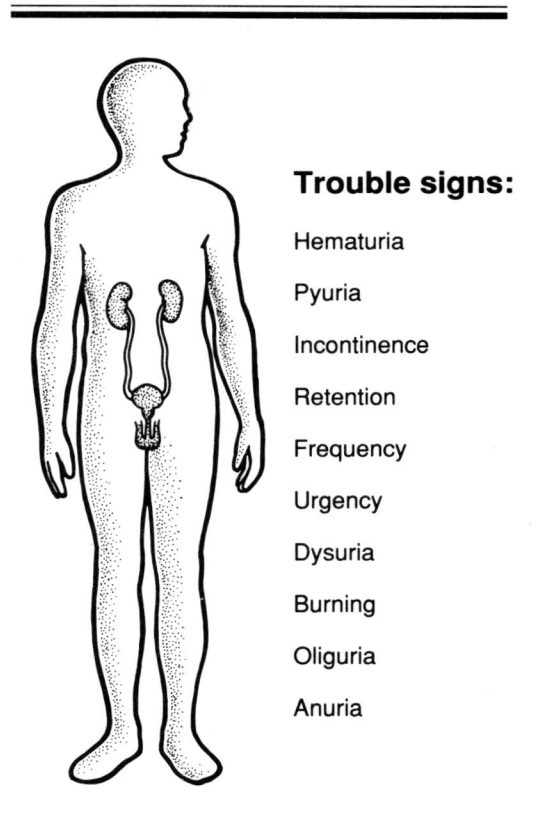

Urgency

Dysuria

Burning

Oliguria

Anuria

Figure 12-4 These symptoms can signal urinary tract disorders or drug side effects.

The first danger in kidney failure is blood poisoning, or **uremia** (*u-re'me-ah*). This is a condition in which the waste products of metabolism build up in the bloodstream because the kidneys are not excreting them properly. These substances can reach poisonous levels. Unless kidney function can be restored, patients with uremia must undergo kidney **dialysis** (Figure 12-5). This is a mechanical filtering of the blood using a dialysis machine.

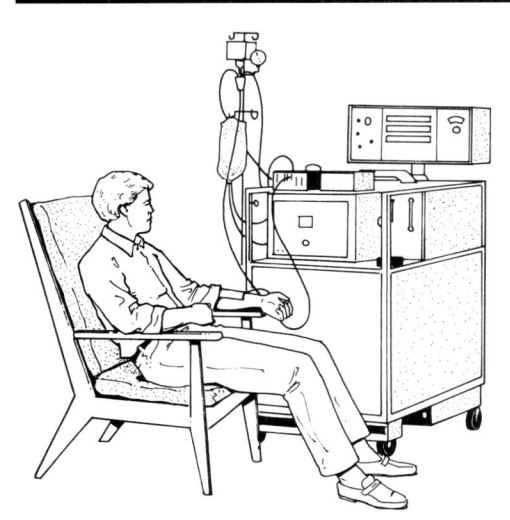

Figure 12-5 Dialysis takes over the blood filtering process for failing kidneys.

Another danger in kidney failure is that drugs are not excreted from the body as rapidly as with healthy kidneys. This is very important to remember when giving medications. The renal system is one of the main ways drugs are removed from the body. A kidney that does not work properly fails to eliminate the drugs as expected, and the drugs build up (cumulate) in the body with each dose. For that reason, dosages must be carefully adjusted and body signs watched closely any time there is a suspected problem with the kidneys.

Some drugs, especially the antibiotics, are damaging to the kidneys. Infections also cause damage. Either of these can lead to kidney failure. But kidney function is also affected by diseases in other parts of the body. These diseases may slow down the work of the kidneys, even though the kidneys themselves are not damaged. For example, in congestive heart failure, not enough blood flows through the kidneys. As a result, the kidneys cannot do a proper job of excreting water and salts. Water is retained in the tissues and swelling occurs.

IMBALANCES OF BODY FLUIDS, ELECTROLYTES, AND pH

The body of an average adult is about 60% water (more in children and less in the elderly). Most of this water is contained within the body cells, but about a quarter of it is in the spaces between cells or in the blood plasma. Maintaining enough water in the body tissues is important, because water is the medium for many chemical exchanges that are crucial to life.

To ensure adequate water, a balance is kept between the fluids taken in (through food and drink) and excreted (through sweat, urine and exhalation). Usually the body does this naturally. But when there is disease, especially disease of the kidneys, the body may not be able to keep the proper balance. This is why it is sometimes necessary to keep track of fluid intake and fluid output (Figure 12-6).

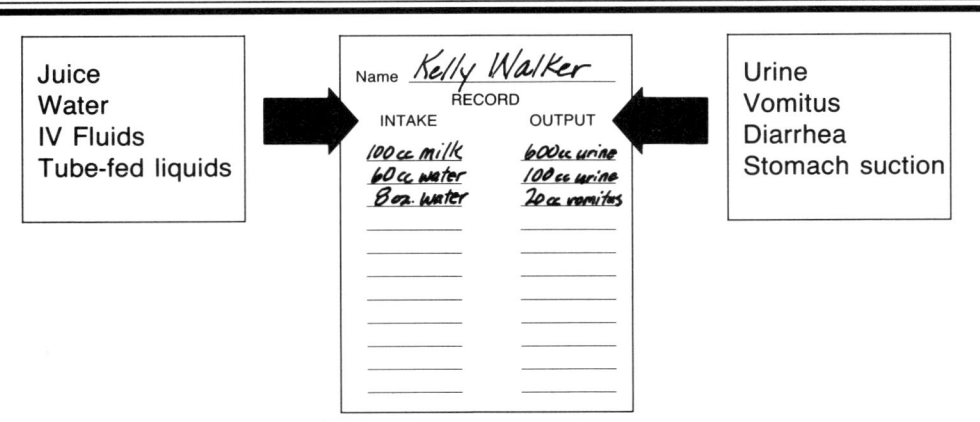

Figure 12-6 Input and output of fluids are recorded to monitor kidney function and fluid balance.

A chart is used to record the quantity of fluids taken in through food, drink, IV infusion, and so on (Figure 12-6). The chart is also used to record the quantity of fluid excreted in the urine and during vomiting. Intake generally exceeds output by 500–800 ml depending on size, activity, and body temperature of the patient because of fluid loss through the skin and breathing. If intake exceeds output by more than 500–800 ml, there may be swelling, or **edema**. If too much water is excreted, the body may become **dehydrated**. Either condition interferes with the proper functioning of the body. By keeping track of fluid intake and output, the medical staff can decide what treatment is necessary to keep the proper balance. A vomiting patient who loses too much water this way may need IV infusions. A person with edema may need a diuretic to make the kidneys excrete more urine.

For the important chemical exchanges of living cells to take place, the water must also contain the proper amount and kind of **electrolytes**. Electrolytes are electrically charged particles (ions) of dissolved salts. They are a means of carrying chemicals through the body fluids. Drugs, nutrients, and oxygen can "hitch a ride" on an electrolyte ion and move between cells and across cell membranes. Because salt attracts water, these salt ions are also a way of holding fluids in the body tissues. The electrolyte ions are potassium, calcium, sodium, magnesium, chloride, bicarbonate, phosphate, and sulfate. All the electrolytes must be present for proper body functioning.

In addition, there must be a proper balance between the amount of fluids (water) and the amounts and kinds of salts. The kidneys are sensitive to both water and salts (Figure 12-7). They compensate for an excess of salts by not allowing salts to be reabsorbed after the blood has been filtered. The unabsorbed salts in turn attract water. Thus both salts and water remain in the kidney tubules, to be carried away through the urinary tract.

The kidneys, then, regulate both the **amount** and the **makeup** of the fluids. Ordinarily, the kidneys are able to keep the right proportion of salts and fluids. However, in disease, kidney malfunction, improper diet, or unusual physical activity, fluid/electrolyte imbalances occur.

Figure 12-7 The kidneys keep a balance between water (H_2O) and electrolyte salts (Na=sodium, Ca=calcium, and K=potassium).

Electrolyte Imbalances

hypokalemia and **hyperkalemia** (*hi'per-kah-le'me-ah*)—too little or too much potassium

hyponatremia and **hypernatremia** (*hi'per-nah-tre'me-ah*)—too little or too much sodium

hypocalcemia and **hypercalcemia** (*hi'per-kal-se'me-ah*)—too little or too much calcium

Another thing that needs to be carefully balanced is the body's pH level. This is the ratio of acids to bases. The body cells need a slightly alkaline environment to function. They cannot tolerate more than very small changes in pH. The body has balancing mechanisms to ensure that strong acids and bases do not upset this balance. The kidneys are very much a part of this process. They are responsible for getting rid of excess acids or bases when the situation requires it. The lungs also assist in this process. When they exhale carbon dioxide, they are eliminating acids from the bloodstream.

Disorders of the acid/base balance are called **acidosis** (*as'i-do'sis*) and **alkalosis** (*al'kah-lo'sis*). Acidosis means too acid an environment for the cells; alkalosis means too alkaline an environment. Drugs may be administered to restore the proper pH. **Acidifiers** (e.g., ammonium chloride and sodium biphosphate) make the pH more acid in the case of alkalosis. **Alkalizers** (e.g., sodium bicarbonate) make the pH more alkaline in the case of acidosis. Acidifiers and alkalizers may be given to prevent pH imbalances caused by certain drugs. They are also given to help certain drugs produce their strongest effects. For example, sodium bicarbonate is given with certain sulfonamides that work best in an alkaline pH. Acidifiers such as cranberry juice or ascorbic acid (vitamin C) may be given with methenamine (*Mandelamine*) to provide an acid urine, which helps the drug work.

DRUGS FOR THE URINARY TRACT AND FLUID IMBALANCES

Urinary Antiseptics (Anti-Infectives)

Some anti-infectives are specially suited for urinary infections because they remain inactive until they are excreted by the kidneys and collect in the urine. These drugs are called **urinary antiseptics** (Figure 12-8).

Figure 12-8 Urinary antiseptics.

Sulfonamides, such as sulfisoxazole (*Gantrisin*) and sulfamethoxazole (*Gantanol*), are most effective for simple urinary infections that have not advanced very far. They are sometimes given in combination with antibiotics and other anti-infectives (e.g., *Septra, Bactrim*). When used in urinary tract infections, sulfonamides must be given with large amounts of fluids to prevent the formation of crystals in the urine.

Ampicillin, nitrofurantoin (*Macrodantin, Furadantin*), and methenamine (*Mandelamine*) are other urinary antiseptics.

Recall from Unit 6 that drug hypersensitivity can be a problem with many of the anti-infectives. Hypersensitivity means that the patient develops a reaction to the drug, something like an allergic reaction, after several doses.

Special analgesics are sometimes given with urinary antiseptics to relieve the pain of infection. Examples of these urinary analgesics are phenazopyridine (*Pyridium*) and ethoxazene (*Serenium*).

Some urinary antiseptics and analgesics can cause changes in the color of the urine, ranging from a deep yellow to reddish or brown. When giving such medications, check the package insert or a drug reference to find out whether you can expect urine discoloration. If so, be sure to forewarn your patient and assure him or her that this is a harmless side effect of the drug.

Urinary antiseptics and analgesics are sometimes administered directly into the bladder. This is done through a urinary catheter and is described in a practice procedure at the end of this unit.

Diuretics

These are drugs that increase the output of water from the body (Figure 12-9). They decrease the reabsorption of salts and water from the kidney tubules, with the result that more urine is produced. Increased urination removes excess water from the system. Diuretics are used to control edema in congestive heart failure. In kidney disorders, diuretics are given to help maintain normal urine production. There are many types of diuretics with different modes of action.

Figure 12-9 Diuretics.

The **thiazides**, a popular group of diuretics, keep the kidneys from reabsorbing sodium, potassium, and chloride. These salts remain in the tubules and attract water. As a result, both these salts and excess water are excreted together. This reduces edema. However, it can cause other problems.

The body cannot stand to lose too much potassium, because potassium is needed for chemical processes inside the cells. Too low a level of potassium (hypokalemia) results in fatigue, muscle weakness, and possibly heart block (a disturbance in the electrical impulses that stimulate the heartbeat). Recall that hypokalemia also potentiates (increases the effect of) the action of digitalis. To avoid these problems, the patient can eat potassium-rich foods such as oranges and bananas. Examples of thiazide diuretics are chlorothiazide (*Diuril*), hydrochlorothiazide (*HydroDiuril, Esidrix*), and methyclothiazide (*Enduron*).

There are also diuretics available that do not prevent the reabsorption of potassium. These are called **potassium-sparing** diuretics. Examples are spironolactone (*Aldactone*) and triamterene (*Dyrenium*). Potassium-sparing diuretics can lead to an **excess** of potassium (**hyperkalemia**), and patients are instructed to avoid potassium-rich foods. The brand-name products *Aldactazide* and *Dyazide* combine a potassium-sparing diuretic with a thiazide.

Two very strong diuretics that prevent reabsorption of both sodium and potassium are furosemide (*Lasix*) and ethacrynic acid (*Edecrin*). There are also carbonic anhydrase inhibitors such as acetazolamide (*Diamox*), and osmotic diuretics such as mannitol (*Osmitrol*).

Replacement Electrolytes and Fluids

Various parenteral and oral preparations are available to replace lost fluids and electrolytes. Potassium (*Slow-K, K-Lyte, Kaon*), calcium (calcium gluconate), magnesium, and other electrolytes can be given orally in the form of tablets and solutions. Or they can be prepared as IV solutions for infusion (Figure 12-10). Intravenous fluids are given routinely before and after surgery to maintain the proper amount and composition of body fluids. Dextrose 5% solution, Ringer's solution, and sodium chloride (saline) solution are fluids commonly administered in IV infusions. Many fluids and electrolytes can be replaced simply by drinking plenty of water and eating a diet rich in potassium, calcium, sodium, magnesium, and so on.

The product information table at the end of this unit gives information on the uses, dosage, action, and side effects of representative drugs that affect the urinary system and fluid imbalances.

GIVING DRUGS THAT AFFECT THE URINARY SYSTEM

Administering Diuretics

The administration of diuretics must be timed so as to avoid keeping the patient up all night going to the bathroom. Check the drug's onset of action so that it takes effect during the daytime. Warn the patient that he or she will be urinating more often than normal because of the diuretic. Make it easy and comfortable for the patient to urinate frequently. Keep a urinal or a bedpan close by for patients who should not get out of bed to go to the lavatory. Keep a bell or a call button handy, too, so that the patient can summon help if needed. One way to make sure a patient gets to the bathroom often enough—and in time—is to set up a schedule. Tell the patient that

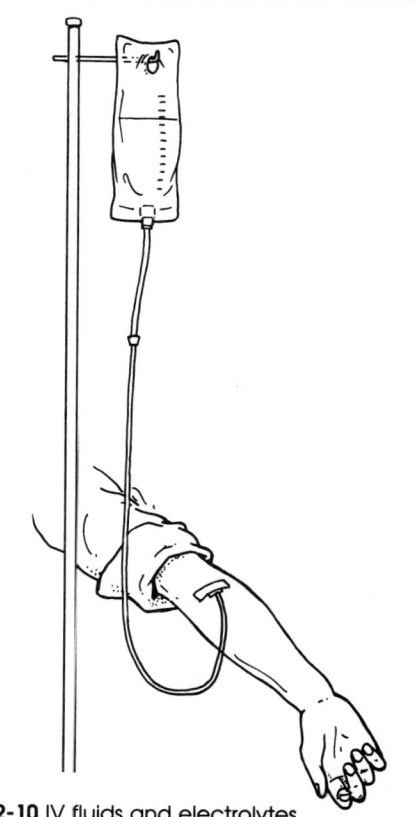

Figure 12-10 IV fluids and electrolytes.

you will come to help every 2 hours, or according to whatever schedule you work out together.

Keep an accurate record of fluid intake and output (Figure 12-11). This is necessary to make sure that the diuretic is working. If it is taking effect, more water should be leaving the body than is taken in. The patient should also be weighed daily to confirm that the diuretic is removing excess water. Weigh at the same time every day. The patient may lose as much as 20 pounds/day.

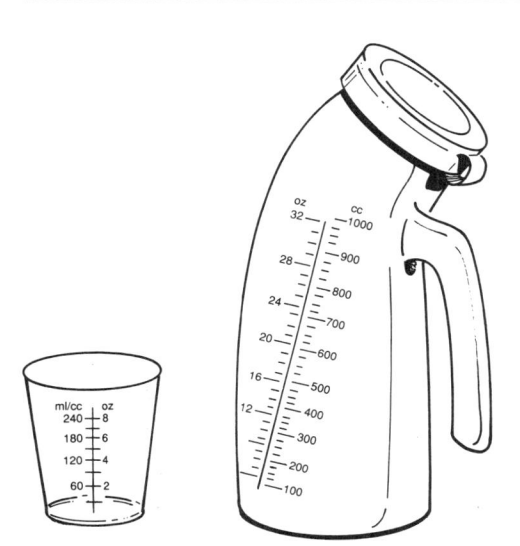

Figure 12-11 Containers for measuring fluid intake and output.

Your observations of the physical condition of the patient are important: swollen arms and legs and possibly a swollen abdomen are signs of edema. If you press your finger into the patient's skin, you will leave a mark that stays indented for some time. When a diuretic is working, you should notice a decrease in the swelling and less pitting of the skin when you press on it.

Be on the alert for side effects signaling an electrolyte imbalance. Diuretics can remove too much potassium and other salts. Look for nausea, thirst, fatigue, dry mouth, muscle weakness, muscle cramps, and any other unusual signs, and chart them. Administer oral potassium as ordered. In severe cases potassium chloride (KCl) may have to be given intravenously.

With some diuretics, the side effect of hypotension is possible. Patients should be cautioned to move slowly when sitting up or standing from a lying-down position to avoid the dizziness due to orthostatic hypotension.

Installing Bladder Medication

A patient with a severe bladder infection may get a buildup of pus and perhaps blood in the bladder. This must be rinsed out from time to time with sterile water. Rinsing the bladder is done by means of a catheter and is called bladder **irrigation**. The same catheter is also used for instilling medication into the bladder; for example, an antibiotic.

An **indwelling** catheter (also called a **retention** or **anchored** catheter) stays inside the bladder for a period of time. It allows urine and pus to drain off into a bag hung at the side of the bed. There are several types of indwelling catheters available with outlets for drainage and irrigation. The Foley catheter (Figure 12-12) is held in place by blowing up a small balloon inside the bladder after inserting the catheter.

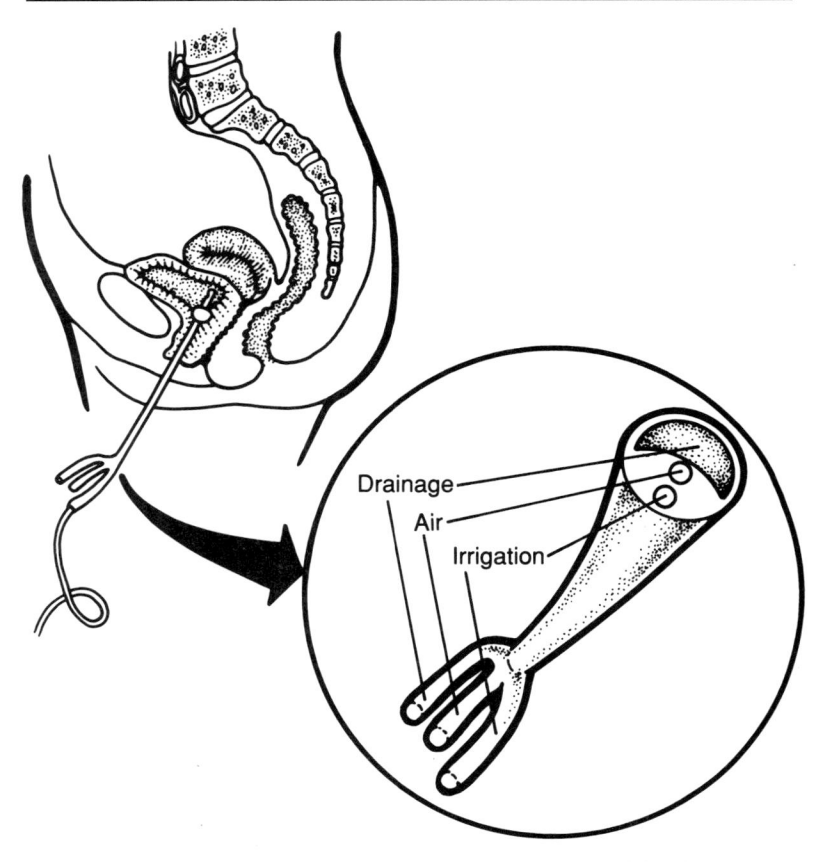

Figure 12-12 An indwelling catheter may be used for administering bladder medications.

Because the catheter opens a passageway between the bladder and the outside environment, sterile technique must be used to avoid letting germs enter the bladder. Special sterile kits are available containing all of the equipment needed for irrigating or instilling medication into the bladder.

The most important things to keep in mind when instilling bladder medications into an indwelling catheter are:

- Follow aseptic procedure: do not let the catheter or medication become contaminated.
- Make sure that the medication is at the proper temperature. Usually room temperature is correct, but check the medication order to be sure.
- Leave the medication in the bladder for the proper amount of time as shown on the medication order.
- Remember to hook up the drainage tube after you have finished giving medication so that urine can be carried away into the drainage bag.
- Give special consideration to the patient's privacy. Draw the curtain around the bed and drape the patient's genital area. You can help ease the patient's embarrassment by being tactful and considerate.

Drugs for the Urinary System and Fluid Balance 291

EXERCISES

A. Fill in the blanks.
1. The organ that is responsible for blood filtration and reabsorption is the __kidney__.
2. Tiny tubes called __nephrons__ make up the cortex of the kidney.
3. In the medulla of the kidney, collecting tubes carry away urea, excess water, and mineral salts. The resulting liquid is called __urine__.
4. The tubes that connect the kidneys to the bladder are the __ureters__.
5. Urine passes out of the body by way of the __urethra__.
6. A full bladder creates the urge to __void__.
7. In 24 hours, the kidneys normally produce about __1500-2000__ ml of urine.
8. About __200-300__ ml of urine are passed during normal urination.

B. List the three functions of the urinary system. _____

C. Define these terms that describe symptoms of urinary tract disorders.
1. hematuria __blood in urine__
2. pyuria __pus in urine__
3. incontinence __unable to control urination__
4. retention __unable to void__
5. dysuria __difficult urination__
6. anuria __absence of urine__

D. Matching. Match medical terms to the definitions.
__c__ 1. mechanical filtering of blood
__a__ 2. blood poisoning due to wastes
__b__ 3. instrument for looking into the urinary tract
__e__ 4. tube for bladder irrigation and medication
__d__ 5. inflammation of the kidney

a. uremia
b. cystoscope
c. dialysis
d. nephritis
e. catheter

E. Short answers.

1. What are electrolytes? Name at least four electrolyte ions.

   Electrically charged ions
   _H, Ca, Na, K_

2. How does the kidney regulate the balance of electrolytes and fluids?

   They don't allow Na to be
   reabsorbed after blood has been filtered

F. From the list below, choose the disorder that best matches each description. Write the name of the disorder in the blank.

   kidney failure   pyelonephritis
   kidney stones   urethritis
   cystitis   edema
   electrolyte imbalance

   1. Mrs. Peach has a painful infection. The doctor has prescribed a urinary antiseptic. _urethritis_

   2. Young Freddy must be put on dialysis to avoid a buildup of toxic waste products in his bloodstream. _kidney failure_

   3. Mr. Bernardi has had painful abdominal spasms for a day due to an obstruction in the ureter. Now the obstructing material has passed into the bladder. His physician will insert an instrument into the bladder to crush and flush out some material. _kidney stones_

   4. Ms. Yamamoto has a severe bladder infection with frequent, painful urination. To keep the bladder empty, a urinary catheter has been inserted. The doctor has ordered regular bladder irrigation and an anti-infective to be administered into the catheter. _cystitis_

   5. Mr. Wincenz has a severe kidney infection that is damaging the nephrons. Antibiotics are being administered with caution so as to avoid further damage that could lead to kidney failure. _pyelonephritis_

   6. Dr. Bland orders a diuretic for a heart patient who is experiencing swelling of the arms and legs. _edema_

   7. After several days on diuretics, the heart patient develops fatigue and muscle weakness. Dr. Bland then orders potassium chloride. _electrolyte imbalance_

G. Tell what each drug category does; for example, Replacement electrolytes *replace lost electrolyte salts.*
   1. Urinary antiseptics __anti-infective of urinary tract__
   2. Diuretics __increase elimination of water through urination__
   3. Acidifiers __pH more acid__
   4. Alkalizers __pH more alkaline__

H. Match the drug names to the drug categories.
   __e__ 1. spironolactone, *Dyrenium*
   __g__ 2. *Lasix, Edecrin*
   __c__ 3. *Diuril, HydroDiuril, Esidrix, Enduron*
   __d__ 4. potassium, calcium, sodium, *Slow-K*
   __h__ 5. *Furadantin*, methenamine, *Gantrisin, Septra*
   __a__ 6. sodium bicarbonate
   __b__ 7. ammonium chloride, sodium biphosphate
   __f__ 8. sodium chloride solution, dextrose solution

   a. alkalizers
   b. acidifiers
   c. thiazide diuretics
   d. replacement electrolytes
   e. potassium-sparing diuretics
   f. replacement fluids
   g. very strong diuretics
   h. urinary antiseptics

I. Match these medical terms that relate to pH and fluid/electrolyte imbalances.
   __a__ 1. shortage of potassium
   __d__ 2. surplus of calcium
   __b__ 3. too little sodium
   __e__ 4. cell environment too acid
   __f__ 5. cell environment too alkaline
   __c__ 6. not enough water retained in the body

   a. hypokalemia
   b. hyponatremia
   c. dehydration
   d. hypercalcemia
   e. acidosis
   f. alkalosis

J. Fill in the blanks.
   1. When a patient is on thiazide diuretics, there is a danger of excreting too much __potassium__, which could result in hypokalemia.
   2. A lack of potassium can be corrected by giving foods such as __bananas__.
   3. When you press the patient's skin, your finger leaves a mark that stays for several minutes. The patient is showing signs of __edema__.
   4. A patient on a diuretic is expected to show a weight __loss__ (gain or loss).
   5. Diuretics should be given at the correct time to avoid inconvenience to the patient. The patient should be told to expect an increase in __urination__.
   6. A catheter that is designed to stay in place over a long period of time is called a(n) __indwelling__ catheter.

7. Rinsing the bladder by means of a catheter is called bladder __irrigation__.

8. When instilling medication into a catheter, use aseptic technique so that __chances of infection lessened__.

9. After administering bladder medication through a catheter, be sure to __reconnect__ the drainage tube.

K. List the types of fluids you would record on an input and output record.

Input: __Water, juice, IV Fluids__

Output: __Urination, vomitus__

ANSWERS TO EXERCISES

A. Fill in the blanks
  1. kidney
  2. nephrons
  3. urine
  4. ureters
  5. urethra
  6. urinate, or void
  7. 1500–2000
  8. 200–300

B. Urinary functions
Excreting waste products of metabolism (urea, mineral salts), regulating the amount of water in the body, and regulating the pH

C. Definitions
  1. blood in the urine
  2. pus in the urine
  3. inability to control urination
  4. inability to urinate even when the bladder is full
  5. painful urination
  6. no production of urine

D. Matching
  1. c
  2. a
  3. b
  4. e
  5. d

E. Short answers
  1. Electrolytes are ions of mineral salts that provide the chemical transport system for cell metabolism. Examples: calcium, sodium, potassium, magnesium, chloride, bicarbonate, phosphate, and sulfate.
  2. By controlling the reabsorption process so that excess electrolytes and fluids are excreted in the urine.

F. Disorders
  1. urethritis
  2. kidney failure
  3. kidney stones
  4. cystitis
  5. pyelonephritis
  6. edema
  7. electrolyte imbalance

G. Drug categories
  1. stop infection in the urinary tract.
  2. increase elimination of water through urination.
  3. make the pH more acid in the case of alkalosis.
  4. make the pH more alkaline in the case of acidosis.

H. Matching drugs
   1. e   5. h
   2. g   6. a
   3. c   7. b
   4. d   8. f

I. Matching fluid imbalances
   1. a   4. e
   2. d   5. f
   3. b   6. c

J. Fill in the blanks
   1. potassium
   2. bananas or oranges
   3. edema
   4. loss
   5. urination
   6. indwelling, anchored, or retention
   7. irrigation
   8. germs do not enter the urinary tract
   9. hook up, or reconnect

K. Recording fluids
   Input: water, juice, IV fluids, gastrostomy fluids
   Output: urine, vomitus, wound drainage, stomach suction, diarrhea

PRACTICE PROCEDURE

INSTILL MEDICATION INTO THE BLADDER THROUGH AN INDWELLING CATHETER

Equipment:

- Physician's order for bladder medication
- Kardex, medicine card, medication record, patient chart
- Medicine tray or cart
- Catheter irrigation/instillation set (Figure 12-13), containing tray or basin (to catch drainage), plastic sheeting, syringe, catheter tip covers, bottle for diluting medication (in some sets), alcohol wipes
- Medication in sterile solution, 50 or 60 cc

_____ 1. Assemble equipment.

_____ 2. Read the physician's order and set up the medication. Check for the "five rights."

_____ 3. Identify the patient following agency policy. Explain what you are going to do. Curtain off the area to provide privacy.

_____ 4. Wash your hands.

_____ 5. Assist the patient to lie down on his or her back, with bent legs spread apart to expose the genital area. Drape the patient so that only the catheter is showing.

_____ 6. Open the sterile packaging of the irrigation set and place it on the bed between the patient's legs. The protective plastic sheeting should be set down on the bed first, with the tray and other items resting on it.

_____ 7. Arrange the catheter tip so that it is hanging over the edge of the tray but not touching the bottom. (This would contaminate the catheter.) Some bladder installation sets have a notched edge on the tray to hold the catheter in place.

_____ 8. Detach the drainage tube from the catheter. (The drainage tube is the one that carries the urine to a bag at the side of the bed.) Cover the exposed end of that tube with the special sterile covering included in the instillation set. This keeps germs from entering the tube while it is detached. Then lay the tube down on the bed, anchoring it with tape or under the mattress so that it does not slide off and drop to the floor.

_____ 9. Lift the end of the catheter and insert the sterile syringe into the opening used for irrigation. Hold the syringe and catheter tube together with the same hand (Figure 12-14). This keeps them from separating when you administer the medication.

_____ 10. Pour the measured amount of medication into the open end of the syringe. Let it drain through the catheter into the bladder. *Do not* force it in with the syringe bulb.

_____ 11. Follow with extra sterile water if ordered.

_____ 12. Before putting down the catheter, clamp it if the medication is to stay in the bladder for a certain period of time. The physician's order should state how long the medication should be retained. If no special length of time is ordered, you may leave the tube unclamped.

_____ 13. Put down the catheter in the same position as before, with the end resting over the edge of the tray but not touching the bottom. If unclamped, the catheter will begin to drain right away. If the catheter is clamped, *remember to unclamp* it after the proper amount of time so that it can drain.

_____ 14. When the medication has drained out, reattach the drainage tube to the end of the catheter. Use a sterile alcohol wipe to clean both the end of the tube and the catheter as you reattach them.

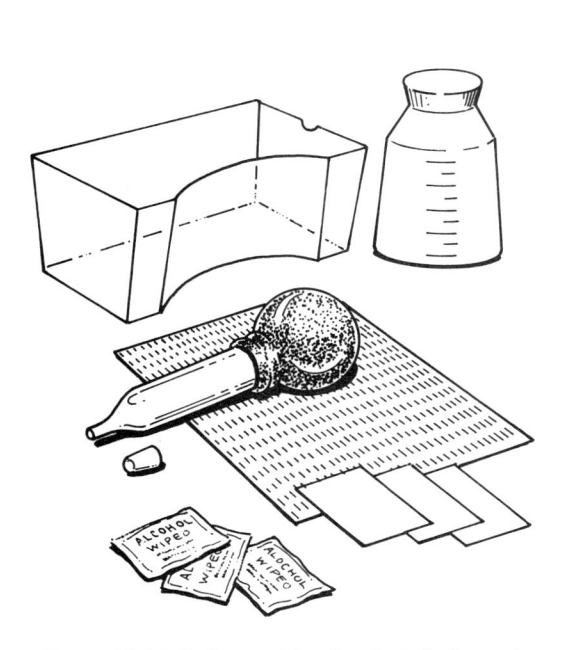

Figure 12-13 Catheter irrigation/installation set for instilling bladder medication.

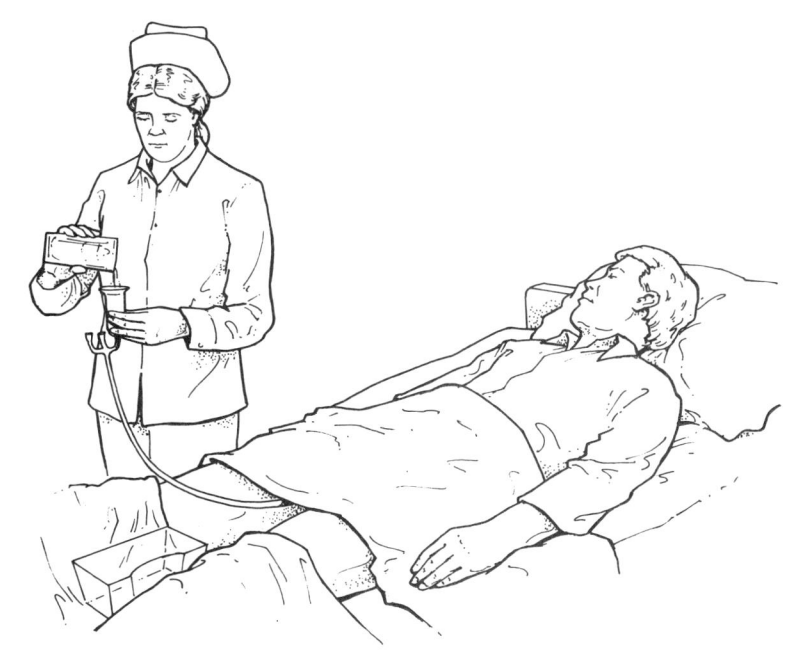

Figure 12-14 Hold the catheter-tube and syringe together while pouring the medication. Note the draping for patient privacy.

_____ 15. Remove and clean or discard the equipment and supplies used.

_____ 16. Give the patient any special instructions and assist him or her into a comfortable position. Make sure the tubing is not pinched or blocked in any way so that urine can drain freely into the collection bag.

_____ 17. Wash your hands.

_____ 18. Chart the medication. If you noticed any unusual substances draining from the bladder or any irritation around the catheter, be sure to chart it and notify your supervisor.

Demonstrate this procedure for the instructor or the nurse in charge.

REPRESENTATIVE DRUGS FOR THE URINARY SYSTEM AND FLUID IMBALANCES

CATEGORY, NAME[a], AND ROUTE	USES AND DISEASES	ACTION	DOSAGE[b] AND SPECIAL INSTRUCTIONS	SIDE EFFECTS AND ADVERSE REACTIONS
Urinary Antiseptics/ Antibacterials/Analgesics				
Sulfisoxazole (*Gantrisin*) Oral, IM, IV, SC	Urinary tract infections (chronic or acute, such as cystitis, pyelitis, and pyelonephritis)	Bacteriostatic, inhibits bacterial synthesis of folic acid	Initial dose: 2–4 g; maintenance: 4–8 g/day divided into 4–6 doses	Blood disorders, skin eruptions, itching, nausea and vomiting, hepatitis, anorexia, headache
Co-Trimazole (*trimethoprim/ sulfamethoxazole*) (*Bactrim, Septra*) Oral, IV	Urinary tract infections	Blocks two consecutive steps in the biosynthesis of nucleic acids and proteins essential for many bacteria	One double-strength tablet, 2 regular-strength tablets, or 4 teaspoons (20 ml) of suspension every 12 hours for 10–14 days	Nausea, vomiting, skin rashes, anorexia, blood disorders, hepatitis, headache, depression
Nitrofurantoin (*Furadantin, Macrodantin*) Oral	Lower urinary tract infections	Kills or stops growth of bacteria in urinary tract	50–100 mg TID or QID; give with food or milk to avoid gastric irritation; rinse mouth after giving liquid form to avoid staining teeth	Anorexia, nausea, diarrhea, yellow to brown discoloration of urine, chest pain, cough
Piperacillin sodium (*Pipracil*) IM, IV	Mixed infections prior to identification of causative organism including urinary tract infections	Inhibits the biosynthesis of cell wall and renders it osmotically unstable	*Complicated urinary infections:* 8–16 g IM or IV (125–200 mg/kg) per day in divided doses q 6–8 hours. *Uncomplicated urinary tract infections:* 6–8 g IM or IV (100–125 mg/kg) per day in divided doses q 6–8 hours	Thrombophlebitis, diarrhea, skin rashes
Ampicillin (*Omnipen, Principen*) Oral, IV	Urinary tract infections (pyelonephritis)	Bactericidal, inhibits cell wall formation	0.5–1 g q 6 hours	Rash, itching, shortness of breath, diarrhea, nausea, vomiting
Tetracycline (*Achromycin, Sumycin*) Oral, IV, IM	Susceptible urinary tract infections	Bacteriostatic, interferes with protein synthesis	250–500 mg q 6 hours; give 1 hour before or 2 hours after meals	Anorexia, nausea, vomiting, diarrhea, rash, superinfection
Phenazopyridine (*Pyridium*) Oral	Urinary tract pain and dysuria due to infections, surgery, injury, or catherization	Anesthetizes mucous membranes of urinary tract	200 mg TID p.c.; found in combination with urinary antiseptics (e.g., Azo Gantrisin, Azo Gantanol)	Reddish-orange discoloration of urine; rarely indigestion, headache
Diuretics				
Hydrochlorothiazide (*Hydro Diuril*) Oral	Edema due to congestive heart failure, cirrhosis of the liver, renal failure, corticosteroid or estrogen therapy; also hypertension	Causes kidneys to excrete more water and mineral salts (sodium chloride, potassium); lowers blood pressure	25–100 mg 1 or 2 times daily; give early in day because of increased urination; monitor weight and fluid intake/output	Gastric irritation, muscle weakness, hypokalemia, orthostatic hypotension, rash
Triamterene (*Dyrenium*) Oral	Edema due to congestive heart failure and other conditions; used with other diuretics for its potassium-sparing effect	Conserves potassium and excretes sodium	Individualized; 50–100 mg in single dose or 2 divided doses, after meals; avoid potassium-rich foods	Diarrhea, nausea, vomiting, weakness, skin rash, dry mouth

REPRESENTATIVE DRUGS FOR THE URINARY SYSTEM AND FLUID IMBALANCES

CATEGORY, NAME[a], AND ROUTE	USES AND DISEASES	ACTIONS	USUAL DOSE[b] AND SPECIAL INSTRUCTIONS	SIDE EFFECTS AND ADVERSE REACTIONS
Furosemide (*Lasix*) Oral, IM, IV	Edema of congestive heart failure and other conditions	A potent diuretic; inhibits reabsorption of sodium	20–80 mg initially and then titrated up to 480 mg/day in patients with severe edematous states	Anorexia, oral and gastric irritation, nausea, vomiting, dizziness, headache, tinnitus and hearing loss, anemia, leukopenia, rash, hypotension
Replacement Electrolytes				
Potassium (*K-Lyte, Slow-K, Kaon*) Oral	Potassium deficiency	Potassium ion replacement	16–25 mEq/day for prevention of hypokalemia; 40–100 mEq/day or more for treatment of potassium depletion	Nausea, vomiting, diarrhea, abdominal distress, hyperkalemia

[a] Brand names given in parentheses are examples only. Check current drug references for a complete listing of available trade name products.

[b] Average adult doses are given. However, dosages are determined by a physician and vary with the purpose of the therapy and the particular patient. The doses presented in this text are for general information only.

Unit 13

Drugs for the Endocrine System

In this unit you will learn about hormones and the glands that manufacture them. You will learn what goes wrong when the glands produce too much or too little of the hormones and how hormone therapy can help correct hormone imbalances. You will learn about the treatment of diabetes and the uses of corticosteroid hormones and hormone-like drugs.

In this unit, you will learn to:

- Define glands and hormones.
- Name the hormones produced by the seven major glands.
- Explain why the pituitary is called the "master gland."
- State the action of each of these hormones or hormonelike drugs: somatotropic hormone, thyroxine, parathormone, corticosteroids, epinephrine (adrenaline) and norepinephrine, insulin, ACTH, and antidiuretic hormone.
- State what hormone is lacking in diabetes mellitus, diabetes insipidus, Addison's disease, and hypothyroidism. Give examples of drugs used for replacement in each case.
- Use correct medical terms in referring to parts of the endocrine system and symptoms of hormone imbalances.
- List the kinds of insulin available for treatment of diabetes mellitus, and give examples of each group.
- Give examples of oral hypoglycemics for diabetes treatment and tell how they work.
- Recognize the symptoms of insulin underdose and overdose, and tell how they are treated.
- Explain why diabetics must have frequent blood or urine tests.
- State what factors affect the diabetic patient's insulin needs.
- Follow specific instructions for parenteral administration of insulin.
- State the actions of glucocorticoids and mineralocorticoids, and give examples.
- List at least three uses of corticosteroids.
- Name five possible side effects of long-term corticosteroid therapy.

ENDOCRINE SYSTEM

The endocrine system is made up of **glands**. These are structures that secrete chemical substances called **hormones**. Hormones regulate many body processes. They are like "chemical messengers." Each hormone carries a particular message as it circulates through the body.

The glands are made up of epithelial tissue that has the ability to trap needed chemicals and combine them to produce hormones. They are like miniature "chemical factories." Because the bloodstream is the main means of distributing hormones, the glands are richly supplied with capillaries that readily transport the manufactured hormones. A complex feedback system governs the secretion of hormones. In healthy people, specific hormones are produced only when needed. Production stops just as soon as the hormones reach the required level in the bloodstream.

Seven glands produce most of the hormones needed to regulate body functions (Figure 13-1). Some glands secrete more than one hormone, but each hormone has its own special job to do. There are a few other structures that also produce hormones but not all are considered glands. These are the thymus, the placenta (in pregnant women), the pineal body, and the hypothalamus area of the brain.

Pituitary Gland

The pituitary (*pi-tu'i-tar'e*), a small gland about the size of a cherry, is located in the skull just below the brain. It has two sections or lobes, each of which produces several hormones. One of these, **somatotropin** (*so'mah-to-tro'pin*) or growth hormone, is important in controlling the growth of the bones and body organs. If too much is produced, the body grows too fast and becomes very large. Too little of this hormone results in stunted growth or dwarfism.

Other hormones produced by the pituitary control the secretions of the sex glands, the thyroid gland, and the adrenal glands. Because it controls the hormone production of other glands, the pituitary is known as the "master gland."

Figure 13-2 shows some of the activities the pituitary hormones regulate. It gives an idea of the wide range of functions performed by hormones.

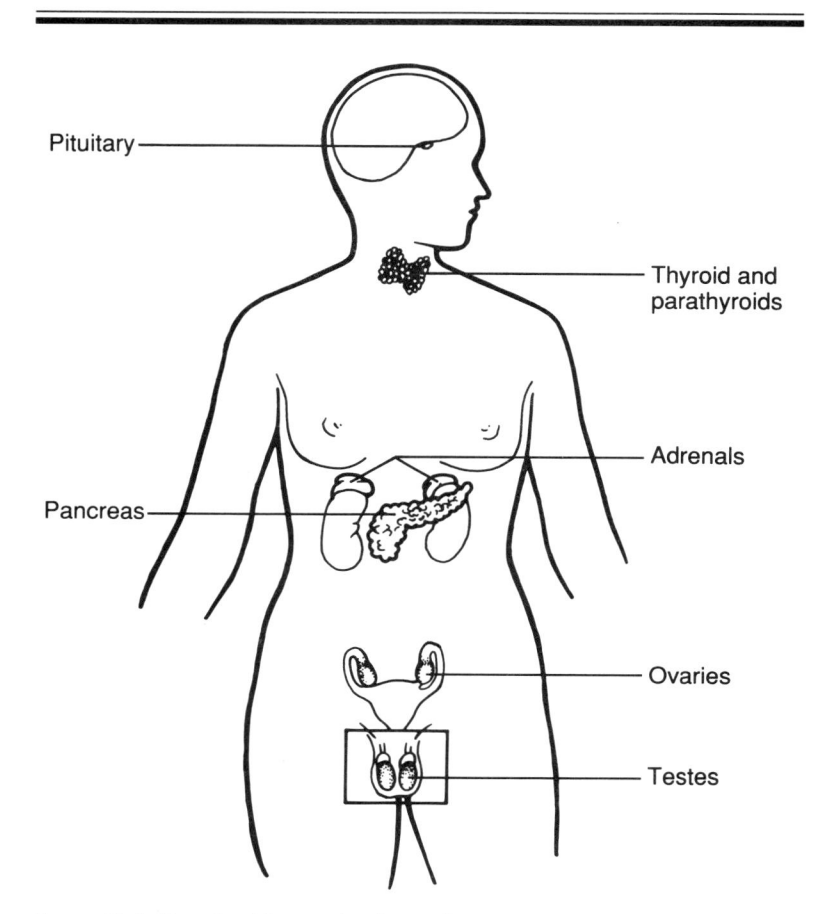

Figure 13-1 Glands of the endocrine system.

Thyroid Gland

This gland is wrapped around the trachea just below the larynx (*lar'inks*) or voice box. It produces the hormone **thyroxine** (*thi-rok'sin*), which controls body metabolism. This is the rate at which all of the cells produce energy (heat, muscle strength, etc.). Thyroxine controls body metabolism by regulating the level of enzyme activity in each cell. When the thyroid produces extra thyroxine, the cells use up glucose and fat at a faster rate; growth and healing speed up; and there is an increase in respiration, heart rate, and nervous and muscular activity. Too little thyroxine causes cell metabolism to slow down.

To produce adequate thyroxine, the thyroid gland needs **iodine**, a mineral that is present in vegetables and seafood. Iodized table salt is available so that people can take in enough iodine to fulfill the needs of the thyroid.

VOCABULARY

acetone: a ketone that is present in the urine of both untreated diabetics and treated diabetics with ketoacidosis; can be detected by a fruity odor on the breath

adrenals: glands sitting atop the kidneys; the inner medulla of each adrenal produces epinephrine and norepinephrine; the outer cortex produces adrenal corticosteroids

antidiabetic agents: insulin and oral hypoglycemics

antidiuretic hormone (ADH): pituitary hormone that promotes reabsorption of water in the kidneys

corticosteroids: hormones produced by the adrenal cortex; have anti-inflammatory action and suppress immune reaction

diabetes insipidus: overexcretion of urine due to lack of antidiuretic hormone

diabetes mellitus: inability of the body cells to utilize sugar due to lack of insulin

diabetic coma: unconsciousness resulting from starvation of body cells in untreated diabetes mellitus

gland: specialized epithelial tissue that secretes hormones

glucagon: hormone secreted by the pancreas that raises the level of blood sugar; counteracts the effects of insulin

glucocorticoids: adrenal corticosteroids that regulate the metabolism of carbohydrates and fats by body cells

glucose: a simple form of sugar that can be "digested" by body cells

glycogen: form of sugar stored in the liver or muscles for release as the body needs it

glycosuria: sugar in the urine

gonads: sex glands; the ovaries and the testes

hormone: chemical substance that regulates many body functions; secreted by glands; each hormone has specific functions

hyperplasia: overdevelopment (e.g., of a gland)

hypoglycemia: low blood sugar; can be the result of insulin overdose or other causes

hypothalamus: portion of the brain linked to the pituitary gland, forming part of the hormone control system

insulin: hormone secreted by the pancreas; regulates the use of sugar by body cells; replacement insulin may be of animal or recombinant DNA origin

insulin shock: hypoglycemia caused by overdose of insulin

iodine: mineral needed by the thyroid to produce thyroxine

islets of Langerhans: structures in the human pancreas that secrete insulin and glucagon

ketoacidosis: acidosis caused by surplus of fatty acids (ketones) in the bloodstream; a complication of diabetes mellitus

ketones: products of incomplete burning of fats; also called fatty acids

mineralocorticoids: adrenal corticosteroids that help regulate the excretion of salts and water by the kidney

NIDDM: Type II diabetes

oral hypoglycemics: drugs that stimulate the pancreas to secrete insulin

parathormone: hormone secreted by the parathyroids; regulates the calcium content of the bloodstream

parathyroids: four glands located behind the thyroid; secrete parathormone

pituitary: gland at the base of the brain; secretes many hormones, including some that stimulate other glands to produce hormones

polyuria: excessive excretion of urine

somatotropic hormone (STH): growth hormone secreted by the pituitary gland

tetany: muscle spasms caused by lack of calcium in the bloodstream

thyroid: gland below the larynx that secretes thyroxine

thyroxine: hormone secreted by the thyroid gland; regulates the speed of metabolism in the body cells

Type I diabetes: previously called juvenile-onset diabetes

Type II diabetes: NIDDM (non-insulin-dependent diabetes mellitus), previously called maturity-onset diabetes

Parathyroid Glands

These are four small glands located behind the thyroid gland. The hormone they produce is called **parathormone**. The calcium content of the blood is controlled by this hormone. A certain amount of calcium is needed in the bloodstream for muscles to work properly. Extra calcium is stored in the bones. When the level of calcium in the blood is low, the parathyroid glands produce parathormone to release stored calcium from the bones. If too much parathormone is manufactured, too much calcium may be taken out of the bones. As a result, the bones may become soft and easy to bend. If too little parathormone is produced, the muscles may go into spasms. This condition, which affects mainly the face and the hands, is called **tetany** (*tet'ah-ne*).

Adrenal Glands (Suprarenals)

The two adrenal glands sit on top of the two kidneys. Each adrenal gland has two layers: an outer **cortex** and an inner **medulla** (*me-dul'ah*). Each layer produces different hormones. One set of hormones, the **corticosteroids** (*kor'ti-ko-ste'roidz*), controls the use of sugars and proteins by the cells (**glucocorticoids**, *gloo'ko-kor'ti-koids*) and regulates the reabsorption of fluids and salts in the kidneys (mineralocorticoids). The corticosteroids thus help the body adapt to changing conditions in the environment.

The other set of adrenal hormones, **epinephrine** (*ep'i-nef'rin*) and **norepinephrine** (*nor'ep-i-nef'rin*), is produced when the body must meet emergency situations. Epinephrine and norepinephrine prepare the body to react to emergencies by stimulating the heartbeat, increasing blood pressure, and releasing extra sugar into the bloodstream. Epinephrine and norepinephrine are produced in the body but are also available as drugs to be administered. Epinephrine made in the body is also known as **adrenaline**. As a drug it is used in the treatment of bronchial asthma, as described in Unit 9. Norepinephrine is used in the emergency treatment of shock because of its ability to constrict the blood vessels.

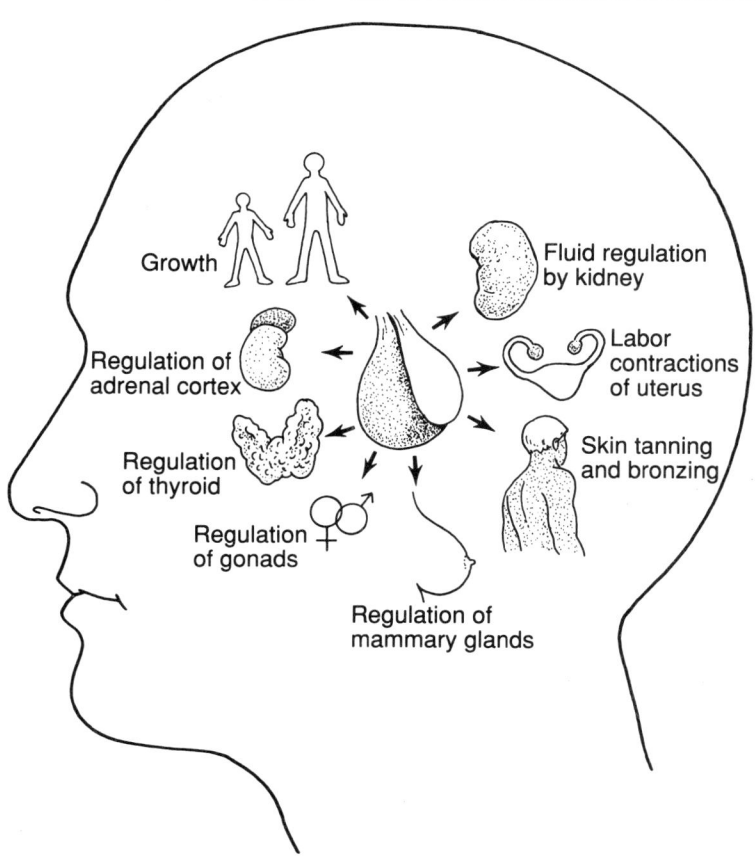

Figure 13-2 Functions of the pituitary hormones. Many of these stimulate other glands to produce hormones.

Pancreas

As noted in Unit 11, the pancreas secretes powerful enzymes as part of the digestive system. It also contains a number of secreting structures that are part of the endocrine system. These structures, scattered throughout the pancreas, are called the **islets of Langerhans**. They secrete two hormones: **insulin** and **glucagon**.

Insulin controls the use of sugar by the cells. It also stimulates the liver to store extra sugar in the form of glycogen. When the pancreas fails to produce insulin, sugar cannot be burned by the cells. Instead, it remains in the bloodstream and is excreted in the urine. This condition is known as **diabetes mellitus**.

The hormone **glucagon** stimulates the liver to release stored sugar into the bloodstream. It is administered in emergencies when diabetic patients have received too much insulin.

Ovaries and Testes

These are the sex glands, or **gonads**. They are responsible for the different physical characteristics of males and females and for the manufacture of sex cells for reproduction. The female gonads are the **ovaries**. The male gonads are the **testes**.

The ovaries, located in the pelvis of the female, secrete the hormones **estrogen** (estrone) and **progesterone**. The testes, held in a pouch between the legs of the male, produce **testosterone**, the male hormone. However, both males and females have both types of hormones in their bodies. These hormones and their uses in drug therapy are described in Unit 14.

Hormone Control System

The level of hormones in the blood is constantly adjusted to meet the body's requirements. A large intake of carbohydrates, for example, stimulates the pancreas to flood the bloodstream with insulin to help reduce the blood sugar level. A complex chemical control system is required to ensure the proper hormone levels. At the center of this control system is the pituitary gland, which stimulates other glands to produce hormones.

The pituitary, in turn, is linked to the brain's control system (the nervous system) by way of the **hypothalamus** (hi'po-thal'ah- mus). This is a portion of the brain stem that lies just behind the pituitary. It is connected to the pituitary by a stalk. The hypothalamus controls such basic body functions as sleep, appetite, and body temperature.

The hypothalamus and pituitary have a kind of partnership in running the hormone chemical message system. The hypothalamus can stimulate or inhibit the pituitary according to conditions inside and outside the body. Because of this link, the endocrine system is influenced by the nervous system. Thus, people's emotions, fears, and moods have an impact on body processes through hormone stimulation as well as nerve stimulation.

Feedback is provided to the control system by the levels of circulating hormones. As mentioned earlier, hormones are distributed throughout the body via the bloodstream. When the proper level of hormone is reached, the pituitary gets a signal from the hypothalamus to stop stimulating hormone production.

To take an example, let's say that the body needs extra sugar and fat for a heavy physical task. The pituitary excretes ACTH (adrenocorticotropic hormone), which is swiftly transported by the bloodstream to the adrenal cortex.

The ACTH then stimulates the adrenal cortex to produce corticosteroids. These help liberate extra sugar and fat for the body to burn for energy. The hypothalamus senses when there are enough corticosteroids in the bloodstream. It then signals the pituitary to "cancel the order" for ACTH. Thus the adrenal cortex stops secreting its hormones until they are again needed (see Figure 13-3).

DISORDERS OF THE ENDOCRINE SYSTEM

Hormones control body processes—growth, metabolism, kidney function, and so forth. Consequently, when there is a disturbance in the production of hormones, the body processes go "out of control." A child whose pituitary produces too much growth hormone grows to be a giant; an adult develops diabetes mellitus because

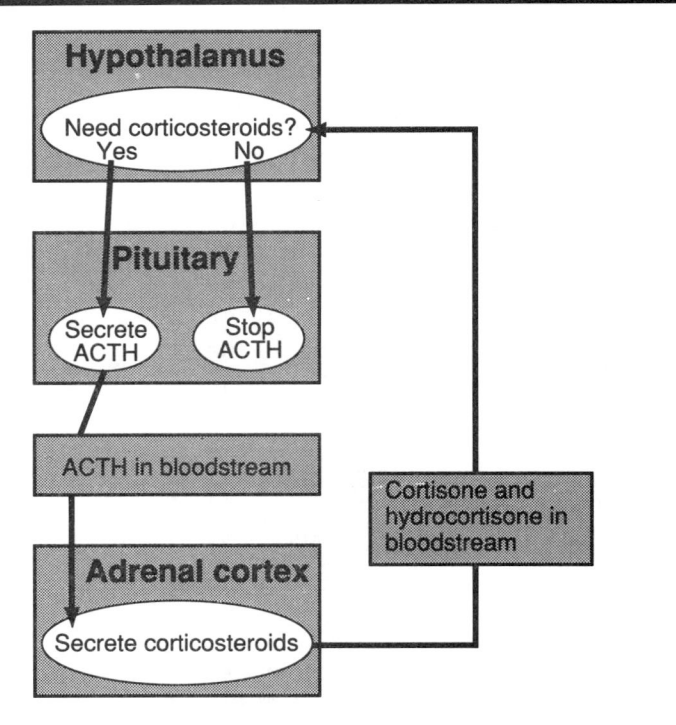

Figure 13-3 Example of a hormone control system.

the pancreas fails to produce enough insulin to maintain sugar metabolism.

The symptoms of endocrine disorders are logically related to the specific hormones that are out of balance. That is, when a certain hormone is lacking, the symptoms show that the body process it regulates is no longer working properly.

Endocrine disorders arise because a gland produces its hormones **too much, too little**, or **too early**. Keep this principle in mind as you study this unit. Table 13-1 lists examples of endocrine disorders and their symptoms. Note that the names of the various disorders usually tell you something about how hormone production has gone wrong. Recall that *hypo* means too little (less than normal) and *hyper*, too much (more than normal).

There are several reasons why a gland might be secreting too much, too little, or too early. One is that the gland may be overdeveloped, a condition called **hyperplasia** (*hi'per-pla'ze-ah*). Or it may contain a tumor. Usually tumors and hyperplasia cause too much hormone production because there are a great many more secreting cells than normal. In these cases, surgery or radiation treatment may be needed to restore the normal hormone balance.

One form of radiation treatment is the radioactive "cocktail." The patient drinks a radioactive material that travels to the gland to destroy the tumor. In the case of a thyroid tumor, for example, the physician can take advantage of the fact that the thyroid traps circulating iodine to use in making thyroxine. A cocktail of radioactive isotopes of iodine can be given so that when they arrive at the thyroid, they destroy the offending cells.

Genetic factors are another reason for gland malfunctions. Some individual are simply born with defective glands or are missing the chemicals necessary for producing hormones. People can inherit tendencies to develop some types of endocrine problems; for example, diabetes mellitus. Genetically caused problems can usually be treated with replacement hormones. Chances for cure are good if these conditions are discovered early enough, before growth and development are permanently affected.

Finally, there may be nothing wrong with a gland at all. The problem may be that the gland is receiving faulty messages from the pituitary. A small tumor on the pituitary, for example, can cause over- or underproduction of the hormones that direct the other glands. Underproduction is diagnosed by administering pituitary hormones to see if they successfully stimulate the other glands. If the problem lies with the pituitary, then either surgery, radiation, or appropriate hormone replacement is required.

HORMONE THERAPY

Hormone replacement is the most common use of hormones in drug therapy. Replacement is necessary whenever hormones are missing because of either genetic defects in the glands, surgical removal of glands, or production of poor-quality hormones. Some hormones and hormonelike drugs are used because of actions that are not related to the endocrine system; for example, the anti-inflammatory action of the adrenal corticosteroids. In this section some of the most common uses of hormones are discussed. Note that most hormones for drug therapy are taken from the bodies of animals: hogs, cattle, sheep, and horses. A few hormones have been synthesized in the laboratory. Recombinant (*re-kom'bi-nant*) DNA technology (genetic engineering) will increase the availability of these important substances.

> **NOTE:**
> Hormones are powerful chemicals that have profound effects on the human body. They must be administered very carefully according to doctors' orders. Often the doses are very small. They may be measured in micrograms (a microgram is one-thousandth of a milligram). The exception is the corticosteroids, which are given in large doses to combat allergic reactions and inflammation.

Table 13-1 Selected Hormones and Their Disorders

HORMONE	FUNCTION	DISORDER	SYMPTOMS	TREATMENT
Pituitary				
Somatotropic hormone (STH)	Regulates growth	Too much—acromegaly	Enlargement of hands, feet, and face	Radiation, surgery
		Too much, too early—gigantism	Growth to an extreme height	Sex hormones
		Too little—dwarfism	Failure to grow to normal height, remaining small and fragile	Somatotropin (growth hormone replacement)
Gonadotropins (FSH, LH)	Regulate development of sex characteristics by stimulating gonads (ovaries and testes) to secrete sex hormones	Too much, too early—sexual precocity	Development of adultlike sex characteristics as young as 5 years old	
		Too little—sexual infantilism	Failure to develop adult sex characteristics during the teens	Hormone replacement
Luteotropic hormone (LTH)	Stimulates mammary glands to produce milk in nursing mothers	Too much at the wrong time—persistent lactation syndrome	Milk produced in non-nursing women	Male hormones
Antidiuretic hormone (ADH)	Regulates reabsorption of water in kidney tubules	Too little—diabetes insipidus	Kidneys do not reabsorb water, resulting in great thirst and production of great quantities of clear urine	Hormone replacement, some diuretics
Thyroid				
Thyroxine (regulated by the thyroid-stimulating hormone (TSH) of the pituitary)	Regulates metabolism (the burning of sugar in the body cells to produce energy)	Too much of either thyroxine or TSH—hyperthyroidism	Nervousness, weight loss, heat intolerance, huge appetite, frequent stools, insomnia, bulging eyes, etc.	Surgery, radioactive iodine "cocktail," antithyroid drugs
		Too little—hypothyroidism (also cretinism and myxedema, depending on when deficiency occurs)	Slowed mental and physical processes, fatigue, hair loss, coldness, constipation, etc.	Hormone replacement
		Poor-quality thyroxine—colloid goiter (other types of goiter have other causes)	Thyroid keeps producing hormone and stores the excess, leading to enlargement of thyroid and swelling in neck	Iodine in food or supplements
Parathyroid				
Parathormone	Releases calcium from bones when blood calcium is low	Too much—hyperparathyroidism	Too much calcium taken out of bones, resulting in bone weakness, deformities, calcium stones in the kidney	Surgery
		Too little—hypoparathyroidism	Muscle spasms (tetany) because of low blood calcium	Hormone replacement

Table 13-1—continued

HORMONE	FUNCTION	DISORDER	SYMPTOMS	TREATMENT
Pancreas				
Insulin	Permits body to burn sugar for energy, regulates storage of sugar in the liver	Too little—diabetes mellitus	Thirst, constant hunger, weight loss, itching, fatigue, changes in vision, slow-healing cuts	Insulin replacement, oral hypoglycemics, management of diet and exercise
Adrenal Cortex				
Mineralocorticoids (aldosterone, desoxycorticosterone)	Regulates salt/water balance in the body by stimulating kidneys to retain sodium and excrete potassium	Too much aldosterone—aldosteronism	Low serum potassium, alkalosis, high blood pressure	Surgery, drugs
Glucocorticoids (cortisone, hydrocortisone)	Stimulate breakdown of protein molecules into carbohydrates	Too much—Cushing's disease	Too much protein breaks down, leading to muscle wasting	Surgery, hormone replacement
		Too little of all the adrenal cortex hormones—acute adrenal crisis, chronic Addison's disease	Shock symptoms in acute cases; in Addison's: weakness, tiredness, changes in skin color, anorexia, gastrointestinal disorders, salt craving	Replacement therapy
Androgenic steroids (small amounts of male and female hormones secreted in both male *and* females)	Thought to contribute to development of sex characteristics (but gonads secrete most of the necessary hormones)	Too much of the wrong sex hormone—feminization of males, virilization of females	Inappropriate sex characteristics (e.g., manliness, deep voice in females; loss of body hair, high voice in males)	Surgery

Drug Management of Diabetes Mellitus

Diabetes mellitus is a condition in which the pancreas does not secrete enough of the hormone insulin. Without enough insulin, the body cannot make proper use of sugar to fuel the cells. As a result, sugar remains in the bloodstream and is excreted in the urine. Meanwhile, the body cells "starve." To compensate, they burn protein and fat. The classic symptoms of diabetes are great hunger and thirst, production of excess urine, weight loss, and weakness. Urine tests reveal large quantities of sugar in the urine.

Diabetes can start in childhood (Type I juvenile type, brittle diabetes) or in adulthood (Type II non-insulin-dependent diabetes). Many older adults develop some degree of diabetes along with the changes of aging. Over time, diabetes causes damage to the tissues and organs of the body. It always carries the danger of complications.

Many mild cases of diabetes can be managed simply by controlling the diet, maintaining a normal body weight, and getting enough exercise to burn off excess blood sugar. Diabetic patients are encouraged to eat small meals throughout the day rather than a few large meals. The idea is to avoid large up- and-down swings in the amount of sugar in the blood. When these measures are not enough to control the diabetes, drug therapy is indicated.

The major drug for Type I diabetes is insulin, which is administered by injection. Several oral drugs are available to control blood sugar in Type II non-insulin-dependent diabetes mellitus (NIDDM).

Insulin—Insulin therapy replaces the missing hormone that enables the body to use sugar (Figure 13-4). More than one preparation of insulin is available, and doctors prescribe different preparations according to individual cases. The dosages are highly individualized and depend on

Figure 13-4 Insulin helps cells burn sugar for energy.

many factors. The insulin preparations are grouped into three basic categories: fast-acting, intermediate-acting, and long-acting. They differ according to how quickly they take effect (onset of action), how soon they reach their peak effect, and how long their effect lasts (duration of action). Table 13-2 summarizes some of these differences.

Popular drugs for diabetes control are the intermediate-acting insulins: lente and NPH. They reach their peak effectiveness in about 9 hours and last up to 24 hours. They are thus convenient for once-a-day doses, usually administered 1/2 hour before breakfast. Some doctors prefer to keep closer control over insulin dosages by using the fast-acting semilente and regular insulins. These are given several times during the day (e.g., 1/2 hour before each meal), and dosages are varied on the basis of frequent urine tests.

Most insulin is derived from beef and pork pancreases. A new product, insulin identical to human hormone (*Humulin N* or *Humulin R*), is now available thanks to advances in genetic engineering.

The diabetic person's need for insulin varies according to diet, amount of exercise, and emotions. All three factors must be kept under control for insulin-replacement therapy to be effective. Changes in these factors affect the dosage requirements for insulin and can lead to over- or underdoses. For this reason, health team members as well as patients must be thoroughly familiar with the symptoms of insulin overdose and underdose.

Too little insulin in the bloodstream is serious and can be fatal if the situation is not caught early and corrected. The first signs are vomiting, excessive thirst, diarrhea, urine containing large amounts of sugar (**glycosuria** *gli'ko-su're-ah*), and (occasionally) increased appetite and eating without weight gain. Later the patient becomes dazed (stuporous), respirations are deep, and the face is dry and flushed. There is a fruity acetone smell to the breath, signaling that the body is burning excessive amounts of fat. This is called **ketoacidosis** (*ke'to-ah-si-do'sis*). If these symptoms go undiag-

Table 13-2 Types of Insulin

CATEGORY	TYPE	SOURCE	ONSET OF ACTION (HOURS)	PEAK EFFECT (HOURS)	DURATION OF ACTION (HOURS)
Fast acting	Regular, *Humulin R*	Beef, pork, human recombinant	1/2	2–3	6–8
	Semilente	Beef, pork	1/2–1	5–7	12–16
Intermediate acting	NPH, *Humulin N*	Beef, pork, human recombinant	1–2	6–12	18–26
	Lente	Beef, pork, human recombinant	1–3	6–12	18–26
Long acting	Ultralente	Beef, pork	4–6	14–24	28–36
	Protamine zinc	Beef, pork	4–6	14–24	26–36

nosed, the person becomes unconscious within a day or two, a condition referred to as **diabetic coma**. The treatment is to administer extra insulin so that the sugar can be burned to fuel the body. Like any disturbance in the acid-base balance of the body, careful treatment by a physician is required.

The opposite situation, too much insulin, is called **hypoglycemia** (*hi'po-gli-se'me-ah*) or **insulin shock**. The symptoms are extreme hunger, nervousness, sweating, heart palpitations, and disturbed vision. They come on as a result of hard physical effort, overly large doses of insulin, or eating too little food. These situations cause all the blood sugar to be burned off so that there is too low a level of sugar in the bloodstream (hypoglycemia). A urine test reveals that there is no sugar in the urine either. Treatment consists of giving sugar in some easily digestible form to increase the blood sugar level quickly (Figure 13-5). In extreme cases, glucose or glucagon may be given parenterally. You should look for signs of insulin shock anywhere from 5 minutes to several hours after a dose of insulin. During the hours of peak effect you should be most watchful for these signs. Keep in mind that the peak effect of any insulin varies according to the individual patient's physical condition and level of activity.

> **NOTE:**
> The term "hypoglycemia" means low blood sugar. Oral hypoglycemics (antidiabetic agents) purposely lower blood sugar to reduce diabetic symptoms. Overdoses of hypoglycemics or of insulin result in drug-induced hypoglycemia, a dangerous adverse reaction. There is another type of hypoglycemia, however, which is unrelated to diabetes. It is responsible for vague symptoms of fatigue, fainting, and weakness. It seems to result from a problem with metabolism and can sometimes be controlled with diet and drugs.

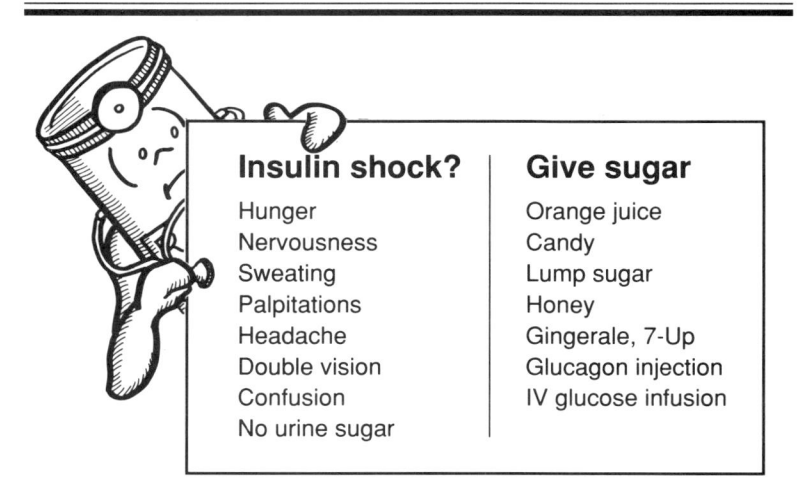

Insulin shock?	Give sugar
Hunger	Orange juice
Nervousness	Candy
Sweating	Lump sugar
Palpitations	Honey
Headache	Gingerale, 7-Up
Double vision	Glucagon injection
Confusion	IV glucose infusion
No urine sugar	

Figure 13-5 Know the signs and treatment of insulin shock when working with a diabetic patient.

The recent development of the **insulin pump** has improved the health of many diabetics and provided them with more freedom. This infusion system, worn on the belt or at the side, has the capability of evening out daily fluctuations in glucose levels better than daily injections (Figure 13-6).

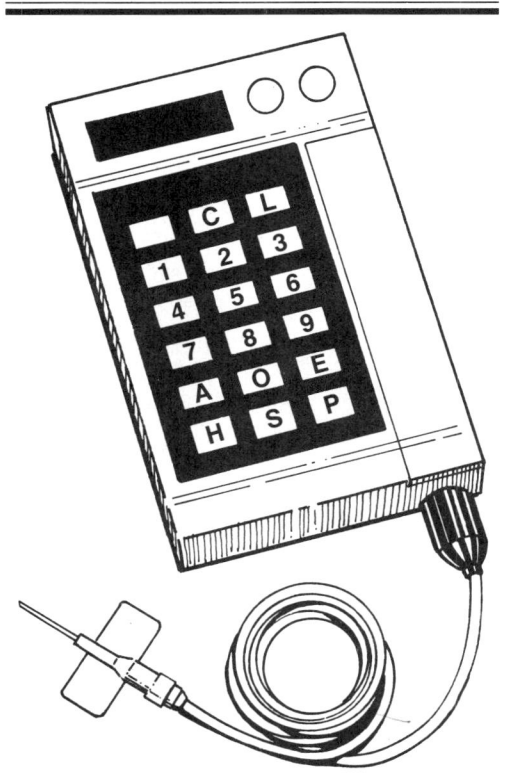

Figure 13-6 The insulin infusion pump has great potential to aid diabetics.

Diabetic patients are largely responsible for giving their own insulin, so they and their families should be educated about all aspects of the disease and its treatment. They must learn new dietary habits and injection and testing procedures. You can help by reinforcing their attempts to moderate their food and exercise and by encouraging them to stay on a regular schedule of medication. Caution them to avoid OTC medications because many of these have a high sugar content. They should also avoid alcoholic beverages.

Oral Hypoglycemics—These drugs are unrelated to insulin and are not oral insulins. They can be used only with certain types of diabetic patients, mainly those who have developed the condition in adulthood and who are overweight. The major oral hypoglycemics are tolbutamide (*Orinase*), chlorpropamide (*Diabinese*), tolazamide (*Tolinase*), and acetohexamide (*Dymelor*) and the newer glipizide (*Glucotrol*) and glyburide (*DiaBeta, Micronase*).

They are used in cases where the pancreas is already producing some insulin. Their effect is to stimulate the pancreas to secrete more insulin so that the body can burn up excess sugar. There is evidence that they may also make the body cells more receptive to the action of insulin. If the dose is too large for the patient's condition, side effects may occur. Those to watch for are nausea and skin eruptions. Table 13-3 summarizes the timing of drug actions for the six major oral hypoglycemics.

Urine and Blood Tests—Most diabetics test urine at home, daily or more often. Urine tests detect sugar, telling the patient how effective their control is. The more sugar in the urine, the less control of the disease.

Tests for sugar in the urine include *Clinitest*, *Diastix*, and *Testape*. The urine must be a freshly voided specimen. The results are recorded on the patient's chart according to the closest color matching the accompanying manufacturer's chart.

Table 13-3 Oral Hypoglycemic Agents for NIDDM (Type II)

	ONSET OF ACTION (HOURS)	PEAK EFFECT (HOURS)	DURATION OF ACTION (HOURS)	DAILY DOSE RANGE[b]
First Generation				
Tolbutamide[a] (*Orinase*)	Rapidly	3–4	24	1–2 g
Tolazamide (*Tolinase*)	Rapidly	3–4	7	250–500 mg
Acetohexamide (*Dymelor*)	Rapidly	3	12–24	250–1500 mg
Chlorpropamide (*Diabinese*)	1	3–6	24	100–750 mg
Second Generation				
Glipizide (*Glucotrol*)	1/2	1–3	Up to 24	Initial 2.5–15 mg Maintenance 15–30 mg
Glyburide (*DiaBeta, Micronase*)	1	4	24 (low levels)	Initial 1.5–5 mg Maintenance 1.5–20 mg

[a] Brand names given in parentheses are examples only. Check current drug references for a complete listing of available trade name products.

[b] *Dosages for the elderly and the debilitated are usually smaller.* Average adult doses are given here. However, dosages are determined by a physician and vary with the purpose of the therapy and the particular patient. The doses presented in this text are for general information only.

A blood test for sugar can be done in the doctor's office or the patient's home with a glucose meter (Figure 13-7). This equipment is accurate and becoming more common as some insurance companies will pay for it.

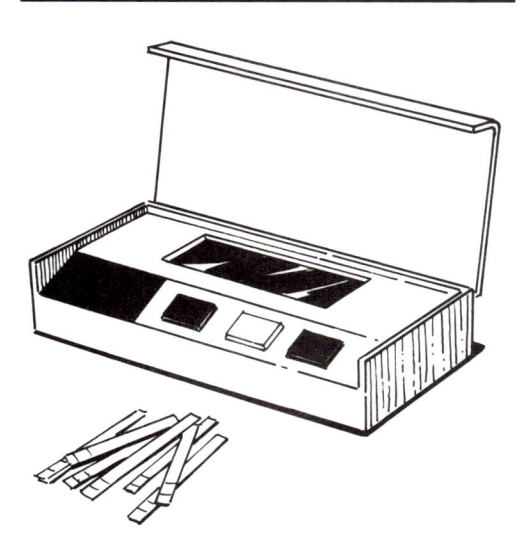

Figure 13-7 Maintaining proper insulin levels is easier and more accurate with recently developed home-use equipment.

Complications of Diabetes

As diabetes progresses, diabetic patients are prone to urinary and vaginal infections and to blood vessel diseases that lead to vision problems, gangrene, foot and leg problems, and dental problems. These complications must be treated separately, keeping in mind that any added drugs may have an impact on the dosage of insulin. Many drugs interact with insulin and oral hypoglycemics, so any drug therapy for these conditions must be carefully planned by a physician. As a member of the health care team, you can assist the patient in the prevention of infection by teaching good habits of skin, foot, and dental care.

Corticosteroids

Corticosteroids are a group of hormones secreted by the adrenal cortex. They are very important to the body, and insufficient production (Addison's disease) can be fatal. There are two major groups of corticosteroids, both having different functions: (1) the **glucocorticoids** (cortisone, hydrocortisone or cortisol), which affect fat and carbohydrate metabolism, and (2) the **mineralocorticoids** (aldosterone, desoxycorticosterone), which regulate the salt/water balance.

The glucocorticoids often included in drug therapy are prednisone (*Deltasone*), prednisolone (*Delta-Cortef*), dexamethasone (*Decadron, Hexadrol*), and methylprednisolone (*Medrol*).

Corticosteroids have many uses. One important use is in hormone replacement therapy. The pituitary may not produce enough ACTH to stimulate corticosteroid production in the adrenal cortex. Or the adrenal cortex itself may not be working properly (Addison's disease). In both cases, corticosteroids can be used to replace the missing hormones.

Large doses of corticosteroids are used in many conditions that are unrelated to adrenal functioning: allergic reactions, skin inflammations, some cancers, autoimmune reactions and suppression of immunity in organ transplant, and eye and respiratory diseases. The main reason for their use in these diseases is that corticosteroids suppress inflammation; that is, the body's normal reaction to irritation or injury (Figure 13-8).

Recall that the inflammation reaction is signaled by redness, warmth to the touch, pain, and swelling. Corticosteroids change the tissue's response to irritation in such a way that these symptoms are reduced.

Figure 13-8 Corticosteroids have many uses, especially in suppressing inflammation, but they can also have serious side effects.

They also reduce fever and itching. Because of their anti-inflammatory action, corticosteroids are often used in chronic inflammatory diseases such as rheumatoid arthritis and rheumatic fever.

When used in small doses for a short time, corticosteroids show few side effects. However, in long-term use and in the large doses required for suppressing inflammation, there are dangers that require careful handling. One problem with corticosteroids is that they mask warning symptoms. Inflammation is suppressed, but the irritation or injury still remains. Tissue destruction can continue even though the symptoms are not obvious. There are other dangers, too: old infections can be reactivated and new infections can start up, but the symptoms will be hidden because the drug suppresses them.

Another problem with long-term corticosteroid therapy is the side effects. Some of these are weight gain, sodium (salt) retention and edema, hypertension, facial rounding ("moon" face), diabetes, easy bruising, thinning of the skin, failure of wounds to heal, psychological changes, ulcers, osteoporosis, and many other effects. In addition, corticosteroid therapy interferes with the feedback between the adrenal glands and the pituitary. After withdrawing corticosteroids, the chemical signal system between the glands takes several months to get back to normal. Consequently, physicians will order gradually smaller doses of a corticosteroid before it is discontinued.

For all of these reasons, doctors try to prescribe the smallest dose possible for the shortest time needed to achieve the desired therapeutic effect. This principle is important, of course, in all drug therapy, but especially so when giving corticosteroids. The doses must be individualized according to each patient's response to the drugs. Those who administer medications must be watchful for side effects. The signs to look for especially are changes in body weight or blood pressure, extreme hunger, severe insomnia, personality changes, and streaking of the skin.

Other Hormones

Thyroid hormone replacement is not uncommon. It is done in cases where the thyroid has been suppressed by radiation or surgery and in hypothyroid conditions such as goiter and myxedema. Natural thyroid hormones are available but the synthetic thyroid hormones are used more frequently: levothyroxine sodium (*Synthroid*), liotrix (*Euthroid*), and liothyronine sodium (*Cytomel*).

The hormone corticotropin (ACTH, *Acthar*) may be given for diagnosing pituitary malfunction and also for stimulating the adrenals to produce glucocorticoids.

Vasopressin tannate (*Pitressin*) is the antidiuretic pituitary hormone (ADH) that regulates the reabsorption of water in the kidneys. It is given to control diabetes insipidus, a disorder in which too much water is excreted in the urine. Vasopressin causes water to be reabsorbed so that the patient urinates normally.

Diagnosis of Hormone Deficiencies

Hormones can be used to find out whether a gland is failing to produce its hormone. Suppose, for example, that the body lacks a certain adrenal hormone. Is this the fault of the pituitary or of the adrenal glands? One way to find out is to administer the pituitary hormone ACTH. If this makes the adrenals secrete the missing hormone, we know that the problem lies with the pituitary—the pituitary has not been secreting enough of its own ACTH to stimulate the adrenals. On the other hand, if the dose of ACTH does *not* stimulate the adrenals, we know that the adrenals are not working properly. In this situation, the patient will likely be put on a regular course of hormone therapy to replace the missing adrenal hormone.

Representative hormones and hormonelike drugs used for replacement therapy and inflammation are given at the end of this unit. Other uses of hormones—for example, in arthritis, cancer therapy, and contraception—are discussed in Units 14 and 15.

ADMINISTERING INSULIN

Insulin is given parenterally, and as a health care worker, you should not administer it unless you are trained and permitted by law to give medications by injection. General instructions on giving injections are provided in Unit 17. The following are special instructions for giving insulin:

- Keep stock supplies of insulin refrigerated to keep them fresh. Before injecting a dose, let it warm to room temperature to reduce the chance of a local reaction.
- Check the expiration date on the package and discard any insulin that is out of date.
- Check insulin that is cloudy to be sure it is okay to administer; i.e., lente and *Humulin N*.
- When giving insulin **suspensions** (e.g., NPH, lente, ultralente), gently rotate the vial between the palms of your hands and turn it end to end several times before drawing up into the syringe.
- Do not shake the vial. If there are any signs of clumping in the vial after you have rotated it gently, discard it.
- Timing is important. The physician will order the insulin to be given at the correct time so that it will reach its peak level when blood sugar is highest.
- Measure insulin very carefully. The proper dose is crucial. To make sure that you have the proper dose, use only an insulin syringe and use the correct syringe size for the strength of insulin. Insulin strength is measured in units (U). Although U80-strength insulin has been used in the past, U100 and U40 are now standard.
- Insulin is usually given subcutaneously or intramuscularly. (Check the label of insulin.) Only regular insulin injection may be given IV. Rotate injection sites to avoid damaging tissues in any one area. Follow a rotation plan as described in Unit 17.
- Be aware of the peak action time for the type of insulin you are giving. That way you can be alert for signs of hypoglycemia and have juice or sugar available if necessary. With long-acting insulin, hypoglycemia may occur during the night, signaled by restless sleep and sweating.

EXERCISES

A. Fill in the blanks.

1. The chemical substances that regulate many body functions are called **hormones**.

2. The structures that combine chemicals to produce hormones are called **glands**.

3. Hormones travel throughout the body by way of the **bloodstream**.

4. The gland that traps iodine while producing its hormone is the **thyroid** gland.

5. The four small glands behind the thyroid are the **parathyroid** glands.

6. The glands that sit on top of the kidneys are the **adrenal** glands.

7. The **pancreas** contains the islets of Langerhans, which secrete insulin and glucagon.

8. In females, sex hormones are produced mainly in the **ovaries**.

9. In males, sex hormones are produced mainly in the **testes**.

10. A tiny gland in the center of the head that controls other glands is the **pituitary**.

11. A part of the brain stem that links the pituitary to the nervous system is the **hypothalamus**.

B. Match these hormones to the jobs they do.

- **d** 1. somatotropic hormone
- **a** 2. thyroxine
- **g** 3. parathormone
- **e** 4. corticosteroids
- **b** 5. epinephrine and norepinephrine
- **h** 6. antidiabetic agents
- **f** 7. ACTH
- **c** 8. antidiuretic hormone (ADH)

a. regulates cell metabolism
b. prepare the body to cope with stress
c. keeps the kidneys from excreting too much urine
d. regulates growth
e. in high doses, suppress inflammation
f. stimulates the adrenal cortex
g. regulates the amount of calcium in the blood
h. enables cells to use sugar

Drugs for the Endocrine System 315

C. Fill in more blanks.

1. Diabetes mellitus is caused by a lack of the hormone __insulin__.
2. Diabetes insipidus is caused by a lack of the __antidiuretic__ hormone.
3. Addison's disease is caused by a long-term lack of __adrenal__ hormones.
4. Hypothyroidism is due to a lack of the hormone __thyroxine__.

D. Define these medical terms.

1. tetany __shaking, tremors__
2. glycosuria __sugar in urine__
3. hypoglycemia __↓ sugar in blood__
4. gonads __secretes sex hormones__
5. hyperplasia __overdevelopment__

E. Below are listed a number of drugs used in the management of diabetes mellitus. Next to each drug, place the letter that tells what drug group it belongs to, as follows:

L = long-acting insulin   F = fast-acting insulin
I = intermediate-acting insulin   O = oral hypoglycemic

__L__ 1. ultralente   __I__ 5. lente
__I__ 2. NPH   __O__ 6. acetohexamide
__O__ 3. Diabinese   __I__ 7. Humulin N
__F__ 4. regular insulin   __O__ 8. tolbutamide

F. Short answers.

1. What is the main action of the oral hypoglycemics?

__Stimulate pancreas__

2. Why must diabetics check their urine regularly with special tests?

__sugar / insulin regulation__

3. What are three factors that bring about changes in the diabetic patient's need for insulin?

4. What is the difference between glucocorticoids and mineralocorticoids?

   gluco - fat/sugar
   mineral - salt/water

5. List all the uses you can think of for corticosteroids.

6. Now list the possible side effects of long-term use of corticosteroids.

G. Diabetic patients on insulin must live with the risk of insulin *overdose* or *underdose*. Decide which of these two problems is signaled by each set of symptoms below. Give the usual treatment for each.

Symptoms	Problem	Give
1. Thirst, much urine, glycosuria, fruity breath, confusion	*diabetic coma*	*insulin*
2. Nervousness, hunger, double vision, sweating, palpitations	*insulin shock*	*sugar*

H. Match these drugs to their uses.

   A 1. ACTH

   D 2. vasopressin tannate

   C 3. *Synthroid*, liothyronine sodium, thyroglobulin

   B 4. Dexamethasone, *Medrol*, prednisone

   a. replacement of pituitary hormone that stimulates production of corticosteroids
   b. inflammatory diseases, allergic reaction, replacement of corticosteroids
   c. thyroid hormone replacement
   d. diabetes insipidus

I. Review the eight special instructions given in the text for administering insulin. List as many as you can here.

___

ANSWERS TO EXERCISES

A. Fill in the blanks
1. hormones
2. glands
3. bloodstream
4. thyroid
5. parathyroid
6. adrenal
7. pancreas
8. ovaries
9. testes
10. pituitary
11. hypothalamus

B. Matching
1. d
2. a
3. g
4. e
5. b
6. h
7. f
8. c

C. More blanks
1. insulin
2. antidiuretic
3. adrenal, or corticosteroid
4. thyroxine

D. Definitions
1. muscle spasms or twitching
2. sugar in the urine
3. low blood sugar
4. ovaries and testes, the sex glands
5. overdevelopment (e.g., of a gland)

E. Drugs for diabetes
1. L
2. I
3. O
4. F
5. I
6. O
7. I
8. O

F. Short answers
1. Oral hypoglycemics stimulate the pancreas to secrete more insulin.
2. If they find sugar in their urine, they know that their bodies are not able to make use of the sugar they have eaten. They must restrict their sugar and/or take more insulin. If they find fatty acids (ketones), this is a signal that they may have ketoacidosis and need more insulin.
3. The main factors are diet, exercise, and emotions. The presence of infection, ketoacidosis, and other disorders are also factors.
4. Glucocorticoids regulate the use of fat and sugar by the body, and mineralocorticoids regulate the salt/water balancing function of the kidneys.
5. Hormone replacement; suppression of immune response; inflammation and allergic reaction; skin inflammations; eye and respiratory diseases.
6. Masked infection, peptic ulcer, round, puffy face, salt retention, weight gain, disturbance of the pituitary/adrenal control system, etc.

G. Insulin risks
1. Problem: Too little insulin, insulin underdose. Give: More insulin.
2. Problem: Insulin shock, insulin overdose. Give: Sugar (orange juice, soft drink, candy, etc.).

H. Drug uses
1. a   2. d   3. c   4. b

I. Administration of insulin
See list of instructions in text.

REPRESENTATIVE HORMONES AND HORMONELIKE DRUGS[a]

CATEGORY, NAME[b], AND ROUTE	USES AND DISEASES	ACTIONS	USUAL DOSE[c] AND SPECIAL INSTRUCTIONS	SIDE EFFECTS AND ADVERSE REACTIONS
Hormones				
Glucagon SC, IM, IV	Severe insulin reaction	Raises blood sugar by stimulating the liver to convert glycogen to glucose	0.5–1 mg; may be repeated 1 or 2 times as ordered; follow physician's instructions for further medication (e.g., IV glucose, insulin)	Nausea, vomiting
Levothyroxine sodium (*Synthroid*) Oral, IV, IM	Hypothyroid conditions such as cretinism, myxedema, goiter, mild hypothyroidism, surgical removal of thyroid gland	Replaces thyroid hormone, stimulates metabolism	Maintenance 0.1–0.2 mg PO daily in single dose, adjusted individually; higher doses in children	Hyperthyroidism or overdose (chest pain, sleeplessness, weight loss, sweating); hypothyroidism or underdose (dry, puffy skin, weight gain, coldness, sleepiness)
Vasopressin tannate (*Pitressin Tannate*) IM	Diabetes insipidus, polyuria due to ADH deficiency	Replaces antidiuretic hormone (ADH) of pituitary; promotes reabsorption of water in the kidneys	0.3–1.0 ml (5 pressor units/ml) as ordered	Hypersensitivity; lethargy and confusion (water intoxication)
Corticosteroids				
Prednisone (*Deltasone*) Oral	Hormone replacement, inflammatory diseases (e.g., arthritis, dermatitis), lymphatic cancer, allergies, ulcerative colitis, kidney disease	Replaces adrenal hormones; suppresses inflammation and immune response	5–60 mg daily (in divided doses) depending on specific disease, adjusted to lowest effective maintenance level. May be given every other day to lessen side effects. Educate patient to maintain personal hygiene so as to avoid infection. Watch for side effects of long-term therapy and chart	Fluid imbalances, edema, hypokalemia, masked infection, stomach pain, rounded ("moon") face, mood changes, and many other side effects
Dexamethasone (*Decadron*) Oral, IV, IM, inhalation	Hormone replacement, inflammatory diseases (e.g., arthritis, dermatitis), lymphatic cancer, allergies, ulcerative colitis, kidney disease, and cerebral edema	Replaces adrenal hormones; suppresses inflammation and immune response; but causes less water retention	0.75–9.0 mg daily PO; up to 10 mg IV	Fluid imbalances; edema, hypokalemia, masked infection, stomach pain, rounded ("moon") face, mood changes, and many other side effects

[a] See also hormones listed in Table 14-2.
[b] Brand names given in parentheses are examples only. Check current drug references for a complete listing of available trade name products.
[c] Average adult doses are given. However, dosages are determined by a physician and vary with the purpose of the therapy and the particular patient. The dose presented in this text are for general information only.

Unit 14

Drugs for the Reproductive System

In this unit you will review the parts of the reproductive system and learn about the hormones produced by the male and female gonads. You will learn what disorders affect this system and which drugs are used to treat them.

In this unit, you will learn to:

- Name the main parts of the male and female internal and external genitalia.

- Use correct medical terms to describe the parts, functions, and disorders of the reproductive system.

- Name the hormones produced by the male and female gonads and tell what they do.

- Describe the actions of gonadotropins, oxytocin, and prolactin.

- Recognize descriptions of major disorders that affect the reproductive system.

- List the main uses of sex hormones in drug therapy.

- State the major side effects of sex hormone therapy.

REPRODUCTIVE SYSTEM

Creating the next generation of human life is the responsibility of the male and female reproductive systems. Of all the body systems, the reproductive system is the least alike in males and females. The two systems have different structures that must work together for reproduction to take place. One basic function of both the male and female systems is to **produce sex cells**. The other function is **engage in sexual intercourse**, the act that makes it possible for those cells to join together. The female system has an added function: to nourish and protect the fetus thus created until it is fully developed for life outside the womb.

The external and internal reproductive organs in both males and females are called **genitalia** (*jen'i-ta'le-ah*). Some of the male and female genitalia have similar functions, but their anatomy is different. The two systems are described separately.

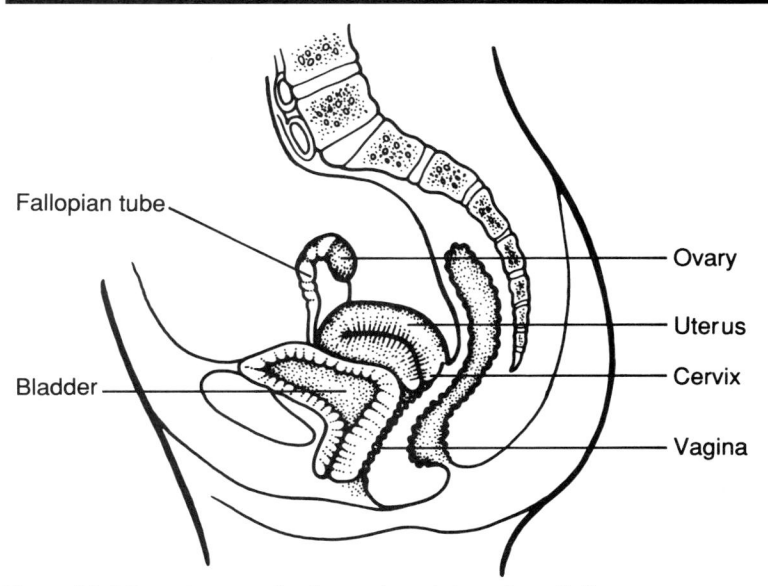

Female Reproductive System

Internal Genitalia—The internal genitalia of the female reproductive system consist of two ovaries, two fallopian tubes, the uterus, and the vagina (Figure 14-1). The **ovaries** are structures that produce female sex cells called **ova** (plural of **ovum**). About once a month, **ovulation** takes place. That is, a single ovum erupts from the surface of one ovary and is swept into a **fallopian tube** (*fal-lo'pe-an*) (also called **uterine tube**) that leads to the uterus. The ovum travels toward the uterus on a trip that takes about 5 days. It is during this trip that, if conditions are right, a male sex cell or sperm may join the ovum to start a new human life. This joining of sex cells is called **fertilization**.

The **uterus** (*u'ter-us*) is designed to hold and nourish the fertilized ovum as it develops. The uterus is shaped like an upside-down pear and is located in the pelvis. It opens through the **cervix** (*ser'viks*) into the **vagina** (*vah-ji'nah*), a barrel-shaped tube. The vagina gives access to the internal genitalia from outside the body. It is through the vagina that sperm may be deposited by the male penis into the female reproductive system.

External Genitalia—The external female genitalia consist of the mons pubis, the labia minora, the labia majora, and the clitoris (Figure 14-2). The **mons pubis** (*monz pu'bis*) is a pad of fat covered with hair located at the front of the body. Just below it are two sets of folds, the **labia** (*la'be-ah*), covering the openings to the vagina and the urethra (a part of the urinary system). Farther toward the back is the opening to the rectum, called the **anus**. The entire female genital area between the vulva and the anus is the **perineum** (*per'i-ne'um*).

At the forward tip of the labia is a tiny bulblike structure called the **clitoris** (*klit'o-*

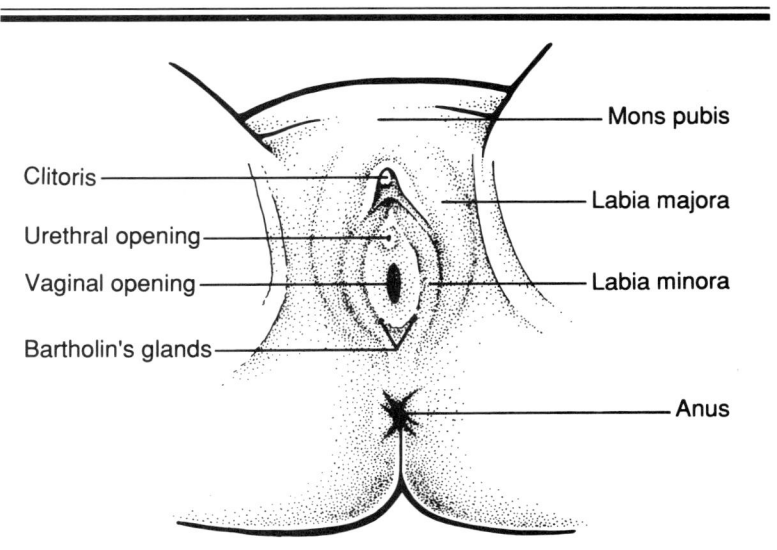

Figure 14-1 Female reproductive system: internal genitalia.

Figure 14-2 Female reproductive system: external genitalia.

VOCABULARY

amenorrhea: failure to menstruate; missed menstrual period

breakthrough bleeding: vaginal bleeding or spotting that occurs at times other than normal menstrual periods

cervicitis: inflammation of the cervix

cervix: entrance of the uterus

dysmenorrhea: painful menstruation

dysuria: difficult or painful urination

endometrium: lining of the uterus

engorgement: filling up of a body part with blood or other fluid, e.g., penis engorgement prior to intercourse, breast engorgement with milk in nursing mothers

estrogen: female hormone

fetus: child developing in the uterus during pregnancy

genitalia: sexual organs, internal or external

gonadotropins: pituitary hormones that stimulate the gonads (ovaries and testes) to secrete hormones

kraurosis: dried condition

labia: two sets of folds surrounding the opening of the vagina

labor: rhythmic contractions of the uterus that push the baby through the vagina during childbirth

menopause: normal end of menstruation in females at the average age of 48

menorrhea: menstruation; also called monthly period, or menses

mons pubis: fatty pad just above the female external genitalia

osteoporosis: declining levels of calcium in bones which can result in fractures

ovaries: female gonads

ovum: female sex cell (plural *ova*: release of these from the ovary is called **ovulation**)

oxytocic: drug that stimulates contractions of the uterus

penis: part of male external genitalia that is used to place sperm in the vagina

perineum: general term for the area of male or female anatomy that is the lowest part of the genitals and the anus

postpartum: after giving birth

progesterone: female hormone

prostate: gland surrounding the male urethra and ejaculatory duct; produces fluids that are combined with sperm to make semen

prostatitis: infection of the prostate gland

receptor sites: a sensory nerve ending that responds to various stimulus

scrotum: sac of skin containing the testes; part of the male external genitalia

sexually transmitted diseases: diseases spread by sexual contact, includes syphilis, gonorrhea, chlamydia, and AIDS

spermatozoa: male sex cells, also called **sperm**

testes: male gonads

testosterone: male hormone (the various forms of testosterone are known collectively as **androgens**)

uterus: part of the female internal genitalia that houses the developing fetus during pregnancy

vaginitis: inflammation of the vagina

vagina: part of the female internal genitalia linking the uterus to the outside of the body; passage into which sperm is deposited and through which a baby is born; also called **birth canal**

---

ris). It is a very sensitive nerve center that helps to make the act of intercourse pleasurable to the woman. Two glands called **Bartholin's glands** (*Bar'to-linz*) are located on either side of the vaginal opening. During sexual excitement, they secrete a lubricating mucus that helps the penis enter the vagina.

Pregnancy and Childbirth—If an ovum is fertilized and manages to attach itself to the lining of the uterus, it begins to develop into a **fetus**, and pregnancy is the result. The fetus is nourished by the mother's blood and cushioned by a surrounding sac of fluid. After approximately 280 days, or 9 months, development is complete and **labor** begins. Rhythmic contractions of the uterus begin to push the baby toward the cervix. The cervix flattens and the baby passes through the vagina (also called the **birth canal**) into the outside world.

While the fetus develops inside the woman's body, changes take place in the **breasts** as well. The breasts are composed of fatty tissue and **mammary** (milk) glands. During pregnancy, they grow larger and the mammary glands prepare to secrete the milk that will nourish the baby through the first few months of life. A few days after birth, the milk glands go into full production, and the breasts swell with milk. The baby can obtain the milk by sucking on the nipples.

Male Reproductive System

The internal genitalia of the male reproductive system consist of two testes, several glands, and a passageway to the outside of the body (Figure 14-3). The **testes** (*tes'tez*) produce millions of tiny sex cells called **spermatozoa** (*sper'mah-to-zo'ah*) or sperm. The sperm collect and mature in a series of coiled tubes called the **epididymis** (*ep'i-did'i-mis*). They then pass through a larger tube, the **vas deferens** (*vas def'er-enz*). The vas deferens leads from the testes to several storage areas called the **seminal vesicles** (*sem'i-nal ves-i-k'lz*) and to the **ejaculatory duct** (*e-jak'u-lah-to're dukt*). This duct passes through the **prostate** (*pros'tat*) **gland** and joins the **urethra** (*u-re'thrah*), a tube leading through the penis to the outside. The prostate gland, the seminal vesicles, and the **Cowper's glands** located on either side of the urethra all produce mucus and fluids that, together with the sperm, make up the **semen**. During ejaculation, a muscular contraction that occurs with a peak of sexual excitement, the semen is propelled out of the body.

The external genitalia include the **scrotum**, a sac of skin in which the two testes are suspended, and the **penis**. During sexual excitement, the spongy tissue of the penis fills up with blood. This makes the penis lengthen and become rigid in preparation for sexual intercourse.

Sex Hormones

A few sex hormones are secreted by the adrenal cortex (see Unit 13), but most come from the male and female sex glands or **gonads** (*go'nadz*).

The female gonads, the ovaries, secrete the hormones **estrogen** (*es'tro-jen*) and **progesterone** (*pro-jes'te-ron*). Estrogen is responsible for the higher voice, breast development, and shapeliness that are characteristic of women. It also stimulates the monthly development of an ovum. If an ovum is fertilized, the ovaries begin to produce progesterone. This prepares the uterus to carry and nourish the fetus as it grows. If the egg is not fertilized, the hormones cause the uterine lining to be shed, resulting in **menstruation** (**menorrhea**, *men'o-re'ah*, or menses). Somewhere between the ages of 42 and 54, the ovaries stop producing estrogen and progesterone, and monthly menstruation ceases. This change in hormone production is known as the **menopause**.

The male gonads, the testes, produce the male hormone **testosterone** (*tes-tos'te-ron*). Testosterone gives men their deeper voice and chest and facial hair. It also stimulates the production of sperm cells.

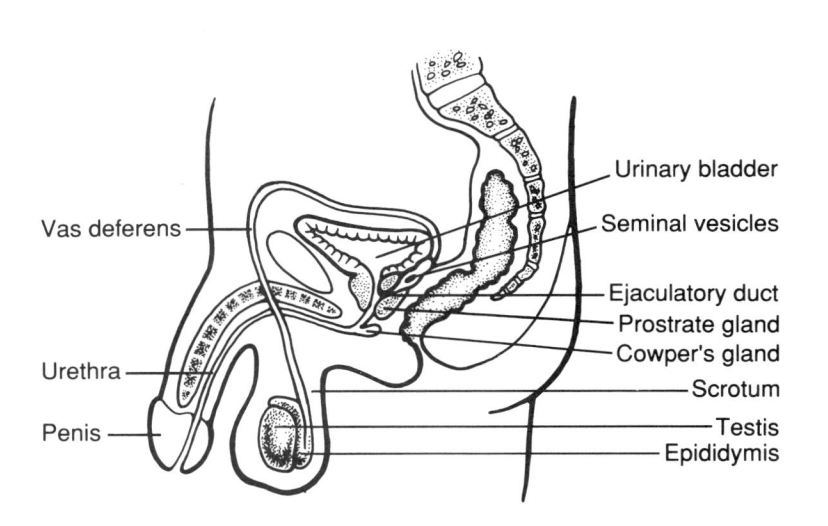

Figure 14-3 Male reproductive system: internal and external genitalia.

NOTE:

Estrogen, progesterone, and testosterone are not single hormones, but represent groups of related hormones. You will see drug references that refer to estrogens, progesterones, progestins, and various forms of testosterone.

Although we say that there are female hormones and male hormones, both kinds of hormones are secreted in every person's body regardless of sex. The sex hormones are closely related to each other chemically. They are all needed because they are involved in other body processes besides sexual development (e.g., growth, bone formation, protein synthesis, storage of minerals).

Pituitary Hormones that Regulate Reproduction

The pituitary hormones FSH (follicle-stimulating hormone) and LH (luteinizing hormone) control several functions of the gonads. For that reason they are also called **gonadotropins** (*gon'ah-do-tro'pinz*). In the female, the two gonadotropins control ovulation and the production of female hormones by the ovaries; in the male, they stimulate the testes to produce sperm and secrete testosterone (Figure 14-4).

Two other pituitary hormones are involved in childbirth (Figure 14-5). **Oxytocin** (*ok'se-to'sin*) stimulates the uterus to start contracting at the beginning of labor. A dose of oxytocin (*Pitocin, Syntocinon*) or a similar, synthetic drug (called an **oxytocic**) may be used to bring about or strengthen labor when a delay would endanger the mother or the child. It may also be given to slow postpartum (after childbirth) bleeding of the uterus. When the baby is born, **prolactin** signals the mammary glands in the female breast to start producing milk. Then oxytocin becomes involved again. It stimulates the mammary glands to "let down" the milk each time the infant begins to nurse.

DISORDERS OF THE REPRODUCTIVE SYSTEM

Vaginal Infections

Vaginal infections are common in women because germs have easy access to the internal organs through the external genitalia. Yeast infection and trichomoniasis (*trik'o-mo-ni'ah-sis*) are the two most common forms of infection. Vaginal infections cause inflammation of the vagina (**vaginitis,** *vaj'i-ni'tis*), and there is an unusual discharge (cheeselike, or foamy and bad-smelling). They also cause itching and burning in the vulvar area. Untreated, they may spread to other organs of the reproductive system, causing further inflammation, e.g., **cervicitis** (*ser'vi-si'tis*), inflammation of the cervix.

A variety of vaginal douches, creams, tablets, and suppositories are available that have antibacterial and antifungal actions. A practice procedure at the end of this unit shows how these are inserted. The specific infecting germ must be identified in the laboratory so that the proper anti-infective can be selected. Some common topical preparations are miconazole (*Monistat 7*), clotrimazole (*Gyne-Lotrimin*), and sulfonamide combinations.

An oral medication, metronidazole (*Flagyl*), is useful in treating trichomoniasis, a protozoan vaginal infection. It is also given to the male sexual partner, because the male sexual organ usually will trap some of the germs and later reinfect the female.

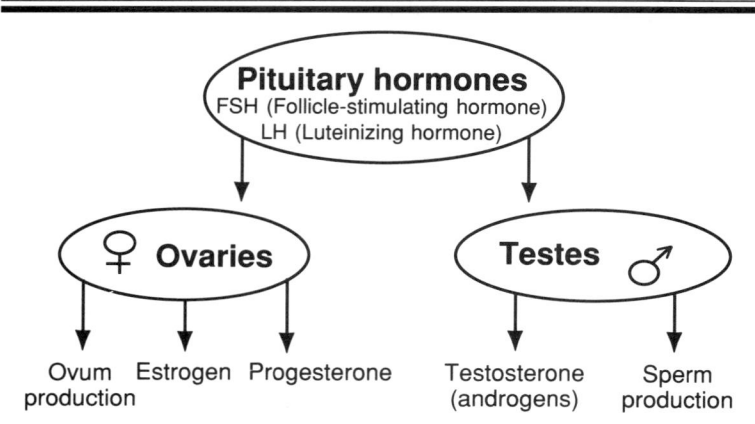

Figure 14-4 Pituitary hormones govern the work of the gonads.

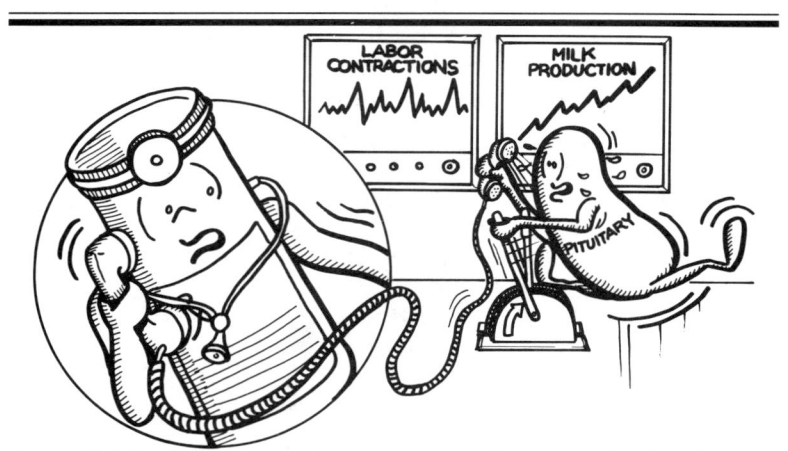

Figure 14-5 The hormones oxytocin and prolactin come into play during childbirth.

Sexually Transmitted Diseases

These diseases represent an important concern in health care. They appear to be increasing in number of diseases and persons infected. In addition, the older infections such as **syphilis** (*sif'i-lis*) and **gonorrhea** (*gon'o-re'ah*) are becoming resistant to some antibiotics. The infections of more recent origin are also difficult to treat and in some instances difficult to diagnose.

Chlamydial (*klah-mid'e-al*) infections are probably the most common but have frequently gone undiagnosed. Infertility and pelvic inflammatory disease (PID) are two serious complications of chlamydial infections.

Trichomoniasis is a vaginal infection that is usually treated with metronidazole (*Flagyl*). **Genital herpes simplex** is a viral infection. There is currently no cure, although acyclovir (*Zovirax*) does relieve symptoms in some patients.

Acquired immune deficiency syndrome (AIDS) is a major health concern for the coming decades. While drugs are available to alleviate some symptoms, research continues for a cure or a vaccine.

The treatment of the sexually transmitted diseases can be especially difficult for the health care worker. Frequently, there are no symptoms, and people are reluctant to discuss existing symptoms and to involve sexual partners in the treatment plan. Prevention is preferable to trying to cure an established infection. Use of condoms by sexually active people has been shown to help prevent the spread of these diseases.

Prostate Diseases

The prostate is the gland that secretes mucus and other substances that help make up semen in the male. Infection of the prostate, **prostatitis** (*pros'tah-ti'tis*), is very common and is signaled by cloudy urine and sometimes blood in the urine. Prostatitis may be a clue to an infection in the bladder (cystitis). Treatment consists of draining the pus from the area, removing the source of infection (e.g., clearing up a bladder infection), and administering anti-infectives.

After age 40, and especially around 60–70, a man's prostate tends to enlarge. As it grows, it can block the urethra and cause difficult or painful urination (dysuria, *dis- u're-ah*). Severe cases require surgery. Prostate cancer is also common, especially in men over age 60. Surgery and radiation therapy are the best treatment if the cancer has not spread. In more advanced cases, female sex hormones help keep the symptoms of prostate cancer under control.

Cancer

All the organs of the male and female reproductive systems can develop malignant tumors. Cancer of the breast and uterus are common in women. Prostate cancer in men has already been mentioned. Tumors of the testicle are rare but very often malignant. Certain cancers—for example, cancer of the breast and prostate—can be controlled through the use of sex hormones.

Infertility

Problems of infertility affect about 15% of couples who wish to have children. Pregnancy is ultimately achieved in about half of the couples who seek treatment.

Infertility in females can be related to cervical mucus, ovulation problems, hormonal imbalances, or endometriosis (*en'do- me'tre-o'sis*). Surgery and drugs can be used to overcome some of these problems. Infertility in the male is usually related to problems with sperm density, motility, or shape or seminal fluid volume or viscosity. Some of the drugs used to overcome infertility problems are clomiphen (*Clomid*), danazol (*Danocrine*), human chorionic gonadotropin (*Pregnyl, Follutein*), and menotropins (*Pergonal*).

USES OF SEX HORMONES IN DRUG THERAPY

The hormones secreted by the gonads—estrogen, progesterone, and testosterone—have other uses besides regulating the organs of reproduction. They are involved in ongoing body processes such as growth, sexual development, bone formation, the storage of minerals, and the building of proteins. They have several uses in drug therapy as well (Figure 14-6). Hormone replacement is one use, but larger doses can be therapeutic for conditions unrelated to a lack of sex hormones. Natural sex hormones for drug therapy are gathered from the bodies of domestic animals. For example, estrogen is collected from the

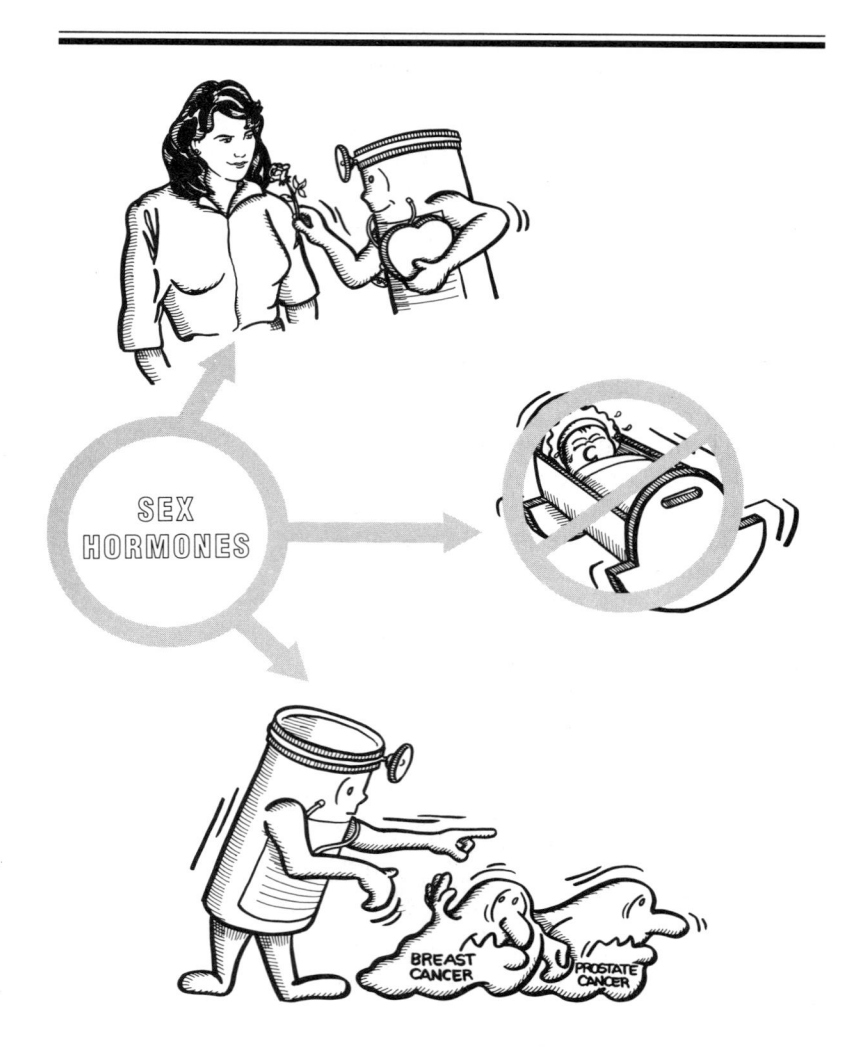

Figure 14-6 Some therapeutic uses of sex hormones: easing effects of menopause, contraception, and controlling cancer of the breast and prostate.

urine of pregnant mares. Synthetic forms are also available.

Representative drugs that affect the reproductive system are given at the end of this unit, including their uses, actions, doses, and side effects.

Estrogen

Estrogen is administered in drug therapy for several reasons. One is to replace female hormones after menopause. At the menopause, the ovaries stop producing female hormones. The pituitary "senses" a lack of these hormones and produces large amounts of gonadotropins in an attempt to stimulate production. As a result, women experience the common discomforts surrounding menopause: "hot flashes," dizziness, and headaches. Small doses of estrogen may be given to reduce these symptoms.

After menopause, estrogen may also be used to prevent bone thinning, brittleness, and spontaneous fracturing (**osteoporosis**, *os'te-o-po-ro'sis*). Osteoporosis may develop at this time because there is less estrogen to stimulate bone cell maintenance. Estrogen is also used to treat failure to menstruate (**amenorrhea**), vaginal inflammation and breast cancer in older women, and prostate cancer in men. Women who do not wish to breast-feed their newborn babies may be given estrogen to "dry up" the milk and prevent swollen breasts (**engorgement**).

The most common side effect of estrogen therapy is nausea, but this often passes with time or with reduced dosages. Breast tenderness and abnormal vaginal bleeding (spotting, breakthrough bleeding) are other side effects of estrogen therapy. To avoid these side effects, estrogen may be administered in cycles—for example, 3 weeks on and 1 week off. The long-term use of estrogen, such as for hormone replacement or menopause symptoms, carries the risk of cancer of the **endometrium** (*en-do-me'tre-um*) (the uterine lining). Estrogen must not be given to pregnant women because it can cause birth defects (congenital anomalies), or it can later cause cancer in the female child.

Many chemical forms of estrogen are available generically. Common forms are estradiol, estrone, and conjugated estrogens (*Premarin*). Topical forms of these drugs are available for application to the vagina to control inflammation after menopause (**senile vaginitis**).

Progesterone

Progesterone, the second female hormone, acts in partnership with estrogen to prepare the body for reproduction. While estrogen stimulates the production of an egg cell in the ovary, progesterone helps prepare the uterus to receive and nourish a fertilized egg. During pregnancy, progesterone also suppresses the production of further egg cells in the ovaries.

Progesterone is given in conditions such as abnormal uterine bleeding, inflammation of the uterine lining (**endometriosis**) dysmenorrhea, and amenorrhea. Side effects of progesterone— nausea, headache, and dizziness—usually go away with continued use. Occasionally a person may develop depression, edema, and apathy while on progesterone. Medroxyprogesterone acetate (*Provera, Depo-Provera*) and megestrol (*Megace*) are synthetic forms of progesterone.

Contraceptives

Perhaps the most widespread use of both estrogen and progesterone is in contraception, the prevention of pregnancy. Oral contraceptives—"the pill"— contain small doses of one or both hormones. These "fool" the pituitary so that it does not stimulate the production of hormones that trigger ovulation. Contraceptives also cause changes in the opening of the uterus, the cervix. The fluids there become sticky, which helps keep sperm from swimming up the uterus to fertilize an ovum. Many brand name combination products contain norgestrel, ethinyl estradiol, ethynodiol diacetate, mestranol, and/or norethindrone.

Contraceptives have many mild side effects such as nausea, breakthrough bleeding, water retention, vaginal infections, and headaches. A more serious problem is the risk of developing blood clots (thrombophlebitis, embolism, etc.). Another concern is the possible link between female hormones and cancer. The long-term effects of oral contraceptives are now under study. It is important to note that oral contraceptive users over the age of 30 who smoke have a greater risk for cardiovascular complications than nonusers.

Testosterone

Like the female sex hormones, the male sex hormones, also called **androgens**, are secreted in both males and females. The main androgen, **testosterone**, is used in replacement therapy for men when the testes are not producing enough hormone for proper development or sexual activity. It also helps relieve the symptoms of breast cancer. Because testosterone promotes the building of body tissues, it may be used to reverse tissue wasting and loss of protein due to burns, surgery, and debilitating diseases that keep patients confined to a chair or bed over long periods of time. When used in women, testosterone can result in masculine side effects (e.g., deepening voice, increased body hair). Its use can also lead to retention of salts and thus edema, which can usually be controlled with diuretics. Examples of testosterones are testosterone propionate and methyltestosterone (*Oreton Methyl*).

EXERCISES

A. Fill in the blanks.

1. Female sex cells, the ova, are produced by the _____.

2. Male sex cells, the sperm, are produced by the _____.

3. The barrel-shaped tube that serves as the birth canal is called the _____.

4. The structure that holds the fertilized ovum while it develops inside the woman's body is the _____.

5. The mons pubis, the clitoris, and the labia are part of the female's external _____.

6. Another name for the vulva is the _____.

7. Lactation occurs when the _____ glands in the breast go into production.

8. The penis and the _____ make up the male external genitalia.

9. The ejaculatory duct passes through the _____ gland, where mucus and other fluids are added to the sperm.

10. Semen leaves the male body through a tube called the _____ which is shared with the urinary system.

B. Match the hormones to the jobs they do in regulating human reproduction.

_____ 1. estrogen

_____ 2. progesterone

_____ 3. testosterone

_____ 4. oxytocin

_____ 5. gonadotropin

_____ 6. prolactin

a. stimulates sperm production and development of deep voice and chest and facial hair
b. acts in partnership with estrogen in regulating ovulation, prepares uterus for pregnancy
c. triggers the onset of labor
d. stimulates development of breasts, shapeliness, and feminine voice
e. stimulates the mammary glands to produce milk
f. tells the ovaries and testes when to secrete sex hormones

C. Define these terms:
1. oxytocic _____

2. dysmenorrhea _____

3. engorgement _____

4. venereal disease _____

5. androgens _____

6. endometrium _____

D. Choose the disorder that best matches each description below. Write the name of the disorder in the blank.

cervicitis senile vaginitis
endometriosis enlarged prostate

1. Nancy B. had an unusual vaginal discharge that caused itching and burning, but she ignored it. Now the doctor says the infection has spread to the opening of the uterus.

   _____

2. Harry J., age 62, is having more and more trouble urinating lately. The doctor thinks something may be blocking the urethra. Harry says this is the same condition that several friends his age have had.

   _____

3. Since menopause, Janice M. has had more trouble than usual with vaginal itching and discharge. Her doctor prescribes small doses of female hormones to help prevent the inflammations.

   _____

4. Akiko N. has an inflammation of the uterine lining, and her doctor has placed her on progesterone therapy.

   _____

E. Short answers
1. List all the therapeutic uses you can think of for sex hormones (both male and female).

   _____

   _____

   _____

2. What are the possible side effects of estrogen therapy (including oral contraceptives)?

_____

_____

3. What are the possible side effects of testosterone therapy?

_____

_____

F. Decide whether each of the following drugs is a female hormone (F) or a male hormone (M). Place an F or an M next to each one.

_____ 1. *Oreton Methyl*
_____ 2. *Premarin*
_____ 3. estradiol
_____ 4. testosterone
_____ 5. *Provera*
_____ 6. conjugated estrogens
_____ 7. methyltestosterone
_____ 8. *Norgestrel*

G. True or false. Circle T if the statement is true, F if it is false.

T F   1. A basic function of the reproductive system is to produce sex cells.
T F   2. It takes 28 days for the ovum to travel to the uterus.
T F   3. Milk is available in the breasts immediately after the baby is born.
T F   4. Spermatozoa are produced in the testes.
T F   5. The source of most sex hormones is the gonads.
T F   6. After an ovum is fertilized, the ovaries produce estrogen.
T F   7. Menopause is when the ovaries stop producing estrogen and begin producing progesterone.
T F   8. Only male hormones are found in males and only female hormones in females.
T F   9. Prolactin is the hormone that tells the breasts to produce milk.
T F 10. Sexually transmitted diseases are all easily treated and cured with drugs.
T F 11. Chlamydial infections are common but have no serious effects.
T F 12. Prostate enlargement is frequently a problem for young men.
T F 13. Dysuria refers to difficult or painful urination.
T F 14. Endometriosis can be a factor in infertility.
T F 15. Osteoporosis is caused by too much estrogen.
T F 16. Nausea is a common side effect of estrogen therapy.
T F 17. Oral contraceptives work by preventing ovulation.
T F 18. Testosterone relieves the symptoms of breast cancer.
T F 19. While taking oral contraceptives, it is a good idea to smoke to avoid weight gain.
T F 20. Androgens is another word for male sex hormones.

ANSWERS TO EXERCISES

A. Fill in the blanks
1. ovaries
2. testes
3. vagina
4. uterus
5. genitalia
6. perineum
7. mammary
8. scrotum
9. prostate
10. urethra

B. Matching
1. d
2. b
3. a
4. c
5. f
6. e

C. Definitions
1. drug that induces or strengthens labor
2. painful menstruation
3. swelling of breasts with milk or of penis prior to intercourse
4. infectious disease spread through sexual contact
5. another name for male sex hormones
6. lining of the uterus

D. Disorders
1. cervicitis
2. enlarged prostate
3. senile vaginitis
4. endometriosis

E. Short answers
1. Easing menopause symptoms, osteoporosis, amenorrhea, prevention of breast engorgement, senile vaginitis, uterine bleeding, endometriosis, contraception, breast and prostate cancer, hormone replacement, reversal of tissue wasting.
2. Nausea, breakthrough bleeding, water retention, vaginal infections, headache, risk of blood clots, possible cancer link, feminization of males.
3. Masculinization of females, water retention.

F. Sex hormones
1. M
2. F
3. F
4. M
5. F
6. F
7. M
8. F

G. True or false
1. T
2. F
3. F
4. T
5. T
6. F
7. F
8. F
9. T
10. F
11. F
12. F
13. T
14. T
15. F
16. T
17. T
18. T
19. F
20. T

PRACTICE PROCEDURE

INSERT VAGINAL MEDICATION

Equipment:

- Medication orders for vaginal medications Kardex, medicine cards, medication record, patient chart
- Medicine tray or cart
- Vaginal medications (practice with one or all four): suppository, ointment, cream, or jelly
- Applicator for inserting medication
- Plastic gloves
- Tissues

_____ 1. Assemble equipment.

_____ 2. Read the medication order and set up medications. Check for the "five rights."

_____ 3. Wash your hands.

_____ 4. Identify the patient. Explain what you are going to do. Have the patient void before beginning the procedure. Curtain off the area for privacy.

_____ 5. Assist the patient into position for insertion. She should lie on her back with knees bent and legs spread apart to expose the perineum. Drape the patient for privacy and warmth.

_____ 6. Put on plastic gloves, and unwrap the suppository or prepare the medication applicator. Suppositories may be inserted either by hand or with a plastic applicator. Creams, ointments, and jellies are inserted with an applicator.

_____ 7. Spread the labia apart and locate the vaginal opening (refer back to Figure 14-2).

_____ 8. Insert the medication.

By hand: Gently insert the suppository about 2–3 inches into the vagina.

By applicator (Figure 14-7): Gently insert the applicator about 2–3 inches inches into the vagina. Push the plunger to release the suppository and withdraw. If inserting ointment, cream, or jelly, slowly withdraw the applicator as you push the plunger. This will deposit the medication along the vaginal canal.

With either method, insert the medication along the back wall of the vagina. The back wall is longer than the forward wall, which has the cervix jutting out of it.

_____ 9. Wipe the vaginal opening with a tissue if necessary, or let the patient do this.

_____ 10. Clean or discard the applicator, and remove and discard your gloves.

_____ 11. Assist the patient back into a comfortable position and give any needed instructions. Provide sanitary pads to soak up vaginal discharge and to avoid staining underclothes.

_____ 12. Wash your hands.

_____ 13. Chart the medication.

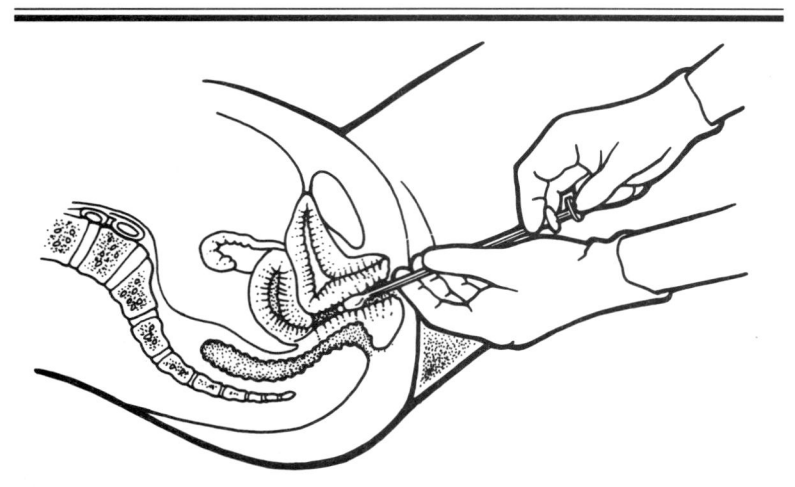

Figure 14-7 Inserting a vaginal suppository with an applicator.

Demonstrate this procedure for the instructor or the nurse in charge.

REPRESENTATIVE DRUGS FOR THE REPRODUCTIVE SYSTEM

CATEGORY, NAME[a], AND ROUTE	USES AND DISEASES	ACTIONS	USUAL DOSE[b] AND SPECIAL INSTRUCTIONS	SIDE EFFECTS AND ADVERSE REACTIONS
Hormones				
Conjugated Estrogens (*Premarin*) Oral, Cream, IV	Menopausal discomfort, atrophic vaginitis, kraurosis vulvae, breast and prostate cancer (palliation)	Replaces estrogen	Atrophic vaginitis: 0.3–1.25 mg daily. Menopause: administer cyclically 3 weeks on and 1 week off. Breast cancer: 10 mg TID for 3 months. Prostate cancer: 1.25–2.5 mg TID	Nausea, breakthrough bleeding, fluid retention
Oxytocin (*Pitocin, Syntocinon*) IV, IM	Initiation of uterine contractions or improvement of them, control of postpartum bleeding	Uterine stimulating actions	10–200 units	Fetal bradycardia, neonatal jaundice, anaphylactic reaction, postpartum bleeding, ruptured uterus, vomiting, fluid retention
Medroxyprogesterone acetate (*Provera*) Oral, IM	Dysfunctional uterine bleeding, amenorrhea	Stops uterine bleeding, stimulates secretions of endometrium	5–10 mg PO 5–10 days; administer with food if gastric upset occurs	Breast tenderness, weight changes, acne, fluid retention, thrombophlebitis, embolism
Norgestrel and ethinyl estradiol (*Ovral, Lo/Ovral*) Oral and Norethindrone and ethinyl estradiol (*Tri-Norinyl*) Oral	Contraception	Suppresses gonadotropins, inhibits ovulation	Follow package directions. Cigarette smoking increases risk of cardiovascular side effects.	Breast tenderness, weight changes, nausea and vomiting, thrombophlebitis, embolism
Methyltestosterone (*Oreton Methyl*) Oral, Buccal	*Male*: hypogonadism *Female*: Postpartum breast engorgement, cancer of the breast	*Male*: Replaces male hormone *Female*: Relieves symptoms	*Male*: 10–40 mg/day PO; 5–20 mg (buccal) *Female*: 80 mg/day PO for 3–5 days or 40 mg/day buccal for breast engorgement; 200 mg/day PO or 100 mg/day buccal for cancer Do not swallow or chew buccal medications. Do not eat, drink, or smoke until buccal medication is dissolved.	*Male*: Jaundice, edema *Female*: Amenorrhea, virilization
Antibacterials				
Miconazole (*Monistat 7*) Suppository, Cream	Local vaginal infections caused by Candida fungus	Fungacidal agent	One suppository or applicator full of cream once daily at bedtime for 7 days. Protect the underclothing.	Vaginal itching and burning, hives, skin rash
Metronidazole (*Flagyl*) Oral, IV	Symptomatic and asymptomatic trichomoniasis	Trichomonacidal agent	2 g given as a single dose or 1 g BID or 250 mg TID for 7 consecutive days. Male partner should be treated also.	Nausea, headache, diarrhea, rarely seizures and peripheral neuropathy

[a] Brand names given in parentheses are examples only. Check current drug references for a complete listing of available trade name products.
[b] Average adult doses are given. However, dosages are determined by a physician and vary with the purpose of the therapy and the particular patient. The doses presented in this text are for general information only.

Unit 15

Drugs for the Musculoskeletal System

In this unit you will review the various parts of the musculoskeletal system and the correct terms used to describe them. You will learn what disorders affect this system and what drugs are helpful.

In this unit, you will learn to:

- Use correct medical terms to describe major parts, functions, and disorders of the musculoskeletal system.
- Recognize descriptions of major disorders that affect the musculoskeletal system.
- Explain the difference between gout, osteoarthritis, and rheumatoid arthritis.
- Describe the actions of drug groups commonly used in the treatment of gout, osteoarthritis, and rheumatoid arthritis and give examples.
- List the side effects of aspirin and tell how they may be controlled.
- Give examples of newer anti-inflammatory agents and their mechanism of action.
- Administer medications to patients with painful musculoskeletal conditions without causing unnecessary discomfort.
- Describe malfunctions of bone marrow and their effects on blood.

MUSCULOSKELETAL SYSTEM

The bones, muscles, and joints make up the musculoskeletal system. This is the system that gives the body its supporting framework and the ability to move. The bones and their connecting joints act like a series of levers. Force is exerted on these levers by the muscles, and the result is movement. Some of the major bones and muscles are shown in Figure 15-1.

Bones

Bones are made up of a special type of connective tissue. Even though they appear to be lifeless, bones are living tissue. The reason for their hardness is that the spaces between bone cells are filled with the mineral **calcium**. Bones start out being relatively soft and pliable in babies. During childhood, calcium is deposited in the spaces between the bone cells, so that the bones gradually harden. Because of their softness, young bones heal more easily than do older ones. Calcium continues to be deposited in the bones throughout life, but it is reabsorbed much faster in older adults, resulting in osteoporosis.

We think of bones mainly as a framework for the muscles, but they perform other important functions as well: they produce blood cells, act as a storage area for calcium and fat, and protect delicate organs of the body. Bones are covered inside and out by membranes that contain blood vessels, lymph vessels, and nerves. When a bone is broken, these membranes aid in the process of healing.

Some parts of bones are made of a soft material called **cartilage**. Cartilage lines every joint and gives shape to the ears and nose. Inside most bones is a spongy type of tissue called **bone marrow**. Red bone marrow manufactures the three formed elements of the blood: all the red blood cells, certain white blood cells, and all the platelets. Yellow bone marrow, found only in the hollow parts of the long bones of the arms and legs, is a storage area for fat. Some bones contain open spaces inside to make them light.

Joints

The places where bones are connected to each other are called joints (Figure 15-2). Joints can be movable, partly movable, or immovable. For example, the elbow joint

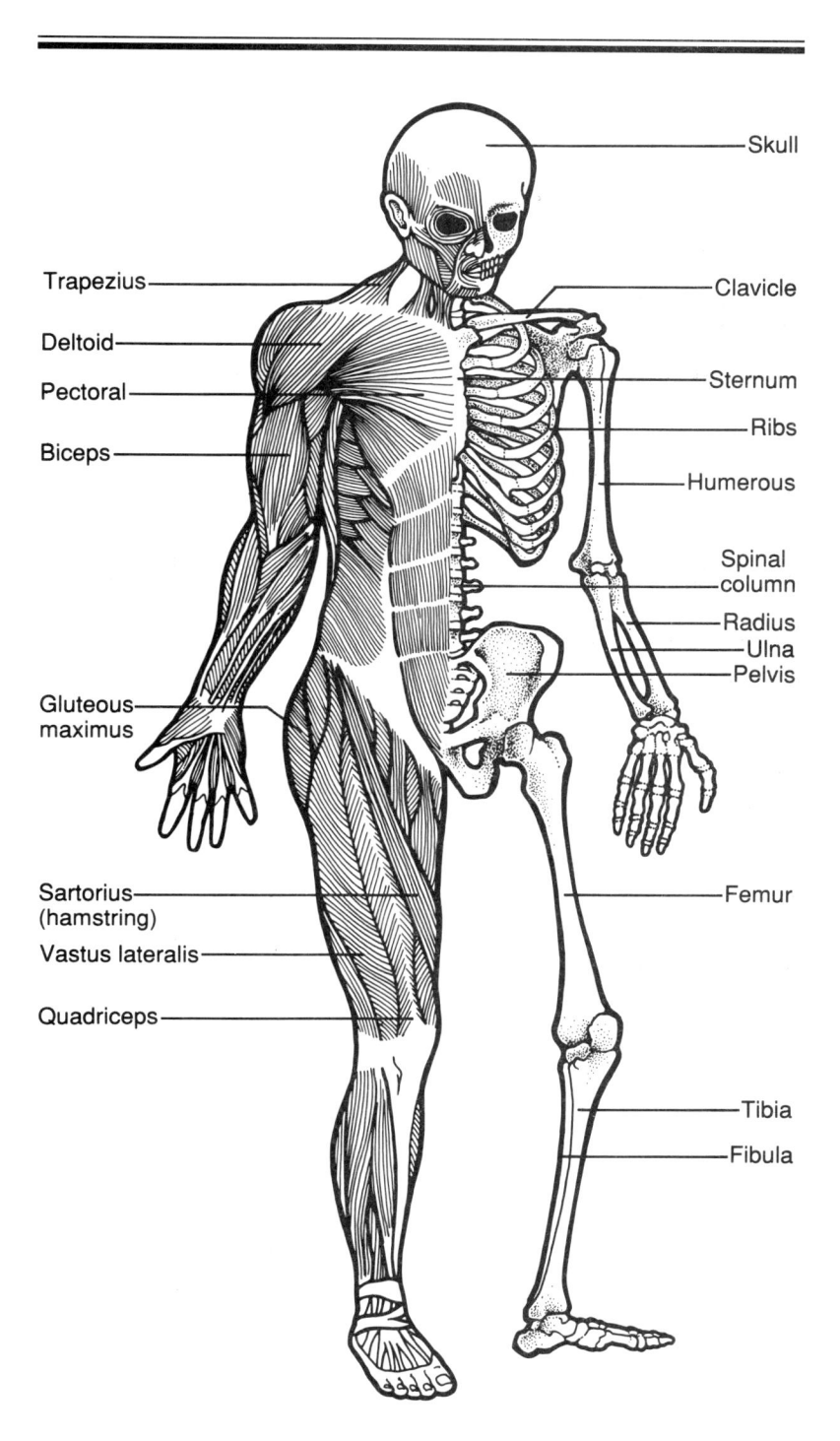

Figure 15-1 The musculoskeletal system, showing major bones and muscles.

is a freely movable joint, and the joints between the four bones of the pelvis are immovable. The ends of bones are covered with soft layers of cartilage that cushion the joints. The bones are held together by **ligaments**, strong bands of connective tissue.

VOCABULARY

alkaline: a base or compound that can neutralize acids

antihyperuricemic: drug that reduces the formation of uric acid

antiarthritic: drug that suppresses inflammation in degenerative diseases of the joints

antipyretic: a drug that reduces fever

arthritis: name for several disorders of the joints, each having different causes and treatments (e.g., gouty arthritis, osteoarthritis, rheumatoid arthritis)

atrophy: wasting and withering away of body tissue (e.g., atrophy of a muscle due to lack of use)

bone marrow depression: slowing down of the blood-cell-building functions of the red tissue inside bones

bursa: small fluid-filled sacs that cushion spots where bones and muscles rub together

enteric coated: tablets that dissolve in intestine and not the stomach

fascia: sheets of tissue that cover the muscles

ligaments: cords of tissue that interconnect bones at the joints

muscle tone: normal slightly contracted state of the skeletal muscles that keeps them prepared for action

osteo: prefix pertaining to the bones

myalgia: muscle pain

orthopedic: pertaining to diseases of the joints and spine

skeletal muscles: muscles responsible for body movement

spontaneous fracture: broken bone not due to trauma; occurs in osteoporosis as a result of bone thinning

synovial capsule: enclosed space between bones at the joints

tendons: cords or bands of tissue that connect muscles to bones

uricosuric: drug that increases excretion of uric acid through the kidneys

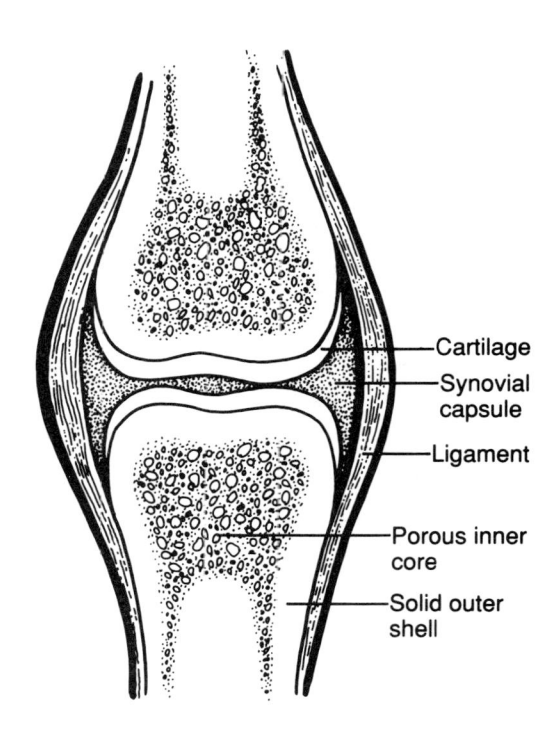

Figure 15-2 Close-up of a joint.

Muscles

The muscles that work together with the bones to allow movement are called **skeletal muscles**. There are two other types of muscle tissue as well:

- Smooth muscle tissue, which lines the gastrointestinal tract, urinary tract, and blood vessels.
- Cardiac muscle tissue, which makes up the heart.

Skeletal muscles are made up of long, thin muscle fibers bundled together with sheets of connective tissue called **fascia** (*fash'e-ah*). The muscles are richly supplied with blood, because they need great quantities of oxygen to generate the energy needed for their heavy work. The more exercise these muscles get, the more blood vessels grow into them to supply the needed nutrients and carry away wastes.

Skeletal muscles are attached to the bones by cords of connective tissue called **tendons**. The muscles exert a force on the bones by contracting, which means that the muscles become shorter and thicker.

When this effort is no longer needed, the muscles relax and assume their normal size.

Muscles that are well-exercised are always a little bit contracted, so that they will be ready for action as needed. This is referred to as **muscle tone**. Poor muscle tone is considered a sign of poor health. If muscles get little or no exercise, they tend to shrink and wither away or **atrophy** (at'ro-fe).

DRUG TREATMENT OF MUSCULOSKELETAL DISORDERS

Physical Injuries

Muscles and bones and their accessory parts are subject to various injuries. **Strains** occur when muscles or tendons are subjected to stress, especially if the stress lasts over a period of time. **Sprains** result from violent stress on a ligament. **Fractures** are breaks in the hard outer portion of bones. The pain associated with strains, sprains, and fractures is treated with analgesics. Otherwise the treatment is medical or surgical.

Osteomyelitis

Osteomyelitis (os'te-o-mi'e-li'tis) is an infection inside a bone, with symptoms usually appearing near a joint. There is pain and tenderness, and fever is present. The infection destroys bone tissue, and pus may drain through the skin. Osteomyelitis is treated with antibiotics. Surgery may be necessary to drain abscesses inside the bone.

Osteoporosis

Osteoporosis (os'te-o-po-ro'sis) appears mainly in women past the menopause. Because of a lack of estrogen, the bones do not produce enough protein to hold the calcium deposits that make bones hard. Consequently, the bones thin out, become abnormally porous, and are easily broken or fracture spontaneously. Osteoporosis can also be brought about by poor nutrition, inactivity in bedridden patients, and diseases like rheumatoid arthritis. Treatment consists of estrogen, calcium supplements, and a diet rich in protein.

Bursitis, Fibrositis, and Synovitis

These are inflammations that arise because of repeated physical stress on the joints or muscles. Bursitis (ber-si'tis) involves the **bursa**, which are small, fluid-filled pouches located between bones and ligaments and between bones and muscles. The bursa are designed to keep these parts from rubbing each other when they move. **Fibrositis** (fi'bro-si'tis) is an inflammation of the muscles, fascia, ligaments, or tendons (also called **tendinitis**, ten'di-ni'tis). **Synovitis** (sin'o-vi'tis) is an inflammation of the cavity surrounding a joint (the **synovial capsule**). All these inflammations produce symptoms of pain, stiffness, redness, and swelling. They are treated with oral analgesics. Sometimes hydrocortisone (a corticosteroid) is injected directly into the inflamed area. The injection reduces inflammation in the local area, while avoiding the systemic effects of an oral corticosteroid. Oral anti-inflammatory drugs such as fenoprofen calcium (*Nalfon*) and naproxen (*Naprosyn*) are also used.

Gout

Gout, or "gouty arthritis," is an inflammation of the joints that starts when there is an excess of **uric acid** in the bloodstream. Uric acid is a normal waste product of cell metabolism. In gout, either the kidneys do not excrete uric acid efficiently or there is a genetic factor that makes the body produce larger amounts of uric acid than normal. Because the uric acid is not completely excreted, crystals of the acid are deposited in the cartilage around the joints. This causes the joints to become red, hot, swollen, and painful. The condition can flare up or become worse with strong emotions or poor eating habits. Uric acid crystals can also form in the urine causing "gravel" or urate stones in the bladder and kidneys.

Chronic gout may be treated with **uricosuric** (u'ri-ko-su'rik) drugs (Figure 15-3). These are drugs that promote the excretion of uric acid, such as sulfinpyrazone (*Anturane*). Or, it may be treated with **antihyperuricemic** drugs, such as allopurinol (*Zyloprim*), which decrease the amount of uric acid produced by the body.

The most common drug for acute attacks of gout is colchicine (with probenecid in

Figure 15-3 Uricosurics help the body excrete excess uric acid.

Colbenemid), made from the root of the autumn crocus. It has the side effects of nausea, vomiting, and diarrhea, but it relieves the pain in the joints within a few hours. The drug can also be used for long-term treatment to prevent attacks of gout. Two other drugs that relieve gout by suppressing inflammation are indomethacin (*Indocin*) and naproxen (*Naprosyn*).

Patients being treated for gout must take many fluids to help wash away the uric acid crystals. Eight glasses of water a day are recommended.

Osteoarthritis

This is a degenerative joint disease, which means that it slowly destroys the joint tissue. It affects mainly the joints of the spine, hip, and knee, which are the weight-bearing joints. Most people over the age of 50 have some form of it, but not all of them show symptoms. As people grow older, the cartilage that cushions the joints begins to thin out and wear away. As a result, the bones rub against each other when the joints are moved. With continual rubbing and scraping, these bones thicken and become knobby or lumpy. Movement becomes painful and stiff. Symptoms are noticed especially toward evening, after a full day's wear and tear on the joints. There is pain and stiffness but usually no inflammation. The treatment consists of resting the joints by taking the weight off them, such as by sitting or lying down. Heat applied to the joints gives some relief, and so do analgesics such as aspirin. In severe cases, hydrocortisone may be injected into a painful joint to counteract inflammation.

Rheumatoid Arthritis

Rheumatoid arthritis, like osteoarthritis, is a degenerative disease of the joints. It is caused not by wear and tear, but by an inflammation of the cartilage in the synovial capsule. It is present in only two people out of one hundred, and few have serious symptoms. The symptoms are pain in the joints (especially of the wrist, fingers, ankles, and other peripheral joints) and stiffness. The stiffness occurs mainly in the morning and improves as the day goes on. There may also be fever, anorexia, weight loss, weakness, easy tiring, and aching muscles. The inflamed joints may feel warm to the touch. As the disease progresses, cartilage is slowly destroyed and the bones may even fuse together, causing loss of movement and sometimes deformity.

There is no specific cure for rheumatoid arthritis. The disease comes and goes, and it occasionally stops all by itself. Some people think it may be a form of autoimmune response, in which the body reacts to its own tissues as if they were "foreign" invaders like allergens and germs. Treatment for rheumatoid arthritis consists of making patients as comfortable as possible using drugs and a variety of physical measures. Heat is an important adjunct treatment, and so is controlled exercise. Exercise is important, because if patients stop moving so as to avoid pain, their muscles will lose tone and the patient will be worse off than before. A surgical procedure called arthroplasty is sometimes used for arthritis patients who cannot move because of badly damaged joints. The ends of the bones are replaced with metal parts or are smoothed and covered with new connective tissue, so that movement of the joint is again possible.

Several types of anti-inflammatory drugs are used to relieve pain and stiffness of rheumatoid arthritis. Together they are known as antiarthritics (Figure 15-4). They cannot stop the destruction of tissue, but they serve to mask the symptoms. Besides suppressing inflammation, many of these drugs also have analgesic and antipyretic actions.

The main antiarthritic is aspirin. It is given in much larger amounts for arthritis than for fever and other types of pain. This is because, in large doses, aspirin has an anti-inflammatory action. Arthritis patients may use up to twenty 5-grain tablets per day, or as many as they can take without getting signs of overdose. These signs include ringing or buzzing in the ears (tinnitus), rapid breathing (tachypnea), dizziness, and severe headache. Aspirin can irritate the stomach, so it is recommended to be taken with food or in enteric-coated form (e.g., *Ecotrin*). Aspirin also affects blood clotting time, so it is used cautiously with persons who are taking anticoagulants.

Other antiarthritics may be given, either alone or along with aspirin. Some of the better known drugs in this category are indomethacin (*Indocin*), ibuprofen (*Motrin*), sulindac (*Clinoril*), naproxen (*Naprosyn*), and fenoprofen (*Nalfon*).

Weekly injections of gold compounds, e.g., aurothioglucose (*Solgana*) and gold sodium thiomalate (*Myochrysine*) are sometimes used, but the toxic effects of gold pose a danger. Gold compounds are usually given when arthritis cannot be controlled by other anti-inflammatory agents. Antimalarial drugs (drugs that treat the disease malaria, e.g., chloroquine) are given orally in some cases. Both gold and antimalarial drugs take up to 6 weeks to show beneficial effects.

The main side effect to watch for with all the antiarthritics is gastrointestinal upset, including stomach pain and gastrointestinal bleeding. Mild stomach upset can usually be avoided by giving the drugs with meals, with a full glass of milk, or with a prescribed antacid.

Oral corticosteroids (e.g., hydrocortisone) may also be given to reduce inflammation in rheumatoid arthritis either alone or in combination with other drugs. Corticosteroids have serious side effects such as bone thinning, diabetes, peptic ulcers, and psychological changes, so the smallest possible doses are administered.

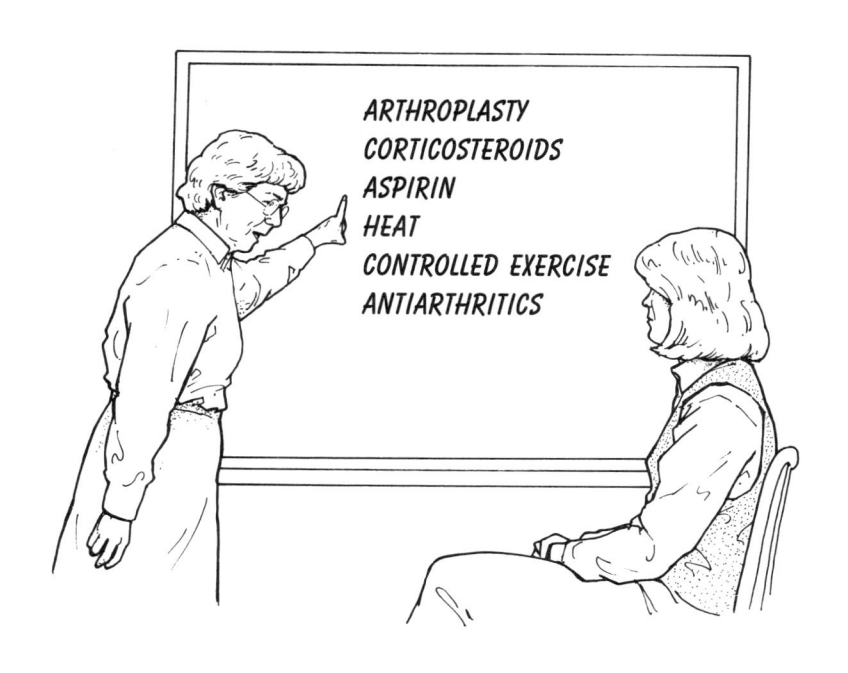

Figure 15-4 Anti-inflammatory drugs (antiarthritics and corticosteroids) and physical measures help keep rheumatoid arthritis symptoms under control.

Muscle Pain

There are many reasons for pain in the skeletal muscles (**myalgia**, *mi-al'je-ah*): overexercise, inflammation, sprains, arthritis, and orthopedic (crippling) conditions. Applications of moist heat, rest, and physical therapy go a long way toward relieving pain that comes from overuse. But doctors sometimes prescribe **muscle relaxants** to relieve muscle pain from arthritis and other musculoskeletal conditions (Figure 15-5). These drugs are really types of sedatives and tranquilizers. Examples are methocarbamol (*Robaxin*), carisoprodol (*Soma*), chlorzoxazone (*Paraflex*; with acetaminophen in *Parafon Forte*), and cyclobenzaprine hydrochloride (*Flexeril*). They affect the central nervous system rather than directly relaxing the muscles. Orphenadrine citrate (*Norflex, Norgesic Forte*) appears to relieve muscle pain by a sedating action. Certain other muscle relaxants (e.g., tubocurarine, a curare alkaloid) are used in preparing patients for some surgeries or for electroshock therapy.

Figure 15-5 Muscle relaxants ease muscle pain through their sedative action.

Bone Marrow Disorders

Because red bone marrow produces most of the important components of the blood, any disorder that affects the bone marrow can create serious problems for the body as a whole. Failure of the bone marrow to produce enough of all three components of the blood is called **aplastic anemia**. Overproduction of white blood cells is called **leukemia** (see Unit 8).

Bone marrow depression is an important and serious adverse reaction linked to many drugs, especially certain antihistamines, tranquilizers, chloramphenicol, phenylbutazone, sulfonamides, antineoplastics, thyroid medications, antidepressants, and diuretics. For this reason, you should be aware of symptoms that indicate that a drug may be affecting the bone marrow:

- **Lack of red blood cells**—weakness, pale skin (pallor), dyspnea
- **Lack of white blood cells**—agranulocytosis, (*ah-gran'u-lo-si-to'sis*)—soreness of mucous membranes in the mouth and throat, fever, chills, extreme fatigue, urinary and vaginal infections
- **Lack of platelets**—bleeding from the gums, nose, or gastrointestinal tract; signs of hemorrhage under the skin, e.g., purpura (*pur'pu-rah*), petechiae (*pe-te'ke-e*), ecchymoses (*ek'i- mo'sez*).

Like any unusual symptoms, these should be charted so that the physician can prescribe alternative drugs or treatment schedules.

Representative drugs used for musculoskeletal disorders are listed at the end of this unit.

CARE OF PATIENTS WITH MUSCULOSKELETAL DISORDERS

Patients with arthritis and other musculoskeletal disorders must live with pain. Sometimes every movement causes them discomfort. Analgesics and anti-inflammatory drugs are designed to relieve this pain, but they cannot remove it completely. When a person is in pain, it is easy to be impatient with those who are trying to help. Keep this in mind when caring for your patients. They hurt, and they may be angry that they must depend on others for routine care such as dressing and eating. There are several things you can do to make things easier:

- Give pain medications on time, following the rules given in Unit 10. This ensures that patients do not have to endure unnecessary pain while waiting for their next dose of medication.
- Handle patients with care. Do not bump against the bed as you prepare to administer medications. If you need to move patients for any reason, do it slowly and support their body parts. Avoid sudden, jarring movements that could cause pain.
- After moving them, reposition body parts in their natural alignment. This will reduce strain on the joints and muscles.
- Attend to psychological needs. Be calm and reassuring. Explain procedures clearly beforehand. Help patients "talk out" the depression and frustration that may come with restricted movement and constant pain.
- Let your actions show that you are aware of the patient's fears and needs. You will be able to do your job better, and the patient will appreciate your help.

Drugs for the Musculoskeletal System

EXERCISES

A. Fill in blanks

1. The musculoskeletal system supports the body and gives it the ability to _____.

2. Bones are connected to each other by means of _____.

3. Bones are living tissue. They get their hardess from deposits of the mineral _____.

4. Bundles of fibers that connect muscles to bones are called _____.

5. The spongy part of the bone where blood cells are produced and fat is stored is called the bone _____.

6. The skull, spinal column, sternum, ribs, and pelvis _____ the vital organs of the head, chest, and abdomen.

7. Smooth muscles allow movement in the gastointestinal tract and blood vessels, while _____ muscles allow movement of the bones.

8. Healthy muscles are slightly contracted at all times. This is called muscle _____.

9. Strains are injuries to muscles and tendons, whereas _____ are injuries to ligaments.

B. Match these drugs to their categories or uses.

1. _____ Ecotrin

2. _____ gold compounds, antimalarial drugs, indomethacin

3. _____ probenecid, Anturane, Zyloprim, colchicine

4. _____ hydrocortisone

5. _____ Robaxin, Flexeril, Soma, Parafon Forte

a. drugs that reduce the formation of uric acid crystals in the joints
b. muscle relaxants
c. corticosteroid sometimes injected into the synovial capsule to reduce joint inflammation
d. anti-inflammatory drugs that relieve rheumatoid arthritis symptoms (noncorticosteroid)
e. enteric-coated aspirin

C. 1. When administering medications to patients with painful musculoskeletal conditions, what can you do to help make them comfortable?

_____

_____

_____

2. List two side effects of giving large doses of aspirin. Tell ways of controlling them.

_____

_____

3. What symptoms can arise when a drug depresses the production of blood cells in the bone marrow?

_____

_____

_____

D. Define

1. atrophy _____

2. myalgia _____

E. Choose the disorder that best matches each description below. Write the name of the disorder on the blank.

osteomyelitis	gout
bursitis	osteoarthritis
osteoporosis	rheumatoid arthritis

1. An elderly patient must eat a diet rich in proteins and calcium, and she is taking small doses of hormones. This is because her bones have become very porous and fracture easily.

_____

2. Minnie J. awakens each day with painful stiffness in her wrists, fingers, and ankles. Her doctor says she has an inflammation in the joints which is causing damage to the ends of the bones. Minnie takes large doses of aspirin along with gold compounds to suppress the inflammation.

_____

3. Jim P. has developed an infection in the leg bone near the knee joint. He is taking antibiotics, and surgery is planned to drain the infected material from the bone.

_____

4. A small fluid-filled pouch in Freda M.'s shoulder joint is inflamed. This is causing swelling, pain, and stiffness. The doctor plans to inject hydrocortisone directly into the joint to reduce the inflammation.

_____

5. Increasing levels of uric acid in George J. is causing crystals to form in the cartilage around the joints. A dose of colchicine relieves the pain in his joints within a few hours.

6. Ben K. finds that his knee and hip joint become painful and stiff toward the end of the day. The doctor suggests taking aspirin and resting the joints by sitting or lying down several times a day.

F. True or false. Circle T if the statement is true and circle F if it is false.

T F 1. Bones are made of minerals and are not really living tissue.
T F 2. After middle age, calcium is no longer deposited in the bones, causing the development of osteoporosis.
T F 3. Myalgia is pain in the skeletal muscles.
T F 4. Blurred vision is the main side effect to be concerned about when administering antiarthritics.
T F 5. Aplastic anemia is a bone marrow disorder.
T F 6. The symptoms of a lack of red blood cells include weakness, pale skin, and dyspnea.
T F 7. Gout is a condition that results from too little uric acid in the bloodstream.
T F 8. Repeated physical stress on the joints or muscles can result in bursititis or fibrositis.
T F 9. Surgery is frequently used to treat osteoporosis.
T F 10. Lack of estrogen is a factor in the development of osteoporosis.
T F 11. Skeletal muscles are attached to the bones by cords of connective tissue called ligaments.
T F 12. Strains occur as a result of violent stress on a ligament.
T F 13. When muscles atrophy, they shrink, get smaller, and wither away.
T F 14. Some joints are immovable.
T F 15. Ligaments are strong bands of connective tissue that hold bones together.
T F 16. In general, muscles need very little oxygen.
T F 17. Platelets are produced in the yellow bone marrow.
T F 18. An inflammation of the synovial capsule is known as synovitis.
T F 19. Crystals of uric acid deposited in the cartilage around joints can cause the joint to become red, hot, swollen, and painful.
T F 20. Rheumatoid arthritis is caused by wear and tear on the joints.

ANSWERS TO EXERCISES

A. Fill in blanks
   1. move
   2. ligaments
   3. calcium
   4. tendons
   5. marrow
   6. protect, support
   7. skeletal
   8. tone
   9. sprains

B. Drugs
   1. e
   2. d
   3. a
   4. c
   5. b

C. 1. Give pain medications on time, move patients carefully, don't bump the bed, meet their psychological needs.
   2. Gastric irritiation; controlled by giving liquids, taking aspirin with food, or taking enteric-coated aspirin. Ringing in the ears, dizziness, severe headache, or rapid breathing; controlled by reducing the dosage.
   3. Weakness, pallor, dyspnea; sore mucous membranes, fever, chills, fatigue; signs of bleeding from the mucous membranes and under the skin.

D. 1. to wither or waste away (as in unexercised muscles)
   2. muscle pain

E. 1. osteoporosis
   2. rheumatoid arthritis
   3. osteomyelitis
   4. bursitis
   5. gout
   6. osteoarthritis

F. True or false
   1. F
   2. F
   3. T
   4. F
   5. T
   6. T
   7. F
   8. T
   9. F
   10. T
   11. F
   12. F
   13. T
   14. T
   15. T
   16. F
   17. F
   18. T
   19. T
   20. F

REPRESENTATIVE DRUGS FOR THE MUSCULOSKELETAL SYSTEM

CATEGORY, NAME[a], AND ROUTE	USES AND DISEASES	ACTIONS	USUAL DOSE[b] AND SPECIAL INSTRUCTIONS	SIDE EFFECTS AND ADVERSE REACTIONS
Anti-inflamatory agents (antiarthritics)				
Aspirin Oral, suppository	Mild to moderate pain, inflammatory diseases (e.g., rheumatoid arthritis, fibrositis)	Reduces pain (analgesic) and inflammation (anti-inflammatory)	Mild pain: 325–650 mg q 4 hours PRN. Rheumatoid arthritis: 3.6–5.4 g daily in divided doses. Give oral forms with food, milk, or full glass of water to avoid stomach irritation	Nausea, stomach pain, indigestion, gastrointestinal bleeding, overdose (ringing in the ears, rapid breathing, dizziness, severe headache)
Ibuprofen (*Motrin*, prescription; *Nuprin, Advil*, OTC)	Rheumatoid arthritis, osteoarthritis, mild to moderate pain	Reduces pain and inflammation	1.2–3.2 g daily, in divided doses, adjusted individually. Give with milk or food if stomach irritation occurs. Takes up to 2 weeks to show effects. If no relief in 2 weeks, consult physician.	Stomach pain, indigestion, dizziness, rash, visual and hearing disturbances, fluid retention, gastrointestinal bleeding
Indomethacin (*Indocin*)	Moderate to severe rheumatoid arthritis including acute flares of chronic disease, moderate to severe ankylosing spondylitis, moderate to severe osteoarthritis, bursitis, or tendonitis, and gouty arthritis	Inhibitor of prostaglandin synthesis; anti-inflammatory agent with ability to relieve pain, swelling, and fever in arthritis	Moderate to severe arthritis: 25 mg BID or TID and if tolerated, increase daily doses 25 or 50 mg until satisfactory response, may give 150–200 mg. Higher doses do not increase effectiveness.	Nausea, indigestion, dizziness, headache, fatigue, tinnitis; consult the PDR for many other side effects. Consult the physician for the patient if necessary.
Fenoprofen calcium (*Nalfon*) Oral	Rheumatoid arthritis and osteoarthritis (acute flares and long-term management)	Nonsteroidal anti-inflammatory with antipyretic and analgesic activity	300–600 mg three or four times a day. The dose can be adjusted as needed	Vomiting, heartburn, diarrhea, GI bleeding, headache, somnolence
Naproxen (*Naprosyn*) Oral	Rheumatoid arthritis, osteoarthritis, ankylosing spondylitis, tendonitis, bursitis, and acute gout	Nonsteroidal anti-inflammatory with antipyretic and analgesic activity	250 or 375 mg morning and evening for rheumatoid arthritis, osteoarthritis, ankylosing spondylitis. For gout: 750 mg, then 250 mg every 8 hours until attack subsides.	GI bleeding, constipation, heartburn, nausea, headache, dizziness, itching, tinnitis, edema
Gold				
Gold sodium thiomalate (*Myochrysine*) Injection	Selected cases of active rheumatoid arthritis; most commonly, patients who have no damage to the joints.	Suppresses synovitis of active rheumatoid arthritis	Weekly injections; 1 wk = 10 mg, 2 wk = 25 mg, 3rd and subsequent injections = 25–50 mg until 1 g for clinical improvement or toxicity	Severe effects are most common after 300–500 mg have been administered; pruritis, rash, dermatitis; mild stomatitis, slight proteinuria. For other adverse reactions, consult the *PDR*. Consult physician for treatment of any side effects.
Auranofin (*Ridaura*) Oral	Definite active rheumatoid arthritis; synovitis in early stage	Modifies disease activity	Daily doses of 6 mg or 3 mg BID, increased to 9 mg after 6 months if response is inadequate	Diarrhea, pruritis, rash, alopecia, conjunctivitis, proteinuria, anemia, leukopenia, eosinophilia, thrombocytopenia

REPRESENTATIVE DRUGS FOR THE MUSCULOSKELETAL SYSTEM

CATEGORY, NAME[a], AND ROUTE	USES AND DISEASES	ACTIONS	USUAL DOSE[b] AND SPECIAL INSTRUCTIONS	SIDE EFFECTS AND ADVERSE REACTIONS
Antihyperuricemics				
Allopurinol (Zyloprim) Oral	Gout, excess uric acid	Suppresses the formation of uric acid by inhibiting the biochemical reactions immediately preceding its formation	200–600 mg/day (in divided doses); start with 100 mg and increase by 100 mg/day to maximal recommended dose of 800 mg or until serum uric acid level of 6 mg/dl is attained. Take with meals and drink 10–12 glasses of fluid daily.	Drowsiness, vomiting, rash, fever, headache
Sulfinpyrazone (Anturane) Oral	Chronic gouty arthritis, intermittent gouty arthritis	Relief from chronic gout	100–200 mg twice daily with meals or milk, individualized	Upper GI disturbances, nausea, rash
Muscle Relaxants				
Carisoprodol (Soma) Oral	Acute, painful musculoskeletal conditions	Blocks the interneuronal activity in the descending reticular formation and spinal cord	350 mg QID	Drowsiness, vertigo, skin rash, fever, tachycardia, nausea, hypotension, leukopenia
Methocarbamol (Robaxin) Oral	Acute, painful musculoskeletal conditions	Central nervous system depression, sedative, relieves pain and stiffness of skeletal muscles	Initial: 1500 mg QID; maintenance: 1000 mg QID	Lightheadedness, dizziness, drowsiness, nausea, rash, pruritis, and other allergic manifestations. Patient should avoid alcohol.
Orphenadrine citrate (Norflex) Oral, IM, IV	Discomfort associated with acute musculoskeletal conditions	Analgesic and anticholinergic actions	100 mg twice daily PO or 60 mg IV or IM (may be repeated every 12 hours)	Dryness of mouth, tachycardia, palpitations, blurred vision, confusion in the elderly

[a] Brand names given in parentheses are examples only. Check current drug references for a complete listing of available trade name products.

[b] Average adult doses are given. However, dosages are determined by a physician and vary with the purpose of the therapy and the particular patient. The doses presented in this text are for general information only.

Unit 16

Medications and the Elderly

In this unit you will learn how the normal physical changes of aging affect pharmacokinetics in the elderly and why this poses special problems for medication administration. You will learn about the social and psychological aspects of aging, so that you can adjust your treatment to best meet elderly patients' needs. Guidelines are presented to help you administer medications properly to elderly patients.

In this unit, you learn to:

- Describe the major changes that take place in the various body systems during aging.

- State why treatment of elderly patients must be individualized according to each person's needs.

- Describe the effects of aging on absorption, distribution, biotransformation, and excretion of drugs.

- Explain how medication orders are usually adjusted to take into account the pharmacokinetics of the older patient.

- Explain why the presence of more diseases in old age makes drug therapy more complicated.

- State what types of adverse reactions health care workers must especially look for in administering drugs to the aged.

- Explain how elderly patients are affected by the attitudes and actions of health care workers.

- List ways that patients can take an active part in their own medication therapy.

- Explain how you can overcome the difficulties of administering medications to the elderly, such as patient misidentification, mistrust of drug therapy, trouble with swallowing pills, hearing and vision problems, patient confusion, memory problems, lazy charting practices, and medication security.

DRUGS AND THE ELDERLY

Regardless of whether you are employed in a nursing home or in another clinical setting, you are likely to find yourself working often with elderly patients. As their bodies age, decreased organ function is a natural occurrence, and they become more prone to disease. Medical assistance is required to help the aged maintain the best health possible. Drugs are often a part of the health maintenance program, and they also play a large part in disease management. The elderly are likely to receive a larger number of drugs than younger adults simply because they tend to have more disorders.

The study of aging is called **gerontology** (*jer'on-tol'o-je*), and the study of diseases of the aged is called **geriatrics** (*jer'e-at'riks*). Because you will be working with the elderly in administering medications, it is important to understand their special problems and needs. It is especially important because the elderly are often given less than the best treatment by those charged with their care. You want to be the best caregiver you know how, and a thorough understanding of the elderly and their drug-related needs is an important step toward that goal (Figure 16-1).

In this chapter we explore the physical, social, and psychological changes that come about with aging; the attitudes of health workers toward aging; the drugs used most commonly with the elderly; and special precautions and procedures to use when giving them medications.

THE PHYSICAL AGING PROCESS

After a certain age, usually about 40, it is normal for the body cells to begin a decline. Nature is programmed to start this decline as soon as its main goal—reproduction—has been fulfilled. As the body cells are lost through aging, the organs that they make up also slow down. Almost every organ loses some of its functioning, although not necessarily enough to require medical help. The body also loses some of its ability to cope with stress. The body's balance-keeping systems are not as finely tuned as before, so stress is longer-lasting and more extreme in old age. Disease and injury are forms of stress that put the body temporarily out of balance. The effect of aging is to make it harder for the elderly to "bounce back" after diseases, even minor diseases such as colds. Healing takes longer and complications are more likely to develop. That is why flu, pneumonia, and broken

Figure 16-1 The physical changes of aging happen at different times in different individuals. Not everyone experiences all these changes to the same degree.

VOCABULARY

collagen: protein making up fibers in connective tissue; builds up in the lung during aging, thus decreasing lung elasticity

geriatrics: the branch of medicine pertaining to the diseases and disorders of old age

gerontology: the study of aging and problems of the aged

---

bones are much more serious for the elderly than for younger adults.

Aging does not occur at exactly the same rate in each person (Figure 16-1). Body systems age at different times and at different rates. There are also wide variations between individuals in the course of aging. For some people, the first sign of aging is loss of visual sharpness—requiring reading glasses, for example. For others it is a slow-down of the digestive system and resulting constipation. They find they must drink prune juice or eat more bran cereals to keep regular bowel habits.

Most people react to aging by being less active than they were before. They take up less strenuous sports and reduce their workload. This is a normal adjustment to the changes of aging. But reducing the level of activity does not and should not mean giving up all activity. With proper health maintenance and proper attitudes in people around them, the elderly can continue to lead an active and rewarding life.

The following is a list of specific changes that may be expected at some time or other in each body system. Now that you have studied each system, you should be able to appreciate how the changes of aging affect the functioning of each system.

- **Integumentary system**

  The skin becomes thinner and dryer and loses its suppleness. The fatty layer under the skin disappears, causing wrinkles and folds and giving less protection against cold and injury. Bruising is more common. Spots of color appear on the skin, and small vessels are likely to burst, causing "spiders." Sweating decreases, and there is less blood flow to the skin. Decubitus ulcers are more of a danger in bedridden patients who are elderly.

- **Cardiovascular system**

  The heart pumps less forcefully and pumps less blood with each beat, even though the number of beats per minute increases. The heart has less ability to gear up for action when the body is under stress. Various parts of the heart and the blood vessels lose their elasticity, and fatty substances may be deposited on the inner layers of arteries. These deposits give more resistance to the pumping action of the heart, so hypertension may develop. There is less blood flow to all parts of the body.

- **Respiratory system**

  A protein called *collagen* (kol'ah-jen) settles in the lungs, lessening their ability to expand. Along with a reduced flow of blood to the lungs, this makes respiration less efficient, and not as much oxygen is supplied to the body. In order to make up for this, an older person must breathe faster than the normal 16–20 times per minute. Breathing is also more shallow.

- **Nervous system**

  Brain cells die off and there is less blood flow to the brain, affecting memory and the ability to make decisions. Confused thinking and changes in personality can result from the poor supply of oxygen to the brain.

- **Sensory system**

  Sensory messages do not come in strong and clear. The eyes have a harder time adjusting to changes in light. The ears do not hear the higher sounds, and hearing aids may be needed. Taste and smell are dulled so that eating is no longer as pleasurable. The sense of touch is dulled. When the senses do not provide as much information as before, the elderly may find themselves confused, especially when in strange surroundings.

- **Gastrointestinal system**

  The secretions and muscular movements of the digestive tract slow down. These changes make food harder to digest and slower to move through the system. Indigestion and constipation are common problems. If teeth are lost or inflamed, eating may be difficult or uncomfortable. The absorption of nutrients from the intestines is less efficient, so nutrition may be affected.

- **Urinary system**

  There is less blood flow to the kidneys, and there are changes within the kidneys themselves. They do not filter the blood as efficiently, so wastes are excreted more slowly. They cannot adapt as quickly as before to changes in the fluid/electrolyte balance.

- **Endocrine system**

  All the glands secrete less of their hormones. As a result, body cell metabolism is not as well-regulated and the body cannot react as quickly to stress. Most of the elderly develop some degree of diabetes.

- **Reproductive system**

  Usually after age 48 or 50, females no longer menstruate or conceive babies. In both men and women, sex hormone production decreases, with resulting physical changes. However, because sexual enjoyment is determined by attitudes and emotions, not just hormones, older people can still enjoy an active sex life.

- **Musculoskeletal system**

  Muscles lose strength and flexibility. The bones become lighter and more porous, so they are more apt to fracture easily and heal slowly. Ligaments and joints are subject to stiffening and thickening. Diseases of bones, joints, and ligaments are more common.

PHARMACOKINETICS IN THE AGED

Let us look at what the changes of aging do to the actions of drugs in the body. Recall from Unit 2 that drugs entering the body undergo four processes: absorption, distribution, biotransformation (metabolism), and excretion. Naturally, the aging of the body systems has an impact on how drugs are absorbed, distributed, biotransformed, and excreted (Figure 16-2). For a person administering medications to the elderly, it is very important to understand these pharmacokinetic effects of aging. This discussion should help you know why you should be particularly watchful for side effects and unusual effects of drugs in the elderly.

Slower Circulation, Slower Absorption

Absorption and distribution are affected mainly by two things: slower blood circulation and slower absorption of oral medications through the intestines. Slower circulation occurs because the heart pumps less efficiently and must work against blood vessels that have lost their elasticity. The stomach and intestines have less of the digestive enzymes that are needed to help drugs break down and be absorbed through the lining. Peristalsis is weaker, so drugs do not reach the intestine as quickly. As a result, drug absorption and distribution are slower and less predictable in the elderly. This means that you cannot be sure that the proper dose is getting to where it is needed in the usual amount of time.

In addition, because of poor circulation, the heart and brain compete with the rest of the body for the blood supply. They demand and get more blood, and other parts of the body are "shorted." Distribution of drugs is affected, because more of the drugs end up in the heart and brain. This can lead to abnormal drug reactions.

Biotransformation or metabolism of drugs is affected by the reduced capacity of the liver. Most drugs are biotransformed in the liver. However, in the elderly the liver produces fewer enzymes to break down the drugs, so they are not biotransformed as quickly or as completely. This means that the drugs stay in effect longer and can build

---

Absorption— **Slower**

Distribution— **Unpredictable**

Biotransformation— **Slower**

Excretion— **Slower**

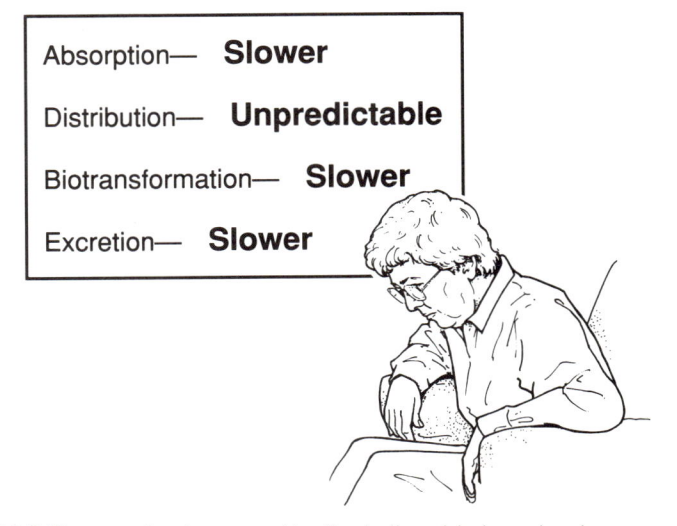

Figure 16-2 Changes in pharmacokinetics in the elderly make drug therapy more complicated and more hazardous.

up in the body with repeated doses. The result may be a cumulative effect and even drug toxicity.

Excretion is affected by changes in kidney function. Reduced blood circulation and changes in the kidney cells combine to make blood filtration slower. Thus drugs are not excreted as quickly. Again, they can build up in the body and show cumulative or toxic effects. Some drugs, such as the urinary antiseptics, do not become active until they are excreted by the kidney. In the elderly these drugs will take longer than usual to show an effect.

Finally, because of the body's lessened ability to keep a balance between all the systems, drugs are more apt to throw the body into wide imbalances. Unusual and even bizarre drug reactions can be expected from time to time. Also, the aged are more sensitive to the effects of certain drugs.

Because of these changes in pharmacokinetics, one must be very careful in administering medications to the elderly. As a general rule, medications for the elderly will be prescribed in smaller doses and will be given farther apart (Figure 16-3). This helps prevent cumulation and toxicity. To aid absorption, adjustments are made in the forms of medication given and in the routes.

More Diseases, Drug Interactions

Two other age-related factors have an impact on the effect of a drug: disease and other drugs. We said that the elderly are more prone to disease and less able to shake it off. If you add disease factors to the age changes already mentioned, the overall picture begins to get complicated. For instance, a diseased kidney or liver, a heart condition, hypertension, any of these can further slow down the handling of drugs by the body. Because the elderly tend to have more diseases, there is a greater chance for adverse drug reactions, especially cumulation.

Consider also the possibilities for drug interactions. The elderly have more ailments, both major and minor, than do younger adults. Thus they are likely to be taking more drugs together. For example, they may routinely take nonprescription laxatives, antacids, or mild stimulants. Any of these can interact with drugs that a doctor may prescribe. It is extremely important for the medical staff to find out what other medications a person may be taking on his or her own, especially OTC medications. For example, it would be a shame to put an older person on a course of tetracyclines for an infection, only to discover later that this patient was taking bicarbonate of soda for an upset stomach. As you know, antacids interfere with the absorption of tetracyclines.

Even more dangerous, take the patient who is on corticosteroids for chronic rheumatoid arthritis, a condition common in old age. Corticosteroids increase the excretion of potassium in the kidneys. Now suppose that the person develops a heart condition requiring digitalis, a cardiac stimulant. A normal dose of digitalis becomes dangerously strong (i.e., is potentiated) when there is little potassium in the body. Cardiac arrhythmias could result from the combined action of the two drugs.

It is the physician's responsibility to avoid wherever possible prescribing drugs that could interact in a harmful way. But, as an added safety precaution, you too should be aware of possible interactions. There are times when the physician must order drugs that are known to interact because the risk of drug interaction is less than the risk of not giving two drugs that the patient needs. At these times all the people who are attending the patient must be especially careful to chart any unusual signs. Examples of important drug interactions that can occur with medications for the elderly are listed in Table 16-1.

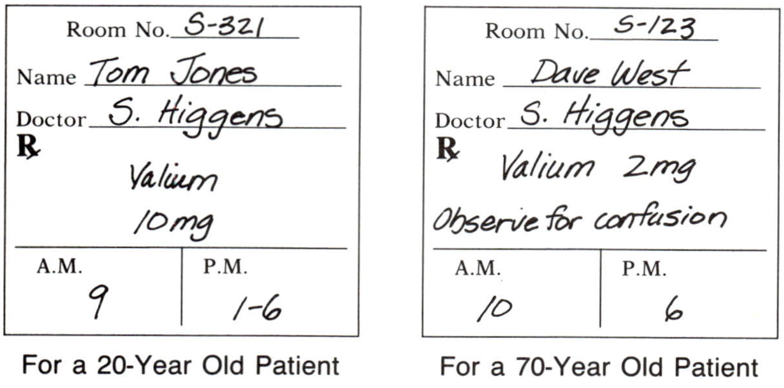

Room No. S-321	
Name *Tom Jones*	
Doctor *S. Higgens*	
℞ Valium 10 mg	
A.M.	P.M.
9	1-6

For a 20-Year Old Patient

Room No. S-123	
Name *Dave West*	
Doctor *S. Higgens*	
℞ Valium 2 mg Observe for confusion	
A.M.	P.M.
10	6

For a 70-Year Old Patient

Figure 16-3 The changes of aging require changes in amount and timing of drug dosages.

Table 16-1 Interactions common in drug therapy with the elderly

DRUGS THAT INTERACT	RESULTS OF COMBINATION
Alcohol + sedatives	Both depress the CNS, can result in toxicity
Antipsychotics + antiparkinsonian agents + antidepressants	All have anticholinergic effects, when combined can cause dry mouth, blurred vision, urine retention, constipation, increased intraocular pressure
Nonsteroidal anti-inflammatory drugs + anticoagulants	Increased anticoagulant effect
Bisacodyl (*Dulcolax*) + antacids	Enteric coating of bisacodyl dissolves in the stomach, causing gastric irritation
Tetracycline + metals (milk, antacids, and other substances containing calcium, magnesium, aluminum, or iron)	Reduced absorption of tetracycline can lessen its effect
Cholestyramine (*Questran*) or cholestipol (*Colestid*) (anticholesteremics) + acidic drugs	Poor absorption of acidic drugs may lessen their effects
Anticholinergics	Slowed peristalsis, slowed gastric emptying, and longer retention in GI tract caused by anticholinergics can affect the absorption of any drug
Salicylates and sulfonylureas	Increased hypoglycemic effect
Cathartics (*laxatives*)	Increased intestinal motility caused by carthartics can decrease absorption of any drug
Antibiotics + food	Presence of food in GI tract slows absorption of antibiotics and can lessen their effects
Warfarin (*Coumadin*) + phenobarbital	Anticoagulant is broken down more quickly, so has less effect; increases risk of thrombus formation
Vitamin D + anticonvulsants ((phenytoin) (*Dilantin*) and phenobarbital)	Vitamin D breaks down more quickly; patient may require Vitamin D supplements
Allopurinol (*Zyloprim*) + mercaptopurine (*Purinethol*) or azathioprine (*Imuran*)	Allopurinol slows breakdown of the other drugs; can lead to toxicity
Salicylates (e.g., aspirin) + acidifiers	Prolongs and possibly increases effects of salicylates, can lead to toxicity
Penicillins + probenecid (*Benemid*)	Excretion of penicillin is blocked; can be a beneficial interaction
Monoamine oxidase inhibitors + sympathomimetics (e.g., amphetamines)	Releases large amounts of norepinephrine; can cause severe headache, hypertension, or arrhythmias
Guanethidine (*Ismelin*) + tricyclic antidepressants or antipsychotics (e.g., chlorpromazine)	Decreases antihypertensive effect of guanethidine; fails to lower blood pressure
Digitalis + diuretics	Diuretics can cause potassium loss, which makes the heart more sensitive to digitalis effects; can cause arrhythmias
Lithium carbonate + diuretics	Loss of sodium increases effects of lithium; can lead to toxicity

The complex pharmacokinetics in the elderly should suggest, then, that you be alert for possible adverse reactions and side effects. You must watch especially for signs of cumulation, toxicity, drug interactions, and unusual effects (Figure 16-4). All your skills of observation and communication are needed to give these patients the safe drug treatment to which they are entitled. Talk with your patients, ask them questions, and carefully notice all their physical and psychological signs. Only with your full cooperation can their needs be met and their safety ensured.

Figure 16-4 Elderly people have more diseases and take more drugs. Keep a close watch on drug effects, because many adverse reactions are possible.

SOCIAL AND PSYCHOLOGICAL ASPECTS OF AGING

Ours is a youth-oriented culture. The elderly here are not held in high regard as they are in some cultures. Frequently, the aged are considered emotional, economic, and social burdens by family, friends, and work associates. Fewer jobs are available to the aged, and retirement may be forced on them. Social activity is reduced because many of their family and friends have moved away or died. All this comes at a time when the aged are faced with physical problems that make them dependent on others for help.

Society's negative attitude toward the elderly carries over into the medical field as well. Physicians sometimes shy away from treating the elderly. One reason is because the elderly are less able to respond to the medical care that doctors can provide. From a doctor's point of view, treating the aged is less "rewarding" than treating younger patients who usually heal more quickly and have a better chance of recovering. Other health care workers fall prey to the same attitudes. Perhaps they cannot accept the fact that they, too, will grow old sometime. Perhaps they view the elderly as less important because of being less youthful and active. Sometimes they seem to forget that the elderly are mature adults who still can think and feel. This causes serious problems in caring for the elderly, especially in long-term care units such as the nursing home.

As a health care provider busy with many demanding chores, you are bound to be tempted into some careless habits where the elderly are concerned. The best way to prevent this is to arm yourself beforehand with a positive attitude. Think through the problems of the elderly, and think through your own reaction to their situation. Take a moment to understand what it means to be an elderly person dependent on others for certain basic needs.

The psychological well-being of the aged depends a great deal on the attitudes of people around them. In our youth-worshipping society, old people are sometimes treated as rejects because they no longer have the bloom and vigor of youth. People who are treated like rejects begin to *feel* like rejects. They lose confidence in themselves and lose interest in living.

A special problem arises because younger adults tend to behave as if the elderly cannot do anything for themselves. Out of kindness or a wish to be helpful, younger adults may take away all the duties and chores that the elderly were used to carrying out. Although younger adults can do some things more quickly and efficiently, that does not mean that they should "take over." When others take over all the cooking, cleaning, and personal care responsibilities, it is no wonder that some older people begin to feel they cannot take care of themselves. They grow more and more dependent on others as their feelings of worthlessness grow, and they shut themselves off from living.

This concept is important to remember when you give medications. The elderly can and should take an active part in their medication therapy. They should be encouraged to take their own medications under your supervision (Figure 16-5). They can pour their own glass of water. They can apply their own ointments. They can help design a plan for remembering to take all their medications. The point is, their health care includes a concern for their mental health. Your treatment of them must leave room for independent effort. Let them do as much as they are capable of doing, even if you could do it more quickly and efficiently. Their mental health depends on your letting them "do for themselves" when they can and want to. Give medical care *with* the patient, not *for* the patient.

Remember, too, that the elderly are *people* first. Just because they are old does not mean they should not be treated courteously and with respect. An important form of respect in giving medications is to individualize treatment. It is a mistake to lump all old people together in the medical treatment they receive. Each person has his or her own pattern of aging and thus a unique set of medical needs.

Finally, be prepared to meet many needs in individual elderly patients. Because of their physical problems and their social isolation, they *will* have more needs than younger patients. They will also have fewer people around to meet those needs, such as family and friends. So you are an important person in their everyday lives. Be supportive of their activities. Encourage them to get the most they can out of life. Love them, help them feel wanted and needed, and help ease their physical and emotional burdens (Figure 16-6). You and your fellow workers have the power to make their lives miserable or rewarding. Do not abuse that power. The more you help them be independent and confident, the less the aged will feel like a burden, both on you and on themselves.

Figure 16-5 Let the elderly take part in their own medication program.

TIPS ON MEDICATING THE ELDERLY

Aging brings changes in the daily patterns of living of older adults. It also brings changes in your responsibilities as a giver of medications. We have discussed some ways of adapting to the psychological and social needs of elderly patients. This section presents some tips that specifically concern the administration of medications. Remember that you must try hard to individualize your treatment of each patient. The physician is responsible for adjusting

Figure 16-6 Take time to talk and to listen. A caring health worker is "good medicine" for an aging patient.

the dosages and routes, but you must adjust your attitude and your nursing care. You must be resourceful, caring, firm, patient, aware, and knowledgeable, as you are the elderly person's "survival kit." The following suggestions may help you adjust your care to the elderly so as to achieve the best drug effect and the best patient cooperation.

- **Identify the "right patient".**

    This first rule of the "five rights" is sometimes more difficult to ensure with the elderly. Lack of oxygen in the brain, drug side effects, and many diseases can cause older people to be confused temporarily about their own identity. You cannot count on identifying them by asking them their name, or even by saying their name and waiting to see if they answer. They may answer to *any* name. Perhaps they simply cannot hear what you said, but want to appear cooperative. The names on their beds or in their clothing are not reliable clues, either. If they are confused, they may wander into the wrong bed and put on someone else's clothing. It is not unusual for patients to lose their identification band, too. If you are in doubt, the only safe way to identify a patient is to ask another staff member who has worked with the patient, such as the nurse in charge.

- **Explain what you are doing**.

    This is one of the most important general rules for administering medications. It should be followed particularly in dealing with the elderly. Everyone likes to be told what to expect, even if they must expect some discomfort. Older people are sometimes fearful of medications and may be distrustful of you. If you explain in a cheerful, positive way why you are there, what medications you are giving, and how you will be giving them, you stand a better chance of getting the patient to cooperate. Remember that the patient's cooperation is to his or her benefit for more than medical reasons. It is a way of allowing the elderly to take an active role in their own care, so that they can keep up their self-confidence and feelings of independence.

- **Be patient, do not rush**.

    Allow the aged to change their position, such as from lying down to sitting up, before administering medications. They will have an easier time swallowing the medication if you do. Give one tablet at a time to swallow, and allow them time between tablets to rest. Rushing them through the medication time will only cause worry and feelings of helplessness. Take the time to treat them as people rather than patients. A slow and easy approach on your part will gain their confidence.

- **Explain what the drug is supposed to do**.

    Many of the elderly mistrust drugs because they grew up in a time when few drugs were used. If you explain in simple terms what the drugs are for, you can increase your patient's cooperation. By explaining the drug effects and benefits, you treat your patients as reasonable, competent adults, as you should. Once again, a slow and easy approach on your part will win you their confidence.

- **Start with the most important medication first**.

    If your patient has trouble taking medications, you want to be sure he or she gets at least the most important one. If any drugs are refused or not taken because of difficulty swallowing, you will, of course, note this on the chart and tell the nurse in charge.

- **Help a patient who has trouble swallowing pills.**

    Suggest placing the medication well to the back of the tongue to make swallowing as easy as possible. Give liquids both before and after administering the medication, using a straw or tube if the patient cannot sit up to drink. If these measures do not work, try crushing and mixing the tablet or capsule contents with applesauce, jello, or juice. But check the package instructions to make sure that the substance you mix it with does not interfere with the drug effect. Diluting or mixing some drugs with food may interfere with absorption and lower the blood level of the drug, thus not giving the desired results. Do not, of course, crush and mix timed-release capsules and enteric coated products. Stay with the patient until all the applesauce or similar soft food is eaten.

- **Assist drug absorption.**

    Oral suspension are absorbed better than suppositories or enteric-coated tablets. They can be absorbed faster by the digestive system, and this prevents a delay in drug action. Give plenty of fluids with the medications to aid absorption. Extra fluids also help with cumulation problems and excretion.

- **When a patient appears confused, assess the reason.**

    Confusion about identity, location, last drug taken, and so on, can come from many sources. There may be a lack of oxygen in the brain. A medication that affects the nervous system may cause the confusion. Or the patient may have psychological problems. Do not automatically assume that the patient is senile or give up trying to communicate with him or her. Consider the drugs he or she is taking. Help the patient focus on what you are saying. Encourage the patient to express his or her needs clearly and to stay in touch with reality.

- **Respect each patient's customs and beliefs.**

    Be sympathetic to patients' cultural and ethnic beliefs and traditions in regard to drug therapy. Be flexible and try to adapt to the patient's requests as much as the physician's orders will allow.

- **Adapt to hearing and vision problems.**

    The elderly may not hear or see as well as younger adults, so you need to adapt your behavior to their special problems. Speak slowly and clearly when giving instructions, and wait for signs of understanding. Stand facing the patient when you speak, so that he or she can read your lips. Write things down, if necessary, and use large letters that can easily be read. Sometimes what seems like mental confusion is merely a sign that the patient cannot hear or see what you are doing or saying. Always keep this possibility in mind, so that you adjust to the situation.

- **Blood and urine tests are important.**

    When ordered, make sure that these are done and the results checked. Many drugs do not have a therapeutic effect until they reach a certain level in the body. The tests are necessary to find out when this point has been reached. A patient who is fearful of tests may accept them better if you explain their importance.

- **Keep eyedrops refrigerated as instructed.**

    Many elderly patients take eyedrops for vision problems, infections, and other disorders. The effectiveness of many eyedrops is lost if they are not refrigerated. Read the package directions and the drug label to determine the proper method of storage.

- **Watch for dangers of OTC drugs.**

    Seemingly harmless OTC drugs, which many elderly patients take, can be dangerous when they accumulate in the body or interact with prescription drugs. Know the combined effects of OTC and prescription drugs so that you can be alert to adverse reactions.

- **Make sure that all ordered medications are given.**

    With the high staff turnover that is common in nursing homes, it is easy to lose track of *who* is giving *what* medications *when*. Parenteral drugs are a special problem, because not everyone is certified to administer them. For example, if you are an uncertified health worker, you may give oral and topical medications, but another staff member must give any required injections. Be sure to tell the appropriate staff member what time the injections are needed and follow up later to be sure that they were given. Injections are easy to overlook but very important for the patient. A good charting system and proper organization can ensure that all ordered medications are received by each patient.

- **Explain the need for medication to asymptomatic patients.**

    Be aware that a patient who has no obvious symptoms may refuse medications. Explain to the patient why some medications (e.g., those for hypertension and infection) must continue to be taken even after the symptoms are under control.

- **Help the elderly remember their medications and instructions.**

    Arrange for your elderly patients to take medications at certain times each day, such as before meals. They may have trouble remembering when they last took their pills. But if they are in the habit of taking them at a regularly scheduled time, they will remember more easily. If special instructions go along with the medications, explain them clearly and simply, but also write them out. Write with large letters, and make sure that the drug bottles are labeled with large letters, too, to make up for poor eyesight in the elderly.

- **Never force a patient to take a medication.**

   You are bound to find some patients, especially elderly psychiatric patients, who will not cooperate in taking their medications. Do not try to force them. If your positive, encouraging attitude and your explanations of the benefits of the drugs do not get the patient to accept a drug, do not push the issue. Instead, report the problem to the nurse in charge and wait for further instructions. In some cases, medications will need to be given parenterally until the patient's cooperation can be secured for oral medication.

- **Keep medications secure.**

   Never leave the medicine room unlocked. Patients may wander by and take medications that can cause them harm. Never leave the medicine cart unattended. Because you will be spending more time with elderly patients in giving their medications, you will have less time to keep an eye on the cart. On the other hand, you do not want to be rushed with the patients. A good solution is to get an attendant to watch the cart while you help the patients. When possible, lock the cart while you are working with patients.

- **Chart medications promptly.**

   Do your charting as soon as you have finished giving the medications. You will have many medications to chart, and you will be tempted to leave the charting until the end of the day. This is a dangerous practice that can lead to medication errors. It can and must be avoided by getting your charting procedures properly organized. The only correct time to chart medications is right after you give them. If a cart is used, the charting form for medications usually is on it for immediate charting.

- **Use caution with PRN medications.**

   When you have a PRN order with a range of doses, try giving the smallest dose first. Often this will be enough to bring about the desired effect. Because of slow absorption and biotransformation, a higher dose may produce unpleasant side effects or adverse reactions. Guard against giving a higher dose of a PRN medication just because a person is confused. The PRN medication may actually be causing the confusion through some effect on the oxygen supply to the brain. Make sure you chart PRN medications immediately. If you put it off until later, someone else may also give the patient another dose of the PRN medication. The patient may not remember that you gave a previous dose. It is easy to overdose a patient accidentally by forgetting to chart PRN medications. You may have performed your task of medication administration as skillfully as possible. You may have followed all the rules and regulations. But there still may come a time when a patient gets the best of you. You may find pills and capsules in pockets, drawers, pillow cases, plants, or anywhere. Report this to the nurse in charge and follow his or her instructions. Just remember to be aware that this will happen and try to prevent it.

EXERCISES

A. The following are situations or scenes that might take place in a nursing home or in a hospital unit that has many elderly patients. Answer the questions briefly, using the principles and guidelines you have studied in this unit.

1. Mr. Jones and Mr. Smith are both 80 years old. Mr. Jones is strong and physically active and enjoys taking walks. He wears glasses to correct his failing vision. He is forgetful sometimes and tends to tell the same jokes over and over again. Mr. Smith, on the other hand, is frail and walks with a cane, but his watchful eyes take in everything that goes on. His mind is sharp, and he entertains the nursing home staff with his views of current political and social events. Why are these men so different in their physical ability and mental alertness, even though they are the same age: What does this mean for their medication therapy?

2. Miss Peach is taking life easier than she used to, because she finds that her energy runs out more quickly now that she is 72. Her breathing has become slightly faster and shallower than before, which the doctor says is normal for a person her age. What changes has her respiratory system probably undergone as a result of aging?

3. Doc Webster is a grand old man who is full of stories about the days when he practiced surgery in a big city hospital. He is taking a number of medications for heart disease and a nervous condition. Today, when you go to his room he does not answer to his name and he has forgotten where he is. It's hard for you to give him his medication instructions, because he can't seem to concentrate on what you are saying. Is he just senile, or are there other reasons why he might appear confused?

4. In giving elderly Mrs. Nimitz her medications, you want to be sure to treat her as an independent, thinking adult. What will you do?

5. Mr. Redbone is under medication for an infection and several other minor disorders. Because of his advanced age, you know that his liver and kidneys are not working as well as they used to. What effect does a weakened kidney or liver have on the way drugs are handled by the body? What adverse reaction should you be on the lookout for?

_____

_____

_____

6. Mrs. Mendoza is suffering from phlebitis and must take an anticoagulant to keep blood clots from forming. She keeps a bottle of aspirin in her purse for occasional arthritic pain. She also has an old bottle of tranquilizers her sister gave her. She hasn't mentioned the aspirin and tranquilizers to her doctor, but she asks you if you think it would be OK to take them when she feels a need to. What should you do?

_____

_____

_____

7. How and why does a doctor usually adjust the normal adult dose when ordering medications for an elderly patient?

_____

_____

_____

8. The nursing home has recently admitted a number of new patients, so that the staff's workload is heavier than usual. You are very busy giving medications and carrying out your other duties. You would like to put off the charting until the end of the day, but you're not sure you should. How will your decision affect the welfare of your patients?

_____

_____

_____

9. A new elderly patient, Mr. Minassian, is getting his first dose of medicine. You are instructing him on the usual side effects of the drug. He is smiling and nodding, but he does not seem to understand what you are saying. What can you do to make sure that he gets the information he needs?

_____

_____

_____

10. Miss Brill sweetly declines any medications you offer her, saying that she doesn't need them. You are worried because you know her blood pressure could become dangerously high if she fails to take the antihypertensive, and she needs her *Dymelor* to control a tendency toward high blood sugar. What should you do?

B. Define the following terms.
   1. geriatrics _____
   2. gerontology _____

C. Drug interactions in the elderly. Reread Table 16-1 carefully. A physician or registered nurse is responsible for monitoring for drug interactions, but other health care providers should be aware of them too. Your task is to understand the meaning of drug interactions and the importance of charting your observations of patient signs that may signal specific interactions.

ANSWERS TO EXERCISES

A. Situations
   1. They differ because people age at different rates, and different body systems age at different times. This means that each man's medication therapy must be individualized according to the sytems that have aged the most.
   2. There has been a gradual loss of elasticity in the lungs because of deposits of the protein collagen. This means less oxygen intake with each breath, so Miss Peach must breathe more often to get the same amount of oxygen as before.
   3. His confusion might be due to the effects of some of the medications on his nervous system. Or, there might be a lack of oxygen in the brain, due to poor circulation that comes with aging.
   4. Let Mrs. Nimitz participate in her own medication plan, pour her own water if she is able, and take her own pills under supervision. You will explain the procedure and the reason for medication so that Mrs. Nimitz is fully informed.
   5. Poor liver function would slow down biotransformation of the drugs, and poor kidney function would slow excretion. The adverse reaction to look out for would be drug cumulation and possibly toxicity.
   6. Inform her that both aspirin and tranquilzers could be dangerous for her while she is on anticoagulants because of drug interactions. Ask her to turn over the medications until the doctor says they are safe to use. She should discard the tranquilizers, since they were prescribed for her sister and not for her.
   7. The dose is usually smaller and given less often, to make up for changes in absorption, distribution, biotransformation, and excretion in the elderly. This is the general rule, but drug treatment must be individualized for each patient.
   8. Putting off the charting until later might lead to medication errors. For example, another staff member may give a patient a PRN medication even though you just gave it an hour ago.
   9. He may have a hearing problem. You could try speaking slowly and clearly, standing so that he can see your face (to read lips). If that does not work, you might try writing down the instructions for him (in large, clear letters). There is also the possibility that he may not understand English, so you might need someone to translate.
   10. Explain what the medications are and what they do. Sit with Miss Brill to gain her confidence and ease her fears. if she still refuses, do not force her to take the medications, but inform the nurse in charge and await further instructions.

B. Definitions
   1. branch of medicine that deals with diseases and disorders of old age
   2. study of the problems of the elderly

Unit 17

Administering Parenteral Medications

In this unit you will learn how to give medications accurately and safely by the parenteral route. You will learn how to handle injection equipment and how to prepare medications for injection. You will learn to locate the proper sites of injections and follow specific injection procedures.

In this unit, you will learn to:

- Define parenteral administration and state the reasons for its use.
- Name and describe the major routes of parenteral administration.
- Identify the parts of a needle and syringe.
- Tell what sizes of needles and syringes are appropriate for different types and sites of injection.
- Accurately identify dosages in calibrated syringes.
- Dispose of injection equipment properly.
- Draw up medications from ampules and viles, using aseptic technique.
- Follow instructions for reconstituting and storing parenteral medications.
- Locate the most common injection sites for intradermal, subcutaneous, and intramuscular administration.
- Explain the reason for site rotation.
- Describe and follow proper procedures for carrying out intradermal, subcutaneous, and intramuscular injections.
- Prevent contamination of medication and maintain asepsis during injection procedures.
- Explain what to do when blood is aspirated during an injection.
- Explain what to do if a needle breaks during parenteral administration.

ORIENTATION TO THE PARENTERAL ROUTE

Parenteral administration is the method of giving drugs by injection using a needle and syringe. It is used in certain situations where other routes would be ineffective or impractical. Since injection puts medication into direct contact with body tissues that contain many blood vessels and capillaries, absorption is more rapid by this route than by the oral, rectal, or topical routes. This makes it a valuable route in emergencies. Certain drugs that can be destroyed by digestive enzymes are given by the parenteral route so that they keep their effectiveness. Injections are also given when patients cannot take oral medications because of difficulty swallowing, nausea or vomiting, intestinal obstructions, or unconsciousness.

The parenteral route is not used unless it is especially important, because the route is more dangerous than others. It involves breaking through the skin's protective covering, which could allow germs to enter body tissues. The rapid absorption that occurs with injection means the dose must be very exact—reactions to overdose can set in very rapidly and may require emergency treatment. Injections done improperly can stretch and injure tissues or hit bones, nerves, and blood vessels, causing pain and possibly serious damage.

Because of the dangers of injury, overdose, and infection, special training and certification are required of people who give medications parenterally. State laws regulate which categories of health care workers are permitted to give injections and what type of certification they must have. If you are not permitted to give injections, never administer drugs parenterally. The law protects your patients from injury, but it also protects you from legal problems.

In Unit 3 you learned about four routes of parenteral administration: intradermal, subcutaneous, intramuscular, and intravenous. These are named according to the type of tissue into which the medication is deposited (Figure 17-1). Recall that **intradermal** means "into the skin" (the layer called the dermis), **subcutaneous** means "into the fatty subcutaneous layer" underlying the skin, and **intramuscular** means "into the muscle." These three routes are described in detail in this unit. **Intravenous** injection and infusion (IV drip) are injections directly into veins. These procedures are not described in this text. They require special training and may be performed only by registered nurses, physicans, and specially licensed technicians. You may, however, be required to assist in setting up an IV infusion or to give a "piggyback" injection into an IV tube under supervision.

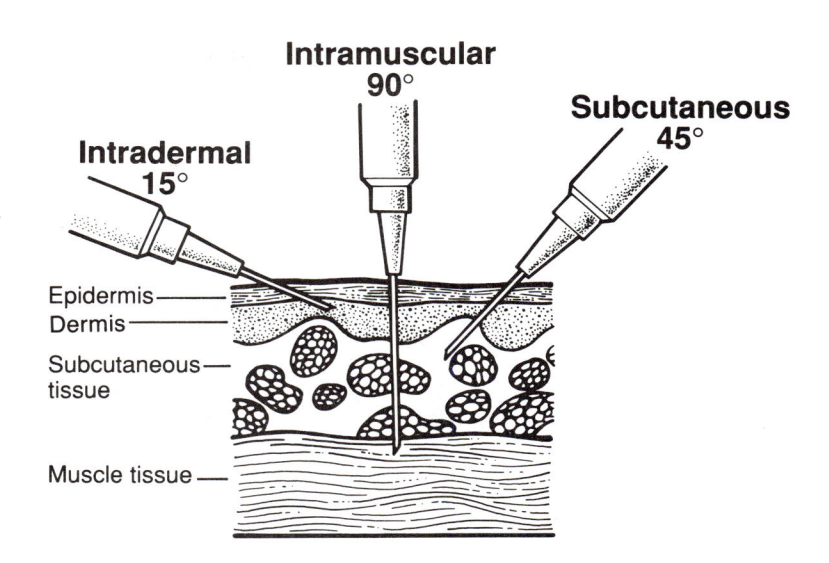

Figure 17-1 Layers of tissue into which medications may be injected.

EQUIPMENT

Parenteral medications are administered using a needle and syringe. You need to be familiar with these pieces of equipment to use them properly.

Syringes

Three types of syringes (Figure 17-2) are used for injecting medications:

- the standard hypodermic syringe
- the insulin syringe
- the tuberculin syringe

The **standard hypodermic syringe** is the most common type and is used with a variety of routes and medications. It is calibrated (marked) in cubic centimeters (cc) and in minims.

The **insulin syringe**, as its name implies, is used for the subcutaneous injection of insulin and is calibrated in units. Insulin

VOCABULARY

acromion process: an extension of the shoulder blade that can be felt at the point where the upper arm meets the shoulder; a landmark for locating the deltoid injection site

aspirate: to draw by suction; to pull back on the syringe plunger to check for entry into a blood vessel

abscess: a buildup of pus enclosed in inflamed tissue

aqueous: thin and watery

anterior: toward the front

barrel: hollow cylinder that makes up the body of a syringe

calibrations: set of marks showing measured amounts on a syringe or other measuring container

extravasation: fluid leaking from a vein into the surrounding tissues

flange: flared part of a syringe barrel; used to steady the syringe while pulling or pushing the plunger

gauge (G): diameter (width) of the lumen of a needle; ranges from 14 to 27 in needles for injection—the smaller the gauge number, the wider the lumen

gluteal arteries: large arteries that supply the muscles of the buttock area

greater trochanter: knob on the upper leg bone (femur) that can be felt where the leg joins the hip; one of the landmarks used for locating the dorsogluteal injection site

hub: broad part of the injection needle that attaches to a syringe

iliac crest: highest point on the hipbone; one landmark used to locate the ventrogluteal injection site

lumen: hollow part of a tube; the part of the needle through which medication flows

necrosis: death of tissue in a living body

needle cover: protective cover on a disposable injection needle that prevents injury and contamination; also called **sheath**

plunger: the part of a syringe used to force medication out under pressure

posterior: toward the back

precipitate: solid particles that separate out from a solution

reconstitute: add liquid to a concentrated substance (e.g., a powdered extract) to make a normal-strength solution

shaft: the long portion of a needle that extends from the point to the hub; also called **cannula** or **stem**

site rotation: the practice of injecting into different locations so as to avoid damaging tissue by repeated injections

sciatic nerve: large nerve in the pelvic (hip) area that carries nerve impulses to and from the legs

stylet: thin wire for cleaning out the lumen of a nondisposable injection needle

superior iliac spines (anterior and superior): landmarks on the front and back of the hipbone; used in locating the dorsogluteal and ventrogluteal injection sites

syringe: device fitted with a hollow needle and plunger (or bulb), used for injecting into or withdrawing fluids from the body

sloughing: dead tissue shedding from a wound or a sore

tracking: backing up of medication in the channel through which a needle entered the tissue

viscous: thick and oily

Z-track: method of displacing the tissues to one side during intramuscular injection to avoid tracking

---

syringes come in 40-unit and 100-unit sizes although the 100-unit syringe is becoming the standard.

The **tuberculin syringe** is designed for intradermal injection of very small amounts of substances in tests for tuberculosis and allergies. It is calibrated in hundredths of cubic centimeters and in minims.

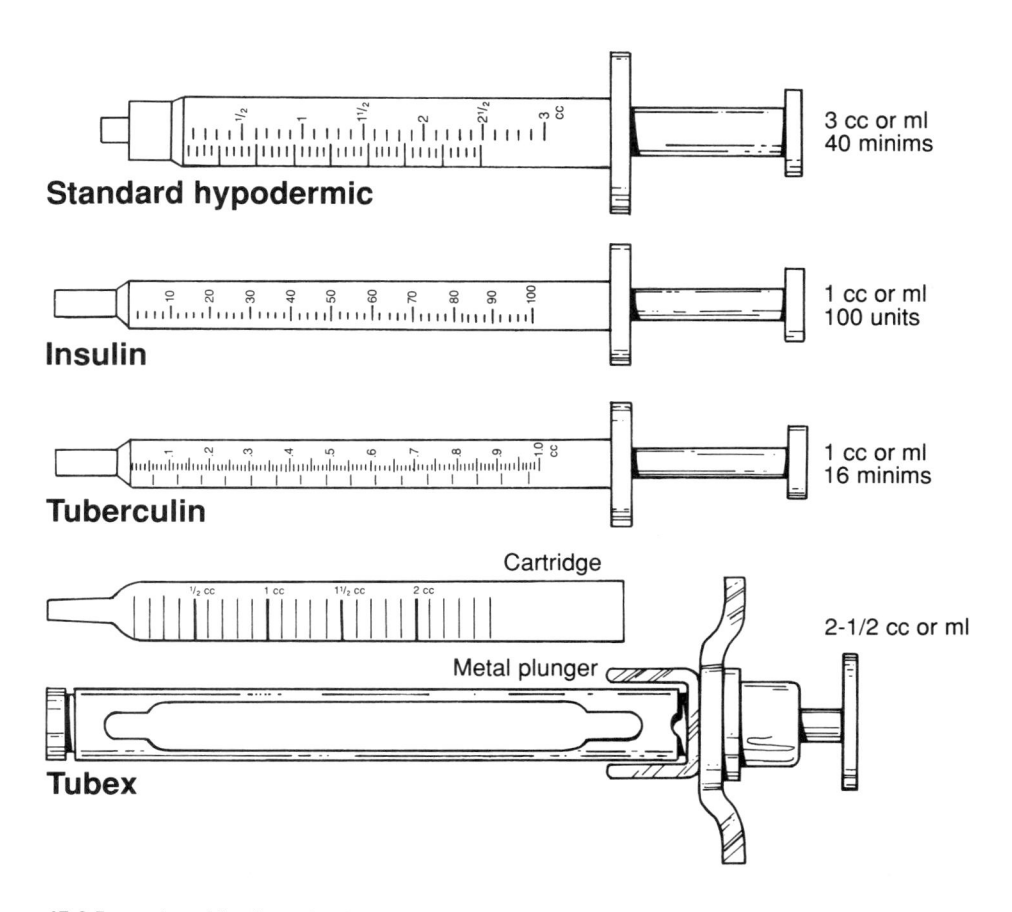

Figure 17-2 Examples of the three basic types of syringes and the Tubex syringe, showing the volumes of medication they hold.

Syringes are sized according to the volume of liquid they can hold. The most common size of the standard syringe is 2½–3-cubic centimeters (cc) or milliliters (ml). Larger syringes of 5–50 cc are also available. These are not usually used for injections, but for adding fluids to IV flasks, for irrigating wounds, and for removing fluids from body cavities.

Syringes are made of disposable plastic or of nondisposable glass. They are packaged either separately or together with needles of appropriate sizes. Disposable syringes and needles are packaged in peel-open paper wrappers. Syringes may be empty or prefilled with specific doses of medication. Prefilled glass cartridges are available for use with a special metal holder and plunger called a Tubex syringe.

The two main parts of a syringe are the **barrel** and the **plunger**. The barrel is a hollow cylinder that holds the medication. The plunger fits snugly in this cylinder and is used to change the pressure within. Pulling the plunger back lowers the air pressure inside the barrel, allowing air or medication to be pulled in from outside. Pushing the plunger in increases the pressure inside the barrel and forces air or medication out.

The barrel, plunger, and other parts of a syringe are identified in Figure 17-3. Obtain sample syringes from your laboratory instructor or the nurse in charge and locate these parts on actual syringes. Memorize the names of the parts so that you will be able to understand instructions given later in this unit.

Needles

Needles for injection are made of metal and are available in various sizes for different purposes. They come packaged with

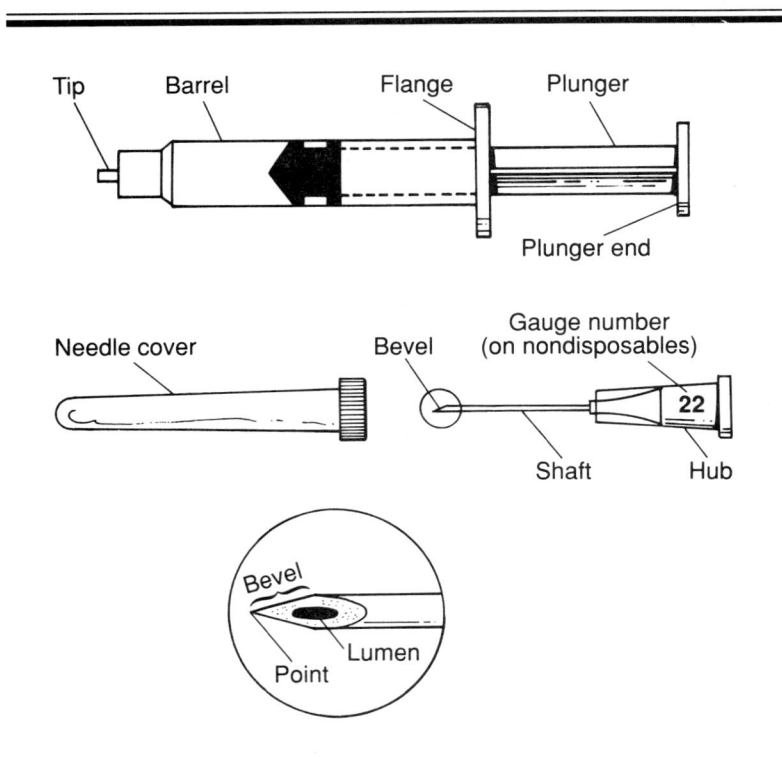

Figure 17-3 Parts of the needle and the syringe.

a protective **needle cover** or **sheath** that keeps them from becoming contaminated. In order to understand how needle size is measured, study the parts of the needle diagrammed in Figure 17-3. The tip of the needle, known as the **point**, breaks through the skin layers. The **bevel** or slanted portion of the needle tip spreads the tissues apart so that the needle can enter smoothly. The longer the bevel, the sharper the needle and the more easily it passes through the tissues. The **shaft** (**stem** or **cannula**) is the long part of the needle. It is embedded in the **hub**, which attaches to the syringe.

Needles are sized according to their **length** and their **gauge** (G). The length of a needle is the distance from the point to the hub—in other words, the length of the shaft. The gauge is the diameter of the **lumen**, which is the hollow part inside the needle through which medication passes. Needle lengths vary from 3/8 inch (1 cm) to 5 inches (13 cm). In general, the shorter lengths (3/8–5/8 inch) are used for subcutaneous and intradermal injections and the longer lengths (1–1 1/2 inches) for intramuscular injections. The longest needles (e.g., 5 inches) are usually used for other purposes such as withdrawing fluids from body cavities.

The choice of a needle length depends in part on the patient's age and body fat. Babies and small children require shorter needles to reach the proper tissues. People with heavy fat deposits require longer needles to reach their muscles (e.g., 2 inches). If a patient is obese or very thin and you are unsure what needle size to use, check with your supervisor.

Needle gauges vary from 14 to 27, with the higher gauges representing thinner needles. For example, a 26-gauge needle has a narrower lumen than a 20-gauge needle. Which gauge to use depends on how thick the medication is. Liquids that are thin and watery are described as **aqueous**, and those that are thick and oily are described as **viscous**. Penicillin and other oil-based solutions are viscous, whereas most other medications are aqueous. Ordinary gauges (22–25G) are used for aqueous medications, but lower numbered gauges (18–20G) must be used with viscous medications, which could easily clog a thinner needle. Package inserts for viscous medications may suggest which gauge to select.

The paper packages on disposable needles are labeled by both length and gauge. Nondisposable needles have the gauge marked on the metal hub. Always be certain that you are using the proper length and gauge of needle for the route and medication being given.

Keeping Injection Equipment Sterile

Because an injection breaks the skin that protects the body from microbes, it is vital that you maintain asepsis when handling needles, syringes, and injectable medications. The parts of a needle and syringe that must be protected from contamination are: the inside of the needle cover, the needle point and shaft, the inside and outside of the hub, the syringe tip, the inside of the syringe barrel, and the plunger. This means that the only parts you may safely touch with your hands are the **outside of the needle cover**, the **outside of the barrel**, the **flange**, and the **plunger end**.

The first step in assembling injection equipment is to check the labels to see whether the needles and syringes are disposable or nondisposable. Disposable equipment is convenient, but reusable equipment may be more economical because it can be sterilized and reused.

Disposable needles and syringes are presterilized and packaged in paper wrappers or plastic containers. To open these, peel back the paper or remove the cover and slide out the contents from that end. If the needle and syringe are packaged separately, attach them as follows: hold the needle cover and twist or press the hub onto the syringe tip, depending on the type of connection. After use, disposable equipment must be discarded in special waste containers for contaminated materials. The needle must be broken before disposal to prevent its being reused.

Nondisposable needles and syringes must be cleaned and sterilized after each use. Flush them immediately after use with cold water, then let them soak in a cleaning solution. Brush or wipe off any remaining medication. If necessary, clear away clogged material inside the needle with a needle wire (**stylet**), inserting it gently from the hub end. Rinse with a cleaning solution and then with alcohol or distilled water. This completes the cleaning operation. Next, the equipment must be sterilized using boiling water, steam (autoclaving), dry heat, ultrasound, or whatever method is available in the central sterilization service of your facility. When attaching or changing a sterile nondisposable needle, use sterile tongs or clamps to hold the needle as you twist or press the hub onto the syringe tip.

DRAWING UP MEDICATIONS

When you are ready to fill a syringe with medication, attach the proper needle, if necessary, and remove the needle cover by pulling it **straight off**. The proper method for filling a syringe depends on whether the medication is contained in an ampule or a vial. Recall that an **ampule** is a single-dose glass container with a bulb that can be broken off at the neck. A **vial** is a small bottle with a rubber stopper through which a needle can be inserted. A vial can contain either a single dose or multiple doses. Remember to check the vial or ampule label against the medicine card as you set up the parenteral medications (Figure 17-4).

Practice procedures at the end of this unit will help you practice the necessary steps so that you can draw up medications smoothly, accurately, and without contaminating the equipment.

From a Vial

To draw medication from a vial, first remove the protective cap. If the vial has been opened previously (e.g., a multiple-dose vial), wipe the rubber stopper firmly in a circular motion with an alcohol wipe (Figure 17-5). This cleans the surface through which the needle will pass, thus guarding against contamination.

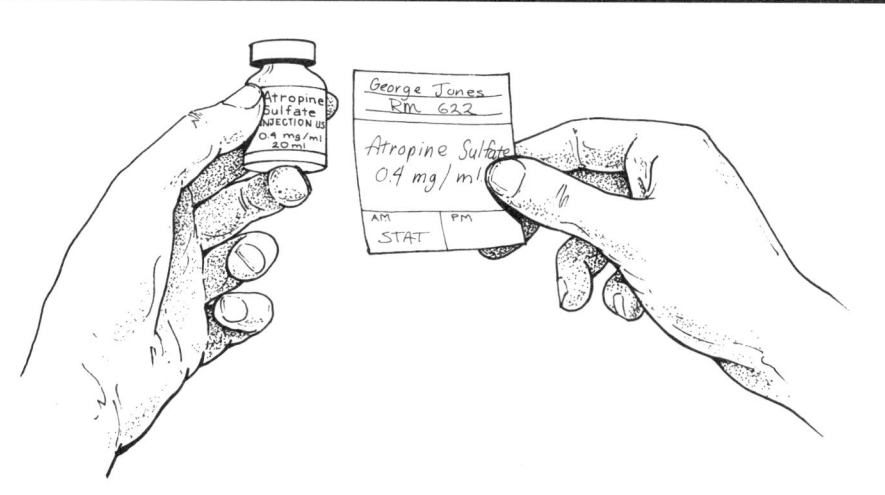

Figure 17-4 Check the drug label against the medicine card (a) as you take it from the storage area, (b) before drawing up the medication, and (c) as you return the bottle to the storage area.

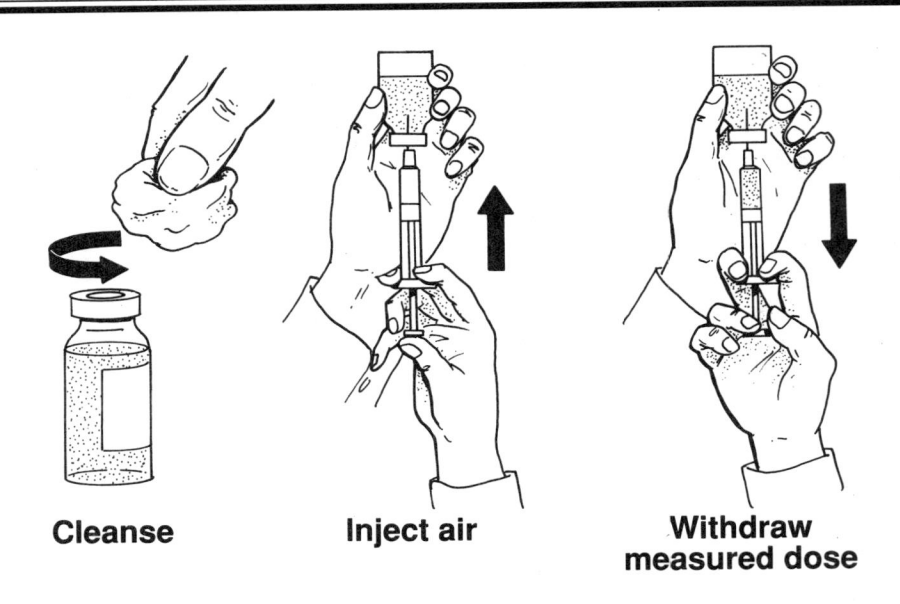

Figure 17-5 Three steps in drawing up medication from a vial.

The air pressure inside the vial is less than the pressure outside. Therefore, some air must be injected into the vial to make the medication easier to withdraw. You should inject an amount of air equal to the volume of medication that you are withdrawing. In other words, if you plan to withdraw 1.5 cc of medication, then you should first inject 1.5 cc of air into the vial. Pull back the stopper to the point marked 1.5 on the calibrated syringe. Then tilt the vial and insert the needle through the rubber stopper. Push in on the plunger to force the air out of the barrel. The vial may be held right side up, tilted, or inverted as you inject the air. Hold the vial securely and do not touch the rubber stopper.

Next, place the needle into the medication and change your hand position to make it easier to pull the plunger. Withdraw the medication by pulling back to the point that marks the exact dose (1.5 cc in our example). Keep the needle below the surface of the liquid, so as to avoid taking in air.

Before taking the needle out of the vial, check for air bubbles in the syringe. Air bubbles keep you from measuring an accurate dose. The tiny bubbles that often collect on the rubber tip of the plunger are no problem. However, if you see larger bubbles in the barrel, hold the syringe straight up at a 90° angle and tap it sharply with your finger. This will cause the bubbles to collect and join together at the tip of the syringe. Force the bubbles out by pushing in slightly on the plunger *and then withdraw more medication.* **Note**: For intramuscular injections, a small bubble (0.2 cc) of air may be added to the syringe after the correct dose of the medication has been drawn up. This use of an air bubble is discussed in this unit.

When you have drawn up the medication, replace the needle cover and assemble the remaining items you need for giving the injection: a medicine card, medication record, or other appropriate record form, and an antiseptic wipe. As long as the needle cover is on, you may place the needle and syringe on a tray or cart without risking contamination.

From an Ampule

To withdraw medication from an ampule, first inspect the ampule to see if there is any medication in the top portion. If so, flick the top with your fingernail to send the medication back into the bottom portion. The neck of the ampule will break along the scoring line, which is usually marked with a colored band. Most ampules today are prescored. However, if you come across one that is not, you will need

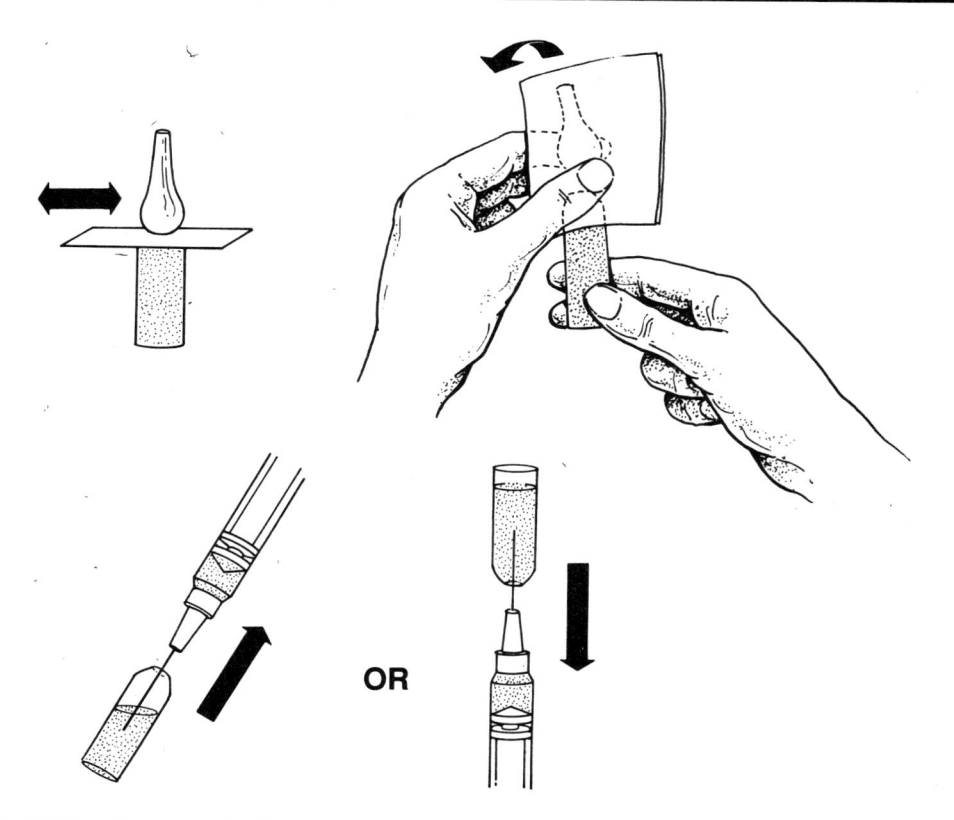

Figure 17-6 Drawing up medication from an ampule.

to score the neck on both sides with a small file. Then, using a piece of clean gauze, paper towel, or tissue to protect your fingers, break the ampule neck with a quick snap (Figure 17-6).

Because the air pressure is the same on the outside and inside of the opened ampule, there is no need to inject air before withdrawing the medication. Insert the needle into the ampule while holding the ampule steady in a tilted or upright position. As you pull back on the plunger, keep the needle submerged in the medication at all times. Some people prefer to invert the ampule while withdrawing the medication. This makes it easier to draw up all medication without getting air bubbles.

No matter which hand position you use, be certain not to touch anything but the outside of the ampule, the outside of the syringe barrel, the flange, and the end of the plunger.

Next, check for air bubbles, replace the needle cover, and assemble the remaining items you need for giving the injection (e.g., medicine card, antiseptic wipe).

Measuring Doses Accurately

To get an accurate dose, pay close attention to the calibrations on the particular syringe you are using. On a 2-cc syringe each mark may represent two-tenths of a cubic centimeter (0.2 cc). Count the number of marks between labeled units of measurement. If there are ten, then each mark measures off one-tenth of the unit. If there are five marks, then each mark measures two-tenths of the unit. If there are five marks, then each mark measures two-tenths of the unit. Figure 17-7 shows how to read the calibrations when with-

Measured Dose

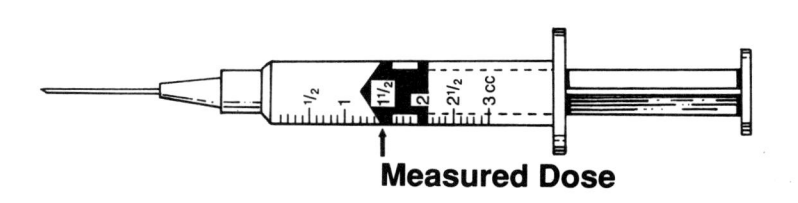

Figure 17-7 The forward edge of the rubber plunger head marks the amount of medication that has been withdrawn.

drawing a measured dose of medication. The spot where the rubber plunger tip makes contact with the barrel is the spot that should be lined up with the desired dosage.

Reconstituting Powdered Drugs

Certain drugs such as the antibiotics are stored in their powdered form because they quickly lose their freshness and effectiveness when in liquid form. These powders come packaged in vials and must be reconstituted before injection. In other words, liquid must be added to make a solution or suspension.

Drug powders are reconstituted using sterile water or saline solution for injection. To find out how much water or saline solution to add, read the directions on the vial label or package insert. Then fill a syringe with the proper measured amount of fluid and inject it into the vial. If you must inject a great deal of fluid into the vial, withdraw some air as you proceed, so that pressure does not build up.

After adding the fluid, shake or rotate the vial to completely dissolve or disperse the medication.

Follow package instructions on whether to shake vigorously or gently. Continue shaking until you do not see any jellylike texture, lumps, or patches of powder along the sides or bottom.

If you have reconstituted a multiple-dose vial, the next step is to write the *time* and *date* of reconstitution on the label. This will tell the staff on other shifts whether this particular solution is still fresh and effective. The unused portion must usually be stored in the refrigerator and be used as soon as possible. The drug package will tell you how long the medication remains effective (a) in dry form (see expiration date), (b) in liquid form when refrigerated, and (c) in liquid form when held at room temperature. If a drug has passed the allowed effectiveness period, discard it.

Also mark the multiple-dose vial with the *strength* of liquid remaining in it (milligrams or units per milliliter). For example, suppose that you reconstituted 1,000,000 units (U) of penicillin G potassium in 9.6 ml of sterile water for injection. You would mark the label to show that the vial contains 100,000 units per milliliter (100,000 U/ml).

Mixing Two Medications in a Syringe

When a patient is to receive more than one medication by injection, it saves discomfort for the patient if both medications can be given in the same injection. However, not all drugs can be mixed with others in the same syringe. Some drugs, when mixed together, will form a precipitate, or granules that cloud the liquid or settle to the bottom. Other drugs may change color when mixed. Either change can signal a loss of effectiveness of the drugs. There may even be no visible change, but the medications may still react together to cancel out each other's effects. Consult a pharmacist or the PDR if you are unsure whether two medications may be mixed.

When premixed unit doses are not available and you wish to mix two drugs that **can** be mixed, use the following procedure. Inject air in both vials equal to the amount of drug to be withdrawn from the vial. Measure the first drug accurately and eliminate air bubbles in the syringe. Then withdraw the second drug. The total amount of liquid in the syringe should be the same as the two individual doses added together (Figure 17-8). If one medication must be withdrawn from a multiple-dose vial, withdraw this medication first. If **both** medications are in multiple-dose vials, change to a fresh needle after withdrawing the first dose. This is done to avoid getting any of the first medication into the second vial.

When mixing different types of insulin in a syringe, you need not change needles, but you must take care not to transfer drops of slower-acting (e.g., NPH) insulin into a vial of fast-acting (regular) insulin. Withdraw the fast-acting or clear insulin first and then the long-acting type. But if you feel uncomfortable about this method, do change needles.

INJECTION SITES

The exact location for an injection depends on whether it is to be subcutaneous, intramuscular, or intradermal. The doctor will have ordered the route but it may be up to you to decide exactly where to administer it. For each parenteral route you have several options. The specific site to choose depends on the build of the patient (thin, fat, heavily muscled), his or her age (infant, young child, average adult, elderly), and the sites of other recently given injections.

Intradermal

Intradermal injections are usually administered into the skin on the inner surface of the lower arm (Figure 17-9). In special cases (e.g., allergy tests), they may also be given in the upper chest area and on the upper back below the shoulder blades.

Very small amounts of medication are given by this route—usually 0.1–0.2 cc—so a tuberculin syringe is used with a 25–26-gauge, 3/8-inch needle. The needle should be held at a 15° angle to the skin. It should pass just below the epidermis into the dermis and be inserted to a depth of 1/8–1/16 inch (you will be able to see the needle point through the skin). As the medication is injected, you should see a small bleb or blister form under the skin. If no bleb forms, withdraw the needle slightly, for you may have gone too deeply. If medication leaks out around the needle as you push the plunger, insert the needle a bit deeper.

Intradermal injections are used to determine exposure to tuberculosis. About 48–72 hours after the intradermal injection of tuberculin, the area is checked for induration and erythema. This procedure is usually called "reading a diagnostic skin test." Induration with erythema is measured to determine exposure to tuberculosis; just erythema without hardness rules out tuberculosis. If the area is less than 5 mm, this is a negative reaction. If the site is 5–10 mm in diameter, this is read as doubtful and another test must be done. If the area is 10 mm or more, this is a positive reaction. A similar test is used for histoplasmosis so it is important to read the directions that come with the medication carefully.

Subcutaneous

The sites for subcutaneous injection are the fatty tissues on the outer upper arm, the front of the thigh, the abdomen, and the upper back below the shoulder blades (Figure 17-10). The most common of these are the arm and the thigh with 1" of fatty tissue. This may be difficult to find on an elderly person so be cautious in choosing an area. Most medication given subcutaneously will absorb slowly due to the lesser vascularity of this tissue compared to muscle tissue. But movement of the area may make absorption faster. Get to know which drugs do this. Check package insert or PDR.

No more than 2 cc of medication may be given subcutaneously. A 2–3-cc syringe is used with a 24–26-gauge, 3/8–5/8-inch needle. The most common needle size for an average adult is 25G 5/8. The needle is inserted at a 45° angle, through the epidermis and the dermis, into the subcutaneous tissue. In some cases, the needle may be inserted at a 90° angle, for example, when the short (3/8-inch) needle is used. In a very obese person, it may be desirable to use a 1-inch needle at a 90° angle. Check with your supervisor on which angle is preferred for specific cases in your health facility.

Intramuscular

The intramuscular route places the needle deep into body tissues where there are nerve bundles, large blood vessels, and bones. Therefore, it is especially important to locate the sites properly. They should be found by touch as well as by sight, using certain prominent bones as landmarks. The advantages of the intramuscular route are:

- A larger amount of medication may be injected—up to 3 cc.
- The muscles can absorb more medication than the other tissues.
- Absorption is quite rapid because the muscles are well-supplied with capillaries.
- Appropriate for oily medications that do not come in oral form.
- Used with uncooperative patients, and those who cannot swallow, to get rapid effect from the drug and to avoid loss of any drug effects.

Intramuscular injections must be made only into the thickest parts of large healthy muscles. There are four possible sites:

- The dorsogluteal sites, both above and to the outside of the buttock area,
- The ventrogluteal sites, both above and to the outside of the buttock area,
- The deltoid site of the upper arm, and
- The vastus lateralis muscle of the thigh (Figure 17-11).

372 Administering Medications

teries. Piercing the sciatic nerve could cause pain and possibly paralysis. The dorsogluteal or posterior gluteal site is the most commonly used intramuscular site in average-sized adults. Two ways of locating the dorsogluteal site are shown in Figure 17-12.

One method is to draw imaginary lines dividing one side of the lower back and buttock area into quarters. The injection is given in the upper outer corner of the upper outer quarter. The other method is to draw an imaginary line between the head of the femur (thigh bone) where it joins the hip (the **greater trochanter**) and the **posterior superior iliac spine** of the hipbone. The injection is given above and to the outside of this line. Study Figure 17-12 carefully and then practice locating the dorsogluteal site on a real person.

When using the dorsogluteal site, the patient should lie in a prone position (on the stomach) with the toes pointed inward or with feet dangling off the edge of the bed. That way, the large muscles of the buttock area will be relaxed. If the prone position is not possible, a side-lying position may be used with the top leg bent.

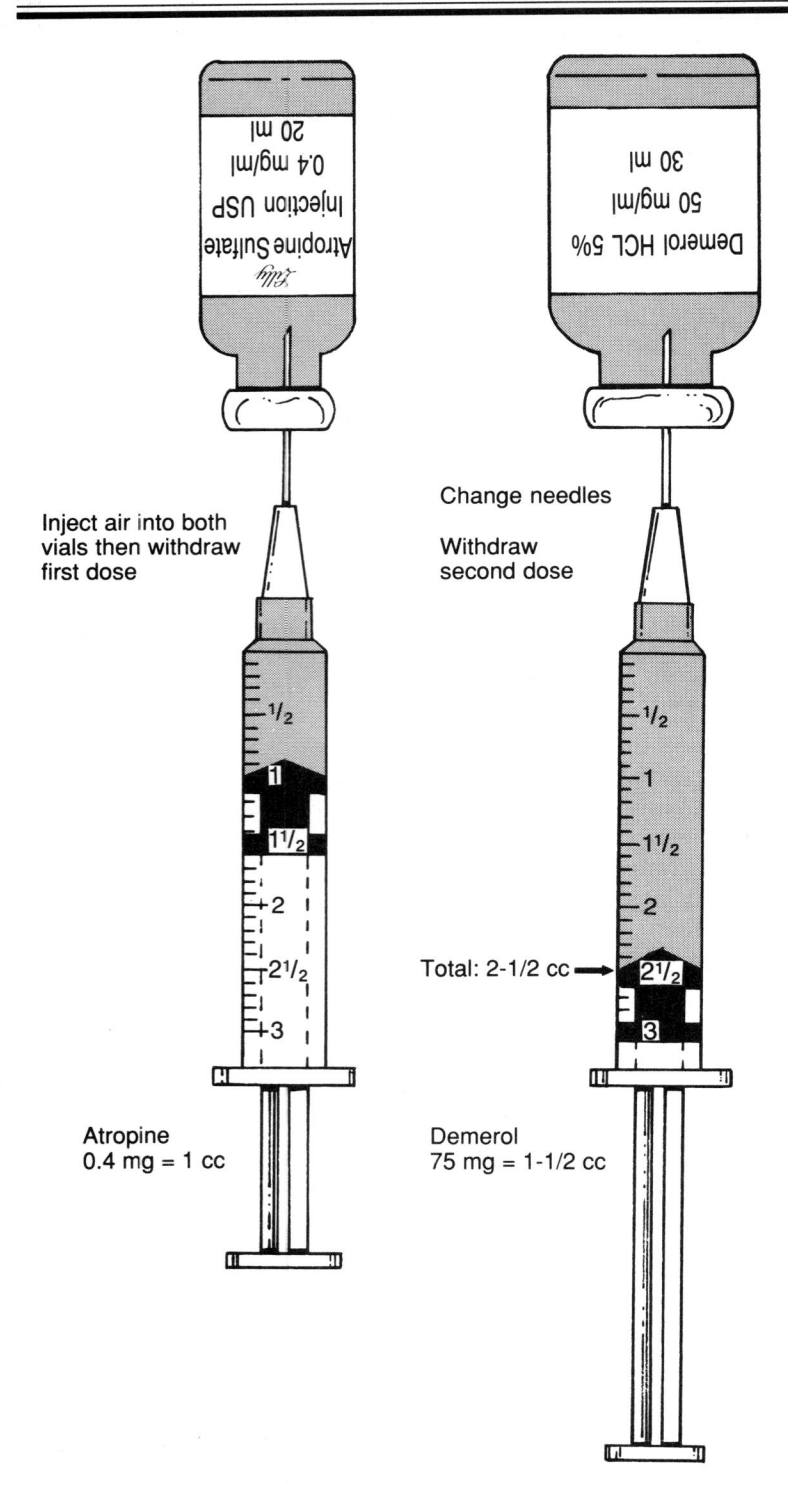

Figure 17-8 Mixing medications in one syringe. Always make certain that the drugs are allowed to be mixed.

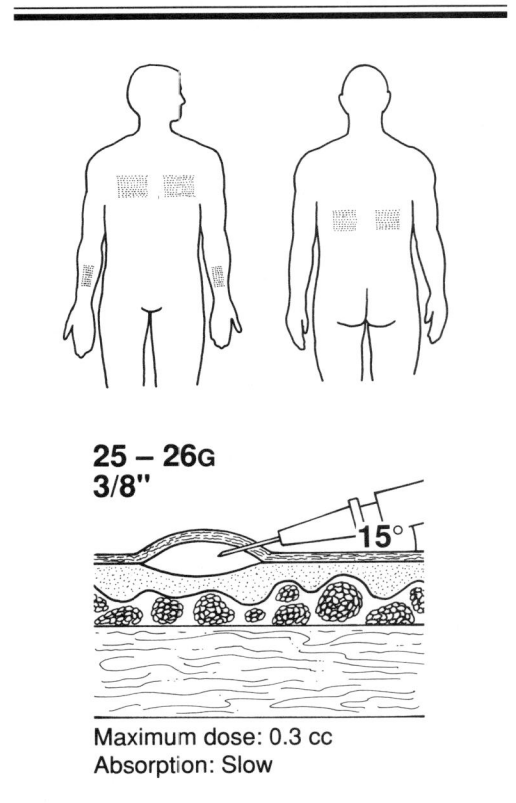

Figure 17-9 The intradermal route.

Maximum dose: 0.3 cc
Absorption: Slow

In the two sites located near the buttock area, the aim is to inject into large muscle masses that are as far away as possible from the **sciatic nerve** and the **gluteal ar-**

The ventrogluteal site is close to the dorsogluteal site but is usually approached from a side-lying position. The site can be located by placing the palm of your hand on the patient's greater trochanter and then feeling for two spots on the hip bone, the **iliac crest** and the **anterior superior iliac spine**. The V formed by touching these spots with your index and third fingers identifies the correct placement of the ventrogluteal injection (Figure 17-13). This site is especially useful when a large amount of medication is to be injected into a patient who must lie flat on his or her back.

The deltoid site is in the deltoid muscle of the outer upper arm, 1–2 inches below the spot where the arm and shoulder join (the **acromion process**.) This is a small site, and it may not have much muscle even in a well-developed body. The maximum amount injected into the deltoid is 1 cc, and a shorter needle (1-inch maximum) is used.

The vastus lateralis site is on the outer upper thigh, in the middle third of the area between the knee and the greater trochanter. This is the preferred site for infants, because their buttock (gluteal) muscles are not well enough developed to safely receive dorsogluteal or ventrogluteal injections.

For intramuscular injections, the needle should be long enough to pass clear through the subcutaneous tissue and deep into muscle tissue. A 21–23-gauge 1–1 1/2-inch needle is usually used, with a 2–3-cc syringe. An 18–20-gauge needle may be used for a viscous medication. The needle is inserted at a 90° angle.

GENERAL PROCEDURE FOR INJECTIONS

Although the various types of injections require different sites, needle sizes, and angles of penetration, certain steps and principles are common to all. With these general instructions in mind, you will be prepared to practice the step-by-step procedures for intradermal, subcutaneous, and intramuscular injections at the end of the unit.

Note: The procedures are described for a right-handed person. If you are left-handed, simply reverse the positions.

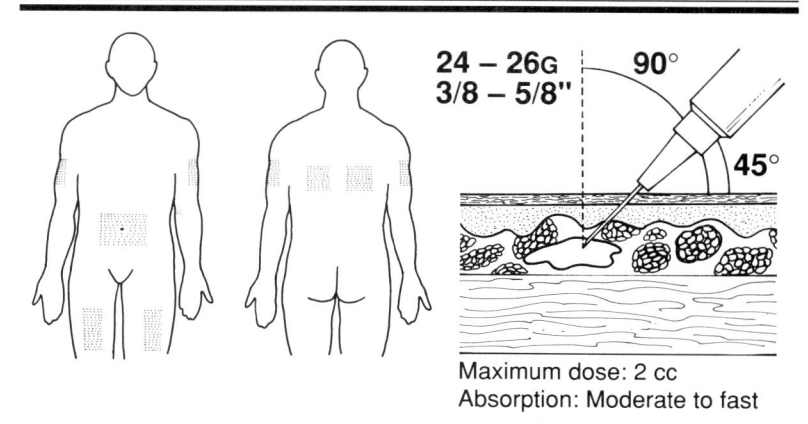

Figure 17-10 The subcutaneous route.

1. Locate and inspect the injection site.

Use the physician's ordered route and the site rotation plan, if any, to determine where an injection should be given. Find that site using both your eyes and your hands. Remove clothing or sheets as necessary to get a full view of the physical landmarks that will help you locate the proper sites. If the injection is to be intramuscular, choose only healthy, heavy muscles that are free of knots and soreness. Inspect the skin carefully for signs of rash, redness, lumps, hair, or birthmarks. Rash or redness may be signs of reactions to previous injections given in that area. **Do not proceed** with the injection if there is a reaction, but chart the appearance of the skin and consult the nurse in charge. Lumps in the skin or underlying muscle suggest that a previous injection was poorly absorbed or caused tissue damage. The next injection should be given at least 1 inch away or in another site.

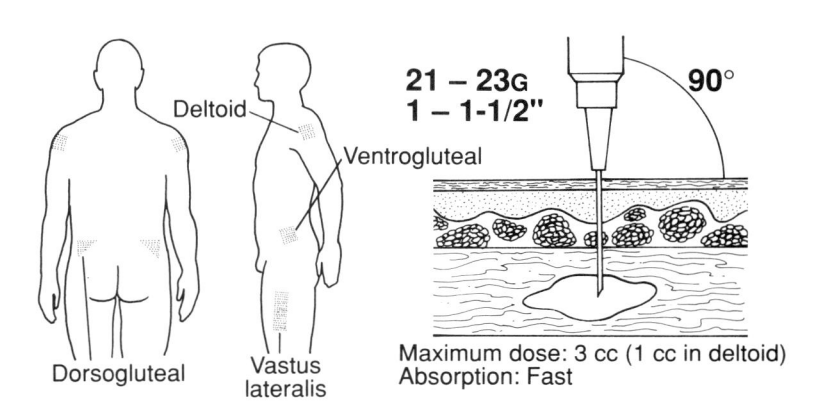

Figure 17-11 The intramuscular route.

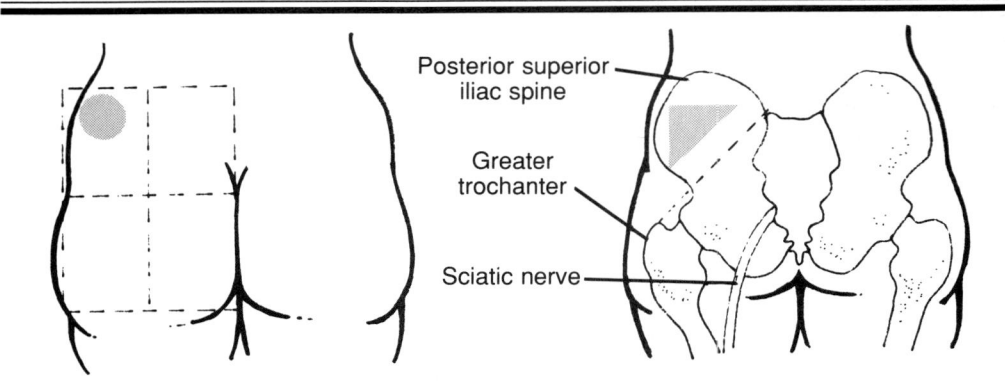

Figure 17-12 Two ways to locate the dorsogluteal site.

2. Disinfect the skin.

Use an antiseptic wipe (e.g., alcohol or *Betadine*) to cleanse the skin so that germs do not enter the body at the injection site. Wipe the skin once with a firm downward stroke, or wipe in a circular motion away from the center. Allow the antiseptic to dry. This is especially important with alcohol, because it can sting if it enters body tissues. Save the antiseptic wipe and hold it between the fourth and little fingers of the left hand. Then it will be handy later when you are ready to withdraw the needle.

3. Stretch and firm the skin.

With your left hand, hold the skin taut. Use your thumb and middle finger to stretch the skin and push it downwards.

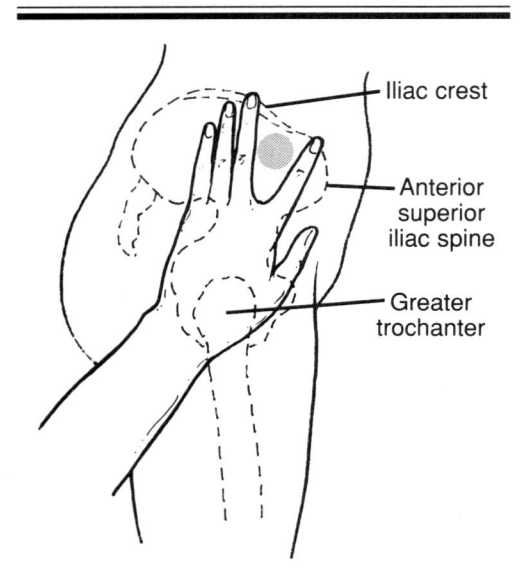

Figure 17-13 Use your hand to feel for the "landmarks" that identify the ventrogluteal site.

Or, when the site is on the arm, grasp the tissue from behind the arm and pull down and back. For the subcutaneous route, a 2- or 3-inch area of skin may be pinched and lifted slightly to pull the subcutaneous tissue away from the muscle layers. This method is especially preferred for patients who are thin. Pulling their skin taut might flatten the subcutaneous tissue too much and cause the injection to reach the muscle. Stretching or pinching firms the skin so that the needle will enter more easily. It also numbs the area slightly so that the injection causes less discomfort. The skin should be held in this way until the needle has been inserted.

4. Insert the needle at the proper angle.

Use the correct angle of insertion for the route, site, and needle size selected. With your right hand, hold the needle and syringe at the correct angle in relation to the skin surface (15°, 45°, or 90°). The bevel should be facing upward. Then insert the needle quickly and smoothly with a firm thrust. The needle should go in almost all the way to the hub. Leave a small part of the shaft visible just in case the needle should break off at the hub. This will make it easier to remove.

5. Release the skin and change hand position.

Lift your left hand so that the skin is no longer stretched or pinched. Move this hand over to support the syringe so that your right hand can operate the plunger. Do not release the syringe from your right hand until your left hand is holding it steady. Any sideward movement of the needle at this step could damage the underlying tissues.

6. Aspirate.

While the needle is fully inserted, pull back slightly on the plunger. This is called **aspirating**. It is a safety check to make sure the needle has not entered a blood vessel. If it is not in a vessel, you will feel some resistance on the plunger and you will not see blood in the syringe. You may then proceed with the injection. However, if the needle *has* entered a vessel, blood will become visible in the syringe as you pull the plunger. If this happens, withdraw the needle slightly and aspirate again. If you see no blood the second time, then you may proceed with the injection. If you do see blood the second time, withdraw the needle and make up a fresh injection. Aspirating is important because medications ordered for subcutaneous and intramuscular injection must not be injected intravenously. If this happened accidentally, it could cause serious harm. There are two cases in which you should not aspirate: (1) intradermal injections, because the needle does not penetrate deep enough to contact large vessels; and (2) anticoagulant injections (e.g., heparin), because aspirating might lead to uncontrolled bleeding.

7. Inject the medication slowly.

Still holding the syringe with your left hand, change your right hand position to push in the plunger. This forces the medication out of the syringe and into the body tissues. It must be injected slowly to avoid overstretching and injuring the tissues. Be certain to inject all the medication by pushing in the plunger fully.

8. Firm the skin and remove the needle.

The skin must once again be firmed so that the needle does not pull the skin as it is withdrawn. Hold the antiseptic wipe (which you tucked between your fingers in Step 1) near the needle and press gently on the skin. Pull the needle out quickly at the same angle as it was inserted. This reduces pain and prevents tissue damage.

9. Massage the site gently (except in certain situations).

Use the antiseptic wipe to massage the area in a gentle, circular motion. This helps spread the medication through the tissues and promotes absorption. This step should be omitted when:

- The medication could stain or irritate tissues.
- Slow absorption is desired.
- The Z-track method (described later) for insulin has been used (the insulin will be absorbed too quickly).
- Heparin was given (a hematoma may develop if small blood vessels rupture).

10. Replace the needle cover and remove and discard equipment.

The needle cover is replaced so that no one is injured while removing the equipment to the disposal area. Be very careful not to insert the needle back in the cover with a lot of force. The needle could go through the cover, allowing you or others to be contaminated. If you used disposable equipment, the needle must be broken before being discarded. The needle and syringe are now contaminated and may not be reused. Many health facilities have a special device for breaking needles and syringes. If one of these is not available, you must dispose of them according to the policy of your facility. Nondisposable equipment must be handled as required by your health facility.

11. Chart the medication.

Be certain to include the specific parenteral route that was used (ID, SC, or IM) and note the location of the injection (right or left arm, right or left dorsogluteal site, etc.).

12. Observe the patient for expected and adverse reactions.

Try to remain with the patient for at least 1 minute, and then check frequently to see how the patient is feeling. The length of time to observe depends on the drug. In certain cases you may have to stay near the patient for a set amount of time (e.g., 20 minutes the first time a person is injected with penicillin). Be alert for the call button of a patient who has recently received an injection. One aim of observation is to see whether the drug is working—whether an analgesic, for example, is successfully relieving pain. The other aim is to spot unexpected side effects and adverse reactions.

Parenteral medications work very quickly compared to oral, rectal, and topical medications, so reactions can occur within minutes of the injection. Systemic adverse reactions may occur due to overdose or allergy. Because these require immediate medical treatment, you should call the supervisor immediately if they occur.

Local reactions result from irritation of the tissues where the drug was injected.

Redness, rash, and lumpiness have already been mentioned as signs of drug sensitivity, tissue irritation, poor absorption, and extravasation. More serious local reactions can result in severe tissue damage, for example, death of tissue (**necrosis**), shedding of skin (**sloughing**), and formation of pus inside the tissues (**abscess**). These conditions require special treatment by a physician. Your duty is to chart and report any unusual signs of inflammation or irritation that appear in the injection area.

The general procedure just outlined includes specific steps required for parenteral administration. In addition to these steps, you should follow the other basic rules for administering medications, such as identifying the patient, explaining the procedure, and assisting the patient into a comfortable position both before and after the injection.

SPECIAL INSTRUCTIONS

Site Rotation

Some people must have injections several times a day, for example, penicillin for a systemic infection. Others, such as insulin-controlled diabetic patients, must have injections daily over a long period of time. If all these injections were to be given in the same site, the tissues might be damaged and scar tissue might form, making further injections difficult. For these reasons, injection sites must be **rotated** according to some pattern that allows the medical staff to keep track of where the last injection was given. Most health agencies adopt a rotation plan such as the one shown in Figure 17-14. This gives them a systematic way of giving regular injections without damaging body tissues. Site rotation is used with subcutaneous and intramuscular injections. Intradermal medications are not usually given over many days.

Prevention of Tracking

As a needle is withdrawn after an injection, it leaves a small channel or **track** where the needle has been. **Tracking** is the leaking of medication into the channel. Medication which did not clear the needle may leak into the track as the needle is pulled out. Or, the pressure of the medication in the tissue where it was injected may force some of the medication to back up into the track. In either case, tracking is not desirable, because the medication may irritate or stain other tissue layers. Penicillin, for example, causes a burning pain if it contacts subcutaneous tissue, and *Imferon* can cause stains. There are several ways to prevent tracking:

- Inject very slowly and wait at least 10 seconds before withdrawing the needle.
- Avoid massaging the injection site, which would increase the pressure on the medication.
- Advise patients to wear loose-fitting clothing and to avoid heavy exercise.
- Use an air bubble or use the Z-track method.

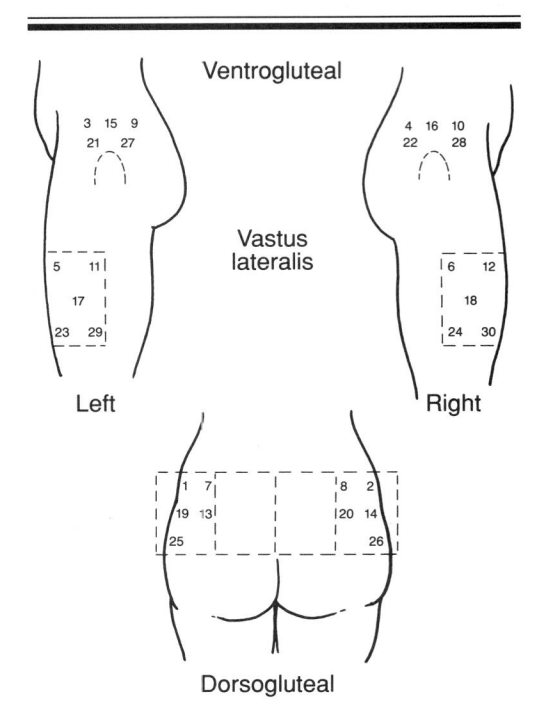

Figure 17-14 Site rotation plan for an IM medication. Numbers show the order and location of injections.

Use of an Air Bubble—Some health facilities recommend the use of an air bubble to prevent tracking in intramuscular injections. In this method, a small amount of air (0.2 cc) is taken into the syringe **after** measuring the correct dose. When the medication is injected, the air bubble leaves the syringe last. It serves to clear the needle of all medication so that none can leak out as the needle is withdrawn. The air bubble also provides a space into which the medication can flow and thus lessen the pressure on surrounding tissues. Finally, the bubble seals off the needle track to block leakage. Check with the person in charge to see whether this is the preferred procedure for intramuscular injections in your facility.

Z-track Intramuscular Injection—The Z-track method of injection may be used to ensure that no medication follows the needle track into subcutaneous tissue (Figure 17-15). In this method, the heel or the outer edge of the hand is used to pull the skin to one side and hold it there during the entire injection procedure. Displacing the skin in this way also moves underlying layers to one side. When the skin is released after withdrawing the needle, the needle track is sealed over as the tissue layers return to their normal position. The Z-track method is specifically required when injecting *Imferon*, *Vistaril*, or anytime you know a drug might back up.

Broken Needles

It is very rare that a needle breaks during an injection, but it can happen and you should be prepared. When a needle breaks, it usually breaks where the shaft joins the hub. If you have followed the proper injection procedure, you will have left a part of the shaft visible. You may then use a sterile clamp or tongs to pull out the needle in the same direction as it entered. If you cannot see the end of the broken needle, keep your eyes on where it entered the skin and grasp a pen or other marker. Mark a circle around the entry site and then contact your supervisor immediately. Do not move the skin or otherwise try to retrieve the needle. It must be removed by a physician. Anytime a needle breaks, you must fill out an incident report or a medication error form. On this form, describe where and how the needle broke and the action taken.

The reason a needle breaks is often because a muscle is suddenly tensed while the needle is being inserted. This can be avoided by placing the patient in a position that holds the muscle in a relaxed position—for example, with the leg flexed for the ventrogluteal site, and with the toes pointed inward or dangling for the dorsogluteal site.

Your Attitude Toward Injections

No matter how skillful you are at giving injections, they are bound to cause fear and discomfort in some patients. This is where psychological factors come into play. You need to explain how and why you are giving the medication, as always. But more than ever, your attitudes toward the procedure and the patient are crucial.

Your attitude toward the patient is important in getting the patient to cooperate in the procedure. Be a good listener and let the patient know that you care about his or her concerns. A relaxed patient who has confidence in you will feel less discomfort than a tense, anxious patient.

Where the procedure itself is concerned, you can only be as confident as the amount of supervised practice you put into learning how to give injections. Practice must, of course, include some feedback on how well you performed the procedure. Once you really understand what you are doing, your confidence will show. The key, then, is to study carefully the theoretical portions of this unit and then practice the injection procedures until you can perform them with 100% accuracy.

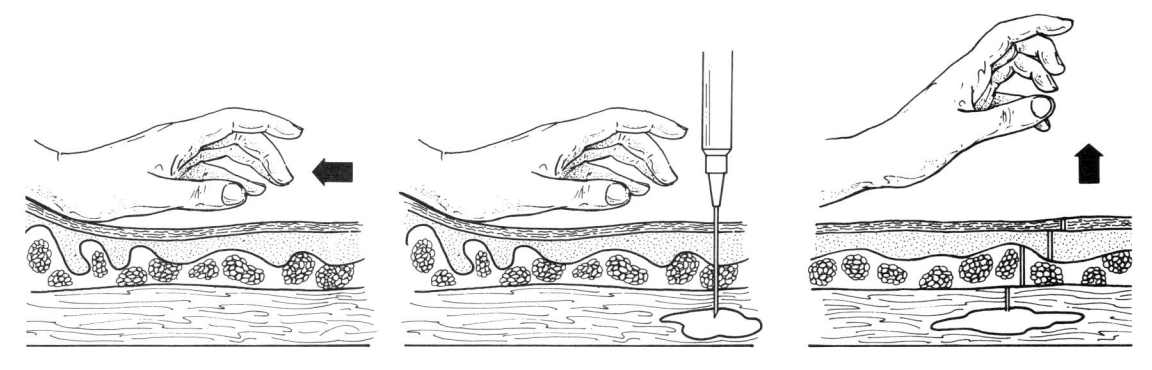

Figure 17-15 The Z-track method prevents the backing up of medication into other tissue layers.

378 Administering Medications

EXERCISES

A. Memorize the basics.

1. Identify the parts of a needle and syringe on the drawing below.

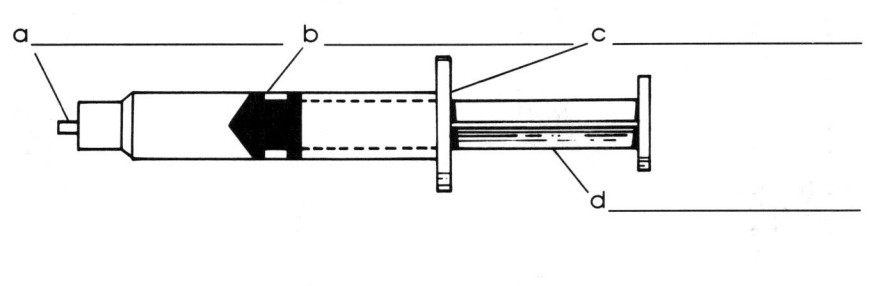

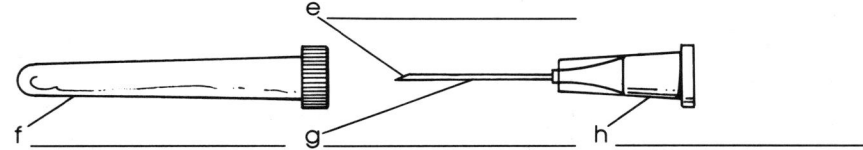

a _____ b _____ c _____

d _____

e _____

f _____ g _____ h _____

2. The syringes below are filled with measured amounts of medication. Tell what the exact dose is in each one.

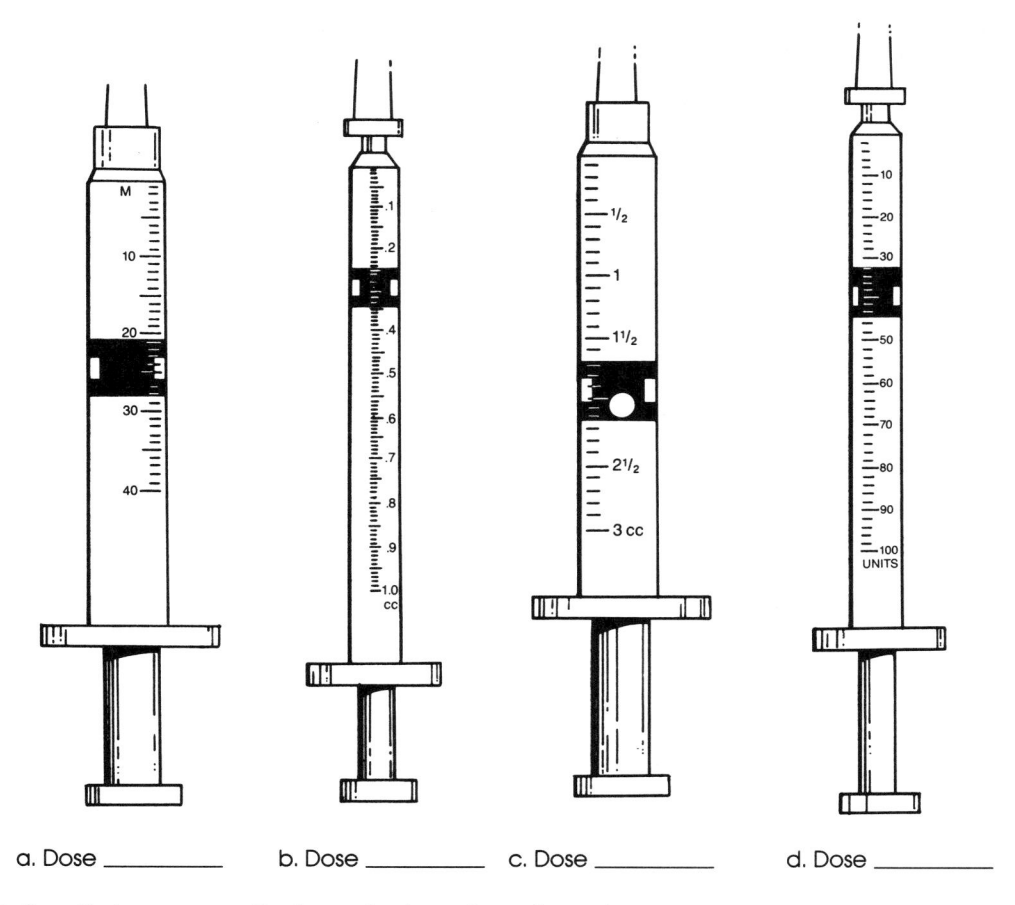

a. Dose _____   b. Dose _____   c. Dose _____   d. Dose _____

3. In Item 2 above, name the type of syringe shown in each case.

a. _____   c. _____

b. _____   d. _____

4. Summarize the information you have learned about parenteral routes and equipment by filling in the blanks in the table below.

	Intradermal	Subcutaneous	Intramuscular
a. Injected into (name tissue layer)	_____	_____	_____
b. Type of syringe	_____	_____ or _____	_____
c. Needle length	_____	_____	_____
d. Needle gauge	_____	_____	aqueous _____ viscous _____
e. Angle of entry	_____	_____	_____

B. Short answers.

1. List at least three reasons why a physician might order a drug to be given by the parenteral route.

   _____

   _____

   _____

2. What is the purpose of site rotation?

   _____

   _____

3. What does it mean to "aspirate" before injecting medication? Why is it done?

   _____

   _____

   _____

4. What should you do if you see blood in the syringe when you aspirate?

   _____

   _____

   _____

5. Many parts of the needle and syringe need to be kept sterile while drawing up medications and giving injections. Place a check mark beside the parts that do not need to be kept sterile (i.e., those you may touch).

   _____ outside needle cover   _____ inside of barrel

   _____ inside needle cover   _____ outside of barrel

   _____ needle point and shaft   _____ plunger

   _____ outside of hub   _____ plunger end

   _____ inside of hub   _____ flange

   _____ syringe tip

C. Define these terms related to injection equipment.

   1. lumen _____

   2. gauge _____

   3. bevel _____

   4. calibrations _____

D. Match sites of injection to routes of injection.

_____ 1. anterior thigh, upper outer arm, abdomen, upper back under shoulder blades

_____ 2. vastus lateralis, deltoid, dorsogluteal, ventrogluteal

_____ 3. inner lower arm, upper chest, upper back under shoulder blades

_____ 4. veins of arms and legs

a. intramuscular
b. intravenous
c. intradermal
d. subcutaneous

E. Fill in the blanks.

1. A knob on the upper leg bone (femus) which is used to help locate the dorsogluteal and ventrogluteal sites is the _____.

2. To "reconstitute" a powdered medication means to add _____ to make a solution or suspension.

3. Injections in the buttock area must be placed very carefully so as to avoid the gluteal arteries and the _____ nerve.

4. Thin, watery liquids that can be given in fine needles (23–27G) are called _____ solutions.

5. Thick or oily liquids that must be given with thicker needles (18–20G) are called _____ solutions.

6. When holding the needle and syringe at the proper angle to the skin, the bevel should be facing _____ (down or up).

7. A medication may back up into the channel through which the needle was inserted into tissue. This is called _____.

8. Nondisposable needles and syringes must be rinsed, cleaned, and _____ before reuse.

9. If a precipitate forms when you mix two medications, the medications are likely to be _____.

10. *Imferon* should not be allowed to track into subcutaneous tissue because it can cause _____.

11. Before drawing up medication from a vial, the rubber stopper must be wiped with _____.

12. When using disposable injection equipment, always _____ the needle before discarding.

13. After drawing up a medication and before replacing the needle cover, always check for _____ in the syringe.

14. Before drawing up a measured amount of medication from a vial, inject an equal amount of _____ into the vial.

15. The neck of an ampule must be _____ before use.

16. The Z-track method prevents tracking because the tissues are _____ before and during the injection.

17. Pulling back on the plunger _____ (raises or lowers) the pressure inside the barrel of a syringe.

18. After reconstituting a powdered drug in a multiple-dose vial, write the _____, _____, and _____ on the label.

F. More short answers.

1. Review the 12 general steps in any injection procedure. Then write them here (from memory, if possible).

   _____

   _____

   _____

   _____

   _____

   _____

   _____

2. List the local reactions that can occur following injections.

   _____

   _____

3. What should you do if the injection site you have chosen is covered with a rash?

4. Why is it desirable to massage the injection site in most cases?

5. What precaution should you take when inserting a needle into tissue so that, in case the needle breaks, you can retrieve it more easily?

6. Why do some people add a small air bubble (0.2 cc) to the syringe before an intramuscular injection?

7. What would you do if a needle broke in your patient's buttock area and you could not see a part of the shaft?

8. How can you avoid broken needles?

9. How do practice and attitude affect your ability to give injections?

ANSWERS TO EXERCISES

A. Basics
   1. a. tip
      b. barrel
      c. flange
      d. plunger
      e. bevel
      f. needle cover or sheath
      g. shaft, stem, or cannula
      h. hub

2. a. 21 minims
   b. 0.25 cc
   c. 1.7 cc
   d. 32 units
3. a. standard hypodermic
   b. tuberculin
   c. standard hypodermic
   d. insulin

4. | | ID | SC | IM |
    |----|----|----|----|
    | a. | skin, dermis | subcutaneous, fatty tissue | muscle |
    | b. | tuberculin | standard hypodermic or insulin | standard hypodermic |
    | c. | 3/8-inch | 3/8–5/8-inch | 1-1½-inch |
    | d. | 25–26G | 24–26G | aqu. 21–23G
visc. 18–20G |
    | e. | 15° | 45° or 90° | 90° |

B. Short answers
   1. Because rapid absorption is desired; because drug is destroyed by digestive juices if taken orally; because patient is unable to swallow, is unconscious, or has nausea, vomiting, or intestinal obstruction.
   2. To avoid damaging tissues and forming scar tissue due to repeated injection in the same place.
   3. To pull back on the plunger and check for blood in the syringe after the needle is inserted into tissue; done to see whether the needle has entered a blood vessel.
   4. Withdraw the needle slightly and aspirate again. If blood is not seen, continue with the injection. If blood is aspirated the second time, make up a new injection and inject elsewhere.
   5. Outside needle cover, outside of barrel, plunger end, flange.

C. Definitions
   1. hollow part inside the needle through which medication flows
   2. diameter of the lumen of an injection needle
   3. slanted part of the needle shaft that tapers down to the point
   4. marks showing equal units of quantity on a syringe or other measurement device.

D. Sites and routes
   1. d
   2. a
   3. c
   4. b

E. Blanks
   1. greater trochanter
   2. liquid (saline or water)
   3. sciatic
   4. aqueous
   5. viscous
   6. up
   7. tracking
   8. sterilized
   9. ineffective
   10. stains
   11. antiseptic, alcohol
   12. break
   13. air bubbles
   14. air
   15. broken off
   16. displaced, moved to one side
   17. lowers
   18. time, date, strength

F. More short answers
   1. See text
   2. Redness, rash, lumpiness, sloughing, necrosis, abscess.
   3. Do not give the injection, but chart the appearance of the skin and consult the nurse in charge.
   4. Massage aids absorption of the medication.
   5. Leave a part of the needle shaft visible.
   6. To seal in the medication and prevent tracking.
   7. Circle the place where the needle entered, using a pen or other marker. Report the incident to the nurse in charge and fill out an incident or accident report form.
   8. Put the patient in a position that keeps the muscles relaxed (e.g., prone, with toes pointed in).
   9. See discussion in text.

PRACTICE PROCEDURE

DRAW UP MEDICATION FROM A VIAL

Equipment:

- Medication order (e.g., regular insulin 60 U SC)
- Kardex, medicine card, medication record, patient chart
- Variety of syringes and needles with covers
- Vial of medication (e.g., 100-unit strength insulin in a multiple-dose vial); check expiration date
- Vials of sterile water for injection (for practice)
- Antiseptic wipes or sponges
- Sterile gauze

_____ 1. Read the medication order and assemble equipment. Check for the "five rights." Read the vial label by holding it next to the medicine card (or Kardex, medication record, or physician's order if medicine cards are not used).

_____ 2. Wash your hands.

_____ 3. Select the proper size needle and syringe for the medication and the route (e.g., for subcutaneous injection of insulin, 100-unit insulin syringe and 25G 5/8-inch needle). If necessary, attach the needle to the syringe.

_____ 4. Check the vial label against the medicine card (or appropriate record) a second time.

_____ 5. Remove the metal or plastic cap from the vial of insulin. If the vial has been opened previously, clean the rubber stopper by applying an antiseptic wipe in a circular motion.

_____ 6. Remove the needle cover (pull it straight off).

_____ 7. Inject air into the vial as follows:
- Hold the syringe pointed upward at eye level. Pull back the plunger to take in a quantity of air that is equal to the ordered dose of medication (60 U in our insulin example).
- Hold the vial upright, tilted, or inverted, according to preference. Take care not to touch the rubber stopper.
- Insert the needle through the rubber stopper of the vial. Inject the air by pushing in the plunger.

_____ 8. Withdraw the medication: Hold the vial and the syringe steady. Pull back on the plunger to withdraw the measured dose of medication. **Measure accurately.** Keep the tip of the needle below the surface of the liquid, otherwise air will enter the syringe.

_____ 9. Check the syringe for air bubbles. Remove them by tapping sharply on the syringe. If you are using an air bubble to prevent tracking, add 0.2 cc of air to the syringe **after** measuring the dose accurately and expelling air bubbles.

_____ 10. Remove the needle from the vial. Replace the sterile needle cover. A nondisposable needle may be laid between two pieces of sterile gauze (follow your agency's policy for handling nondisposables).

_____ 11. Check the vial label against the medicine card (or appropriate record) for a third time.

_____ 12. Place the filled needle and syringe on a medicine tray or cart, with an antiseptic wipe and the medicine card (or appropriate record). The dose is now ready for injection.

_____ 13. Return multiple-dose vials to the proper storage area (cabinet or refrigerator). Dispose of unused medication in a single-dose vial according to your agency's procedure. (Remember, disposal of a controlled substance must be witnessed and the proper forms signed).

Demonstrate this procedure for the instructor or the nurse in charge.

PRACTICE PROCEDURE

DRAW UP MEDICATION FROM AN AMPULE

Equipment:

- Medication order (e.g., *Demerol* 50 mg IM stat)
- Kardex, medicine card, medication record, patient chart
- Variety of syringes and needles with covers
- Ampule of medication (e.g., 1-ml ampule of *Demerol* containing 100 mg/ml); check expiration date
- Ampules of sterile water for injection (for practice)
- Sterile gauze
- Antiseptic wipes or sponges

_____ 1. Read the medication order and assemble equipment. Check for the "five rights." Read the ampule label by holding it next to the medicine card (or Kardex, medication record, or physician's order if medicine cards are not used).

_____ 2. Wash your hands.

_____ 3. Select the proper size needle and syringe for the medication and the route (e.g., a 2½-cc standard hypodermic syringe and 22G 1½ needle for IM injection of *Demerol*). If necessary, attach the needle to the syringe.

_____ 4. Check the ampule label against the medicine card (or other appropriate record) for a second time.

_____ 5. Shake or tap down any medication in the top of the ampule.

_____ 6. Score the neck of the ampule if it is not prescored. Then break the neck of the ampule. Use a piece of clean gauze, paper towel, or tissue to protect your fingers.

_____ 7. Remove the needle cap from the needle and syringe.

_____ 8. Withdraw the medication. Insert the needle into the open end of the broken ampule. Pull back on the plunger and remove a measured dose of medication. The ampule may be held right side up or tilted sideways and quickly inverted, according to the preferred procedure in your agency. **Measure accurately.** (If using the sample order of *Demerol*, draw up 0.5 mL of the drug).

_____ 9. Check the syringe for air bubbles. Remove them by tapping sharply on the syringe. (If you are using an air bubble to prevent tracking, add 0.2 cc of air to the syringe **after** measuring the dose accurately and expelling air bubbles).

_____ 10. Replace the needle cover. A nondisposable needle may be laid between two pieces of sterile gauze (follow your agency's policy for handling nondisposables).

_____ 11. Check the ampule label against the medicine card (or appropriate record) for a third time.

_____ 12. Place the filled needle and syringe on a medicine tray or cart with an antiseptic wipe and the medicine card (or appropriate record). The dose is now ready for injection.

_____ 13. Discard the unused portion of the ampule according to your agency's procedure. If you are disposing of a controlled substance such as *Demerol*, have someone witness the disposal and sign the proper form).

Demonstrate this procedure for the instructor or the nurse in charge.

PRACTICE PROCEDURE

ADMINISTER INTRADERMAL INJECTION

Equipment:

- Medication order for an intradermal preparation (e.g., Mantoux test for tuberculosis)
- Kardex, medicine card, medication record, patient chart
- Vial or ampule of medication for ID injection; check expiration date
- Sterile needle, 26-gauge 3/8-inch (26G 3/8) with cover
- Sterile tuberculin syringe
- Sterile antiseptic wipes
- Medicine tray
- Needle and syringe breaker, if available
- Container for disposal of contaminated materials
- Plastic dummy or arm for practice injections

____ 1. Read the medication order and check for the "five rights."

____ 2. Assemble equipment and prepare the injection. Use sterile technique and measure accurately.

____ 3. Identify the patient following agency policy. Explain what you are going to do.

____ 4. Assist the patient into a comfortable position that allows access to the injection site (lower inner arm, upper back, or upper chest).

____ 5. Inspect the injection site. Inject only into healthy skin free of rash, redness, or lumps.

____ 6. Cleanse the site with an antiseptic wipe and allow to dry.

____ 7. With one hand, pull the skin taut by spreading the fingers or by pulling from behind the inner arm.

____ 8. With the other hand, hold the needle at a 15° angle to the skin surface. Insert the needle quickly and gently just under the outer layer of skin. Insert it to a depth of 1/8–1/16 inch. **Do not** aspirate.

____ 9. Release the skin and steady the syringe.

____ 10. Inject the medication slowly and fully. You should see a small blister or bleb form just under the skin.

____ 11. Withdraw the needle gently and quickly. Replace the needle cover.

____ 12. Wipe the skin again with the antiseptic.

____ 13. Dispose of the equipment properly, breaking disposable needles.

____ 14. Chart the medication.

____ 15. Instruct the patient if he or she must report a skin reaction within several days.

Demonstrate this procedure for the instructor or the nurse in charge.

PRACTICE PROCEDURE

ADMINISTER SUBCUTANEOUS INJECTION

Equipment:

- Medication order for a subcutaneous preparation
- Kardex, medicine card, medication record, patient chart
- Vial or ampule of medication prepared for subcutaneous injection; check expiration date
- Sterile needle, size 25 gauge 5/8-inch (25G 5/8) or 27G ½–1-inch with cover
- Sterile syringe, size 2–3 cc
- Sterile antiseptic wipes
- Medicine tray
- Needle and syringe breaker, if available
- Container for disposal of contaminated materials
- Plastic dummy, arm, torso for practice injections.

_____ 1. Read the medication order and check for the "five rights."
_____ 2. Assemble equipment and prepare the injection. Use sterile technique and measure accurately.
_____ 3. Identify the patient following agency policy. Explain what you are going to do.
_____ 4. Assist the patient into a comfortable position that allows access to the injection site (outer upper arm, upper back, anterior thigh).
_____ 5. Inspect the injection site. If rash or redness is present, chart and report to your supervisor and do not give the injection. If lumps are present, inject at least 1 inch away or choose another site.
_____ 6. Cleanse the site with an antiseptic wipe and allow to dry. Secure the wipe between your fourth and little fingers for later use.
_____ 7. With one hand, lift and pinch the skin and subcutaneous tissue between the thumb and finger, or spead the skin between two fingers. For a thin person, use only the pinching method. For an obese person, simply spread the skin taut.
_____ 8. With the other hand, hold the needle at a 45° angle to the skin, bevel side up. (With a 3/8-inch needle or with an obese person, use a 90° angle). Insert the needle quickly and smoothly. Leave 1/8-inch of the needle shaft showing.
_____ 9. Release the pinched tissue and use this hand to steady the inserted needle and syringe. Be careful not to move the needle from side to side.
_____ 10. Aspirate, using your free hand to pull back on the plunger. If no blood appears, proceed with the injection. If a small amount of blood appears, withdraw the needle slightly and aspirate again. If blood still appears, prepare a new injection with fresh equipment and move to another site.
_____ 11. Inject the medication slowly. Push the plunger all the way in to inject the full dose.
_____ 12. Withdraw the needle quickly, firming the skin with the antiseptic wipe held near the needle. Pull the needle at the same angle (45° or 90°) as it was inserted. Put the cover back on the needle for safety.
_____ 13. Massage the site gently with the antiseptic wipe if this is appropriate. (It is not appropriate with insulin or heparin.)
_____ 14. Dispose of the equipment properly, breaking disposable needles.
_____ 15. Chart the medication: name, dosage, route, site, and time.
_____ 16. Observe the patient frequently (or as ordered) to make sure that the medication is working and that there are no adverse reactions. Subcutaneous injections usually take 30 minutes or more to absorb. Instruct the patient in any necessary self-care and advise the patient to rest quietly for at least a few minutes.

Demonstrate this procedure for the instructor or the nurse in charge.

PRACTICE PROCEDURE

NOTE: *This procedure is geared to the average adult. Equipment must be adjusted for infants, young children, and the elderly. If you wish to practice the Z-track method, follow the special instructions in the text.*

ADMINISTER INTRAMUSCULAR INJECTION

Equipment:
- Medication order for aqueous intramuscular preparation
- Kardex, medicine card, medication record, patient chart
- Vial or ampule of medication prepared for IM injection; check expiration date
- Sterile needle, size 22-gauge 1½-inch (22G 1½) with cover (1-inch size for the deltoid site)
- Sterile syringe, size 2½–3 cc
- Sterile antiseptic wipes
- Medicine tray
- Needle and syringe breaker, if available
- Container for disposal of contaminated materials
- Plastic dummy or torso for practice injections and standard injection procedure.

____ 1. Read the medication order and check for the "five rights."
____ 2. Assemble equipment and prepare the injection. Add a 0.2-cc air bubble to the syringe after measuring the medication, if this method is used in your agency.
____ 3. Identify the patient following agency policy. Explain what you are going to do.
____ 4. Assist the patient into a comfortable position that allows access to the injection site (dorsogluteal, ventrogluteal, deltoid, or vastus lateralis).
____ 5. Inspect the injection site for signs of redness, rash, or lumps. If rash or redness is present, chart and report to your supervisor and **do not** give the injection. If a lump is present, make the injection at least 1 inch away or choose another site.
____ 6. Cleanse the site with an alcohol wipe and allow to dry.
____ 7. With one hand, spread the skin taut between two fingers.
____ 8. With the other hand, hold the needle at a 90° angle to the skin, bevel side up. Insert the needle quickly and smoothly, with a firm thrust. Leave 1/8-inch of the needle shaft showing.
____ 9. Release the taut skin and use this hand to steady the inserted needle and syringe. Be careful not to move the needle from side to side.
____ 10. Aspirate, using your free hand to pull back on the plunger. If no blood appears, proceed with the injection. If blood appears, withdraw the needle slightly and aspirate again. If blood still appears, prepare a new injection with fresh equipment and move to another site.
____ 11. Inject the medication slowly. Push the plunger all the way in to inject the full dose.
____ 12. Withdraw the needle quickly, firming the skin with the antiseptic wipe held near the needle. Pull out at the same 90° angle as the needle entered. Replace the needle cover.
____ 13. Massage the site with the antiseptic wipe. (You may have the patient exercise the muscle gently to increase absorption.)
____ 14. Dispose of the equipment properly, breaking disposable needles.
____ 15. Chart the medication.
____ 16. Observe the patient frequently (or as ordered) to make sure there are no adverse reactions. Instruct the patient as to any necessary self-care and advise the patient to rest quietly for at least a few minutes.

Demonstrate this procedure for the instructor or the nurse in charge.

Drugs and Pharmacology

AMA Drug Evaluations. 1986. Chicago: American Medical Association.

Drug Information. 1987. Bethesda, MD: American Society of Hospital Pharmacists.

Facts and Comparisons. 1988. St. Louis: Facts and Comparisons, Inc.

Goodman and Gilman's The Pharmacological Basis of Therapeutics. 1985. New York: Macmillan.

Handbook of Nonprescription Drugs. Washington, DC: American Pharmaceutical Association.

Hitner, H., and Nagle, B.T. 1987. *Basic Pharmacology for Health Occupations.* Mission Hills, CA: Glencoe Publishing.

Lippincott's Nurses' Drug Manual. 1986. Philadelphia: Lippincott.

Physicians' Desk Reference. Oradell, NJ: Medical Economics Company. (New edition published yearly)

United States Pharmacopeia Dispensing Information. 1985. Rockville, MD: United States Pharmacopeial Convention.

United States Pharmacopeia. 25th ed./*National Formulary.* 16th ed. 1985. Rockville, MD: United States Pharmacopeial Convention.

Medical Terms

Dorland's Illustrated Medical Dictionary. 26th ed. Philadelphia: Saunders.

Encyclopedia and Dictionary of Medicine, Nursing, and Allied Health. 1983. Philadelphia: Saunders.

Fisher, J.P. 1988. *Basic Medical Terminology.* 3rd ed. Mission Hills, CA: Glencoe Publishing.

Mosby's Medical and Nursing Dictionary. 1983. St. Louis: Mosby.

Stedman's Medical Dictionary. 24th ed. Baltimore: Williams & Wilkins.

Taber's Cyclopedia Medical Dictionary. 1981. 14th ed. Philadelphia: Davis.

Mathematics

Curren, A.M. 1979. *Math for Meds.* 3rd ed. Seal Beach, CA: Wallcur.

Medici, G.A. 1980. *Drug Dosage Calculations.* Englewood Cliffs, NJ: Prentice-Hall.

Moon, R.G. 1977. *Basic Arithmetic.* 2nd ed. Columbus, OH: Merrill.

Olsen, J.L., and Ablon, L.J. 1983. *Medical Dosage Calculations.* 3rd ed. Menlo Park, CA: Benjamin/Cummings.

Skelley, E.G. 1982. *Medications and Mathematics for the Nurse.* 5th ed. Albany, NY: Delmar.

Anatomy and Physiology

Anthony, C.P., and Thibodeau, G. 1984. *Structure and Function of the Body.* 7th ed. St. Louis: Mosby.

Gray's Anatomy. 1973. Philadelphia: Saunders.

Memmler, R.L., and Wood, D.L. 1983. *Structure and Function of the Human Body.* 3rd ed. Philadelphia: Lippincott.

Disease Conditions

Memmler, R.L., and Wood, D.L. 1983. *The Human Body in Health and Disease.* 5th ed. Philadelphia: Lippincott.

The Merck Manual. 15th ed. 1987. Rahway: Merck Sharp & Dohme Research Laboratories.

Nursing Procedures

Caldwell, E., and Hegner, B. 1985. *Health Care Assistant.* Albany, NY: Delmar.

Kozier, B., and Erb, G.L., 1983. *Fundamentals of Nursing.* 2nd ed. Menlo Park, CA: Addison-Wesley.

Lewis, L.W. 1983. *Fundamental Skills in Patient Care.* 3rd ed. Philadelphia: Lippincott.

Lippincott Manual of Nursing Practice. 4th ed. Philadelphia: Lippincott.

Special Topics

Stevens, M.K. 1975. *Geriatric Nursing for Practical Nurses.* 2nd ed. Philadelphia: Saunders.

Trissel, L.A. 1983. *Handbook of Injectable Drugs.* Bethesda, MD: American Society of Hospital Pharmacists.

USAN and USP Dictionary of Drug Names. 1988. Rockville, MD: United States Pharmacopeial Convention, Inc.

Williams, S.R. 1984. *Mowry's Basic Nutrition and Diet Therapy.* 7th ed. St. Louis: Mosby.

Periodicals

American Journal of Nursing. Professional Journal of the American Nurses' Association, 555 W. 57th Street, New York, NY 10019.

Geriatric Nursing: American Journal of Care for the Aging. 555 W. 57th Street, New York, NY 10019.

Journal of Practical Nursing: The Voice of Practical/Vocational Nursing. National Association for Practical Nurse Education and Service, Inc., 254 W. 31st Street, New York, NY 10001.

Pharmacy Times. Pharmacy Times, Inc., 80 Shore Road, Port Washington, NY 11050.

R N. Medical Economics, Inc., Litton Industries, Oradell, NJ 07649.

A

Abbreviations, medication
forms, 47
routes, 52
Abnormal sounds,
breathing, 206
Abscess, 364
Absorption, 28–30
changes in the elderly, 351
drugs through skin, 163
Abused drugs, 40
Accumulation, drug, 31
Acetaminophen, 235
Acetazolamide, 288
Acetohexamide, 310
Acetone, 302
Acetylcholine, 226–227
Acetylcysteine, 222
Achromycin, 139, 298
Acid, 282
Acid-fast germs, 137
Acidifier, 282, 286
Acidosis, 282, 286
Acne, 158, 160
Acoustic nerve, 230
Acquired immune deficiency
syndrome (AIDS), 136, 325
Acromegaly, 306
Acromion process, 364, 373
ACTH, 304, 312
Acthar, 312
Actidil, 209
Actifed, 209
Action, 28
Active ingredients, 47–48
Acyclovir, 325
A & D Ointment, 163
Addiction, 39
Addison's disease, 307, 311
ADH, 302, 306, 312
Adipose tissue, 30, 32
Adjunctive, definition, 178
Administration considerations,
anti-infectives, 137
drug, five rights, 109
factors, effect on, 32
oral, 52
Adrenal cortex, 307, 311
Adrenal corticosteroids, 305
Adrenal glands, 302, 303
Adrenaline, 303
Adrenocorticotropic
hormone, 304
Adriamycin, 142
Adrucil, 154
Adsorbent, 254
Adverse reactions, 28, 35
Advil, 235, 345
Aeroseb HC, 174
Aerosol, 204
Afrin, 208, 222
Age, adjusting dose, 78
effect on drug action, 32
Aging process, 349
effect on drug action, 32
social and psychological
effects, 354

Agranulocytosis, 340
AIDS, 325
Air bubble, in parenteral
administration, 376
Alcohol, 40, 49, 353
and sedatives, 37
solutions, 49
Alcoholics, drugs, 239
Aldactazide, 288
Aldactone, 185, 288
Aldomet, 185, 198
Aldosterone, 307, 311
Aldosteronism, 307
Alfentanil, 16
Alimentary canal, 253
Alkalizers, 282, 287
Alkalosis, 259, 282, 286
Alkylating agents, 142, 154
Allerest, 210
Allergen, 204
Allergic reactions, 35
corticosteroids, 311
tetracycline, 139
Allergy, 28
penicillin, 139
tests, 55
Allopurinol, 337, 346, 353
Alopecia, 132
Alprazolam, 250
Aludrox, 260, 278
Alveolar sacs, 203
Alveoli, 203, 204
Amantadine, 237
Ambulatory patient, 48
Amenorrhea, 322, 326
Amikacin, 139
Amikin, 139
Amiloride, 185
Aminoglycosides, 139
Aminophylline, 210
Amitriptyline, 234, 249
Ammonium chloride, 286
Amoxicillin, 139
Amoxil, 139
Amphetamines, 16, 40, 226, 234, 353
Amphojel, 264
Amphotericin B, 162
Ampicillin, 139, 287, 298
Ampule, 98
drawing up medication, 368
Anal rectal ridge, 254, 265
Analgesics, 158, 226, 235, 249, 298
Anaphylaxis, 28, 132, 139
Anatomy, 4
Anchored catheter, 282, 289
Androgenic steroids, 307
Anemia, 178, 184
Anesthesia, 226, 236
Anesthetic gases, 31
Anesthetics, 175
Angina pectoris, 178, 183, 185, 187
Animals, as drug sources, 3
Anorexia, 206, 254, 257
Anorexiants, 254, 263
Antacids, 254, 259, 278, 353

and tetracycline, 37
interaction with tetracycline, 139
Antagonism, 28, 37, 38
Antepar, 263
Anterior superior iliac spine, 372
Antianemics, 178, 188
Antianxiety drugs, 235, 249
Antiarrhythmics, 183, 187, 199
Antiarthritics, 336, 338, 345
Antibacterials, 162, 174, 298, 333
Antibiotics, 27, 132, 136, 138, 153, 154, 353
automatic stop order, 104
in cancer treatment, 142
side effects, 138
Antibodies, 28, 35, 132, 135, 181
gamma globulin, 140
Anticholesteremics, 186, 353
Anticholinergics, 234, 254, 261, 278, 353
Anticoagulants, 178, 187, 200, 353
automatic stop order, 104
Anticonvulsants, 226, 232, 237, 250, 353
Antidepressants, 234, 249, 353
Antidiabetic agents, 302
Antidiarrheals, 254, 262, 278
Antidiuretic hormone (ADH), 302, 306, 312
Antidote, 28
Antiemetics, 254, 261
Antiflatulents, 254, 260
Antifungals, 158, 162, 174
Antigen, 28
Antihistamines, 27, 158, 162, 204, 209, 222
Antihypertensives, 178, 184, 185, 199
side effects, 186
Antihyperuricemics, 336, 337, 346
Anti-inflammatory drugs, 158, 162, 173, 338, 345
Anti-infectives, 132, 136, 162, 174
table, 153
Antilipemics, 178, 184, 186
Antimalarial drugs, 339
Antimetabolites, 142, 154
Antiminth, 263
Antinauseants, 264, 278
Antineoplastics, 132, 142
table, 154
Antiparasitics, 254, 263
Antiparkinsonian agents, 237, 251, 353
Antipruritics, 158, 162, 173
Antipsychotics, 226, 250, 353
Antipyretics, 226, 336
effects, 238
Antiseptics, 158, 162, 175
Antispasmodics, 254, 261, 278
Antitubercular drugs, 223

Antitussives, 204, 208, 222
Antivert, 261, 278
Anturane, 337, 346
Anuria, 282, 284
Anus, 254
Anusol, 264
Apical pulse, 178, 187
Aplastic anemia, 340
Apnea, 204, 206
Apothecary, 72
Apothecaries' system, 71
and metric systems, conversions, 76
units, 72
Application, skin drugs, 165
Apresoline, 185
Aqua-Mephyton, 201
Arabic numerals, 72
Aramine, 185, 198
Arco-Lase Plus, 262
Aristocort, 162, 173
Arrhythmias, 178, 183, 186
Artane, 237
Arterial blood, 181
Arteries, 177
Arteriosclerosis, 178, 184
Artery, 178
Arthritis, 336
Aseptic techniques, 132, 136
Aspirating, parenteral administration, 374
Aspirin, 34, 235, 339, 345
Assay, 4
Asthma, 35, 54, 204, 207, 210
Astringents, 158, 161, 173, 254
Atarax, 162
Atenolol, 198
Atherosclerosis, 178, 184
Athlete's foot, 160, 162
Atomizers, 54, 204, 213
Atromid-S, 186
Atropine sulfate, 261
Atrophy, 336
Auranofin, 345
Auricle, 230
Aurothioglucose, 339
Autoclave, 132, 144
Autoclaving, 367
Autoimmune reactions, corticosteroids, 311
Automatic stop order, 48, 59, 104
Autonomic nervous system, 226, 228
Axon, 227
Azathioprine, 353

B

Baby Magic, 163
Baciguent, 163
Bacteria, 134
Bacterial infections, 135
infections, skin, 160
pneumonia, 206
Bactericidals, 132
activity, 138
Bacteriostatic activity, 132, 138

Index

Bactine, 174
Bactrim, 140, 153, 287, 298
Bandages, 166
Banthine, 261
Barbiturates, 16, 32, 40, 226, 235
  automatic stop order, 104
Barrel, 364
Bartholin's glands, 322
Base, 282
Bedsores, 158, 160
Belching, 257
Belladonna, 261
Belladonna tincture, 48
Bellergal, 262
Benadryl, 209
Benadryl elixir, 48
Benemid, 353
Benign, definition, 132
Bentyl, 262, 278
Benylin, 209, 210, 222
Benylin DM, 208
Benzalkonium chloride, 162
Benzedrex, 208
Benzocaine, 162, 175
Benzodent, 264
Benzodiazepines, 226
Benzoic acid, 162
Benzonatate, 222
Benztropine, 237, 251
Betadine, 162, 163, 175, 264
Betamethasone, 162, 173
Bevel, 366
Bile, 254
BiNCU, 154
Bioassay, 4
Bioavailability testing, 8
Biocidal activity, 132
Biogenetic engineering, as drug source, 5
Biostatic activity, 132
Biosynthesis, 132
Biotransformation, 28–32
Birth canal, 322
Bisacodyl, 262, 278, 353
Bismuth, 262
Bi-SoDol, 264
Bladder, 282
  infection, 325
  medication, installation, 289
Bleomycin, 142
Blistex, 264
Blood, 181
  circulation in the cardiovascular system, 177
  diseases, 184
  disorders, chemotherapy, 141
  disorders, chloramphenicol, 139
  pressure (BP), 178, 180
  pressure, normal and variations, 180
  sugar, 307
  tests, glucose levels, 310
  vessels, 30, 177
  vessel diseases, 183
  vessels, skin, 157
Bloodstream, 29

Blurred vision, 230
Body cells, 27
Body systems, 131, 133
Body water, 133
Boils, 160
Bone marrow, 184, 335
  depression, 336, 340
  disorders, 340
Bones, 335
Bonine, 261, 264
Bradycardia, 178
Bradykinesia, 231
Brain, 225, 227
Brand names, 5, 7
Breakthrough bleeding, 322
Breast cancer, 325
Breathing difficulties, 189, 206
  exercises, 211
Breathlessness, 182
Brethine, 210
Brittle diabetes, 307
Broad-spectrum antibiotics, 137
Broken needles, 377
Bronchi, 203–204
Bronchioles, 203, 204
Bronchitis, 207
Bronchodilators, 204, 207, 210, 223
Bronchopulmonary disorders, 206
Bronkaid, 210
Buccal administration, 54
Bucladin-S, 261
Buclizine, 261
Bulk formers, 262
Bumetanide, 185
Bumex, 185
Burns, 160
Burping, 257
Bursa, 336–337
Bursitis, 337
Butabarbital, 16

C

Caladryl, 163, 173
Calamine, 50, 163
  and diphenhydramine, 173
Calan, 199
Calciparine, 200
Calcium, 134, 288, 335
Calcium gluconate, 288
Calculations, dose, 70
  parenteral therapy, 79
Calibrations, 364
Camphor spirit, 48
Cancer, 325
  and chemotherapy, 140
  cells, 27
  corticosteroids, 311
  disease effects, 143
  drugs, 130
  patient, care, 142
  respiratory tract, 207
  side effects, 143
  treatment, 141
  tumors, 140

Cannula, 364, 366
Cantil, 262
Capillaries, 28, 30, 177, 178
Capoten, 185
Capsules, 51
  calculating the correct number, 76
Captopril, 185
Carbamazepine, 237, 251
Carbidopa and levodopa, 251
Carbohydrates, 134
Carbol-fuchsin, 173
Carbon dioxide, 178
Carbonic anhydrase inhibitors, 288
Cardiac arrest, 28, 178, 182
Cardiac arrhythmias, 183
Cardiac drugs, 177
Cardiac glycosides, 178, 186, 198
Cardiac muscle tissue, 336
Cardiovascular complications, oral contraceptives, 327
  disorders, 182
  drugs, side effects and adverse reactions, 189
  system, aging, 350
  system, drugs, 176
  system drugs, summary, 190
  system drugs, table, 198–201
Cardizem, 199
Carisoprodol, 339, 346
Carminatives, 260
Carmustine, 142, 154
Cartilage, 335
Cascara sagrada, 262
Cas-Evac, 262, 264
Castellani's Paint, 173
Caster oil, 262
Cathartics, 254, 262, 278, 353
Catheter, 282, 283
Celestone, 162
Cells, body, types, 131
  molecules, 27
  reproduction, 131
  reproduction in cancer, 141
Centimeter, 72
Central nervous system (CNC), 225
Cephalexin, 139
Cephalosporins, 139
Cephalothin, 139, 153
Cerebellum, 227
Cerebral cortex, 227
Cerebral stimulants, 234
Cerebrovascular accident (CVA), 226, 232
Cerebrum, 227
Cerumen, 226, 230
Ceruminous glands, 157
Cervicitis, 322, 324
Cervix, 321, 322
Charting, 98
  medications, 111
  on medication records, 112
  topical drugs, 166
  nursing homes, 115
Chemical dependence, 39

Chemical drug effect, 34
Chemical name, 4, 7
Chemical reactions, 30
Chemical reactions in body, role of water, 133
Chemical synthesis, as drug source, 5
Chemotherapy, 132
  side effects, 141
Cheracol, 210
Cheracol with codeine, 16
Chest pain, 182, 183, 206
Childbirth, 322
Children's doses, calculation, 78
Chlamydial infections, 135, 325
Chlor-Trimeton, 209, 210
Chloral hydrate, 16, 236, 250
Chlorambucil, 142
Chloramphenicol, 139
Chlordiazepoxide, 16, 249
6-Chloro-3, 4-dihydro-2H-1,2,3-benzothiadiazine-7-sulfonamide 1,1-dioxide, chemical drug name, 6
Chloroform, 31
Chloroquine, 339
Chlorothiazide, 185, 199, 288
Chlorpheniramine, 209, 223
Chlorpromazine, 236, 250, 353
Chlorpropamide, 310
Chlorzoxazone, 339
Cholangitis, 258
Cholecystitis, 258
Cholesterol levels, 186
Cholestipol, 353
Cholestyramine, 186, 353
Cholinomimetics, 234
Choloxin, 186
Choroid layer, 229
Circulatory system, 177
Cirrhosis, 33, 258
Clearasil, 163
Clinical considerations, respiratory drugs, 211
Clinitest, 310
Clinoril, 339
Clitoris, 321
Clofibrate, 186
Clomid, 325
Clomiphen, 325
Clotrimazole, 162, 174, 324
CNS, 226
CNS depressants, 233, 235
CNS stimulants, 233, 234
Coagulants, 178, 188, 200
Coatings, tablets, 51
Cobalt, 27
Cocaine, 16, 40
Cod liver oil emulsion, 50
Codeine, 208, 222, 235
Cogentin, 237, 251
Colace, 263, 264, 278
Colbenemid, 338
Colchicine, 338
Colds, 210
Colestid, 186, 353
Colestipol, 186

Collagen, 350
Colorado tick fever, 134
Coma, 226, 230
Compazine, 261, 278
Complications, diabetes, 311
Comprehensive Drug Abuse Prevention and Control Act of 1970, 14
Computers, drug administration data, 107
Comtrex, 210
Concentration, 48
Congestive heart failure, 183
Conjugated estrogens, 326, 333
Conjunctiva, 226, 229
Conjunctival sac, 226
Conjunctivitis, 140, 232
Connective cells, 131
Constipation, 257
Contac, 210
Contact dermatitis, 158, 159
Containers, for measurements, 75
Contaminated, definition, 98
Contraception, 326
  use of drugs, 5
Contraceptives, 4, 6, 327
Contractions, 178, 180
Contraindications, 4
Controlled substances, 4, 104, 105
  cabinet, 100
  definition, 15
  disposal, 101
  medicine cart, 101
Controlled Substances Act of 1970, 14, 16
Controlling cancer, 326
Conversion factor, 78
Conversions, 72
  different measurement systems, 74
  in dosage calculations, 77
  metric and apothecaries' systems, 76
  metric system, 74
  24-hour clock, 58
Convulsions, 226, 230, 232
Cordran, 162
Corn Huskers, 163
Cornea, 229
Coricidin D, 210
Coronary arteries, 179
  disease, 183
Corpuscles, 178, 181
Correctol, 264
Cort-dome, 174
Cortef Rectal Itch, 174
Corticosteroids, 158, 160, 231, 302, 303, 311, 318, 339
  automatic stop order, 104
  in skin disorders, 162
  long-term effects, 312
Corticotropin, 312
Cortisol, 311
Cortisone, 307, 311
Cortisporin, 139, 153, 162, 233, 251

Cosmegen, 142, 154
Co-trimoxazole, 153, 298
Cough suppressants, 208
Coughing, 205
Coumadin, 187, 200, 353
Counterirritant, 48
Cowper's glands, 323
Cranial, 226
Craniosacral division, 228, 229
Cretinism, 306
Cruex, 162
Crystodigin, 186, 198
Cubic centimeter, definition, 73
Culture and sensitivity test, 132, 137
Cumulation, 28
  symptoms, 36
  treatment, 36
Cure, use of drugs, 5
Cushing's disease, 307
Cutdown, 178
Cuticura Medicated, 163
Cutdown, 185
Cyanocobalamin, 184, 188
Cyanosis, 28, 178, 182
Cyclizine, 261
Cyclobenzaprine hydrochloride, 339
Cyclopar, 153
Cyclophosphamide, 142
Cyproheptadine, 209
Cystitis, 282, 284, 325
Cystoscope, 282, 283
Cytarabine, 142
Cytomel, 312
Cytoplasm, 132, 133, 227
Cytosar-U, 142
Cytoxan, 142
Cytotoxic drugs, 142

D

Dactinomycin, 142, 154
Dalmane, 236, 250
Danazol, 325
Dandruff, 158, 160
Danocrine, 325
Darbid, 261
DEA, 4, 15
  number, 59
Decadron, 311, 318
Decimal fractions, 73
Decongestant, 204, 208, 222
Decubitus ulcers, 158, 160
Defecation, 254, 262
Dehydration, 282
Delacort, 174
Delayed-release capsules, 51
  tablets, 51
Delta-Cortef, 311
Deltasone, 311, 318
Demerol, 235, 249
Demulcents, 212
Dendrites, 227
Depakene, 237
Dependence, 28
Depo-Provera, 327

Depressants, 40, 104
Depression, 226
Dermacort, 174
Dermatitis, 158, 159
Dermoplast, 163
Dermatology, 158
Dermis, 157, 158
Desenex, 162, 163
Desitin, 163
Desoxycorticosterone, 307, 311
Dexamethasone, 311, 318
Dextromethorphan, 208
Dextrothyroxine sodium, 186
DiaBeta, 310
Diabetes insipidus, 302, 306
Diabetes mellitus, 302, 303, 307
Diabetic coma, 302, 309
Diabinese, 310
Diagnosis, use of drugs, 5
Dialysis, 282, 285
Diamox, 288
Diaphragm, 205
Diastix, 310
Diastolic pressure, 178, 180
Diazepam, 16, 249
Dibucaine, 162
Dicumarol, 187, 200
Dicyclomine, 262, 278
Diethylpropion, 264
Di-Gel, 261, 264
Digestants, 254, 260
Digestive system, 253
Digital pressure, 239
Digitalis, 177, 183, 353
  drug use, 3
  products, 186
Digitalization, 178, 186
Digitoxin, 186, 198
Digoxin, 186, 199
Dilantin, 237, 250, 353
Diltiazem hydrochloride, 199
Dimenhydrinate, 261, 278
Dimetane, 209
Dimetapp, 209
Diphenhydramine, 209, 222
Diphenoxylate, 278
Diphenoxylate HCl with atropine sulfate, 16
Diplopia, 226, 232
Diprosone, 162
Disease conditions, effect on drug action, 32
  prevention, 5
Disinfectants, 132, 144, 158, 162
Disposal of drugs, 100
Disposable materials, use in controlling infections, 144
Disposable needles and syringes, 367
Disposing of unused drugs, 101
Distribution, drug, 29, 30
Diuretics, 34, 178, 183, 185, 199, 282, 287, 298, 353
Diuril, 185, 199, 288
Diverticulitis, 259
Diverticulosis, 259
Dizziness, 230

DNA, 4
Docusate, 278
Donnagel, 262, 264
Dopar, 237
Dopram, 234
Dosage calculation, drugs, 70, 76, 77
Dosage calculations with conversions, 77
Dosage forms, 47
  liquids, 47
  semiliquids, 47
  semisolids, 51
  solids, 51
Dosage range, 71, 72
Dosages, 71
Doses, 4
  adjusting for age, 78
  adjusting for weight, 79
  for children, calculation, 78
  parenteral, 369
Doxapram hydrochloride, 234
Doxorubicin, 142
Doxycycline, 139
Drug Enforcement Administration, 15
Drug-related disorders, 39
Drugs, 4
  abuse, 28, 39, 239
  accumulation, 31
  action, 27, 29, 31, 34
  action, administration factors, 32
  administration, five rights, 109
  administration, isolation patients, 144
  administration, role of computers, 107
  allergy, symptoms, 35
  allergy, treatment, 35
  card, 4
  card sample, 14
  cards, preparation, 13
  classifications, 16
  cart, setting up, 107
  cost, 8
  cumulation, 36
  dependence, symptoms, 39
  dependence, treatment, 39
  disposal, 100
  effects, 27, 34
  elderly, 348
  excretion, 31
  for chemotherapy, 141
  for pain, 238
  forms, 47
  history, 32
  hypersensitivity, 35
  interactions, 37
  interactions, elderly, table, 353
  interactions, in the elderly, 352
  interactions, symptoms, 38
  interactions, treatment, 38
  laws, 15–17
  legislation, 14

Index

names, 6
ordering from hospital pharmacy, 97
ordering, nursing homes, 99
packaging, 99
parenteral administration, 362
powdered, reconstitution, 370
references, 8
routes, 53
sources, 3
standards, 6
storage, 100
therapy, 5
therapy, sex hormones, 325
tolerance, 36
uses, 5
Drug-taking history, effect on drug action, 33
Dram, 72
Dramamine, 261, 264, 278
Dressings, 166
Dristan, 210
Drixoral, 209
Drolban, 142, 154
Dromostanolone, 142, 154
Drop factor, 72
Dry cough, 208
Dry weight equivalents, 75
Dulcolax, 262, 264, 278, 353
Duodenal ulcer, 258
Duodenum, 253–254
Dwarfism, 306
Dyazide, 288
Dymelor, 310
Dyrenium, 185, 199, 288, 298
Dyskinesia, 226
Dysmenorrhea, 322
Dyspnea, 28, 178, 182, 206
Dysrhythmia, 178, 183
Dysuria, 282, 284, 322

E

Ear, 229
 diagram, 230
 disorders, 233
 medications, 240, 251
Eardrum, 226
Ecchymosis, 158, 166, 340
Eczema, 158–159
Edecrin, 185, 288
Edema, 28, 158, 159, 178, 282, 286
E.E.S., 139
Effersyllium, 263
Ejaculatory duct, 323
EKG, 178
Elasticity, 178, 180, 205
Elavil, 234, 249
Elderly, changes in nervous system, 230
 drug absorption, 30
 drug interactions, 352
 drugs, 348
 heart disease, 182
 liver function, 31
 medication tips, 355
 social and psychological aspects, 354
Electrical conduction system, heart, 179
Electricity, heartbeat, 179
Electrolytes, 282, 285, 286
 imbalances, 286
Electrocardiogram (EKG), 178
Electrocardiograph (EKG), 179
Elixir of terpin hydrate and codeine, 209
Elixirs, 48–49
Elixophyllin, 210, 223
Embolism, 178, 184
Embolus, 184
Emesis, 254, 257
Emergency drugs, 239
Emergency orders, 57
Emetics, 254, 261
Emollients, 263
Emotional condition, effect on drug action, 33
Emotional dependence, 39
Emphysema, 204, 207
Empirin-Compound with Codeine, 235
Emulsions, 50
E-Mycin, 139, 153
Encephalitis, 232
Endocrine system, aging, 351
 drugs, 300
Endometriosis, 325–326
Endometrium, 322, 326
Enduron, 288
Engineering, biogenetic, as drug source, 5
Enteric-coated capsules, 51
 drugs, 48
 tablets, 51, 336
Enteritis, 259
Environment, 32
Environmental conditions, effect on drug action, 33
Enzymes, 28, 30, 253, 254
Ephedrine, 210
Epidermis, 157–158
Epididymis, 323
Epiglottis, 203, 204
Epilepsy, 231
Epinephrine, 30, 207, 210, 223, 303
Epithelial cells, 131, 158
Equanil, 249
Equivalents, 72
 apothecaries' system, 72
 different measurement systems, 75
 household system, 74
 metric system, 74
Ergotamine tartrate, 54
Error form, 98
Eructation, 254, 257
Erythema, 158–159
Erythrocin, 139
Erythrocytes, 131
Erythromycins, 139, 153
Esidrix, 185, 288
Eskalith, 236
Esophagus, 253–254
Estradiol, 326
Estrogen, 304, 322–324, 326
Estrone, 326
Ethacrynic acid, 185, 288
Ethambucol, 207
Ethchlorvynol, 236
Ether, 31
Ethinyl estradiol, 327
Ethosuximide, 237
Ethoxazene, 287
Ethynodiol diacetate, 327
Euphoria, 28
Euthroid, 312
Excretion, 28–29, 31
Exhalation, 203, 205
Ex-Lax, 262, 264
Expectorants, 204, 208, 222
Expiration date, 98
External auditory meatus, 230
External genitalia, female, 321
Extract, 48
Extrapyramidal reaction, 226, 236
Extravasation, 132, 364
Eyes, 229
 diagram, 229
 diseases, corticosteroids, 311
 disorders, 232
 medications, 239, 251
Eye medications, 251
 ointments, 50
Eyelid, 229

F

FDA, 4, 14
FDCA, 4, 14
FSH, 306, 324
Facial nerves, 230
Fainting, 182
Fallopian tube, 321
Fascia, 336
Fastin, 264
Fatigue, 182, 189
Fats, 134
Feces, 254
Federal drug laws, 16
Female reproductive system, 321
 diagram, 321
Fenethylline, 16
Fenoprofen, 339, 345
Feosol, 188, 200
Fer-In-Sol, 188, 200
Ferrous sulfate, 188, 200
Fertilization, 321
Fetus, 322
Fever, corticosteroids, 312
Fibrillation, 183
Fibrositis, 337
Fiorinal, 235
First-degree burns, 160
Flagyl, 324, 333
Flange, 364
Flatus, 257
Fletcher's Castoria, 262
Flexeril, 339
Flight or fight system, 229
Fluidextracts, 48–49
Fluids, balance, drugs, 280
 imbalances, drugs, table, 298
 tissue, 133
 respiratory conditions, 212
Fluocinonide, 162
Fluorouracil, 27, 142, 154
Fluoxymesterone, 142
Fluphenazine, 236, 250
Flurandrenolide, 162
Flurazepam, 16, 236, 250
Foley catheter, 289
Follicle, 158
Follicle-stimulating hormone, 324
Follutein, 325
Food, and anti-infectives, 138
Food and Drug Administration, 14
Food, Drug, and Cosmetic Act, 14
Food, effects on drug absorption, 38
Forceps, 158
Forms, patient chart, 111
Forms of medication, 47
Formula, 72
Fraction, 72
Fractures, 337
Freezone, 163
Frequency, 282, 284
Fulvicin, 174
Fulvicin P/G, 162
Function, human body, 131
Fungal organisms, 161
Fungi, 134
Fungicide, 158
Fungizone, 162
Fungus, 158
 infections (mycoses), 135
 infections, skin, 160
Furadantin, 287, 298
Furosemide, 185, 288, 299

G

Garamycin, 139, 160
Gallbladder, 254, 256
 disorders, 258
Gallstones, 258
Gamma globulin, 140
Gantanol, 140, 287
Gantrisin, 140, 153, 287, 298
Gas exchange, 203
 in the cardiovascular system, 177
Gastric gavage, 254, 265
Gastric irritation, anti-infectives, 138
Gastric lavage, 254
Gastritis, 258
Gastroscope, 254, 258
Gastrostomy tube, 254, 265
Gastrointestinal drugs, table, 278–279
 system, aging, 350

system, drugs, 252
tract, 254
Gauge (G), 364, 366
Gelatin, 48
film, 201
hemostatics, 201
sheath, capsules, 51
sponge, 188
Gelfoam, 188
Gels, 50
Gelusil, 260, 264, 278
Generic names, drugs, 6–7
Generic prescription, 57
Generics, 4
Genetic factors, effect on drug action, 32
Genital herpes simplex, 325
Genitalia, 322
Gentamicin, 139, 160
Gentian violet, 263
Geriatrics, 349
Germs, 134
Gerontology, 349
Giantism, 306
Gingivitis, 258
Gland, 302
Gland malfunctions, 305
Glaucoma, 232
Glipizide, 310
Glomerulus, 281
Glomeruli, 282
Glossopharyngeal nerves, 230
Glucagon, 302, 303, 318
Glucocorticoids, 302, 303, 307, 311
Glucose, 302
meter, 311
Glucotrol, 310
Gluteal arteries, 364, 371
Glutethimide, 16
Glyburide, 310
Glycogen, 302
Glycosuria, 302, 308
Gold compounds, 339
Gold sodium, 345
Gold sodium thiomalate, 339
Gonadotropins, 306, 322, 324
Gonads, 302, 304, 323
Gonorrhea, 138–139, 325
Gout, 337
Gouty arthritis, 337
Grain, 72
Gram, 72
Gram-negative microbes, 137
Gram-positive microbes, 137
Gram stain, 132
Grand mal epilepsy, 232
Greater trochanter, 364, 372
Griping, 257
Griseofulvin, 162, 174
Guaifenesin, 208
Guanethidine, 353
Gum disorders, 258
Gyne-Lotrimin, 324

H

Habituation, 28, 39
Hair follicle, skin, 157
root, skin, 157
hair shaft, skin, 157
Halcion, 236, 250
Haldol, 250
Haley's M-O, 264
Hallucinogens, 28, 40, 239
Haloperidol, 250
Halotestin, 142
Handbook of Nonprescription Drugs, 8
Hardening of the arteries, 184
Hashish, 16
Hay fever, 35, 210
Head and Shoulders, 163
Healing, 131
Health maintenance, 4, 6
use of drugs, 5
Heart, 177
attack, 28
depressants, 179, 187, 199
disease, aging, 182
muscle, 186
stimulants, 186, 198
Heartbeat, 179
Heartburn, 257
Hematinics, 178, 188, 200
Hematoma, 178
Hematuria, 282, 284
Hemoglobin, 178, 181, 184
Hemolytic diseases, 184
Hemoptysis, 178, 182, 205, 207
Hemorrhage, 178, 182, 184, 188, 205
Hemorrhoids, 162, 259
Hemostatics, 178, 188
Heparin, 3, 187
Heparin calcium, 200
Hepatitis, 258
Hepatotoxicity, 132
Heroin, 16
Hexadrol, 311
Hg, 178
High blood pressure, 180
Histamine, 28, 35, 158, 162, 209
Hives, 159
Hoarseness, 206
Hodgkin's disease, 141, 184
Hormones, 154, 301, 302, 333
control system, 304
deficiencies, diagnosis, 312
disorders, table, 306
in cancer treatment, 142
table, 318
Hospital infections, 136
Hospital pharmacy, ordering drugs, 97
Household system, 71, 74
Hub, 364, 366
Human chorionic gonadotropin, 325
Humulin N, 308
Humulin R, 308
Hydralazine, 185
Hydrochlorothiazide, 185, 288, 298
Hydrocortisone, 162, 307, 311, 339
HydroDiuril, 185, 288, 298
Hydroxyzine, 162
Hyperacidity, 254, 258
Hypercalcemia, 282, 286
Hyperkalemia, 282, 286, 288
Hypernatremia, 282, 286
Hyperoxygenation, 213
Hyperplasia, 302, 305
Hyperpnea, 204, 206
Hyperpotassemia, 282
Hypersensitivity, 28–29, 132, 138, 140
Hypertension, 178, 180, 184, 187
Hyperthyroidism, 306
Hyperventilation, 204, 206
Hypnotics, 40, 226
Hypocalcemia, 282, 286
Hypodermic syringe, 363
Hypoglycemia, 302, 309
Hypoglycemics, oral, 310
Hypokalemia, 187, 282, 286
Hyponatremia, 282, 286
Hypopotassemia, 282
Hypotension, 28, 178, 180
Hypothalamus, 302, 304
Hypothyroidism, 306
Hypoxia, 213, 226
Hytone, 174

I

Ibuprofen, 30, 235, 339, 345
Idiosyncrasy, 28, 35
symptoms, 36
treatment, 36
Iliac crest, 364, 372
Ilosone, 139
Ilotycin, 153
Imferon, 188
Imipramine, 234, 249
Immune system, 134
Immunity, 132, 135
Immunization, 132, 136
Impetigo, 160
Impulses, 226–227
Imuran, 353
Incident report, 98, 117
forms, 116
Incontinence, 282, 284
Inderal, 187, 199, 200
Indications, 5
Indigestion, 257
Indocin, 338, 339, 345
Indomethacin, 338, 339, 345
Indwelling catheter, 282, 289
Infections, 132, 136, 160
and immunity, 134
drugs, 130
patients at risk, 136
renal, 284
special precautions, 144
Infectious disease, 132, 134
table, 135
Infertility, 325
Inflammation, 158–159
Infusion, 48
INH, 223
Inhalation, 48, 205
administration, 54
therapy, 210
Inhalers, 54
Initial dose, 189
Injections, general procedure, 373
point, 178
sites, 370
Inoculation, 132
Insertion, 48
Insomnia, 226, 231
Instillation, 48, 54
Insufflation, 48, 54
Insulin, 3, 27, 256, 302, 303, 307
administration, 313
pump, 309
shock, 302, 309
syringe, 363
types, 308
Integument, 157, 158
Integumentary system, 157
aging, 350
Interactions, anticoagulants, 188
therapeutic, 38
Intercellular fluid, 133
Intermittent infusion set, 187
Intermittent positive pressure breathing (IPPB) apparatus, 204, 213
Internal genitalia, female, 321
Intestinal disorders, 140
motility, 254, 257
parasites, 259
Intra-arterial administration, 55
Intracardiac administration, 55
Intracutaneous administration, 55
Intradermal administration, 55
injections, 371
Intramuscular administration, 55
route, 371
Intraosseous administration, 55
Intraspinal administration, 55
Intrathecal administration, 55
Intravenous (IV) drip, 48
infusion, 55
injection, 55
therapy, dosage calculations, 79
Iodine, 301–302
Ipecac Syrup, 264
IPPB, 204, 213
Iris, 229
Iron, 181, 184
preparations, 188
side effects, 188
Irregular heartbeats, 182
Irrigation, 48, 54, 282
Irritable bowel, 259
Islets of Langerhans, 302, 303
Ismelin, 353
Isolation, 132, 136

patients, special procedures, 144
procedures, 143
Isoniazid, 207, 223
Isopropamide iodide, 261
Isoproterenol, 210, 223
Isopto Carpine, 232, 251
Isordil, 185, 198
Isosorbide dinitrate, 185, 198
Isuprel, 210, 223
Itching, 159, 166
  corticosteroids, 312
IV drip, 55
Ivy Dry Cream, 163

J

Jaundice, 254, 258
Jock itch, 160
Johnson's Medicated Powder, 163
Joints, 335
  diagram, 336

K

Kaolin, 262
Kaon, 288, 299
Kaopectate, 262, 264
Kardex, 98, 103
  file, 102
Keflex, 139
Keflin, 139
Kemadrin, 237
Kenalog, 162
Keratin, 158–159, 161
Keratolytic, 158, 161, 173
Keratosis, 158–159
Keri, 163
Ketoacidosis, 302, 309
Ketones, 302
Kidneys, diagram, 281
  disease, effect on drug response, 32
  failure, 284
  function, 31
  stones, 284
Kilogram, 72
K-Lyte, 187, 288, 299
Kolantyl, 260, 264
Kraurosis, 322
Kwell, 163

L

Labeling instructions, 59
Labia, 322
Labor, 322
Lacrimal gland, 226, 229
Lacrimal sac, 239
Lanolin, 48, 50
Lanoxin, 186, 199
Large intestine, 256
Larodopa, 237
Larotid, 139
Larynx, 203–204, 206
Lasix, 185, 288, 299
Laws, drug use, 16
Laxative, 254, 262, 353
Legality, patient chart, 111
Legend drugs, 5

Legionnaires' disease, 139
Lens, 229
Lente insulin, 308
Lesions, 158–159
Leukemia, 141, 178, 184, 340
Leukeran, 142
Leukocytes, 132, 135, 181
  as defense, 134
Leukopenia, 132
Levin tube, 254, 265
Levophed, 185, 198
Levothyroxine, 318
Levothyroxine sodium, 312
Levodopa, 237
LH, 306, 324
Librax, 262
Librium, 249
Lice, 161
Lidex, 162
Ligaments, 336
Lindane, 163
Liniments, 50
  administration, 50
Liothyronine sodium, 312
Liotrix, 312
Liquid dosage forms, 47
Liquid volume equivalents, 75
Liter, 72
Lithane, 236
Lithium carbonate, 236, 353
Lithonate, 236
Liver, 254, 256
  cell, diagram, 27
  disease, effect on drug response, 32
  disorders, 258
  function, elderly, 31
Loading dose, 189
Local effects, 34
Lomotil, 262, 278
Lomustine, 142
Long-term medications, 238
Loop diuretics, 185
Lo/Ovral, 333
Lopressor, 185, 199
Lotions, 50
  administration, 50
Lotrimin, 162, 174
Lovastatin, 186
Low blood sugar, 309
Lozenges, 52
LSD, 16, 40
LTH, 306
Lubricants, 263
Lumen, 364
Lung cancer, 207
Luteinizing hormone, 324
Luteotropic hormone, 306
Lymph, 178
  diseases, 184
  nodes, 181
  vessels, 181
Lymphatic system, 181, 184
Lysergic acid diethylamide, 16

M

Maalox, 260, 264, 278
Maalox Plus, 261
Macrodantin, 287, 298
Mafenide, 160
Mafenide acetate, 162, 174
Magmas, 50
Magnesium and aluminum, 278
Main effect, 28
  drug, 34
Maintenance dose, 189
Malaria, 134
Male reproductive system, 323
  diagram, 323
Malignant, definition, 132
  tumors, 140
Mammary glands, 157, 158, 323
Mandelamine, 287
Mannitol, 288
Marezine, 261, 264
Marijuana, 16, 40
Math review: fractions, 80
Measles, 136
Measurement, drugs, 70
  systems, 71
  systems, conversions, 74
  system equivalents, 75
Measuring containers, relative sizes, 75
Mebendazole, 263
Mechanism of action, anti-infectives, 136
Mechlorethamine, 142, 154
Meclizine, 261, 278
Medicaid, 17
Medicare, 17
Medicated bath, 166
Medications, 5
  elderly, 348
  errors, reporting forms, 117
  introduction, 2
  order, 55, 102
  order form, 98
  order, possible errors, 59
  record, 98, 102, 103, 112
  record form, 24-hour clock, 105
  therapy, 46–61
  setting up, 107
Medicine cards, 98, 102, 103
  cart, 98, 101
  room, 98, 100
  tray, 101
  tray, setting up, 107
Medi-Quick, 163
Medrol, 311
Medroxyprogesterone acetate, 327, 333
Medulla, 281
Megace, 327
Megestrol, 327
Meniere's disease, 233
Meninges, 226
Meningitis, 138, 139, 143, 232
Menopause, 322–323
Menorrhea, 322–323

Menotropins, 325
Menstruation, 323
Mental state, effect on drug action, 33
Meperidine, 16, 30, 235, 249
Mephentermine, 185
Mephyton, 188, 201
Meprobamate, 236, 249
Mercaptopurine, 142, 154, 353
Mercurochrome, 162
Mercury (Hg), 178, 180
Merthiolate, 162
Mestranol, 327
Metabolism, 5, 28, 142
  drug, diagram, 30
Metamucil, 263, 264, 278
Metaraminol, 185, 198
Metastasis, 132
Meter, 73
Methadone, 16, 235
Methantheline bromide, 261
Methaqualone, 16
Methenamine, 287
Methicillin, 153
Methocarbamol, 339, 346
Methoxamine, 185
Methyclothiazide, 288
Methylphenidate, 16, 234, 249
Methyldopa, 185, 199
Methylprednisolone, 311
Methyltestosterone, 327, 333
Metolazone, 185
Metoprolol, 185, 199
Metric system, 71, 73
  and apothecaries' system, conversions, 76
  doses, 73
  system, units, 7
Metronidazole, 324, 333
Mevacor, 186
Miconazole, 324, 333
Micro K, 187
Microbes, 132, 134
Microgram, 72
Micronase, 310
Microorganisms, 132, 134
Micturition, 282
Migraine headache, 54
Milk glands, 31
Milk, interaction with tetracycline, 139
Milk of magnesia, 50
Milligram, 72
Milliliters, 72–73
  calculating the correct number, 76
Milpath, 262
Mineralocorticoids, 302, 303, 307, 311
Minerals, 133
  as drug sources, 3
Minim, 72
Miltown, 236
Misuse of drugs, 40
Mites, 161
Mithracin, 142
Mixture, 48
Monistat 7, 324, 333

Monoamine oxidase (MAO) inhibitors, 234, 353
Mons pubis, 321–322
Moon face, corticosteroids, 312
Morphine, 16, 34, 235
Motrin, 235, 339, 345
Mouth, 253
Mucolytics, 204
Mucomyst, 208, 222
Mucous membrane, 48, 164, 208
   as barrier, 134
Mucus, 204
   respiratory diseases, 211
Multiple-dose packages, 99–100
Multiple sclerosis, 231
Mumps, 143
Muscles, 336
   atrophy, 337
   cells, 131
   pain, 339
   relaxants, 346
   tone, 336, 337
Musculoskeletal system, aging, 351
   diagram, 335
   drugs, 334
   drugs, table, 345–346
Mustargen, 142
Myalgia, 336, 339
Myasthenia gravis, 231
Mycitracin, 163
Mycobacterium tuberculosis, 207
Mycolog, 162
Mycostatin, 162, 174
Mydriatics, 232
Myelin sheath, 226–227, 231
Mylanta, 261, 264
Mylicon, 261, 278
Myocardial infarction, 178, 182, 183
Myocardium, 177, 186
Myochrysine, 339, 345
Mysoline, 237

N

Nafcillin, 139
Nalfon, 339, 345
Nalorphine, 30
Naprosyn, 338, 339, 345
Naproxen, 338, 339, 345
Narcolepsy, 234
Narcotics, 5, 40, 226, 235, 239
   antitussives, 208, 222
   automatic stop order, 104
Nardil, 234
Narrow-spectrum antibiotics, 132, 137
Nasal catheter, 213
Nasal cavities, 203–204
Nasogastric tube, 254, 265
Nausea, 257
Nebulizers, 54, 204, 213
Necrosis, 364

Needles, 365
   cover, 364
Neoloid, 262
Neomycin, 139
Neomycin sulfate, polymyxin B, and bacitracin, 162
Neo-Polycin, 162, 163
Neosporin, 139, 162, 163
Neosporin ophthalmic, 251
Neostigmine, 231
Neo-Synephrine, 185, 208, 210, 222
Nephritis, 282, 284
Nephrons, 281, 282
   diagram, 283
   units, 31
Nerve cells, 131
   diagram, 227
Nerve end, skin, 157
Nervous system, aging, 350
   drugs, 224
   drugs, table, 249–251
Neuralgia, 232
Neuritis, 232
Neurons, 226, 227
   fibers, 227
Niacin, 186
Nicrobid, 186
Nicotine, 40
NIDDM, 302, 307
Nifedipine, 185, 199
Nit, 158
Nitro-Bid, 198
Nitrofurantoin, 287, 298
Nitrogen mustards, 142
Nitroglycerin, 30, 54, 179, 183, 185, 198
Nitrosoureas, 142
Nitrostat, 185, 198
Noctec, 236, 250
Nonnarcotic antitussives, 208, 222
Nonproductive cough, 208, 212
Nonsteroidal anti-inflammatory drug, 235, 353
Norepinephrine, 185, 198, 227, 303
Norethindrone, 327
   and ethinyl estradiol, 333
Norflex, 339, 346
Norgesic Forte, 339
Norgestrel, 327
   and ethinyl estradiol, 333
Nose, 230
   drops, 213
Novahistine, 16
Noxema, 163
NP 27, 163
NPH insulin, 308
Numzident, 264
Nupercainal, 162, 163, 264
Nuprin, 235, 345
Nurses' notes, 98, 112, 113
Nursing home clinic charts, 115
Nursing home, drug ordering, 99
Nutracort, 174

Nystatin, 162, 174
Nystatin-triamcinolone-gramicidin, 162

O

Occlusive bandage, 164
Occlusive dressing, 158
Official names, drugs, 5–7
Ointments, 50
   skin, 165
Olfactory cells, 230
Oliguria, 282, 284
Omnipen, 139, 298
Oncovin, 142
Opium, 16, 40
Optic nerves, 229
Orabase, 264
Oral hypoglycemics, 302, 310
Oral route, 52
Order sheet, drugs, 97
Oreton Methyl, 327, 333
Organs, 132–133
Orinase, 310
Ornade, 209
Orphenadrine citrate, 339, 346
Orthopedics, 336
Orthopnea, 204, 206
Orthostatic hypotension, 179, 186
Osmitrol, 288
Osmotic diuretics, 288
Osteoarthritis, 338
Osteomyelitis, 337
Osteoporosis, 322, 326, 335, 337
OTC drugs, definition, 15
Otitis, 233
Outpatients, 48, 57
Ovaries, 304, 321, 322
Overdose, 28, 36
   and toxicity, symptoms, 37
   and toxicity, treatment, 37
Over-the-counter (OTC) drugs, 5
Ovral, 333
Ovulation, 321
Ovum, 322
Oxacillin, 139
Oxazepam, 16
Oxybenzone, 160
Oxycodone, 235
   and aspirin, 249
Oxygen, 213
   inhalation therapy, 211
   mask, 213
   tent, 213
Oxymetazoline, 208, 222
Oxytocics, 322, 324
Oxytocin, 54, 324, 333

P

PABA, 160
Pacemaker cells, 179
Package inserts, 5, 13
Packing, unit or multiple dose, 100
Palpitations, 179, 182

Pancreas, 254, 256, 303, 307
Pancreatitis, 259
Para-aminobenzoic acid (PABA), 160
Paraflex, 339
Paralysis, 226, 230
Parasite, 158
Parasitic infections, 135
Parasiticides, 158, 163
Parasympathetic division, 229
Parasympathetic nervous system, 226
Parasympatholytics, 234
Parasympathomimetics, 234
Parathormone, 302, 303, 306
Parathyroids, 302, 303, 306
Paregoric, 48
Parenteral administration, 55
   general procedure, 373
Parenteral medication, administration, 362
Parenteral therapy, 79
Parepectolin, 16
Parkinson's disease, 231
Parkinson's drugs, 237
Pastes, 48, 50
Patency, 187
Patient chart, 111, 112
Patient considerations, skin disorders, 165
Patient history, 98
   sheet, 111
Pathogens, 132, 134
Pathology, 5
PDR, 5
Pectin, 262
Pediculicides, 161, 163
Pediculosis, 158, 161
Pelvic inflammatory disease (PID), 325
Penicillin, 136–138, 353
   allergy, 139
Penicillin G and probenecid, 38
Penicillin G potassium, 138, 153
Penicillin V, 138
Penicillinase, 132, 139
Penis, 322–323
Pentazocine, 235, 249
Pentids, 138, 153
Pentobarbital, 16, 235
Pen-Vee, 138
Peptic ulcer, 258
Pepto-Bismol, 262, 264
Percodan, 249
Percussion, 204, 211
Pergonal, 325
Periactin, 209
Peri-Colace, 263
Perineum, 321–322
Peripheral nervous system, 225–226
Peristalsis, 229, 253, 254, 257
Peritonitis, 259
Periwinkle plant (vinca), 142
Pernicious anemia, 188
Petechiae, 158, 166, 340

Petrolatum, 48
Peyote, 16
pH, 28, 282
 balance, 281
 imbalance, 285
Pharmaceuticals, 5
Pharmacists, 8
Pharmacodynamics, 3, 5, 26–40
 and body cells, 27
Pharmacokinetics, 5
 elderly, 351
Pharmacology, 5
 definition, 3
Pharmacy, 3, 5
 ordering drugs, 97
 requisition, 98
Pharynx, 203–204
Phazyme, 261
Phenazopyridine, 287, 298
Phendimetrazine, 16
Phenelzine sulfate, 234
Phenergan, 209, 222, 261
Phenergan expectorant with codeine, 209
Phenobarbital, 16, 235, 237, 353
 elixir, 48
Phenolax, 262
Phenolphthalein, 262
Phenothiazines, 236
Phentermine, 264
Phenylephrine, 185, 208, 222
Phenylpropanolamine, 208, 222
Phenytoin, 237, 250, 353
Phillips' Milk of Magnesia, 264
Phlebitis, 179, 183
Phlegm, 204
Photodermatitis, 158, 166
Photophobia, 240
Photosensitivity, 133, 139
Physical changes, effects on drugs, 349
Physical dependence, 39
Physical techniques, mucus drainage and breathing, 211
Physical therapy, 231
Physicians' Desk Reference (PDR), 8
Physician's order sheet, 48, 55, 56
Physiology, 5
Phytonadione, 188, 201
PID, 325
Pilocarpine, 232, 251
Piperacillin, 298
Piperazine, 263
Pipracil, 298
Pitocin, 333
Pitressin, 312, 318
Pituitary, 301, 302, 306
 hormones, reproduction, 324
 problems, 312
Placebo, 28
 effect, 28, 33, 238
Placidyl, 236
Plantain weed, 263
Plants, as drug sources, 3
Plasma, 179, 181

Platelets, 179, 181
Pleura, 204
Pleurisy, 207
Plicamycin, 142
Plunger, 364
Pneumonias, 206
Policy, drug disposal, 101
Polyps, 259
Polymyxin B, 251
Polymyxin B-neomycin-gramicidin-hydrocortisone, 153
Polypharmacy, 33
Polyuria, 302
POMR, 98, 114
Pore, skin, 157
Posterior superior iliac spine, 372
Postpartum, 322
Postural drainage, 204, 211
Potassium, 288, 299
Potassium chloride, 34
Potassium levels, 187
Potassium-sparing diuretics, 185, 288
Potentiation, 28, 37
Povan, 263
Povidone-iodine, 162, 175
Powders, 51
Powdered drugs, reconstitution, 370
Precautions, 5
Precipitate, 364
Prednisolone, 311
Prednisone, 311, 318
Prefixes, metric system, 73
Pregnancy, 322
Pregnyl, 325
Premarin, 326, 333
Preparation H, 264
Prescription, 5, 48
 blank, 55, 57
 drugs, definition, 15
Prevention, use of drugs, 5
Primatene Mist, 210, 223
Primidone, 237
Principen, 139, 298
Principles of charting, 115
P R N, 59
Pro re nata, 59
Pro-Banthine, 261, 278
Probenecid, 353
Probenecid and penicillin G, 38
Problem-oriented medical record (POMR), 114
Problems, parenteral therapy, 79
Procainamide, 187, 200
Procardia, 185, 199
Prochlorperazine, Proctofoam, 174
Proctoscope, 255, 258
Procyclidine, 237
Productive cough, 204, 208
Progesterone, 304, 322–324, 326–327
Progress notes, 114

Prolactin, 324
Prolixin, 236, 250
Promethazine, 6, 209, 222
Pronestyl, 187, 200
Proof of the care, chart, 111
Proof-of-use record, 98
 controlled substances, 106
Propagest, 208, 222
Propantheline, 261, 278
Propoxyphene, 16
Propranolol, 179, 185, 187, 199, 200
Proprietary names, 5, 7
Propylhexadrine, 208
Prostaphlin, 139
Prostate, 322
 cancer, 325
 diseases, 325
 gland, 323
Prostatitis, 322, 325
Protamine zinc insulin, 308
Protective isolation, 143
Protectives, 158, 161
Proteins, 134
Proteolytics, 204, 208
Prothrombin time, 188
Protozoa, 134
Protozoan infections, 135
Provera, 327, 333
Pruritus, 158, 159
Psilocyn, 16
Psorex, 163
Psoriasis, 158, 160
Psychiatric patients, 239
Psychological dependence, 39
 support, skin conditions, 164
Psychology, 5
Psychosis, 226
Psyllium, 263, 278
Pulmonary edema, 182, 205
 embolism, 207
Pulse, 179, 180
 normal rate, 181
Pupil, 229
Pure Food and Drug Act, 14
Purgatives, 255, 262
Purinethol, 154, 353
Purodigin, 198
Purple foxglove, drug use, 3
Purpura, 340
Pus, 135
Pyelonephritis, 282, 284
Pyorrhea, 258
Pyrantel pamoate, 263
Pyridium, 287, 298
Pyrvinium pamoate, 263
Pyuria, 282, 284

Q

Questran, 186, 353
Quibron Plus, 210
Quinidine, 187, 199
Quinora, 187

R

Radiation, cancer, 141
Rebound effect, 204, 208
Receptor, 226
 sites, 322
Rectal administration, 54
 suppositories, 52
Rectum, 255
Red blood cells, 181
Reddening, 159
References, 5
Refills, 59
Refrigeration, drugs, 100
Regular insulin, 308
Remission, 133, 142
Reorder sheet, drugs, 99
Replacement electrolytes, 288, 299
Replacement therapy, hormones, 305
Reproductive system, aging, 351
 drugs, 320
 drugs, table, 333
Reservoirs, 28, 30
Resistance, 133
 antibiotics, 137
Resorcinol, 161
Respiration, 203–205
 rate, 205
Respiratory diseases, corticosteroids, 311
 drugs, administration, 211
 isolation, 143
 stimulants, 234
 system, aging, 350
 system disorders, 205
 system, drugs, 202
 system drugs, table, 222–223
 therapists, 213
 therapy, 212
Response to drugs, factors, 32
Retention, 282, 284
 catheter, 282, 289
Retina, 229
Reverse isolation, 143
Rhabdomyosarcoma, 133
Rheumatic fever, corticosteroids, 312
Rheumatoid arthritis, 338
 corticosteroids, 312
Rhinitis, 208
Rickettsiae, 134
Rickettsial infections, 135
Ridaura, 345
Rifampin, 207
Rigidity, 231
Ringworm, 162
 of the groin, 160
 of the scalp, 160
Ritalin, 234, 249
Robaxin, 339, 346
Rolaids, 264
Roman numerals, 72
Romilar, 210
Routes of administration, 30, 52–53

effect on drug action, 33
Routine drugs, 98
Routine responsibilities, 96–117
Rx, 57

S

Salicylates, 353
Salicylic acid, 160–162, 173
Saline, cathartics, 262
Saliva, 48, 204, 255
Salivary glands, 253
Salt, 133
Satellite pharmacy, 98
Scabicide, 158, 161, 163
Scabies, 158, 161
Scaling, 159
Schedule I drugs, 16
Schedule II drugs, 16
Schedule III drugs, 16
Schedule IV drugs, 16
Schedule V drugs, 16
Schedules, anti-infectives, 138
  chemotherapy, 141
Sciatic nerve, 364, 371
Sclera, 229
Scopolamine hydrobromide, 261
Scored tablets, 51
Scrotum, 322–323
Seasonal rhinitis, 208
Sebaceous gland, skin 157
Sebisol, 163
Seborrhea, 160
Seborrheic dermatitis, 158, 160
Sebum, 157–158
Secobarbital, 16, 235
Second-degree burns, 160
Sedatives, 40, 226, 353
  and alcohol, 37
  and tranquilizers, 239
  hypnotics, 235, 237, 249
Seizures, 227, 231
Seldane, 209, 223
Selenium sulfide, 160
Self-terminating orders, 48, 59, 104
Selsun Blue, 160, 163
Semen, 323
Semilente insulin, 308
Semiliquid dosage forms, 47
Seminal vesicles, 323
Semisolid dosage forms, 51
Semisynthetic penicillin, 139
Senile vaginitis, 326
Senna, 262
Senokot, 262, 264
Senokot-S, 263
Sensacort, 174
Senses, 229
  organs, 225
  receptors, 157, 158, 229, 230
Sensitivity, 29, 138
Sensory system, aging, 350
  drugs, 224
  drugs, table, 249–251
Septra, 153, 287, 298
Serenium, 287

Setting up medications, 107
Set up drugs, 98
Sex, effect on drug action, 32
  hormones, 323
Sexually transmitted
  diseases, 322, 325
Shaft, 364, 366
Shock, 28, 29, 184
Side effects, 5, 29, 34
  antibiotics, and
    sulfonamides, 138
  antihypertensives, 186
  iron, 188
  skin drugs, 166
  sulfonamides, 140
Sigmoidoscope, 255
Silvadene, 162, 175
Silver sulfadiazine, 162, 175
Simethicone, 260
Sinarest, 210
Sinemet, 237, 251
Single-dose packages, 99
Sinusitis, 208
Site rotation, 364, 376
Size, effect on drug action, 32
Skeletal muscles, 336
Skin, as protection, 134
  cancer, 160
  cross section of layers, 157
  diseases, 159
  disorders, 159
  drug absorption, 163
  drugs, 156
  drugs, table, 173–175
  infections, 160
  inflammations, corticosteroids, 311
  medications, 166
  parts, 157
  rashes, 35
Slipstream nebulizer, 213
Sloughing, 364
Slow-K, 187, 288, 299
Small intestine, 253
Smooth muscle tissue, 336
SOAP, 98
Sodium bicarbonate, 259, 287
Solarcaine, 162, 163, 175
Solbar, 160
Solgana, 339
Solid dosage forms, 51
Solutions, 47, 48
Soma, 339, 346
Somatotropic hormone
  (STH), 302, 306
Somatotropin, 301
Somophyllin, 210
Spasm, 204
Spastic colitis, 259
Spastic colon, 259
Sperm, 322
Spermatozoa, 322–323
Sphygmomanometer, 179–180
Spinal cord, 225, 227
Spinal meningitis, 134
Spirits, 48, 49
Spirochetal infections, 135
Spironolactone, 185, 288

Spleen, 179, 182
Spontaneous fracture, 336
Sprains, 337
Sprays, 51, 213
Sputum, 204–205
Standard medical
  abbreviations, 60
Standards, 5
Standing orders, 48, 59
Staphcillin, 139, 153
Staphylococcal infections, 136
Stat order, 48
State drug laws, 17
Stelazine, 236, 250
Stepwise approach, antihypertensive therapy, 185
Sterile, 48
Sterility, injection
  equipment, 55
  parenteral administration, 366
Stethoscope, 205
Stimulants, 27, 40, 104, 239, 249
  cathartics, 262
Stock supply, 98, 101
Stoma, 255, 265
Stomach, 253
  tubes, 265
Stomatitis, 143, 258
Stools, 254
Storage of drugs, 100
Strep throat, 139, 208
Streptomycin, 139, 207, 223
Strict isolation, 143
Stri-Dex Medicated Pads, 163
Strip label, 98
  drugs, 99
Strains, 337
Stroke, 184, 226, 232
Structure, human body, 131
Stupor, 227, 231
Stye, 232
Stylet, 364, 367
Subcutaneous injections, 371
Subcutaneous layer, skin, 159
Subcutaneous route, 55
Subjective-objective-
  assessment-plan (SOAP), 115
Sublingual administration, 54
Suctioning, respiratory
  diseases, 211
Sudafed, 210
Sudoriferous glands, 157
Sulfa drugs, 139
Sulfadiazine, 140
Sulfamethoxazole, 140, 287
Sulfamylon, 140, 160, 162, 174
Sulfinpyrazone, 337, 346
Sulfisoxazole, 140, 153, 287, 298
Sulfonamides, 133, 136, 139, 287, 324
  side effects, 138
Sulfonylureas, 353
Sulfur, 161
Sulindac, 339
Sumycin, 139, 298

Summary of events,
  chart, 115
Sunburns, 162
Superinfection, 133, 161
Superior iliac spines, 364
Suppositories, 52, 265
Suppression of immunity,
  corticosteroids, 311
Suprarenals, 303
Surfak, 263
Surgery, cancer, 140
Suspensions, 47–48
Sustained-release tablets
  and capsules, 51
Sweat duct, skin, 157
Sweat glands, 157
Swelling, 159, 183
Symmetrel, 237
Sympathetic division, 228
Sympathetic nervous
  system, 227
Sympatholytics, 234
Sympathomimetics, 234
Symptoms, endocrine
  disorders, 305
  GI disorders, 256
  skin disorders, 159
Synacort, 174
Synalar, 162
Synapse, 227
Synergism, 37
Synovial capsule, 336
Synovitis, 337
Synthesis, chemical, as
  drug source, 5
Synthroid, 312, 318
Syntocinon, 333
Syphilis, 138, 325
Syringes, 363–364
  diagram, 365
  mixing two drugs, 370
  parts, 366
Syrups, 5
Systemic effects, 34
Systems, 133
Systems of measurement, 71
Systolic pressure, 179–180

T

Tablets, 51
  calculating the correct
    number, 76
Tachycardia, 179, 183
Tachypnea, 205–206
Talwin, 235, 249
Tardive dyskinesia, 227, 236
Tarry stools, 255
Taste buds, 230
Tear ducts, 229
Technical language, 13
Tedral, 209
Tegretol, 237, 251
Tegrin, 163
Teldrin, 209, 223
Temaril, 162, 173
Tendinitis, 337
Tendons, 336–337

Index

Tenormin, 199
Tenuate, 264
Terbutaline, 210
Terfenadine, 209, 210, 223
Terpin hydrate, 208
Tessalon, 222
Testape, 310
Testes, 304, 322, 323
Testosterone, 304, 322–324, 327
Tetany, 302–303
Tetracycline, 139, 298, 353
  and antacids, 37
  interaction with antacids and dairy products, 139
Theophylline, 210, 223
Therapeutic drugs, 5
Therapeutic effect, 34
Therapeutic uses, sex hormones, 326
Therapy, 5
Thiazides, 179, 185, 287, 288
Thimerosal, 162
Thioridazine, 236
Third-degree burns, 160
Thoracolumbar division, 228
Thorazine, 236, 250, 261
Thrombin, 188
Thrombophlebitis, 179, 183
Thrombosis, 179, 183
Thrombus, 183
Thymus gland, 231
Thyroid, 301, 302, 306
  hormone replacement, 312
Thyroid-stimulating hormone, 133
Thyroxine, 301–302, 306
Time, 32
  abbreviations, 60
  of day, effect on drug action, 33
  24-hour clock, 58
Timed-release tablets and capsules, 51
Tinactin, 162, 163
Tinctures, 48–49
  of iodine, 48
  of merthiolate, 48
Tinea capitis, 160
Tinea cruris, 160
Tinnitus, 227
Tissues, 133
  fluid, 133
  layers, 363
Tobramycin, 137
Tofranil, 234, 249
Tolazamide, 310
Tolbutamide, 310
Tolerance, 29
  symptoms, 36
  treatment, 36
Tolinase, 310
Tolnaftate, 162
Tongue, 230
Tooth disorders, 258
Topical administration, 54
  anesthetics, 162
  corticosteroids, 162, 173
  drugs, charting, 166

  medications, respiratory passages, 213
  medications, skin, 161
Torecan, 261
Toxic effects, alkylating agents, 142
Toxicity, 36–37
Trachea, 203, 205
Tracking, 364
  prevention, 376
Trade name drugs, 5–7
Tranquilizer, 227
Transdermal, 179
Transdermal system, nitroglycerin, 195
Treatment, cancer, 140
Treatment, use of drugs, 5
Tremor, 227, 230, 231
Trench mouth, 258
Triamcinolone, 162, 173
Triaminic, 210
Triamterene, 185, 199, 288, 298
Triazolam, 236, 250
Trichomoniasis, 324–325
Tricyclic antidepressants, 234, 353
Trifluoperazine, 250
Trihexyphenidyl, 237
Trimeprazine, 162, 173
Trimethoprim/sulfamethoxazole, 298
Tri-Norinyl, 333
Troches, 52
TSH, 133, 306
Tubercle bacillus, 207
Tuberculin syringe, 364
  in tests, 55
Tuberculosis, 143, 207
Tubocurarine, 339
Tumors, 133, 232, 259
Tums, 264
24-hour clock, 58
Tylenol, 235
Tylenol with codeine, 16, 235
Type I diabetes, 302, 307
Type II diabetes, 302, 307

U

Ulcerations, 159
Ulcerative colitis, 259
Ulcers, 255, 258
Ultralente insulin, 308
Unguentine, 163
Unipen, 139
Unit, 72
Unit-dose packages, 100
United States Pharmacopeia Dispensing Information, 8
United States Pharmacopeia/National Formulary (USP/NF), 6
Units (U) of antibiotics and hormones, 74
  of measurement, 71
Unusual effects, 35
Urea, 161, 281, 282
Uremia, 285

Ureteritis, 284
Ureters, 281–282
Urethra, 281–282, 323
Urethral suppositories, 52
Urethritis, 284
Urgency, 282, 284
Uric acid, 337
Uricosuric drugs, 337
Urinary antiseptics, 282, 287, 298
  frequency, 282
  system, aging, 351
  system drugs, 280
  system, drugs, table, 298
  tract infections, 140, 284
Urination, 282
Urine, 282
Urine tests, and glucose levels, 310
Urticaria, 159
U.S. Food and Drug Administration, 6
USAN, 5
USP DI, 5, 8
USP/NF, 5
Uterine tube, 321
Uterus, 321–322

V

Vaccinations, 55, 133
Vagina, 321–322
Vaginal administration, 54
  infections, 324
  suppositories, 52
Vaginitis, 322, 324
Valisone, 162, 173
Valium, 249
Valproic acid, 237
Varicose veins, 179, 184
Vas deferens, 323
Vaseline, 163
Vasoconstrictors, 179, 185, 198
Vasodilators, 179, 184, 185, 198
Vasopressin, 312, 318
Vasoxyl, 185
V-Cillin K, 138
Veins, 177, 179
Velban, 142
Venous blood, 181
Ventilator, 205, 211
Verapamil hydrochloride, 199
Verbal orders, 57
Vermox, 263
Vertigo, 227, 230
Vial, 98
  drawing up medication, 367
Vibramycin, 139
Vicks Formula 44, 210
Villi, 255–256
Vinblastine, 142
Vincristine, 142
Viral pneumonia, 206
Virus infections, 135
Viruses, 134
Visceral, 227
Vital signs, 205
Vitamin D, 353

Vitamin K, 188, 201
Vitamins, 134
Voice box, 203
Voiding, 282
Volume, 72
Vomiting, 257

W

Warfarin, 187, 200, 353
Water, in body, 133
Weight, dosage adjustment, 79
Welts, 159
White blood cells, 134, 181
Withdrawal symptoms, 29, 39
Wound preparation, 164
Wyamine, 185

X

Xanax, 250

Y

Yeast infection, 324
Yellow bone marrow, 335
Yellow fever, 136

Z

Zarontin, 237
Zaroxolyn, 185
Zephiran, 162, 163
Zetar, 163
Zinc oxide, 163
Zinc pyrithione, 160
Zinc undecylenate, 162
Ziradryl, 163
Zovirax, 325
Z-track, 364
Z-track intramuscular injection, 377
Zyloprim, 338, 346, 353